Among the Mormons

AMONG THE MORMONS

Historic Accounts
by Contemporary Observers

Edited by

William Mulder and A. Russell Mortensen

UNIVERSITY OF NEBRASKA PRESS · LINCOLN

Foreword

═══════════

TO MOST PEOPLE the Mormons are still the dark side of the moon. Yet for a century and a quarter now they have been a standard curiosity both at home and abroad. Today a Mormon girl is crowned Miss America, a Mormon apostle named to the President's cabinet, and the great Tabernacle Choir from Salt Lake City wins the applause of Europe in an unprecedented tour. But news about the Mormons was at one time more sensational and on occasion the country's chief diversion. Even before polygamy appeared on the scene to give the Republicans of 1856 a cause and a slogan, Mormon calamities in Missouri and Illinois reached the ears of Congress and, through the newspapers, enlisted the sympathies of the nation. The Mormon flight to the Rocky Mountains in the wake of manifest destiny had important consequences for western history, and kept the Mormons thereafter constantly in the wind.

Their notoriety won them an attention in the press, European as well as American, out of all proportion to their numbers. The "Letter from Great Salt Lake City" became a familiar feature in *The New York Times*, which through the years frequently editorialized on "The Mormon Question" or "The Situation in Utah." Every major magazine in the United States and in England, where Mormon proselyting was most successful, sooner or later published articles on the Mormons—from Dickens's gossipy *All the Year Round* to the staid *Edinburgh Review*. Though they often abandoned discussion for diatribe, these articles reflected an interest in Mormon affairs that never flagged. *The Saturday Evening Post* and *Holiday* carry on the tradition in our own time, while the learned journals have discovered in Mormonism a ripe field for scholarship.

Most popular in the monthlies were the reports of visitors to Mormon country, Stanleys back from darkest Africa. Readers of *Putnam's* in 1855, for example, could turn the page from Irving's "Life of Washington" or Longfellow's "Song of Hiawatha" to Mrs. B. G. Ferris's serialized "Life among the Mormons" and thrill at her descriptions of Zion as a "Botany Bay of society." As a book, her letters were advertised the next year in the end pages of Frederick Law Olmsted's *A Journey in the Seaboard Slave States*, symbolic of the way the country divided its attention between slavery and polygamy, the twin relics of barbarism. Harriet Beecher Stowe appropriately shed tears at the reports coming from Utah, as harrowing as anything in *Uncle Tom's Cabin.*

Travelers' tales fed an imagination hungry to hear dime-novel adventures, and did much to produce the popular image of the Mormons at worst as degraded, at best as God-fearing and industrious but deluded fanatics. Curious observers sought them out early. Hardly a travel book about America after 1830 failed to mention them. All sorts of visitors called on Joseph Smith, the American Mohammed, and after his death on Brigham Young, the American Moses, to ponder the daring experiments of their millennial community. Proper Bostonians, an Adams and a Quincy no less, descended on Nauvoo the Beautiful in 1844 to find its prophet-founder a challenging enigma. Emerson, venturing far west in 1871, paid Brigham Young his respects and thought unavoidably of Father Abraham; the Mormons, he said, were an afterclap of Puritanism. While Sir Richard Burton, dashing British adventurer fresh from Mecca and ready for the holy City of the Saints, discovered oriental parallels everywhere. Whatever their conclusions, the visitors always found the Mormons intriguing, and their reports, whether elaborate book-length studies like Hepworth Dixon's *New America* or the chance letter of a Forty-Niner passing through the Valley of the Great Salt Lake, make vivid reading today. More than history, they mirror the attitudes and opinions which often determined the course of history.

The record collected here from the buried columns of old newspapers, obscure memoirs, out-of-print books, forgotten periodicals, and hitherto unpublished letters is as varied as it is vital. It begins with Joseph Smith's own story of the rumored gold plates, and with his neighbors' recollections and ridicule. The rumors fan out into the burnt-over district of up-state New York, where religious excitement had already singed many a soul since the Great Revival. They creep into Lucius Fenn's letter, written from Seneca County to Birdseye Bronson in Connecticut early in 1830, about a new bible that speaks of the "Millenniam day" and tells "when it is a going to take place." Once the new church is founded the religious press is full of letters to the editor about the Mormonites and their New Jerusalem, all eager to pass on the latest incredulities. A freewheeling evangelist like Nancy Towle, taking the Erie Canal rest cure, encounters the Mormons in Kirtland, Ohio, as they are about to depart for Independence, the land they hope to make their inheritance. Soon the columns of local papers in Missouri, hating Mormon presumptions, flame with charges and countercharges and ring with ultimatums that erupt in civil warfare. Petitions besiege the state legislature, and citizens' committees pass resolutions painting a seditious image of the Mormons, while the Yankee Mormons for their part leave no doubt about what they think of the Missouri Pukes.

For a while the reports brighten when the Mormons take refuge in Illinois, where Whig and Democrat alike curry their favor. A young lawyer named Abe Lincoln votes for their city charter. As President he will treat them as he did green stumps in a clearing: "I plow around them." A circuit judge named Stephen A. Douglas on more than one occasion acquits their warrant-ridden prophet. A future mayor of Boston visits Nauvoo, the booming Mormon capital on the Mississippi. When the old Missouri hatreds catch up with the prophet and a mob shoots him down, a country doctor clears his conscience and writes his daughter an eye-witness reminiscence of the tragedy; while from Philadelphia an aroused humanitarian hastens to Winter Quarters to succor the evacuated Saints, sees their abandoned city, and writes its classic epitaph.

In the Rocky Mountains the Mormons seek a refuge from their enemies but find themselves instead athwart a national highway to California, and soon Forty-Niners are describing the miracle of life in the desert, a wonder as great as gold in El Dorado. After them come the government surveyors like Howard Stansbury and Captain John Gunnison, who leave their good names on the map and in Mormon memory. Not so the first federal officials, who promptly quarrel with their constituents and carry tales of treason back to Washington that keep Utah a vassal territory for over forty years and make the *Congressional Globe* read like lurid fiction. "The Mormons," delegate William H. Hooper complains in 1870, "are the most vigorously lied about people on earth." The busybody Horace Greeley has to see for himself and calls on Brigham Young for a famous interview, which he reports at length in the columns of his New York *Tribune*.

The soldiers, the carpetbaggers, and the crusaders who follow in the official wake all have an ax to grind and see the Mormons henceforth as a problem. Professional reformers are bent equally on saving the poor coolies of San Francisco and the plural wives of Salt Lake City. Samuel Bowles, crusading editor of the Springfield *Republican*, tags along with Speaker of the House Schuyler Colfax on a transcontinental junket after the Civil War and is convinced Utah faces the country with another irrepressible conflict. Mormon immigrants in his eyes are the dregs of ignorant Europe, nourishing Mormon power and iniquity. But Charles Dickens, as the "Uncommercial Traveler," observes a shipload of them aоout to embark from London and finds them, in their class, the pick and flower of England.

Meanwhile a few serene and guileless outsiders such as Eliza Cumming, wife of the governor who replaces Brigham Young, write home charming letters that tell more about what life among the Mormons is really like than pouches full of official reports and books of reform. At the other extreme, a callow Sam Clemens and his clowning contemporary, Artemus Ward, with one eye on the lecture platform, crack standard jokes about the Mormons and gaily perpetuate the world's outlandish image of them.

After 1869 the completed transcontinental railroad brings the curious in droves, forerunners of the modern tourist, eager to gawk at Brigham Young and count the number of bedroom gables in his house. A few see more than polygamy: Phil Robinson sees the inner workings of the United Order co-operatives, and Captain John Codman gets out of Salt Lake and into the settlements to see irrigation transforming the desert. Others go to the famed Salt Lake Theatre, the "cathedral in the desert," or listen to a Mormon sermon in that architectural curiosity, the great Tabernacle; or, like Mrs. Thomas L. Kane, they visit "twelve Mormon homes." After the death of Brigham Young in 1877, travelers can no longer boast an interview with the Lion of the Lord, but the anti-polygamy crusade keeps their reports lively. All are preoccupied with the strife between Mormon and Gentile, the struggle to "liberate" and "Christianize" Utah and bring it to unsullied statehood. It was a poor traveler who did not see a Mormon wife in distress.

But by 1900 Florence A. Merriam can spend a genteel summer in a Mormon village with its sense of an era past, and describe it in the elegiac manner of New England's local colorists. The new century, except for the brief skirmish during the investigation of Mormon Senator Reed Smoot in 1903, finds the Mormon capital the hustling center of scenic America rather than the storm center of religious and political controversy.

It is a long way from the earliest rumors about Joseph Smith's angelic visitations to tourists' views of a society that, after 125 years, is the fruit of those visions. Through its loose chronological arrangement, with introductions providing a thread of narrative, the present anthology reflects the distance and the change. Wherever possible, the brief commentary introducing each selection tells enough about an observer and the circumstances of his visit to explain allusions or a particular bias and give them a setting.

A single volume cannot begin to include all the contemporary accounts,

Foreword

but the obvious polemic and plainly bad reporting of so many of them can be sacrificed without regret. What is left makes, we hope, a collection rich and representative. Omissions within given selections are faithfully indicated. A few observations by Mormons themselves fill gaps that the outside observers left. What may seem repetition now and again is simply a familiar subject seen through another pair of eyes or at a different period, making possible some interesting comparisons. The portraits of Joseph Smith and Brigham Young are particularly numerous, but therefore perhaps all the more valuable, like the different Washingtons that have come down to us.

As far as we know we play no favorites. The Mormons, who are "human beings by birth and saints only by adoption," were great enough to make a considerable stir in history, and the great can afford a few eccentricities.

It is a pleasure to acknowledge the well-wishes of many friends for this collection and the valuable contributions of some, whose help has ranged from a casual suggestion to tireless footwork in ferreting out materials. Dale L. Morgan and Stanley S. Ivins have been especially generous, and the staff of the Utah State Historical Society have been particularly devoted: John James, Jr., Patricia Tull Marti, Tula Murphy, Jane Stites, and Dorothy Summerhays. For a variety of services, always given when we needed them most, we thank Leonard J. Arrington, Eileen S. Barr, George Ellsworth, Mary Lythgoe, Mary Muller, Bryce Nelson, Dorothy Roberts, and Karen M. Russell. Special thanks go to our wives, Gweneth G. Mulder, who typed the whole manuscript, and Florence Mortensen, whose good sense never failed. Finally, we are greatly indebted to Henry Robbins of the editorial staff at Alfred A. Knopf, Inc., for his criticisms and for seeing the work through press, and to Alfred A. Knopf himself, for initially encouraging the idea of the book and for his patience while we prepared the manuscript.

Salt Lake City　　　　　　　　　　　　　WILLIAM MULDER
May 1957　　　　　　　　　　　　　　　A. RUSSELL MORTENSEN

Contents

Contents

Contents

Contents

Among the Mormons

Prologue

THE MORMONS [1]

Robert P. Tristram Coffin

———

Joseph Smith, when he was young,
Saw a golden censer swung,

In the sunset saw two wings
Full of eyes and shining things.

Among the pumpkins in a field
He found a great book, seven-sealed.

Treading furrows Joseph trod
Walked a twilit, comely god.

The beards on New York farmers' jaws
Grew too heavy for small laws.

A Moses or an Abraham
Felt that nations in him swam.

Each Noah and each Hezekiah
Grew white stallions of desire.

Their hearts were spreading tents and wines,
Promised lands, and concubines.

"Bring Urim, Thummim, bring the Ark!"
Cried each belated patriarch.

Brigham Young and Joseph Smith
Called the roll of men of pith.

[1] "The Mormons" is reprinted here from *Collected Poems* by Robert P. Tristram Coffin, by permission of The Macmillan Co.; copyright 1939 by The Macmillan Co.

3

Out of bondage, out of Goshen,
Moved a mighty human ocean.

Illinois and young Missouri
Spurned them from their gates in fury.

Vultures, Indians, and guns
Played about old Abram's sons.

Through the prairie grass they stalked
Leaving bones the sunlight chalked.

At their van by night and day
A god in flames blazed out the way.

The bisons saw them, and they churned
Earth to thunder as they turned.

Mountains rose but never quailed them,
For the hosts of Mormon scaled them.

They burst into a land of salt,
"Here is Canaan, faithful, halt!"

They threw the plowshares from the wagons,
They turned the desert into flagons,

Turned the alkali to grain,
And God applauded and sent rain.

Sons and daughters rose like corn,
The Lord exalted Mormon's horn.

He spun the world four thousand years
Back to Jacob and his steers.

For a season the Lord sped them
For the courage that had led them.

Then he smiled and spun again
The earth upon his golden chain.

Prologue

And the new age caught them up,
Stilled the psaltery, drained the cup.

Mormon's wings grew heavy lead,
And he sank his graying head

On the knees where living bone
Turned to very ancient stone.

All the million eyes grew dim
With the age that crept on him.

Gone the tents and wives and pride,
And the youngest god had died.

Cosmos heard his dying cry,
"Ulla! ulla!" down the sky.

The mammoth and the mastodon
Hailed his spirit coming wan

To the pasture out of space
Where the great dead gods have place.

Bel and Dagon, thundering Thor,
Tiu, the maniac of war.

Gone the concubines and pride,
The oldest god of all had died.

I · GENESIS

I · Genesis

The Times of Joseph Smith

THE MORMON PROPHET'S CAREER was brief but crowded. The fourteen years from the founding of his church in western New York in 1830 to his death in Illinois in 1844 assume an importance reflected in the fullness of the following pages. What otherwise seems a disproportionate amount of space for so short a span is nothing less than the contemporary record of events which determined Mormonism's course for the next hundred years. In his rise from village seer to conscious prophet and presidential candidate, and in his progress from Palmyra to Nauvoo, "the great emporium of the West," Joseph Smith stood out in an age already full of the uncommon doings of common men. A powerful original mind, but untaught by the lessons of history, as Josiah Quincy found him, he came at length to regard himself, in Whittier's words, as "a miracle and a marvel." He provoked deep loyalties and rankling hatreds. The hatreds finally destroyed him; the loyalties kept alive his movement after him.

Early Mormonism was a movement in a very real sense. It developed quickly from a sect into a society endowed with energies and a sense of destiny which kept it constantly in motion. Joseph Smith's unfolding theology seemed tuned to all the reform fiddles of the times. He filled the breathless years with experiments in theocracy and communitarianism and temperance and polygamy, with expectations of millennium and the Second Coming, with worldwide evangelism and practical programs of emigration and colonization, with aspirations and nonconformities which the frontier, despite its vaunted individualism, could not abide. The years run like a fugue. The successive beginnings and trials in Ohio, Missouri, and Illinois frantically pursue each other in contrapuntal repetitions of the same theme, rising to moments of climax until the dominant swell of triumph and tragedy in Nauvoo. The life of the city and very nearly the whole movement ebbs with the martyred prophet's own. What began in supernatural wonder ends in all too human misery.

9

Vitality marks the period as much as motion. The energy was part of the movement, giving it continuity despite one crisis after another. Every trial was the Lord's test of his chosen remnant. The schisms that shattered Mormonism time and again, more critical than inroads from without, only attest its strength. They were signs of the seriousness with which converts and dissenters took their salvation, ready to stake their souls on points of doctrine which a later, less Biblical generation could treat with indifference.

The ensuing narratives by Joseph Smith's intimate disciples—both the loyal and the disaffected, by frontier editors following his fortunes, and by observers aroused by the Mormon commotion, have been selected to interpret as well as report the absorbing chronicle of the 1830's and early 1840's. They reach into the background of the 1820's when there were as yet no Mormons but only forerunners and foreshadowings. The selections serve to establish a sense of place as well as of personalities, and to recapture the excitement of novel ideas as they spurred believers to action and the skeptical to scorn and opposition. In short, they recover the immediate response of the country to each new turn in the incredible fortunes of early Mormonism.

An American Prophet's Own Story

THOUGH HE ONCE ASSERTED that no man knew his history, Joseph Smith left ample if baffling sources for it. His autobiography, a public life edited as the History of the Church *in six volumes, still leaves him an enigma. In 1844, two months before his death, he said: "I don't blame anyone for not believing my history. If I had not experienced what I have, I could not have believed it myself."*

He was a legend long before he committed his own story to print in 1842 in a famous letter to John Wentworth, editor of the Chicago Demo-crat. Remarkable for its economy, the letter affords a swift review of the earliest visions, the discovery and content of the Book of Mormon *record, the rise of an evangelical religion embracing restoration, millennium, and the Second Coming, and its rapid spread in the United States and abroad. On his own assertions Mormonism takes its official and unquestioning stand as a divinely inspired movement.*

An American Prophet's Own Story

Known familiarly in Mormon history as "The Wentworth Letter," it is reproduced here from Times and Seasons *(Nauvoo, Illinois), in which it was originally published on March 1, 1842. The letter concludes with thirteen articles of faith which have become Mormonism's creed in brief, by now familiar the world over, for they are quoted on the back of missionary calling cards in many languages.*

Joseph Smith was thirty-seven when he addressed Mr. Wentworth with such lofty confidence. He was riding a wave of power and influence in Nauvoo that had made the Almighty himself, as the prophet boasted, his right-hand man. But in two short and troubled years the wave spent itself, ending with the prophet's murder in Carthage, Illinois, on June 27, 1844.

I was born in the town of Sharon, Windsor County, Vermont, on the 23d of December, A.D. 1805. When ten years old my parents removed to Palmyra, New York, where we resided about four years, and from thence we removed to the town of Manchester.

My father was a farmer and taught me the art of husbandry. When about fourteen years of age I began to reflect upon the importance of being prepared for a future state, and upon enquiring the plan of salvation I found that there was a great clash in religious sentiment; if I went to one society they referred me to one plan, and another to another; each one pointing to his own particular creed as the *summum bonum* of perfection: considering that all could not be right, and that God could not be the author of so much confusion I determined to investigate the subject more fully, believing that if God had a church it would not be split up into factions, and that if he taught one society to worship one way, and administer in one set of ordinances, he would not teach another principles which were diametrically opposed. Believing the word of God I had confidence in the declaration of James: "If any man lack wisdom let him ask of God who giveth to all men liberally and upbraideth not and it shall be given him." I retired to a secret place in a grove and began to call upon the Lord. While fervently engaged in supplication my mind was taken away from the objects with which I was surrounded, and I was enwrapped in a heavenly vision and saw two glorious personages who exactly resembled each other in features, and likeness, surrounded with a brilliant light which eclipsed the sun at noon-day. They told me that all religious denominations were believing in incorrect doctrines, and that none of them was acknowledged of God as his church and kingdom. And I was expressly commanded to "go not after them," at the same time receiving a promise that the fulness of the gospel should at some future time be made known unto me.

On the evening of the 21st of September, A.D. 1823, while I was praying unto God, and endeavoring to exercise faith in the precious promises of scripture, on a sudden a light like that of day, only of a far purer and more glorious appearance and brightness, burst into the room; indeed the first sight was as though the house was filled with consuming fire; the appearance produced a shock that affected the whole body; in a moment a personage stood before me surrounded with a glory yet greater than that with which I was already surrounded. This messenger proclaimed himself to be an angel of God sent to bring the joyful tidings, that the covenant which God made with ancient Israel was at hand to be fulfilled, that the preparatory work for the second coming of the Messiah was speedily to commence; that the time was at hand for the gospel, in all its fulness to be preached in power, unto all nations that a people might be prepared for the millennial reign.

I was informed that I was chosen to be an instrument in the hands of God to bring about some of his purposes in this glorious dispensation.

I was also informed concerning the aboriginal inhabitants of this country, and shown who they were, and from whence they came; a brief sketch of their origin, progress, civilization, laws, governments, of their righteousness and iniquity, and the blessings of God being finally withdrawn from them as a people was made known unto me: I was also told where there was deposited some plates on which were engraven an abridgment of the records of the ancient prophets that had existed on this continent. The angel appeared to me three times the same night and unfolded the same things. After having received many visits from the angels of God unfolding the majesty and glory of the events that should transpire in the last days, on the morning of the 22d of September, A.D. 1827, the angel of the Lord delivered the records into my hands.

These records were engraven on plates which had the appearance of gold, each plate was six inches wide and eight inches long and not quite so thick as common tin. They were filled with engravings, in Egyptian characters and bound together in a volume, as the leaves of a book with three rings running through the whole. The volume was something near six inches in thickness, a part of which was sealed. The characters on the unsealed part were small, and beautifully engraved. The whole book exhibited many marks of antiquity in its construction and much skill in the art of engraving. With the records was found a curious instrument which the ancients called "Urim and Thummim," which consisted of two transparent stones set in the rim of a bow fastened to a breastplate.

Through the medium of the Urim and Thummim I translated the record by the gift and power of God.

In this important and interesting book the history of ancient America is unfolded, from its first settlement by a colony that came from the tower of Babel, at the confusion of languages, to the beginning of the fifth century of the Christian era. We are informed by these records that America in ancient times has been inhabited by two distinct races of people. The first were called Jaredites and came directly from the tower of Babel. The second race came directly from the city of Jerusalem, about six hundred years before Christ. They were principally Israelites, of the descendants of Joseph. The Jaredites were destroyed about the time that the Israelites came from Jerusalem, who succeeded them in the inheritance of the country. The principal nation of the second race fell in battle towards the close of the fourth century. The remnant are the Indians that now inhabit this country. This book also tells us that our Saviour made his appearance upon this continent after his resurrection, that he planted the gospel here in all its fulness, and richness, and power, and blessing; that they had apostles, prophets, pastors, teachers and evangelists; the same order, the same priesthood, the same ordinances, gifts, powers, and blessing, as was enjoyed on the eastern continent, that the people were cut off in consequence of their transgressions, that the last of their prophets who existed among them was commanded to write an abridgment of their prophecies, history &c., and to hide it up in the earth, and that it should come forth and be united with the Bible for the accomplishment of the purposes of God in the last days. For a more particular account I would refer to the *Book of Mormon*, which can be purchased at Nauvoo, or from any of our travelling elders.

As soon as the news of this discovery was made known, false reports, misrepresentation and slander flew as on the wings of the wind in every direction, the house was frequently beset by mobs and evil designing persons, several times I was shot at, and very narrowly escaped, and every device was made use of to get the plates away from me, but the power and blessing of God attended me, and several began to believe my testimony.

On the 6th of April, 1830, the "Church of Jesus Christ of Latter-Day Saints," * was first organized in the town of Manchester, Ontario County, state of New York. Some few were called and ordained by the spirit of

---

* Originally "Church of Christ" (*Ed. note*).

revelation, and prophecy, and began to preach as the spirit gave them utterance, and though weak, yet were they strengthened by the power of God, and many were brought to repentance, were immersed in the water, and were filled with the Holy Ghost by the laying on of hands. They saw visions and prophesied, devils were cast out and the sick healed by the laying on of hands. From that time the work rolled forth with astonishing rapidity, and churches were soon formed in the states of New York, Pennsylvania, Ohio, Indiana, Illinois and Missouri; in the last named state a considerable settlement was formed in Jackson County; numbers joined the church and we were increasing rapidly; we made large purchases of land, our farms teemed with plenty, and peace and happiness was enjoyed in our domestic circle and throughout our neighborhood; but as we could not associate with our neighbors—who were many of them of the basest of men and had fled from the face of civilized society to the frontier country to escape the hand of justice—in their midnight revels, their sabbath breaking, horseracing, and gambling, they commenced at first to ridicule, then to persecute, and finally an organized mob assembled and burned our houses, tarred, and feathered, and whipped many of our brethren and finally drove them from their habitations; who houseless, and homeless, contrary to law, justice and humanity, had to wander on the bleak prairies till the children left the tracks of their blood on the prairie. This took place in the month of November [1833], and they had no other covering but the canopy of heaven, in this inclement season of the year; this proceeding was winked at by the government, and although we had warrantee deeds for our land and had violated no law, we could obtain no redress.

There were many sick, who were thus inhumanly driven from their houses, and had to endure all this abuse and to seek homes where they could be found. The result was, that a great many of them being deprived of the comforts of life, and the necessary attendances, died; many children were left orphans; wives, widows; and husbands widowers. Our farms were taken possession of by the mob, many thousands of cattle, sheep, horses, and hogs, were taken and our household goods, store goods, and printing press, and type were broken, taken, or otherwise destroyed.

Many of our brethren removed to Clay [County] where they continued until 1836, three years; there was no violence offered but there were threatnings of violence. But in the summer of 1836, these threatnings began to assume a more serious form; from threats, public meetings were called, resolutions were passed, vengeance and destruction were threatened, and affairs again assumed a fearful attitude. Jackson county

14

was a sufficient precedent, and as the authorities in that county did not interfere, they boasted that they would not in this, which on application to the authorities we found to be too true, and after much violence, privation and loss of property we were again driven from our homes.

We next settled in Caldwell and Daviess counties, where we made large and extensive settlements, thinking to free ourselves from the power of oppression, by settling in new counties, with very few inhabitants in them; but here we were not allowed to live in peace, but in 1838 we were again attacked by mobs, an exterminating order was issued by Gov. Boggs, and under the sanction of law an organized banditti ranged through the country, robbed us of our cattle, sheep, horses, hogs &c., many of our people were murdered in cold blood, the chastity of our women was violated, and we were forced to sign away our property at the point of the sword, and after enduring every indignity that could be heaped upon us by an inhuman, ungodly band of marauders, from twelve to fifteen thousand souls—men, women, and children— were driven from their own fire sides, and from lands that they had warrantee deeds of, houseless, friendless, and homeless (in the depth of winter), to wander as exiles on the earth or to seek an asylum in a more genial clime, and among a less barbarous people.

Many sickened and died, in consequence of the cold and hardships they had to endure; many wives were left widows, and children orphans, and destitute. It would take more time than is allotted me here to describe the injustice, the wrongs, the murders, the bloodshed, the theft, misery and woe that has been caused by the barbarous, inhuman, and lawless proceedings of the state of Missouri.

In the situation before alluded to we arrived in the state of Illinois in 1839, where we found a hospitable people and a friendly home, a people who were willing to be governed by the principles of law and humanity. We have commenced to build a city called "Nauvoo" in Hancock County. We number from six to eight thousand here besides vast numbers in the county around and in almost every county of the state. We have a city charter granted us and a charter for a legion the troops of which now number 1500. We have also a charter for a university, for an agricultural and manufacturing society, have our own laws and administrators, and possess all the privileges that other free and enlightened citizens enjoy.

Persecution has not stopped the progress of truth, but has only added fuel to the flame; it has spread with increasing rapidity. Proud of the cause which they have espoused and conscious of their innocence and of the truth of their system, amidst calumny and reproach have the elders of this church gone forth, and planted the gospel in almost every state in the Union; it has penetrated our cities, it has spread over our villages, and has caused thousands of our intelligent, noble, and patriotic citizens to obey its divine mandates and be governed by its sacred truths. It has also spread into England, Ireland, Scotland and Wales: in the year of 1839 where a few of our missionaries were sent over five thousand joined the standard of truth; there are numbers now joining in every land.

Our missionaries are going forth to different nations, and in Germany, Palestine, New Holland, the East Indies, and other places, the standard of truth has been erected: no unhallowed hand can stop the work from progressing; persecutions may rage, mobs may combine, armies may assemble, calumny may defame, but the truth of God will go forth boldly, nobly, and independent till it has penetrated every continent, visited every clime, swept every country, and sounded in every ear, till the purposes of God shall be accomplished and the great Jehovah shall say the work is done.

We believe in God the Eternal Father, and in his son Jesus Christ, and in the Holy Ghost.

We believe that men will be punished for their own sins and not for Adam's transgression.

We believe that through the atonement of Christ all mankind may be saved by obedience to the laws and ordinances of the Gospel.

We believe that these ordinances are 1st, Faith in the Lord Jesus Christ; 2d, Repentance; 3d, Baptism by immersion for the remission of sins; 4th, Laying on of hands for the gift of the Holy Ghost.

We believe that a man must be called of God by "prophecy, and by laying on of hands" by those who are in authority to preach the gospel and administer in the ordinances thereof.

We believe in the same organization that existed in the primitive church, viz: apostles, prophets, pastors, teachers, evangelists &c.

We believe in the gift of tongues, prophecy, revelation, visions, healing, interpretation of tongues &c.

We believe the Bible to be the word of God as far as it is translated correctly; we also believe the *Book of Mormon* to be the word of God.

We believe all that God has revealed, all that he does now reveal, and we believe that he will yet reveal many great and important things pertaining to the kingdom of God.

We believe in the literal gathering of Israel and in the restoration of the Ten Tribes. That Zion will be built upon this continent. That Christ will reign personally upon the earth, and that the earth will be renewed and receive its paradisiac glory.

We claim the privilege of worshipping Almighty God according to the dictates of our conscience, and allow all men the same privilege let them worship how, where, or what they may.

We believe in being subject to kings, presidents, rulers, and magistrates, in obeying, honoring and sustaining the law.

We believe in being honest, true, chaste, benevolent, virtuous, and in doing good to *all men;* indeed we may say that we follow the admonition of Paul "we believe all things, we hope all things," we have endured many things and hope to be able to endure all things. If there is any thing virtuous, lovely, or of good report or praise worthy we seek after these things. Respectfully &c.,

Joseph Smith

A Yankee Household

NEW ENGLAND IS FULL of famous families: the Adamses, the Quincys, the Cabots—and the Smiths and the Macks, in their way equally remarkable. It has been popular to make of Joseph Smith's immediate ancestors a study in disintegration, to see in them a decline, a breakdown of the conservative values of the first 150 years after they came to Massachusetts. They seem an expression of the restlessness that crossed the Alleghenies into the hinterland of New York after the Revolution and went to seed in the greater moral, social, and religious freedom of the frontier. They were poor, ignorant, incompetent drifters— thus the popular image. The log-cabin origins of Joseph Smith's contemporary Abraham Lincoln seem romantic, while the humble circumstances of the Smiths are made a reproach.

Actually they were not very different from the thousands who joined the great migration of the depression years after the war of 1812 and left sterile New England hills for the rumored bounty of the western wilderness. Joseph Smith, Sr., who once taught school, had a "handsome farm" in Vermont when Lucy Mack, whose mother was a schoolteacher, married him, bringing with her a dowry of a thousand dollars. But Jo-

seph was badly worsted when he speculated in exporting ginseng root to China and had to sell his farm and use his wife's dowry to pay his debts, starting them on a long wandering from one place to another, one misfortune to another. Their crops failed three years in succession until in 1816, the "historic year without a summer," they had had enough.

Lucy Mack Smith, with considerable spirit, relates below how she started out from Norwich, Vermont, in a covered buckboard to join her husband. Joseph had gone ahead, bound for the Ohio country, but had stopped instead at Palmyra, New York, where real estate was already touched by the Erie Canal fever and cost dear. The Smiths eventually lost their land in Manchester, just across the line from Palmyra—the hundred acres Lucy describes—after meeting all but the final payment. In a futile attempt to gain time and prevent foreclosure, they secured sixty signatures from among the neighbors attesting their good repute and industry. One season they won the town's fifty-dollar bounty for boiling down the most sugar from their trees.

Lucy Smith dictated her anecdotal reminiscences in 1845, when she was nearly seventy, to Martha Jane Knowlton Coray at Nauvoo. Mrs. Coray left one copy of the manuscript, called "The History of Mother Smith, by Herself," with Lucy and took another to Utah, which she gave to Brigham Young. Orson Pratt, one of Brigham Young's apostles, secured the Smith family manuscript on his way to England, where he published it in Liverpool in 1853 as Biographical Sketches of Joseph Smith the Prophet, and His Progenitors for many Generations. *Twelve years later Brigham Young declared it unauthorized and ordered it suppressed and destroyed. An official version did not appear until 1901, when it was called* History of the Prophet Joseph. *It was revised and reissued as late as 1945 as* History of Joseph Smith by His Mother. *The first selection below comes from the rare Liverpool edition.*

One other selection supplements Lucy Smith's. Though by a contemporary, it was written after the Smith family had won considerable notoriety and it mingles subjective judgments with factual reminiscence. O. Turner wrote his recollections in 1851 in History of the Pioneer Settlement of Phelps and Gorham's Purchase, and Morris' Reserve (*Rochester, 1851*).

I

Mr. Smith now determined to plant once more, and if he should meet with no better success than he had the two preceding years, he would then go to the state of New York, where wheat was raised in abundance.

A Yankee Household

The next year an untimely frost destroyed the crops, and being the third year in succession in which the crops had failed, it almost caused a famine. This was enough; my husband was now altogether decided upon going to New York. He came in, one day, in quite a thoughtful mood, and sat down; after meditating some time, he observed that, could he so arrange his affairs, he would be glad to start soon for New York with a Mr. Howard, who was going to Palmyra. . . .

After his departure, I and those of the family who were of much size, toiled faithfully, until we considered ourselves fully prepared to leave at a moment's warning. We shortly received a communication from Mr. Smith, requesting us to make ourselves ready to take up a journey for Palmyra. In a short time after this, a team came for us. . . .

Having traveled a short distance, I discovered that Mr. Howard, our teamster, was an unprincipled and unfeeling wretch, by the way in which he handled both our goods and money, as well as by his treatment of my children, especially Joseph. He would compel him to travel miles at a time on foot, notwithstanding he was still lame. We bore patiently with his abuse, until we got about twenty miles west of Utica, when one morning, as we were getting ready to continue our journey, my oldest son came to me and said, "Mother, Mr. Howard has thrown the goods out of the wagon, and is about starting off with the team." Upon hearing this, I told him to call the man in. I met him in the bar-room, in the presence of a large company of travelers, both male and female, and I demanded his reason for the course which he was taking. He told me the money which I had given him was all expended, and he could go no further.

I then turned to those present and said, "Gentlemen and ladies, please give your attention for a moment. Now, as sure as there is a God in heaven, that team, as well as the goods, belong to my husband, and this man intends to take them from me, or at least the team, leaving me with eight children, without the means of proceeding on my journey." Then turning to Mr. Howard, I said, "Sir, I now forbid you touching the team, or driving it one step further. You can go about your own business; I have no use for you. I shall take charge of the team myself, and hereafter attend to my own affairs." I accordingly did so, and proceeding on our journey, we in a short time arrived at Palmyra, with a small portion of our effects, and barely two cents in cash.

When I again met my husband at Palmyra, we were much reduced—not from indolence, but on account of many reverses of fortune, with which our lives had been rather singularly marked. Notwithstanding our misfortunes, and the embarrassments with which we were surrounded, I was quite happy in once more having the society of my husband, and in throwing myself and children upon the care and affection of a tender companion and father.

We all now sat down, and counselled together relative to the course which was best for us to adopt in our destitute circumstances, and we came to the conclusion to unite our strength in endeavoring to obtain a piece of land. Having done considerable at painting oil-cloth coverings for tables, stands, etc., I set up the business, and did extremely well. I furnished all the provisions for the family, and besides this, began to replenish our household furniture, in a very short time, by my own exertions.

My husband and his sons, Alvin and Hyrum, set themselves to work to pay for one hundred acres of land, which Mr. Smith contracted for with a land agent. In a year, we made nearly all of the first payment, erected a log house, and commenced clearing. I believe something like thirty acres of land were made ready for cultivation the first year. . . . When the time for making the second payment drew nigh, Alvin went from home to get work, in order to raise the money, and after much hardship and fatigue, returned with the required amount. This payment being made, we felt relieved, as this was the only thing that troubled us; for we had a snug log-house, neatly furnished, and the means of living comfortably. It was now only two years since we entered Palmyra, almost destitute of money, property, or acquaintance. The hand of friendship was extended on every side, and we blessed God, with our whole heart, for his "mercy, which endureth for ever.". . .

The following spring, we commenced making preparations for building another house, one that would be more comfortable for persons in advanced life.

II

Joseph Smith, the father of the prophet . . . first settled in or near Palmyra village, but as early as 1819 was the occupant of some new land on "Stafford street" in the town of Manchester, near the line of Palmyra. Here the author remembers to have first seen the family, in the winter of '19, '20, in a rude log house, with but a small spot underbrushed around it. "Mormon Hill" is near the plank road about half way between the villages of Palmyra and Manchester. The elder Smith had been a Universalist, and subsequently a Methodist; was a good deal of a smatterer in Scriptural knowledge: but the seed of revelation was sown on

20

weak ground; he was a great babbler, credulous, not especially industrious, a money digger, prone to the marvelous; and withal, a little given
to difficulties with neighbors, and petty lawsuits. . . .

Mrs. Smith was a woman of strong uncultivated intellect; artful and
cunning; imbued with an illy regulated religious enthusiasm. . . . she
gave out that such and such ones—always fixing upon those who had
both money and credulity—were to be instruments in some great work
of new revelation. . . .

Joseph Smith, Jr., afterwards "Jo Smith". . . was lounging, idle . . .
and possessed of less than ordinary intellect. The author's own recollections of him are distinct ones. He used to come into the village of Palmyra with little jags of wood, from his backwoods home; sometimes pa-
tronizing a village grocery too freely; sometimes find an odd job to do
about the store of Seymour Scovell; and once a week he would stroll
into the office of the old Palmyra Register, for his father's paper. How
impious, in us young "dare Devils" to once and a while blacken the face
of the then meddling inquisitive lounger—but afterwards Prophet, with
the old fashioned balls, when he used to put himself in the way of the
working of the old fashioned Ramage press! . . .

But Joseph had a little ambition; and some very laudable aspirations;
the mother's intellect occasionally shone out in him feebly, especially
when he used to help us solve some portentous questions of moral or
political ethics, in our juvenile debating club, which we moved down to
the old red schoolhouse on Durfee street, to get rid of the annoyance
of critics that used to drop in upon us in the village; and subsequently,
after catching a spark of Methodism in the camp meeting, away down
in the woods, on the Vienna road, he was a very passable exhorter in
evening meetings.

Dreams and Visions, Signs and Wonders

THE DREAMS AND VISIONS *of Joseph Smith's father, his mother,
and his maternal grandfather were often startling anticipations of his
own divinings. His family's allegorical temper, ready to read a supernatural sign in every unusual occurrence, their prayers and miraculous heal-*

ings, and their heightened expectations based on Biblical prophecy were all reminiscent of the Puritans. John Bunyan's idiom, combining realism and symbol, echoes in the descriptions of their dreams, where the language is scriptural, the color local.

The selection that follows samples this richly imaginative and visionary family endowment. Solomon Mack, Joseph's grandfather, in his old age wrote a lively chapbook, Narrative of the Life of Solomon Mack *(Windsor, 1810), which has been called "an Iliad of woes" for its unrelieved catalog of sufferings and accidents, fever sores, smallpox, falling fits, and broken bones which overtook him during a long life as backwoodsman in Connecticut, sutler in the French and Indian War, artilleryman in the Revolution, sailor to Liverpool, and privateersman in Long Island Sound. All of these adventures he turned to pious account, for at seventy-six he experienced a remarkable religious conversion, became zealous, and often visited the schools to talk to the young on religion. Residents of Gilsum, New Hampshire, remembered him as an old man riding about town on a side-saddle.*

In the 76th year of my age, I was taken with the Rheumatism and confined me all winter in the most extreme pain for most of the time. I under affliction and dispensation of providence, at length began to consider my ways, and found myself destitute of knowledge to extole me to enquire. My mind was imagining, but agitated. I imagined many things; it seemed to me that I saw a bright light in a dark night, when contemplating on my bed which I could not account for, but I thought I heard a voice calling to me again. I thought I saw another light of the same kind, all which I considered as ominous of my own dissolution. I was in distress that sleep departed from my eyes and I literally watered my pillow with tears that I prayed eagerly that God would have mercy on me. . . .

Another night soon after I saw another light as bright as the first, at a small distance from my face, and I thought I had but a few moments to live, and not sleeping nights, and reading, all day I was in misery; well you may think I was in distress, soul and body. At another time, in the dead of the night I was called by my christian name, I arise up to answer to my name. The doors all being shut and the house still, I thought the Lord called and I had but a moment to live. . . . I have often thought that the lights which I saw were to show me what a situation I was in. . . . The calls, I believe, were for me to return to the Lord who would have mercy on me.

Grace Abounding and Religious Revival

THE IMMEDIATE SPUR *to Joseph Smith's youthful religious awakening was a revival in Palmyra—in 1820 as he later told it, in 1823 as his brother William recalled it. It was not a wild affair—not marked by the excesses of the Kentucky frontier—but rather a mild excitement, one in a series of stirrings recurrent in western New York since the Great Revival of 1787–1805. They were times when, according to a local historian, the gospel was "simply preached, plainly, fully, earnestly, affectionately, and constantly." Palmyra, settled for thirty years by 1820, was too stable to take to the barks and the jerks; but it was in the heart of the "burnt-over district" and there were frequent awakenings in its individual churches, occasions when, moved by "abundant and importunate prayer" and an "effusion of the Holy Spirit . . . many were reforming in hope, while multitudes were inquiring the way of salvation."*

A significant prelude to Joseph Smith's rejection of the churches in the midst of this revival was his family's life-long soul-searching and independency. His paternal grandfather, Asael Smith, of Topsfield, Massachusetts, was liberal in his views, leaning, if at all, toward the Universalists, while some of his children attended the Congregational church. Asael could not reconcile Scripture with the conflicting creeds of the sects. Some years before his death in Vermont in 1830, he wrote the charge to his family which is reproduced as the first selection below from Joseph Fielding Smith's Essentials in Church History *(Salt Lake City, 1922). To "search the scriptures and consult sound reason" became a major theme in Mormonism.*

Joseph Smith's mother likewise maintained her independency, despite the efforts of Methodist exhorters and Presbyterian ministers. Like Anne Hutchinson before her, she refused to acknowledge any spiritual authority greater than Scripture and her private convictions. A brother, Jason Mack, became a Seeker at sixteen, "believing that by prayer and faith the gifts of the gospel, which were enjoyed by the ancient disciples of Christ, might be attained." He looked for God in some later time to manifest his power "as He had anciently done—in signs and wonders." For Lucy, Joseph's vision ended the search for a restoration of the "ancient order."

23

In the second selection below, taken from William Smith on Mormonism (*Lamoni, Iowa, 1883*), *William describes his brother Joseph debating the same question that had plagued their mother and grandfather
before him. William's reminiscences had the benefit of his brother's own
account, which he nevertheless confuses, confounding the vision of the
Father and the Son with the visit of the angel Moroni. But the passage
supplies interesting details about the revival and the family's reaction to
Joseph's disclosures.*

I

And first to you, my dear wife, I do with all the strength and power
that is in me, thank you for your kindness and faithfulness to me, be-
seeching God who is the husband of the widow, to take care of you and
not to leave you nor forsake you, or suffer you to leave nor forsake him,
nor his ways. Put your whole trust solely in him, he never did nor never
will forsake any that trust in him. . . . And now my dear children, let
me pour out my heart to you and speak first of immortality in your souls.
Trifle not in this point; the soul is immortal; you have to deal with an
infinite Majesty; you go upon life and death, therefore in this point be
serious. Do all to God in a serious manner; when you think of him, speak
of him, pray to him, or in any way make your addresses to his great
Majesty, be in good earnest. Trifle not with his name or with his attributes, nor call him to witness to any thing but is absolute truth, nor
then, but when sound reason or serious consideration requires it. And as
to religion, I would not wish to point out any particular way for you; but
first I would wish you to search the scriptures and consult sound reason
and see if they (which I take to be two witnesses that stand by the God
of the whole earth) are not sufficient to evince to you that religion is a
necessary theme. . . .

For the public.—Bless God that you live in a land of liberty and bear
yourselves dutifully and conscionably towards the authority under which
you live. See God's providence in the appointment of the Federal Constitution and hold union and order precious jewels.

II

In 1822 and 1823, the people in our neighborhood were very much
stirred up with regard to religious matters by the preaching of a Mr.
Lane, an Elder of the Methodist Church, and celebrated throughout the
country as a "great revival preacher."

My mother, who was a very pious woman and much interested in the welfare of her children, both here and hereafter, made use of every means which her parental love could suggest, to get us engaged in seeking for our souls' salvation, or (as the term then was) "in getting religion." She prevailed on us to attend the meetings, and almost the whole family became interested in the matter, and seekers after truth. I attended the meetings with the rest, but being quite young and inconsiderate, did not take so much interest in the matter as the older ones did. This extraordinary excitement prevailed not only in our neighborhood but throughout the whole country. Great numbers were converted. It extended from the Methodists to the Baptists, from them to the Presbyterians; and so on until finally, all the sects became engaged in it; and it became quite the fashion to "get religion." My mother continued her importunities and exertions to interest us in the importance of seeking for the salvation of our immortal souls, until almost all of the family became either converted or seriously inclined.

After the excitement had subsided, in a measure, each sect began to beat up for volunteers; each one saying, "We are right," "Come and join us," "Walk with us and we will do you good," etc. The consequence was that my mother, my brothers Hyrum and Samuel, older than I, joined the Presbyterian Church. Joseph, then about seventeen years of age, had become seriously inclined, though not "brought out," as the phrase was, [and] began to reflect and inquire, which of all these sects was right. Each one said that it was right; which he knew could not be the case; and the question then was which one of the whole taught the true gospel of Jesus Christ, and made known the plan of salvation. If he went to one he was told they were right, and all others were wrong. If to another, the same was heard from them. Each professed to be the true church. This did not satisfy him, as he was aware that there could be but one way of entering into the Kingdom of Heaven, and that there was but one "straight and narrow path," etc. All this however was beneficial to him, as it urged him forward, and strengthened him in the determination to know for himself of the certainty and reality of pure and holy religion. He continued in secret to call upon the Lord for a full manifestation of his will, the assurance that he was accepted of him, and that he might have an understanding of the path of obedience.

At length he determined to call upon the Lord until he should get a manifestation from him. He accordingly went out into the woods and falling upon his knees called for a long time upon the Lord for wisdom and knowledge. While engaged in prayer a light appeared in the heavens, and descended until it rested upon the trees where he was. It appeared like fire. But to his great astonishment, did not burn the trees. An angel then appeared to him and conversed with him upon many things. He told him that none of the sects were right; but that if he was faithful in keeping the commandments he should receive, the true way should be made known to him; that his sins were forgiven. . . .

The next day I was at work in the field together with Joseph and my eldest brother Alvin. Joseph looked pale and unwell, so that Alvin told him if he was sick he need not work; he then went and sat down by the fence, when the angel again appeared to him, and told him to call his father's house together and communicate to them the visions he had received, which he had not yet told to any one; and promised him that if he would do so they would believe it. He accordingly asked us to come to the house, as he had something to tell us. After we were all gathered, he arose and told us how the angel appeared to him; what he had told him as written above; and that the angel had also given him a short account of the inhabitants who formerly resided upon this continent, a full history of whom he said was engraved on some plates which were hidden, and which the angel promised to show him. He continued talking to us sometime. The whole family were melted to tears, and believed all he said. Knowing that he was very young, that he had not enjoyed the advantages of a common education; and knowing too, his whole character and disposition, they were convinced that he was totally incapable of arising before his aged parents, his brothers and sisters, and so solemnly giving utterance to anything but the truth. All of us, therefore, believed him, and anxiously awaited the result of his visit to the hill Cumorah, in search of the plates containing the record of which the angel told him.

"Something Is a Going to Take Place"

ON FEBRUARY 12, 1830, Lucius Fenn of Covert, New York, wrote a letter to an old neighbor in Winchester, Connecticut. Along with antimasonry, intemperance, and the considerable stir religion was making that winter in the lake country, a book being printed at Palmyra, some *fifty miles away, was the news of the day. It was a bible, Fenn wrote, concealed for fourteen hundred years and now revealed to a man who could not read at all in English but who could read its gold leaves which told of "the Millenniam day" and "when it is a going to take place." It was all very singular in a time of "general solemnity upon the people in these parts," and Fenn could only hope there would be "a greater outpouring of the spirit than ever."*

Lucius Fenn's letter to Birdseye Bronson is a rare piece of Americana. Never before published, it is the oldest known contemporary evidence, other than newspaper notices, of the rumors that preceded the appearance of the Book of Mormon itself: "there was it is said an angel appeared. . . ." Papers in western New York had been publishing advance notices of the book since the previous June, describing it as the Golden Bible and even reproducing its preface and its opening chapters. Fenn's letter indicates how rapidly such news had become common knowledge and reflects what the papers had been saying about the forthcoming book's strange origin and miraculous translation. The terms "Mormons" and "Mormonism," of course, do not appear in his letter. They did not become current until after the publication of the Book of Mormon on March 26, 1830, and the formation of Joseph Smith's "Church of Christ" shortly after on April 6.

It is significant that Fenn should mention the persecution of the Freemasons in western New York, an attack marked by lurid exposures, hysteria, and violence. After 1827 it grew to extraordinary proportions, the fanatic antimasonic agitation spreading into Ohio, Pennsylvania, and New England to become the equally fanatic Antimasonic Party which promoted the early political fortunes of figures like Thurlow Weed, Thaddeus Stevens, and William H. Seward. Mormonism was to experience the same blind prejudice and mass hatred that greeted Masonry: alarmists ironically denied both of them free speech, freedom of association, and freedom of religion in the name of liberty. Like Freemasonry, Mormonism bred suspicion because to nativists it seemed secret, undemocratic, and subversive of American institutions.

Pertinent parts of the Lucius Fenn letter are reproduced below through the courtesy of the William Robertson Coe Collection of Western Americana at Yale University Library, which holds the original manuscript. Mr. Stanley S. Ivins of Salt Lake City kindly made his photostat copy of the original available for transcribing and helped to decipher a sometimes puzzling hand. Spelling and punctuation, but not the idiom, have been standardized for clarity.

I · GENESIS

Dear Sir

I have been very anxious to hear from Winchester this some time but I do not expect to unless I write first. . . . It is always the case, in every place there is something to make hard feelings. We have had some trouble in this State for 2 or 3 years back. Freemasonry has done something or the freemasons here made a great deal of trouble and talk for some time past and it has come to that, we do not have any of them in any kind of office not even and in some churches they have turned them out of the church. But it has at present not been the subject as much as has been. They have now something else to talk about. Now the subject is this—the cold sober societies are now the conversations. Now I think myself that there is need enough of them. We think that it has done good and we are in hopes that it will do more for I think that it is of a very great importance and there ought to be something done to stop the progress of intemperance, for it has gone to a great extent in this country and we hope that we shall in some measure stop its progress. This will do for a while and this will be an old story and then we will try something else. There is something that has taken place lately that is mysterious to us. It is this—there has been a bible found by 3 men but a short distance from us which is something remarkable we think. There was it is said an angel appeared to these 3 men and told them that there was a bible concealed in such a place and if one of them would go to that place he would find it. He went and found as the angel said. It was in a stone chest. What is most to be wondered at is this that the man that found it could not read at all in the English language but he read this bible and nobody else cannot. It has been concealed there for fourteen hundred years. It is written on a kind of gold leaf. It is the same that ours is only there is an addition to it. They are a printing it in Palmyra. It is expected that it will come out soon so that we can see it. It speaks of the Millenniam [sic] day and tells when it is a going to take place and it tells that the man that is to find this bible his name is Joseph and his father's name is Joseph. Some people think that it is all a speculation and some think that something is a going to take place different from what has been. For my part I do not know how it will be but it is something singular to me. As it respects religion there has been considerable of an attention paid to it this winter between these lakes and there has been considerable many as we humbly hope have been renewed by the grace of God. There is a general solemnity upon the people generally in these parts and we hope that there will be a greater out-

28

pouring of the spirit than ever. So now you see I have given you short account of what is a doing here. . . . We should like to see you all very much indeed but we do not expect to very soon for it seems to me the most like home of any place that I ever lived, but the land is nothing to be compared to this for this is the best that I ever saw in my life I think. But the people are not so respectable as they are amongst you but we cannot expect to have every thing exactly right always. I do not know as I have any thing else to write at present only as I said before you must answer me and give our respects to all of our friends. These few lines are from your

friend   Lucius Fenn

N B Direct your letter to Covert, Seneca County, State of Newyork to be left at Chauncy Pratt's post office and it will certainly come.

A *Farmer's Excitement*

WHAT WAS SINGULAR *news in Lucius Fenn's letter had been common talk in and around Palmyra for some time. As much as any one, Martin Harris had noised the word about. The town, which respected him as a quick-tempered and disputatious but prosperous farmer who knew his Bible by heart, was amazed at his endorsement of a visionary with a seer stone. He had become friendly with the Smith family in 1826 and "very sanguine in his belief," according to his wife, "that Joseph could see in his stone anything he wished." When Harris mortgaged his farm for $3,000 to pay for an edition of 5,000 copies of the* Book of Mormon *at E. B. Grandin's printshop, neighbors thought him daft. Nothing daunted, Harris provisioned the prophet while he worked on his book, even serving for a time as his scribe. He took a copy of some "caractors" drawn from the plates to antiquarian Samuel L. Mitchell of Rutgers and Charles Anthon, professor of classics at Columbia, hoping to secure a certificate attesting the authenticity of the transcript as "reformed Egyptian." When they turned the simple farmer out, he was only the more convinced the work was of God.*

To his unbelieving wife Lucy it was all a trial. Several years later she

*swore in an affidavit how "unreasonable" he had become. Once "indus-
trious, attentive to his domestic concerns, and thought to be worth about
ten thousand dollars," she could only grieve at this attachment to Joseph
Smith: "Whether the Mormon religion be true or false, I leave the world
to judge, for its effects upon Martin Harris have been to make him more
cross, turbulent and abusive to me." They finally separated; Martin followed the Mormons to Kirtland, Ohio, where he had a falling out and
was lost to the church: "I never left the church; the church left me." In
1869 a Mormon missionary found him still in Ohio and brought him out
to Utah, where he often retold the story of his intimate role as "one of
the original Mormons," as he described himself. His grave in Clarkston,
Utah, is frequently visited by those who honor him as one of the "Three
Witnesses" to the Book of Mormon.*

*The selection below is taken from an interview with Martin Harris
held in Ohio in January, 1859, and published in Tiffany's Monthly (New
York) in two installments in May and June the same year.*

The first time I heard of the matter, my brother Presarved Harris, who
had been in the village of Palmyra, asked me if I had heard about Joseph Smith, jr., having a golden bible. My thoughts were that the money-
diggers had probably dug up an old brass kettle, or something of the
kind. I thought no more of it. This was about the first of October, 1827.
The next day after the talk with my brother, I went to the village, and
there I was asked what I thought of the Gold Bible? I replied, The
Scripture says, He that answereth a matter before he heareth it, it is
foolishness unto him. I do not wish to make myself a fool. I don't know
anything about it. Then said I, what is it about Joe's Gold Bible?
They then went on to say that they put whiskey into the old man's [Jo-
seph Smith, Sr.] cider and got him half drunk, and he told them all
about it. They then repeated his account, which I found afterwards to
agree substantially with the account given by Joseph. Then said I to
them, how do you know that he has not got such gold plates? They replied, "Damn him! angels appear to men in this enlightened age! Damn
him, he ought to be tarred and feathered for telling such a damned lie!"
Then I said, suppose he has told a lie, as old Tom Jefferson said, it did
[not] matter to him whether a man believed in one god or twenty. It
did not rob his pocket, nor break his shins. What is it to us if he has
told a lie? He has it to answer for if he has lied. If you should tar and
feather all the liars, you would soon be out of funds to purchase the material.

I then thought of the words of Christ, The kingdom divided against itself cannot stand. I knew they were of the devil's kingdom, and if that is of the devil, his kingdom is divided against itself. I said in my heart, this is something besides smoke. There is some fire at the bottom of it. I then determined to go and see Joseph as soon as I could find time.

A day or so before I was ready to visit Joseph, his mother came over to our house and wished to talk with me. I told her I had no time to spare, she might talk with my wife, and, in the evening when I had finished my work I would talk with her. When she commenced talking with me, she told me respecting his bringing home the plates, and many other things, and said that Joseph had sent her over and wished me to come and see him. I told her that I had a time appointed when I would go, and that when the time came I should then go, but I did not tell her when it was. I sent my boy to harness my horse and take her home. She wished my wife and daughter to go with her; and they went and spent most of the day. When they came home, I questioned them about them. My daughter said, they were about as much as she could lift. They were now in the glass-box, and my wife said they were very heavy. They both lifted them. I waited a day or two, when I got up in the morning, took my breakfast, and told my folks I was going to the village, but went directly to old Mr. Smith's. I found that Joseph had gone away to work for Peter Ingersol to get some flour. I was glad he was absent, for that gave me an opportunity of talking with his wife and the family about the plates. I talked with them separately, to see if their stories agreed, and I found they did agree. When Joseph came home I did not wish him to know that I had been talking with them, so I took him by the arm and led him away from the rest, and requested him to tell me the story, which he did as follows. He said: "An angel had appeared to him, and told him it was God's work.". . . Joseph had before this described the manner of his finding the plates. He found them by looking in the stone found in the well of Mason Chase. The family had likewise told me the same thing.

Joseph said the angel told him he must quit the company of the money-diggers. That there were wicked men among them. He must have no more to do with them. He must not lie, nor swear, nor steal. He told him to go and look in the spectacles, and he would show him the man that would assist him. That he did so, and he saw myself, Martin Harris, standing before him. That struck me with surprise. I told him I wished him to be very careful about these things. "Well," said he, "I saw you standing before me as plainly as I do now." I said, if it is the devil's work I will have nothing to do with it; but if it is the Lord's, you can have all the money necessary to bring it before the world. He said the angel told him that the plates must be translated, printed and sent before the world. I said, Joseph, you know my doctrine, that cursed is every one that putteth his trust in man, and maketh flesh his arm; and we know that the devil is to have great power in the latter days to deceive if possible the very elect; and I don't know that you are one of the elect. Now you must not blame me for not taking your word. If the Lord will show me that it is his work, you can have all the money you want.

While at Mr. Smith's I hefted the plates, and I knew from the heft that they were lead or gold, and I knew that Joseph had not credit enough to buy so much lead. I left Mr. Smith's about eleven o'clock and went home. I retired to my bedroom and prayed God to show me concerning these things, and I covenanted that if it was his work and he would show me so, I would put forth my best ability to bring it before the world. He then showed me that it was his work, and that it was designed to bring in the fullness of his gospel to the gentiles to fulfill his word, that the first shall be last and the last first. He showed this to me by the still small voice spoken in the soul. Then I was satisfied that it was the Lord's work, and I was under a covenant to bring it forth.

The excitement in the village upon the subject had become such that some had threatened to mob Joseph, and also to tar and feather him. They said he should never leave until he had shown the plates. It was unsafe for him to remain, so I determined that he must go to his father-in-law's in Pennsylvania. He wrote to his brother-in-law Alvah Hale, requesting him to come for him. I advised Joseph that he must pay all his debts before starting. I paid them for him, and furnished him money for his journey. I advised him to take time enough to get ready, so that he might start a day or two in advance: for he would be mobbed if it was known when he started. We put the box of plates into a barrel about one-third full of beans and headed it up. I informed Mr. Hale of the matter, and advised them to cut each a good cudgel and put into the wagon with them, which they did. It was understood that they were to start on Monday; but they started on Saturday night and got through safe. This was the last of October, 1827. It might have been the first of November.

Village Seer

LONG BEFORE Martin Harris befriended him Joseph Smith had won a considerable local reputation as an imaginative youth with awesome powers of second sight. By means of a luminous stone he could locate lost articles and look deep into the earth for buried treasure. His family took pride in his powers, which he himself took seriously. Before the golden plates started him on a religious career, he had frequently been called upon to display his rural divining. As far as Chenango County, two days' journey away, they had heard, as his mother put it, that "he possessed certain means by which he could discern things invisible to the natural eye."

Villagers who did not appreciate his creative talents, his rich fantasy, simply considered him an abandoned liar. Parson Reed warned him one day he "was going to hell for his lying habits." But Daniel Hendrix, who set type for the Book of Mormon, *remembered him as jovial, easy-going, quick to make warm friends, a "romancer of the first water," a good talker who would have made "a fine stump speaker" with training. "I never knew so ignorant a man as Joe was to have such a fertile imagination." As prophet, Joseph deliberately cultivated his transcendentalism: "I am a rough stone. The sound of the hammer and chisel was never heard on me until the Lord took me in hand. I desire the learning of heaven alone."*

The selection below recalls something of the youth who was a natural seer before he became a conscious prophet. Joseph Smith's apologists wince unnecessarily at his early activities. Digging for money was neither uncommon nor disreputable. The Palmyra Herald *on July 24, 1822, quoted the Montpelier (Vermont)* Watchman *as saying that "We could name, if we pleased, at least five hundred respectable men, who do, in the simplicity and sincerity of their hearts, verily believe that immense treasures lie concealed upon our green mountains; many of whom have been for a number of years, most industriously and perseveringly engaged in digging it up."*

The selection that follows is an unusual account of young Joseph's encounter with the law in 1826 in South Bainbridge, later Afton, where he had gone at the request of Josiah Stoal (here called Isaiah Stowell) to hunt for Spanish silver. W. D. Purple published his recollections of the trial, based on notes made at the time, in the Chenango Union (Norwich, New York), on May 2, 1877. They are reproduced here from a notarized typescript copy made from an original issue of the Union too spoiled by water damage to photostat.

It was while working for Mr. Stoal that Joseph boarded at the home of Isaac Hale in Harmony, Pennsylvania, at the Great Bend of the Susquehanna, where he met Hale's daughter Emma and eloped with her—she was of age—to New York. The father-in-law remained unimpressed by Joseph's later role as prophet; he sourly remembered that Joseph at his marriage had said he had given up what he called "glass-looking" and had promised to work hard for a living.

More than fifty years since, at the commencement of his professional career, the writer spent a year in the present village of Afton, in this County. It was then called South Bainbridge, and was in striking contrast with the present village at the same place. It was a mere hamlet, with one store and one tavern. The scenes and incidents of that early day are vividly engraven upon his memory, by reason of his having written them when they occurred, and by reason of his public and private rehearsals of them in later years. He will now present them as historical reminiscences of old Chenango, and as a precursor of the advent of the wonder of the age, Mormonism.

In the year 1825 we often saw in that quiet hamlet, Joseph Smith, Jr., the author of the Golden Bible, or the Book of Mormon. He was an inmate of the family of Deacon Isaiah Stowell, who resided some two miles below the village, on the Susquehanna. Mr. Stowell was a man of much force of character, of indomitable will, and well fitted as a pioneer in the unbroken wilderness that this country possessed at the close of the last century. He was one of the Vermont sufferers, who for defective titles, consequent on the forming a new State from a part of Massachusetts in 1791, received wild lands in Bainbridge. He had been educated in the spirit of orthodox puritanism, and was officially connected with the first Presbyterian church of the town, organized by Rev. Mr. Chapin. He was a very industrious, exemplary man, and by severe labor and frugality had acquired surroundings that excited the envy of many of his less fortunate neighbors. He had at this time grown up sons and daughters to share his prosperity and the honors of his name.

About this time he took upon himself a monomaniacal impression to seek for hidden treasures which he believed were buried in the earth. He hired help and repaired to Northern Pennsylvania, in the vicinity of Lanesboro, to prosecute his search for untold wealth which he believed to be buried there. Whether it was the "Ninety bars of gold/ and dollars many fold" that Capt. Robert Kidd, the pirate of a preceding century, had despoiled the commerce of the world, we are not able to say, but that he took his help and provisions from home and camped out on the black hills of that region for weeks at a time was freely admitted by himself and family.

What success, if any, attended these excursions is unknown, but his hallucinations adhered to him like the fabled shirt of Nessus and had entire control over his mental character. The admonition of his neighbors, the members of his church, and the importunities of his family had no impression on his wayward spirit.

There had lived a few years previous to this date, in the vicinity of Great Bend, a poor man named Joseph Smith, who, with his family, had removed to the western part of the State, and lived in squalid poverty near Palmyra, in Ontario County. Mr. Stowell, while at Lanesboro, heard of the fame of one of his sons, named Joseph, who, by the aid of a magic stone, had become a famous seer of lost or hidden treasures. These stories were fully received into his credulous mind, and kindled into a blaze his cherished hallucination. Visions of untold wealth appeared through this instrumentality, to his longing eyes. He harnessed his team, and filled his wagon with provisions for "man and beast," and started for the residence of the Smith family. In due time he arrived at the humble log-cabin, midway between Canandaigua and Palmyra, and found the sought for treasure in the person of Joseph Smith, Jr., a lad of some eighteen years of age. He, with the magic stone, was at once transferred from his humble abode to the more pretentious mansion of Deacon Stowell. Here, in the estimation of the Deacon, he confirmed his conceded powers as a seer by means of the stone which he placed in his hat and, by excluding the light from all other terrestial things, could see whatever he wished, even in the depths of the earth. This omniscient attribute he firmly claimed. Deacon Stowell and others as firmly believed it. Mr. Stowell, with his ward and two hired men, who were, or professed to be, believers, spent much time in mining near the State line on the Susquehanna and many other places. I myself have seen the evidences of their nocturnal depredations on the 'face of Mother Earth, on the Deacon's farm, with what success "this deponent saith not."

In February, 1826, the sons of Mr. Stowell, who lived with their father, were greatly incensed against Smith, as they plainly saw their father squandering his property in the fruitless search for hidden treasures, and saw that the youthful seer had unlimited control over the illusions of their sire. They made up their minds that "patience had ceased to be a virtue," and resolved to rid themselves and their family from this incubus, who, as they believed, was eating up their substance and depriving them of their anticipated patrimony. They caused the arrest of Smith as a vagrant, without visible means of livelihood. The trial came on in the above mentioned month, before Albert Neeley, Esq., the father of Bishop Neeley of the State of Maine. I was an intimate friend of the Justice, and was invited to take notes of the trial, which I did. There was a large collection of persons in attendance, and the proceedings attracted much attention.

The affidavits of the sons were read, and Mr. Smith was fully examined by the Court. . . . He said when he was a lad, he heard of a neighboring girl some three miles from him, who could look into a glass and see anything however hidden from others; that he was seized with a strong desire to see her and her glass; that after much effort he induced his parents to let him visit her. He did so, and was permitted to look in the glass, which was placed in a hat to exclude the light. He was greatly surprised to see but one thing, which was a small stone, a great way off. It soon became luminous, and dazzled his eyes, and after a short time it became as intense as the mid-day sun. He said that the stone was under the roots of a tree or shrub as large as his arm, situated about a mile up a small stream that puts in on the South side of Lake Erie, not far from the New York and Pennsylvania line. He often had an opportunity to look in the glass, and with the same result. The luminous stone alone attracted his attention. This singular circumstance occupied his mind for some years, when he left his father's house, and with his youthful zeal traveled west in search of this luminous stone.

He took a few shillings in money and some provisions with him. He stopped on the road with a farmer, and worked three days, and replenished his means of support. After traveling some one hundred and fifty miles he found himself at the mouth of the creek. He did not have the glass with him, but he knew its exact location. He borrowed an old ax and a hoe, and repaired to the tree. With some labor and exertion he found the stone, carried it to the creek, washed and wiped it dry, sat down on the bank, placed it in his hat, and discovered that time, place and distance were annihilated; that all the intervening obstacles were removed, and that he possessed one of the attributes of Deity, an All-Seeing-Eye. He arose with a thankful heart, carried his tools to their owner, turned his feet towards the rising sun, and sought with weary limbs his long deserted home.

On the request of the Court, he exhibited the stone. It was about the size of a small hen's egg, in the shape of a high-instepped shoe. It was composed of layers of different colors passing diagonally through it. It was very hard and smooth, perhaps by being carried in the pocket.

Joseph Smith, Sr., was present, and sworn as a witness. He confessed at great length all that his son had said in his examination. He delineated his characteristics in his youthful days—his visions of the luminous stone in the glass—his visit to Lake Erie in search of the stone—and his wonderful triumphs as a seer. He described very many instances of his finding hidden and stolen goods. He swore that both he and his son were mortified that this wonderful power which God had so miraculously given him should be used only in search of filthy lucre, or its equivalent in earthly treasures, and with a long-faced, "sanctimonious seeming," he said his constant prayer to his Heavenly Father was to manifest His will concerning this marvelous power. He trusted that the Son of Righteousness would some day illumine the heart of the boy, and enable him to see His will concerning Him. These words have ever had a strong impression on my mind. They seemed to contain a prophetic vision of the future history of that mighty delusion of the present century, Mormonism. The "old man eloquent" with his lank and haggard visage—his form very poorly clad—indicating a wandering vagabond rather than an oracle of future events, has, in view of those events, excited my wonder, if not my admiration.

The next witness called was Deacon Isaiah Stowell. He confirmed all that is said above in relation to himself, and delineated many other circumstances not necessary to record. He swore that the prisoner possessed all the power he claimed, and declared he could see things fifty feet below the surface of the earth, as plain as the witness could see what was on the Justice's table, and described very many circumstances to confirm his words. Justice Neeley soberly looked at the witness and in a solemn, dignified voice, said, "Deacon Stowell, do I understand you as swearing before God, under the solemn oath you have taken, that you *believe* the prisoner can see by the aid of the stone fifty feet below the surface of the earth, as plainly as you can see what is on my table?" "Do I *believe* it?" says Deacon Stowell, "do I believe it? No, it is not a matter of belief. I positively know it to be true.". . . It is hardly necessary to say that, as the testimony of Deacon Stowell could not be impeached, the prisoner was discharged, and in a few weeks he left the town.

Greene, April 28, 1877

"We Hear You Have a Gold Bible"

WORD THAT Joseph Smith had an ancient treasure piqued the curiosity of the countryside. The greedy were for finding it if it were a reality; the pious for persuading the Smiths it was a delusion. Lucy Mack Smith describes many stratagems the family used to outwit the ransackers: they buried, or faked the burial of, the box of plates in a barrel of meal, in a hollow birch log in the woods, in flax stowed in the loft, under the hearth, under the floor of a cooper's shop, until, as Martin Harris relates in an earlier selection, Joseph Smith fled to Harmony, Pennsylvania, with them hidden in a cask of beans.

No one ever saw the plates, except eleven selected witnesses, who saw them with their "spiritual eyes." No one could look upon them with natural sight and live. Intimates "hefted" them, felt their outlines, and guessed at the shape of the Urim and Thummim beneath a covering cloth, but never took a furtive look. As translator, Joseph always sat behind a curtain and dictated, at first to his wife Emma and to Martin Harris, who showed 116 pages of the manuscript to his skeptical wife, only to have her confiscate and destroy them, bringing the work to a prolonged standstill.

In the spring of 1829, Oliver Cowdery, a district schoolteacher originally from Vermont, came to board with the elder Smiths in Manchester, heard of Joseph's marvel, and went to Harmony to serve as his scribe. The dictating went forward rapidly. "These days," Cowdery remembered, "were never to be forgotten—to sit under the sound of a voice dictated by the inspiration of heaven, awakened the utmost gratitude of this bosom. Day after day I continued, uninterrupted, to write from his mouth, as he translated with the Urim and Thummim, or, as the Nephites would have said, 'Interpreters,' the history or record called the 'Book of Mormon.'"

38

"We Hear You Have a Gold Bible"

*When in June, 1829, Joseph Smith in spite of the scoffers actually
did produce a book-length manuscript and obtained a copyright as
"Author and Proprietor," efforts turned to preventing its publication.
Egbert B. Grandin of Palmyra at first refused to undertake the book;
Thurlow Weed, editor of the* Advertiser *in Rochester, also turned it
down. When Martin Harris agreed to mortgage part of his farm for the
required $3,000, Grandin reconsidered and in July, 1829, began setting
type, with the manuscript brought him in sections and always closely
guarded.*

*Lucy Smith describes some of the opposition below, the passages
coming, as before, from her* Biographical Sketches.

The printing went on very well for a season, but the clouds of persecution again began to gather. The rabble, and a party of restless religionists, began to counsel together, as to the most efficient means of putting
a stop to our proceedings.

About the first council of this kind was held in a room adjoining
that in which Oliver [Cowdery] and a young man by the name of
Robinson were printing. Mr. Robinson, being curious to know what
they were doing in the next room, applied his ear to a hole in the
partition wall, and by this means overheard several persons expressing
their fears in reference to the Book of Mormon. One said, "it was destined
to break down everything before it, if not put a stop to," and, "that it
was likely to injure the prospects of their ministers," and then inquired,
whether they should endure it. "No, no," was the unanimous reply. It
was then asked, "how shall we prevent the printing of this book?" Upon
which it was resolved by the meeting, that three of their company should
be appointed to go to the house of Mr. Smith, on the following Tuesday
or Wednesday, while the men were gone to their work, and request
Mrs. Smith to read the manuscript to them; that, after she had done
reading it, two of the company should endeavor to divert her attention
from it to some other object, while the third, seizing the opportunity,
should snatch it from the drawer, or wherever it should be kept, and
commit it immediately to the flames.

"Again," said the speaker, "suppose we fail in this, and the book is
printed in defiance of all that we can do to the contrary, what means
shall we then adopt? Shall we buy their books and allow our families
to read them?" They all responded, "No." They then entered into a
solemn covenant, never to purchase even a single copy of the work, or

permit one member of their families to buy or read one, that they might thus avert the awful calamity which threatened them. . . .

On the fourth day subsequent to the afore-mentioned council, soon after my husband left the house to go to his work, those three delegates appointed by the council, came to accomplish the work assigned them. Soon after they entered, one of them began thus:—

"Mrs. Smith, we hear that you have a gold bible; we have come to see if you will be so kind as to show it to us?"

"No, gentlemen," said I, "we have no gold bible, but we have a translation of some gold plates, which have been brought forth for the purpose of making known to the world the plainness of the Gospel, and also to give a history of the people which formerly inhabited this continent." I then proceeded to relate the substance of what is contained in the Book of Mormon, dwelling particularly upon the principles of religion therein contained. I endeavored to show them the similarity between these principles, and the simplicity of the Gospel taught by Jesus Christ in the New Testament. "Notwithstanding all this," said I, "the different denominations are very much opposed to us. The Universalists are alarmed lest their religion should suffer loss, the Presbyterians tremble for their salaries, the Methodists also come, and they rage, for they worship a God without body or parts, and they know that our faith comes in contact with this principle."

After hearing me through, the gentlemen said, "Can we see the manuscript, then?"

"No, sir," replied I, "you cannot see it. I have told you what it contains, and that must suffice."

He made no reply to this, but said, "Mrs. Smith, you and the most of your children have belonged to our church for some length of time, and we respect you very highly. You say a good deal about the Book of Mormon, which your son has found, and you believe much of what he tells you, yet we cannot bear the thoughts of losing you, and they do wish—I wish, that if you do believe those things, you would not say anything more upon the subject—I do wish you would not."

"Deacon Beckwith," said I, "if you should stick my flesh full of faggots, and even burn me at the stake, I would declare, as long as God should give me breath, that Joseph has got that Record, and that I know it to be true."

At this, he observed to his companions, "You see it is of no use to say anything more to her, for we cannot change her mind." Then, turning to me, he said, "Mrs. Smith, I see that it is not possible to persuade you out of your belief, therefore I deem it unnecessary to say anything more upon the subject."

"No, sir," said I, "it is not worth your while."

=====

Governor Harding's Recollection

CURIOUSLY ENOUGH, a future governor of the Territory of Utah happened to be in Palmyra in 1829 in E. B. Grandin's printshop at the moment proof of the title page of the Book of Mormon *was struck; at the Smith home, moreover, he listened to passages read aloud from the original manuscript. Stephen S. Harding of Milan, Indiana, wrote letters on two different occasions recollecting the events of his 1829 visit, one on June 1, 1867, published in Pomeroy Tucker's* Origin, Rise, and Progress of Mormonism *(New York, 1867), and the other, in greater detail, in February, 1882, reproduced here from Thomas Gregg,* The Prophet of Palmyra *(New York, 1890).*

By 1882 Judge Harding was an octogenarian and in feeble health, but sharp in memory. His brief term as governor of the Territory of Utah (for one year, from June, 1862, to July, 1863) was marked by an unfortunate turn from initial good feeling between him and the Mormons to bitter misunderstanding, a circumstance which certainly did not soften his view of early Mormonism as ignorant and superstitious. His reference to the Brookville Enquirer's *notice about the Golden Bible as early as 1827 is evidence to believers that Joseph Smith did not fake his chronology of discovery.*

In the summer of 1829, I resolved to return to the place of my nativity, in the vicinity of Palmyra, N.Y. It was from this place that my father had emigrated in the spring of 1820, with his large family, to the newly admitted State of Indiana. This was before the days of railroads, and I took stage from Cincinnati for Cleveland, from Cleveland down the lake shore for Buffalo, where I saw, for the first time, the great canal, only recently completed. On this I took passage for Palmyra. . . .

When I left my home in the West, I had never heard of Mormonism, by that name. When I was a student at Brookville, in the fall of 1827,

41

the Brookville *Enquirer* was laid upon my table, when my eye fell upon a paragraph, credited to some Eastern paper, of the finding of a book of metallic plates, called the "Golden Bible." It was found by a young man by the name of Joe Smith, who had spent his time for several years in telling fortunes and digging for hidden treasures, and especially for pots and iron chests of money, supposed to have been buried by Captain Kidd. This paragraph interested me more at the time from the fact that all this had happened near the village of Palmyra, N.Y. I had at the time no certain recollection as to who this "Joe Smith" was, but remembered having seen a long-legged, tow-headed boy of that name, who was generally fishing in the mill-pond at Durfee's grist-mill, on Mud Creek, when my elder brother and I went to mill. This boy was about three years older than myself, and it turned out that he was the veritable finder of the "Golden Bible."

Of course the paragraph in the *Enquirer* passed without further notice at the time, and the whole subject was forgotten, until I found myself in the very neighborhood where the thing had happened. At that time the *Book of Mormon* had not been printed, and no Mormon church had been organized. I do not believe that such a thing as the latter had ever been seriously contemplated, and that the publication of the *Book of Mormon* had for its object only the making of money, by publishing and putting on sale a book that could be readily sold as a curiosity at a high profit. Nevertheless, there was something so unusual in the affair, that it excited a good deal of curiosity and comment. . . .

Upon my return to Palmyra, and learning that Martin Harris was the only man of any account, as we say in the West, among all of his near associates, it was but natural that I should seek an early interview with him. I found him at the printing office of the Wayne *Sentinel* in Palmyra, where the *Book of Mormon* was being printed. He had heard several days before of my arrival in the neighborhood, and expressed great pleasure at seeing me. A moment or two after, I was introduced to Oliver Cowdery, Joseph Smith, Sen., and then to the young "Prophet" himself.

Here was a most remarkable quartette of persons. I soon learned that at least three of them were in daily attendance at the printing-office, and that they came and went as regularly as the rising and setting of the sun. I have the authority of Martin Harris himself, who stated that some one hundred and fifty pages, more or less, of the original manuscript of the *Book of Mormon* had been stolen, lost, or destroyed, by some evil-minded person, and that the angel of the Lord had appeared to young

Joseph and informed him that the devil had appeared in the form of a man or woman, and had possessed himself of the sacred MS.; and Joseph had been commanded by the angel to thenceforth always have at least three witnesses to watch over it when in the hands of the printers. This was the reason given me at the time by Harris, why at least three persons should bring the MS. to the office immediately after sunrise, and take it away before sunset in the evening.

After my introduction to Cowdery and the Smiths, I entered into conversation with them—especially with Cowdery and the father of the prophet. But young Joe was hard to be approached. He was very taciturn, and sat most of the time as silent as a Sphynx, seeming to have no recollection of ever having seen me when fishing in Durfee's mill-pond. This young man was by no means of an ordinary type. He had hardly ever been known to laugh in his childhood; and would never work or labor like other boys; and was noted as never having had a fight or quarrel with any other person. But notwithstanding this last redeeming trait, he was hard on birds' nests, and in telling what had happened would exaggerate to such an extent, that it was a common saying in the neighborhood: "That is as big a lie as young Joe ever told."

He was about six feet high, what might be termed long-legged, and with big feet. His hair had turned from tow-color to light auburn, large eyes of a bluish gray, a prominent nose, and a mouth that of itself was a study. His face seemed almost colorless, and with little or no beard. . . .

I had arrived at the printing-office about nine in the morning, and after my interview with Harris, and introduction, as aforesaid, I spent an hour or two with E. B. Grandin and Pomeroy Tucker, proprietor and foreman of the *Sentinel*. From these gentlemen I learned many particulars that were new to me. I expressed a desire to read the manuscript then in process of being printed; but was informed by them that that was hardly possible, inasmuch as a few sheets only at a time were used as copy in the hands of the printers; and that probably Cowdery and Smith would have no objection to reading it to me, if I would give them an opportunity without interfering with their duties at the office.

It was now noon, and I went home with my cousin (Mr. Tucker) to dinner. On returning to the office, I found Harris, Cowdery, and the Smiths had remained, substituting a lunch for a regular dinner. My intimacy with them was renewed, and Harris talked incessantly to me on the subject of dreams, and the fearful omens and signs he had seen in the heavens. Of course I became greatly interested, and manifested a desire to hear the miraculous MS. read; and it was agreed that I should go out with them to the house of the elder Smith, and remain over night. In the mean time, I remarked that but one at a time left the printing office, even for a short period.

The sun had now got down to the roofs of the houses, and the typos had laid by their work. Each page of the MS. that had been used as copy was delivered to Cowdery, and we prepared to return to Smith's. We arrived at our destination a few minutes before sunset. The Smith residence consisted of a log house, not exactly a cabin. Upon our arrival, I was ushered into the best room in company with the others. In a few moments I was left alone, my companions having gone out on private business. An interview with the family was being held by them in the other part of the house. It was not long before they returned, accompanied by Lucy Smith, the Prophet's mother. She came close to me, and taking me by the hand, said: "I've seed you before. You are the same young man that had on the nice clothes, that I seed in my dream. You had on this nice ruffled shirt, with the same gold breast-pin in it that you have now. Yes, jest ezactly sich a one as this!"—suiting the action to the word, taking hold of the ruffle, and scrutinizing the pin closely. It was not long till she left the room, and I, following to the door, saw two stout, bare-footed girls, each with a tin bucket of red raspberries. Soon after, the old man announced that supper was ready. We went into the other part of the house, where supper was waiting, consisting of brown bread, milk, and abundance of fine raspberries before mentioned. There was no lack of these, and if any left the table without a really good supper, it was not the fault of the hostess. She, good soul—full sister to all her sex—began to make excuses, saying: "If I had only known what a nice visitor I was goin' to have, I would have put on the table flour bread, and not ryn' Injun."

I remarked that it needed no excuses; that the supper was good enough for a king, and that the berries on the table were better than could be bought in any city in America. Beside being true, this had the effect of quieting the feelings of the old lady.

It was now time to begin the reading of the manuscript, and we retired to the room we had occupied. This was before the days of lucifer matches, and there being no fire, it took some time before a light could be brought into the room. This was done by our good hostess, who set upon the table a tin candlestick with a tallow dip in it, remarking: "This is the only candle I can find in the house; I thought I had two, but mabby the rats has eat it up."

Cowdery commenced his task of reading at the table, the others sitting around. The reading had proceeded for some time, when the candle began to spit and splutter, sometimes almost going out, and flashing up with a red-blue blaze. Here was a phenomenon that could not be mistaken. To say that the blaze had been interrupted by the flax shives that remained in the tow wicking, would not do; but Martin Harris arrived at a conclusion "across lots": "Do you see that," said he, directing his remark to me and the old lady, who sat beside him. "I know what that means; it is the Devil trying to put out the light, so that we can't read any more." "Yes," replied the old lady; "I seed 'im! I seed 'im! as he tried to put out the burnin' wick, when the blaze turned blue."

The tallow dip shortened at such a fearful rate that the further reading had to be abandoned. It was now past ten, and the other members of the family retired. The MS. was carefully put away, and directions given as to where we were to sleep. In the meantime Mother Smith loaded a clay pipe with tobacco, which she ground up in her hands; a broom splint was lighted in the candle, and the delicious fumes issued in clouds from the old lady's mouth.

She now began to talk incessantly for the little time that remained, and told me at some length the dream that she had, when I appeared before her, "in the nice suit of clothes and ruffled shirt," as she expressed it; and continued: "You'll have bad dreams, mebby, to-night; but don't git skeered; the angel of the Lord will protect you."

After breakfast, in the morning, Mother Smith followed me as I arose from the table, and plied me with questions as to whether I had had dreams, and whether I had seen a vision that "skeered" me. I told her I had a dream, but so strange that I could not tell it to her or any one else. The fact was communicated to Harris and the rest. All saw that I looked sober, and I determined to leave them in doubt and wonder.

We started back to Palmyra, Cowdery bearing in his hand the sacred scroll. Martin was exceedingly anxious that I should give him at least some glimpse of the strange things I had seen in my dream. I told him that was impossible, and I began to doubt whether I ought to tell it to any human being. They all became interested in my reply; and the prophet himself, forgetting his taciturnity, said: "I can tell you what it was. I have felt just as you do. Wait, and the angel of the Lord will open your eyes." Here we parted and I returned to the home of my brother. . . .

About four weeks afterwards I again visited Palmyra, and spent part of the day in the printing-office, where I found the prophet, Cowdery, and Harris again. The latter took me by the hand with a grip and a shake that were full of meaning; even the prophet himself shook hands with me, looking me steadily in the eye as if new ideas possessed him in regard to myself; and it was evident that my dream had been repeated to these people, and that it was a puzzle to them all.

In the meantime the printing of the *Book of Mormon* was proceeding. There was abundant evidence that the proof sheets had been carefully corrected. The printing was done on a lever press of that period; and when a sufficient number of pages for the entire edition of five thousand copies had been completed, the type had to be distributed. This was a slow process in comparison with what is done in a jobbing office of to-day. Mr. Tucker, the foreman, had just received from Albany a font of new type, and had set up with his own hands the title page of the *Book of Mormon*, and preparations were now ready for the first impression. About this time the prophet's father also came in. He, too, had evidently heard of my dream, and shook my hand most cordially. Mr. Grandin and two or three typos were present, as if curious in seeing the first impression of the title page. Tucker took up the ink-balls and made the form ready; then laying the blank sheet upon it, with one pull at the lever the work was done; then taking the impression, looked at it a moment, passed it to Cowdery, who scanned it carefully, and passed it to the prophet himself, who seemed to be examining every letter, and without speaking gave it into the hands of his father and Harris. It was then returned to Tucker. Of course we all looked at it with more or less curiosity, and the work was pronounced excellent. Tucker, who was my cousin, then handed it to me, saying: "Here, Steve, I'll give this to you. You may keep it as a curiosity." I thanked him, and put it carefully in my pocket.

Pedlar's Progress

WITH THE Book of Mormon *a reality, however satirically received by the press, Joseph Smith on April 6, 1830, formed a little company of believers into a Church of Christ, an American church with its own scripture. By June it numbered thirty, with the Smith family in Man-*

chester, the Peter Whitmer family in Fayette, and Martin Harris and Oliver Cowdery its mainstays. Oliver took the canal route east "with a load of 'Gold Bibles,'" as the Palmyra Reflector *put it, "under command to declare the truth (according to Jo Smith) in all the principal cities of the Union." Joseph himself sought out old friends in the Susquehanna country, where he won a small following and got his first taste of persecution. His brother Samuel meanwhile, with a knapsack full of copies of the* Book of Mormon *to sell at $1.25, set out as missionary. In her* Biographical Sketches, *excerpted below, his mother preserves his recital of what befell him.*

The new gospel spread by contact as well as rumor. The Book of Mormon *was its contagious carrier. The most notable consequence of Samuel's peddling that first summer of the "new dispensation" was the conversion of Brigham Young, one in a dramatic series of conversions touched off when young Samuel, on a hunch, left a copy with a reluctant Reverend Greene.*

On the thirtieth of June, Samuel started on the mission to which he had been set apart by Joseph, and in traveling twenty-five miles, which was his first day's journey, he stopped at a number of places in order to sell his books, but was turned out of doors as soon as he declared his principles. When evening came on, he was faint and almost discouraged, but coming to an inn, which was surrounded with every appearance of plenty, he called to see if the landlord would buy one of his books. On going in, Samuel enquired of him, if he did not wish to purchase a history of the origin of the Indians.

"I do not know," replied the host, "how did you get hold of it?"

"It was translated," rejoined Samuel, "by my brother, from some gold plates that he found buried in the earth."

"You d—d liar!" cried the landlord, "get out of my house—you shan't stay one minute with your books."

Samuel was sick at heart, for this was the fifth time he had been turned out of doors that day. He left the house, and traveled a short distance, and washed his feet in a small brook, as a testimony against the man. He then proceeded five miles further on his journey, and seeing an apple tree a short distance from the road, he concluded to pass the night under it; and here he lay all night upon the cold, damp ground. In the morning, he arose from his comfortless bed, and observing a small cottage at no great distance, he drew near, hoping to get a little refreshment. The only inmate was a widow, who seemed very poor. He asked her for food, relating the story of his former treatment. She prepared him victuals, and, after eating, he explained to her the history of the Book of Mormon. She listened attentively, and believed all that he told her, but, in consequence of her poverty, she was unable to purchase one of the books. He presented her with one, and proceeded to Bloomington, which was eight miles further. Here he stopped at the house of one John P. Greene, who was a Methodist preacher, and was at that time about starting on a preaching mission. He, like the others, did not wish to make a purchase of what he considered at that time to be a non-sensical fable; however, he said that he would take a subscription paper, and, if he found anyone on his route who was disposed to purchase, he would take his name, and in two weeks, Samuel might call again, and he would let him know what the prospect was of selling. After making this arrangement, Samuel left one of his books with him, and returned home. At the time appointed, Samuel started again for the Rev. John P. Greene's, in order to learn the success which this gentle-man had met with in finding sale for the Book of Mormon. This time, Mr. Smith and myself accompanied him, and it was our intention to have passed near the tavern, where Samuel was so abusively treated a fort-night previous, but just before we came to the house, a sign of small-pox intercepted us. We turned aside, and meeting a citizen of the place, we enquired of him, to what extent this disease prevailed. He answered, that the tavern keeper and two of his family had died with it not long since, but he did not know that any one else had caught the distemper, and that it was brought into the neighborhood by a traveler, who stopped at the tavern over night.

This is a specimen of the peculiar disposition of some individuals, who would purchase their death for a few shillings, but sacrifice their soul's salvation rather than give a Saint of God a meal of victuals. According to the word of God, it will be more tolerable for Sodom and Gomorrah, in the day of judgment, than for such persons.

We arrived at Esquire Beaman's, in Livonia, that night. The next morning Samuel took the road to Mr. Greene's, and finding that he had made no sale of the books, we returned home the following day. . . .

After relating to us the success he [Samuel] had met with at Canan-daigua, he gave us an account of his third mission to Livonia:

"When I arrived at Mr. Greene's," said he, "Mrs. Greene informed me that her husband was absent from home, that there was no prospect of selling my books, and even the one which I had left with them, she expected I would have to take away, as Mr. Greene had no disposition to purchase it, although she had read it herself, and was much pleased with it. I then talked with her a short time, and, binding my knapsack upon my shoulders, rose to depart; but, as I bade her farewell, it was impressed upon my mind to leave the the book with her. I made her a present of it, and told her that the Spirit forbade me taking it away. She burst into tears, and requested me to pray with her. I did so, and afterwards explained to her the most profitable manner of reading the book which I had left with her; which was, to ask God, when she read it, for a testimony of the truth of what she had read, and she would receive the Spirit of God, which would enable her to discern the things of God. I then left her, and returned home."

I shall now turn aside from my narrative, and give a history of the above book. When Mr. Greene returned home, his wife requested him to read it, informing him very particularly with regard to what Samuel had said to her, relative to obtaining a testimony of the truth of it. This, he, for a while, refused to do, but finally yielded to her persuasions, and took the book, and commenced perusing the same, calling upon God for the testimony of his Spirit. The result of which was, that he and Mrs. Greene were in a short time baptized. They gave the book to Phineas Young, Mrs. Greene's brother, who read it, and commenced preaching it forthwith. It was next handed to Brigham Young, and from him to Mrs. Murray, his sister, who is also the mother of Heber C. Kimball's wife. They all received the work without hesitancy, and rejoiced in the truth thereof. Joseph Young was at this time in Canada, preaching the Methodist doctrine; but, as soon as Brigham became convinced of the truth of the Gospel, as contained in the Book of Mormon, he went straightway to his brother Joseph, and persuaded him to cease preaching Methodism, and embrace the truth, as set forth in the Book of Mormon, which he carried with him.

Thus was this book the means of convincing this whole family, and bringing them into the Church, where they have continued faithful members from the commencement of their career until now. And, through their faithfulness and zeal, some of them have become as great and honorable men as ever stood upon the earth.

Parley Parker Pratt Seeks Salvation

THE EARLIEST MORMONS *were forerunners as well as followers of Joseph Smith, whose miraculous narrative seemed only the natural outcome of their own seeking. Parley Parker Pratt's* Autobiography, *a classic of American religious literature, reflects the state of mind which made ready converts of so many dissatisfied sectarians in the New York, Pennsylvania, and Ohio country. Born in 1807 in Burlington, Otsego County, in upstate New York, Pratt was plagued early by all the religious doubts and longings of the "burnt-over district." As a boy of twelve he read Revelation on the first resurrection and felt "an inexpressible anxiety to secure to myself a part in a resurrection so glorious. I felt the weight of worlds—of eternal worlds resting upon me."*

In 1826, when the following selection opens, he was nineteen years of age, and discouraged. He had lost a seventy-acre farm at Oswego on Lake Ontario when he could find no market for his crop, and he had been as yet unable to testify to "an experience of religion" which would admit him to the Baptist Society. "Weary and disconsolate," he fled civilization, like Cooper's Leatherstocking, and sought a forest retreat in Ohio. But his encounter with Joseph Smith in 1830 marked the beginning of an eventful career as missionary, writer, and colonizer among the Mormons. He converted his brilliant brother Orson Pratt, who became the foremost theologian of the new faith; and on his first mission "into the wilderness" in 1830, Parley won over the influential Sidney Rigdon and his Reformed Baptists, a large-scale conversion which made Kirtland, Ohio, the first Mormon headquarters.

Joseph Smith called him "Archer of Paradise": his eloquent books like Voice of Warning *and* Key to Theology, *and his hymns, articles, and tracts for* The Latter-day Saints' Millennial Star, *which he edited in England, were effective arrows in his quiver of divinity. They provided basic formulations of the prophet's doctrines of Zion and the Second Coming. As one of Joseph Smith's close circle of twelve apostles, Pratt participated in all of Mormonism's major experiences in Ohio, Missouri, Illinois, and England, and, under Brigham Young, in the Far West. On May 13, 1857, he was killed by desperadoes on the Arkansas frontier*

50

and became in the eyes of his people "another great apostle and martyr of the nineteenth century."

The following passage, which concludes with an eloquent portrait of the prophet, is taken from The Autobiography of Parley Parker Pratt, *edited by his son Parley P. Pratt (New York, 1874). The Autobiography has gone through four editions.*

In the autumn of 1826 I resolved to bid farewell to the civilized world—where I had met with little else but disappointment, sorrow and unrewarded toil; and where sectarian divisions disgusted and ignorance perplexed me—and to spend the remainder of my days in the solitudes of the great west, among the natives of the forest.

There, at least, thought I, there will be no buying and selling of lands—no law to sweep all the hard earnings of years to pay a small debt—no wranglings about sects, and creeds, and doctrines. I will win the confidence of the red man; I will learn his language; I will tell him of Jesus; I will read to him the Scriptures; I will teach him the arts of peace; to hate war, to love his neighbor, to fear and love God, and to cultivate the earth. Such were my resolutions.

In October, 1826, I took leave of my friends and started westward. I paid most of my money in Rochester for a small pocket Bible, and continued my journey as far as Buffalo. At this place I engaged a passage for Detroit, on board a steamer; as I had no money, I agreed to work for the same.

After a rough passage and many delays, I was at length driven by stress of weather to land at Erie, in Pennsylvania; from whence I travelled by land till I came to a small settlement about thirty miles west of Cleveland, in the State of Ohio. The rainy season of November had now set in; the country was covered with a dense forest, with here and there a small opening made by the settlers, and the surface of the earth one vast scene of mud and mire; so that travelling was now very difficult, if not impracticable.

Alone in a land of strangers, without home or money, and not yet twenty years of age, I became discouraged, and concluded to stop for the winter; I procured a gun from one of the neighbors; worked and earned an axe, some breadstuff and other little extras, and retired two miles into a dense forest and prepared a small hut, or cabin, for the winter. Some leaves and straw in my cabin served for my lodging, and a good fire kept me warm. A stream near my door quenched my thirst; and fat venison, with a little bread from the settlements, sustained me for food. The storms of winter raged around me; the wind shook the forest, the wolf howled in the distance, and the owl chimed in harshly to complete the doleful music which seemed to soothe me, or bid me welcome to this holy retreat. But in my little cabin the fire blazed pleasantly, and the Holy Scriptures and a few other books occupied my hours of solitude. Among the few books in my cabin, were McKenzie's travels in the Northwest, and Lewis and Clark's tour up the Missouri and down the Columbia rivers.

Spring came on again; the woods were pleasant, the flowers bloomed in their richest variety, the birds sung pleasantly in the groves; and, strange to say, my mind had become attached to my new abode. I again bargained for a piece of forest land; again promised to pay in a few years, and again commenced to clear a farm and build a house.

I was now twenty years of age.

I resolved to make some improvements and preparations, and then return to my native country, from which I had been absent several years. There was one there whom my heart had long loved, and from whom I would not have been so long separated, except by misfortune. . . . [Pratt returns to Canaan, Columbia County in New York to court Miss Thankful Halsey, whom he marries on September 9, 1827. He brings her back to his Ohio clearing.]

Eighteen months had passed since our settlement in the wilderness. The forest had been displaced by the labors of the first settlers for some distance around our cottage. A small frame house was now our dwelling, a garden and a beautiful meadow were seen in front, flowers in rich profusion were clustering about our door and windows; while in the background were seen a thriving young orchard of apple and peach trees, and fields of grain extending in the distance, beyond which the forest still stood up in its own primeval grandeur, as a wall to bound the vision and guard the lovely scene. Other houses and farms were also in view, and some twenty children were returning from the school actually kept by my wife, upon the very spot where two years before I had lived for months without seeing a human being.

About this time one Mr. Sidney Rigdon came into the neighborhood as a preacher, and it was rumored that he was a kind of Reformed Baptist, who, with Mr. Alexander Campbell, of Virginia, a Mr. Scott, and some other gifted men, had dissented from the regular Baptists, from whom they differed much in doctrine. At length I went to hear him, and what was my astonishment when I found he preached faith in Jesus Christ, repentance towards God, and baptism for remission of sins, with the promise of the gift of the Holy Ghost to all who would come forward, with all their hearts, and obey this doctrine!

Here was the *ancient gospel* in due form. Here were the very principles which I had discovered years before; but could find no one to minister in. But still one great link was wanting to complete the chain of the ancient order of things; and that was, the *authority* to minister in holy things—the apostleship, the power which should accompany the form. This thought occurred to me as soon as I heard Mr. Rigdon make proclamation of the gospel. . . .

After hearing Mr. Rigdon several times, I came out, with a number of others, and embraced the truths which he taught. We were organized into a society, and frequently met for public worship.

About this time I took it upon me to impart to my neighbors, from time to time, both in public and in private, the light I had received from the Scriptures concerning the gospel, and also concerning the fulfilment of the things spoken by the holy prophets. I did not claim any authority as a minister; I felt the lack in this respect; but I felt in duty bound to enlighten mankind, so far as God had enlighted me.

At the commencement of 1830, I felt drawn out in an extraordinary manner to search the prophets, and to pray for an understanding of the same. My prayers were soon answered, even beyond my expectations; the prophecies of the holy prophets were opened to my view; I began to understand the things which were coming on the earth—the restoration of Israel, the coming of the Messiah, and the glory that should follow. I was so astonished at the darkness of myself and mankind on these subjects that I could exclaim with the prophet: surely, "*darkness covers the earth, and gross darkness the people.*"

I was all swallowed up in these things. I felt constrained to devote my time in enlightening my fellow men on these important truths, and in warning them to prepare for the coming of the Lord. . . . [In August, 1830, Pratt and his wife close out their wilderness home and proceed to Cleveland, where they take passage on a schooner bound for Buffalo, and from there set out for Albany by canal boat. At Newark, a small town 100 miles from Buffalo, Pratt takes leave of his wife "for a season," feeling he has "a work to do" in the region.]

It was early in the morning, just at the dawn of day; I walked ten miles into the country, and stopped to breakfast with a Mr. Wells. I proposed to preach in the evening. Mr. Wells readily accompanied me through the neighborhood to visit the people, and circulate the appointment.

We visited an old Baptist deacon by the name of Hamlin. After hearing of our appointment for evening, he began to tell of a *book*, a STRANGE BOOK, A VERY STRANGE BOOK! in his possession, which had been just published. This book, he said, purported to have been originally written on plates either of gold or brass, by a branch of the tribes of Israel; and to have been discovered and translated by a young man near Palmyra, in the State of New York, by the aid of visions, or the ministry of angels. I inquired of him how or where the book was to be obtained. He promised me the perusal of it, at his house the next day, if I would call. I felt a strange interest in the book. I preached that evening to a small audience, who appeared to be interested in the truths which I endeavored to unfold to them in a clear and lucid manner from the Scriptures. Next morning I called at his house, where, for the first time, my eyes beheld the BOOK OF MORMON—that book of books . . . which was the principal means, in the hands of God, of directing the entire course of my future life.

I opened it with eagerness, and read its title page. I then read the testimony of several witnesses in relation to the manner of its being found and translated. After this I commenced its contents by course, I read all day; eating was a burden, I had no desire for food; sleep was a burden when the night came, for I preferred reading to sleep.

As I read, the spirit of the Lord was upon me, and I knew and comprehended that the book was true, as plainly and manifestly as a man comprehends and knows that he exists. My joy was now full, as it were, and I rejoiced sufficiently to more than pay me for all the sorrows, sacrifices and toils of my life. I soon determined to see the young man who had been the instrument of its discovery and translation.

I accordingly visited the village of Palmyra, and inquired for the residence of Mr. Joseph Smith. I found it some two or three miles from the village. As I approached the house at the close of the day I overtook a man who was driving some cows, and inquired of him for Mr. Joseph Smith, the translator of the *Book of Mormon*. He informed me that he now resided in Pennsylvania; some one hundred miles distant. I inquired for his father, or for any of the family. He told me that his father had gone a journey; but that his residence was a small house just before me; and, said he, I am his brother. It was Mr. Hyrum Smith. I informed him of the interest I felt in the Book, and of my desire to learn more about it. He welcomed me to his house, and we spent the night together; for neither of us felt disposed to sleep. We conversed most of the night, during which I unfolded to him much of my experience in my search after truth. . . .

In the morning I was compelled to take leave of this worthy man and his family—as I had to hasten back a distance of thirty miles, on foot, to fulfill an appointment in the evening. As we parted he kindly presented me with a copy of the Book of Mormon. I had not yet completed its perusal, and was glad indeed to possess a copy of my own. I travelled on a few miles, and, stopping to rest, I commenced again to read the book. . . . I esteemed the Book, or the information contained in it, more than all the riches of the world. Yes; I verily believe that I would not at that time have exchanged the knowledge I then possessed, for a legal title to all the beautiful farms, houses, villages and property which passed in review before me, on my journey through one of the most flourishing settlements of western New York. . . .

I now returned immediately to Hyrum Smith's residence, and demanded baptism at his hands. I tarried with him one night, and the next day we walked some twenty-five miles to the residence of Mr. Whitmer, in Seneca County. Here we arrived in the evening, and found a most welcome reception.

This was the family, several of whose names were attached to the *Book of Mormon* as witnesses—Mr. Joseph Smith having translated much of the book in Whitmer's chamber.

I found the little branch of the church in this place full of joy, faith, humility and charity. We rested that night, and on the next day, being about the 1st of September, 1830, I was baptized by the hand of an Apostle of the Church of Jesus Christ, by the name of Oliver Cowdery. This took place in Seneca Lake, a beautiful and transparent sheet of water in Western New York.

A meeting was held the same evening, and after singing a hymn and prayer, Elder Cowdery and others proceeded to lay their hands upon my head in the name of Jesus, for the gift of the Holy Ghost. After which I was ordained to the office of an Elder in the Church, which included authority to preach, baptize, administer the sacrament, administer the Holy Spirit, by the laying on of hands in the name of Jesus Christ and to take the lead of meetings of worship.

I now felt that I had authority in the ministry. . . .

I now commenced my labors in good earnest [among his kin at the old homestead]. I addressed crowded audiences almost every day, and the people who had known me from a child, seemed astonished—knowing that I had had but little opportunity of acquiring knowledge by study; and while many were interested in the truth, some began to be filled with envy, and with a lying, persecuting spirit. My father, mother, aunt Van Cott, and many others, believed the truth in part; but my brother Orson, a youth of nineteen years, received it with all his heart, and was baptized at that time, and has ever since spent his days in the ministry. . . .

Having lifted a warning voice to multitudes in all this region of country, I now took leave, and repaired again to the western part of New York, and to the body of the Church.

On our arrival, we found that brother Joseph Smith, the translator of the *Book of Mormon*, had returned from Pennsylvania to his father's residence in Manchester, near Palmyra, and here I had the pleasure of seeing him for the first time.

He received me with a hearty welcome, and with that frank and kind manner so universal with him in after years.

On Sunday we held meeting at his house; the two large rooms were filled with attentive listeners, and he invited me to preach. I did so, and afterwards listened with interest to a discourse from his own mouth, filled with intelligence and wisdom. We repaired from the meeting to the water's edge, and, at his request, I baptized several persons.

President Joseph Smith was in person tall and well built, strong and active; of a light complexion, light hair, blue eyes, very little beard, and of an expression peculiar to himself, on which the eye naturally rested with interest, and was never weary of beholding. His countenance was ever mild, affable, beaming with intelligence and benevolence; mingled with a look of interest and an unconscious smile, or cheerfulness, and entirely free from all restraint or affectation of gravity; and there was something connected with the serene and steady penetrating glance of his eye, as if he would penetrate the deepest abyss of the human heart, gaze into eternity, penetrate the heavens, and comprehend all worlds.

He possessed a noble boldness and independence of character; his manner was easy and familiar; his rebuke terrible as the lion; his benevolence unbounded as the ocean; his intelligence universal, and his language abounding in original eloquence peculiar to himself—not polished—not studied—not smoothed and softened by education and refined by art; but flowing forth in its own native simplicity, and profusely abounding in variety of subject and manner. He interested and edified, while, at the same time, he amused and entertained his audience; and none listened to him that were ever weary with his discourse. I have even known him to retain a congregation of willing and anxious listeners for many hours together, in the midst of cold or sunshine, rain or wind, while they were laughing at one moment and weeping the next. Even his most bitter enemies were generally overcome, if he could once get their ears.

I have known him when chained and surrounded with armed murderers and assassins who were heaping upon him every possible insult and abuse, rise up in the majesty of a son of God and rebuke them, in the name of Jesus Christ, till they quailed before him, dropped their weapons, and, on their knees, begged his pardon, and ceased their abuse.

In short, in him the characters of a Daniel and a Cyrus were wonderfully blended. The gifts, wisdom and devotion of a Daniel were united with the boldness, courage, temperance, perseverance and generosity of a Cyrus. And had he been spared a martyr's fate till mature manhood and age, he was certainly endued with powers and ability to have revolutionized the world in many respects, and to have transmitted to posterity a name associated with more brilliant and glorious acts than has yet fallen to the lot of mortal. As it is, his works will live to endless ages, and unnumbered millions yet unborn will mention his name with honor, as a noble instrument in the hands of God, who, during his short and youthful career, laid the foundation of that kingdom spoken of by Daniel, the prophet, which should break in pieces all other kingdoms and stand forever.

Away to the Ohio

"ALL ETERNITY IS PAINED," declared the prophet in the beginning of 1831, "and the angels are waiting the great command to reap down the earth, to gather the tares that they may be burned." But the Lord would lead the Saints to a refuge, a land of promise which they and their children should possess forever as an "inheritance." Zion would be established somewhere in the west. For the present the church would gather in and around Kirtland, Ohio, where the Campbellites were proving hospitable to the new gospel. Their celebrated preacher Sidney Rigdon had embraced it and had come east to see the prophet. Now, in January, 1831, Joseph Smith and his wife accompanied Rigdon on

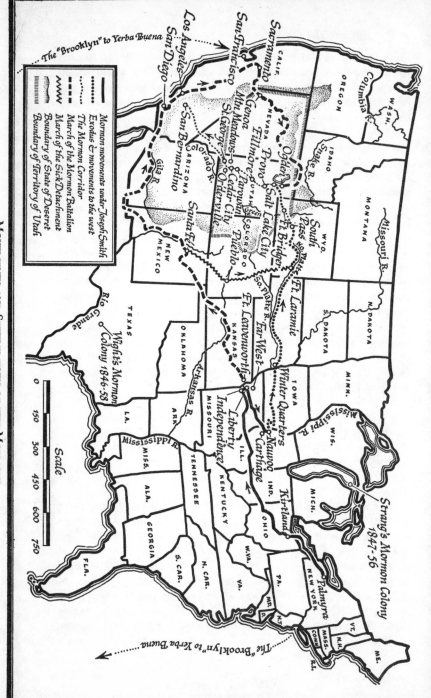

MOVEMENTS AND SETTLEMENTS OF THE MORMONS

his return to Kirtland, calling on the New York believers to follow them—to sell or rent their farms and bring their poor with them. On January 6 Mother Smith wrote her brother Solomon in Gilsum, New Hampshire: "There have been three hundred added to the Church in Ohio within a few weeks, and there are some added to this Church almost daily. The work is spreading very fast. . . . We expect to go away to the Ohio early in the spring."

The prophet's westward urge, expressed in the doctrines of gathering and of inheritance, came in the wake of a momentous missionary journey that Oliver Cowdery, the recently converted Parley Pratt, and two companions undertook in the fall of 1830. On that preaching tour of four months and 1,500 miles they had converted Sidney Rigdon, raised up churches all over the Western Reserve, presented the Book of Mormon *to three Indian tribes who thanked them for "this news concerning the book of our forefathers," and, penetrating the wilderness of upper Missouri, had come at length to Independence, then little more than a trading post on the westernmost frontier of the United States. Pratt gave an enthusiastic report of the expedition to Joseph Smith, who was already in Kirtland and finding the place very much to his liking. But Missouri, heartland of the continent, was Old Eden in the prophet's theology, and there, he determined, the Saints would build their New Jerusalem. Ohio and Missouri thus became the dual stage of Mormon action for the better part of the 1830's.*

Newspapers like the antimasonic Telegraph *at Painesville, Ohio, on the shores of Lake Erie not far from Kirtland, observed the coming of the Mormons with a lively, irreverent interest. But perhaps the earliest account about the Mormons at Kirtland to appear in a book was Nancy Towle's. Her description of her visit in September, 1831, forms part of* Vicissitudes Illustrated *(Portsmouth, N.H., 1833), the record of her experiences as a free-lance evangelist in both Europe and America. A former New Hampshire schoolmistress, Nancy Towle had been "bearing public testimony" since 1821, moving freely among the denominations and traveling extensively in Canada, New England, and the east. Two years before her Kirtland visit she had been to England, where she was called "an elect lady" and "a person of piety and usefulness." She even ventured into Ireland to inveigh against "popish errors."*

As the account below opens, she had made her way from Boston to Albany, thence by canal boat to Buffalo, and down Lake Erie to Painesville. Her punctuation, rather freely given to dashes, has here been modified.

To the state of Ohio, I desired to go. . . . A very singular people (both of origin and practice) had attracted my attention, whose particular place of gathering, at this time, was there. I had heard much of the people, and in many places the excitement I found considerably in their favor; but many were *halting between two opinions* respecting them, and wishing to be informed. . . .

Accordingly I took the steam-boat in company with Elizabeth, and we travelled down the Lake, and landed at Painesville, Ohio. From thence we went direct to Kirtland, where we met with the people referred to, and were entertained of E. Marsh, from the city of Boston. Just as we reached the place (which appeared providential), all of their chief Elders arrived home: so that we had every opportunity of informing ourselves respecting them, which was desirable. . . . To the faith of the Apostles, some of them profess already to have attained; particularly Mr. S——, whom they call their "Seer." He could do many wonderful things.

They believe . . . "That a day of great wrath, is bursting upon all the kindred, of the earth; and that, in *Mount Zion, and in Jerusalem,* alone, *shall be deliverance in that day,"* (even in the land, which the Lord Jesus had given to them, for a dwelling-place, *and an everlasting posses-sion*). The place where they then had their stay was not the 'Land of Promise'—but *that* lay on the western boundary of the State of Missouri, in which place they were then assembling, and where they believed, in process of time, they should have a temple, and a city, of great magnificence and wealth; and that shortly, they should increase, and tread down all their enemies, and bruise them beneath their feet. After which period, Christ Jesus should descend, and reign with them, personally one thousand years upon the earth. And then their enemies should be loosed for a season (or, as one said to me, for the space of three months) when should take place the General Judgment and the "final consummation of all things."

These things, accordingly, they had prevailed on some thousands to believe. Of their numbers, I found ministers of different persuasions: and some, it appeared, who had once been eminent for piety. I found, also, many men of both influence and wealth. Husbands, who had left their wives: and wives, that had left their husbands. Children, that had left their parents; and parents, their children;—that they might be *"accounted worthy,"* as they said, *"to escape all the things that should come to pass and to stand before the Son of Man."*

On the evening that we arrived, they had a meeting for *searching hearts*, which we were too weary to attend. The next day (which was the Sabbath) we had the privilege of going to hear them—but they allowed us to say nothing. We were present at their communion season; also by the river side, where the ordinance of baptism was administered. Thus, through all their exercises I had followed them for one day, with the strictest scrutiny. . . .

As a people, wherefore in common with the world, I will do them the justice to say, I saw nothing indecorous: nor had I an apprehension of any thing of the kind. But in their public performances, I no more looked upon them as sanctioned by the Lord of Hosts than if they had merely intended to mimic the work of the Lord. Rather, to the contrary, I viewed the whole with the utmost indignation and disgust: and as a mere profanation and sacrilege of all religious things.

I really viewed it strange that so many men of skill should be thus duped of them. I pitied and loved them too, believing that many had actually intended forsaking all for Christ. . . .

Having by this time understood that they could neither *flatter*, nor *frighten* us, to their belief, they then undertook by threats, if possible, to *drive* us thereto: and said one—

Phelps, "You are *in the gall of bitterness, and the strong bonds of iniquity*. And I have authority to say to you, 'You shall not be saved, unless you believe that Book!' "

"If I had the Book, Sir, I would burn it!". . .

Ques. "Mr. Smith, can you, in the presence of Almighty God, give your word by oath that an Angel from Heaven shewed you the place of those Plates?—and that you took the things contained in that Book from those plates? And at the direction of the Angel, you returned said Plates to the place from whence you had taken them?"

Ans. "I will not swear at all!"

Upon this, being about to leave the place, he turned to some women and children in the room and lay his hands upon their heads (that they might receive the Holy Ghost) when "Oh!" cried one to me, "What blessings you do lose! No sooner, his hands fell upon my head than I felt the Holy Ghost as *warm-water* go over me!"

But I was not such a stranger to the spirit of God as she imagined—that I did not know its effects, from that of *warm-water*! And I turned to Smith, and said, "Are you not ashamed of such pretensions? You, who are no more than any ignorant plough-boy of our land! Oh! blush at such abominations! and let shame, forever cover your face!"

He only replied, by saying, "The gift has returned back again as in former times, to illiterate fishermen." So he got off, as quick as he could. He recollected himself, wherefore, and returned to pass the compliment of "Good-by!" A good-natured, low-bred sort of a chap that seemed to have force enough to do no one any harm. Another of their Elders threatened to put us off the ground, and that he would have no more such blasphemy there. I said, "Sir, you need not trouble yourself to do that; we will go without. We were invited to this place by the woman of the house; and did not think of being carried out by any other person."

We attended a meeting of Presbyterians, on Monday evening, and were invited to join them in prayer and exhortation. That we accordingly did, with a degree of satisfaction. Two christian people came in the next morning and invited us to Perry. To which place we rejoiced to go, believing that God had sent them.

As we left the Mormonites (for so they are called), a number of families started for the "Promised-Land." One turned to us, with much apparent animation, and said, "We are now going to that Land, which is to be our dwelling-place, forever-more!" And they renewed their charge to us, That if we could not see with them, to be careful, and not oppose them. I returned, "I shall think it my duty to speak, and write against you, wherever I may go!"

At Perry, I spoke in a school-house; where all seemed to hear with much surprise. Next night I spoke at the Methodist Chapel in Painesville. There we found some husbands and wives at variance about Mormonism. The one, detesting such a mass of absurdities (or rather the evils resulting therefrom) had burned the Book—while the other wished to unite with the people and held the same as sacred. I now rejoiced that I could give them such advice, if heeded, as would prevent the unhappy division (if not the ruin of themselves) before it was too late: and I now understood more especially, why duty had led me hither. Because, as I found, Here were many staggered at these things that dared not for their lives oppose them; neither did they dare embrace them.

―――――

"I Certainly Should Have Gone into the Water"

"THE MORMONITES, *in some places, seem to be swallowing Campbellites, Universalists, &c," wrote one correspondent from Portage County,
Ohio. And another, calling himself "A Presbyterian," wrote from near-by
Chester expressing his amazement: "Would you believe me if I should
tell you that many methodists, and methodist ministers, and some baptists and presbyterians have joined them? Such is the fact, yes sir, they
have been down through the ice in the mill-pond and their sins are all
washed away, and they are clothed with self righteousness as with a gar-
ment."*

*As much as anything it was Sidney Rigdon's eloquence that won them
over. The former Disciple gave Mormonism a persuasive voice. How
persuasive, Frederic G. Mather recounts in the following episode taken
from "The Early Days of Mormonism," which appeared in* Lippincott's
Magazine *(Philadelphia) in August, 1880.*

*Rigdon became Joseph Smith's intimate counselor from the moment
of their meeting, each respecting the other's gifts. Tanner and licensed
preacher, Rigdon had left the Regular Baptists in 1824 to join Alexander
Campbell and Walter Scott in forming the Disciples, better known as
Campbellites. Once he accepted the* Book of Mormon *and the prophet's
authority, he was easily at home in Mormonism's restorationist theology.
In Ohio he once suffered a savage tarring and feathering along with the
prophet. In Missouri, where he helped to settle new Mormon colonies, his
eloquence got him into even more serious trouble: his Fourth of July sermon at Far West in 1838 served notice on the anti-Mormons that the
church would brook molestation no longer but would take to the sword,
a threat which provoked an extermination order from Governor Boggs.
In Illinois he contributed to the rise of Nauvoo, where he served as
councilman, city attorney, and postmaster.*

*The prophet found him "a great and good man," but vain and unstable,
and finally rejected him as counselor in 1843, saying he had carried
Brother Sidney on his back long enough. Yet the next year Rigdon ran
for Vice-President with the prophet as President on the Mormon ticket
in the national elections. He was in Pittsburgh campaigning when Joseph*

*Smith was killed. He hurried back to Nauvoo to assume leadership of
the church, but the church rejected him in favor of Brigham Young. Ex-
communicated in 1844, Rigdon backtrailed to Pennsylvania and finally
to Friendship, New York, where he died in 1876.*

A very clear idea of his [Sidney Rigdon's] religious power may be
gained by the following statement of Judge John Barr, ex-sheriff of Cuyahoga county, Ohio, and a most excellent authority on the history of the
Western Reserve. The statement has never been made public hitherto:
"In 1830 I was deputy sheriff, and, being at Willoughby (now in Lake
county) on official business, determined to go to Mayfield, which is seven
or eight miles up the Chagrin River, and hear Cowdery and Rigdon on
the revelations of Mormonism. Varnem J. Card, the lawyer, and myself
started early Sunday morning on horseback. We found the roads crowded
with people going in the same direction. Services in the church were
opened by Cowdery with prayer and singing, in which he thanked God
fervently for the new revelation. He related the manner of finding the
golden plates of Nephi. He was followed by Rigdon, a famous Baptist
preacher, well known throughout the eastern part of the Western Reserve
and also in Western Pennsylvania. His voice and manner were always
imposing. He was regarded as an eloquent man at all times, and now he
seemed fully aroused. He said he had not been satisfied in his religious
yearnings until now. At night he had often been unable to sleep, walking
and praying for more light and comfort in his religion. While in the midst
of this agony he heard of the revelation of Joe Smith, which Brother
Cowdery had explained: under this his soul suddenly found peace. It
filled all his aspirations. At the close of a long harangue in this earnest
manner, during which every one present was silent, though very much
affected, he inquired whether any one desired to come forward and be
immersed. Only one man arose. This was an aged 'dead-beat' by the
name of Cahoon, who occasionally joined the Shakers, and lived on the
country generally. The place selected for immersion was a clear pool in
the river above the bridge, around which was a beautiful rise of ground
on the west side for the audience. On the east bank was a sharp bluff
and some stumps, where Mr. Card and myself stationed ourselves. The
time of baptism was fixed at 2 p.m. Long before this hour the spot
was surrounded by as many people as could have a clear view. Rigdon
went into the pool—which at the deepest was about four feet—and after
a suitable address, with prayer, Cahoon came forward and was immersed.
Standing in the water, Rigdon gave one of his most powerful exhorta-

tions. The assembly became greatly affected. As he proceeded he called for the converts to step forward. They came through the crowd in rapid succession to the number of thirty, and were immersed, with no intermission of the discourse on the part of Rigdon. Mr. Card was apparently the most stoical of men—of a clear, unexcitable temperament, with unorthodox and vague religious ideas. He afterward became prosecuting attorney for Cuyahoga county. While the exciting scene was transpiring below us in the valley and in the pool, the faces of the crowd expressing the most intense emotion, Mr. Card suddenly seized my arm and said, 'Take me away!' Taking his arm, I saw that his face was so pale that he seemed to be about to faint. His frame trembled as we walked away and mounted our horses. We rode a mile toward Willoughby before a word was said. Rising the hill out of the valley, he seemed to recover, and said, 'Mr. Barr, if you had not been there I certainly should have gone into the water.' He said the impulse was irresistible."

―――――

Tar and Feathers

SECTARIAN JEALOUSY OF THE MORMONS occasionally erupted in violence, disturbing the peace of the Western Reserve. In his person Joseph Smith, like the religion he founded, bred strong loyalties and deep hatreds. The animosity of apostates was particularly virulent, especially of those who had been won to Mormonism through belief in miracles and then became disillusioned in their expectations. Converts Ezra Booth and Simonds Ryder of Ohio—Booth a former Methodist preacher and Ryder a former Campbellite—became especially bitter. Booth wrote a series of spiteful and damaging letters (which were published in E. D. Howe's Mormonism Unvailed *[sic] in 1834); but Ryder laid vengeful hands on the prophet. Ryder complained that the letter commissioning him to preach for the Mormons spelled his name "Rider"; if the Spirit could err in spelling, it might have erred in calling him to the ministry as well. On March 24, 1832, he and a disgruntled gang fell upon Joseph Smith and Sidney Rigdon in Hiram, Ohio, not far from Kirtland, where the prophet and his family were living with Father John Johnson. Joseph describes their savagery in his journal, published in the documentary* History of the Church (*Salt Lake City, 1902*), *edited by B. H. Roberts, from which the following passages are taken. The twins he mentions were adopted babies not yet a year old.*

On the 24th of March, the twins before mentioned, which had been sick of the measles for some time, caused us to be broken of our rest in taking care of them, especially my wife. In the evening I told her she had better retire to rest with one of the children, and I would watch with the sicker child. In the night she told me I had better lie down on the trundle bed, and I did so, and was soon after awakened by her screaming murder, when I found myself going out of the door, in the hands of about a dozen men; some of whose hands were in my hair, and some had hold of my shirt, drawers and limbs. The foot of the trundle bed was towards the door, leaving only room enough for the door to swing open. My wife heard a gentle tapping on the windows which she then took no particular notice of (but which was unquestionably designed for ascertaining whether or not we were all asleep), and soon after the mob burst open the door and surrounded the bed in an instant, and, as I said, the first I knew I was going out of the door in the hands of an infuriated mob. I made a desperate struggle, as I was forced out, to extricate myself, but only cleared one leg, with which I made a pass at one man, and he fell on the door steps. I was immediately overpowered again; and they swore by G—, they would kill me if I did not be still, which quieted me. As they passed around the house with me, the fellow that I kicked came to me and thrust his hand, all covered with blood, into my face and with an exulting hoarse laugh, muttered: *"Ge, gee, G— d— ye, I'll fix ye."*

They then seized me by the throat and held on till I lost my breath. After I came to, as they passed along with me, about thirty rods from the house, I saw Elder Rigdon stretched out on the ground, whither they had dragged him by his heels. I supposed he was dead. I began to plead with them, saying, "You will have mercy and spare my life, I hope." To which they replied, "G— d— ye, call on yer God for help, we'll show ye no mercy"; and the people began to show themselves in every direction; one coming from the orchard had a plank; and I expected they would kill me, and carry me off on the plank. They then turned to the right, and went on about thirty rods further; about sixty rods from the house, and thirty from where I saw Elder Rigdon, into the meadow, where they stopped, and one said, "Simonds, Simonds" (meaning, I supposed, Simonds Ryder), "pull up his drawers, pull up his drawers, he will take cold." Another replied: *"Ain't ye going to kill 'im? ain't ye going to kill 'im?"* when a group of mobbers collected a little way off, and said: "Simonds, Simonds, come here"; and "Simonds" charged those who had hold of me to keep me from touching the ground (as they had done all the time), lest I should get a spring upon them. They held a council, and as I could occasionally overhear a word, I supposed it was to know whether or not it was best to kill me. They returned after a while, when I learned that they had concluded not to kill me, but to beat and scratch me well, tear off my shirt and drawers, and leave me naked. One cried, "Simonds, Simonds, *where's the tar bucket?"* "I don't know," answered one, *"where 'tis, Eli's left it."* They ran back and fetched the bucket of tar, when one exclaimed, with an oath, *"Let us tar up his mouth";* and they tried to force the tar-paddle into my mouth; I twisted my head around, so that they could not; and they cried out, *"G— d— ye, hold up yer head and let us giv ye some tar."* They then tried to force a vial into my mouth, and broke it in my teeth. All my clothes were torn off me except my shirt collar; and one man fell on me and scratched my body with his nails like a mad cat, and then muttered out: *"G— d— ye, that's the way the Holy Ghost falls on folks!"*

They then left me, and I attempted to rise, but fell again; I pulled the tar away from my lips, so that I could breathe more freely, and after a while I began to recover, and raised myself up, whereupon I saw two lights. I made my way towards one of them, and found it was Father Johnson's. When I came to the door I was naked, and the tar made me look as if I were covered with blood, and when my wife saw me she thought I was all crushed to pieces, and fainted. During the affray abroad, the sisters of the neighborhood had collected at my room. I called for a blanket, they threw me one and shut the door; I wrapped it around me and went in. . . .

My friends spent the night in scraping and removing the tar, and washing and cleansing my body; so that by morning I was ready to be clothed again. This being the Sabbath morning, the people assembled for meeting at the usual hour of worship, and among them came also the mobbers; viz.: Simonds Ryder, a Campbellite preacher and leader of the mob; one McClentic, who had his hands in my hair; one Streeter, son of a Campbellite minister; and Felatiah Allen, Esq., who gave the mob a barrel of whiskey to raise their spirits. Besides these named, there were many others in the mob. With my flesh all scarified and defaced, I preached to the congregation as usual, and in the afternoon of the same day baptized three individuals.

The next morning I went to see Elder Rigdon, and found him crazy, and his head highly inflamed, for they had dragged him by his heels, and those, too, so high from the ground that he could not raise his head from the rough, frozen surface, which lacerated it exceedingly; and when he saw me he called to his wife to bring him his razor. She asked him what he wanted of it; and he replied, to kill me. Sister Rigdon left the room, and he asked me to bring his razor; I asked him what he wanted of it, and he replied he wanted to kill his wife; and he continued delirious some days. The feathers which were used with the tar on this occasion, the mob took out of Elder Rigdon's house. After they had seized him, and dragged him out, one of the banditti returned to get some pillows; when the women shut him in and kept him a prisoner some time.

During the mobbing one of the twins contracted a severe cold, continued to grow worse until Friday, and then died. The mobbers were composed of various religious parties, but mostly Campbellites, Methodists and Baptists, who continued to molest and menace Father Johnson's house for a long time.

Land of Promise

MORMONISM'S WESTWARD DRIFT fulfilled a grand design which the prophet had made explicit in a series of revelations even before leaving New York. The Saints were to prepare a holy city, like Enoch's of old, where they were to gather to await the Second Coming; then "for the space of a thousand years shall the earth rest." The poor, he said, should have "a land of promise, a land flowing with milk and honey." The Mormons believed literally that the meek shall inherit the earth.

Accordingly, they looked hopefully to Jackson County, Missouri, where Oliver Cowdery and his missionary companions had wintered while Parley Pratt made his report to Joseph Smith in Kirtland. The prophet and Sidney Rigdon themselves journeyed to Independence in the summer of 1831, sending a corps of twenty-eight Mormon elders in pairs before them on foot, by stage, and by steamboat to call a wicked generation to repentance and raise up churches along the way. They rendezvoused in

Independence in July and were shortly joined by some twenty families from Colesville, New York, who had come all the way as a congregation. These settled in Kaw Township on the edge of the prairie twelve miles southwest of Independence. In Independence itself the brethren chose a lot not far from the courthouse as a site for a temple. It was to be the center of the land of Zion, which Sidney Rigdon dedicated for the gathering of the Lord's people.

The gathering was to be a practical work of colonization. They were to buy up the land to the westward; Sidney Gilbert was appointed church agent to receive money and purchase lands; Edward Partridge as bishop was to divide them into inheritances as Mormon settlers arrived; and W. W. Phelps, former editor of the antimasonic Phoenix in New York, was to be "printer and publisher to the church in Zion." Zion was a going concern, though the beginnings were humble enough: several families lived through the first long winter in an open, unfinished log room without windows and with only the frozen ground for a floor, subsisting on beef and bread made of coarse corn meal. And the congregation at Zion's first Sunday service mirrored the rawness and variety of the American frontier. It was a motley gathering of settlers, vagabond Indians, renegades, traders, and Negro slaves. The Mormons themselves, exclusively from the North, seemed an alien presence among so many Southerners. Here was a portent of future conflict.

In the first passage below, taken from the documentary History of the Church (Salt Lake City, 1902), Joseph Smith gives his impressions of the society and the country during his visit in 1831. His description reflects confidence that his people would erect a city that would be the crowning glory of the western world. For it was written "The law shall go forth from Zion."

The second and third selections are drawn from the contemporary press.

I

Our reflections were many, coming as we had from a highly cultivated state of society in the east, and standing now upon the confines or western limits of the United States, and looking into the vast wilderness of those that sat in darkness; how natural it was to observe the degradation, leanness of intellect, ferocity, and jealousy of a people that were nearly a century behind times, and to feel for those who roamed about without the benefit of civilization, refinement, or religion; yea, and exclaim in the language of the Prophets: "When will the wilderness blossom as the rose? When will Zion be built up in her glory, and where will Thy temple stand, unto which all nations shall come in the last days?". . .

The country is unlike the timbered states of the East. As far as the eye can reach the beautiful rolling prairies lie spread out like a sea of meadows; and are decorated with a growth of flowers so gorgeous and grand as to exceed description; and nothing is more fruitful, or a richer stockholder in the blooming prairie than the honey bee. Only on the water courses is timber to be found. There in strips from one to three miles in width, and following faithfully the meanderings of the streams, it grows in luxuriant forests. The forests are a mixture of oak, hickory, black walnut, elm, ash, cherry, honey locust, mulberry, coffee bean, hackberry, boxelder, and bass wood; with the addition of cottonwood, butterwood, pecan, and soft and hard maple upon the bottoms. The shrubbery is beautiful, and consists in part of plums, grapes, crab apple, and persimmons.

The soil is rich and fertile; from three to ten feet deep, and generally composed of a rich black mould, intermingled with clay and sand. It yields in abundance, wheat, corn, sweet potatoes, cotton and many other common agricultural products. Horses, cattle and hogs, though of an inferior breed, are tolerably plentiful and seem nearly to raise themselves by grazing in the vast prairie range in summer, and feeding upon the bottoms in winter. The wild game is less plentiful of course where man has commenced the cultivation of the soil, than in the wild prairies. Buffalo, elk, deer, bear, wolves, beaver and many smaller animals here roam at pleasure. Turkeys, geese, swans, ducks, yea a variety of the feathered tribe, are among the rich abundance that grace the delightful regions of this goodly land—the heritage of the children of God.

The season is mild and delightful nearly three quarters of the year, and as the land of Zion, situated at about equal distances from the Atlantic and Pacific oceans, as well as from the Allegheny and Rocky mountains, in the thirty-ninth degree of north latitude, and between the sixteenth and seventeenth degrees of west longitude, it bids fair—when the curse is taken from the land—to become one of the most blessed places on the globe. The winters are milder than the Atlantic states of the same parallel of latitude, and the weather is more agreeable; so that were the virtues of the inhabitants only equal to the blessings of the Lord which He permits to crown the industry of those inhabitants, there would be a measure of the good things of life for the benefit of the Saints, full, pressed down, and running over, even an hundredfold. The disadvantages here, as in all new countries, are self-evident—lack of mills and schools; together with the natural privations and inconveniences which the hand of industry, the refinement of society, and the polish of science, overcome.

But all these impediments vanish when it is recollected what the Prophets have said concerning Zion in the last days; how the glory of Lebanon is to come upon her; the fir tree, the pine tree, and the box tree together, to beautify the place of His sanctuary, that He may make the place of His feet glorious. Where for brass, He will bring gold; and for iron, He will bring silver; and for wood, brass; and for stones, iron; and where the feast of fat things will be given to the just; yea, when the splendor of the Lord is brought to our consideration for the good of His people, the calculations of men and the vain glory of the world vanish, and we exclaim, "Out of Zion the perfection of beauty, God hath shined."

Joseph Smith

II

September 17, 1831.

THE MORMONITES.—We learn from the Plainsville Gazette, that this infatuated people are again in motion. In their own cant phrase, "they are going to inherit the promise of God to Abraham and his seed." Their destination is some indefinite spot on the Missouri river, they say about 1500 miles distant. About eighty of them have recently been ordained, and some of them have gone; others are about going, two and two, part by the western rivers and part by land, to their distant retreat, far away from the cheering voice of civilized man. Those who have disposed of their property go now, and such as have no property are making market for it so eagerly as often to disregard pecuniary interests, and all are to follow with all convenient dispatch. They still persist in their power to work miracles. They say they have often seen them done— the sick are healed and the lame walk, devils are cast out—and these assertions are made by men heretofore considered rational men, and men of truth. The Gazette expresses the opinion that although the leaders of this sect are gross imposters, a great portion of its members are sincere and honest.

Some of the leaders of this sect, we are told, passed through this place two or three weeks since, on their return to Ohio. We understand, that they have determined to migrate to Jackson County, on the extreme edge of this State; for which purpose they have purchased a sufficiency of land whereupon to locate the whole of the believers of Mormonism. We have some hope that the latter part of the paragraph may be true; as in any other event, we should not rejoice much in the acquisition of so many deluded, insane enthusiasts. [*Missouri Intelligencer & Boon's Lick Advertiser* (Columbia), September 17, 1831.]

III

Lyman, N.H., April 28, 1832.

There has been in this town, and vicinity, for about a week, two young men from the westward, who are Mormonites; and are daily giving to the people lectures on the subject of their religion, as they call it. They say they are commanded by God to preach to this generation, and say to them, that all who do not embrace their faith and mode of worship, forsake their friends, houses, and lands, and go with them to a place of safety, which is in the state of Missouri, where they are about building a city, will be destroyed by the sword, famine, pestilence, earthquakes, &c., and that reformation, repentance, and faith, unless it be accompanied with a speedy removal to their city of refuge, will be of no avail.

They state that they do not *guess* at this, but they *absolutely* know it, by a revelation from Heaven, through the immediate ministrations of Angels.

They, however, recommend to the people who have property, to sell the same, and take the avails with them. . . . [*Independent Messenger* (Boston), June 7, 1832.]

━━━━━━

New Jerusalem: Letter from Independence

A BAPTIST CLERGYMAN living at Independence saw the discrepancy between Zion the ideal and Zion the reality. B. Pixley, having observed the Mormons for over a year since their arrival in Jackson County, felt sure that "The very materials of which the society is composed must at length produce an explosion."

One of the explosive elements was the doctrine of inheritances with its corollary "law of consecration and stewardship," to which Pixley alludes as "the idea of equality." In Kirtland early in 1831 Joseph Smith had proposed that his ideal community practice the consecration of property and a system of stewardships which put the management of the temporal affairs of the church in the hands of a presiding bishop. Every

72

man was to give his property unreservedly to the bishop with a binding covenant and to receive in return a deeded inheritance according to his need which became his stewardship to manage independently. Surpluses from his management were to go into the bishop's storehouse for obtaining inheritances for the poor. It was an ideal intended to make the Saints equal in temporal as in spiritual matters. Only on these terms could Zion be sanctified.

But the doctrine of inheritances, applied in Missouri, led to extravagant expectations on the part of poor converts, selfishness rather than sacrifice on the part of some of those who were better off, and tragic misunderstanding on the part of non-Mormon neighbors. The old settlers feared that the Mormons claimed Missouri by divine right. The Evening and the Morning Star, *Mormon monthly at Independence, deplored these abuses and impressions, but they were fatal. Serious trouble was less than a year away.*

Pixley's letter of October 12, 1832, to the editor of the Christian Watchman, *reproduced below from the* Independent Messenger (*Boston, Mass.*) *of November 29, 1832, a Universalist organ, was widely reprinted, appearing in papers as scattered as the* Missouri Intelligencer *of Columbia and the* American Eagle *of Westfield, New York.*

SIR,—Dwelling as I do among a people called Mormonites, and on the very land which they sometimes call Mount Zion, at other times the New Jerusalem—and where, at no distant period, they expect the re-appearing of the Lord Jesus to live and reign with them on earth a thousand years—I have thought perhaps it might be a part of duty to inform those who may feel interested in relation to this subject, that although there has, from first to last, four or five hundred Mormonites in all—men, women and children—arrived at this place, yet there is no appearance here different from that of other wicked places. The people eat and drink, and some get drunk, suffer pain and disease, live and die like other people, the Mormons themselves not excepted. They declare that there can be no true church where the gift of miracles, of tongues, of healing, &c. are not exhibited and continued. Several of them, however, have died, yet none have been raised from the dead. And the sick, unhappily, seem not to have faith to be healed of their diseases. One woman, I am told, declared in her sickness, with much confidence, that she should not die, but here live and reign with Christ a thousand years; but unfortunately she died, like other people, three days after. They tell indeed of working miracles, healing the sick, &c. &c. these things, how-

ever, are not *seen* to be done, but only *said* to be done. People, therefore, who set their faces for the Mount Zion of the West (which by the
by is on a site of ground not much elevated), must calculate on being
disappointed, if they believe all that is said of the place, or expect much
above what is common in any new country of the West.

Of the Mormons as a sect, I am prepared to say but little, except that
they seem to be made up of people of every sect and kind, Shakers,
Baptists, Methodists, Presbyterians and Campbellites, and some have
been of two or three of these different sects before they became Mormonites. Their best prerequisite for the reception of their expected
Saviour, it should seem for the most part, is their poverty. There is
no doubt but that some suffer for want of the necessaries of life, and in
this respect not a little imitate the good Lazarus. But they have no fellow-
ship for Temperance societies, Bible societies, Tract societies, or Sunday
school societies.

Their first, best, great and celebrated preacher, Elder Rigdon, tells
us the Epistles are not and were not given for our instruction, but for
the instruction of a people of another age and country, far removed
from ours, of different habits and manners, and needing different teaching; and that it is altogether inconsistent for us to take the Epistles written
for that people at that age of the world, as containing suitable instruction
for this people at this age of the world. The Gospels too, we are given
by them to understand, are so mutilated and altered as to convey little
of the instruction which they should convey. Hence we are told a new
revelation is to be sought—is to be expected, indeed is coming forthwith.
Our present Bible is to be altered and restored to its primitive purity,
by Smith, the present prophet of the Lord, and some books to be added
of great importance, which have been lost.

They profess to hold frequent converse with angels; some go, if we may
believe what they say, as far as the third heaven, and converse with the
Lord Jesus face to face. They baptize, saying, "I John, the Messenger,
baptize thee, &c." More secretly, they are said to impart to their converts the gift of the Holy Ghost. They profess to know where the ark of
the Covenant, Aaron's rod, the pot of Manna, &c. now remain hid.
They who can believe all this, will no doubt expect a Saviour soon, and
without hesitation will worship the first object that may be proclaimed
and presented to them for that purpose.

The last preaching I heard of theirs was a most labored discourse; its
object was to prove that this place, here fixed upon by the Mormons
as their location, is the very Mount Zion so often mentioned in Scripture.

74

This alone, it should seem, would be a sufficient index to the *head* or the *heart* of the preacher, and the belief of it a sufficient index to the *reading* and *understanding* of the hearers.

Their possessions here are small, very small, compared with their numbers; something less, I believe, than four sections of land, which would cost but little more than three thousand dollars. Twenty acres is the portion assigned for each family to use and improve while they continue members of the society; but if they leave they are to go out empty. Some in comfortable circumstances at the East have spent or given to the society their little all in coming to this land of promise, and now find themselves in no very enviable circumstances, looking here and there for labor, and women going to wash for their neighbors of the world to supply themselves with the necessaries of life.

The idea of equality is held forth; but time will show that some take deeds of property in their own name, and those too of the most zealous and forward in the cause and prosperity of the society. And perhaps they do not pretend, like Ananias and Sapphira, to have given all to the society; yet it is a point of duty they most rigidly enjoin on all their proselytes to cast their all into the common stock. Under these circumstances, it needs no prophetic eye to foresee that there will soon be a murmuring of the Greeks against the Hebrews. Indeed there already begins to be some feeling and some defection arising from this subject. There is much reason to believe they cannot hold together long. With Theudas, it is more than probable they will soon be scattered and brought to nought.

The very materials of which the society is composed must at length produce an explosion. Yet judging from the past, and from what our Saviour has told us of the future, that there should be false Christs and false Prophets, showing signs and wonders so as to deceive, if it were possible, the very elect, we may well look on this new sect as ominous of the latter day approaching, and calling upon all to watch and pray, and to give good heed to the word of our Saviour, where he says, "Go ye not after them, nor follow them."

Yours, &c.   B. PIXLEY.

Independence, Jackson Co. Mo. Oct. 12, 1832.

Trouble in Jackson County

BY JULY, 1833, *the Mormons numbered 1,200 in their new settlements in Jackson County, Missouri, which they called Zion. The Evening and the Morning Star, which they founded in June, 1832—the first Mormon periodical and the westernmost publication in the United States—warned them: "Let not your flight be in haste, but let all things be prepared before you." The church was not a common-stock concern, it said, neither was Missouri a Canaan which latter-day Israel had to conquer by the sword. Money was to be sent to the bishop, lands purchased, and preparations made for their coming. But, as John Corrill, one of their leading elders, wrote later, they ignored the regulation and "the church got crazy to go up to Zion." Some converts sought loaves and fishes. Others had to be brought down from the clouds where they saw themselves already meeting the Savior. They considered themselves the meek who should inherit the earth, making their Missouri neighbors uneasy, all the more because the Mormons favored the "free people of color." It was a touchy point in Missouri.*

The old settlers saw the county filling up with northern emigrants, mostly poor. Afraid the Mormons would soon become a majority and rule the county, the old settlers at first offered to sell out to the Mormons, who were willing but too poor to buy. Exasperated, the old citizens found voice in extremists like Reverend Finis Ewing, head of the Cumberland Presbyterians: "The 'Mormons' are the common enemies of mankind and ought to be destroyed."

At the same time the Mormons were plagued by troubles within. A dissenter sued the bishop for fifty dollars. As a member, he had sent the money from Ohio "to purchase an inheritance for himself and the saints of God in Zion in these last days," only to find that the bishop had drawn the deed in his own name. The Star *explained this as common procedure; the bishop held the property for the church. The fifty dollars had been a consecration, a deed of gift no more returnable than donations to missionary societies or colleges in other churches. But the Missouri court found for the plaintiff, who, lamented the* Star, *"shortly after denied the faith and ran away on Sunday," to spread a further bad opinion about the Mormons. Other dissenters withdrew, vexing the church with lawsuits.*

Meanwhile, there were incidents between Mormons and Missourians. As early as 1832 houses had been stoned and shot at, a haystack burned, families insulted. In April, 1833, some 300 old settlers met at Independence to decide on a course of action, but the meeting ended in drunken disagreement, a typical "Missouri row." On July 4th they circulated a set of resolutions called the "Secret Constitution" setting forth their grievances against the Mormons. On July 20th they met at the courthouse in Independence and issued an ultimatum: a committee waited upon the Mormon leaders and required them to shut up all their workshops, their store, and their printing office, and agree to leave the county. The Mormons required time to give an answer. Given only fifteen minutes, they refused to comply with the proposals.

The committee took the refusal back to the courthouse, where the assembly voted to demolish the printing office, which they did forthwith, tarring and feathering Bishop Edward Partridge and one of the elders. Three days later several hundred mobsters appeared to continue the work of destruction. Mormon leaders offered their lives if they would spare the church, but the Missourians answered no, that every man should answer for his own life or leave the county. The Mormons agreed to leave, some in January, the remainder in the spring of 1834. For a few months the old settlers were appeased.

Missouri's anti-Mormon outrages were the counterpart of the anti-abolition violence breaking out all over the country. Two years late respectable Bostonians dragged the abolitionist William Lloyd Garrison through the streets by a rope, intending to hang him; in 1837 mobsters in Alton, Illinois, murdered Elijah Lovejoy after twice destroying his emancipationist press. "Is not this a free state?" Lovejoy had asked, echoing the Mormons. "Have I not a right to claim the protection of the laws?"

The following account from the Missouri Intelligencer and Boon's Lick Advertiser (*Columbia*) *of August 10, 1833, presents the minutes and resolutions of the meeting of July 20th. In the demolition of their printing press the Mormons lost the greater part of the first edition of their* Book of Commandments, *a collection of the revelations of Joseph Smith, later revised and reissued as* The Doctrine and Covenants. *An original copy of the* Book of Commandments *sells today for $1,500.*

At a meeting of the citizens of Jackson County, Missouri, called for the purpose of adopting measures to rid themselves of the set of fanatics called Mormons, held at Independence on the 20th day of July, 1833, which meeting was composed of gentlemen from every part of the country, there being present between four and five hundred persons. . . .

This meeting, professing to act, not from the excitement of the moment, but under a deep and abiding conviction that the occasion is one that calls for cool deliberation, as well as energetic action, deem it proper to lay before the public an expose of our peculiar situation, in regard to this singular sect of pretended christians, and a solemn declaration of unalterable determination to amend it.

The evil is one that no one could have foreseen, and is therefore unprovided for by the laws, and the delay incident to legislation would put the mischief beyond remedy.

But little more than two years ago, some two or three of these people made their appearance on the Upper Missouri and they now number some 1,200 souls in this county, and each successive autumn and spring pours forth its swarm among us, with a gradual falling off in the character of those who compose it; until it seems that those communities from which they come, were flooding us with the very dregs of their composition. Elevated as they mostly are but little above the condition of our blacks, whether in regard to property or education, they have become a subject of much anxiety on that part, serious and well grounded complaints having been already made of their corrupting influence on our slaves.

We are told, and not by the ignorant alone, but by all classes of them, that we (the Gentiles) of this country are to be cut off, and our lands appropriated by them for inheritances. Whether this is to be accomplished by the hand of our destroying Angel, the judgements of God, or the arm of power, they are not fully agreed among themselves.

Some recent remarks in the "Evening and Morning Star," their organ, in this place, by their tendency to moderate such hopes and repress such desires, show plainly that many of this deluded and infatuated people have been taught to believe that our lands are to be taken from us by the sword. From the same "Star" we learn that for the want of more honest or commendable employment, many of their society are now preaching through the state of New York, Ohio, and Illinois and that their numbers are increasing beyond every rational calculation; all of whom are required, as soon as convenient, to come up to Zion, [the] name they have thought proper to confer on our little village. Most of those who have already come, are characterized by the profoundest ignorance, the grossest superstitions, the most abject poverty. Indeed it is a subject of regret by the "Star" itself, that they have come, not only unable to buy an inheritance, which means some fifteen acres of wild land, for each family, but destitute of the means of procuring bread and meat. When we reflect on the extensive field in which this sect is operating . . . it requires no gift of prophecy to tell that the day is not far distant, when the government of the county will be in their hands. When the Sheriff, the Justices, and the county Judges will be Mormons, or persons willing to court their favor from motives of interest or ambition. What would be the fate of our lives and property, in the hands of jurors and witnesses who do not blush to declare and would not upon occasion hesitate to swear that they have wrought miracles and supernatural cures; have converse with God and His angels; and possess and exercise the gift of Divination and of unknown tongues and fired with the prospect of obtaining inheritances without money and without price, may be better imagined than described.

One of the means resorted to by them, in order to drive us to emigrate, is an indirect invitation to the free brethren of color in Illinois to come up like the rest to the land of Zion . . . to claim and exercise the rights of citizenship. Contemporaneous with the appearance of this article, was the general expectation among the brethren here, that a considerable number of this degraded class were only waiting this information before they set out on their journey. With the corrupting influence of these on our slaves and the stench both physical and moral, that their introduction would set off in our social atmosphere, and the vexation that would attend the civil rule of these fanatics, it would require neither a visit from the destroying angel, nor the judgements of an offended God, to render our situation here, insupportable. True, it may be said, and truly no doubt that the fate that has marked the rise and fall of Joanna Southcote and Ann Lee will also attend the progress of Jo. Smith; but this is not copiate to our fears, for when the fabric falls the *rubbish* will remain.

Of their pretended revelations from Heaven—their personal intercourse with God and his Angels—the maladies they pretend to heal by the laying on of hands—and the contemptible gibberish with which they habitually profane the Sabbath and which they dignify with the appellation of unknown tongues, we have nothing to say. Vengeance belongs to God alone. But as to the other matters set forth in this paper, we feel called on by every consideration of self-preservation, good society, public morals, and the fair prospects, that if not blasted in the germ, await this young and beautiful country, at once to declare, and we do hereby most solemnly declare:

1. That no Mormon shall in future move and settle in this county.

2. That those now here, who shall give a definite pledge of their intention within a reasonable time to remove out of the county, shall be allowed to remain unmolested until they have sufficient time to sell their property and close their business without any material sacrifice.

3. That the editor of the "Star" be required forthwith to close his office, and discontinue the business of printing of this county; and as to all other stores and shops belonging to the sect their owners must in every case strictly comply with the terms of the second article of this declaration, and upon failure, prompt and efficient measures will be taken to close the same.

4. That the Mormon leaders here, are requested to use their influence in preventing any further emigration of their distant brethren to this county, and to counsel and advise their brethren here to comply with the above requisition.

5. That those who fail to comply with the above requisitions, be referred to those of their brethren who have the gift of divination, and of unknown tongues to inform them of the lot that awaits them.

Which address being read and considered was unanimously adopted. And thereupon it was resolved that a committee of twelve be appointed forthwith to wait on the Mormon leaders, and see that the foregoing requisitions are complied with by them; and upon their refusal, that said committee do, as the organ of the county, inform them that it is our unwavering purpose and fixed determination, after the fullest consideration of all consequences and responsibilities under which we act, to use such means as shall insure their full and complete adoption.

"Excitement, Anxiety and Alarm"

THE MORMONS CONSIDERED *the July agreement illegal and not binding. It had been made under duress and, after two or three months of quiet, they petitioned the state government to prevent their forced evacuation of Jackson County, Governor Daniel Dunklin told them they must appeal to the courts, an empty comfort because the civil officers* and influential citizens of Jackson—the judge of the county court, the justices of the peace, the constable and his deputies, the doctors, the lawyers, and the merchants—were all signers of the agreement seeking to drive the Mormons out. Four lawyers from neighboring Clay County undertook their case. "Here let me remark," wrote John Corrill, a later dissenter, "that up to this time the Mormons had not so much as lifted a finger, even in their own defence, so tenacious were they for the precepts of the gospel—'turn the other cheek.'"

Incensed that the Mormons should attempt to stay, the old citizens took to night depredations, pulling down their houses and whipping their men. The Mormons prepared for self-defense, but they were badly armed. On November 4, 1833, they met the Missourians above the Blue, eight or nine miles from Independence. Three or four were killed on both sides in the skirmish and several wounded. The news reached Independence a little after dark, where several Mormons were undergoing a sham trial. So great was the excitement that the court had to shut the prisoners up in jail for their own protection. Lyman Wight, supposing them unjustly imprisoned and about to be shot, marched into Independence with 150 Mormons, only to give up their arms when they learned the situation.

The Mormons all left Jackson County during the winter. Some went briefly to Van Buren County; some backtrailed east. Most of them crowded the Missouri bottoms in wretched privation and crossed the Missouri River north into Clay County, where they were hospitably received. They were not permitted to return to Jackson County, even to settle up their business. The old settlers burned down over two hundred empty Mormon houses in the spring to finish their winter's work.

Rumors and confused alarms meanwhile overspread the countryside. B. Pixley, writing from Independence on November 7, 1833, describes below what he called "a serious moment" in the conflict. Pixley, Baptist preacher and missionary to the Indians, was himself no friend of the Mormons and bore tales from house to house which did them no good. His present letter, addressed to the editors of the New York Observer, is taken from the Christian Watchman of Boston, where it was reprinted on December 13, 1833. The riotous incidents, in some accounts called "Regulating the Mormonites," were widely reported in the nation's press.

Independence, (Mo.) Nov. 7, 1833

Gentlemen—For several days past this place has exhibited a scene of the most excitement, anxiety and alarm. Yesterday and the day before there were more than 200 citizens under arms, the stores were shut, and business mostly suspended. You probably already know that a new sect of religionists called *Mormons* have been emigrating in considerable numbers, and settling in this place, and that their preaching, in which they maintain that they inhabit "the Mount Zion spoken of in Scripture"; that the present inhabitants would be driven off unless they sold to the Mormons and went off peaceably—that they, the Mormons, should possess the country, together with their inviting free negroes from all parts of the country to come and join them, and their pretended power to work miracles and speak with tongues—all these things taken together, aroused so much indignation in the minds of the inhabitants, that they assembled last summer, according to appointment, without noise or riot, or drunkenness, but with deliberate purpose, and pulled down the printing office (a brick building), and drew the roof into the highway. They were about to proceed to the same act of violence against the store, when a parley took place, and the parties came to terms of accommodation. The Mormons were to close up their business, and were all to move away before another summer; while the other party bound themselves to pay all damages done to the printing office, &c.

Thus peace was made, and so the matter stood until a few days since, when it was found not only that the Mormons did not intend to move according to agreement, but that they were arming themselves, and threatened to kill if they should be molested. This provoked some of the more wild and ungovernable among us to improper acts of violence, such as breaking in upon the Mormon houses, tearing off the covering &c. On this the Mormons began to muster, and exhibit military preparations. Two gentlemen, passing peaceably through the settlement on Saturday evening, were hailed, and commanded to advance and give the countersign. But as they could not do this, they were put under arrest in what was called the guard house, and kept prisoners until morning.

On Sunday, I believe, some shots were exchanged, the Mormons having given the first fire and wounded one man. On Monday a party of the inhabitants, some of them armed, went toward the Mormon settlement, mostly for the purpose of inquiry, and to learn whether the Mormons would attempt to attack them. These were led into ambuscade and fired upon by the Mormons before they arrived at their settlement, and two men were killed on the spot. This little party of inhabitants, said to be eleven in number, retreated before about fifty or sixty Mormons but, after the Indian mode, from tree to tree fired back upon the pursuers, till the Mormons had three killed (among whom was one of their elders) and several wounded. This was about sunset.

The same night the Mormons pretended to have had a revelation from heaven (for you must know that these people regulate their conduct by revelations direct from heaven) *to arise and pursue and destroy their enemies.* In obedience to the mandate from above (for nothing else it should seem but such an extraordinary belief could have led them to such an extraordinary line of conduct), they were discovered under arms to the number of about one hundred and fifty advancing on Tuesday morning to the town of Independence. The alarm was given, and mounted horsemen, from all quarters, flew to the place of conflict, and advanced to meet the Mormons half a mile out of town. It was a serious moment; many hearts, no doubt, palpitating with fear, and as many more, not looking at consequences, panting for the onset. But happily the Mormon courage failed under a view of superior numbers, and they were induced to deliver up their arms and retire; but I am sorry to add that such was the ungovernable and unmanly conduct of some in our community, that it was with the utmost difficulty that the civil authorities could protect their prisoners from being massacred on the spot. Even now the Mormons who are peaceably moving off, are under the necessity of being guarded by the civil authorities to protect them from the violence which otherwise they would have the greatest reason to fear. In justice, however, to a goodly number of the community, I must remark that the sufferings of the Mormons, and especially the women and children, in being obliged to move off so suddenly at this season of the year, has excited much lively sympathy and humane feeling, and some have made very liberal contributions for their relief. Although in the meantime, they cannot but condemn the course of the Mormons, and deprecate the evils which must arise to any community where such principles are evolved, and designs manifested, by arbitrary means, by blood and violence, to build up the kingdom of the Redeemer.

B. Pixley.

Zion's Camp

AROUSED BY THE OUTRAGES in Missouri, Joseph Smith in February, 1834, hurried an appeal to Mormon churches throughout the east to send men and materials to the aid of the exiles. "We learn," said the Painesville (Ohio) Telegraph, "that some Davids or Goliaths are to be dispatched immediately by the prophet to the relief of the brethren in the wilderness." In May about 150 men, "the strength of the Lord's house," rendezvoused at New Portage, Ohio, about fifty miles from Kirtland, ready to redeem Zion. Known as Zion's Camp, they loaded twenty wagons with supplies and, with the prophet incognito, marched through Indiana and central Illinois, conducting military drill along the way. If they could not repossess their lands they could at least make of them a burying ground.

They arrived, augmented to nearly 200, in Clay County in June. At Fishing River they were spared an encounter with an equal force of Missourians who were prevented by a storm from crossing over from Jackson County. All sorts of inflammatory rumors had preceded the Mormons, and the Jackson people were prepared: "We have no doubt," said the Liberty Enquirer, "but the citizens of Jackson are determined to dispute every inch of ground, burn every blade of grass, and suffer their bones to bleach on their hills, rather than the Mormons shall return to Jackson county."

Seeing the temper of the Missourians, and with his own camp struck by cholera, the prophet turned to negotiation. There were proposals and counterproposals. The people of Jackson County offered to buy out the Mormons at an agreed evaluation plus 10 per cent, or to sell out to them on the same terms, within thirty days. The Mormons, if they sold out, were to stipulate that no one of their number would ever enter the county again. But the Mormons could not buy out the whole Jackson County population, and on such short notice; and "to sell our land would amount to a denial of our faith." They proposed that the matter be turned over to twelve arbitrators, six from each side, who would determine the worth of the property of those who could not live with the

Mormons in the county; these would be bought out within a year, less the damages owing the Mormons, also to be determined by the committee. "We want to live in peace with all men, and equal rights is all we ask."

But the negotiations foundered. The prophet returned to Kirtland advising his people to continue quietly in Clay and lay their case "before the world, to be weighed in the balance of public opinion." To him the show of loyalty of Zion's Camp was a sufficient sacrifice, which the Lord accepted as he had accepted the spirit of Abraham's offering of Isaac. From the stalwarts in the Camp he chose his first Quorum of Twelve Apostles, among them Brigham Young. In Clay County, the Mormons fared peacefully until the summer of 1836.

Zion's Camp, a unique expedition in the history of the American frontier, attracted a good deal of newspaper notice, as it marched from Ohio to Missouri, arousing speculation that the "Mormon War" was about to be renewed. Some of this commentary is sampled below.

I

The Mormon war in Missouri is about to be renewed. Gen. Joe Smith took up his line of march from this county on Monday last, with a large party of his fanatical followers, for the seat of war.—This expedition has been a long time in active preparation. Soon after the outrages committed upon the members of the sect last Nov. in Missouri, the prophet here sent forth his general orders, which he pretended was a revelation from God, for all his able bodied men to repair to the scene of difficulty. His preachers were sent forth to all parts of the country among their proselytes, with a printed copy of the revelation in their pockets, reiterating and magnifying all the tales of woe which had befallen "*the church*" in the "promised land." Like Peter the Hermit, in the days of the crusades, they have made every effort to stir up the holy zeal of the "warriors, my young men, and they that are of middle age also," to the combat. They have been made to believe it was a direct command from the Supreme Being, which could not be disobeyed. For several months past they have been collecting munitions of war for the crusade. Dirks, knives, swords, pistols, guns, powder-horns, &c. &c. have been in good demand in this vicinity. Some have equipped themselves with four or five pistols. The prophet, it is said, has a sword over *four feet* long. When he is fully equipped for battle, he will probably put on the huge spectacles (said to be 8 or 10 inches between the glasses) which he pretended to have dug up with his gold bible—they will no doubt answer the purposes of a spy-glass. Then look out, Missourians! But we apprehend the General will take good care of number one. The whole number which are on the move to "expel the infidels from the holy land," they say is about 500. The day before leaving head-quarters, the prophet harangued his troops in person, informing them that he was ready for martyrdom in attestation of his pretensions, and that he expected to be killed; but he had not yet finished his course.

People unacquainted with this delusion will be ready to enquire how they manage their pecuniary affairs in fitting out such expeditions. What they purchase of "the world" their credit is always first offered in payment, or part payment. They have a common fund, which can always be increased by saying "the Lord has need of it." [Painesville (Ohio) *Telegraph,* May 9, 1834.]

II

The excitement which existed in this country about the time the Mormons from Ohio arrived, has entirely subsided. Many of them have returned to the east, and the rest are scattered about throughout the country, and are actively engaged in assisting the citizens in saving their crops of wheat, &c. We rather think that the WAR is over! [Liberty *Enquirer,* quoted in *Missouri Intelligencer and Boon's Lick Advertiser,* July 19, 1834.]

"By No Means Men of Weak Minds"

MISSOURI WAS *a tale of woe, but in Ohio the Mormons prospered—for a while. In Kirtland, their growing headquarters, they built their first temple. It was begun in poverty in 1833 and completed in 1836 at a cost of $40,000—although the donations from congregations throughout the church fell short by $14,000, leaving a debt which proved prelude to other financial troubles. Meanwhile the temple served as a school of the prophets where the leading elders gathered for instruction. From three to four hundred of them came to Kirtland in the fall and early winter of 1835 to "seek learning and study the best books, and get a knowledge of countries, kingdoms, languages, &c," which, according to*

"By No Means Men of Weak Minds"

John Corrill, one of the visiting elders from upper Missouri, "inspired them with an extravagant thirst after knowledge." A solemn assembly in March, 1836, was particularly memorable, when the brethren washed each other's feet and anointed each other with oil, pronounced mutual blessings, and served the sacrament, "in which," said Corrill, "they partook of the bread and wine freely, and a report went abroad that some of them got drunk: as to that every man must answer for himself. A similar report . . . went out concerning the disciples at Jerusalem, on the day of pentecost."

A letter from James H. Eells of Elyria, Ohio, on April 1, 1836, describes some of these heady developments with grudging admiration. It appeared originally in the New-York Evangelist, *and was extracted by the* Christian Journal *of Exeter, New Hampshire, of April 21, 1836, from which it is taken here by way of Dale L. Morgan's file of Mormon transcripts from the religious press.*

[Kirtland, 1836]

Br. *Leavitt*—I have often wondered that so little is said or known of the Mormons, who are now making progress in this country. There certainly has not a more extraordinary religious sect sprung up since the time of Mahomet. They are generally thought too contemptible even to be noticed. But I think this is a mistake.

The Kirtland imposture has collected a considerable number of followers, not less, they say, than twenty thousand. I have just made a visit to the settlement at Kirtland, where about one thousand are located. There they have erected, and nearly completed, a huge stone temple at an expense of forty thousand dollars. Its dimensions are sixty by eighty feet, and fifty feet high. It is of no earthly order of architecture, but the Prophet says it is exactly according to the pattern showed him, though it is by no means equal to that in splendor, from the want of means. It appears to be of two stories, having two rows of gothic windows running round it, besides windows projecting from the roof for the attic story. The first floor is the place of worship, and is completed in a very showy style, with four rows of pulpits at each end, having three pulpits in a row. These twelve pulpits rise behind and above one another, and are designed, the uppermost row, as they say, for the bishop and his counsellors; the second for the priest and his counsellors; the third for the teachers, and the fourth, or lowest, for the deacons. Each end is provided in the same manner. The body of the house is occupied with slips, but the seats in them are movable, so that the audience can sit facing either end of the room. Over the division between each of the rows of pulpits hangs a painted canvass, rolled up to the ceiling, and to be let down at pleasure, so as to conceal the dignitaries behind from the audience. Similar curtains, or as they are called, "veils," are disposed of over the room, so that it can at any time be divided into four apartments to carry on the objects of the imposture. Every thing about the temple is evidently designed to strike the senses and attract curiosity, and at the dedication, which is to take place next Sabbath, most astonishing "glories" are promised and expected by the faithful. The second floor, and the attic loft are designed for a seminary, literary and theological! which is expected to have the manual labor system attached to it.

The Mormons appear to be very eager to acquire education. Men, women and children lately attended school, and they are now employing Mr. [Joshua] Seixas, the Hebrew teacher, to instruct them in Hebrew; and about seventy men in middle life, from twenty to forty years of age, are most eagerly engaged in the study. They pursue their studies alone until twelve o'clock at night, and attend to nothing else. Of course many make rapid progress. I noticed some fine looking and intelligent men among them. Some in dress and deportment have all the appearance of gentlemen, yet the majority are exceedingly ignorant. They all profess a great deal of piety. And in this respect they equal the Mahometans themselves. They abound in prayers and other acts of devotion. Many of them are converts from the Baptist and Methodist sects, but none, or next to none from the Presbyterian church; and aside from the delusion of Mormonism, they have the appearance of being devout Christians. They are by no means, as a class, men of weak minds. Perhaps most fanatics and visionaries have intellects peculiarly though perversely active. . . .

The rise and progress of this extraordinary delusion, shows religious teachers the importance of having sound instruction imparted along with high excitement, that men may have some other evidence on which their faith rests, than the *impulses* of their own unstable minds. And the fact that scarcely a convert has been made from Presbyterian ranks (a fact which the fanatics ascribe to their *pride*) is certainly highly creditable to that denomination.

James H. Eells.

—————

Pride and Apostasy in Ohio

IN KIRTLAND the Mormons ran with the tide of speculation which swept the country in 1836 and 1837. It brought them disaster in the financial panic that followed shortly after Van Buren became President. In debt on their temple, overextended in land purchases, and caught short in an abortive banking operation, they saw their bubble of prosperity quickly burst. "Evil surmising, fault-finding, disunion, dissension and apostasy," as Joseph Smith himself recalled it, followed on the heels of bankruptcy.

In June, 1837, the prophet said the Lord revealed that "something new must be done for the salvation of His Church," and he despatched Heber C. Kimball, a Vermont potter, and three others on a mission to England, the first Mormon mission abroad. Born in desperation, it proved to be Mormonism's greatest strength: by its centenary in Great Britain, Mormonism had won 126,593 converts. Over 52,000 of these had emigrated to Zion—most of them to Utah, but 5,000 came early enough to help build up Nauvoo.

Meanwhile factions tore the society apart in Kirtland until, early in January, 1838, the prophet—after a series of fist-fights and court actions —and Sidney Rigdon had to flee by night for their lives. They went to Far West, Missouri, a thriving Mormon town.

John Corrill, an early convert in Ohio who had been one of the first to go to Jackson County and who had been recalled to supervise completion of the temple, describes the events leading to the breakup of the Kirtland community, and its aftermath. The excerpts below are taken from A Brief History of the Church of Christ of Latter Day Saints (St. Louis, 1839), which he wrote shortly after leaving the Mormons and while serving as a member of the Missouri legislature, where he nevertheless continued to defend them.

And now I return to Kirtland with my story. After finishing the house of the Lord so far as to have it ready for the solemn assembly, the church found itself something like fifteen or twenty thousand dollars in debt, as near as I can recollect. As the house had been built by faith, as they termed it, they must now continue their faith and contrive some means to pay the debt. Notwithstanding they were deeply in debt, they had so managed as to keep up their credit, so they concluded to try mercantile business. Accordingly, they ran in debt in New York, and elsewhere, some thirty thousand dollars, for goods, and, shortly after, some fifty or sixty thousand more, as I was informed; but they did not fully understand the mercantile business, and, withal, they suffered pride to arise in their hearts, and became desirous of fine houses, and fine clothes, and indulged too much in these things, supposing for a few months that they were very rich. They also spent some thousands of dollars in building a steam mill, which never profited them anything. They also bought many farms at extravagant prices, and made part payment, which they afterwards lost, by not being able to meet the remaining payments. They also got up a bank, for which they could get no charter, so they issued their paper without a charter, and, of course, they could not collect their pay on notes received for loans, and, after struggling with it awhile, they broke down.

During their mercantile and banking operations they not only indulged in pride, but also suffered jealousies to arise among them, and several persons dissented from the church, and accused the leaders of the church with bad management, selfishness, seeking for riches, honor, and dominion, tyrannising over the people, and striving constantly after power and property. On the other hand, the leaders of the church accused the dissenters with dishonesty, want of faith and righteousness, wicked in their intentions, guilty of crimes, such as stealing, lying, encouraging the making of counterfeit money, &c.; and this strife or opposition arose to a great height, so that, instead of pulling together as brethren, they tried every way in their power, seemingly, to destroy each other; their enemies from without rejoiced at this, and assisted the dissenters what they could, until Smith and Rigdon finally were obliged to leave Kirtland, and, with their families, came to Far West, in March or April, 1838.

During this strife some of the elders became tired of this scene, and left Kirtland; P. P. Pratt went to the city of New York, where he built up a church. . . .

In order to pay the debts in New York, and elsewhere, many of the church in Kirtland turned out their farms and stripped themselves of property, took orders on the bishop in Far West, and, in their poverty followed Smith and Rigdon to Far West as soon as practicable.

Far West, Missouri

THE MORMONS HAD LEFT *Jackson County like Noah's dove, look-ing for a place to rest their feet. They lighted on Clay County, across the Missouri River, where the citizens received them humanely, assured by Mormon promises that they considered Clay only a temporary asylum. After two and a half years of Mormon occupation, Clay became uneasy, and on June 29, 1836, its leading citizens met at the courthouse in Lib-erty to review the situation. The complaints against the Mormons were familiar: theirs was a peculiar religion for this age; they were eastern people whose habits and speech differed from the Missourians; they were opposed to slavery; they regarded the Indians as part of God's chosen people destined to inherit Missouri. True or false, said the citi-zens, these characteristics had the same effect "in exciting our commu-nity." They feared that these deep-seated differences would lead to open conflict, and they called on the Mormons to leave the county vol-untarily. Out of gratitude, they said, the Saints should remove them-selves.*

In a mass meeting called to consider the petition of the Clay citizens, the Mormons denied they had any disposition either to meddle with slavery or to traffic with the Indians. But they made a "covenant of peace" to leave Clay and accepted the citizens' offer to raise money by subscription in each township to help them resettle.

The Mormons selected sparsely settled northern Missouri and began arriving at Shoal Creek in October. They petitioned for a county of their own which they called Caldwell, with Far West its county seat. By the fall of 1838 they opened two thousand farms in the county, or some 250,000 acres bought from the federal government for $318,000. At Far West, they built 150 houses, four dry-goods stores, three family groceries, half a dozen blacksmith's shops, and two hotels; excavated for a temple 120 by 80 feet; and moved the schoolhouse to the center of the square to be used as church, town hall, and courthouse as well. The school sec-tion of land sold for $7.90 an acre, providing a school fund of about $5,000. The town forbade saloons. A church conference in October, 1837, voted not to support any shops selling spirituous liquors, tea, coffee, or *tobacco—an early observance of the Mormon dietary law known as the Word of Wisdom, making Far West a unique temperance town in hard-drinking Missouri.*

In The Missouri Persecutions *(Salt Lake City, 1900), excerpted below, Mormon historian Brigham H. Roberts visits Far West long after its decline and reflects on it as a classic memory.*

The town plat of Far West as first laid off embraced a square mile, but afterwards additions were made as the population increased. In the center of the town a large public square was laid off, approached by four main roads running east and west, north and south, each a hundred feet wide. Eventually the blocks were so laid off that each block contained four acres, divided into four lots. Far West was located in the western part of Caldwell County, about eight miles west of the present county seat—Kingston. The town site is the highest swell in that high rolling prairie country, and is visible from a long distance.

Standing on what used to be the public square of Far West, on the occasion of my visit there in 1884, I obtained an excellent view of all the surrounding country. Vast fields of waving corn and meadow land were stretched out on all sides, as far as the eye could see. Several towns and villages, with their white church spires gleaming in the sun-light, were in plain view, though from five to ten miles distant. Away to the east is Kingston, the present county seat of Caldwell; further to the northeast is Breckenridge, Hamilton and Kidder; to the west is Plattsburg, and south is the quaint village of Polo. All these places are within easy vision from the site of Far West, and increase the grandeur of the scene.

The site chosen for Far West is the finest location for a city in the county, but notwithstanding all the advantages of the location, Far West has been abandoned. In the fall of 1838 it was a thriving town of some three thousand inhabitants, but to-day nothing remains except the house of the Prophet Joseph, now owned by D. F. Kerr, and one portion of the Whitmer Hotel, now used as a stable. This is all that remains of the buildings, at Far West, erected by the hands of the saints. A few farm houses have been built in the vicinity since their expulsion from Missouri, and a quarter of a mile from the public square stands a neat white Methodist church.

Nothing but an excavation one hundred and ten feet by eighty, enclosed in an old field, with a large rough unhewn stone in each corner, now marks the spot that was once the pretentious public square of Far West. This excavation was made on the 3rd of July, 1837, and was intended for the basement of the temple the saints expected to erect there. . . .

Standing on this consecrated ground and viewing the few relics that are left to remind us that the saints once lived here, one naturally falls into a sad reverie. It is true we are not surrounded by the fallen columns of ruined temples; or the ruins of splendid palaces, or massive walls, such as one would meet with at Babylon, Jerusalem, Rome or Athens. It is not the ruins of an antique or celebrated civilization that inspires one's sadness over Far West. But there one sits in the midst of the ruined prospects and blighted hopes of the saints of God, instead of in the midst of broken columns, ponderous arches, and crumbling walls.

The chief interest about Far West, of course, is the fact that it was the theatre where were enacted those stirring scenes which add another black page to the history of Missouri.

Sidney Rigdon's Ultimatum

WITH THE ARRIVAL of a Kirtland remnant in Missouri in 1838, Mormon settlement expanded into surrounding counties. In Carroll they founded DeWitt and in Daviess they laid out a town the prophet called Adam-ondi-Ahman, "the valley of God, in which Adam blessed his children," more commonly known as Diahman. Daviess citizens feared its growth would injure Gallatin, their county seat; once more the Mormons seemed sure to overrun the country, and the old settlers did not relish living "under the laws and administration of Joe Smith." Lyman Wight, moreover, an uncontrollable Mormon apostle whom the prophet called "the wild ram of the mountains," frequently boasted—when there was as yet no mob—what the Mormons would do if the mob did not let them alone.

Meanwhile the Mormon community at Far West was plagued by dissent. Even old intimates like Oliver Cowdery and David Whitmer, two Book of Mormon witnesses, were read out of the church. In June Sidney Rigdon delivered what was afterward called his "salt sermon," in which he made clear he considered the dissenters salt that had lost its savor and fit only to be literally trodden under foot. On the strength of that,

93

eighty-four churchmen signed a document ordering the dissenters to leave Caldwell County within three days or suffer a "more fatal calamity." It was the beginning of an effort by a close band of misguided loyalists called Danites to enforce unity, to separate the chaff from the wheat within the church, ironically applying to their own brethren the same terrorizing tactics the Missourians had applied to the Mormons. The church as a whole knew this society only as legitimate companies of tens and fifties organizing to meet eventual mobs. Mormon history is still in shadow on the work of these early extremists.

Not content with giving sharp warning to dissenters within, the inordinate Rigdon turned on the outsiders in the peroration of his Fourth of July sermon at Far West. Provoked beyond measure by signs that the old, senseless hatreds were about to pour out on them again, he announced that this time the Mormons would not turn the other cheek. The faithful were carried away in the belief that God would protect them, no matter how numerous their enemies. At the close of the oration, his assembly in the square shouted "Hosannah, hosannah, hosannah! Amen, Amen, Amen!" three times over, approving a suicidal policy that would only split the church and provoke a civil war with Missouri.

Sidney Rigdon's disastrous ultimatum was published in pamphlet form and reprinted in newspapers far and wide as "a curious document" to become the excited topic of the day. Its unbridled climax is reproduced below from Oration delivered by Mr. S. Rigdon, on the 4th of July, 1838. At Far West, Caldwell County, Missouri *(Far West, Mo., 1838), with the permission of the Chicago Historical Society.*

Many of us, in times past, were rich, but for Jesus' sake and at the command of our God we have become poor, because he became poor for our sakes; so in like manner, we follow his example, and become poor for his sake.

And as Moses left Egypt not fearing the wrath of the king, and refused to be called the son of Pharoah's daughter, choosing rather to suffer affliction with the people of God, than enjoy the pleasures of sin for a season . . . so do we choose to suffer with the people of God, rather than enjoy the flatteries of the world for a season.

It is not because we cannot, if we were so disposed, enjoy the honors and flatteries of the world, but we have voluntarily offered them in sacrifice, and the riches of the world also, for a more durable substance. Our God has promised us a reward of eternal inheritance. . . . The promise is sure, and the reward is certain. It is because of this, that we have taken the spoiling of our goods. Our cheeks have been given to the smiters, and our heads to those who have plucked off the hair. We have not only when smitten on one cheek turned the other, but we have done it, again and again, until we are wearied of being smitten, and tired of being trampled upon. We have proved the world with kindness, we have suffered their abuse without cause, with patience, and have endured without resentment, until this day, and still their persecutions and violence does not cease. But from this day and this hour, we will suffer it no more.

We take God and all the holy angels to witness this day, that we warn all men in the name of Jesus Christ, to come on us no more forever; for from this hour, we will bear it no more, our rights shall no more be trampled upon with impunity. The man or the set of men, who attempts it, does it at the expense of their lives. And that mob that comes on us to disturb us, it shall be between us and them a war of extermination, for we will follow them, till the last drop of their blood is spilled, or else they will have to exterminate us: for we will carry the seat of war to their own houses, and their own families, and one party or the other shall be utterly destroyed.—Remember it then all *Men!*

We will never be the aggressors, we will infringe on the rights of no people; but shall stand for our own until death. We claim our own rights, and are willing that all others shall enjoy theirs.

No man shall be at liberty to come into our streets, to threaten us with mobs, for if he does, he shall atone for it before he leaves the place, neither shall he be at liberty, to vilify and slander any of us, for suffer it we will not in this place.

We therefore, take all men to record this day, that we proclaim our liberty on this day, as did our fathers. And we pledge this day to one another, our fortunes, our lives, and our sacred honors, to be delivered from the persecutions which we have had to endure for the last nine years, or nearly that. Neither will we indulge any man, or set of men, in instituting vexatious law suits against us, to cheat us out of our just rights, if they attempt it we say wo be unto them.

We this day then proclaim ourselves free, with a purpose and a determination, that never can be broken, "no never! *no never!!* NO NEVER!!!"

"A True Narrative of Causes"

AN ELECTION EPISODE at Gallatin, Daviess County, on August 6, 1838, touched off a series of alarms and skirmishes between Missourians and Mormons which shortly threw the whole state into an uproar. The earliest exchange was satirically called "Squire Black's War" in the press because Justice Adam Black accused an armed "Mormon posse" of forcing him on pain of death to sign an agreement that he would not prosecute them in any lawless acts; whereupon a William Peniston, who had declared the Mormons should not be allowed to vote, swore out a complaint against Joseph Smith, Lyman Wight, and others before circuit judge Austin A. King charging them with insurrection.

What actually happened in this first phase of what became a civil war is retold more or less accurately in a communication from Liberty, Clay County, which appeared in the Western Star *on September 14 and was reprinted in the* Missouri Argus *of St. Louis on September 27, 1838, from which it is taken here. "Lyman Wright" should be read "Lyman Wight."*

Liberty, Mo., Sept. 14.

We desire in the statement we are about to make, to give the true narrative of the causes which have produced the difficulty between the Mormons and the citizens of Daviess county, as well as to give all that has occurred respecting the movements of both parties since the first difficulty took place.

At the election in Daviess county, a citizen objected to a Mormon's voting, which brought about angry words—the Mormon was struck with a club, and in return used the same weapon himself; and before the affair terminated, several on both sides were engaged, and knives freely used. No person was killed, but some cut and bruised. The excitement did not terminate with the fight. Shortly afterwards Joe Smith, Lyman Wright, and other Mormon leaders collected a large force in Caldwell, and went into Daviess county to protect the Mormons residing there. They went armed and equipped for war, but they say their intention was peace, and if what we hear be true, respecting the paper which they presented to Adam Black, a justice of the peace, for his signature, a very different face has been placed upon the transaction to that B. swore to. The paper Smith presented to Black was to the effect that, inasmuch as it was anticipated that difficulties would grow out of the fight at the election, between the Mormons and the citizens of Daviess, he (Black) as justice of the peace, pledged himself that he would take lawful notice of any unlawful proceedings of either party—Smith representing to Black, that if he would sign such a paper, he would show it to his own people and to others, and that it would have an effect to prevent difficulties.

We understand that the facts elicited at the trial of Smith and Wright (who gave themselves up, and were heard before the Judge of our Circuit Court last week), completely stamped the certificate of Black, Cumstock, and others, with falsehood. After the trial of Smith and Wright, it was believed that difficulties had ceased, but not so. The people of Daviess county had sent letters and messengers to other counties, in order to raise men to drive all the Mormons out of Daviess, and many from other counties had gone to their aid. The Mormons seeing this, made preparations also. When, seeing the crisis at which things were arriving, the judge of our Circuit, Hon. Austin A. King, asked General D. R. Atchinson to raise 1,000 men in his Division, and forthwith march into Daviess, to keep the peace, and prevent bloodshed. . . .

We are not apprehensive that anything serious will take place, though both parties have become much excited.

————

Civil War in Missouri

THE "MORMON WAR" in Missouri, which cost the Mormons every- thing they had and the state an official appropriation of $200,000 for its military role in it, was a confused tragedy. Once started, the drama, with all its ironies and contradictions and moments when chance might so easily have given events a happier turn, moved to its fateful close: from 12,000 to 15,000 Mormons finally and officially were harried out of the state and Joseph Smith himself was in chains on charge of treason and under sentence to be shot. It was "bloody Missouri" long before it was *"bloody Kansas," and the issues were in part the same: "Mormonism, emancipation and abolitionism must be driven from our State."*

In the civil strife neighboring counties behaved like sovereign states, conducting border warfare and threatening invasion and counterinvasion. The Missourians meant to drive the Mormons "from Daviess to Caldwell, and from Caldwell to hell." And the Mormons were equally determined to "make clean work now and expel the mob from Daviess and then from Caldwell." One inflammatory incident led to another. Rumor and exaggeration ran riot, defense was often mistaken for aggression, and fear and hatred decided each new blow. With both Missourians and Mormons taking the law into their own hands, mob and militia became indistinguishable, and Governor Lilburn W. Boggs himself declared: "The quarrel is between the Mormons and the mob, and they can fight it out." Both sides had become too desperate to listen to reason.

The furor lasted nearly three months, from the election incident at Gallatin on August 6, 1838, to the surrender of the Mormons at Far West on October 31. By then 3,000 men were under arms, with, as one paper quipped, "no scarcity of generals." By then the Mormon colony at De Witt, where the Kirtland refugees were still camped in wagons, had been forced to evacuate to Far West; Adam-ondi-Ahman had been besieged and would have to evacuate in ten days; Mormon stock had been slaughtered and crops destroyed and outlying settlers mercilessly abused; the Mormons had captured an ammunition train and fallen unknowingly on the militia instead of the mob; the Mormons had been accused of pillaging Gallatin and burning Millport; Governor Boggs had charged them with open rebellion and issued an extermination order; marauding regulators had massacred Mormon settlers at Haun's Mill; and now, at Far West, the Mormons gave up their leaders to the state for trial, promised to leave Missouri, and pledged their lands to pay for the costs of the war.

The selections that follow reflect the excited temper of the times, with messengers flying about like Paul Reveres to rouse the countryside and minute skirmishes blown up into spectacular battles. Austin A. King, one of the letter-writers below, was judge of the circuit court in the fifth judicial district at Richmond and conducted several of Joseph Smith's hearings, but he was hardly a judicial observer. He speaks all the more for the Missourian point of view in an intensely partisan conflict which to the Mormons seemed only a grand conspiracy to rob them of their improved lands. The issues, unfortunately, were not so diabolically simple.

I

The following intelligence is quite alarming. The letter which we give below was received yesterday by Saint Peters, which left Glasgow about day-light on Monday morning, the 7th instant. The letter was written about the hour of the boat's leaving. The writer is one of the most respectable citizens of the upper country, his statements may be relied upon.

In addition to the above, we understand that a messenger bearing despatches to his Excellency Governor Boggs, arrived in the City yesterday. What the contents of the despatches were, or what orders his Excellency has taken, we have not learned. We believe that this intestine war will not be settled without a fight, and the quicker they have it, the better for the peace and quiet of the country. If the Governor thinks proper to order out the troops again, we suggest that he give the call to the St. Louis Grays. Equipped and drilled as they are, they would be more effective than twice their number of raw militia, besides it would save calling out so many Major Generals, &c.

GLASGOW, Oct. 7th, 1838

Gentlemen,—As one of a committee of six from the counties of Howard and Chariton, appointed to visit the county of Carroll, where the disturbance exists between the Mormons and the citizens and to examine into the causes, and to endeavor to effect a reconciliation between the parties, I have thought proper to communicate to you the facts as they exist. The Mormons reside at a town, six miles above the mouth of Grand River, called De Witt. For the last week some citizens of Carroll, and others from Saline and Chariton counties, to the number of about two hundred persons, have been assembled within one mile of De Witt, all well armed, and have one piece of artillery, threatening every day to attack the Mormons in De Witt; in fact on the 4th of July there was an attack made and many guns fired from both sides, but only one man wounded of the mob party as they are called. We were there on yesterday, and endeavored to bring about a reconciliation between the parties; the citizens proposed that if the Mormons would leave the country and not return again, they would pay them back the amount their property cost, with 10 per cent interest thereon, and return them the amount of their expenses in coming and going out of the county. The Mormons replied that ever since they had been a people they had been driven from place to place, and they had determined they should be driven no more and that they had determined, every one of them to die on the ground. There are 100 families of Mormons who are there and are now encamped with their wagons in town, having just arrived; what number of men they have we could not ascertain, but presume they have considerable assistance from their principal town—Far West—in Caldwell county, about 60 or 80 miles distance, within the last 24 hours their number have increased so much that the mob have declined an attack until reinforced from other counties. A Messenger has just arrived, who left there at day-light this morning, and reports that the guard was fired upon by Mormons about 1 o'clock last night, and continued until the time he left, but no one had been shot of the mob. Some 20 or 30 from our county have volunteered their assistance. The commanders of the mob are Dr. Austin (Gen.) and Col. Jones. The Mormons are commanded by Hinkle. I don't think I have ever saw more resolute or determined men than the Mormons. It was our unanimous opinion that if some force sufficient to suppress them does not interpose immediately, there will be great slaughter and many lives lost—some of our first citizens have engaged in it. Our country is in great excitement in consequence of it, and there is no telling where it will end.

> Your obedient servant,
>
> WM. F. DUNNICA.

[*Missouri Republican Daily* (St. Louis), October 11, 1838.]

II

> Richmond, Oct. 24, 1838.

Dear Sir [Governor Boggs]:

As Mr. Williams will be to see you in reference to our Mormon difficulties, and will be able to say to you perhaps all that can be said, I have deemed it my duty not withstanding, to give you such information as I have sought and obtained; and it is such that I assure you may be relied on. Our relations with the Mormons are such, that I am perfectly satisfied that the arm of the Executive authority is too weak to give peace to the country. Until lately, I thought the Mormons were disposed to act only on the defensive; but their recent conduct shows that they are the aggressors, that they intend to take the law into their own hands. Of their recent outrages in Daviess you have doubtless heard much already. Of their course of conduct there I will give you the general facts; for to give particulars would far transcend the limits of a letter. On Sun-

100

day, before they marched into Daviess, Jo Smith made known his views to the people, and declared the time had come when they would avenge their own wrongs, and that all who were not for them, that their property should be forfeited, and their lives also be forfeited.

With this declaration and much else said by Smith to excite the people present—the next day was set to meet to see who was for them and who against them, and render such severe penalties, that there was none, I learn, who did not turn out, and about 300 or 400 men, with Smith at their head, marched into Daviess. This was on Tuesday; the next day was the snowstorm, and Thursday they commenced their ravages upon the citizens, driving them from their homes and taking their property. Between 80 and 100 men went to Gallatin pillaging houses and the store of Mr. Strollings [Stollings], and the post-office, and then burnt the houses. They carried off the spoils on horse back and wagons, and now have them, I understand, in a storehouse, near their camp. Houses have been robbed of their contents—beds, clothing, furniture, &c. And all deposited, and they call it, "a consecration to the Lord." —At this time there is not a citizen in Daviess except Mormons. Many have been driven without warning, others have been allowed a few hours to start. The stock of the citizens have been seized upon, killed and salted by hundreds; and from 50 to 100 wagons are now employed in hauling in the corn from the surrounding country. They look for a force against them, and consequently preparing for a siege, building block houses, &c. They have lately organized themselves into a band of what they call "Danites," who are sworn to obey their leading men in whatever they say or do, right or wrong—and further, to put to instant death those who will betray them. There is another band of twelve called the "Destructives," whose duty it is to watch the movements of men and of communities, and to avenge themselves for supposed wrongful movements against them, by privately burning houses, property, and even laying in ashes towns, &c. . . .

The Mormons expect to settle the affair at the point of the sword, and I am well warranted in saying to you that the people in this quarter of the State look to you for that protection, which they believe you will afford, when you have learned the facts. I do not pretend to advise your course, nor make any suggestions other than what I have stated; that it is utterly useless for the civil authorities to pretend to interpose. The Country is in great commotion, and I can assure you that either with or without authority, something will shortly have to be done.

I hope you will let me hear from you by the return of Mr. Williams, and if you should come up the country shortly it will give me pleasure to take the trouble to see you.

I am, very respectfully,

AUSTIN A. KING.

[*Missouri Argus* (St. Louis), November 8, 1838.]

"Exterminate or Expel Them!"

AN EXAGGERATED REPORT of a Mormon brush with Missouri militia under a Captain Bogart on October 25 reached Richmond, where it was fully believed the Mormons were on their way to sack and burn the city. Richmond sent to near-by Lexington for help. Lexington responded with "one hundred well armed and daring men," and Judge E. M. Ryland sent an express to two men on their way to the capitol at Jefferson urging them to hurry and spread the news en route and to send couriers into surrounding counties to raise volunteers. Judge Ryland warned they must go "prepared with the full determination to exterminate or expel" the Mormons from the state.

On the strength of this message and the false reports that the Mormons had burned Gallatin and Millport, Governor Lilburn W. Boggs two days later issued his infamous extermination order to General John B. Clark of the state troops, which made explicit an old intention in Missouri. The governor's order is reproduced below from John Corrill, A Brief History of the Church of Christ of Latter Day Saints (*St. Louis, 1839*).

Head Quarters of the Militia, City of Jefferson,
October 27th, 1838.

Sir—Since the order of the morning to you, directing you to cause four hundred mounted men to be raised within your division, I have received by Amos Rees, of Ray county and W. C. Williams, Esq., one of my aids, information of the most appalling nature, which entirely changes the face of things, and places the Mormons in the attitude of an open and avowed defiance of the laws, and of having made war upon

102

the people of this State. Your orders are, therefore, to hasten your operations and endeavour to reach Richmond, in Ray county, with all possible speed. The Mormons must be treated as enemies, and must be exterminated, or driven from the State if necessary for the public peace. If you can increase your forces, you are authorised to do so to any extent you may consider necessary. I have just issued orders to Maj. Gen. Willock, of Marion county, to raise five hundred men, and to march them to the northern part of Daviess, and there unite with General Doniphan, of Clay, who has been ordered with five hundred men to proceed to the same point, for the purpose of intercepting the retreat of the Mormons to the north. They have been directed to communicate with you by express: you can also communicate with them if you find it necessary. Instead, therefore, of proceeding as at first directed, to reinstate the citizens of Daviess in their homes, you will proceed immediately to Richmond, and there operate against the Mormons. Brig. Gen. Parks, of Ray, has been ordered to have four hundred men of his brigade in readiness to join you at Richmond. The whole force will be placed under your command.

Gen. John B. Clark, Fayette, Howard Co.

(Signed) L. W. Boggs, Com. in Chief.

Massacre at Haun's Mill

THREE DAYS AFTER Governor Boggs's extermination order, thirty Mormon families collected at Haun's Mill on Shoal Creek felt its terror. A band of marauders, "fighting on its own hook," descended on them, men, women, and children scattering for shelter into the woods and, fatally for them, into a blacksmith shop. Nineteen men and boys were killed, some brutally, and a dozen wounded. One of the regulators shot down Thomas McBride, an old Revolutionary soldier, with his own gun, then hacked him savagely with a corn knife. Another, after the massacre, found a nine-year-old boy cowering under the bellows in the blacksmith shop. He shot him through the head, boasting later that "Nits will make lice, and if he had lived he would have become a Mormon." The guerrillas rifled the hamlet, hauling off goods and wagons and taking perhaps a dozen horses. One man carried away an empty ten-gallon keg, which he held before him on his saddle and beat as a drum. Another took a woman's bonnet for his sweetheart. "The keg and bonnet incident," records a sober history of Caldwell County, "will indicate the spirit in which this 'campaign' was waged against the saints." The survivors, not knowing what to expect, hastily threw the dead into an unfinished well and withdrew to Far West.

Joseph Young, an eyewitness, describes the fateful October 30th in the section below. Young had arrived at Haun's Mill from Kirtland only two days before. He had been warned upon reaching upper Missouri that he was in danger of being stopped by armed men if he proceeded. "I was not willing, however, while treading my native soil, and breathing republican air, to abandon my object, which was to locate myself and family in a fine, healthy country." His affidavit is excerpted here from a Mormon documentary collection, History of the Church of Jesus Christ of Latter-day Saints (*Salt Lake City, 1902*), *edited by B. H. Roberts.*

It was about four o'clock, while sitting in my cabin with my babe in my arms, and my wife standing by my side, the door being open, I cast my eyes on the opposite bank of Shoal creek and saw a large company of armed men, on horses, directing their course towards the mills with all possible speed. As they advanced through the scattering trees that stood on the edge of the prairie they seemed to form themselves into a three square position, forming a vanguard in front.

At this moment, David Evans, seeing the superiority of their numbers, (there being two hundred and forty of them, according to their own account), swung his hat, and cried for peace. This not being heeded, they continued to advance, and their leader, Mr. Nehemiah Comstock, fired a gun, which was followed by a solemn pause of ten or twelve seconds, when, all at once, they discharged about one hundred rifles, aiming at a blacksmith shop into which our friends had fled for safety; and charged up to the shop, the cracks of which between the logs were sufficiently large to enable them to aim directly at the bodies of those who had there fled for refuge from the fire of their murderers. There were several families tented in the rear of the shop, whose lives were exposed, and amidst a shower of bullets fled to the woods in different directions.

After standing and gazing on this bloody scene for a few minutes, and finding myself in the uttermost danger, the bullets having reached

104

the house where I was living, I committed my family to the protection of heaven, and leaving the house on the opposite side, I took a path which led up the hill, following in the trail of three of my brethren that had fled from the shop. While ascending the hill we were discovered by the mob, who immediately fired at us, and continued so to do till we reached the summit. In descending the hill, I secreted myself in a thicket of bushes, where I lay till eight o'clock in the evening, at which time I heard a female voice calling my name in an under tone, telling me that the mob had gone and there was no danger. I immediately left the thicket, and went to the house of Benjamin Lewis, where I found my family (who had fled there) in safety, and two of my friends mortally wounded, one of whom died before morning. Here we passed the painful night in deep and awful reflections on the scenes of the preceding evening.

After daylight appeared, some four or five men, who with myself, had escaped with our lives from the horrid massacre, and who repaired as soon as possible to the mills, to learn the condition of our friends, whose fate we had but too truly anticipated. When we arrived at the house of Mr. Haun, we found Mr. Merrick's body lying in the rear of the house, Mr. McBride's in front, literally mangled from head to foot. We were informed by Miss Rebecca Judd, who was an eye witness, that he was shot with his own gun, after he had given it up, and then cut to pieces with a corn cutter by a Mr. Rogers of Daviess county, who keeps a ferry on Grand river, and who has since repeatedly boasted of this act of savage barbarity. Mr. York's body we found in the house, and after viewing these corpses, we immediately went to the blacksmith's shop, where we found nine of our friends, eight of whom were already dead; the other, Mr. Cox, of Indiana, struggling in the agonies of death and soon expired. We immediately prepared and carried them to the place of interment. The last office of kindness due to the remains of departed friends, was not attended with the customary ceremonies or decency, for we were in jeopardy, every moment expecting to be fired upon by the mob, who, we supposed, were lying in ambush, waiting for the first opportunity to despatch the remaining few who were providentially preserved from the slaughter of the preceding day. However, we accomplished without molestation this painful task. The place of burying was a vault in the ground, formerly intended for a well, into which we threw the bodies of our friends promiscuously. Among those slain I will mention Sardius Smith, son of Warren Smith, about nine years old, who, through fear, had crawled under the

105

bellows in the shop, where he remained till the massacre was over, when he was discovered by a Mr. Glaze, of Carroll county, who presented his rifle near the boy's head, and literally blowed off the upper part of it. Mr. Stanley, of Carroll, told me afterwards that Glaze boasted of this fiend-like murder and heroic deed all over the country.

The number killed and mortally wounded in this wanton slaughter was eighteen or nineteen. . . . Miss Mary Stedwell, while fleeing, was shot through the hand, and, fainting, fell over a log, into which they shot upwards of twenty balls.

To finish their work of destruction, this band of murderers, composed of men from Daviess, Livingston, Ray, Carroll, and Chariton counties, led by some of the principal men of that section of the upper country . . . proceeded to rob the houses, wagons, and tents, of bedding and clothing; drove off horses and wagons, leaving widows and orphans destitute of the necessaries of life; and even stripped the clothing from the bodies of the slain. According to their own account, they *fired seven* rounds in this awful butchery, making upwards of sixteen hundred shots at a little company of men, about thirty in number. I hereby certify the above to be a true statement of facts, according to the best of my knowledge.

JOSEPH YOUNG.

The Mormons Surrender

FAR WEST, the Mormon capital in Missouri, capitulated on October 31, 1838, after a night of suspense following the massacre at Haun's Mill. John Corrill, a member of the Missouri legislature and one of the Mormon negotiators, describes the surrender and its aftermath below. Secretly dismayed with the desperate course the Mormons had lately pursued, Corrill shortly left them. Mormons accuse him and Colonel Hinkle of betraying Joseph Smith into the hands of the state by accepting the terms of surrender without consulting the prophet. But the prophet had told them to "sue for peace like a dog," and was ready to give himself up rather than have the troops fall upon his people. Corrill

106

stoutly maintains that the Mormon leaders knew the terms of peace, and that they realized there was no way out but to submit.

This account is drawn from A Brief History of the Church of Christ of Latter Day Saints, which John Corrill published at St. Louis the next year. The petition he refers to was an attempt on the part of the Mormons to have the legislature remove the conditions they had pledged to observe at the time of surrender. It never came to a vote. Neither did a bill to provide for the investigation of "the late disturbances in the State of Missouri." Introduced in January, 1839, it was tabled in February until July, by which time the Mormon departure was a fait accompli and Missouri was saved the trouble.

This order [of Governor Boggs] greatly agitated my mind. I expected we should be exterminated without fail. There lay three thousand men, highly excited and full of vengeance, and it was as much as the officers could do to keep them off from us any how; and they now had authority from the executive to exterminate, with orders to cut off our retreat, and the word Mormons, I thought, included innocent as well as guilty; so of course there was no escape for any. These were my first reflections on hearing the order. But General Lucas soon said that they would be more mild than the order required; that if we would give up the heads of the church to be punished; surrender our arms; give up all our property (those who had taken up arms) to pay the debts of the whole church and the damages done in Daviess and elsewhere; and then all leave the State forthwith, except those retained to be punished, they would spare our lives, and protect us out of the State. The sun was then about two hours high, and he gave us till sunset to make up our minds and deliver the prisoners. A gentleman of note told me that if these men were suffered to escape, or if they could not be found, nothing could save the place from destruction and the people from extermination. We knew that General Lucas had no authority, and his requirements were illegal; for he was out of the bounds of his division, and the Governor's order was to General Clark, and not to him: but there was no other way for the Mormons but to submit. We immediately went into town and collected Joseph Smith, jr., Sidney Rigdon, Lyman Wight, Parley P. Pratt, George W. Robertson together, and told them what the Governor's order and General Lucas required. Smith said if it was the Governor's order, they would submit, and the Lord would take care of them. So we hurried with them as fast as possible to the place appointed. We met General Lucas, with his army, but a short distance from town. He had made every arrangement to surround and destroy the place; but the prisoners delivered themselves up, and General Lucas, with the army and prisoners, returned to their camp. These prisoners were to be retained as hostages till morning, and then, if they did not agree to the proposals, they were to be set at liberty again. I suppose they agreed to the proposals, for they were not set at liberty. Next morning, General Lucas marched his army near to town, and Colonel Hinkle marched out the Mormons, who gave up their arms, about six hundred guns, besides swords and pistols, and surrendered themselves as prisoners. I would here remark, that a few days previous to this, news had frequently come to Far West that they were soon to be attacked, and Caldwell county destroyed: so the judge of the county court had ordered Col. Hinkle with the militia to guard the county against invasion. They turned out and organized under this order, and in this situation surrendered to Gen. Lucas. A guard was placed around Far West to keep all things secure, and Gen. Parks, with an army, was sent to Adamondiaman, where there were about one hundred and fifty armed Mormons, who surrendered to him and gave up their arms. The five prisoners who first surrendered, together with Amasa Lyman and Hiram Smith, who had been added to them, remained in the camp until Friday morning, when Gen. M. Wilson, of Jackson, started with the prisoners and arms to Independence. The troops were then discharged, except a guard around town.

On Saturday evening or Sunday morning, Gen. Clark arrived with fourteen hundred mounted men, and said there were six thousand more within a day's march, but they were turned back. Previous to the arrival of Gen. Clark, the Mormons were gathered together and about five hundred made to sign a deed of trust, in which five commissioners were appointed, to whom they deeded all their property in trust for the use of all the creditors of the church, and also to pay all the damages done by the Danites, and the overplus, if any, was to be refunded. Gen. Clark ratified what Gen. Lucas had done, and kept the town well guarded, and permitted none to go out, except now and then one to see their families and then return again. However, in a day or two, he gathered up all the Mormon prisoners and selected forty or fifty, such as he thought, from the best information he could get, ought to be punished, and put them in a store and had them guarded over night. He then withdrew the guard from town and let the remainder go free, but the next day marched with the prisoners to Richmond, where Gen. Lucas had been previously ordered to return the prisoners and arms he had taken to Independence. In Richmond, they guarded the prisoners, seven of whom (the leaders) they put in irons, and held a court of enquiry before Judge King over them; after which they retained thirty-six for trial, and let the rest, between twenty and thirty, go free. Those retained for trial were charged with various crimes—treason, murder, arson, burglary, robbery, and larceny. Gen. Clark, before leaving Far West, sent Gen. Wilson to Adamondiaman with a sufficient force, and he so regulated matters there as to have all the Mormons leave Daviess county except a very few, who were to see to the property, &c. The Mormons from Daviess mostly went to Caldwell.

The prisoners charged with treason and murder were confined in jail, in Liberty and Richmond, and the rest let to bail. During this campaign, many reports were circulated concerning the misconduct of the soldiers, but how far they were true I am not able to say, but I thought at the time, the officers tried to keep good order among the troops, and that whatever abuse was practiced on the Mormons ought to have been charged on the individuals that did it, and not upon the officers or community at large. It was said that women were insulted and even ravished, but I doubt the truth of the latter. Some were insulted; yet, as soon as the officers were informed, they set guards to prevent further insult. Two men that were taken prisoners were struck on the head, one was badly hurt and the other killed. The man who killed him accused him of having abused his family and burned his house; but on returning home he found his house had not been burned at all. Why he was not committed for trial, I never knew. Many others were taken prisoners, but generally were well treated and set free without injury. There was much corn, cattle, fodder, &c., used for the army, but the officers said the State would pay for it. There were some instances of soldiers shooting cattle, hogs and sheep, merely for sport, when they did not want them for food, but this, I understood, was contrary to the officers' orders. There were also several cases in which persons were plundered of horses and other property, even clothing and furniture out of houses, by the soldiers, but they alleged that they were looking after and getting their property back which had been taken from them. I have been told that the same has been practised, more or less, by companies passing through the county, since the troops have been withdrawn. Others, to whom they were indebted, have taken their property for debts, until they are literally stripped, and are at this time in a miserable, destitute situation. The Legislature, on hearing of their situation, appropriated two thousand dollars for their relief, as well as for the relief of the destitute in Daviess. A number of the Mormons met, and appointed a committee who drew up a petition in their behalf, to the Legislature, setting forth a short history of their difficulties, from their first settlement in Jackson county to the present time, and praying the Legislature to rescind the Governor's exterminating order, under which they were compelled to leave the State, and also release them from the deed of trust made in duress; pay them for their arms or return them, and pay them for their arms taken from them, as well as other damages sustained by them in Jackson county, and let them have the privilege of living in the State. (When Col. Pitcher took their arms in Jackson, he agreed to return them as soon as they left the county, but this he refused to do even on the Governor's order for them.) Some two hundred families have left Caldwell county, and others are preparing to go, but some are desirous to stay in the State; and their object in getting up the petition was to be relieved from their expelling contract, so that men should not have the privilege of abusing them under a legal pretence, thinking it was right because they agreed to leave the state, though that contract was strictly illegal. This petition I presented to the Legislature on the 19th December. It produced some excitement in the House and was laid on the table for the present.

Flight from Missouri

AFTER THE MORMONS grounded their arms at Far West, a summary court martial sentenced Joseph Smith, his brother Hyrum, Sidney Rigdon, and four other leaders to be shot the next morning in the public square in sight of their families and their people "as an example." When General A. W. Doniphan denounced such an execution as cold-blooded murder and threatened to remove his troops if it were carried out, General S. D. Lucas of Jackson County changed his mind and had the prisoners taken to Independence. The troops paraded them through the streets, heaped them with abuse, and finally turned them over in chains to civil authorities in Richmond, where fifty-nine other Mormons were charged with "treason, murder, arson, larceny, theft, and stealing": treason, for having fought the State of Missouri; murder, for the death of several militiamen; and arson, larceny, theft, and stealing, for their counter-depredations. Judge Austin A. King found Mormon belief in the superiority of Christ's kingdom over any worldly authority "a strong point for treason."

After a series of prejudiced hearings in which most of the Mormon witnesses were spirited away, five prisoners were indicted for treason and committed to jail in Liberty, and five for murder and committed in Richmond. From Liberty the prophet wrote that "the murders at Haun's Mill, the exterminating order of Governor Boggs, and the one-sided rascally proceedings of the Legislature, have damned the State of Missouri to all eternity." Missouri, in fact, did not really know what to do with him and at length, after six months, the governor himself connived at his escape. When in April, 1839, the prisoners in Liberty were given a mittimus for Boone County, the sheriff and his guards deliberately got drunk and told them to make good their freedom. Within a few days the prophet was among friends in Illinois. Certain factions in Missouri continued to prosecute him—they sought his extradition from Illinois, and warrants and kidnapping attempts beset him all during the Nauvoo period.

By the time Joseph Smith reached Illinois, from 12,000 to 15,000 Mormon refugees had left Missouri, most of them making their way to the countryside around Quincy, Illinois, and to the Half Breed Tract in Iowa. The destitute were saved largely through the emerging leadership of Brigham Young, president of the Council of Twelve, who covenanted "never to desert the poor who are worthy" until all had been delivered out of the hands of their oppressors. He established corn desposits eastward across Missouri from Far West to the Mississippi and arranged for ferriage at strategic points. By April, 1839, the evacuation was complete and Mormons were finding employment among the friendly people of Illinois and were already dreaming of a new capital.

The Daily Missouri Republican below takes note of Joseph Smith's escape; and an item from the Cleveland Herald suggests how the Mormon expulsion had captured the sympathy of the country.

I

The celebrated Mormon leader, Joseph Smith, who has so long been in confinement in the upper part of Missouri, arrived in town [Quincy, Illinois] on Monday last. He and four of his companions, consisting of Lyman Wight, Caleb Baldwin, Hiram Smith and Alexander McRae, escaped from the guard which was taking them from Daviess to Boone

111

county for trial. The guard got drunk and fell asleep, in one night of their travel, and the prisoners, knowing that they could not expect justice in any courts of upper Missouri, very properly turned their backs upon their persecutors and left them alone in their iniquity. We had supposed from the stories and statements we had read of "Jo Smith" (as he is termed in the papers) to find him a very illiterate, uncouth sort of a man; but from a conversation, we acknowledge an agreeable disappointment. In conversation he appears intelligent and candid, and divested of all malicious thought and feeling towards his relentless persecutors. There are five more of the Mormons in confinement in Ray county jail.

Query. Will Governor Boggs offer a reward for the apprehension of the fugitives or will he demand them from Gov. Carlin? [*Daily Missouri Republican* (St. Louis), May 3, 1839, quoting a Quincy, Illinois, paper.]

II

It is an old saying "that the blood of the martyrs is the seed of the church." The persecutions and war of extermination waged on the Mormons by the people and government of Missouri have justly awakened much sympathy for the followers of Smith and Rigdon. In New Jersey, Mormonism has taken root, and is extending its borders to several neighborhoods. A number of persons have been converted to the Mormon faith, and the zeal of its teachers has been strengthened by former persecutions and is now increased by accessions of converts. We notice that Mr. Green, the Mormon preacher who excited so much feeling in Cincinnati by his recital of the sufferings and attempted extermination of this sect in Missouri, is now in New York city seeking for contributions in aid of the women and children, who without fault or crime, have been turned houseless and homeless upon the world. Mr. Green is deputed by the society, and seems to be favorably received in New York.

[Cleveland *Herald,* quoted in Painesville (Ohio) *Telegraph,* September 26, 1839.]

Beginnings in Illinois

GENERAL JOHN B. CLARK *had advised the Mormons at Far West to scatter, warning that the old calamities would befall them if they congregated in exclusive settlements. But "gathering" was the heart of Mormonism, and it was not long before they laid foundations for a new capital. The prophet's arrival in Quincy was the signal for action. In May he led a committee which bought several hundred acres of farm-land, on terms, from Dr. Isaac Galland at Commerce, Illinois, a swampy hamlet of six houses clustered on the edge of a great bend of the Mississippi 190 miles above St. Louis. It was the beginning of Nauvoo the Beautiful, a name "carrying with it also," the prophet said, "the idea of rest."*

"The place was literally a wilderness," he wrote. "The land was mostly covered with trees and bushes, and much of it was so wet that it was with the utmost difficulty that a footman could get through, and totally impossible for teams. Commerce was unhealthy, very few could live there; but believing that it might become a healthy place by the blessing of heaven to the Saints, and no more eligible place presenting itself, I considered it wisdom to make an attempt to build up a city."

On December 25, 1839, the Cleveland Herald *could observe, "These persecuted people are going ahead." An early visitor writing to the Alexandria* Gazette *describes Nauvoo's beginnings, the astonishing recovery of the Mormons and their expansion into Iowa and the country surrounding Nauvoo, and their unique political position. He reports Joseph Smith's outspoken opinion of President Van Buren, whom the prophet had sought out in Washington in a fruitless effort to persuade the federal government to vote the Mormons compensation for their Missouri losses. The account is excerpted below from the Quincy* Whig, *which reprinted it on October 17, 1840. Two months later Nauvoo was formally incorporated. The Illinois legislature, with Abraham Lincoln voting "aye," granted it a municipal charter with extraordinary privileges which made it a virtual city-state. Both Democrats and Whigs were eager to curry Mormon favor. With Joseph Smith mayor and lieutenant-*

general of a Mormon arm of the state militia in the form of the Nauvoo Legion, he seemed at last safe from the snares of his enemies.

Since the Mormons were expelled from the State of Missouri, they have purchased the town of Commerce, a situation of surpassing beauty, at the head of the lower rapids, on the Illinois shore of the upper Mississippi river. The name of the place they recently changed to Nauvoo, the Hebrew term for Fair or Beautiful. Around this place, as their centre, they are daily gathering from almost every quarter; and several hundred new houses, erected within the last few months, attest to the passing traveller the energy, industry, and self-denial with which the community is imbued. They have also obtained possession of extensive lands on the opposite side of the river, in that charming portion of Iowa Territory known as the "Half Breed Reservation"; and there, upon the rolling and fertile prairies, they are rapidly selecting their homes and opening their farms. As the traveller now passes through those natural parks and fields of flowers, which the hand of the Creator seems to have originally planned there for the inspection of his own eye, he beholds the cabins, dotted down in the most enchanting perspective either on the borders of the timber, or beside the springs and streams of living water, which are interspersed on every hand.

Nor are they unmindful of their interests abroad, while they are thus accomplishing so much at home. No sect, with equal means, has probably ever suffered and achieved more in so short a time. Their elders have not only been commissioned and sent forth to every part of our own country, but they have left their families and friends behind them, and gone to Europe, and even to the Holy Land, to reveal the wonders of the "new and everlasting covenant" to preach the dispensation of the fullness of time. . . .

It was a beautiful morning towards the close of April last, when the writer of the foregoing sketch, accompanied by a friend, crossed the Mississippi river, from Montrose, to pay a visit to the prophet. As we approached his house, we saw him ride up and alight from his beautiful horse; and handing the bridle to one of his followers in attendance, he waited in front of his gate to receive us. A number of principal men of the place soon collected around, apparently anxious to hear the words which fell from his lips. His bearing towards them was like one who had authority; and the deference which they paid him convinced us that his dominion was deeply seated in the empire of their consciences. To our minds, profound knowledge of human nature had evidently taught him that, of all principles, the most omnipotent is the religious principle; and to govern men of certain classes, it only is necessary to control their religious sentiments. . . .

Thinking this a proper time to propose a few inquiries relative to some of his peculiar tenets, I observed that it was commonly reported of him, that he believed in the personal reign of the Messiah upon earth, during the millennial era.

"I believe in no such thing," was his reply. "At the opening of the period, I believe that Christ will descend; but will immediately return again to heaven. Some of our elders," he continued, "before I had found time to instruct them better, have unadvisedly propagated some such opinions; but I tell my people that it is absurd to suppose that Christ 'will jump out of the frying pan into the fire.' He is in a good place now, and it is not to be supposed that he will exchange it for a worse one."

Not a little shocked by the emblem employed by the Prophet, we descended from his chamber, and the conversation turned upon his recent visit to Washington, and his talk with the President of the United States. He gave us distinctly to understand that his political views had undergone an entire change; and his description of the reception given him at the executive mansion was any thing but flattering to the distinguished individual who presides over its hospitalities.

"Before he had heard the story of our wrongs," said the indignant Prophet, "Mr. Van Buren gave us to understand that he could do nothing for the redress of our grievances lest it should interfere with his political prospects in Missouri. *He is not as fit,*" said he, "*as my dog, for the chair of state;* for my dog will make an effort to protect his abused and insulted master, while the present chief magistrate will not so much as lift his finger to relieve an oppressed and persecuted community of freemen, whose glory it has been that they were citizens of the United States."

"You hold in your hands," I observed, "a large amount of political power, and your society must exert a tremendous influence, for weal or woe, in the coming elections."

"Yes," said he, "I know it; and our influence, as far as it goes, we intend to use. There are probably not far short of an hundred thousand souls in our society, and the votes to which we are entitled throughout the Union must doubtless be extensively lost to Mr. Van Buren."

Not being myself disposed in any way to intermeddle in party politics I made no definite reply; but immediately taking leave we returned to Montrose, abundantly satisfied that the Society over which he presides has assumed a moral and political importance which is but very imperfectly understood.

Charlotte Haven Writes Home from Nauvoo

CHARLOTTE HAVEN *of Portsmouth, New Hampshire, arrived in Nauvoo in December, 1842, to find that "at least a third of the Mormons are English," an exaggerated estimate but evidence that immigration had already made an impact. She stayed a year, living with a brother and his wife Elizabeth and becoming a lively member of the city's Gentile minority, which she called "our little society." She must have been an attractive young woman, for she describes many balls and socials to which, though not a Mormon, she was invited. And when she took her first walk in the city, passing by the temple, she said, "I verily believe every man at work cutting stone laid down his tools and gazed at me as I passed."*

Her letters to her family provide intimate glimpses of Nauvoo's social life. Nine of them, extending from January 3, 1843, to October 15, 1843, were published in the Overland Monthly (San Francisco) *for December, 1890, as "A Girl's Letters from Nauvoo," from which the following highlights have been taken.*

I

City of Nauvoo,
Jan. 3, 1843.

. . . At eleven o'clock we came in full sight of the City of the Saints, and were charmed with the view. We were five miles from it, and from our point of vision it seemed to be situated on a high hill, and to have a dense population; but on our approach and while passing slowly through the principal streets, we thought that our vision had been magnified, or distance lent enchantment, for such a collection of miserable houses and hovels I could not have believed existed in one place. Oh, I thought, how much real poverty must dwell here! Suddenly we missed our traveling companion,—on looking back we beheld her sprawling on the ground, having sprung from the stage as it passed her house.

As we neared our little white cottage with green blinds, we saw, coming very fast across a vacant lot, a strange looking man, making eager gesticulations. He seemed to be covered with snow-flakes, and a woman was following close behind. In a moment we recognized brother, and saw that the snowflakes were feathers. "Oh, Henderson!" we both exclaimed; "have the Mormons already treated you with a coat of tar and feathers?"

"No," he laughingly replied. He and the woman, Mrs. Conklin, were having some feather beds filled for us, and seeing the stage, without regard to appearances, hastened to greet us.

The stage left us at the kitchen door. The introduction to this room was discouraging enough—full of smoke from a fire just kindled in the fire-place, no furniture except a red chest and a box of crockery, upon which was extended a half venison, flanked by a basket of vegetables, and sundry parcels of groceries. The only redeeming appendage was a forlorn old bachelor, who stood with his back to the fire and hands crossed before him. Brother introduced him to us as Judge Emmons, adding that he had just engaged to "eat him,"—a Western term used for board without lodging. We glanced into the other rooms,—a large box stove in what is parlor and dining room, a bedstead without bedding in the bed room,—that was all!

Judge Emmons . . . suggested that a search be made in his old quarters to see if some pieces of furniture might remain undisposed of. So we immediately dispatched him and brother for it. They soon returned with a table, three chairs, a coffee-pot and mill, two large tin dippers, and a *spider*. This last our grandmothers might have called a bake-kettle; it has three legs and an iron cover, which is covered with hot coals when anything is baking.

Brother had engaged a girl, but she could not come yet, so Mrs. C. kindly offered to get dinner for us and our boarder,—a herculean task it seemed to me, with the fire-place and such cooking utensils; but we had a nice dinner,—venison, hot biscuits, potatoes roasted in the ashes, etc.,—for we were awfully hungry. . . .

As darkness came on we were reminded that our lamps were at Warsaw, and the stores a mile away. Fortunately we had candles, and H. improvised candlesticks by making holes in the biscuits left from dinner. The next day he got two small blocks of wood, and now we have two new shining tin candlesticks. Dr. Weld, another of the stranded bachelors, having gone his round of patients, passed the evening with us, but both gentlemen took their departure before nine o'clock, and we went to bed—on the two feather beds with husk beds beneath. I had mine on the parlor floor and slept comfortably. . . .

But my paper is so full and crowded I fear you cannot read it, and I have not said half I wanted to. Love to all, and Happy New Year. Don't forget Grandma and children.

Affectionately yours,
Charlotte.

II

Nauvoo, Jan. 22, 1843.

My Dear Sister Isa:

. . . Last Sabbath there was preaching at the Prophet's house. Having not a little curiosity to see and hear this strange man, who has attracted so many thousands of people from every quarter of the globe, the Judge and myself sallied forth. We had not proceeded far when a large horse-sled, with a little straw on the bottom upon which were seated men and women, stopped before us; one of the men asked us to get on, and by a little crowding we placed ourselves among them and were borne along with the multitude that were thronging to hear their beloved leader. Such hurrying! one would have thought it was the last opportunity to hear him they would ever have, although we were two hours before the services were to commence. When the house was so full that not another person could stand upright, the windows were opened for the benefit of those without, who were as numerous as those within.

Joseph Smith is a large, stout man, youthful in his appearance, with light complexion and hair, and blue eyes set far back in the head, and expressing great shrewdness, or I should say, cunning. He has a large head and phrenologists would unhesitatingly pronounce it a bad one, for the organs situated in the back part are decidedly the most prominent. He is also very round-shouldered. He had just returned from Springfield, where he has been upon trial for some crime of which he was accused while in Missouri, but he was released by habeas corpus. I, who had expected to be overwhelmed by his eloquence, was never more disappointed than when he commenced his discourse by relating all the incidents of his journey. This he did in a loud voice, and his language and manner were the coarsest possible. His object seemed to be to amuse and excite laughter in his audience. He is evidently a great egotist and boaster, for he frequently remarked that at every place he stopped going to and from Springfield people crowded around him, and expressed surprise that he was so "handsome and good looking." He also exclaimed at the close of almost every sentence, "That's the idea!" I could not but with wonder and pity look upon that motley and eager crowd that surrounded me, as I thought, "Can it be possible that so many of my poor fellow-mortals are satisfied with such food for their immortal souls?" for not one sentence did that man utter calculated to create devotional feelings, to impress upon his people the great object of life, to teach them how they might more faithfully perform their duties and endure their trials with submission, to give them cheering or consoling views of a divine providence, or to fit them for an eternal life beyond the grave. . . .

There are two more Gentile brethren arrived in the city, and they will be quite an agreeable acquisition to our little society, Dr. Higbee and Mr. Skinner, a lawyer. They dined with us a few days ago on roast turkey, which was cooked by being suspended by a string from the mantel-piece, with the "spider" beneath to catch the gravy. It was pronounced excellent by all. Our "spider" is now cast into the shade by a Yankee Notion cooking stove; our bread candle-sticks were superseded by blocks of wood, then flat-bottomed tin candle-sticks, and now we are at the height of our ambition with glass lamps and spirit gas, for our trunks and furniture arrived yesterday. . . .

I believe I have mentioned that H. has formed an acquaintance with a Mormon family named Haven, who claim relationship and I believe we really have the same ancestors in Richard and Susanna Haven who settled at Lynn. There is a son who is a Methodist preacher. They came from Hopkinton, Mass.

> Yours affectionately,
> Charlotte,

III

> Venus, *alias* Commerce, *alias* Nauvoo.
> March 5, 1843.

My dear brother and sister:

. . . Notwithstanding cold and mud, we have passed a pleasant winter, our society being mostly confined to our little Gentile band. A few other acquaintances we have made, Hiram Kimball's family, who lived here when it was Commerce—Mrs. K's mother has become a Mormon and Mrs. K is leaning that way—then, at the post-office, the Rigdon family. We enter a side door leading into the kitchen, and in a corner near the door is a wide shelf or table, on which against the wall is a sort of cupboard with pigeon-holes or boxes—this is the post-office. In this room, with the great cooking stove at one end, the family eat and sit. Mrs. R. when I go for the mail always invites me to stop and rest, which after a cold, long walk I am glad to do, thus opening an acquaintance with Elder Sidney Rigdon, the most learned man among the Latter Day Saints. He is past fifty and is somewhat bald and his dark hair slightly gray. He has an intelligent countenance, a courteous manner, and speaks grammatically. He talks very pleasantly about his travels in this country and Europe, but is very reticent about his religion. I have heard it stated that he was Smith's chief aid in getting up the Book of Mormon and creed. He is so far above Smith in intellect, education, and secretiveness, that there is scarcely a doubt that he is at the head in compiling it. I looked over his library—on some bookshelves in the kitchen. It was a very good student's collection—Hebrew, Greek, and Latin lexicons and readers, stray volumes of Shakespeare, Scott, Irving's works, and a number of other valuable books. He studied for the ministry in his youth, then was employed in a newspaper office. His wife is always busy with domestic labor. They have five daughters.

The only party I have attended in this Holy City was at their house. Here is a copy of the invitation. You will observe the date was a year ago. However, we concluded it was a slight mistake, as the Judge received an invitation somehow with this year's date.

NAUVOO Feb 20 1842

The company of Mr Mrs and Miss Haven
is Solicited to attend a party at the
hous of Mr Rigdon on Thursday the 24
inst at three oclock P M

Sarah Rigdon
Eliza Rigdon

The Judge called me, and we trudged off. We were met at the P. O. door by Miss Sarah; her mother, who was paring potatoes near the stove, came forward, the venerable Elder stood behind the cook stove (which was in full operation) dressed in his Sunday best suit, the highest and stiffest shirt collar, and a white heckerchief with ends flowing over his shoulders. By his side was a very fine, stylish gentleman with gold spectacles whom he introduced to me as Mr. Marr—" A descendant of the Earl of Mar," occurred to me. He is a native of Portland, Me., and a last year's graduate of the Cambridge Law School.

Charlotte Haven Writes Home from Nauvoo

Leaving my escort in the kitchen, I was ushered into the next room—where lo! there was a large quilting frame, around which sat eight of the belles of Nauvoo, to each of whom I was introduced, then a seat was assigned me near the head of the frame, and equipped with needle, thread, and thimble, I quilted with the rest. But not a word was said, and fearing my presence had checked hilarity, I offered a few kindly remarks, only to be answered with "Yes, Marm," or "No, Marm." It was quite embarrasing, when my next neighbor timidly whispered, "We talk in the evening."

So I was stilled and put all my energy on the quilt, which was finished and taken out of the frame by six o'clock. The door to the kitchen or living room was then thrown open and we were ushered in. The scene, how changed! Through the whole length of the room, from the post-office to the stove, a table extended, loaded with a substantial supper, turkey, chicken, beef, vegetables, pies, cake, etc. To this we did silent justice.

Leaving the family to clear away, we young people returned to the other room and placed ourselves like wall-flowers. Gentlemen soon came in in groups, and when all were assembled, Mr. Rigdon came in, shook hands with the gentlemen, then placed himself in the middle of the room, and taking a gentleman by his side, commenced introductions, "Mr. Monroe,—Miss Burnett, my daughter, Miss Marks, Miss Ives, my daughter, Miss Ivens, Miss Bemis, my daughter from La Harpe, Miss Haven, my daughter."

Mr. Monroe retires and another gentleman is called up and the ceremony repeated, until all the strangers had been introduced. Then Mr. R. says, "Is there any other gentleman who has not been introduced?" when a Mr. Ives came forward and pointing with his finger, "I have not been introduced to that lady (Miss Haven) and that (Miss Bemis)."

This ceremony over, all seemed more joyous; songs were sung, concluding with the two little girls singing several verses of the Battle of Michigan, deaconed out to them line by line by their elder sister, Miss Nancy. Then followed an original dance *without music*, commencing with marching and ending with *kissing!* Merry games were then introduced, The Miller, Grab, etc., not at all of an intellectual order; so I suggested Fox and Geese, which was in vogue with us ten years ago. It took well. Brother says he called at the office during the evening, and the Elder was urging his wife to look in upon the young people. He heard him say that he had been half over the world but never had seen anything equal to this in enjoyment. At nine o'clock we went out to a second edition of supper, and then the games were renewed with vigor. We left about ten. The Miss Rigdons, who called on us the next day, said the party did not break up till twelve. . . .

This evening with the Judge I shall go either to Mrs. H. Kimball's, or to a prayer meeting, for you must know the saints take an interest in our spiritual welfare, by sending us to read the Book of Mormon, The Voice of Warning, and the Book of Covenants, and invite us to attend prayer meetings.

We are having beautiful sunsets these days, and from our parlor window we have an extensive western view; and later on in the night the heavens are all aglow with light from the prairie fires. Between the river and the Iowa bluffs eight or ten miles west, ten to twenty fires are started burning the refuse grass and straw preparatory to putting in spring crops. Often I sit up a long time after going to my room, watching these long lines of fire as they seem to meet all along the horizon. The sun is down and darkness is fast gathering, so I must close with much love from

Your sister
Charlotte.

IV

City of Nauvoo, May 2, 1843.

My dear home friends:

. . . The plain between us and the river, embracing twelve acres or more, is covered with luxuriant grass looking bright and green. For the last week or so it has presented a lively appearance from the parade and exercises of the companies of the Nauvoo Legion. This military organization comprises between two and three thousand soldiers, part of whom belong to the State. It is divided into two cohorts, and then subdivided into regiments and companies, and is intended to represent a Roman legion. These parades are preparatory to the grand annual parade on the 6th of this month, to take place on the prairie a few miles out, when Joseph, the commander-in-chief, inspects the troops. It is expected that all the élite of the city will be present on this grand gala day. We understand there is to be a cavalcade of ladies with nodding plumes. Miss Ell (she is very, very tall) will lead the van and present a banner. Dr. H. has invited me to view this imposing scene, and if nothing better offers I shall go, and expect much amusement.

Last Sunday morning the Judge came in and soon proposed a walk, for it was a balmy spring day, so we took a bee-line for the river,

122

down the street north of our house. Arriving there we rested awhile on a log, watching the thin sheets of ice as they slowly came down and floated by. Then we followed the bank toward town, and rounding a little point covered with willows and cottonwoods, we spied quite a crowd of people, and soon perceived there was a baptism. Two elders stood knee-deep in the icy cold water, and immersed one after another as fast as they could come down the bank. We soon observed that some of them went in and were plunged several times. We were told that they were baptized for the dead who had not had an opportunity of adopting the doctrines of the Latter Day Saints. So these poor mortals in ice-cold water were releasing their ancestors and relatives from purgatory! We drew a little nearer and heard several names repeated by the elders as the victims were douched, and you can imagine our surprise when the name George Washington was called. So after these fifty years he is out of purgatory and on his way to the "celestial" heaven! It was enough, and we continued our walk homeward.

A new Masonic Lodge was installed in this place last Thursday. Most of the chief men here are Masons. With the Judge I went to the Temple, where the solemn services were held, and there we waited nearly two hours before the procession with a fine band of music made its appearance. First were the invited guests, most of whom were "female women folks," wives and sisters of Masons, then the Masons in full regalia. Mr. Rigdon, by far the ablest and most cultivated of the Mormons, gave us a brief but very fine address, then followed the inauguration ceremony, which was quite simple, a hymn was sung, and the procession again formed with the invited guests in the rear, and marched to a vacant lot opposite brother's store. Here the Masons parted right and left forming two long rows, and the ladies marched between and seated themselves in an interesting row down one side of the table,—and we saw no more. All went off in fine style, as the Mormons say, and brother, who was one of the guests, said that the feast was sumptuous,—a whole hog barbecued in a trench. . . .

H. and L. send love. The boy grows finely and is quite handsome, his mother says. Remember me most affectionately to all inquiring friends, and believe me

Your aff.
Charlotte.

"Great Events Have Transpired": Politics and Polygamy

ON JULY 2, 1843, *Charlotte Haven wrote in a suddenly more serious vein. Nauvoo had seen some excitement with the arrest of Joseph Smith on the old Missouri charges, and a mass meeting bristling with arms had debated what action to take. Charlotte describes the prophet's triumphal return. She did not know that in a comic-opera sequence he had turned the tables on his captors and succeeded in having them taken into custody for false arrest: from the Nauvoo courts the prophet could always secure a writ of habeas corpus.*

The episode illustrates the absolute powers of Nauvoo as a private commonwealth, able to decide any cases arising under the statutes in its municipal court. It was an overdose of power which, as events proved, the prophet could not stand. His bravado increased with his strength until at length he flung caution to the winds, as Sidney Rigdon had done in Far West. He even issued an ordinance prescribing punishment for anyone using language disrespectful of the church; he insisted that no Illinois law could become valid in Nauvoo until it bore his signature; he bargained the Mormon vote with rival parties before each election; and he asked Congress to erect his city into a federal territory free of state control.

In successive steps, like the ruse Charlotte Haven describes in the second letter below, the Mormons alienated both Democrats and Whigs, leaving themselves surrounded by a solid ring of political enemies. Even more disastrous was the schism created within the church by the prophet's revelation in July, 1843, sanctioning polygamy for a secret few. Charlotte's letter of September 8, 1843, speaks her incredulity at what turned out to be all too true. The division proved fatal, leading to Joseph Smith's death by violence and the dissolution of Mormonism's bright promise in Nauvoo.

The following significant excerpts from her July and September letters are taken from "A Girl's Letters from Nauvoo," which appeared originally in the Overland Monthly *(San Francisco) for December, 1890.*

124

"Great Events Have Transpired": Politics and Polygamy

I

Nauvoo, July 2nd [1843.]

. . . Great events have meanwhile transpired, throwing our little City of the Saints into the greatest commotion and excitement. I seldom attend the Mormon meetings, but last Sunday afternoon I went to the grove to hear Hyrum Smith, Joseph's elder brother, an illiterate man; the preaching consisted mostly of low anecdotes and boasting of the strength of their church, with quotations from the Bible thrown in promiscuously. Toward the close a dispatch was brought him that Joseph, who was visiting friends near Rock Island, had been arrested by a band of Missourians.

When Hyrum read the message aloud, every man, woman, and child, were on their feet in an instant, pressing towards the platform, and it was with difficulty that he could quiet them. He appointed a meeting at six o'clock to take means for Joseph's release. I walked home as fast as possible, for immediately the whole city seemed to be in arms, guns and pistols firing, swords glistening in every direction like a sudden outburst of 4th of July, men, women, and children, gathering in groups talking loud and warlike.

At the appointed time five thousand men were on the spot, ready to rescue their prophet in any way their leader might suggest. He warned them against excitement, told them to go peaceably, to take nothing but secret arms, "for," says he, "He that seeth in secret will reward you openly." Such was their zeal that within two hours after the news of Joseph's arrest three hundred men were on board of a steamboat headed for Rock Island, and three hundred more on horseback and in wagons started for the same place. A patrol was organized, and a special guard to protect the chief elders from falling into the hands of any stray Missourian. Brother had occasion to go to the store in the evening and I went with him. Three times on our return we were hailed with "Halt," by armed sentinels. I somehow had no fear, but was glad to reach home.

Today Joseph was brought home in triumph, having suffered a few days' imprisonment in an old barn, from which he escaped, I am told, by giving some Masonic sign, before his friends arrived. I wish you could have seen the procession as it passed through the city; Joseph with his wife, Sister Emma, as she is called, led the van; she with white nodding plumes, followed by a half-mile of the populace in every wheeled vehicle that could be mustered, drawn by horses and oxen. In one buggy were Mr. Heringshaw, Mrs. Goodwin, and myself, and in a large wagon our Gentile brethren, Goodwin, Emmons, Haven, Weld, and the two Mr. Mars, who had displayed on one side of their vehicle "Peace and Harmony." The Prophet was quite overcome with emotion, even to shedding tears, at this unexpected show of sympathy from his non-followers. I have not yet fully learned the cause of the arrest, but believe it to be concerning the attempted murder of Gov. Boggs some years ago in Missouri. All is as quiet now as if nothing had happened.

Mrs. Case returned to Q. [Quincy] last week. I had several talks with her and Mr. H. upon their doctrine, but in no way can I be a Mormon. With my best wishes and God's blessing, I remain

Yours lovingly,
Charlotte.

II

Nauvoo, Sept 8.

My dear friends at home:

. . . We have been reading Dickens's notes on America, sent us by Mrs. D. of Quincy. We admire Dickens much, he has a keen sense of our national peculiarities which he paints in sparkling humor, yet he delineates the wild and beautiful scenery of ———— with graphic accuracy. You know H. and E. were on the boat with him down the Ohio and had several conversations with him. He certainly describes most faithfully travel on canals and our great Western rivers.

A few Sabbaths ago Joseph announced to his people that the gift of prophecy was taken away from him until the Temple and Nauvoo House should be finished, but that his mantle had fallen on his brother Hyrum, to whom it belonged by birthright, and he charged his people to obey implicitly all the commands revealed to Hyrum. We hear that he has already had some wonderful revelations not yet made public, but that a few of the elders put their heads together and whisper what they dare not speak aloud. What it is we can only surmise by faint rumors. A month ago or more one of the Apostles, Adams by name, returned from a two years' mission in England, bringing with him a wife and child, although he had left a wife and family here when he went away, and I am told that his first wife is reconciled to this certainly at first unwelcome guest to her home, for her husband and some others have reasoned with her that plurality of wives is taught in the Bible, that Abraham, Jacob, Solomon, David, and indeed all the old prophets and good men, had several wives, and if right for them, it is right for the Latter Day Saints. Furthermore, the first wife will always be first in her husband's affection and the head of the household, where she will have a larger influence. Poor, weak woman!

I cannot believe that Joseph will ever sanction such a doctrine, and should the Mormons in any way engraft such an article on their religion, the sect would surely fall to pieces, for what community or State could harbor such outrageous immorality? I cannot think so meanly of my sex as that they could submit to any such degradation.

Our Gentile friends say that this falling of the prophetic mantle on to Hyrum is a political ruse. Last winter when Joseph was in the meshes of the law, he was assisted by some politicians of the Whig party, to whom he pledged himself in the coming elections. Now he wants the Democratic party to win, so Hyrum is of that party, and as it is revealed for him to vote, so go over all the Mormons like sheep following the bell sheep over a wall. Nauvoo, with its 15,000 inhabitants, has a vote that tells in the State elections, and all summer politicians, able men of both parties, have been here making speeches, caressing and flattering.

Yesterday being parade day, to show a little attention to our guest, brother engaged a team and carried us out on the prairie to view the troops. There were over 2,000 men, it was said, divided into four divisions, and when marching in line with two bands of music they made quite an imposing appearance. Their costumes, for I can't say uniforms, were more fantastic than artistic. They were quite picturesque, certainly, for every officer and private consulted his individual taste; no two were alike. Nearly all had some badge, stripe, or scarf, of bright color. Some wore the breeches and knee-buckles of a hundred years ago. I thought if some Eastern military company would send out discarded uniforms, they might make a good speculation. However, they went through their drill, marching, counter-marching, and forming squares and other military combinations, very nicely.

This is probably the last letter I shall write to you in our little cottage, for we move in two or three weeks to our new brick house, a block beyond the Temple. Business is coming up that way. Love to all.

Your affectionate sister,
Charlotte.

"If We Are not Molested"

TWO SISTERS from New England, both members of the church, arrived in Nauvoo with their husbands in the fall of 1843 thinking to make it their permanent home. But their letters to their parents, Calvin and Abigail Hall of Sutton, Massachusetts, also Mormons, betray an early apprehension at the state of affairs already hinted at by Charlotte Haven. The sisters, Martha Hall, who married Mormon elder Jesse Haven (not a relative of Charlotte), and Sarah Hall, who married an Irish convert, Isaac Scott, reacted differently. Martha's faith proved a match for every setback; Sarah revolted, believing the church had apostatized from the original faith. Their letters trace their divergent courses.

The two extracted below, the earliest after their arrival, are already portentous. They form part of a series of eleven letters edited by George F. Partridge and published in the New England Quarterly *for December, 1936, as "The Death of a Mormon Dictator: Letters of Massachusetts Mormons, 1843–1848." They are reprinted here with the permission of the* New England Quarterly. *Partridge has modernized the spelling and punctuation. Passages from other letters will be presented hereafter where they illuminate the narrative of events leading to and following Joseph Smith's martyrdom.*

I

Nauvoo, Illinois, Dec. 27, 1843.

Dear Father and Mother:

. . . November 6: Arrived at Nauvoo about noon. It is much the handsomest situation I have seen on the Mississippi. I can assure you we were all tired of traveling and glad to get on shore. I have had but one night of sound sleep since I left. There is a great deal of noise on the boats.

Monday, December 18: I suppose you have been looking for a letter from one of us before this, but I did not go to housekeeping till the eighth of this month. I visited till then among Mr. Haven's friends, and wanted to wait till I got to housekeeping before I wrote. We live in a new brick house, upstairs.

Mr. Haven is teaching school here. Sarah is teaching about three miles out. Nauvoo looks much better than I expected; it is quite a pleasant place, but every thing is very different from what it is at the East. The soil differs much from any thing I ever saw. I have not seen a stone or any gravel in the place. The mud here sticks to my feet just like paste. There are quarries near by where they get stone for building. We shall soon have a fine city here if we are not molested. The river here is about a mile and a half wide. There are some quite large islands here. Many have gone out to live on them; they return in the spring. . . .

December 21: I suppose you will hear that there is trouble among us before you get this. The Missourians seem determined not to let us alone. They keep kidnaping our people. It is not safe for them to go out of Nauvoo. One of our men was kidnaped last night; he was over to Montrose [Iowa] on business. The civil authorities have taken one of the kidnapers; he is under three thousand dollars bond; we are going to send to our governor to have him send to the governor of Missouri for the release of our people. I expect he will not give them up unless our governor will give up Joseph Smith. I don't think they will ever have the pleasure of taking him. God will ere long come out in vengeance against them.

I can say I like Nauvoo, and had rather be here than at the East even if we are driven. I could never advise any to come here but true-hearted Mormons. We know that if we suffer affliction with the people of God, we shall also reign with them. We know that the saints of God in all ages have suffered, and the Bible says that we shall suffer persecution. It is true that this is the place to try people. The church in Sutton thinks they have trials but they know no more about them than infants. I wish my friends were all Mormons and were here. I know they would enjoy themselves. I never heard such good preaching in my life as I have since I came here. We have some *very* smart men. I wish, father, you and mother would write me a long letter.

Martha.

II

Vicinity of Nauvoo, April 13, 1844.

Dear Mother:

. . . I had a school this winter, between thirty and forty different scholars some of them larger than myself. I suppose you are thinking that

I have taken a long school; however I never enjoyed myself better. We live in a little white cottage two and a half miles on a straight line from the Temple and three-quarters of a mile from the Mississippi. It is very pleasant a summer's evening to walk along its banks; they are high above the river, and there are beautiful ravines below. I am learning to ride horseback; we rode about two miles the other evening along the river and it was delightful. The boats we can hear from the house as they pass up and down. We crossed the river to Fort Madison in Iowa in a ferry-boat the other day.

We go to meeting near the Temple every Sunday. I do love to hear the *Prophet* preach; there was over thirty baptized last Sunday in the river. Joseph baptized quite a number of them; there was about fifteen thousand [hundred?] people at meeting; we have the meetings in a grove near the Temple. A great many thousand people attended the conference. It closed on Tuesday last.

Father Scott expects to go to Ireland this summer to preach the gospel. He and his family were in Missouri the time the church were driven. He is an high priest. It is twenty-five years since they left Ireland for America. I firmly believe that this work is of God and that it will roll on in spite of wicked men and devils.

Mother you think you have trials but I can tell you there is nothing there to try your faith; I mean comparatively speaking. I never fully understood the place in holy writ where the Lord says he will have a tried people until I came here with the Church. Sometimes I almost fear that I shall give up but by the help of the Lord I mean to endure to the end. You know little concerning the Church, I can assure you; I think that if the saints were as wise before they start as after they get here, many would not have faith enough to come. *A word to the wise is sufficient.* Dear Mother pray for me that I may be of the household of faith. . . .

There was scarcely a night during the winter but what I dreamed of you and was back there with you but I always thought I was coming back and often thought I was waiting for you to come back with me.

Sarah Scott.

═══════════

Two Boston Brahmins Call on the Prophet

PERHAPS THE MOST *distinguished visitors to Nauvoo in 1844 were Charles Francis Adams and his cousin Josiah Quincy. Adams was the son of former President John Quincy Adams and the father of Henry Adams. Thirty-six and a member of the Massachusetts house of representatives at the time of his visit, he later established the anti-slavery* Boston Whig, *became Free-Soil candidate for Vice-President, served a term in Congress, and during the Civil War served with distinction as Lincoln's Minister to England. Before his death in 1886 he edited the many-volumed* Works of John Adams *and the* Memoirs of John Quincy Adams.

Josiah Quincy was one of a confusing number of Quincys with the same name. A family portrait in 1860 shows five generations together, four Josiahs among them, and three of them at one time or another mayors of Boston. The Josiah Quincy (1802–1882) who visited Nauvoo and who himself became mayor of Boston the next year, was the son of the Josiah Quincy who was mayor of Boston from 1823 to 1828 and President of Harvard from 1829 to 1845.

Both Adams and Quincy kept journals, recording their chance stopover at Nauvoo only forty-three days before Joseph Smith met his death. Quincy's "ten closely written pages" of notes formed the basis of his chapter on Joseph Smith in Figures of the Past (*Boston, 1883*), *which brought together separate papers Quincy had previously printed in* The Independent. *The chapter, except for some editorializing on the "Mormon question" in the 1880's, is reproduced below from the first edition.*

It is by no means improbable that some future text-book, for the use of generations yet unborn, will contain a question something like this: What historical American of the nineteenth century has exerted the most powerful influence upon the destinies of his countrymen? And it is by no means impossible that the answer to that interrogatory may be thus written: *Joseph Smith, the Mormon Prophet.* And the reply, absurd as it doubtless seems to most men now living, may be an obvious commonplace of their descendants. History deals in surprises and paradoxes quite as startling as this. The man who established a religion in this age of free debate, who was and is to-day accepted by hundreds of thousands as a direct emissary from the Most High—such a rare human being is not to be disposed of by pelting his memory with unsavory epithets. Fanatic, impostor, charlatan, he may have been; but these hard names furnish no solution to the problem he presents to us. Fanatics and impostors are living and dying every day, and their memory is buried with them; but the wonderful influence which this founder of a religion exerted and still exerts throws him into relief before us, not as a rogue to be criminated, but as a phenomenon to be explained. . . . Ten closely written pages of my journal describe my impressions of Nauvoo, and of its prophet, mayor, general, and judge; but details, necessarily omitted in the diary, went into letters addressed to friends at home, and I shall use both these sources to make my narrative as complete as possible. I happened to visit Joseph Smith in company with a distinguished gentleman, who, if rumor may be trusted, has been as conscientious a journal-writer as was his father. It is not impossible that my record may one day be supplemented by that of my fellow-traveller, the Hon. Charles Francis Adams.

It was on the 25th of April, 1844, that Mr. Adams and myself left Boston for the journey to the West which we had had for some time in contemplation. I omit all account of our adventures—and a very full account of them is before me—until the 14th of May, when we are ascending the clear, sparkling waters of the Upper Mississippi in the little steamboat "Amaranth." With one exception we find our fellow-passengers uninteresting. The exception is Dr. Goforth. A chivalric, yet simple personage is this same doctor, who has served under General Jackson at the battle of New Orleans and is now going to Nauvoo, to promote the election of the just nominated Henry Clay. It is to this gentleman we owe our sight of the City of the Saints, which, strangely enough, we had not intended to visit. Though far from being a Mormon himself, Dr. Goforth told us much that was good and interesting about this strange people. He urged us to see for ourselves the result of the singular political system which had been fastened upon Christianity, and to make the acquaintance of his friend, General Smith, the religious and civil autocrat of the community. "We agreed to stop at Nauvoo," says my journal, "provided some conveyance should be found at the landing which would take us up to General Smith's tavern, and prepared our baggage for this contingency. Owing to various delays, we did not reach the landing till nearly midnight, when our friend, who had jumped on shore the moment the boat stopped, returned with the intelligence that no carriage was to be had, and so we bade him adieu, to go on our way. But, as we still lingered upon the hurricane deck, he shouted that there was a house on the landing, where we could get a good bed. This changed our destiny, and just at the last moment we hurried on shore. Here we found that the 'good bed' our friend had promised us was in an old mill, which had been converted into an Irish shanty. However, we made the best of it, and, having dispossessed a cat and a small army of cockroaches of their quarters on the coverlet, we lay down in our dressing-gowns and were soon asleep."

We left our lowly bed in the gray light of the morning, to find the rain descending in torrents and the roads knee-deep in mud. Intelligence of our arrival had in some mysterious manner reached General Smith, and the prophet's own chariot, a comfortable carryall, drawn by two horses, soon made its appearance. It is probable that we owed the alacrity with which we were served to an odd blunder which had combined our names and personalities and set forth that no less a man than ex-President John Quincy Adams had arrived to visit Mr. Joseph Smith. Happily, however, Dr. Goforth, who had got upon the road before us, divided our persons and reduced them to their proper proportions, so that no trace of disappointment was visible in the group of rough-looking Mormons who awaited our descent at the door of the tavern. It was a three-story frame house, set back from the street and surrounded by a white fence, that we had reached after about two miles of the muddiest driving. Pre-eminent among the stragglers by the door stood a man of commanding appearance, clad in the costume of a journeyman carpenter when about his work. He was a hearty, athletic fellow, with blue eyes standing prominently out upon his light complexion, a long nose, and a retreating forehead. He wore striped pantaloons, a linen jacket, which had not lately seen the washtub, and a beard of some three days' growth. This was the founder of the religion which had been preached in every quarter of the earth. As Dr. Goforth introduced us to the prophet, he mentioned the parentage of my companion. "God bless *you*, to begin with!" said Joseph Smith, raising his hands in the air and letting them descend upon the shoulders of Mr. Adams. The benediction, though evidently sincere, had an odd savor of what may be called official familiarity, such as a crowned head might adopt on receiving the heir presumptive of a friendly court. The greeting to me was cordial—with that sort of cordiality with which the president of a college might welcome a deserving janitor—and a blessing formed no part of it. "And now come, both of you, into the house!" said our host, as, suiting the action to the word, he ushered us across the threshold of his tavern.

A *fine-looking man* is what the passer-by would instinctively have murmured upon meeting the remarkable individual who had fashioned the mould which was to shape the feelings of so many thousands of his fellow-mortals. But Smith was more than this, and one could not resist the impression that capacity and resource were natural to his stalwart person. I have already mentioned the resemblance he bore to Elisha R. Potter,* of Rhode Island, whom I met in Washington in 1826. The likeness was not such as would be recognized in a picture, but rather one that would be felt in a grave emergency. Of all men I have met, these two seemed best endowed with that kingly faculty which directs, as by intrinsic right, the feeble or confused souls who are looking for guidance. This it is just to say with emphasis; for the reader will find so much that is puerile and even shocking in my report of the prophet's conversation that he might never suspect the impression of rugged power that was given by the man.

On the right hand, as we entered the house, was a small and very comfortless-looking bar-room; all the more comfortless, perchance, from its being a dry bar-room, as no spiritous liquors were permitted at Nauvoo. In apparent search for more private quarters, the prophet opened the door of a room on the left. He instantly shut it again, but not before I perceived that the obstacle to our entrance was its prior occupancy by a woman, in bed. He then ran up-stairs, calling upon us to follow him, and, throwing open a door in the second story, disclosed three Mormons in three beds. This was not satisfactory; neither was the next chamber, which was found, on inspection, to contain two sleeping disciples. The third attempt was somewhat more fortunate, for we had found a room which held but a single bed and a single sleeper. Into this apartment we were invited to enter. Our host immediately proceeded to the bed, and drew the clothes well over the head of its occupant. He then called a man to make a fire, and begged us to sit down. Smith then began to talk about himself and his people, as, of course, we encouraged

---

* Elisha Reynolds Potter, Sr. (1764–1835) was a blacksmith, farmer, and practicing lawyer who served some thirty years in the Rhode Island legislature and was four times elected to Congress. "Wherever he went he was a conspicuous figure, by reason of his gigantic stature, vigorous personality, and keen wit." *Dictionary of American Biography* (*Ed. note*).

him to do. He addressed his words to Mr. Adams oftener than to me, evidently thinking that this gentleman had or was likely to have political influence, which it was desirable to conciliate. Whether by subtle tact or happy accident, he introduced us to Mormonism as a secular institution before stating its monstrous claims as a religious system. Polygamy, it must be remembered, formed no part of the alleged revelations upon which the social life at Nauvoo was based; indeed, the recorded precepts of its prophet were utterly opposed to such a practice, and it is, at least, doubtful whether this barbarism was in any way sanctioned by Smith. Let a man who has so much to answer for be allowed the full benefit of the doubt; and Mormonism, minus the spiritual wife system, had, as it has to-day, much that was interesting in its secular aspects. Its founder told us what he had accomplished and the terrible persecutions through which he had brought his people. He spoke with bitterness of outrages to which they had been subjected in Missouri, and implied that the wanton barbarities of his lawless enemies must one day be atoned for. He spoke of the industrial results of his autocracy in the holy city we were visiting, and of the extraordinary powers of its charter, obtained through his friend, Governor Ford. The past had shown him that a military organization was necessary. He was now at the head of three thousand men, equipped by the State of Illinois and belonging to its militia, and the Saints were prepared to fight as well as to work. "I decided," said Smith, "that the commander of my troops ought to be a lieutenant-general, and I was, of course, chosen to that position. I sent my certificate of election to Governor Ford, and received in return a commission of lieutenant-general of the Nauvoo Legion and of the militia of the State of Illinois. Now, on examining the Constitution of the United States, I find that an officer must be tried by a court-martial composed of his equals in rank; and as I am the only lieutenant-general in the country, I think they will find it pretty hard to try me."

At this point breakfast was announced, and a substantial meal was served in a long back kitchen. We sat down with about thirty persons, some of them being in their shirt-sleeves, as if just come from work. There was no going out, as the rain still fell in torrents; and so, when we had finished breakfast, the prophet (who had exchanged his working dress for a broadcloth suit while we lingered at the table) proposed to return to the chamber we had quitted, where he would give us his views of theology. The bed had been made during our absence and the fire plentifully replenished. Our party was now increased by the presence of the patriarch, Hiram Smith; Dr. Richards, of Philadelphia, who seemed to be a very modest and respectable Mormon; Dr. Goforth; and a Methodist minister, whose name I have not preserved. No sooner were we seated than there entered some half-dozen leaders of the sect, among whom, I think, were Rigdon and Young; but of their presence I cannot be positive. These men constituted a sort of silent chorus during the expositions of their chief. They fixed a searching, yet furtive gaze upon Mr. Adams and myself, as if eager to discover how we were impressed by what we heard. Of the wild talk that we listened to I have preserved but a few fragments. Smith was well versed in the letter of the Scriptures, though he had little comprehension of their spirit. He began by denying the doctrine of the Trinity, and supported his views by the glib recitation of a number of texts. From this he passed to his own claims to special inspiration, quoting with great emphasis the eleventh and twelfth verses of the fourth chapter of Ephesians, which, in his eyes, adumbrated the whole Mormon hierarchy. The degrees and orders of ecclesiastical dignitaries he set forth with great precision, being careful to mention the interesting revelation which placed Joseph Smith supreme above them all. This information was plentifully besprinkled with cant phrases or homely proverbs. "There, I have proved that point as straight as a loon's leg." "The curses of my enemies run off from me like water from a duck's back." Such are the specimens which my journal happens to preserve, but the exposition was constantly garnished with forcible vulgarisms of a similar sort. The prophet referred to his miraculous gift of understanding all languages, and took down a Bible in various tongues, for the purpose of exhibiting his accomplishments in this particular. Our position as guests prevented our testing his powers by a rigid examination, and the rendering of a few familiar texts seemed to be accepted by his followers as a triumphant demonstration of his abilities. It may have been an accident, but I observed that the bulk of his translations were from the Hebrew, which, presumably, his visitors did not understand, rather than from the classical languages, in which they might more easily have caught him tripping.

"And now come with me," said the prophet "and I will show you the curiosities." So saying, he led the way to a lower room, where sat a venerable and respectable-looking lady. "This is my mother, gentlemen. The curiosities we shall see belong to her. They were purchased with her own money, at a cost of six thousand dollars"; and then, with deep feeling, were added the words, "And that woman was turned out upon the prairie in dead of night by a mob." There were some pine presses fixed against the wall of the room. These receptacles Smith opened, and disclosed four human bodies, shrunken and black with age. "These are mummies," said the exhibitor. "I want you to look at that little runt of a fellow over there. He was a great man in his day. Why, that was Pharaoh Necho, King of Egypt!" Some parchments inscribed with hieroglyphics were then offered us. They were preserved under glass and handled with great respect. "That is the handwriting of Abraham, the Father of the Faithful," said the prophet. "This is the autograph of Moses, and these lines were written by his brother Aaron. Here we have the earliest account of the Creation, from which Moses composed the First Book of Genesis." The parchment last referred to showed a rude drawing of a man and woman, and a serpent walking upon a pair of legs. I ventured to doubt the propriety of providing the reptile in question with this unusual means of locomotion. "Why, that's as plain as a pikestaff," was the rejoinder. "Before the Fall snakes always went about on legs, just like chickens. They were deprived of them, in punishment for their agency in the ruin of man." We were further assured that the prophet was the only mortal who could translate these mysterious writings, and that his power was given by direct inspiration.

It is well known that Joseph Smith was accustomed to make his revelations point to those sturdy business habits which lead to prosperity in this present life. He had little enough of that unmixed spiritual power which flashed out from the spare, neurasthenic body of Andrew Jackson. The prophet's hold upon you seemed to come from the balance and harmony of temperament which reposes upon a large physical basis. No association with the sacred phrases of Scripture could keep the inspirations of this man from getting down upon the hard pan of practical affairs. "Verily I say unto you, let my servant, Sidney Gilbert, plant himself in this place and establish a store." So had run one of his revelations, in which no holier spirit than that of commerce is discernible. The exhibition of these august relics concluded with a similar descent into the hard modern world of fact. Monarchs, patriarchs, and parchments were very well in their way; but this was clearly the nineteenth century, when prophets must get a living and provide for their relations. *"Gentlemen,"* said this *bourgeois* Mohammed, as he closed the cabinets, *"those who see these curiosities generally pay my mother a quarter of a dollar."*

The clouds had parted when we emerged from the chamber of curiosities, and there was time to see the Temple before dinner. General Smith ordered a capacious carriage, and we drove to that beautiful eminence, bounded on three sides by the Mississippi, which was covered by the holy city of Nauvoo. The curve in the river enclosed a position lovely enough to furnish a site for the Utopian communities of Plato or Sir Thomas More; and here was an orderly city, magnificently laid out, and teeming with activity and enterprise. And all the diligent workers, who had reared these handsome stores and comfortable dwellings, bowed in subjection to the man to whose unexampled absurdities we had listened that morning. . . . Near the entrance to the Temple we passed a workman who was laboring upon a huge sun, which he had chiselled from the solid rock. The countenance was of the negro type, and it was surrounded by the conventional rays.

"General Smith," said the man, looking up from his task, "is this like the face you saw in vision?"

"Very near it," answered the prophet, "except" (this was added with an air of careful connoisseurship that was quite overpowering)—"except that the nose is just a thought too broad."

The Mormon Temple was not fully completed. It was a wonderful structure, altogether indescribable by me. Being, presumably, like something Smith had seen in vision, it certainly cannot be compared to any ecclesiastical building which may be discerned by the natural eyesight. It was built of limestone, and was partially supported by huge monolithic pillars, each costing, said the prophet, three thousand dollars. Then in the basement was the baptistry, which centered in a mighty tank, surrounded by twelve wooden oxen of colossal size. These animals, we were assured, were temporary. They were to be replaced by stone oxen as fast as they could be made. The Temple, odd and striking as it was, produced no effect that was commensurate with its cost. Perhaps it would have required a genius to have designed anything worthy of that noble site. The city of Nauvoo, with its wide streets sloping gracefully to the farms enclosed on the prairie, seemed to be a better temple to Him who prospers the work of industrious hands than the grotesque structure on the hill, with all its queer carvings of moons and suns. This, however, was by no means the opinion of the man whose fiat had reared the building. In a tone half-way between jest and earnest, and which might have been taken for either at the option of the hearer, the prophet put this inquiry: "Is not here one greater than Solomon, who built a Temple with the treasures of his father David and with the assistance of Huram, King of Tyre? Joseph Smith has built his Temple with no one to aid him in the work."

On returning to the tavern, dinner was served in the kitchen where we had breakfasted. The prophet carved at one end of the board, while some twenty persons, Mormons or travellers (the former mostly coatless), were scattered along its sides. At the close of a substantial meal a message was brought to the effect that the United States marshal had arrived and wished to speak to Mr. Adams. This officer, as it turned out, wanted my companion's advice about the capture of some criminal, for whom he had a warrant. The matter was one of some difficulty, for, the prophet being absolute in Nauvoo, no man could be arrested or held without his permission. I do not remember what was the outcome of this interview, which was so protracted that it caused Mr. Adams to miss one of the most notable exhibitions of the day.

"General Smith," said Dr. Goforth, when we had adjourned to the green in front of the tavern, "I think Mr. Quincy would like to hear you preach." "Then I shall be happy to do so," was the obliging reply; and, mounting the broad step which led from the house, the prophet promptly addressed a sermon to the little group about him. Our numbers were constantly increased from the passers in the street, and a most attentive audience of more than a hundred persons soon hung upon every word of the speaker. The text was Mark xvi. 15, and the comments, though rambling and disconnected, were delivered with the fluency and fervor of a camp-meeting orator. The discourse was interrupted several times by the Methodist minister before referred to, who thought it incumbent upon him to question the soundness of certain theological positions maintained by the speaker. One specimen of the sparring which ensued I thought worth setting down. The prophet is asserting that baptism for the remission of sins is essential for salvation. *Minister.* Stop! What do you say to the case of the penitent thief? *Prophet.* What do you mean by that? *Minister.* You know our Saviour said to the thief, "This day shalt thou be with me in Paradise," which shows he could not have been baptized before his admission. *Prophet.* How do you know he wasn't baptized before he became a thief? At this retort the sort of laugh that is provoked by an unexpected hit ran through the audience; but this demonstration of sympathy was rebuked by a severe look from Smith, who went on to say: "But that is not the true answer. In the original Greek, as this gentleman (turning to me) will inform you, the word that has been translated paradise means simply a place of departed spirits. To that place the penitent thief was conveyed, and there, doubtless, he received the baptism necessary for his admission to the heavenly kingdom." The other objections of his antagonist were parried with a similar adroitness, and in about fifteen minutes the prophet concluded a sermon which it was evident that his disciples had heard with the heartiest satisfaction.

In the afternoon we drove to visit the farms upon the prairie which this enterprising people had enclosed and were cultivating with every appearance of success. On returning, we stopped in a beautiful grove, where there were seats and a platform for speaking. "When the weather permits," said Smith, "we hold our services in this place; but shall cease to do so when the Temple is finished." "I suppose none but Mormon preachers are allowed in Nauvoo," said the Methodist minister, who had accompanied our expedition. "On the contrary," replied the prophet, "I shall be very happy to have you address my people next Sunday, and I will insure you a most attentive congregation." "What! do you mean that I may say anything I please and that you will make no reply?" "You may certainly say anything you please; but I must reserve the right of adding a word or two, if I judge best. I promise to speak of you in the most respectful manner." As we rode back, there was more dispute between the minister and Smith. "Come," said the latter, suddenly slapping his antagonist on the knee, to emphasize the production of a triumphant text, "if you can't argue better than that, you shall say all you want to say to my people, and I will promise to hold my tongue, for there's not a Mormon among them who would need my assistance to answer you." Some back-thrust was evidently required to pay for this; and the minister, soon after, having occasion to allude to some erroneous doctrine which I forget, suddenly exclaimed, "Why, I told my congregation the other Sunday that they might as well believe Joe Smith as such theology as that." "Did you say Joe Smith in a sermon?" inquired the person to whom the title had been applied. "Of course I did. Why not?" The prophet's reply was given with a quiet superiority that was overwhelming: "Considering only the day and the place, it would have been more respectful to have said Lieutenant-General Joseph Smith." Clearly, the worthy minister was no match for the head of the Mormon church. . . .

I should not say quite all that struck me about Smith if I did not mention that he seemed to have a keen sense of the humorous aspects of his position. "It seems to me, General," I said, as he was driving us to the river, about sunset, "that you have too much power to be safely trusted to one man." "In your hands or that of any other person," was the reply, "so much power would, no doubt, be dangerous. I am the only man in the world whom it would be safe to trust with it. Remember, I am a prophet!" The last five words were spoken in a rich, comical aside, as if in hearty recognition of the ridiculous sound they might have in the ears of a Gentile. I asked him to test his powers by naming the successful candidate in the approaching presidential election. "Well, I will prophesy

that John Tyler will not be the next President, for some things are possible and some things are probable; but Tyler's election is neither the one
nor the other." We then went on to talk of politics. Smith recognized the
curse and iniquity of slavery, though he opposed the methods of the
Abolitionists. His plan was for the nation to pay for the slaves from the
sale of the public lands. "Congress," he said, "should be compelled to take
this course, by petitions from all parts of the country; but the petitioners
must disclaim all alliance with those who would disturb the rights of
property recognized by the Constitution and foment insurrection." It
may be worth while to remark that Smith's plan was publicly advocated,
eleven years later, by one who has mixed so much practical shrewdness
with his lofty philosophy. In 1855, when men's minds had been moved to
their depths on the question of slavery, Mr. Ralph Waldo Emerson declared that it should be met in accordance "with the interest of the
South and with the settled conscience of the North. It is not really a
great task, a great fight for this country to accomplish, to buy that property of the planter, as the British nation bought the West Indian slaves."
He further says that the "United States will be brought to give every
inch of their public lands for a purpose like this." We, who can look back
upon the terrible cost of the fratricidal war which put an end to slavery,
now say that such a solution of the difficulty would have been worthy
a Christian statesman. But if the retired scholar was in advance of his
time when he advocated this disposition of the public property in 1855,
what shall I say of the political and religious leader who had committed
himself, in print as well as in conversation, to the same course in 1844? If
the atmosphere of men's opinions was stirred by such a proposition when
war-clouds were discernible in the sky, was it not a statesmanlike word
eleven years earlier, when the heavens looked tranquil and beneficent?

General Smith proceeded to unfold still further his views upon politics.
He denounced the Missouri Compromise as an unjustifiable concession
for the benefit of slavery. It was Henry Clay's bid for the presidency.
Dr. Goforth might have spared himself the trouble of coming to Nauvoo
to electioneer for a duellist who would fire at John Randolph, but was
not brave enough to protect the Saints in their rights as American citizens.
Clay had told his people to go to the wilds of Oregon and set up a government of their own. Oh yes, the Saints might go into the wilderness and
obtain justice of the Indians, which imbecile, time-serving politicians
would not give them in the land of freedom and equality. The prophet
then talked of the details of government. He thought that the number of
members admitted to the Lower House of the National Legislature

should be reduced. A crowd only darkened counsel and impeded business. A member to every half million of population would be ample. The powers of the President should be increased. He should have authority to put down rebellion in a state, without waiting for the request of any governor; for it might happen that the governor himself would be the leader of the rebels. It is needless to remark how later events showed the executive weakness that Smith pointed out—a weakness which cost thousands of valuable lives and millions of treasure; but the man mingled Utopian fallacies with his shrewd suggestions. He talked as from a strong mind utterly unenlightened by the teachings of history. Finally, he told us what he would do, were he President of the United States, and went on to mention that he might one day so hold the balance between parties as to render his election to that office by no means unlikely.

Who can wonder that the chair of the National Executive had its place among the visions of this self-reliant man? He had already traversed the roughest part of the way to that coveted position. Born in the lowest ranks of poverty, without book-learning and with the homeliest of all human names, he had made himself at the age of thirty-nine a power upon earth. Of the multitudinous family of Smith, from Adam down (Adam of the "Wealth of Nations," I mean), none had so won human hearts and shaped human lives as this Joseph. His influence, whether for good or for evil, is potent to-day, and the end is not yet.

I have endeavored to give the details of my visit to the Mormon prophet with absolute accuracy. If the reader does not know just what to make of Joseph Smith, I cannot help him out of the difficulty. I myself stand helpless before the puzzle.

"A Portentous Aspect": The Nauvoo Expositor
Is Destroyed

ON JUNE 16, 1844, Isaac Scott wrote his wife's parents, Calvin and Abigail Hall of Sutton, Massachusetts, startling news. For two years past, he said, Joseph Smith had taught strange doctrine that now was breaking the church and the community wide open. Scott's letter is historic, a firsthand account of events that led directly to the prophet's undoing and threw the whole countryside into an uproar.

A number of dissenters, among them some high officials unable to go along with Smith's demagoguery and his private sanction of a plurality of wives, started an opposition press, the Nauvoo Expositor. *Its first issue on June 7, 1844,* denounced the prophet's high-handedness and immorality, demanded the unconditional repeal of the city charter "to correct the abuses of the unit power," and announced the organization of a reform church. Joseph Smith moved swiftly against the seceders. As mayor he called an emergency meeting of the city council, which declared the newspaper a nuisance and ordered it destroyed. Three days later the marshal smashed the press and confiscated all available copies of the first issue.

The editors fled to Carthage, the county seat, breathing vengeance. They swore out a warrant for the prophet's arrest, listing the grievances which saw not only Mormons and anti-Mormons opposed but also the Mormons divided against each other: freedom of the press, polygamy, and political dictatorship. Feeling ran high and it looked like another war of extermination, with Carthage and Nauvoo poised and fearful of marches on each other. The Scott letter concludes on an ominous note: "There is a report that a mob is coming to Nauvoo," a report, however, which proved unfounded.

The letter follows, reproduced with the permission of the New England Quarterly, where it was originally published as one of a series in December, 1936.

Vicinity of Nauvoo, June 16, 1844.

My Dear Father and Mother:

. . . Because of the things that *are* and *have been* taught in the Church of Latter Day Saints for two years past which now assume a *portentous aspect*, I say because of these things we are in trouble. And were it not that we wish to give you a fair unbiased statement of facts as they really exist, we perhaps would not have written you so soon. But we feel it to be our duty to let you know how things are going on in *this land of boasted liberty*, this Sanctum-Sanctorum of all the Earth, the City of Nauvoo. The elders will likely tell you a different tale from what I shall as they are positively instructed to deny these things abroad. But it matters not to us what they say; our object is to state to you the *truth*, for we do not want to be guilty of *deceiving any one*. We will now give you a correct statement of the doctrines that are taught and practised in the

Church according to our own knowledge. We will mention three in particular.

A plurality of Gods. A plurality of *living* wives. And unconditional sealing up to eternal life against *all sins* save the shedding of innocent blood or consenting thereunto. These with many other things are taught by Joseph, which we consider are *odious* and doctrines of devils.

Joseph says there are Gods above the God of this universe as far as he is above us, and if He should transgress the laws given to Him by those above Him, He would be hurled from his Throne to hell, as was Lucifer and all his creations with him. But God says there is no other God but himself. Moses says he is the *Almighty* God, and there is none other. David says he knows of no other God. The Apostles and Prophets almost all testify the same thing.

Joseph had a revelation last summer purporting to be from the Lord, allowing the saints the privilege of having ten living wives at one time, I mean certain conspicuous characters among them. They do not content themselves with young women, but have seduced married women. I believe hundreds have been deceived. Now should I yield up your daughter to such wretches?

Mr. Haven [Scott's brother-in-law] knows these statements are correct, for they have been taught in the quorum to which he belongs by the highest authority in the Church. He has told me that he does not believe in these teachings but he does not come out and oppose them; he thinks that it will all come out right. But we think God never has nor never will sanction such proceedings, for we believe he has not changed; he says *"I am God I change not."* These things we can not believe, and it is by Sarah's repeated request that I write this letter.

Those who can not swallow down these things and came out and opposed the doctrine publicly, have been cut off from the Church without any lawful process whatever. They were not notified to trial neither were they allowed the privilege of being present to defend themselves; neither was any one permitted to speak on their behalf. They did not know who was their judge or jury until it was all over and they delivered over to all the buffetings of Satan; although they lived only a few rods from the council room. These are some of their names: William Law, one of the first Presidency; Wilson Law, brigadier general; Austin Coles, president of the High Council; and Elder Blakesly, who has been the means of bringing upwards of one thousand members into the Church. He has been through nearly all the states in the Union, the Canadas, and England preaching the Gospel. Now look at the great sins they have committed, the Laws' un-Christian-like conduct—Blakesly and others, *Apostasy*. If it is apostasy to oppose such doctrines and proceedings as I have just mentioned (which are only a few of the enormities taught and practised here), then we hope and pray that *all* the Church may apostatize.

After they had been thus shamefully treated and published to the world they went and bought a printing press determined to defend themselves against such unhallowed abuse. It cost them six hundred dollars. [They] commenced their paper, but Joseph and his clan could not bear the truth to come out; so after the first number came out Joseph called his Sanhedrin together; tried the press; condemned it as a nuisance and ordered the city marshal to take three hundred armed men and go and burn the press, and if any offered resistance, to *rip them from the guts to the gizzard*. These are his own words. They went and burnt the press, papers, and household furniture. The Laws, Fosters, Coles, Hickbies [Higbees], and others have had to leave the place to save their lives. Those who have been thus unlawfully cut off have called a conference; protested against these things; and reorganized the Church. William Law is chosen President; Charles Ivans [Ivins], bishop, with the other necessary officers. The Reformed Church believed that Joseph has transgressed in his priestly capacity and has given himself over to serve the devil, and his own lusts. We will endeavor to send you a paper and you can then judge for yourselves. They had only commenced publishing the dark deeds of Nauvoo. A hundredth part has not been told yet.

[The letter was written up to this point by Isaac Scott, husband of Sarah. The rest is in his wife's hand.]

The people of the state will not suffer such things any longer. But I am sorry that the innocent must suffer with the guilty. I believe there are hundreds of honest hearted souls in Nauvoo, but none of them I think have forgotten what they were once taught: that cursed is he that putteth his trust in man. It would offend some of them more to speak irreverently of Joseph, than it would of God himself. Joseph says that he is a God to this generation, and I suppose they believe it. Any one needs a throat like an open sepulchre to *swallow down* all that is taught here. There was an elder once wrote in confidence to a friend in England; told him the state of the Church here, and they showed it to some of the elders there, and they wrote back to the heads of the Church, and it caused him a great deal of trouble. I think if you would once come here, you would not put so much confidence in all who go by the name of Mormons.

I am very much obliged for the pin ball; I think it is very pretty, and

145

it comes from Mother so far, from old Massachusetts. I shall appreciate it highly. My health has been very good since I came to the West notwithstanding it is a sickly part of the country. I enjoy myself *well* this summer. My husband is every thing I could wish, and I hope we may live all the days of our appointed time together. Joseph had two balls last winter and a dancing-school through the winter. There was a theatre established in the spring; some of the twelve took a part—Erastus Snow and many of the leading members of the Church. Dear Mother, I hope the time is not far distant when we can enjoy each other's society, but when and where I suppose time only will determine. There is a report that a mob is coming to Nauvoo.

Sarah Scott

Martyrdom at Carthage

WITH THE COUNTRYSIDE AROUSED over the destruction of the Expositor, *Governor Thomas Ford, with good if vacillating intentions, called out the militia and hurried from Springfield to hold the lid down, if possible, on an explosive situation. He pledged Joseph and Hyrum Smith safe conduct to Carthage. They had gone through the forms of arrest, habeas corpus, trial, and acquittal before the singular municipal court of Nauvoo of which the prophet was judge, jury, counsel, and prisoner, and had promptly sent the deputy sheriff back to Carthage with his warrants, and with admonitions. Faced with a second summons and the mounting anger of Hancock County, they had crossed the Mississippi intending flight to the west, but friends, fearful Nauvoo would be laid waste if they did not surrender, prevailed on them to return. "If my life is of no use to my friends," the prophet said, "it is of no use to me." The brothers rode into Carthage and were lodged for their own protection in jail.*

To his dismay the Governor found the militia rabidly anti-Mormon. He ordered it dispersed except for a protective guard. But a company from Warsaw, disgruntled at the order, converted itself into a mob which stormed the jail—the guard yielding easily as if by design—and shot the prophet and his brother to death, leaving a companion, apostle John

146

Taylor, badly wounded. Their fury spent, the mobsters—now awe-stricken citizens—beat a retreat to Warsaw and, fearing reprisal, hastily ferried their families to the Missouri side of the river. But the Mormons were too paralyzed for vengeance.

An eyewitness of these turbulent events was Dr. Thomas L. Barnes, a long-time resident of Carthage, who attended the wounded and became reluctantly involved in the aftermath. In 1897, in his eighty-sixth year, he wrote his daughter, Miranda Barnes Haskett, two frank letters recalling the slaying. In the following excerpt from his letter of November 6, 1897, the erratic spelling and punctuation of the self-taught country doctor have been standardized, but not his grammar. By his own account he "practiced for a while without a diploma," but he eventually graduated from a course of lectures at the University of Missouri. His rugged practice often took him on twenty-four-hour calls on both sides of the Mississippi, when he would ride at night and cross it in a skiff "where it was a mile wide," but "in this way," he wrote his daughter, "I soon established a fair reputation as a physician."

Transcripts of the letter were obtained through the kindness of Dr. Elmer Belt of Los Angeles and Mrs. Bertha Martin of Santa Rosa, California, by whose courtesy it is excerpted here.

November 6, 1897

Well, Mirand, I suppose you would like me to tell you something about the killing of the Smiths and what led to it.

Some person made complaint under oath before a justice of the peace charging Jo Smith with some grave offence. I do not now remember what the offence was. A warrant was issued by the justice of the peace, and given to a constable to serve. I met the constable on his way to Nauvoo to serve the writ; I told [him] I would go with him, which I did. He served the writ on the accused without any trouble. As was usual in such cases, where a grave charge is made against a prominent person, almost every person in the vicinity would soon know it.

The city authorities was granted by their *Charter* as they supposed unlimited authority.

They issued a writ of habeas corpus—I believe that is what they called the writ, and took the accused out of the constable's hands and set him at liberty. While this proceeding was going on, in conversation with Mr. Smith he said to me he was not guilty of that nor any other crime. Said he, let them charge me with any crime. I do not care what it is. I can prove that I was not there and did not do it. I said to him, if they will fix the time and place. He answered as a matter of course or words to that effect.

Well the constable returned to Carthage and made his return of his warrant.

That fact that the municipal authorities of Nauvoo had set the authorities of the State at defiance, and taken a man charged with crime out of the hands of an officer of the law, caused great excitement all over that part of the state. Public meetings were held, inflammatory speeches were made in more than one place in the county. The Governor was petitioned to send the military of the state to enforce obedience to the law. The Governor sent some two or three companies of the state troops into the county. A part of the militia rendezvoused at Carthage and a part at Warsaw. It was arranged that on a certain day they were to march to Nauvoo. They all professed to be ready and anxious to fight, if needs be kill, and drive the Mormons out of the county. In the meantime Smith had surrendered himself to the officers of the law. The Governor disbanded the soldiers that was at Carthage, and sent word to them at Warsaw, who was then on the march for Nauvoo.

When they got the disbanding order many of them were indignant at the Governor, resigned their offices and formed themselves into a mob determined to have satisfaction of the Smiths any way, whether by authority of law or by violence. The men that were willing to set all laws aside and have the life of the Smiths at any cost formed a new company and started to Carthage where the Smiths, Jo and Hyram, John Taylor, the editor of the Mormon paper, and Willard Richards, private secretary to Jo Smith, were. Joseph Smith was presumably in the hands of the constable and the others, his friends, were with him too in charge of an officer.

The under sheriff and jailor lived in the jail. The jail was a two-story stone house. The lower story and part of the upper story was occupied by the jailor and his family. The jail proper was in the north end of the building upstairs divided off into cells. The front room upstairs was a kind of a family room. At the head of the stairs there was two doors, one entering into the family room, and the other entering into the jail proper.

I have tried to be a little particular in describing the house so as to give you an idea of the way the mob got to their victims.

I said this new company or mob as they really were had some understanding of some of the citizens of our town. I want you to know and believe, my daughter, that I had nothing do with the murder of the Smiths, or any other person, and during all the excitement I never did any thing to any one that I would not under like circumstances they should do to me.

I said I thought some of our citizens, citizens of Carthage I mean, were party to the whole matter. One of them, a prominent man and a man of influence, came to me just before the cowardly murder was committed, and asked me to go out on the road toward Nauvoo and see what was going on out that way. I went, and John Wilson, an old citizen, and Doctor Morrison, a prominent physician, went with me.

We went about three miles from Carthage on the Nauvoo road, where we had a fine view of the country all around—the country being prairie all around. We could see very plain where the Carthage and Warsaw road was. We saw going on that road quite a company going hurriedly in the direction of Carthage. It was not long till we could see quite a number on the same road going toward Warsaw. We then went back to Carthage to report, and what did we find? Such a sight as I hope never to see again.

When we saw that company going to and from Carthage my suspicions was aroused that all was not right. Afterward my suspicions was strengthened from the fact that a guard of the "Carthage Grays," a part of a military company, had been left in charge of the accused to protect and keep them safe, whose sworn duty it was to protect their prisoner, as well as it was to keep him from running off. They were there I dont know just how many, I think from six to ten men, on guard when the mob came rushing on them. They fired blank cartridges over the heads of the mob, as I afterwards learned from some one of the guard. My impression is that they were equal guilty as any one of the mob. Excuse me for calling the murderers of the Smiths a mob; I think that is the right name to call them, though I believe, I do not know it, that you had an uncle in the affair.

Well after the brave guards had fired their blank cartridges on the mob and was taken prisoners, the mob rushed upstairs to where the Smiths, Taylor and Richards were enjoying themselves. Some said they were sipping their wine. Whether that is true or not I do not know. At any rate they were comfortably situated, and they had a right to suppose safely protected by the laws of the great State of Illinois.

When the false guard had made their hypocritical assault on the other part of the mob (I look upon them as being equally guilty as those that came from Warsaw), they the attacking party rushed upstairs with murder in their hearts to where the accused were, tried to break open the door which it appears was held shut by all of the men, when the mob commenced firing their loaded arms through the door. It appears that one of the balls in the commencement of the attack passed through a panel of the door and hit Hyram in his neck which probably broke his neck; he fell back and died, as I was informed, instantly. When I went in to the room shortly afterwards his head was laying against the wall on the other side from the door.

It is supposed when Hyram fell the door was partially opened by the attacking party. So much so at any rate that I was informed that Jo Smith had what was common then, what was and probably is now called one of Allen's poker boxes. It is said, and there is no doubt but what it is true, that he slipped his hand through the opening of the door and hit a young man from Warsaw about his neck or shoulder, which made it convenient for the young man to remain for a while in Missouri.

The attacking party forced the door open and commenced firing at Smith. It is said they must have hit him and probably disabled him, as he staggered across the floor to the opposite side of the room, where there was a window. It is said that there he gave the hailing sign of the distress of a Mason, but that did him no good. In the room behind him was armed men, furious men, with murder in their hearts. Before him around the well under the window there was a crowd of desperate men, as he was receiving shots from behind, which he could not stand, in desperation he leaped or rather fell out of the window near the well, where he breathed his last. When I found him soon afterwards he was laying in the hall at the foot of the stairs where his blood had as I believe left indelible stain on the floor.

I suppose by this time you are anxious to know what became of Taylor and Richards? Was they also killed, no they were not. Taylor was severely wounded, Richards was not hurt.

Shall I try to describe the wounds that Taylor received and got over them? Well let me tell you where we found him; I cannot impress your mind of his appearance as he appeared to us when we were called to him by the jailor.

We found him in a pile of straw. It appeared that a straw bed had been emitted [?] in the cell where he was when we found him. He was very much frightened as well as severely wounded. It took strong persuading of the jailor, as well as our positive assurance that we meant him no harm, but was desirous of doing him some good. He finally consented to come out of his cell. When we examined him we found that he had been hit by four balls. One ball had hit him in his forearm and passed down and lodged in the hand between the phalanges of his third and fourth fingers. Another hit him on the left side of the pelvis cutting through the skin and tissue leaving a superficial wound that you could lay your hand in. A third ball passed through his thigh lodging in his [illegible]. A fourth ball hit his watch, which he had in the fob in his pantaloons. Which I suppose the Mormons have today, to show the precise time that their great *Leader* was killed.

The wounds had bled quite freely, the blood had had time to coagulate, which it had done, and where the clothes & straw came in contact they all adhered together so that [when] Mr. Taylor came out his self-sought cell he was a pitiable looking sight. We took the best care of him we could till he left us. He got well but never paid us for skill or good wishes.

You want to know what has become of Richards. He was not hurt. You will ask how did it happen that his comrade so badly treated and he came off without receiving any damage whatever.

It was in this way, as I suppose I think he told me so. The four braced themselves against the door to keep the mob out. He stood next to the hinges of the door so when the door opened it would turn back against the wall that divided the room that they were in from the prison room. So when they crowded the door open it shut him up against the wall and he stood there and did not move till the affair was all over. So they did not see him.

After we were through with Taylor I went to Richards and I said to him, Richards what does all this mean? Who done it? Said he, doctor I do not know, but I believe it was some Missourians that came over and have killed brothers Joseph and Hyrum and wounded brother Taylor. Said I to him, do you believe that? He said I do. Says I, will you write that down and send it to Nauvoo? He said he would if he could get any person to take it. I told him if he would write it I would send it.

He wrote the note. I found the man that took it to Nauvoo.

Shall I tell you any more?

Your father

Thomas Barnes

Aftermath: "The Church Is Now Divided"

"THE COURSE THEY TOOK," wrote Isaac Scott of the prophet and his brother, "roused the indignation of saint and sinner that held sacred the laws and institutions of our country. I told them the morning after they done the deed it would cause them tears before their corn would silk, which came to pass." The disillusioned Scotts wrote home to New England expressions of the dismay and division which beset the Mormons after Joseph Smith's martyrdom. Sarah found her mother unswayed, while she herself felt the church had abandoned its first principles. She and her husband eventually joined one of the splinter groups under James J. Strang, who retired to Wisconsin as a new promised land and enjoyed a colorful but brief career as seer and revelator to a small flock who thought of themselves as original Mormons.

The following extracts are taken from the series of letters Isaac and Sarah Scott wrote to Sarah's parents in Sutton, Massachusetts, originally published in the New England Quarterly *for December, 1936. They are reprinted here with the permission of the* New England Quarterly.

I

Nauvoo, Illinois, July 22, 1844.

My Dear Father and Mother:

Having an opportunity to send to the East by the way of brother Eames, who expects to return in a few weeks, I thought I would improve it and send you a few lines. I suppose you received our letter and was somewhat prepared, when you heard of the dreadful murder of Joseph and Hyrum Smith in Carthage jail. Little did we think that an event like that would ever transpire. The Church believed that he would be acquitted as he had been on former occasions, and Joseph prophesied in the last *Neighbor* that was published before his death that they would come off victorious over them all, as sure as there was a God in Israel. Joseph also prophesied on the stand a year ago last conference that he could not be killed within five years from that time; that they could not kill him till the Temple would be completed, for that he had received an unconditional promise from the Almighty concerning his days, and he

152

set Earth and Hell at defiance; and then said, putting his hand on his head, they *never* could kill this Child. But now that he *is* killed some of the Church say that he said: unless he gave himself up. My husband was there at the time and says there was no conditions whatever, and many others testify to the same thing.

I suppose you have heard from Mr. Haven and Martha before this and have learned their mind concerning Joseph and Hyrum, but I can not help believing that had they been innocent, that the Lord would not have suffered them to fall by the hands of wicked murderers. I believe they would have been living men to-day, had they been willing for others to enjoy the same liberties they wish themselves.

The governor [Thomas Ford] visited Nauvoo the day that Joseph and Hyrum were killed and made a speech. He told the people of Nauvoo the burning of that press was arbitrary, unlawful, unconstitutional, and that they had hurt themselves more than ten presses could have injured them in ten years. . . .

Who the vile murderers were I suppose never will be known till the day when all flesh shall stand before God to answer for the deeds done in the body. Many of the Mormons lay it to the Missourians, others to the apostates, as they call them. If it is apostasy from Mormonism to come out against the doctrines of more Gods than one, more wives than one, and many other damnable heresies that they have taught, I hope and pray that I and all the rest of the Church may become apostates. . . .

Dear Mother: I have seen some sorrowful days since I left you and some happy ones. But I can tell you it is a sorrowful time here at present. Those that stood up for Joseph before his death are getting divided among themselves. . . .

August 9: Yesterday I attended a conference in Nauvoo. I suppose Martha will give you the particulars of it. The twelve were appointed to take charge of all the concerns of the Church both spiritual and temporal. Brigham Young said if he had been here, he wouldn't have consented to give Joseph up and he would be damned if he would give himself up to the law of the land. He would see them all in hell first; the Church [sic], and then he said he would see all Creation in Hell before he would. These statements are correct, and they needn't any [of them] attempt to deny them. If they do, they are ignorant of the matter or they are wilful liars. . . .

Sarah Scott

153

Nauvoo, February 6, 1845.

My dear Father and Mother:

. . . I find by your letter that my first letter to you surprised you, and I suppose my second had a still worse effect upon your mind by the way you wrote after receiving it, because I told you the truth concerning those doctrines that I know have been taught in the Church. I did not write from hearsay concerning those doctrines, as you represented, but from actual knowledge. But now because their iniquity has come to light and God's judgments have overtaken them, they deny that they were ever taught. But I say they are liars, and the truth is not in them. I am sorry it grieved you so because I can not believe in a man having ten or a dozen wives at a time. I did not know it was a part of Mormonism until I came to Nauvoo. You say that you are sorry I have turned against the Church and seem to think I have denied Mormonism, but did I not state in my letter my decided belief in it? I believe I did; and still believe Mormonism unadulterated with *Spiritual wifeism,* and the like, is of God and will prevail. . . .

Dear Mother, you seem to me to be preparing your mind to receive these strange things should they be presented to you; you quote a passage to try and prop their frail tenement, but read a little farther and you will find that to us there is but one living and true God. You seem to be sorry that you advised me to come West, but I am glad, for by so doing I have been an eye and ear witness to their proceedings. Had I not have come, I might have been as you are, knowing nothing of their teachings in Zion; but I am here, have heard and seen for myself and know verily what I write to be true. . . .

Stealing has been carried on to an alarming extent in and about Nauvoo last fall and this winter. They first began to steal from the dissenters and raised the cry that the dissenters did it themselves to bring persecution on the Church, but after a while a few of the good Mormon souls were caught in it; three have been taken to Carthage Jail, and more will likely follow. Father Scott and his daughter had a large washing stole from them last fall. I believe there are many sincere souls in Nauvoo that are desiring to serve God in an acceptable way, that have sacrificed their all for the truth and are willing to spend and be spent in laboring to bring forth and establish Zion in these last days. But when the head is sick, the whole heart is faint.

The first night I stopped in Nauvoo I slept in an old crazy log cabin where I could lay and count the stars, and although there was a fire-place big enough to roast an ox, I thought I should froze to death. This room rents for twenty-four dollars a year. Nauvoo abounds with such rooms. I have known many a family living in this way with a large family of children—only just one room, no cellar, no cupboards, a room and a fire-place without a crane is all that many have. It was just such a one where I boarded last winter. We live by ourselves now and have a room and a bedroom and a good large cooking-stove, and I feel myself pretty well off at that. We have a good cow and have sold two or three pounds of butter a week through the winter, besides supplying ourselves.

Write as soon as you get this and send me a paper as often as you can

Sarah S. Scott.

III

Nauvoo, March 1, 1845.

Dear Brother:

. . . The Church is now divided, and part go for Sidney Rigdon and William Law, the only Presidents left the Church. The other part hold to the Twelve, who arrogate to themselves the authority to lead the Church. Rigdon and Law are honorable, virtuous men; therefore you see they would not do to [sic] teach polygamy, adultery, fornication, perjury etc. which *is* and *has been* abundantly taught in the Church. I have heard it taught, I presume, an hundred times; I will be mistaken if Nauvoo before long don't be laid as waste as ever Jerusalem was; the wickedness of this people exceeds anything on record. The Temple, if ever finished, will be a splendid edifice. The steam-boats have been running on the river for some time past.

You may, perhaps, wonder that I write so plain about the Mormons and ask the question: "Isn't Scott a Mormon?" Yes, he is; but not a latter day saint. The difference between a Mormon and L.D.S. is great: the Mormons believe in *original Mormonism,* while the L.D. Saints believe and practise the doctrines above named. The Church cut me off in Missouri for no crime only opposing Daniteism, stealing, swearing, lies *etc.* I have seen them there *steal* thousands of dollars worth of property and heard them afterwards swear in court they did not do it. They have tried to get me to join them since, but I could not do it under such circumstances. Write when convenient.

Yours *etc.*

Isaac Scott.

Whittier Attends a Mormon Conventicle

MORMON MISSIONARIES FOUND in the blood of the martyred prophet even more eloquent testimony of his divine calling, and they preached his gospel with renewed energy. John Greenleaf Whittier, the Quaker poet, was in his thirties and already something of a national figure as abolitionist and teller of New England legends, when on an impulse he attended a Mormon service in Lowell, Massachusetts. He found the young preacher still in mourning in memory of the fallen prophet. Whittier wrote a vivid description of the occasion (with some incidental observations on the motivation of Mormon converts) which was published as "A Mormon Conventicle" in Howitt's Journal and reprinted in Littell's Living Age for October–December, 1847, from which it is taken here.

Passing up Merrimack-street the other day, my attention was arrested by a loud earnest voice, apparently engaged in preaching, or rather "holding forth," in the second story of the building opposite. I was in the mood to welcome anything of a novel character, and following the sound, I passed up a flight of steps leading to a long, narrow and somewhat shabby room, dignified by the appellation of Classic hall.

Seating myself, I looked about me. There were from fifty to one hundred persons in the audience, in which nearly all classes of this heterogeneous community seemed pretty fairly represented, all listening with more or less attention to the speaker.

He was a young man with dark enthusiastic complexion, black eyes and hair; with his collar thrown back, and his coat cuffs turned over, revealing a somewhat undue quantity of "fine linen," bending over his coarse board pulpit, and gesticulating with the vehemence of Hamlet's player, "tearing his passion to rags." A band of mourning crape, fluttering with the spasmodic action of his left arm, and an allusion to "our late beloved brother JOSEPH SMITH," sufficiently indicated the sect of the speaker. He was a *Mormon*—a saint of the latter days.

His theme was the power of faith. Although evidently unlearned and innocent enough of dealing in such "abominable matters as a verb or a noun, which no Christian ear can endure," to have satisfied Jack Cade himself, there was a straight-forward vehemence and intense earnestness in his manner, which at once disarmed my criticism. He spoke of Adam, in Paradise, as the lord of this lower world—"For," said he, "water couldn't drown him, fire couldn't burn him, cold couldn't freeze him —nothing could harm him, for he had all the elements under his feet. And what, my hearers, was the secret of this power? His faith in God: that was it. Well, the devil wanted this power. He behaved in a mean, *ungentlemanly way*, and deceived Eve, and lied to her, he did. And so Adam lost his faith. And all this power over the elements that Adam had, the devil got, and has it now. He is the prince and power of the air, *consequently*, he is master of the elements and lord of this world. He has filled it with unbelief, and robbed man of his birthright, and will do so until the hour of the power of darkness is ended, and the mighty angel comes down with the chain in his hand to bind the old serpent and dragon."

Another speaker, a stout black-browed "son of thunder," gave an interesting account of his experience. He had been one of the apostles of the Mormon Evangel, and had visited Europe. He went in faith. He had "but three cents in his pocket" when he reached England. He went to the high professors of all sects, and they would not receive him; they pronounced him "damned already." He was reduced to great poverty and hunger: alone in a strange land; with no one to bid him welcome. He was on the very verge of starvation. "Then," said he, "I knelt down and I prayed in earnest faith, 'Lord, give me this day my daily bread.' O, I tell ye, I *prayed with a good appetite;* and I rose up, and was moved to go to a house at hand. I knocked at the door, and when the owner came, I said to him, 'I am a minister of the Lord Jesus Christ, from America. I am starving—will you give me some food?' 'Why, bless you, yes,' said the man, 'sit down and eat as much as you please.' And I did sit down at his table, blessed be God: but my hearers, he was not a professor; he was not a Christian, but one of Robert Owen's infidels. The Lord reward him for his kindness."

In listening to these modern prophets, I discovered, as I think, the great secret of their success in making converts. They speak to a common feeling; they minister to a universal want. They contrast strongly the miraculous power of the gospel in the apostolic time with the present state of our nominal Christianity. They ask for the signs of divine power; the faith, overcoming all things, which opened the prison doors of the apostles, gave them power over the elements, which rebuked disease and death itself, and made visible to all the presence of the living God. They ask for any declaration in the Scriptures that this miraculous power of faith was to be confined to the first confessors of Christianity. They speak a language of hope and promise to weak, weary hearts, tossed and troubled, who have wandered from sect to sect, seeking in vain for the primal manifestations of the divine power.

In speaking of Mormonism as a delusion, I refer more particularly to the apocryphal book of Mormon. That the great majority of the "Latter Day Saints" are honest and sincere fanatics, I have no reason to doubt. They have made great sacrifices and endured severe and protracted persecution for their faith. The reports circulated against them by their unprincipled enemies in the west are in the main destitute of foundation. I place no dependence upon charges made against them by the ruffian mob of the Mississippi valley, and the reckless slave-drivers, who, at the point of the bayonet and bowie-knife, expelled them from Missouri, and signalized their Christian crusade against unbelievers by murdering old men, and violating their innocent wives and daughters. It is natural that the wrong-doers should hate those whom they have so foully injured.

The Prophet himself, the master-spirit of this extraordinary religious movement, is no more. He died by the hands of wicked and barbarous men, a martyr—unwilling, doubtless, but still a martyr—of his faith. For after all, Joe Smith could not have been wholly insincere. Or, if so in the outset, it is more than probable that his extraordinary success, his wonderful power over the minds of men, caused him to seem a miracle and a marvel to himself; and, like Mohammed and Napoleon, to consider himself a chosen instrument of the eternal power.

In the "Narrative of an Eye-witness of the Mormon Massacre," published in a Western paper, I was a good deal impressed by the writer's account of the departure of the prophet from "the holy city" to deliver himself up to the state authorities at Warsaw. It was well understood, that in so doing, he was about to subject himself to extreme hazard. The whole country round about was swarming with armed men, eager to imbrue their hands in his blood. The city was in a fearful state of alarm and excitement. The great Nauvoo legion, with its two thousand strong of armed fanatics, was drawn up in the principal square. A word from the prophet would have converted that dark silent mass into desperate and unsparing defenders of their leader, and the holy places of their faith. Mounted on his favorite black horse, he rode through the glittering files, and with words of cheer and encouragement, exhorted them to obey the laws of the state, and give their enemies no excuse for persecution and outrage. "Well," said he, as he left them, "they are good boys, if I never see them again." Taking leave of his family, and his more intimate friends, he turned his horse, and rode up in front of the great temple, as if to take a final look at the proudest trophy of his power. After contemplating it for a while in silence, he put spurs to his horse, in company with his brother, who, it will be recollected, shared his fate in the prison, dashed away towards Warsaw, and the prairie horizon shut down between him and the city of the saints for the last time.

Once in the world's history we were to have a Yankee prophet, and we have had him in Joe Smith. For good or for evil, he has left his track on the great pathway of life; or, to use the words of Horne, "knocked out for himself a window in the wall of the nineteenth century," whence his rude, bold, good-humored face will peer out upon the generations to come. But the prophet has not trusted his fame merely to the keeping of the spiritual. He has incorporated himself with the enduring stone of the great Nauvoo temple, which, when completed, will be the most splendid and imposing architectural monument in the new world. With its huge walls of hewn stone—its thirty gigantic pillars, loftier than those of Baalbec—their massive caps carved into the likeness of enormous human faces, themselves resting upon crescent moons, with a giant profile of a face within the curve—it stands upon the highest elevation of the most beautiful city site of the west, overlooking the "Father of Waters"—a temple unique and wonderful as the faith of its builder, embodying in its singular and mysterious architecture, the Titan idea of the Pyramids, and the solemn and awe-inspiring thought which speaks from the Gothic piles of the middle ages.

II · EXODUS

II · Exodus

The Flight into the Wilderness

THE DEATH OF JOSEPH SMITH threw the Mormons for a time into deep dejection and touched off a struggle for power within the ranks that made for schism and confusion. Lyman Wight led a colony off to Texas, James J. Strang declared Wisconsin a new land of promise, and the ineffectual Sidney Rigdon retired with a remnant to Pennsylvania. But the mantle of the prohet fell on Brigham Young, strong-minded president of the Council of the Twelve, who dealt heavily with the schismatics and quickly magnetized the pieces of Joseph's kingdom. He carried most of the church with him in his decision to remove to the far West.

With sheriffs hounding him and factions multiplying, Joseph Smith himself had contemplated such a move. He once predicted that the Saints would yet become a mighty people in the Rocky Mountains. He had read Frémont with lively interest. In February, 1844, he had proposed to send a small exploring expedition to Oregon and California to "hunt out a good location . . . where we can build a city in a day, and have a government of our own, get up into the mountains, where the devil cannot dig us out. . . ." The next month he had asked Congress to authorize him to raise 100,000 armed volunteers "to extend the arm of deliverance to Texas; to protect the inhabitants of Oregon from foreign aggressions and domestic broils; . . . to open the vast regions of the unpeopled west and south to our enlightened and enterprising yeomanry." Politicians had urged Mormon occupation of the West—it seemed good riddance at a safe distance and at the same time a way to put their disturbing energy at the service of the country. Stephen A. Douglas himself was "ripe for Oregon and the California" and said he would resign his seat in Congress "if he could command the force that Mr. Smith could." Governor Thomas Ford of Illinois approached Brigham Young to suggest "a matter in confidence—California now offers a

163

field for the prettiest enterprise that has been undertaken in modern time. . . . Why would it not be a pretty operation for your people to go out there . . . and establish an independent government . . . ?"

Brigham Young and the Council determined to send a scouting expedition to the Rockies, but the unhallowed haste of the anti-Mormons, by now a political faction in full cry, prevented such a disciplined move, and the first of the Mormons were harried out of Nauvoo in the winter of 1845–6 in spite of an agreement they would be given until "grass grows and water runs." The Mormons now became the Camp of Israel, clinging to Brigham Young, unwilling to let him or the Twelve out of their sight and obstructing saner plans to prepare the way before them. The thousands who evacuated Nauvoo, after the wolf hunts and house-burnings and hazings, created an appalling refugee emergency. They erected way-station settlements across Iowa, the vanguard planting crops for the rear to harvest. At Winter Quarters on the Missouri, Brigham Young finally managed, in the spring of 1847, to get a genuine pioneer company off to the Great Basin.

Meanwhile the government granted their request to form a battalion for the war with Mexico, which meant soldiers' pay and provisions to help outfit the ragged camp. And meanwhile Mormons in the eastern states were uprooting, some coming overland to join the exodus, others organizing to go by sea, one group, the *Brooklyn* company, making a remarkable voyage around the Horn and reaching the Pacific coast a year before the main body of the Mormons arrived in the Valley of the Great Salt Lake.

In this three-pronged movement the Mormons committed themselves dramatically to the mainstream of America's westering in 1846, the momentous year of decision. More than ever they regarded themselves as the modern Israel, a people in flight from Egypt seeking their promised land and living their Exodus as they would live their Chronicles in the New Canaan. They gave themselves a pioneer heritage that after a century is often mistaken as the whole of the Mormon story. No displaced persons ever found a surer place in history.

Though it was only three years from the death of Joseph Smith to the arrival of the pioneer vanguard in Salt Lake Valley, the years were full, and they are fully reported—from an eyewitness account of the first wagons making their way across the wintry Mississippi to a description of life in the Mormon encampments among the Omahas. The outstanding observer for the period is Colonel Thomas L. Kane, whose discourse on the Mormons before the Philadelphia Historical Society in

1850 is a literary as well as historical classic. The pages in the ensuing section record a saga today considered typically American, though ironically it came to pass because the Mormons seemed at the time so alien.

━━━━━━

"As Soon as Grass Grows and Water Runs"

"IT IS A SETTLED THING," reported the Quincy Whig in September, 1845, "that the public sentiment of the state is against the Mormons, and it will be in vain for them to contend against it . . . it is their duty to obey the public will, and leave the state as speedily as possible." A series of "wolf hunts" and houseburnings, with friendly Jack Mormons as well as the Mormons themselves the victims, had been giving force to that sentiment for months, until Sheriff J. B. Backenstos of Hancock County had to call upon "all law-abiding citizens as a posse comitatus . . . to give their united aid in suppressing the riotous and in maintaining the supremacy of the laws." In his opinion "the Mormon community have acted with more than ordinary forbearance—remaining perfectly quiet, and offering no resistance, when their dwellings, other buildings, and stacks of grain, &c., were set on fire in their presence, and they have forborne until forbearance is no longer a virtue."

Anti-Mormon conventions in Quincy and Carthage passed formal resolutions demanding that the Mormons remove the next spring, and urging patience on the part of the hotheads. Brigham Young, acting for the Mormon Council of Twelve, agreed to leave "as soon as grass grows and water runs" and for a point "so remote that there will not need to be a difficulty with the people and ourselves." He agreed to have "no more seed time nor harvest among our people in this county, after gathering their present crops." But he stipulated that the citizens should help them sell or rent their properties, that "all men will let us alone with their vexatious law suits, so that we may have the time, for we have broken no law; and help us to cash, dry goods, groceries, good oxen, milch cows, beef cattle, sheep, wagons, mules, harnesses, horses, &c., in exchange for our property, at a fair price, and deeds given at payment, that we may have the means to accomplish a re-

moval, without the suffering of the destitute, to an extent beyond the endurance of human nature." The citizens accepted the proposition as unconditional, pledging not to hinder or obstruct the Mormons in their efforts to sell, but not obliging themselves to assist.

Even that coldblooded and minimum concession was violated. Governor Ford in October admitted that "The spirit of the people . . . is up, and the signs are very evident that an attempt will be made by the surrounding counties to drive them [the Mormons] out." The Mormons might think themselves strong enough to defend themselves, but did they, he asked, want to live in a state of continued war? Confessing he had no legal power to enforce it, he asked Stephen A. Douglas to intercede and urge their early and voluntary departure.

The Mormons felt obliged to give their oppressors a dramatic token of their good faith: in the dead of winter a vanguard left Nauvoo, crossed the frozen Mississippi, and camped at Sugar Creek, Iowa. Most of the leadership were with the advance, an assurance to Illinois that the Mormons were evacuating for good. The Daily Missouri Republican *of February 13, 1846, describes below the beginnings of what would become a great exodus.*

We gather from several articles in the Warsaw *Signal*, and other quarters, that a portion, if not the whole, of the Mormons intend soon to commence their pilgrimage for California. That they should begin their journey so early in the season—before the winter has terminated, and long before grass shall appear, upon which to subsist their cattle and horses—is hazardous, and likely to be attended with severe trials and much suffering. But it is stated that from ten to twelve hundred have already crossed the river from Nauvoo, and are encamped on Sugar Creek, Iowa, seven miles distant. Among them were the *Twelve*, the High Council, all the principal men of the church, and about one hundred females. They were several days and nights in getting across the river. It is said to be the plan of the leaders to send this company forward as a *pioneer corps*. They are to proceed about five hundred miles westward, where they are to halt, build a village, and put in a spring crop. They are to remain there until those who follow in the spring reach them—when another pioneer company will start for a point five hundred miles still further west, where they will stop, build a village, and put in a fall crop. The company remaining behind will, in the spring, move on to this second station; and in this manner they hope to accomplish the long journey which is in contemplation. Many of those who now go as pioneers, are to return, so soon as their crop is in, for their families. There is a spice of romance about this arrangement for their journey—an apparent indifference to the sufferings which they must undergo—a confidence in the plans and orders of their church leaders—which must attract some portion of the public sympathy, even though it be undeserved. Their future journeyings will be observed with interest.

It is said in the *Signal*, that *the Twelve* crossed the river on Sunday night, apparently apprehensive of some visitation from officers who might interfere with their departure. They left behind them, as agents for the sale of the remaining property, A. Babbitt, Fulmer, and Heywood, formerly of Quincy.

Maj. Warren, who has been in command of the Illinois Militia stationed during the winter in Hancock county, has issued an address to the citizens of that county. In this address, he says:

"That he has learned with much regret, that a body of men, some twelve in number, have assumed the authority, of notifying a number of families, to make preparation to leave the county by the first of May next, on pain of being burned out, and this, too, as they said, upon the authority of Gov. Ford. Looking forward, as I now do, to the consummation in good faith, of the compromise effected last fall by Gen. Hardin, Majors Douglass, McDougall and myself, and believing as I do, that it is the duty of all good citizens and lovers of good order to abide by that compromise, and to avoid all causes of excitement, I feel it my duty to declare, that all persons engaged in notifying citizens at this time to leave, are *violators of the peace*, amenable to the law of the land, and thus they ought to be punished to the utmost extent of the law. The declaration that they were authorized to give such notice by Gov. Ford is *false* and *slanderous*. And I hereby pledge myself, and the force under my command, to move at a moment's warning, to put down all violence and breaches of the peace, and to assist in the execution of all proper legal process, let it come from what party it may, either Mormon or Anti-Mormon; and further, *advise* all good citizens (if aggressions are made upon their persons or property, when there is no chance to procure the assistance of the Volunteers) to defend their persons and property with powder and lead."

The *Signal* also condemns any attempt to interfere with the compromise between the two parties in that county.

"So On Our Way to California"

THE MORMONS WERE irrepressible, as the following "Mormon Song" published "by request" in the Missouri Whig *of Palmyra on April 2, 1846, suggests. "Old Sharp" was Tom Sharp, editor of the Warsaw Signal, a rabid Mormon hater who had taken part in the assault on Carthage jail. "Williams" was Col. Levi Williams, leader of the anti-Mormon force from Warsaw that had killed the prophet and his brother. "Our Governor" was Thomas Ford, who to the Mormons seemed cowardly and ineffectual. A good many songs, the verses set to familiar tunes, were inspired by the exodus. Most famous would be William Clayton's "Come, Come, Ye Saints," frequently sung by the Mormon Tabernacle Choir today, with its heartening chorus, "All is well, all is well."*

Mormon Song

Early next Spring we'll leave Nauvoo,
And on our journey we'll pursue,
We'll go and bid the mob farewell
And let them go to heaven or hell.

Chorus:

So on our way to California,
In the Spring we'll take our journey;
Far above the Arkansas fountain
We'll pass across the Rocky Mountain.

The robbers now have done their best,
Old Sharp and Williams amongst the rest;
They burned our houses and our goods,
And left our sick folks in the woods.

Below Nauvoo, in the Green Plains,
They burned our houses and our grains;
If we fought they all were bent
To raise for help the Government.

168

> Our Governor he is so small
> He has no room for a soul at all;
> He never can be damn'd or blest
> If Heaven or hell should do their best.
>
> The old settlers who claim the soil
> They surely thought to take the spoil,
> And then a scrape they did begin,
> But not much money have brought in.
>
> Since it is so we have to go
> And leave the City of Nauvoo,
> I hope you'll all be strong and stout,
> And then the mob can't back you out.

A City for Sale

THE MONTHS FOLLOWING the departure of the Mormon vanguard from Nauvoo early in 1846 transformed the city into a great wagon shop and supply depot making ready for total evacuation. A reporter for the Daily Missouri Republican at St. Louis has left a graphic description of the unprecedented scene as the Saints put their beloved city on the block. A group of French Icarians at length made the largest purchases, hoping to establish a communitarian society where the Mormon utopia had failed.

The account, which makes interesting allusions to splinter movements among the Mormons, is taken from the issue for May 13, 1846, by which time the advance party, calling itself the Camp of Israel, had made its way some two hundred miles west of Nauvoo into Iowa territory. The vanguard did not, as the report speculates, push on to the mountains that season, although that had been the original intention.

A few days ago, to satisfy ourselves of the actual state of affairs at Nauvoo, and to ascertain whether the Mormons were really disposed to leave the country, in conformity with their agreement last fall, we spent last Friday, Saturday and a portion of Sunday, in the city and surrounding country.

The city and country presents a very altered appearance since last fall. Then, the fields were covered with, or the barns contained, the crops of the season. Now, there are no crops, either growing or being planted. In many instances, the fences have been destroyed, houses have been deserted, and the whole aspect of the country is one of extreme desolation and desertion. At nearly every dwelling, where the owners have not sold out and moved off, preparations were making to go. Nearly every workshop in the city has been converted into a wagon maker's shop. Even an unfinished portion of the Temple is thus used, and every mechanic appears to be employed in making, repairing or finishing wagons, or other articles necessary for the trip. Generally, they are providing themselves with light wagons, with strong, wide bodies, covered with cotton cloth—in some instances painted, but mostly white. These are to be met with in every direction, and contribute greatly to the singular and mournful appearance of the country.

They appear to be going in neighborhoods, or companies, of four to six and ten wagons, and some of them are tolerably well provided with teams and provisions, but a very large portion present the appearance of being illy provided for so long a trip. Many of them are going with poor teams, and an amount of provisions insufficient for their subsistence for two months, if so long. Indeed, the stock of provisions for the whole company, so far as one may judge from appearance, cannot sustain the crowd until the fall, much less support them through the coming winter. If they should fail to make a good crop this year, at the stopping place, it cannot be otherwise than that many of them, especially the women and children, and the aged and decrepit, must be sorely pressed by starvation, if many of them do not literally perish from famine in the plains. They take with them their milch cows and their teams, being chiefly oxen. These will furnish food in the last resort. But, even with this resource, they have a very scanty supply. Of those whose condition is calculated to arouse sympathy, are a number of women, many of whom have large families of children, inadequately provided with provisions, &c., and without the assistance or protection of any male person. How they expect to get through the journey, we cannot conceive. The Church may give them some protection and assistance, but in all the preliminary preparations, and in setting out on the journey, these women seemed to rely upon themselves and their children, when they happened to be of an age to render any aid whatever.

A City for Sale

In the midst of this scene, in which there is presented an abandonment of their homes, the breaking up of social relations, a sacrifice of property, and inability to procure the necessary equipments and provisions—with an indefinite journey before them, a journey of months, probably years through plains and over mountains, occupied by Indians, and destitute of the assistance which might be expected in a civilized country—the spectator cannot fail to be struck with the lightness of heart, apparent cheerfulness, and sanguine hopes with which families bid adieu to their friends, and set out on their journey. Occasionally, the reverse of this is met with, but the great mass go forth, sustained and cheered by the promises of their leaders, and, strange as it may seem, a most devout conviction of the truth of their religion, and the rewards which they are to receive from heaven for their present sacrifice. No sect of religious enthusiasts were ever more firmly convinced of the entire truth of their creed than these people. Their trials and privations they regard as a species of martyrdom, which they must not shrink from, and for which they will be spiritually and temporally rewarded in due season. Their enthusiasm, or fanaticism, is stimulated by songs and hymns, in which their men, women and children join, and containing allusions to their persecutions; and the names of Oregon and California, and the hopes that await them, are mingled with their religious belief and expectations.

As a stranger passes through he will find himself frequently beset, mostly by women and children, with inquiries, "Do you wish to purchase a house and lot?" "Do you wish to buy a farm?" and thereupon, if any disposition is signified, he will be pressed and entreated to go and examine, and all the advantages, cheapness, &c., will be fully explained. The frequency and earnestness manifested everywhere, in the city and country, indicate the great anxiety which they entertain to get off. They are effecting some sales, but, from the sacrifices they are making, one would suppose the number and amount of transfers would be greater than they are. In the city, houses and lots are selling at from two to five and ten hundred dollars, which must have cost the owners double that sum. They are willing to sell for cash, or oxen or cattle, or to exchange for such articles of merchandise as they can barter or carry away with them. The most cases, they can give good titles. The number of purchasers is not in proportion to the property in market, nor near as large as was anticipated, from the profitable speculations which they offer, and the kind of property which they are willing to receive in payment. Farmers in other sections, it appears to us, would make profitable investments by exchanging their surplus stock for houses and lots in Nauvoo, or for farms. . . . Authority has been given to the Trustees to sell the Temple itself. Their original purpose was to lease it for a term of years, for some religious or literary purpose. Now they propose to sell it, and thus cut off the last and only motive which could exist to induce them to stay at Nauvoo, or return to it at any future time. The Temple is a stupendous building. . . . So far as room and convenience are requisite, it would answer well for a college or an asylum.

The members of the Church are not at peace even among themselves. A number, including Mrs. Emma Smith, the widow of Joe Smith, and his brother, deny the jurisdiction, and complain greatly of the conduct of the Council of Twelve—who have assumed and exercised the supreme authority since the death of the Prophet. This party, we believe, recognize the spiritual power of the new Prophet, [James J.] Strang, of Voree, Wisconsin Territory, but look forward to the time when a son of Joe, a lad of twelve or fourteen years of age, shall assume the position in the Church which his father occupied. This party do not contemplate removing with the other, but most of them will either join Strang, in Wisconsin Territory, or go to other parts.

They are crossing the river every day from Nauvoo, and a large number cross at Madison. Bad roads and high waters have detained them. It is difficult to arrive at the number who have crossed and are on the way. The first party, which crossed the river in February, have progressed as far as the east fork of Grand river, about 200 miles west of Nauvoo, within the Territory of Iowa. This party are styled the *Camp of Israel,* and have with them the Council of Twelve and most of the leading men of the Church. From the best information we could obtain, this Camp includes about 3000 souls. Between the Camp and the Mississippi river, there is said to be about 1500 wagons. Major Warren, who, on Friday last, visited the Camps within ten miles of Montrose, estimates the number of teams at about one thousand. Allowing five or six souls to a wagon—and the estimate is a reasonable one—it would give about seven thousand persons between the Mississippi and Grand river.

The first party have selected a temporary resting place on the east fork of Grand river, in the edge of a grove, which is free from underbrush. The soil is said to be very rich, and easily broken up and cultivated. Here they will enclose a large field—about 2300 acres—and leave that portion of their people who are not prepared to travel further, to plant and cultivate a crop, which is to be gathered for the subsistence of those who come on later in the season. Another portion of the camp will move two or three hundred miles further on, and select a second site, and put in a crop of buckwheat, and such roots and plants as grow rapidly, and will mature late in the season. After sowing this, those having provisions to subsist themselves through the winter, and teams sufficiently strong, will move further westward, or cross the mountains, if practicable. A body of several hundred, having the stoutest teams and the most ample supply of provisions, have been sent forward, with instructions to push directly across the mountains, and explore the territories of Oregon, California and Vancouver's Island, and upon their report it will depend where the Church will be re-established. This party, it is believed, have crossed the Missouri about sixty miles above St. Josephs, and are already some distance on the road to Oregon. From the camp on Grand river—says a letter from the Twelve to the Church at Nauvoo—the trading men have been sent out into Platte and the adjoining counties, to exchange whatever they can spare for oxen, cows and provisions. They complain, however, that the price of everything is high.

In and about Nauvoo, and throughout Hancock county, there is every indication that the citizens, or Anti-Mormons, with few exceptions, are satisfied that the Mormons are going, and are disposed to let them get off without further difficulty. There are, however, some few turbulent spirits in the county—for these broils have not been without their effects on the morals of individuals—and particularly some young men, who are willing, at any sacrifice, to keep up the excitement. A few nights ago, a Mr. Rea was dragged from his bed by four or five persons, stripped, and most severely beaten, but whether it was the act of the Anti-Mormons, or of one of the divisions of the Mormon church, we understood from the officers, was doubtful. The doors of other individuals have been placarded with notices to leave, &c., and on Saturday evening last, a number of persons assembled at Pontosuc, reported at about one hundred and fifty, who are said to have been under much excitement, and resolved to visit Nauvoo on the 16th inst. and burn down the houses and drive out all those who had not already left. These proceedings were universally condemned by the more intelligent and respectable portion of the Anti-Mormon party, and the movement appeared to excite no uneasiness on the part of Major W. B. Warren, who had had the command of the State troops stationed in the county for the past seven months. Maj. Warren is well satisfied, that a large majority of the Mormons will leave as soon as they can dispose of their property. He has dismissed all his company except ten or twelve, two of whom are stationed at Carthage, and the remainder are with him at Nauvoo. He has established regulations by which he will hereafter ascertain, weekly, the number of teams and persons crossing the river, so that the public will be able to determine how fast the Mormons are leaving. . . . He will remain in Nauvoo until about the first of June.

"We Have Sold our Place for a Trifle"

AN INTIMATE LOOK at the uprooting described in the previous selection comes from Martha Haven writing from Nauvoo to her mother in Sutton, Massachusetts in July, 1846. Her mother, Abigail Hall, had come to Nauvoo on a visit to her daughters Martha and Sarah and had received a "patriarchal blessing." Now she had returned, her faith as unshaken by the upheaval within the church as Martha's, though Sarah had become an active dissenter. While Sarah and her husband, Isaac Scott, went to Burlington, Wisconsin, to join the Strangites—to become in turn disillusioned with them—Martha and Jesse Haven prepared to go west with the Camp of Israel. Martha's letter describes these preparations, a little current in the mighty mainstream of the exodus. The verses she enclosed add a good deal of folk interest, summing up the spirit in which the Mormons accepted their latest misfortunes. The letter is reproduced below with permission of the New England Quarterly, *where it was published December, 1936, as one of a series in "The Death of a Mormon Dictator: Letters of Massachusetts Mormons, 1843–1848," edited by George F. Partridge.*

Nauvoo, July 4, 1846.

My dear dear Mother:

The joy of meeting and the pain of separating have passed, and I am again alone. I have been very anxious to hear from you, to know how you got home. I should have written long before this had I known where to have told you to direct your letters. We think soon of going to Farmington, Iowa. We shall probably stay there till fall; so direct your letters there till you hear to the contrary. My health has been growing poorer since you left. Have been to meeting but once since

"We Have Sold our Place for a Trifle"

I went with you, have not felt able to go. Mr. Haven talks of boxing our things ready for the wilderness and boarding if he can get a good place for me. Farmington is about twenty-five miles from here on the Des Moines River. Sister Sarah was in two or three times after you left; she made me her last visit the twenty-fifth of May; said they should start their journey the twenty-seventh.

We have sold our place for a trifle to a *Baptist minister*. All we got was a cow and two pairs of steers, worth about sixty dollars in trade. He bought Joel's and Brother Palmer's and pays in trade, except Joel's mortgage; he had to pay that in money, of course. Brother Palmer gets a very nice cow and pair of steers for his part. Joel gets a horse and buggy and then there is a colt and harness which he and Mr. Haven own between them. I like to have forgot them. You see I can't write straight; so I will stop and rest.

July 5: I will now try to conclude my letter. We have again been troubled with mobbers, between sixty and a hundred collected a few weeks ago. They drove a number of farming settlers into Nauvoo and whipped several men, some of them so bad that they have since died. They swore that they would enter the City, destroy the Temple and drive [out] the remaining inhabitants. Sheriff McIntosh [Backenstos] sent them word that if they did not go home, he would come out with an armed force and disperse them at the point of the bayonet. At this intelligence they fled. They say they will come again after harvest. Our people are leaving as fast as possible.

Give my love to all my brothers and sisters; tell them to write as often as possible, and I will do the same. I feel thankful that I have had the privilege of having a visit from my *dear* Mother. I can tell you I felt lonesome enough after I got home from the river the day you started. Mr. Haven went down the next morning as soon as he was up; carried your comb and some bread, but found you gone.

Martha S. H. Haven.

1. *Come go with me, come go with me*
   Ye Saints of God come go with me
   The time is come we must away
   To distant lands where God shall say
   No longer let us linger here.
   The world is doomed to woe and fear
   This Gentile race the Priesthood hates
   We have no home within the States
   Let us away to seek our rest
   Our home's not here; it's in the West.

2. *My kindred come, come go with me,*
   All friends of truth where'er you be;
   Ye poor, ye lame, ye halt, ye blind;
   Ye need not one be left behind.
   Come go with me, I'm Westward bound
   Where mobbers blasts shall never sound;
   Where truth will spread and justice flow;
   Where party sects will never grow;
   Where God shall be our priest and king;
   And Saints to him their offerings bring.

3. *Come, then, oh come; no more delay;*
   The Spirit whispers, haste away.
   This Nation now has sealed its doom
   And soon with wrath will be o'erthrown.
   The Prophet's blood has stained the land;
   He fell by cruel mobbers hands.
   Although the rulers pledged their faith
   That he, with them, should be kept safe,
   Their pledge they broke; they spilt his blood,
   And forced his Spirit back to God.

4. *We'll go away from this vain world*
   With freedom's banners wide unfurled
   To a land of peace and liberty
   Beside the great Pacific Sea.
   There we will sing in joyful strains,
   And shout Hosanna o'er the plains
   Where mobs and strife shall be no more
   Upon the great Pacific shore,
   Sweet praises to our God will give
   While in our peaceful tents we live.

5. *We'll bid adieu to party clan*
   And rend asunder all their bands;
   We'll leave them to their wretched fate
   Because they do the Gospel hate.
   We'll leave these scenes of strife and woe
   To milder climes we all will go,
   Where right will rule and justice reign;
   We there will break this Gentile chain;
   No more we'll wear their cursed yoke
   For God has said it shall be broke.

6. *Then come, ye Saints, no longer stay.*
   In forty six we'll move away

> *Our God shall be our constant aid*
> *His arm is bare, be not afraid;*
> *The journey's great and arduous, too,*
> *But dread it not; there's peace in view.*
> *Though wicked men may rage and foam,*
> *The silent West shall be our home*
> *God says he'll be our guide and shield*
> *And for his Saints his power will wield.*

It makes me very nervous to write; so I have to do it by littles. The mob are trying again to see what they can do. They have driven a few more into the City. Some of the new settlers have been baptized and want to sell and go with us.

July 7: I have a stout girl of fifteen to help me. She is one of the kind that never can see anything that is to be done. We shall only keep her till we can do better. Tell me whether Mr. B—— mistrusts that this is more than one sheet. I thought I would try it once. I wish I could see you all before leaving. Farewell for the present. May health attend you all!

Martha S. Haven.

The Camp of Israel

THE MORMONS HAD *originally intended in the spring of 1846 to send "out into the western country . . . a Company of Pioneers, consisting of young, hardy men, with some families . . . to be furnished with an ample outfit . . . a printing press, farming utensils of all kinds, with mill irons and bolting cloths, seeds of all kinds, grain, etc." The pioneers would put in a spring crop, build houses, prepare for those who would come as soon as grass could sustain teams and stock. They were to proceed west until they found a good place to make a crop, "in some good valley in the neighborhood of the Rocky Mountains, where they will infringe upon no one, and not be likely to be infringed upon." Should the President of the United States recommend the erection of block houses and stockade forts on the route to Oregon, the Mormons would undertake that work, for "under our peculiar circumstances, we*

177

*can do it with less expense to the government than any other people."
And, to prove their patriotism had not been "overcome by fire, by
sword, by daylight nor by midnight assassinations," they were prepared
to sustain the claims of the United States to Oregon. All these proposals
were outlined in a circular of the Nauvoo High Council on January
20, 1846.*

*But the premature exodus from Nauvoo changed a pioneer expedi-
tion into an overwhelming tide of displaced persons. The Mormons became the Camp of Israel, strung out across Iowa in a unique combination of temporary settlements and people in motion, sustaining each
other. A correspondent of the Hancock (Illinois) Eagle describes this
amazing organization in an account briefed by the Daily Missouri Republican of July 15, 1846, from which it is taken here.*

Late from the Mormon Camp.—The Hancock *Eagle*, of Friday last,
notices the arrival there of Mr. S. Chamberlain, who left the most distant camp of the Mormons at Council Bluffs on the 26th ult, and on
his route passed the whole line of Mormon emigrants. He says that the
advance company of the Mormons, with whom were the *Twelve*, had
a train of one thousand wagons, and were encamped on the east bank
of the Missouri River, in the neighborhood of the Council Bluffs. They
were employed in the construction of boats, for the purpose of crossing
the river.

The second company had encamped temporarily at station No. 2,
which has been christened Mount Pisgah. They mustered about three
thousand strong, and were recruiting their cattle preparatory to a fresh
start. A third company had halted for a similar purpose at Garden
Grove, on the head waters of Grand River, where they have put in
about 2000 acres of corn for the benefit of the people in general. Between Garden Grove and the Mississippi River, Mr. Chamberlain counted
over one thousand wagons *en route* to join the main bodies in advance.

The whole number of teams attached to the Mormon expedition,
is about three thousand seven hundred, and it is estimated that each
team will average at least three persons, and perhaps four. The whole
number of souls now on the road may be set down in round numbers
at twelve thousand. From two to three thousand have disappeared from
Nauvoo in various directions. Many have left for Council Bluffs by the
way of the Mississippi and Missouri rivers—others have dispersed to
parts unknown; and about eight hundred or less still remain in Illinois.
This comprises the entire Mormon population that once flourished in

Hancock county. In their palmy days they probably numbered between fifteen and sixteen thousand souls, most of whom are now scattered upon the prairies, bound for the Pacific slope of the American continent.

Mr. Chamberlain reports that previously to his leaving, four United States military officers had arrived at the Mount Pisgah camp, for the purpose of enlisting five hundred Mormons for the Santa Fe campaign. They were referred to Headquarters at Council Bluffs, for which place they immediately set out. It was supposed that the force would be enrolled without delay. If so, it will furnish Col. Kearney with a regiment of well disciplined soldiers who are already prepared to march.

Mr. Chamberlain represents the health of the traveling Mormons as good, considering the exposure to which they have been subjected. They are carrying on a small trade in provisions with the settlers in the county, with whom they mingle on the most friendly terms.

The Mormon Battalion

ELDER JESSE C. LITTLE'S *appointment to preside over the Mormon mission in the eastern states in January, 1846, instructed him to "take every honorable advantage of the times" he could. "If our government shall offer any facilities for emigrating to the western coast, embrace those facilities, if possible." The Mormons hoped for a commission, by land, to build forts on the road to Oregon or, by sea, to procure the freight of any provisions or naval stores the government might be sending to any part of the Pacific. In May Elder Little went to Washington to see what he could do.*

It proved an opportune moment. Congress had just declared war on Mexico and planned to form an Army of the West at Fort Leavenworth under Colonel, soon General, S. W. Kearney to invade New Mexico and ultimately co-operate with the Pacific fleet. The obvious way to assist the Mormons and the government at the same time was to enlist Mormon men, arm and equip them, and establish them in California to defend the country.

The Mormons were not fighting men, said Elder Little, but they would act "as one man" on behalf of the United States in the land to which they were going. On June 5 President Polk told him the Mormons would be protected in California and that 500 to 1,000 of his people should be taken into the service, officered by their own men. Col. Thomas L. Kane of Philadelphia, lawyer and humanitarian who had befriended Elder Little, offered to carry the War Department's order to Fort Leavenworth. Captain James Allen carried the offer to the Mormon camps, pointing out the material advantages of a year's enlistment.

Enlistment meant a year's advance clothing allowance of $42 per man, or $21,000 for the battalion, a windfall to secure stores and supplies for their families. But enlistment was not an unmixed blessing for the Mormon camps. It meant a loss of able-bodied young men needed to herd the stock, drive the teams, and pioneer the way. It meant delaying the march to the Great Basin for another year. Brigham Young and his council weighed the issues. Reassured that they would be permitted to dwell on Indian lands meanwhile and that the government's intentions were benevolent, they urged enlistment. "If there are not young men enough," said Brigham, "we will take old men, and if they are not enough, we will take women!" Colonel Kane describes below the farewell ball for the companies raised at Council Bluffs. The passage is taken from his lecture before the Historical Society of Pennsylvania which was published as The Mormons *in 1850.*

The Battalion, raised to full strength of 500 from the several camps across Iowa, reported to Fort Leavenworth on August 1. Early in October it reached Santa Fe, where Lt. Col. Philip St. George Cooke took command. He was not impressed: "It was enlisted too much by families; some were too old and feeble, and some too young; it was embarrassed by many women; it was undisciplined; it was much worn by traveling on foot, and marching from Nauvoo, Illinois; their clothing was very scant . . . their mules were utterly broken down . . . and animals were scarce. . . ." But by the time the Battalion reached San Diego on January 29, 1847, following a route which the Southern Pacific Railroad travels today, Cooke could pay his men a handsome tribute.

After their tour of duty, most Battalion men made their way to the Valley of the Great Salt Lake to join their families, who had meanwhile come west with the main body of Mormon pioneers. Some of them, scattering for employment in California, were among the workmen who discovered flakes of gold in the mill race they were building for John Sutter on the American River. The Mormon Battalion has had a modern revival among the Sons of Utah Pioneers who, numbering

180

*more officers than privates, love to parade in the blue and gold uni-
forms they imagine their ancestors wore.*

At the commencement of the Mexican war, the President considered
it desirable to march a body of reliable infantry to California at as
early a period as practicable, and the known hardihood and habits of
discipline of the Mormons were supposed peculiarly to fit them for
this service. As California was supposed also to be their ultimate destination, the long march might cost them less than other citizens. They
were accordingly invited to furnish a battalion of volunteers early in
the month of July.

The call could hardly have been more inconveniently timed. The
young, and those who could best have been spared, were then away
from the main body, either with pioneer companies in the van, or,
their faith unannounced, seeking work and food about the northwestern
settlements, to support them till the return of the season for commencing emigration. The force was therefore to be recruited from among
the fathers of families, and others whose presence it was most desirable
to retain.

There were some, too, who could not view the invitation without
jealousy. They had twice been persuaded by (State) government authorities in Illinois and Missouri, to give up their arms on some special
appeals to their patriotic confidence, and had then been left to the
malice of their enemies. And now they were asked, in the midst of an
Indian country, to surrender over five hundred of their best men for
a war-march of thousands of miles to California, without the hope of
return till after the conquest of that country. Could they view such a
proposition with favor?

But the feeling of the country triumphed. The Union had never
wronged them. "You shall have your battalion at once, if it has to be a
class of Elders," said one, himself a ruling Elder. A central "mass meeting" for council, some harangues at the more remotely scattered camps,
an American flag brought out from the store-house of things rescued,
and hoisted to a tree mast—and, in three days, the force was reported
mustered, organized, and ready to march.

There was no sentimental affection at their leave-taking. The afternoon before was appropriated to a farewell ball; and a more merry
dancing rout I have never seen, though the company went without
refreshments, and their ballroom was of the most primitive. It was the

custom, whenever the larger camps rested for a few days together, to make great arbors, or boweries, as they called them, of poles, and brush, and wattling, as places of shelter for their meetings of devotion or conference. In one of these, where the ground had been trodden firm and hard by the worshipers of the popular Father Taylor's precinct, we gathered now the mirth and beauty of the Mormon Israel.

If anything told the Mormons had been bred to other lives, it was the appearance of the women, as they assembled here. Before their flight, they had sold their watches and trinkets as the most available resource for raising ready money; and, hence, like their partners, who wore waistcoats cut with useless watch pockets, they, although their ears were pierced and bore the loop-marks of rejected pendants, were without ear-rings, finger-rings, chains, or brooches. Except such ornaments, however, they lacked nothing most becoming the attire of decorous maidens. The neatly darned white stocking, and clean, bright petticoat, the artistically clear-starched collar and chemisette, the something faded, only because too well washed, lawn or gingham gown, that fitted modishly to the waist of the pretty wearer—these, if any of them spoke of poverty, spoke of a poverty that had known its better days.

With the rest, attended the Elders of the Church within call, including nearly all the chiefs of the High Council, with their wives and children. They, the gravest and most trouble-worn, seemed the most anxious of any to be the first to throw off the burden of heavy thoughts. Their leading off the dancing in a great double cotillion, was the signal bade the festivity commence. To the canto of debonair violins, the cheer of horns, the jingle of sleigh bells, and the jovial snoring of the tambourine, they did dance! None of your minuets or other mortuary processions of gentles in etiquette, tight shoes, and pinching gloves, but the spirited and scientific displays of our venerated and merry grandparents, who were not above following the fiddle to the Foxchase Inn, or Gardens of Gray's Ferry. French fours, Copenhagen jigs, Virginia reels, and the like forgotten figures executed with the spirit of people too happy to be slow, or bashful, or constrained. Light hearts, lithe figures, and light feet, had it their own way from an early hour till after the sun had dipped behind the sharp sky-line of the Omaha hills. Silence was then called, and a well cultivated mezzo-soprano voice, belonging to a young lady with fair face and dark eyes, gave with quartette accompaniment a little song, the notes of which I have been unsuccessful in repeated efforts to obtain since—a version of the text, touching to all earthly wanderers:

The Mormon Battalion

*"By the rivers of Babylon we sat down and wept.
We wept when we remembered Zion."*

There was danger of some expression of feeling when the song was over, for it had begun to draw tears! but breaking the quiet with his hard voice, an Elder asked the blessing of heaven on all who, with purity of heart and brotherhood of spirit had mingled in that society, and then all dispersed, hastening to cover from the falling dews. All, I remember, but some splendid Indians, who, in cardinal scarlet blankets and feathered leggings, had been making foreground figures for the dancing rings, like those in Mr. West's picture of our Philadelphia treaty, and staring their inability to comprehend the wonderful performances. These loitered to the last, as if unwilling to seek their abject homes.

Well as I knew the peculiar fondness of the Mormons for music, their orchestra in service on this occasion astonished me by its numbers and fine drill. The story was, that an eloquent Mormon missionary had converted its members in a body at an English town, a stronghold of the sect, and that they took up their trumpets, trombones, drums, and hautboys together, and followed him to America.

When the refugees from Nauvoo were hastening to part with their table ware, jewelery, and almost every other fragment of metal wealth they possessed that was not iron, they had never thought of giving up the instruments of this favorite band. And when the battalion was enlisted, though high inducements were offered some of the performers to accompany it, they all refused. Their fortunes were with the camp of the tabernacle. They had led the farewell service in the Nauvoo temple. Their office now was to guide the monster choruses and Sunday hymns; and like the trumpets of silver, made of a whole piece, "for the calling of the assembly, and for the journeying of the camps," to knoll the people into church. Some of their wind instruments, indeed, were uncommonly full and pure-toned, and in that clear, dry air could be heard to a great distance. It had the strangest effect in the world, to listen to their sweet music winding over the uninhabited country. Something in the style of a Moravian death-tune blown at day-break, but altogether unique. It might be when you were hunting a ford over the great Platte, the dreariest of all wild rivers, perplexed among the far-reaching sand bars, and curlew shallows of its shifting bed —the wind rising would bring you the first faint thought of a melody; and as you listened borne down upon the gust that swept past you a cloud of the dry sifted sands, you recognized it—perhaps a home-loved theme of Henry Proch or Mendelssohn. Mendelssohn Bartholdy, away there in the Indian marches!

═══════════════

The Voyage of the Brooklyn

WHILE THE CAMP OF ISRAEL pitched its tents across Iowa on the way west and the Mormon Battalion marched off to California along the Santa Fe trail, another Mormon exodus took place by sea. A company of 238 (70 men, 68 women, and 100 children) cleared New York harbor aboard the sailship Brooklyn on February 4, 1846, rounded the Horn, and on July 31 went ashore at Yerba Buena in San Francisco Bay, the first colonists to strengthen American occupation of what had lately been Mexican territory. Ironically, they had sought to leave the United States for good. "There's that damned flag again!" their leader Samuel Brannan is supposed to have said, though one member of the company remembered that at sight of it "All hearts felt more cheerful and secure."

Fully outfitted with everything from sawmill irons to a printing press, they settled New Hope on the north bank of the Stanislaus not far from the San Joaquin, but disagreements and uncertainty about the intent of the main body of the church shortly broke up the colony. Sam Brannan, impatient and perturbed, crossed the Sierras in the summer of 1847, encountered Brigham Young with the pioneer vanguard west of Fort Bridger, and vainly tried to persuade him to make California his destination.

A little more than half the Brooklyn company eventually made their separate ways to the Salt Lake Valley; the rest remained in California, most of them losing their identity as Mormons, though a few joined later Mormon colonies at San Bernardino and in Arizona. Brannan himself, a tarnished and unstable leader in Mormon eyes, became a principal actor in much of California's early drama: he founded the California Star, participated in the discovery of gold and the wild speculations in San Francisco real estate (Brannan Street is named after him), invested in mines, milling, and railroads, became a large-scale distiller, a landed proprietor in both California and Sonora, Mexico, and was known at one time as the richest man in California. But he became dissolute, ruined his family and his health, and lost his fortune. He died *"a sorry wreck"* in Sonora in 1889. His spectacular career has made him a perennially favorite character in novels about the Mormons.

The firsthand narrative of the Brooklyn expedition excerpted below comes from Edward C. Kemble, a printer who was one of the very few non-Mormons among the passengers. His recollections appeared in the Sacramento Daily Union on September 11, 1866, as "Twenty Years Ago. The 'Brooklyn Mormons' in California," and in two nostalgic sketches called "Yerba Buena—1846," which were published in the Union on August 26 and October 14, 1871.

In the year 1845 there was published at No. 7 Spruce Street, in the city of New York, a weekly newspaper, which bore the pretentious title of *The Prophet.* . . . The publisher of the Mormon paper in New York was a young printer who, some time in the year of which I write, came on from the West. . . . This young man was introduced as Elder Brannan, and whatever his footing at first, he was not long in making his mark among the brethren. A sallow, cadaverous, hard-featured man, debilitated by a long attack of Western fever, and so feeble as scarcely to be able to stand at "case" or perform an ordinary day's work, he was, nevertheless, a power among the dull, pliant minds about him, and clearly from the start the "coming man" who was to revolutionize the little world of which the Prophet was the central luminary. The vigor, boldness and ability with which he went straight to his work were irresistible, and very soon he had placed himself at the head of the society in New York, preaching on Sundays and quite carrying captive his hearers with his nervous, impassioned declamation, editing and attending to the publication of his paper and in active correspondence with the Mormon authorities at Nauvoo on the subject of the proposed exodus in the spring. . . . At the time of which I write the Mormons were actively but secretly planning a march to the Pacific and the occupation of a portion of the region then known as the Mexican province of Alta California. Through their agents in New York, the Nauvoo authorities commenced the organization of an expedition by sea to the California coast, which was destined to be the vanguard of the great army of Mormons to be set in motion toward the Pacific the following spring.

Then commenced the fitting out of this expedition and the preparations for departure on the long voyage. The publisher of *The Prophet* fell almost naturally into the place of leader and chief organizer. . . .

On the 6th of February the expedition was ready to sail. For several days previous the members had been gathering into the city from distant parts. Nearly all the New England and Middle States were represented, the emigrants being mostly farmers and mechanics from the rural districts, persons in decent circumstances, but who had probably sacrificed most of their worldly goods in securing the passage of themselves and families and procuring an outfit for the journey and for a start in life after their arrival. They were generally Americans and intelligent, though few among them, from their leader down, made any pretense to education. Nearly all the trades were represented and a goodly assortment of all the implements and utensils of domestic industry, including some of the most recent improvements in husbandry, had been purchased with the company fund and stowed on board the *Brooklyn*. They were of course abundantly supplied with firearms, for a military organization had been contemplated from the outset, and some of the newest patterns of revolving guns and pistols were in their hands. Cases of muskets, also, enough to arm every man, woman and child on board were added to more peaceful freight, together with quantities of powder and lead. In short, the company was thoroughly prepared and self-reliant for all the emergencies of settlement in a new and possibly hostile country. They had provisions enough for their subsistence until a new crop should be planted and gathered, with the aid of fish and game of their prospective dominions of which the most extravagant stories were told. They had a small library for use on board the ship, but which, if I am not mistaken, was the gift of some one of the charitable Societies of New York, and as a crowning triumph of the genius of civilization which directed their efforts, they had taken on board with them a press, type and entire office material of *The Prophet* newspaper, two of the printers (mere boys) employed on the paper adhering to its fortunes and accompanying this first Yankee press on its mission to California.

The total number of souls on board the *Brooklyn*, exclusive of the ship's officers and crew, was 238, of which number a little over one-half were women and children. With perhaps a dozen exceptions all were Mormons, and to their credit it must be said that whatever their religion may have at that time taught on the subject of polygamy or the spiritual-wife doctrine, as it was known, practically the system was utterly ignored. Nor was the moral or religious standing of such as assented to its "orthodoxy" enhanced in the estimation of their fellow

"Saints." The married men of the company were each the husband of one wife, the three or four elders who had the spiritual charge of the flock were men of good report, in their domestic relations at least, the wives, and widows were orderly and well behaved, the young women, of whom there were fifteen or twenty in the company, were modest and discreet, and probably no emigrant ship ever crossed the ocean— certainly none ever sailed to California—whose female passengers at the end of a long voyage preserved reputations as unspotted as did those of the *Brooklyn*. The entire "between decks" of the vessel, fore and aft, was filled up with small staterooms, and though the smallness of the ship necessitated the closest storage consistent with the health of the passengers, there was rarely an infraction of discipline or decorum among the members of the company, even in the most trying times, such as were occasioned by heat or stress of weather.

The *Brooklyn* moved out from her pier on a pleasant winter afternoon, and a strange spectacle her appearance presented to the eyes of wondering New Yorkers. Ship loads of emigrants arriving from foreign countries were scenes of daily occurrence, but a vessel crowded with emigrating Americans departing for a distant and almost unknown shore was a sight of rarer if not unprecedented novelty. The wharf was crowded with the friends and relatives of the voyagers, and a dense mass of spectators drawn by curiosity and gazing in apparent astonishment skirted the piers and hung upon the shipping in the vicinity. To the oft repeated inquiry who they were and whither they were going, few among the outside crowd were able to give an intelligent reply. The *Brooklyn* deck was of course the scene of lively excitement and affectionate leave-taking. The crowd on shore kept up their spirits by giving them repeated parting cheers, which those on board duly acknowledged in kind, and even essayed to tip them a song and chorus, the latter having reference to the enterprise on which they were starting out. I remember but a stanza of this song, which was set to a lively quickstep popular at the time. It was supposed to be the affectionate exhortation of the departing Saint to some female disciple to join him in his western venture:

> *Sister, see yon evening star*
> *Shining o'er the hills afar!*
> *Shines it not for you and me,*
> *Over the California sea?*

and then the chorus:

> *Rejoice! rejoice! the wilderness shall bloom!*

187

When in the Narrows and nearly opposite Fort Lafayette the *Brooklyn* hoisted at her main a signal on which was inscribed in large letters, Oregon, which was dimly understood by members of the company to be a sort of blind, intended to deceive Uncle Sam; and as that worthy old gentleman did not at that time enjoy to a very eminent degree the respect of the Mormon community because of his alleged indifference to their complaints of persecution, the ruse of naming Oregon as their place of destination was secretly applauded on board the *Brooklyn* as very clever and commendable. . . .

The voyage of the *Brooklyn* commenced under no very favoring circumstances. Three days out of New York the ship caught a severe gale, greatly adding to the discomforts of the passengers, most of whom had never been in sight of blue water before. Their trials increased as they drew near the line. The *Brooklyn* was a dull sailer, and her space between decks close and ill-ventilated. Besides, the cooking conveniences were limited, and frequently during heavy weather it was with greatest difficultly meals could be served. The sick were a great care, and the want of proper medical attendance aggravated their sufferings and increased the hardships of all on board. It was at first attempted to institute a sort of camp discipline; guards were set and the company was called up and mustered at meal times by drum beat. But this was found impracticable, and indeed for a few weeks every species of routine and system seemed alike unavailable. After crossing the equator, however, and getting into steadier weather, better order was evoked, and the daily life on shipboard shaped itself to suit the necessities of the situation, and thenceforward the journey had fewer trials, except from wearisomeness. The leader chose to himself three counselors, who were also charged with the administration of government and co-operation in the direction of company affairs. Petty officers, stewards, assistants, table-waiters, etc., were appointed, and the whole company divided into "watches," from which each night alternately guards or watchmen were detailed to exercise the customary vigilance against fire, and also to keep an eye to the good order and decorum of the various members of the company. Every evening, when the weather permitted, the company were assembled for prayers, and on Sunday there was preaching, generally by the Elder in charge of the expedition. I should mention one circumstance which, though trifling, did not fail to provoke comment, though it may scarcely be said to have disturbed the "gentle concord" between the company and their leader. Soon after leaving port the latter exchanged the rude pine table, tin plate, iron spoon and coarse fare of the company for a seat at the better provided board of the Captain of the ship, nor did he go back again to the common fare until the vessel reached her destination. . . .

Cape Horn was doubled without experiencing any greater hardships than intensely cold weather could inflict on a ship's company destitute of facilities for securing sufficient artificial warmth. But off the coast of Chile the *Brooklyn* took a gale which blew her back nearly abreast of the Cape again. The captain of the ship was an exceedingly nervous man, though a good seaman, and if the Mormons had possessed less faith in their being ultimately allowed to reach the promised land for which they were steering, it might have been sorely tried on this occasion, as the Captain announced to them that the ship was in exceeding peril—that he had done all he could for their safety, and gave them no encouragement to believe that she would outlive the storm. However, on the third day the gale abated, and not many days after, the ship made her first land and cast anchor in the little bay which the island of Juan Fernandez offers the visiting navigator. The stoppage was made for wood and water, and the time was improved by the passengers of the *Brooklyn* in never-to-be-forgotten rambles among the picturesque little valleys and mountains which, to those who have ever seen them, imparted to the boyhood's story *Robinson Crusoe* associated with the island deeper interest and beauty. Not the least among the attractions for which the spot is famous are its abundant fishing grounds, and for variety and quantity it would be hard to imagine their superior. The catching and salting of as many barrels of these fish as they would require for the rest of the journey, filled up the week of their stay here as agreeably as the visitors could desire, and now the *Brooklyn* resumed her journey, laying her course for the Sandwich Islands. . . .

At Honolulu the *Brooklyn* colonists experienced a kind reception and their expedition was the theme of every tongue. Anticipating the curiosity and inquisitiveness which would be excited among the islanders regarding the plans of the voyagers and the peculiarities of their religious faith, their leader had impressed them with the necessity of caution and reticence long before the ship arrived in port, and had even undertaken to frame answers for the most obvious questions suggested in the minds of strangers. For example, they were taught to reply to the question, "What is Mormonism?" that it was to mind one's own business. But the courteous treatment which the *Brooklyn* passengers met with disarmed them of meditated churlishness and made their short stay among the hospitable residents of Honolulu the most delightful episode of their long voyage. . . . It was at Honolulu that the *Brooklyn* people first heard that war had been declared by the United States against Mexico. The frigate *Congress*—one of the victims of the rebel iron-clad *Merrimac* in the late war—was in port en route to "the Coast," as California and Oregon were then familiarly designated by the islanders. In the interviews which took place between the Mormon leaders and the officers of the *Congress* the former learned with blank dismay that the seizure of California was contemplated by the United States, if indeed the order for the capture of its seaport towns had not been already executed. Strangely such a possible obstruction of their plans of sovereignty as one of the issues of a war with Mexico, loudly talked of when they left the United States, had never been imagined by the *Brooklyn* colonists. In all their long voyage the contingency had never once been discussed. There were long faces and wrathful words, which in these days would have been counted as disloyal, and whispered consultations under the ship's hatches at the assembling for prayers the evening these unpleasant tidings were made known. Nor was the news made more agreeable by the intimation frequently thrown out during the remainder of their stay at the Islands that they would be expected to render assistance in the conquest of the country to which they were going. The arms they held in their hands they were ready enough to use, as originally intended, for their own protection, or for any needful acquisitions under the banner of the church. But to help establish the authority of the United States again over them was a very wide departure from their original plans, if not in direct antagonism with their designs. They hoped the purposes of the United States might have been misapprehended, or that the design, if made at all, would be restricted to the seaport towns of California, and be temporary in its operations.

Thus hoping for the best, but preparing for the worst, the *Brooklyn* colony again set sail, this time to complete their voyage and make a landing for the last time, wherever that should be. . . .

The ship left Honolulu on the 2d of July. The "time-honored Fourth" was not forgotten, though it is hard to say whether it was from force of association or from motives of policy, the Mormons wishing doubtless, to stand well with the Captain and crew of their transport. At noonday the company was mustered on deck and a volley fired, which was the extent of the demonstrative rejoicings on board. On the 31st of July . . . early in the morning, through the thick haze, the shores of California were descried amid great exultation and glad but anxious heart-beatings, and by three o'clock in the afternoon the *Brooklyn* was at anchor off the town of Yerba Buena.

The ship landed her colony of 238 men, women and children on the beach of Yerba Buena during the first days of August, 1846. When the tide served, the ship's launch and small boat set them ashore bag and baggage, on a strip of good, firm land between Clay and Washington streets, thirty yards from the line of the stores on the west side of Montgomery Street, and about six feet below its hard earth level; at low tide the boats touched at the foot of the rocky bluff known later as Clark's Point. . . .

I look through my "loophole" on the busy scene of the *Brooklyn* landing. The beach is strewn with goods and implements, such as never before were landed on this wild coast. There were Yankee plows of which I will venture to say not a dozen had ever before been introduced into California . . . and there were harrows landed from the *Brooklyn* over which even many "foreigners" in Yerba Buena scratched their wise polls in puzzled meditation on their uses; for the youthful Californian of that period of agriculture had never been combed by the harrow. Scythes, grain-cradles, hoes and rakes, and all that in those days made up the complete outfit of the husbandmen, with various mechanic implements and dairy utensils, covered the landing, and are being dragged on Yankee wheels by hand-power up the long hill at Washington Street. In an inclosed space in the rear of the houses, near the junction of this street with Montgomery, the Mormon colony first pitched its tents; a few families are lodged in the few vacant houses about town. Headquarters are established at the adobe building on Dupont Street between Clay and Washington, where were stored the company's goods and implements. And now the campfires are lighted and the new life in this strange land begins. . . .

The *Brooklyn* colony set about their labor of preparing new homes with heavy hearts. A few abandoned the field in the outset and returned to the East in the first ship that sailed out of the harbor. Others separated from the company of the faithful and set up for themselves. The first school opened in Monterey, then the capital of the country, was established by a seceder from the *Brooklyn* colony. Two or three unprotected females opened pie shops in Yerba Buena. But the main body of Mormons formed themselves into a Farming, Trading and Manufacturing company, elected a board of officers, and inaugurated their existence as a corporate body by taking a contract to supply a certain number of saw-logs from the Redwoods near Bodega for Captain Smith's mills at that point. The *Brooklyn* had been chartered to load at Bodega, and a few weeks after their landing in California a select party of woodchoppers from the *Brooklyn* company found themselves again on board the old ship on their way up the coast. About the same time the new organization bought a ship's longboat, and sent her sloop-rigged up the San Joaquin, with a party on board to make the first venture in farming, and formed the first settlement in the San Joaquin valley.

And now comes the story of the mill on Clay Street, from which was sent forth the first issue of the press in the embryo mistress of the Pacific. I doubt if ever a babe born in a mill was more royally couched. The first impress of the types was laid upon satin. It was the programme of a reception given to Commodore Stockton by the citizens of Yerba Buena, on the occasion of his arrival from the lower coast. The babe was born about the first of October, 1846. The old mill was about the largest frame structure in town. . . . On the ground floor there had been set up—how many years before I know not—a single run of stones worked by mule power arastra-wise. The second floor or loft was reached by a crazy staircase on the outside. The Mormons hired the building soon after their arrival, and set one of their number to work with a mule, grinding wheat for the company. Let me pause for a moment to masticate the tough wheat-cake of my recollection. Flour, even of the lowest unbolted grade, it never for a moment aspired to be called. It had a conscience as well as a hide, and just dropped from the mill a dirty mess of partially cracked wheat of a very inferior and damaged quality. That was our bread—our very ill bread—of those times that tried men's teeth. It was a fitting accompaniment to the herb tea and the wormy jerked beef—our unchangeable diet. . . .

Up those outside stairs, with incredible difficulty and no small danger of being buried beneath their wreck, with the frame of a No. 4 Washington press across our stomachs, my fellow printer and I lifted and pushed and dragged that *Star* printing machine. The name of the intended paper had been cut in wood six months before in the City of New York; yea, some of the type (a column Brandreth pill advertisement) had been set. We had half a dozen pairs of cases of old Long Primer and Brevier type, and two or three small fonts of job type. These, with the press, were set up in the loft of the mill, and the first printing office in the Bay of San Francisco was ready for business.

Communique on Displaced Persons

WHILE THE MORMONS were making history on far-flung frontiers, Nauvoo fell victim to a final insult in the form of an assault by impatient anti-Mormons. They actually laid siege to the city and fought what the papers called the battle of Nauvoo. The city was already desolate. Of 2,500 houses not a tenth were inhabited, and most of these by so-called New Settlers, who, to their discomfort, were frequently mistaken for Mormons and had to bear the brunt of the September attack. The last of the Mormons crossed the Mississippi at gunpoint, more hastily and less well prepared than the vanguard companies early in the year. A correspondent calling himself Che-mo-ko-mon describes their evacuation in the Burlington (Iowa) Hawkeye for September 24, 1846.

DEAR HAWK—My powers of description are totally inadequate to give your readers any just conception of the "scenes" that now present themselves on every hand in this vicinity. On either shore of the Mississippi may be seen a long line of tents, wagons, cattle, &c. with numberless wretched specimens of humanity. Since the armistice or "treaty" the Mormons are crossing in almost breathless haste. Three or four "flats" are running constantly, both day and night. This morning, Saturday, 19th, at the solicitation of Capt. Vrooman, of the Fort Madison Guards, I crossed the river from Montrose, to take a peep at this city of Desolation. We proceeded to the Mansion House, where we met with a small detachment of soldiers and a number of strangers. From thence we went to the Temple. On entering the vestibule of this renowned edifice, a singular spectacle presented itself. The seats of the High Priests of the "Twelve" and of the "Seventy" were occupied by a grim visaged soldiery. Some lay sleeping on their "arms," and others lay rolled up in their blankets. On every hand lay scattered about in beautiful confusion, muskets, swords, cannon balls, and terrible missiles of death. Verily thought I, how are the *holy* places desecrated! I thought of old Oliver Cromwell, when he drove the horses of his army through the "cloisters" of the Worcester Cathedral, and appropriated the Baptismal fount as a manger.

193

II · EXODUS

I am penning this scrawl to you in the upper seat of the Sanctuary. Over my head there is a large inscription in gold letters "The Lord is our sacrifice"; on my right lie three soldiers asleep, resting on their arms—my feet are resting on a pile of chain shot—and a keg of powder, just discovered, lies at my elbow.

I left the Temple "solitary and alone," to perambulate the desolate city. All was stilled and hushed as the charnel house. Not a human being was seen. Houses appeared suddenly deserted, as though the inmates had precipitately fled from a pestilence or the burning of a volcano. Some had windows open and the flowers blooming on the casements, but no fair hand was there, and no breath was heard, save the rustling zephyrs of heaven. It appeared as if the vengeance of the Almighty rested upon this doomed city.

I roamed over the vast Parade Ground where, four years ago, I beheld the *soi disant* "Prophet" review his Legion of 3000 strong, in all the "pride and circumstance" of military glory. Where now is the Prophet? Let the plains of Carthage answer. And where the multitudes that shouted hozannas to his name?

Verily thought I, "truth is stranger than fiction." I returned again through the desolate streets to the Mansion House. One solitary being, with a child in her arms, stood at the corner of a street, and saluted me with an imploring and almost frantic look.

"Pray, sir, are you one of the committee?" said she.

When I replied that I was a stranger, her eyes filled with tears. She related her history. 'Tis soon told, and is the history of hundreds.

"We came from Yorkshire, England. My husband died eighteen months after our arrival. He gave all his money to the church."

"Where are your friends?" said I.

"I have none—not one. The soldiers say I must leave in two hours. This child is sick and my other is a cripple." She had flour enough for but one dinner!

On the Montrose side of the Mississippi, many of the scenes were heartrending. I stopped at the door of one tent, arrested by the subdued sobs of a young mother, whose heart was broken with grief. By her side lay her infant, a corpse. She had neither friend or relative to bury her child, nor a mouthful of food to eat.

I was informed that Gen. Brockman, to his honor be it spoken, conducted with marked discretion and humanity; and the night the army took possession of the city, not a rail was disturbed or a particle of property molested. Although they encamped adjoining an extensive orchard of choice fruit, not a hand was laid upon it. The boat is leaving for Montrose and I must drop my pen. Perhaps more anon from your faithful chronicler.

―――――

Epitaph for Nauvoo

IN TWO GRAVE CRISES *Thomas Leiper Kane proved so remarkable a conciliator between the Mormons and the rest of the country that both sides paid him tribute. To Brigham Young he was "the good, the generous, the energetic and talented little Colonel," and in an annual message to Congress President James Buchanan praised the "pure benevolence" of his contribution to "the pacification" of Utah Territory in 1858. Kane was the best friend the Mormons ever had and the country's most reliable informant.*

He was born on January 27, 1822, in Philadelphia, the son of federal judge John Kintzing Kane and brother of Elisha Kent Kane, the Arctic explorer. Kane was only twenty-four when Mormon elder Jesse Little called on his father en route to Washington to acquaint the government with the plight of the Mormons and seek permission to raise a Mormon battalion for the expedition against Mexico. Young Kane, already something of a humanitarian, immediately dropped his law clerkship and headed west to give what help he could. He carried with him President Polk's orders to General Stephen W. Kearney at Ft. Leavenworth to raise the requested battalion.

Kane stayed some time with Brigham Young and the main Mormon encampment near Council Bluffs on the Missouri. His informative, vigorous, and urgent letters interceded with the Superintendent of Indian Affairs at St. Louis on behalf of the Mormons. He endorsed their request for permission to reside temporarily on Indian lands, and acquainted the War Department, the President, and the eastern press with the injustices done to the Mormons. He described their destitution, their loyalty in volunteering a battalion for the Mexican war, and their intention to unburden the United States of any anxiety concerning them by going to the Rocky Mountains. Kane says he was instrumental in persuading Brigham Young to choose the Great Basin for the final settlement rather than the San Francisco or Sacramento regions.

195

On his return east he visited the temporary settlements in Iowa along what came to be known as the Mormon Road. On the banks of the Mississippi he came upon the refugee camps most recently expelled from Nauvoo. Crossing the river, he walked about the deserted Mormon capital.

Back in Philadelphia, Kane resumed his law clerkship. He served as a United States commissioner in eastern Pennsylvania, worked for abolition, and became an agent of the Underground Railroad. Meanwhile, he continued to champion the Mormons. In 1850 he spoke on "The Mormons" before the Pennsylvania Historical Society, recounting his experiences of 1846. And he wrote President Polk, the War Department, and Horace Greeley, among others, comprehensive accounts of the Mormon situation. He told Greeley in 1847: "As you call upon me to state explicitly what are the wants of these applicants for our charity, I answer you explicitly, everything." He called the attention of the country at large to the "appreciable influence" the Mormons could exert upon the national welfare: "Their men are careful agriculturists or skilful artisans educated chiefly in Great Britain or the Atlantic States of the North—hardy, enterprising and industrious as a matter of religion as well as habit." They would develop a region rich in natural resources and, as a militia "respectable above the average," give the United States an advantage there in "future military operations."

In 1857 he reappeared among his old friends in Utah as the President's special emissary to mediate between the Mormons and federal officials, averting open conflict in the so-called "Utah Rebellion." In the Civil War Kane rose to brigadier-general; he raised a regiment of hunters and loggers known as the "Bucktails" and distinguished himself at Chancellorsville. He paid Utah another visit in 1872, this time with his wife and two sons, wintering with Brigham Young in St. George. At Brigham Young's death in 1877, Kane once more came west to pay his old friend a final tribute. Kane died on December 26, 1883.

The following selection is taken from The Mormons *(Philadelphia, 1850).*

A few years ago, ascending the Upper Mississippi in the autumn when its waters were low, I was compelled to travel by land past the region of the Rapids. My road lay through the Half-Breed Tract, a fine section of Iowa, which the unsettled state of its land-titles had appropriated as a sanctuary for coiners, horse-thieves, and other outlaws. I had left my steamer at Keokuk, at the foot of the Lower Fall, to hire a carriage, and to contend for some fragments of a dirty meal with the swarming flies, the only scavengers of the locality. From this place to where the deep water of the river returns, my eye wearied to see everywhere sordid, vagabond and idle settlers; and a country marred, without being improved, by their careless hands.

I was descending the last hill-side upon my journey, when a landscape in delightful contrast broke upon my view. Half encircled by a bend of the river a beautiful city lay glittering in the fresh morning sun; its bright new dwellings, set in cool, green gardens, ranging up around a stately dome-shaped hill, which was crowned by a noble marble edifice, whose high tapering spire was radiant with white and gold. The city appeared to cover several miles; and beyond it, in the background, there rolled off a fair country, chequered by the careful lines of fruitful husbandry. The unmistakable marks of industry, enterprise, and educated wealth everywhere, made the scene one of singular and most striking beauty.

It was a natural impulse to visit this inviting region. I procured a skiff, and, rowing across the river, landed at the chief wharf of the city. No one met me there. I looked and saw no one. I could hear no one move; though the quiet everywhere was such that I heard the flies buzz, and the water-ripples break against the shallow of the beach. I walked through the solitary streets. The town lay as in a dream, under some deadening spell of loneliness, from which I almost feared to wake it; for plainly it had not slept long. There was no grass growing up in the paved ways; rains had not entirely washed away the prints of dusty footsteps.

Yet I went about unchecked. I went into empty workshops, ropewalks and smithies. The spinner's wheel was idle; the carpenter had gone from his work-bench and shavings, his unfinished sash and casing. Fresh bark was in the tanner's vat, and the fresh-chopped lightwood stood piled against the baker's oven. The blacksmith's shop was cold; but his coal heap, and ladling pool, and crooked water-horn were all there, as if he had just gone off for a holiday. No work-people anywhere looked to know my errand. If I went into the gardens, clinking the wicket-latch loudly after me, to pull the marigolds, heartsease, and lady-slippers, and draw a drink with the water-sodden well-bucket and its noisy chain; or, knocking off with my stick the tall, heavy-headed dahlias and sunflowers, hunted over the beds for cucumbers and love-apples—no one called out to me from any opened window, or dog sprang forward to bark an alarm. I could have supposed the people hidden in the houses, but the doors were unfastened; and when at last I timidly entered them, I found dead ashes white upon the hearths, and had to tread a-tiptoe, as if walking down the aisle of a country church, to avoid arousing irreverent echoes from the naked floors.

On the outskirts of the town was the city graveyard; but there was no record of plague there, nor did it anywise differ much from other Protestant American cemeteries. Some of the mounds were not long sodded; some of the stones were newly set, their dates recent, and their black inscriptions glossy in the mason's hardly-dried lettering ink. Beyond the graveyard, out in the fields, I saw, in one spot hard by where the fruited boughs of a young orchard had been roughly torn down, the still smouldering embers of a barbecue fire, that had been constructed of rails from the fencing round it. It was the latest sign of life there. Fields upon fields of heavy-headed yellow grain lay rotting ungathered upon the ground. No one was at hand to take in their rich harvest. As far as the eye could reach, they stretched away—they sleeping too in the hazy air of autumn.

Only two portions of the city seemed to suggest the import of this mysterious solitude. On the southern suburb, the houses looking out upon the country showed, by their splintered wood-work and walls battered to the foundation, that they had lately been the mark of a destructive cannonade. And in and around the splendid Temple, which had been the chief object of my admiration, armed men were barracked, surrounded by their stacks of musketry and pieces of heavy ordnance. These challenged me to render an account of myself, and why I had the temerity to cross the water without a written permit from a leader of their band.

Though these men were generally more or less under the influence of ardent spirits, after I had explained myself as a passing stranger, they seemed anxious to gain my good opinion. They told the story of the Dead City: that it had been a notable manufacturing and commercial mart, sheltering over 20,000 persons; that they had waged war with its inhabitants for several years, and had finally been successful only a few days before my visit, in an action fought in front of the ruined suburb; after which, they had driven them forth at the point of the sword. The defense, they said, had been obstinate, but gave way on the third day's bombardment. They boasted greatly of their prowess, especially in this battle, as they called it; but I discovered they were not of one mind as to certain of the exploits that had distinguished it, one

198

of which, as I remember, was, that they had slain a father and his son, a boy of fifteen, not long residents of the fated city, whom they admitted to have borne a character without reproach.

They also conducted me inside the massive sculptured walls of the curious Temple, in which they said the banished inhabitants were accustomed to celebrate the mystic rites of an unhallowed worship. They particularly pointed out to me certain features of the building, which, having been the peculiar objects of a former superstitious regard, they had, as matter of duty, sedulously defiled and defaced. The reputed sites of certain shrines they had thus particularly noticed; and various sheltered chambers, in one of which was a deep well, constructed, they believed, with a dreadful design. Beside these, they led me to see a large and deep-chiselled marble vase or basin, supported upon twelve oxen, also of marble, and of the size of life, of which they told some romantic stories. They said the deluded persons, most of whom were emigrants from a great distance, believed their Deity countenanced their reception here of a baptism of regeneration, as proxies for whomsoever they held in warm affection in the countries from which they had come. That here parents "went ino the water" for their lost children, children for their parents, widows for their spouses, and young persons for their lovers; that thus the Great Vase came to be for them associated with all dear and distant memories, and was therefore the object, of all others in the building, to which they attached the greatest degree of idolatrous affection. On this account, the victors had so diligently desecrated it, as to render the apartment in which it was contained too noisome to abide in.

They permitted me also to ascend into the steeple, to see where it had been lightning-struck the Sabbath before; and to look out, east and south, on wasted farms like those I had seen near the city, extending till they were lost in the distance. Here, in the face of pure day, close to the scar of the Divine wrath left by the thunderbolt, were fragments of food, cruses of liquor, and broken drinking vessels, with a bass drum and a steamboat signal bell. . . .

It was after nightfall, when I was ready to cross the river on my return. The wind had freshened since the sunset, and, the water beating roughly into my little boat, I headed higher up the stream than the point I had left in the morning, and landed where a faint glimmering light invited me to steer.

Here, among the dock and rushes, sheltered only by the darkness,

199

without roof between them and the sky, I came upon a crowd of several hundred human creatures, whom my movements roused from uneasy slumber upon the ground.

Passing these on my way to the light, I found it came from a tallow candle, in a paper funnel shade, such as is used by street venders of apples and peanuts, and which, flaring and guttering away in the bleak air off the water, shone flickeringly on the emaciated features of a man in the last stage of a bilious, remittent fever. They had done their best for him. Over his head was something like a tent, made of a sheet or two, and he rested on a but partially ripped open old straw mattress, with a hair sofa cushion under his head for a pillow. His gaping jaw and glazing eye told how short a time he would monopolize these luxuries; though a seemingly bewildered and excited person, who might have been his wife, seemed to find hope in occasionally forcing him to swallow awkwardly measured sips of the tepid river water, from a burned and battered bitter-smelling tin coffee-pot. Those who knew better had furnished the apothecary he needed; a toothless old bald-head, whose manner had the repulsive dullness of a man familiar with death scenes. He, so long as I remained, mumbled in his patient's ear a monotonous and melancholy prayer, between the pauses of which I heard the hiccup and sobbing of two little girls who were sitting upon a piece of drift-wood outside.

Dreadful, indeed, was the suffering of these forsaken beings; bowed and cramped by cold and sunburn, alternating as each weary day and night dragged on, they were, almost all of them, the crippled victims of disease. They were there because they had no homes, nor hospital, nor poor-house, nor friends to offer them any. They could not satisfy the feeble cravings of their sick; they had not bread to quiet the fractious hunger-cries of their children. Mothers and babes, daughters and grand-parents, all of them alike, were bivouacked in tatters, wanting even covering to comfort those whom the sick shivers of fever were searching to the marrow.

These were Mormons, famishing in Lee County, Iowa, in the fourth week of the month of September, in the year of our Lord 1846. The city—it was Nauvoo, Illinois. The Mormons were the owners of that city, and the smiling country around. And those who had stopped their ploughs, who had silenced their hammers, their axes, their shuttles, and their workshop wheels; those who had put out their fires, who had eaten their food, spoiled their orchards, and trampled under foot their thousands of acres of unharvested bread; these were the keepers of their dwellings, the carousers in their temple, whose drunken riot insulted the ears of their dying. . . .

They were, all told, not more than six hundred and forty persons who were thus lying on the river flats. But the Mormons in Nauvoo and its dependencies had been numbered the year before at over twenty thousand. Where were they? They had last been seen, carrying in mournful train their sick and wounded, halt and blind, to disappear behind the western horizon, pursuing the phantom of another home.

The Mormon Encampments

IN THE FOLLOWING EXCERPT from Col. Thomas L. Kane's discourse on the Mormons, he comes upon them in July, 1846, on the banks of the Missouri and describes his two-months' stay at the Papillon camp on the west side of the river. He provides a graphic picture of daily camp life among an uprooted yet ordered community and reviews their trailmaking across Iowa. Kane knew firsthand the wretched sickness produced in the "Misery Bottoms," for he himself became so ill of "nervous, billious fever" he could not hold a pen. In August Brigham Young wrote the command at Ft. Leavenworth to send medical aid "sparing no time, or expense for change of horses or breaking of carriages." Mormon esteem for Kane was so great they named their settlement on the eastern banks of the Missouri Kanesville in his honor, for several years an important way-station for western immigrants.

Delayed by their own wants, and by their exertions to provide for the wants of others, it was not till the month of June that the advance of the emigrant companies arrived at the Missouri. This body, I remember, I had to join there, ascending the river for the purpose from Fort Leavenworth, which was at that time our frontier post. The Fort was the interesting rendezvous of the Army of the West, and the headquarters of its gallant chief, Stephen F. Kearney, whose guest and friend I account it my honor to have been. . . .

Almost at the outset of my journey from Fort Leavenworth, while yet upon the edge of the Indian border, I had the good fortune to fall in with a couple of thin-necked sallow persons, in patchwork pantaloons, conducting northward wagon loads of Indian corn, which they had obtained, according to their own account, in barter from a squatter for some silver spoons and a feather bed. Their character was disclosed by their eager request of a bite from my wallet; in default of which, after a somewhat superfluous scriptural grace, they made an imperfect lunch before me off the softer of their corn ears, eating the grains as horses do, from the cob. I took their advice to follow up the Missouri; somewhere not far from which, in the Pottawatamie country, they were sure I would encounter one of their advancing companies.

I had bad weather on the road. Excessive heats, varied only by repeated drenching thunder squalls, knocked up my horse, my only traveling companion, and otherwise added to the ordinary hardships of a kind of life to which I was as yet little accustomed. I suffered a sense of discomfort, therefore, amounting to physical nostalgia, and was, in fact, wearied to death of the staring silence of the prairie, before I came upon the objects of my search.

They were collected a little distance above the Pottawatamie Agency. The hills of the "High Prairie" crowding in upon the river at this point, and overhanging it, appear of an unusual and commanding elevation. They are called the Council Bluffs, a name given them with another meaning, but well illustrated by the picturesque congress of their high and mighty summits. To the south of them, a rich alluvial flat of considerable width follows down the Missouri, some eight miles, to where it is lost from view at a turn, which forms the site of the Indian town of Point aux Poules. Across the river from this spot the hills recur again, but are skirted at their base by as much low ground as suffices for a landing.

This landing, and the large flat or bottom on the east side of the river, were crowded with covered carts and wagons; and each one of the Council Bluff hills opposite, was crowned with its own great camp, gay with bright white canvas, and alive with the busy stir of swarming occupants. In the clear blue morning air the smoke streamed up from more than a thousand cooking fires. Countless roads and by-paths checkered all manner of geometric figures on the hill sides. Herd boys were dozing upon the slopes; sheep and horses, cows and oxen, were feeding around them, and other herds in the luxuriant meadow of the then swollen river. From a single point I counted four thousand head of cattle in view at one time. As I approached the camps, it seemed to me the children there were to prove still more numerous. Along a little creek I had to cross were women in greater force than *blanchisseuses* upon the Seine, washing and rinsing all manner of white muslins, red flannels, and parti-colored calicoes, and hanging them to bleach upon a greater area of grass and bushes than we can display in all our Washington Square.

Hastening by these, I saluted a group of noisy boys, whose purely vernacular cries had for me an invincible home-savoring attraction. It was one of them, a bright-faced lad, who hurrying on his jacket and trowsers, fresh from bathing in the creek, first assured me I was at my right destination. He was a mere child; but he told me of his own accord where I had best go seek my welcome, and took my horse's bridle to help me pass a morass, the bridge over which he alleged to be unsafe.

There was something joyous for me in my free rambles about this vast body of pilgrims. I could range the wild country wherever I listed, under safeguard of their moving host. Not only in the main camps was all stir and life, but in every direction, it seemed to me I could follow "Mormon Roads," and find them beaten hard, and even dusty, by the tread and wear of the cattle and vehicles of emigrants laboring over them. By day, I would overtake and pass, one after another, what amounted to an army train of them; and at night, if I encamped at the places where the timber and running water were found together, I was almost sure to be within call of some camp or other, or at least within sight of its watch-fires. Wherever I was compelled to tarry, I was certain to find shelter and hospitality, scant, indeed, but never stinted, and always honest and kind. After a recent unavoidable association with the border inhabitants of Western Missouri and Iowa, the vile scum which our own society, to apply the words of an admirable gentleman and eminent divine, "like the great ocean washes upon its frontier shores," I can scarcely describe the gratification I felt in associating again with persons who were almost all of Eastern American origin—persons of refined and cleanly habits and decent language—and in observing their peculiar and interesting mode of life; while every day seemed to bring with it its own especial incidents, fruitful in the illustration of habits and character. . . .

The most striking feature . . . of the Mormon emigration was undoubtedly their formation of the Tabernacle Camps and temporary Stakes or Settlements, which renewed, in the sleeping solitudes everywhere along their road, the cheering signs of intelligent and hopeful life.

I will make this remark plainer by describing to you one of these camps, with the daily routine of its inhabitants. I select at random, for my purpose, a large camp upon the delta between the Nebraska and Missouri, in the territory disputed between the Omaha and Otto and Missouri Indians. It remained pitched here for nearly two months, during which period I resided in it.

It was situated near the Petit Papillon, or Little Butterfly River, and upon some finely rounded hills that encircle a favorite cool spring. On each of these a square was marked out; and the wagons as they arrived took their positions along its four sides in double rows, so as to leave a roomy street or passage-way between them. The tents were disposed also in rows, at intervals, between the wagons. The cattle were folded in high-fenced yards outside. The quadrangle inside was left vacant for the sake of ventilation, and the streets, covered in with leafy arbor work, and kept scrupulously clean, formed a shaded cloister walk. This was the place of exercise for slowly recovering invalids, the day-home of the infants, and the evening promenade of all.

From the first formation of the camp all its inhabitants were constantly and laboriously occupied. Many of them were highly educated mechanics and seemed only to need a day's anticipated rest to engage at the forge, loom, or turning-lathe, upon some needed *chore* of work. A Mormon gunsmith is the inventor of the excellent repeating rifle, that loads by slides instead of cylinders; and one of the neatest finished fire-arms I have ever seen was of this kind, wrought from scraps of old iron, and inlaid with the silver of a couple of half-dollars, under a hot July sun, in a spot where the average height of the grass was above the workman's shoulders. I have seen a cobbler, after the halt of his party on the march, hunting along the river bank for a lapstone in the twilight, that he might finish a famous boot-sole by the camp fire; and I have had a piece of cloth, the wool of which was sheared, and dyed, and spun, and woven, during a progress of over three hundred miles.

Their more interesting occupations, however, were those growing out of their peculiar circumstances and position. The chiefs were seldom without some curious affair on hand to settle with the restless Indians; while the immense labor and responsibility of the conduct of their unwieldy moving army, and the commissariat of its hundreds of famishing poor, also devolved upon them. They had good men they called Bishops, whose special office it was to look up the cases of extremest suffering; and their relief parties were out night and day to scour over every trail.

The Mormon Encampments

At this time, say two months before the final expulsion from Nauvoo, there were already, along three hundred miles of the road between the city and our Papillon camp, over two thousand emigrating wagons, besides a large number of nondescript turn-outs, the motley make-shifts of poverty, from the unsuitably heavy-cart, that lumbered on mysteriously, with its sick driver hidden under its counterpane cover, to the crazy, two-wheeled trundle, such as our own poor employ for the conveyance of their slop-barrels, this pulled along, it may be, by a little dry-dugged heifer, and rigged up only to drag some such light weight as a baby, a sack of meal, or a pack of clothes and bedding.

Some of them were in distress from losses upon the way. A strong trait of the Mormons was their kindness to their brute dependents, and particularly to their beasts of draught. They gave them the holiday of the Sabbath whenever it came round: I believe they would have washed them with old wine, after the example of the emigrant Carthaginians, had they had any. Still, in the Slave-coast heats under which the animals had to move, they sometimes foundered. Sometimes, too, they strayed off in the night, or were mired in morasses; or oftener were stolen by Indians, who found market covert for such plunder among the horse-thief whites of the frontier. But the great mass of these pilgrims of the desert was made up of poor folks, who had fled in destitution from Nauvoo, and been refused a resting-place by the people of Iowa.

It is difficult fully to understand the state of helplessness in which some of these would arrive, after accomplishing a journey of such extent, under circumstances of so much privation and peril. The fact was, they seemed to believe that all their trouble would be at an end if they could only come up with their comrades at the Great Camp. For this they calculated their resources, among which their power of endurance was by much the largest and most reliable item, and they were not disappointed if they arrived with these utterly exhausted. . . .

Beside the common duty of guiding and assisting these unfortunates, the companies in the van united in providing the highway for the entire body of emigrants. The Mormons have laid out for themselves a road through the Indian Territory, over four hundred leagues in length, with substantial, well-built bridges, fit for the passage of heavy artillery, over all the streams, except a few great rivers where they have established permanent ferries. The nearest unfinished bridging to the Papillon Camp was that of the Corne à Cerf, or Elk Horn, a tributary of the Platte, distant may be a couple of hours' march. Here, in what seemed to be an incredibly short space of time, there rose the seven great piers and abutments of a bridge, such as might challenge honors for the entire public-spirited population of Lower Virginia. The party detailed to the task worked in the broiling sun, in water beyond depth, and up to their necks, as if engaged in the perpetration of some pointed and delightful practical joke. The chief sport lay in floating along with the logs, cut from the overhanging timber up the stream, guiding them till they reached their destination, and then plunging them under water in the precise spot where they were to be secured. This, the laughing engineers would execute with the agility of happy, diving ducks.

Our nearest ferry was that over the Missouri. Nearly opposite the Pull Point, or Point aux Poules, a trading post of the American Fur Company, and village of the Pottawatamies, they had gained a favorable crossing, by making a deep cut for the road through the steep right bank. And here, without intermission, their flat-bottomed scows plied, crowded with the wagons, and cows, and sheep, and children, and furniture of the emigrants, who, in waiting their turn, made the woods around smoke with their crowding camp fires. But no such good fortune as a gratuitous passage awaited the heavy cattle, of whom, with the others, no less than 30,000 were at this time on their way westward; these were made to earn it by swimming. . . .

After the sorrowful word was given out to halt, and make preparation for winter, a chief labor became the making hay; and with every day dawn brigades of mowers would take up the march to their positions in chosen meadows, a prettier sight than a charge of cavalry, as they laid their swaths, whole companies of scythes abreast. Before this time the manliest, as well as the most general daily labor, was the herding of the cattle; the only wealth of the Mormons, and more and more cherished by them, with the increasing pastoral character of their lives. A camp could not be pitched in any spot without soon exhausting the freshness of the pasture around it; and it became an ever recurring task to guide the cattle, in unbroken droves, to the nearest place where it was still fresh and fattening. Sometimes it was necessary to go farther, to distant ranges which were known as feeding grounds of the buffalo. About these there was sure to prowl parties of thievish Indians; and each drove therefore had its escort of mounted men and boys, who learned self-reliance and heroism, while on night guard alone, among the silent hills. But generally the cattle were driven from the camp at the dawn of the morning, and brought back thousands together in the evening, to be picketed in the great corral or enclosure, where beeves, bulls, cows and oxen, with the horses, mules, hogs, calves, sheep and human beings, could all look together upon the red watch-fires, with the feeling of security when aroused by the Indian stampede, or the howlings of the prairie wolves at moonrise.

When they set about building their winter houses, too, the Mormons went into quite considerable timbering operations, and performed desperate feats of carpentry. They did not come ornamental gentlemen or raw apprentices, to extemporize new versions of Robinson Crusoe. It was a comfort to notice the readiness with which they turned their hands to woodcraft; some of them, though I believe these had generally been bred carpenters, wheel-wrights, or more particularly boat-builders, quite outdoing the most notable *voyageurs* in the use of the ax. One of these would fell a tree, strip off its bark, cut and split up the trunk in piles of plank, scantling, or shingles; make posts, and pins, and pales —everything wanted almost of the branches; and treat his toil from first to last with more sportive flourish than a schoolboy whittling his shingle.

Inside the camp, the chief labors were assigned to the women. From the moment, when after the halt, the lines had been laid, the spring-wells dug out, and the ovens and fireplaces built, though the men still assumed to set the guards and enforce the regulations of police, the Empire of the Tented Town was with the better sex. They were the chief comforters of the severest sufferers, the kind nurses who gave them in their sickness those dear attentions with which pauperism is hardly poor, and which the greatest wealth often fails to buy. And they were a nation of wonderful managers. They could hardly be called housewives in etymological strictness; but it was plain that they had once been such, and most distinguished ones. Their art availed them in their changed affairs. With almost their entire culinary material limited to the milk of their cows, some store of meal or flour, and a very few condiments, they brought their thousand and one receipts into play with a success that outdid for their families the miracle of the Hebrew widow's cruise. They learned to make butter on a march by the dashing of the wagon, and so nicely to calculate the working of barm in the jolting heats that, as soon after the halt as an oven could be dug in the hill-side and heated, their well-kneaded loaf was ready for baking, and produced good leavened bread for supper. . . .

Every day closed as every day began, with an invocation of the divine favor; without which, indeed, no Mormon seemed to dare to lay him down to rest. With the first shining of the stars, laughter and loud talking hushed, the neighbor went his way, you heard the last hymn sung, and then the thousand-voiced murmur of prayer was heard, like bubbling water falling down the hills. . . .

In the camp nearest us on the west, which was that of the bridging party near the Corne, the number of its inhabitants being small enough to invite computation, I found as early as the 31st of July, that 37 per cent of its inhabitants were down with the fever, and a sort of strange scorbutic disease, frequently fatal, which they named the Black Canker. The camps to the east of us, which were all on the eastern side of the Missouri, were yet worse fated.

The climate of the entire upper "Misery Bottom," as they term it, is, during a considerable part of summer and autumn, singularly pestiferous. . . . The Mormons were scourged severely. . . . The fever prevailed to such an extent that hardly any escaped it. They let their cows go unmilked. They wanted for voices to raise the psalm of Sundays. The few who were able to keep their feet, went about among the tents and wagons with food and water, like nurses through the wards of an infirmary. Here at one time the digging got behind hand; burials were slow; and you might see women sit in the open tents keeping the flies off their dead children, some time after decomposition had set in.

In our own camp, for a part of August and September things wore an unpleasant aspect enough. Its situation was one much praised for its comparative salubrity; but, perhaps, on this account, the number of cases of fever among us was increased by the hurrying arrival from other localities of parties in whom the virus leaven of disease was fermented by forced travel.

But I am excused sufficiently the attempt to get up for your entertainment here any circumstantial picture of horrors, by the fact, that at the most interesting season, I was incapacitated for nice observation by an attack of fever—mine was what they call the congestive—that it required the utmost use of all my faculties to recover from. I still kept my tent in the camp line; but, for as much as a month, had very small notion of what went on among my neighbors. I recollect overhearing a lamentation over some dear baby, that its mother no doubt thought the destroying angel should have been specially instructed to spare.

I wish, too, for my own sake, I could forget how imperfectly one day I mourned the decease of a poor Saint, who, by clamor, rendered his vicinity troublesome. He, no doubt, endured great pain; for he groaned shockingly till death came to his relief. He interfered with my own hard-gained slumbers, and I was glad when death did relieve him.

———

Winter Quarters among the Indians

BRIGHAM YOUNG'S *destination was the Great Basin, as he repeatedly made clear long before the Saints finally arrived in the Valley of the Great Salt Lake. On August 9, 1846, he assured President Polk that in their exile the Mormons were embarked on "a journey which we design shall end in a location west of the Rocky Mountains, and within the Basin of the Great Salt Lake, or Bear river valley, as soon as circumstances shall permit, believing that to be a point where a good living will require hard labor, and consequently will be coveted by no other people, while it is surrounded by so unpopulous but fertile a country."*

It was a shrewder choice than California, though allusions to California abound in the literature. But "California" was an inclusive term, with its eastward boundaries undetermined. When the Mormons sang John Taylor's lively verse, "The Upper California, O that's the land for me,/ It lies between the mountains and the great Pacific sea," they were thinking of the Rocky Mountains.

Meanwhile the Mormons had to tarry on both sides of the Missouri River, among the Pottawatamies on the east and the Omahas on the west. The western encampment became known officially as Winter Quarters, near present-day Florence, Nebraska, and served as the starting point for the vanguard of 143 picked men and 3 women in 70 horse-drawn wagons who left in April, 1847, to plant first crops in the Salt Lake Valley. A company of nearly 2,000 in 566 wagons left Winter Quarters in time to arrive in the Valley in September. Col. Thomas L. Kane vividly portrays the pact-making with the Indians which permitted the temporary existence of Winter Quarters, and notes the mutual sympathy of Indians and Mormons growing out of their common identity as dispossessed peoples. The selection comes from his lecture on the Mormons in Philadelphia in 1850.

II · EXODUS

Though the season was late, when the Mormons first crossed the Missouri, some of them moved forward with great hopefulness, full of the notion of viewing and choosing their new homes that year. But the van had only reached Grand Island and the Pawnee villages, when they were overtaken by more ill news from Nauvoo. Before the summer closed, their enemies set upon the last remnant of those who were left behind in Illinois. They were a few lingerers, who could not be persuaded but there might yet be time for them to gather up their worldly goods before removing, some weakly mothers and their infants, a few delicate young girls, and many cripples and bereaved and sick people. These had remained under shelter, according to the Mormon statement at least, by virtue of an express covenant in their behalf. If there was such a covenant it was broken. A vindictive war was waged upon them, from which the weakest fled in scattered parties, leaving the rest to make a reluctant and almost ludicrously unavailing defense, till the 17th day of September, when 1,625 troops entered Nauvoo, and drove all forth who had not retreated before that time.

Like the wounded birds of a flock fired into toward nightfall, they came straggling on with faltering steps, many of them without bag or baggage, beast or barrow, all asking shelter or burial, and forcing a fresh repartition of the already divided rations of their friends. It was plain now, that every energy must be taxed to prevent the entire expedition from perishing. Further emigration for the time was out of the question, and the whole people prepared themselves for encountering another winter on the prairie.

Happily for the main body, they found themselves at this juncture among Indians who were amicably disposed. The lands on both sides of the Missouri, in particular, were owned by the Pottawatamies and Omahas, two tribes whom unjust treatment by our United States had the effect of rendering most auspiciously hospitable to strangers whom they regarded as persecuted like themselves.

The Pottawatamies, on the eastern side, are a nation from whom the United States bought, some years ago a number of hundred thousand acres of the finest lands they have ever brought into market. . . . They were under [a] second sentence of transportation when the Mormons arrived among them.

They were pleased with the Mormons. They would have been pleased with any whites who would not cheat them, nor sell them whisky, nor whip them for their poor gipsy habits, nor bear themselves indecently

210

toward their women, many of whom, among the Pottawatamies, especially those of nearly unmixed French descent, are singularly comely, and some of them educated. But all Indians have something like a sentiment of reverence for the insane, and admire those who sacrifice, without apparent motive, their worldly welfare to the triumph of an idea. They understand the meaning of what they call a great vow, and think it the duty of the right-minded to lighten the votary's penance under it. To this feeling they united the sympathy of fellow-sufferers for those who could talk to them of their own Illinois, and tell the story how from it they also had been ruthlessly expelled.

Their hospitality was sincere, almost delicate. Fanny Le Clerc, the spoiled child of the great brave, Pied Riche, interpreter of the Nation, would have the pale-face Miss Devine learn duets with her to the guitar; and the daughter of substantial Joseph La Framboise, the interpreter of the United States—she died of the fever that summer—welcomed all the nicest young Mormon Kitties and Lizzies, and Jennies and Susans, to a coffee feast at her father's house, which was probably the best cabin in the river village. They made the Mormons at home, there and elsewhere. Upon all their lands they formally gave them leave to tarry just so long as should suit their own good pleasure.

The affair, of course, furnished material for a solemn council. Under the auspices of an officer of the United States, their chiefs were summoned, in the form befitting great occasions, to meet in the dirty yard of one Mr. P. A. Sarpy's log trading house, at their village. They came in grand toilet, moving in their fantastic attire with so much *aplomb* and genteel measure, that the stranger found it difficult not to believe them high-born gentlemen, attending a costumed ball. . . . When the red men had indulged to satiety in tobacco smoke from their peace pipes, and in what they love still better, their peculiar metaphoric rodomontade, which, beginning with the celestial bodies, and coursing downwards over the grandest sublunary objects, always managed to alight at last on their Grandfather Polk, and the tenderness for him of his affectionate colored children; all the solemn funny fellows present, who played the part of chiefs, signed formal articles of convention with their unpronounceable names.

The renowned chief, Pied Riche—he was surnamed Le Clerc on account of his remarkable scholarship—then arose, and said:

"My Mormon Brethren—The Pottawatamie came, sad and tired, into this unhealthy Missouri Bottom, not many years back, when he was taken from his beautiful country beyond the Mississippi, which had abundant game and timber, and clear water everywhere. Now you are driven away, the same, from your lodges and lands there, and the graves of your people. So we have both suffered. We must help one another, and the Great Spirit will help us both. You are now free to cut and use all the wood you may wish. You can make all your improvements, and live on any part of our actual land not occupied by us. Because one suffers, and does not deserve it, is no reason he shall suffer always, I say. We may live to see all right yet. However, if we do not, our children will.—*Bon jour.*"

And thus ended the pageant. I give this speech as a morsel of real Indian. It was recited to me after the treaty by the Pottawatamie orator in French, which language he spoke with elegance. *Bon jour* is the French, Indian, and English hail and farewell of the Pottawatamies.

The other entertainers of the Mormons at this time, the Omahas, or Mahaws, are one of the minor tribes of the Grand Prairie. Their great father, the United States, has found it convenient to protect so remote a dependency against the over-powering league of the Dahcotahs or Sioux, and has judged it dangerous, at the same time, to allow them to protect themselves by entering into a confederation with others. Under the pressure of this paternal embarrassment and restraint, it has therefore happened, most naturally, that this tribe, once a powerful and valued ally of ours, has been reduced to a band of little more than a hundred families; and these, a few years more will entirely extinguish. . . .

The pauper Omahas were ready to solicit as a favor the residence of white protectors among them. The Mormons harvested and stored away for them their crops of maize; with all their own poverty, they spared them food enough besides, from time to time, to save them from absolutely starving; and their entrenched camp, to the north of Omaha villages, served as a sort of breakwater between them and the destroying rush of the Sioux.

This was the Head Quarters of the Mormon Camps of Israel. The miles of rich prairie, enclosed and sowed with the grain they could contrive to spare, and the houses, stacks, and cattle shelters, had the seeming of an entire county, with its people and improvements transplanted there unbroken. On a pretty plateau, overlooking the river, they built more than seven hundred houses in a single town, neatly laid out with highways and byways, and fortified with breast-work, stockade, and block-houses. It had, too, its place of worship, "Tabernacle of the

Congregation," and various large workshops, and mills and factories, provided with water power.

They had no camp or settlement of equal size in the Pottawatamie country. There was less to apprehend here from Indian invasion; and the people scattered themselves, therefore, along the rivers and streams, and in the timber groves, wherever they found inviting localities for farming operations. In this way many of them acquired what have since proved to be valuable pre-emption rights.

Upon the Pottawatamie lands, scattered through the border regions of Missouri and Iowa, in the Sauk and Fox country, a few among the Ioways, among the Poncahs in a great company upon the banks of the *L' Eau qui Coule,* or Running Water River, and at the Omaha winter quarters, the Mormons sustained themselves through the heavy winter of 1846–1847. It was the severest of their trials. . . .

This winter was the turning-point of the Mormon fortunes. Those who lived through it were spared to witness the gradual return of better times. And they now liken it to the passing of a dreary night, since which they have watched the coming of a steadily brightening day.

"These Western Moves Are Hard on Cattle"

AMONG THE REFUGEES at Winter Quarters were Martha and Jesse Haven, last heard from in the summer of 1846 as they prepared to leave Nauvoo. On January 3, 1848, Martha wrote her mother a brief but engaging letter. Once again she provides an intimate glimpse of the Mormon experience. By this time two thousand of her fellow believers had already gone on to the Salt Lake Valley. The summer would see a steady emptying of the temporary settlements in Iowa and Nebraska; Winter Quarters, having served its usefulness, would be abandoned within a few months. The Mormons could not overstay on Indian lands. Martha herself remained for a time in one of the Iowa encampments while her husband answered a mission call to South Africa. "Have no uneasiness on my account," she wrote him. The following letter is reprinted with the permission of the New England Quarterly, where it was published in the issue of December, 1936.

II · EXODUS

My dear, dear Mother:

After almost despairing of ever hearing from home again, I at last received your most welcome letter.

Our little black cow could not stand the journey here; she laid down and refused to travel before we got to the last settlement. Mr. Haven went back and made out to get her to the settlement where he got four dollars for her. I can tell you, Mother, these western moves are hard on cattle as well as on the people.

I should have answered your letter sooner but I have again been sick, but the God of all the earth will do right.

Tell Catherine if she has an opportunity: if she will send me a toothbrush, I will remember it and try to reward her sometime; there are none here.

We now expect to leave this place in May or June for the Mountains. There is a plenty of salt and saleratus there; they are both white and nice; our pioneers brought back considerable. I have had some of both to use.

May your lives and health all be spared and may the day come when we shall all meet again. Tell Henry I have got the first lock of hair that was ever cut from his head and shall always keep it; I often take a look at it and wish that I could see its former owner.

Mr. Haven's health is good; he sends his respects to all. He is toiling hard to make a fit-out for the Mountains. If I can have health, I can stand hardships very well. This place has got to be vacated in the coming summer. I expect the [sectarian] missionaries are at the bottom of it; they will have their reward. We have done a great many thousand dollars worth of work here, which will be of great service to them, such as digging wells, fencing, and breaking the ground.

I expect all of Mr. Haven's folks will go on when we do. Truly, we have no abiding City. The ensign is to be reared upon the mountains and *all* Nations to flow unto it. We are not going to a remote corner of the earth to hide ourselves far from it. Do write me a long letter before I leave here. My best love to Father, Brothers and Sisters, From your affectionate daughter

Martha S. H. Haven

III · CHRONICLES AND JUDGES

III · Chronicles and Judges

The Times of Brigham Young

A GAIN, as in the days of ancient Israel, a whole people were on the move to a new and promised land. The vanguard of these modern Israelites, sent to spy out the land, rode out upon the eastern benchland of the great valley of the New Canaan on July 21, 1847. Two days later Orson Pratt, the leader of the advance company, called the camp together and dedicated the land to the service of the Lord. On the following day, the 24th, Brigham Young himself arrived to make official the first entry of the Mormon pioneers into the Valley of the Great Salt Lake. This date ever since has been celebrated as the founding of the Mormon empire in the Far West.

For the first time in all their movings, from New York to Ohio to Missouri to Illinois and now to the Rocky Mountains, the Saints were the initial settlers and masters of the lands they proposed to occupy. In this inland fastness, a thousand miles from anywhere, empty and uninviting, it was hard to believe that the westward-running tide of humanity let loose by the discovery of gold in the foothills of the Sierras would so soon overrun the peaceful and remote outposts of the newly marked-out Mormon country. Mormons were not alone in America's westward trekking in 1846 and '47, but the trickle of these years became a flood in '49 and after, and the Mormon-Gentile struggle began all over again. Only this time it was under different conditions and somewhat on Mormon terms.

In Deseret for a while they established a pure theocracy, the first since the Puritan commonwealth of Massachusetts Bay. "If they'll let us alone for ten years," said Brigham Young, referring to the Gentiles, "I'll ask no odds of them." He had his ten years, but barely, for 1857 brought a succession of crises. In the summer, President James Buchanan, swayed by reports that the Mormons were in a state of rebellion, sent a new governor under military escort to replace Brigham Young. In September, with Johnston's Army on its way and Mormon feelings running a high fever, some Mormon fanatics, joined by some Indians, massacred a train of California-bound Arkansas emigrants at Mountain Meadows. A shocked nation, all the more convinced that the Mormons were seditious, cried for retribution. Early in 1858, after a winter of anxiety and preparations for a scorched earth defense of Zion, Brigham and his people accepted their first Gentile governor and United States troops entered the Kingdom.

But the change in administration was nominal. The Mormons were still in the saddle and could take President Buchanan's subsequent "pardon" with the humor it deserved. They had won a moral victory. Though their theocracy was dissolved, they could still indulge the traditional American desire to govern themselves and resist long and bitterly any rule imposed from afar.

The times of Brigham Young, aside from the political warrings, saw the Mormons conquer the land, colonizing and consolidating a country of imperial proportions. It was a harsh land, clean and bright, with distances that hurt the eyes. It was not lush like the humid East, but a country that could be made fertile with patience, toil, and water. The immigration of thousands of converts from all over the world provided a select population, heavily British and Scandinavian, who strengthened the Yankee brotherhood.

Brigham Young meanwhile perfected the organization of the church and became its president, filling Joseph Smith's role of "prophet, seer, and revelator." The salty Heber C. Kimball and the scholarly Dr. Willard Richards served him as counselors, making a New England triumvirate. Brigham Young was a pragmatist, but he saw the things of this world in the light of eternity, claiming always that he simply followed where the visionary Joseph had led. Not revelation but a practical trial of ideas already revealed marked his administration; it led to a control of the temporal as well as spiritual affairs of his people that was nearly complete. A spectacular example was his bold promotion of polygamy, practiced as an open secret for a decade and in 1852 publicly avowed as sacred doctrine and declared a necessary adjunct to celestial salvation. Another example was the consecration movement of the middle 1850's, which sought to have the faithful deed their properties to the church to avoid resale to outsiders. It lasted only briefly during a burning revival or "reformation" which called for rebaptism and rededication to Zion's unity.

The man who directed Mormon destinies for over a quarter of a century fascinated contemporaries, who drew countless portraits. Sir Richard Burton, British adventurer, saw him in 1860 in his prime. Brigham Young was fifty-nine at the time, and he looked "about forty-five."

"Altogether the Prophet's appearance was that of a gentleman farmer in New England—in fact, such as he is: his father was an agriculturist and revolutionary soldier, who settled 'down East.' He is a well-preserved man; a fact which some attribute to his habit of sleeping, as the Citizen Proudhon so strongly advises, in solitude. His manner is at once affable and impressive, simple and courteous: his want of pretension contrasts favorably with certain pseudo-prophets that I have seen, each and every one of whom holds himself to be a 'Logos' without other claim save a semi-maniacal self-esteem. He shows no signs of dogmatism, bigotry, or fanaticism, and never once entered—with me at least—upon the subject of religion. He impresses a stranger with a certain sense of power; his followers are, of course, wholly fascinated by his superior strength of brain. It is commonly said there is only one chief in Great Salt Lake City, and that is 'Brigham.' His temper is even and placid; his manner is cold—in fact, like his face, somewhat bloodless; but he is neither morose nor methodistic, and, where occasion requires, he can use all the weapons of ridicule to direful effect, and 'speak a bit of his mind' in a style which no one forgets. He often reproves his erring followers in purposely violent language, making the terrors of a scolding the punishment in lieu of hanging for a stolen horse or cow. His powers of observation are intuitively strong, and his friends declare him to be gifted with an excellent memory and a perfect judgment of character. If he dislikes a stranger at the first interview, he never sees him again. Of his temperance and sobriety there is but one opinion. His life is ascetic: his favorite food is baked potatoes with a little buttermilk, and his drink water: he disapproves, as do all strict Mormons, of spirituous liquors, and never touches any thing stronger than a glass of thin Lagerbier; moreover, he abstains from tobacco. . . .

The times of Brigham Young, strictly speaking, were not over until his death in 1877. But the following selections bring the period to a close in 1865, at the moment when the nation, fresh from its triumph over slavery, determined to do something about the Mormons and polygamy. "We have done a bigger job in the South," a New Englander told a British traveler in 1866, "and we shall now fix things up in Salt Lake City." Brigham Young remained on the scene for another dozen years, still dominating his society, but the days of his supremacy were past. He had been challenged before, but now the whole energy of the nation turned to the solution of the Mormon problem, so long neglected in the events leading to the Civil War. The completion of the transcontinental railroad in 1869, ending Mormon isolation, signalized the new era. Never again was Mormon hegemony so complete in the land it had hoped to make its exclusive inheritance.

The accounts that follow recover much of the drama of those times— the drama of the land itself, and of the insuppressible people on it. The presettlement explorers, the Forty-Niners, the military and civil officials and their wives, the veteran travelers from abroad, the casual visitors, and the professional journalists all have a story to tell. Some looked with sympathy and others with distaste, but all found the scene absorbing.

====

The Spanish Padre and the Valley of Paradise

THE MORMONS WERE, of course, the first permanent settlers in Deseret, but they were not the first to visit or describe it. Nearly three quarters of a century before, in the year of the Declaration of Independence, the famous Escalante Expedition made an extended reconnaissance of the area in the search for a satisfactory route between the old Spanish colony of New Mexico and the recently established capital of Monterey in Alta California. Father Silvestre Velez de Escalante, the journalist of the expedition, wrote perhaps the first recorded eyewitness description of the land and its aboriginal inhabitants. What to the permanent settlers of a later period was forbidding desert was to Escalante and his companions a paradise. Utah Valley, which lies immediately south of the Valley of the Great Salt Lake, seemed particularly bounteous.

In his own report to the king, Captain Miera y Pacheco, mapmaker of the party, was enthusiastic about the valley with its large body of fresh water and its numerous rivers and meadows. "This is the most pleasing, beautiful, and fertile site in all New Spain. It alone is capable of maintaining a settlement with as many people as Mexico City, and of affording its inhabitants many conveniences, for it has everything necessary for the support of human life." But the official diarist, Escalante, has left the best and most detailed description. Significant portions of the Escalante Journal have been translated into English and published during the past century, including Philip Harry, "The Journeyings of Father Escalante, 1776," in J. H. Simpson, Explorations Across the Great Basin of Utah in 1859 (Washington, 1876); W. R. Harris, The Catholic Church in

The Spanish Padre and the Valley of Paradise

Utah (*Salt Lake City, 1909*); *and twice by the Utah State Historical Society: the Herbert S. Auerbach translation in 1943 and Herbert E. Bolton's* Pageant in the Wilderness, *in Vol. 18 of the* Utah Historical Quarterly (*1950*), *from which the present excerpts are reprinted through the courtesy of the society.*

The plain of the valley must be from southeast to northwest, sixteen Spanish leagues long (which are the leagues we use in this diary), and from northeast to southwest, ten or twelve leagues. It is all clear and, with the exception of the marshes on the shores of the lake, the land is of good quality, and suitable for all kinds of crops.

Of the four rivers which water the valley, the first on the south is that of Aguas Calientes [today the Spanish Fork], in whose wide meadows there is sufficient irrigable land for two good settlements. The second, which follows three leagues to the north of the first and has more water, could sustain one large settlement or two medium-sized ones with an abundance of good land, all of which can be irrigated. This river, which we named Rio de San Nicolás [today Hobble Creek], before entering the lake divides into two branches, and on its banks besides the cottonwoods there are large sycamores. Three and one-half leagues northwest of this river is the third, the country between them being of level meadows with good land for crops. It carries more water than the two foregoing streams, and has a larger cottonwood grove and meadows of good land, with opportunities for irrigation sufficient for two or even three good settlements. We were close to it on the twenty-fourth and twenty-fifth, and we named it Rio de San Antonio de Padua [today the Provo]. We did not reach the fourth river although we could see its grove of trees. It is northwest of the Rio de San Antonio and has in this direction a great deal of level land which is good, judging from what has been seen. They told us that it has as much water as the others, and so some ranchos or pueblos could be established on it. We named it Rio de Santa Ana [today the American Fork]. Besides these rivers, there are many pools of good water in the plain and several springs running down from the sierra.

What we have said regarding settlements is to be understood as giving to each one more lands than are absolutely necessary, for if each pueblo should take only one league of agricultural land, the valley would provide for as many pueblos of Indians as there are in New Mexico. Because, although in the directions indicated above we give the size mentioned, it is an understatement, and on the south and in other directions there are very spacious areas of good land. In all of it there are good and very abundant pastures, and in some places it produces flax and hemp in such quantities that it looks as though they had planted it on purpose. The climate here is good, for after having suffered greatly from the cold since we left the Rio de San Buenaventura [today the Green], in all this valley we felt great heat both night and day.

Besides these most splendid advantages, in the nearby sierras which surround the valley there are plentiful firewood and timber, sheltered places, water and pasturage for raising cattle and horses. . . . Toward the south and southwest close by there are two other extensive valleys, also having abundant pasturage and sufficient water. The lake, which must be six leagues wide and fifteen leagues long, extends as far as one of these valleys. It runs northwest through a narrow passage, and according to what they told us, it communicates with others much larger.

This lake of Timpanogotzis [today Utah Lake] abounds in several kinds of good fish, geese, beaver, and other amphibious animals which we did not have an opportunity to see. Round about it are these Indians, who live on the abundant fish of the lake, for which reason the Yutas Sabuaganas call them Come Pescados [Fish Eaters]. Besides this, they gather in the plain grass seeds from which they make atole, which they supplement by hunting hares, rabbits and fowl of which there is great abundance here. There are also buffalo not very far to the north-northwest, but fear of the Cumanches prevents them [the Come Pescados] from hunting them. Their habitations are chozas or little huts of willow, of which they also make nice baskets and other necessary utensils. In the matter of dress they are very poor. The most decent clothing they wear is a buckskin jacket and long leggings made of the same material. For cold weather they have blankets made of the skins of hares and rabbits. They speak the Yuta language but with notable differences in the accent and in some of the words. They have good features and most of them have heavy beards. In all parts of this sierra to the southeast, southwest and west live a large number of people of the same tribe, language, and docility as these Lagunas, with whom a very populous and extensive province could be formed. . . .

The other lake with which this one communicates, according to what they told us, covers many leagues, and its waters are noxious and extremely salty, for the Timpanois assure us that a person who moistens any part of his body with the water of the lake immediately feels much itching in the part that is wet. Round about it, they told us, live a numerous and peaceful nation called Puaguampe, which in our ordinary speech means "Witch Doctors" and who speak the Cumanche language. Their food consists of herbs. They drink from several fountains or springs of good water which are around the lake, and they have houses of grass and earth (the earth being used for the roofs). . . .

The Timpanogotzis were so-called from the lake on which they live, which they call Timpanogó, and this is the special name of this lake, for the name or word with which they designate any lake in general is "pagariri." This one must be six leagues wide and fifteen leagues long to the narrows and the junction with the large one.

On the Eve of Settlement

DURING A BRIEF GENERATION *after the Escalante Expedition the land was crossed and recrossed by mountain men, by travelers on the Old Spanish Trail, and by government explorers and other wanderers in the wastelands of the Far West. Beginning in the early 1840's, an ever increasing number of overland travelers to the Pacific passed through what is now Utah—a good many just the year before the Mormon hegira. Most famous of the overlanders of 1846 was the tragic Donner party, which approached the future Mormon heartland by the same route the Pioneers of 1847 would follow.*

Traveling a few days ahead of the Donners was a party which included a young Swiss immigrant, Heinrich Lienhard. Lienhard entered the Great Salt Lake Valley from the north, via Weber Canyon and the east littoral of the lake through present Davis County. He was impressed by what he saw—the Great Salt Lake, the mountains, and the land itself. Two days later, while passing the southern end of the lake, Lienhard and his companions decided to go for a swim. His journal account of that adventure may be the first description of swimming in the great inland sea. Published in Zurich in 1898, his journal has appeared only in piecemeal translation in the United States. The following passages are taken from West from Fort Bridger, *published in Vol. 19 of the* Utah Historical Quarterly *(1951), which contained that portion of the journal which describes his traversing of the Great Basin. The selections printed here*

*are reproduced through the courtesy of the Utah State Historical So-
ciety.*

On the 7th [of August] we reached the flat shore of the magnificent
Salt Lake, the waters of which were clear as crystal, but as salty as the
strongest salt brine. It is an immense expanse of water and presents
to the eye in a northeasterly [northwesterly] direction nothing but sky
and water. In it there are a few barren islands which have the appearance
of having been wholly burnt over. The land extends from the mountains
down to the lake in a splendid inclined plane broken only by the fresh
water running down from ever-flowing springs above. The soil is a rich,
deep black sand composition [loam] doubtless capable of producing
good crops. The clear, sky-blue surface of the lake, the warm sunny
air, the nearby high mountains, with the beautiful country at their foot,
through which we on a fine road were passing, made on my spirits an
extraordinarily charming impression. The whole day long I felt like singing and whistling; had there been a single family of white men to be
found living here, I believe that I would have remained. Oh, how unfortunate that this beautiful country was uninhabited! . . .

On August 9 we continued our journey south, to round the lake in a
westerly direction farther on; Ripstein, an American named Bunzel, and
I were somewhat in advance of our wagons and came to a place where
the road passed close to the lake. The morning was so delightfully warm
and the absolutely clear water so inviting that we soon resolved to take
a salt water bath. The beach glistened with the whitish-gray sand which
covered it, and on the shore we could see the still-fresh tracks of a bear,
notwithstanding which we soon had undressed and were going down
into the salty water. We had, however, to go out not less than a half
mile before the water reached our hips. Even here it was still so transparent that we could see the bottom as if there were no water whatever
above it, yet so heavy that we could hardly tread upon the bottom
with our feet; it was here quite a trick to stand even on tiptoe. I confidently believe that one who understood only a little of swimming could
swim the entire length of the 70-mile-long lake without the slightest danger of drowning. I was a poor swimmer, Ripstein none at all, and he
could lay himself on his back, so that fully half of his body emerged above
the clear salt brine. Had I [not] known that in ordinary water I sank
lightly beneath the surface, I would have supposed that I had become
an absolutely first-rate swimmer, [for] I could assume every conceivable
position, without the least danger. I could in a sitting position swim on

224

my side, swim on my back, and I believe one could make a competent somersault without special effort, for by giving only a slight push with the foot against the bottom, one could leap high up. Since my hair was thick, hanging down to my shoulders, when I lay on my back, I had to hold high a great part of my body before my head came under water. For learning to swim, no water in the whole world is so well adapted as the Salt Lake; here, at the mouth of an inflowing fresh water stream where one could choose gradually lighter water, one could safely learn how to be a perfect swimmer. I swam nearly the whole distance back, yes, one could easily swim in water which was hardly more than 1½ feet deep. Only a single feature had the swimming in this lake that was not conducive to pleasure; this consisted in the fact that when one got a little water in one's eye, it occasioned a severe burning pain; and after we reached the shore and dressed ourselves without first washing in unsalted water, being desirous of hastening on, we soon experienced an almost unbearable smarting or itching over the whole body where the salt water had filled up all the crevices of the skin with an all-enveloping deposit of salt.

The Promised Land

CONTRARY TO THE EXPRESSIONS of early observers, the traditional view of the Great Basin is that it was sterile and barren. In official Mormon history it was desert. Only God's beneficent smile upon his chosen people in their new-found promised land would make the desert "blossom as the rose." But at least some of the original pioneers of 1847 did not share this fiction. The English convert, William Clayton, lately a private secretary to the Prophet Joseph Smith and now an historian of the pioneer camp under the leadership of Brigham Young, found himself on July 22 with a small group, slightly ahead of the main body, at the mouth of Emigration Canyon overlooking the Valley of the Great Salt Lake. His Journal, *published in Salt Lake City in 1921, records his enthusiasm on that memorable occasion.*

While the brethren were cutting the road, I followed the old one to the top of the hill and on arriving there was much cheered by a handsome view of the Great Salt Lake lying, as I should judge, from twenty-five to thirty miles to the west of us; and at eleven o'clock I sat down to contemplate and view the surrounding scenery. There is an extensive, beautiful, level looking valley from here to the lake which I should judge from the numerous deep green patches must be fertile and rich. The valley extends to the south probably fifty miles where it is again surrounded by high mountains. To the southwest across the valley at about twenty to twenty-five miles distance is a high mountain, extending from the south end of the valley to about opposite this place where it ceases abruptly leaving a pleasant view of the dark waters of the lake. Standing on the lake and about due west there are two mountains and far in the distance another one which I suppose is on the other side of the lake, probably from sixty to eighty miles distance. To the northwest is another mountain at the base of which is a lone ridge of what I should consider to be rock salt from its white and shining appearance. The lake does not show at this distance a very extensive surface, but its dark blue shade resembling the calm sea looks very handsome. The intervening valley appears to be well supplied with streams, creeks and lakes, some of the latter are evidently salt. There is but little timber in sight anywhere, and that is mostly on the banks of creeks and streams of water which is about the only objection which could be raised in my estimation to this being one of the most beautiful valleys and pleasant places for a home for the Saints which could be found. Timber is evidently lacking but we have not expected to find a timbered country. . . . For my own part I am happily disappointed in the appearance of the valley of the Salt Lake, but if the land be as rich as it has the appearance of being, I have no fears but the Saints can live here and do well while we will do right. When I commune with my own heart and ask myself whether I would choose to dwell here in this wild looking country amongst the Saints surrounded by friends, though poor, enjoying the privileges and blessings of the everlasting priesthood, with God for our King and Father; or dwell amongst the gentiles with all their wealth and good things of the earth, to be eternally mobbed, harassed, hunted, our best men murdered and every good man's life continually in danger, the soft whisper echoes loud and reverberates back in tones of stern determination; give me the quiet wilderness and my family to associate with, surrounded by the Saints and adieu to the gentile world till God says return and avenge you of your enemies.

"The Garden of Joseph"

ON OCTOBER 12, 1849, *after a little over two years in the Valley, Brigham Young and his counselors issued an official report of conditions in Zion. The "second General Epistle of the Presidency of the Church of Jesus Christ of Latter-Day Saints . . . to the Saints Scattered throughout the Earth," excerpted below, was published in the* Frontier Guardian *(Kanesville, Iowa), on December 26, 1849, and in the* Millennial Star *(Liverpool), April 5, 1850. It ran the gamut of political, religious, social, and economic developments, touching on the establishment of a militia, the organization of formal government, the departure and arrival of missionaries, the passing through of Forty-Niners, the development of agriculture, the creation of an emigration fund, and the construction of buildings, public and private.*

While full of information about Deseret at the end of the second year, the epistle must be read with some caution. Its tone is completely optimistic with little or no reference to the trials and hardships which attended the life of the early settlers and which form such an important part of pioneer folklore today. In fact, according to the letter, disease and death had been practically banished from Zion: "The health of the Saints in the valley is good, and it is so seldom that anyone dies, we scarce recollect when such an event last occurred." The epistle is, obviously and simply, but importantly, official propaganda, advertising the new country in very special terms for very special colonists. It is a résumé of accomplishments accompanied by a plea for the Saints to "gather" to Zion: "Brethren, come from the States, from the nations, come! and help us to build and grow, until we can say, enough—the valleys of Ephraim are full." Significantly, the epistle expresses the hope that Deseret will be admitted into the Union "free and independent like our sister States"—a hope that would be disappointed.

Greetings:—Beloved brethren, since our communication of April, many events interesting in their nature, as relating to the progress of truth, and the happiness of the faithful have transpired, and we improve the earliest moment to write of the same, that the hearts of all may be united with us in praise to Israel's God for the fulfilment of His promises, and of the prophecies in these last days.

On the 12th of April, Elder Amasa Lyman left this place in company with several brethren for Western California, carrying our former epistle; and Capt. Allen Compton started with a mail containing the same, for the States, two days after; and although the snow was unusually deep, and had been long considered impassible, we are happy in having learned that Brother Compton and the little band of the brethren accompanying him, arrived safe in Kanesville after a speedy and toilsome journey.

The heat of summer began to be exhibited at mid-day about the middle of April, which rapidly dispersed the snow upon the mountains, though more or less continues in sight of our beautiful valley perpetually, and the weather continued variable until the 23rd of May, when it was very severe, accompanied by a heavy fall of snow, and was followed the succeeding day by a severe frost; since which time the weather has been mild and warm, generally, with occasional slight frosts in the valley every month and almost every week, until the last, when two or three successive and severe frosts put an end to vegetation generally.

The Nauvoo Legion has been re-organized in the valley, and it would have been a source of joy to the Saints throughout the earth, could they have witnessed its movements on the day of its great parade; to see a whole army of mighty men in martial array, ground their arms, not by command but simply by request, repair to the temple block, and with pick and spade open the foundation for a place of worship, and erect the pilasters, beams and roof, so that we now have a commodious edifice 100 by 60 feet, with brick walls, where we assemble with the Saints from Sabbath to Sabbath, and almost every evening in the week, to teach, counsel, and devise ways and means for the prosperity of the Kingdom of God: and we feel thankful that we have a better house or bowery for public worship the coming winter, than we have heretofore had any winter in this dispensation.

The inhabitants of this great Basin have instituted a provisional state of government, adopted a constitution, elected officers, and we anticipate that, at the next session of Congress, we shall be admitted into the Union, free and independent like our sister States. Our city lies near the Great Salt Lake, which borders on the west on an extensive desert which runs through the Basin from north to south. We call our new state, Deseret.

A number of the brethren left here in May, and established a ferry on the Upper Platte during the high water, and another company opened a ferry at each crossing of Green river. Both companies have returned in safety, and we anticipate the same ferries will be re-opened in season for the emigration next spring.

The 24th of July was a day long to be remembered by all present in this valley, and all Saints who shall learn of our celebration, as the anniversary of the arrival of the Pioneers two years previous. To behold twelve or fifteen hundred feet of tables, filling the bowery and all adjoining grounds, loaded with all luxuries of the field and gardens, and nearly all the varieties that any vegetable market in the world could produce, and to see the seats around those tables filled and re-filled by a people who had been deprived of those luxuries for years by the cruel hand of oppression, and freely offering seats to every stranger within their borders, and this too, in the valley of the mountains, a thousand miles from civilization, where two years before nought was to be found save the wild root of the prairie, and the mountain cricket, was a theme of unbounded thanksgiving and praise to the Giver of all good, as the dawning of a day when the children of the Kingdom can sit under their own vines and fig-trees and inhabit their own houses, having none to make them afraid. May the time be hastened when the scattered Israel may partake of such like banquets from the garden of Joseph.

Thousands of emigrants from the States to the Gold Mines have passed through our city this season, leaving large quantities of domestic clothing, wagons, &c., in exchange for horses and mules, which exchange has been a mutual blessing to both parties.

The Elders who received appointments for foreign missions last spring, were generally detained in the valley, to raise grain and locate their families, until recently. . . .

The direct emigration of the Saints to this place will be some five or six hundred wagons this season, besides many who came in search of gold, have heard the Gospel for the first time and will go no farther, having believed and been baptized.

Sept. 28th, fourteen or fifteen of the brethren arrived from the gold country, some of whom were very comfortably supplied with the precious metal, and others, who had been sick, came as destitute as they went on the ship *Brooklyn* in 1846. That there is plenty of gold in Western California is beyond doubt, but the valley of the Sacramento is an unhealthy place, and the Saints can be better employed in raising grain, and building houses in this vicinity, than digging for gold in the Sacramento, unless they are counselled so to do. The true use of gold is for paving streets, covering houses and making culinary dishes, and when the Saints shall have preached the Gospel, raised grain and built up cities enough, the Lord will open up the way for a supply of gold to the perfect satisfaction of His people; until then, let them not be over anxious, for the treasures of the earth are in the Lord's store house, and He will open the doors thereof, when and where He pleases.

The grain crops in the valley have been good this season; wheat, barley, oats, rye, and peas, more particularly. The late corn and buckwheat, and some lesser grains and vegetables, have been materially injured by the recent frost; and some early corn at Brownsville, forty miles north, a month since; and the buckwheat was severely damaged by hail at the Utah settlement, sixty miles South about three weeks since; but we have great occasion for thanksgiving to Him who giveth the increase, that He has blest our labors, so that with prudence we shall have a comfortable supply for ourselves, and our brethren on the way, who may be in need, until another harvest; but we feel the need of more laborers, for more efficient help, and multiplied means of farming and building at this place. We want men. Brethren, come from the States, from the nations, come! and help us to build and grow, until we can say, enough— the valleys of Ephraim are full.

Any of the brethren, master workmen in cotton or woollen factories, who will come on with their means, machinery, and hands to work it, will meet a warm reception, and have every possible facility rendered them to prosecute their business, for we need such establishments in our midst.

The Bowery was crowded on the 6th of Oct. Conference, so that the cry was "our place is not large enough." A sweet and heavenly influence prevailed, and much important business was transacted, as may be seen more particularly by the minutes accompanying this.

It was decided to locate a town or city at Brownsville [today's Ogden], and also at Utah [valley], near the settlements now existing, the Presidency having previously visited those places and selected sites.

Early in the fall we sent messengers to Sandpitch valley, who selected a place for a settlement, about 200 miles South of this, and we expect that from 50 to 100 families will start for that place in a few days. They also discovered a plentiful supply of good rock, or mountain salt, toward the contemplated settlement.

The walls of our Council house are nearly completed. The baths at the warm spring house are in progress; the foundation is laid, and brick prepared for an extensive store house and granary; and no exertions are wanting on our part to push forward the public works, as fast as tithing and means are put in our hands; and we are happy to say that an increasing spirit of liberality and faithfulness is daily manifest among the Saints.

About one month since we suggested the propriety of creating a perpetual fund for the purpose of helping the poor Saints to emigrate to this place, agreeably to our covenants in the Temple that we would "never cease our exertions, by all the means and influence within our reach, till all the Saints who were obliged to leave Nauvoo should be located at some gathering place of the Saints." The Council approved of the suggestion, and a committee was immediately appointed to raise a fund by voluntary contribution to be forwarded east next mail. The October Conference sanctioned the doings of the committee, and appointed Brother Edward Hunter, a tried, faithful, and approved Bishop, a general agent to bear the perpetual emigrating funds to the States, to superintend the direction and appropriation thereof, and return the same to this place with such poor brethren as shall be wisdom to help.

We wish all to understand, that this fund is PERPETUAL, and is never to be diverted from the object of gathering the poor to Zion while there are Saints to be gathered, unless He whose right it is to rule shall otherwise command. Therefore we call upon President Orson Hyde and all the Saints, and all benevolent souls everywhere, to unite their gold, their silver, and their cattle, with ours in this perpetual fund, and co-operate with Bishop Hunter in producing as many teams as possible, preparatory for next spring's emigration, and let the poor who are to be helped, go to work with their might, and prepare wagons of wood for their journey. Such wagons, without any iron, now exist in this valley, that have come from the states, having done good business; and so great has been the influx of wagons this season, that they are cheap, and iron comparatively plentiful.

This perpetual fund is to be under the special direction of the presidency at all times, and as soon as Bishop Hunter shall return with the same and his freight of Saints to this place, the cattle and teams will be disposed of to the best advantage, and the avails, with all we can add to it, will be sent forth immediately on another mission, and we want you all prepared to meet it and add to it, and so would we continue to increase it from year to year, until, "when a nation is born in a day," they can be removed the next, if the Lord will; therefore, ye poor and meek of the earth, lift up your heads and rejoice in the Holy One of Israel, for your redemption draweth nigh; but in your rejoicing be patient, for

231

though your turn to emigrate may not be the first year, or even the second, it will come, and its tarryings will be short, if all the Saints who have, will be as liberal as those in the valley.

All the apostles now in the valley have had missions assigned to them. Elder John Taylor, accompanied by Curtis E. Bolton and John Pack, goes to France; Elder Lorenzo Snow to Italy, accompanied by Joseph Toronto; Elder Erastus Snow to Denmark, accompanied by Peter Hanson, and will start in about a week, passing through the States. Elder Franklin D. Richards, accompanied by John S. Higbee, George B. Wallace, Job Smith, H. W. Church, Joseph W. Johnson, Joseph W. Young, and Jacob Gates, will go with the mission to England, to co-operate with President Orson Pratt; Elder John Forsgreen will go out at the same time on a mission to Sweden. For wise purposes Elder P. P. Pratt's mission to the Western Islands will be deferred until spring.

Elder Orson Pratt is doing a great work in England, and the cause of truth is advancing rapidly in all her home dominions, and the rejoicing of the Saints here causes Satan to howl, for he is compelled to be subject to the power of the Highest. Elder Woodruff's is located in Cambridge Port, Massachusetts, and has been comforting and instructing the Saints in Canada and the Eastern States the past year. If Elder Woodruff now will gather up all the Saints in his vicinity, and come with them to this place, he will do a great work, and will be opening the way for a visit to those nations who have both eyes and ears, and are crying to the Elders of Israel, "Come, tell us of the things of God, for we have heard that God is with you.". . .

Brother Parley P. Pratt is opening a new road through the range of mountains from the Weber to this place, which is already so far advanced that this fall's emigration will pass over it. This road will be accomplished at a great expense, and will be a great blessing to the emigrating brethren, and together with bridges in the valley, over the Weber and Ogden fork, all of which we expect will be completed before the next emigrating season, will shorten the distance and greatly facilitate the progress of travellers.

The health of the saints in the valley is good, and it is so seldom that any one dies, we scarce recollect when such an event last occurred. . . .

While kingdoms, governments, and thrones, are falling and rising; revolutions succeeding revolutions; and the nations of earth are overturning; while plague, pestilence and famine, are walking abroad; and whirlwind, fire, and earthquake, proclaim the truth of prophecy, let the

Saints be faithful and diligent in every duty, and especially in striving to stand in chosen places, that they may watch the coming of the Holy One of Israel. We remain your brothers in the New Covenant.

> BRIGHAM YOUNG.
> HEBER C. KIMBALL.
> WILLARD RICHARDS.

Great Salt Lake City, Deseret, Oct. 12th, 1849

Forty-Niners

IN THE ISOLATION of the Rocky Mountains the Mormons hoped only to be left alone. But on January 24, 1848, six months to the day following the arrival of the pioneers in Utah, gold was discovered at Coloma on the south fork of the American River. Ironically, Mormons themselves, members of the Mormon Battalion, shared in the discovery. The news was slow to get around, but by spring of the next year the Gold Rush was on. The Mormons soon found themselves, instead of isolated, fairly astride the great highroad to the Pacific, and the unwilling hosts to thousands bound for the gold fields. Salt Lake City became a renowned Halfway House in the Wilderness.

Lost in the greater excitement of gold was another event of considerable significance. Technically the Mormons had settled in Mexican territory, although the Mexicans were hardly aware of it and perhaps cared less. On February 2, 1848, nine days after the discovery of gold, the Mexican War came to an end with the signing of the treaty of Guadalupe Hidalgo, and Utah along with other vast areas of the Far West and Southwest became United States territory.

To be sure, not all of the Argonauts of 1849 and after took the route through the Valley of the Great Salt Lake, but enough of them—from 5,000 to 8,000—did to exert a tremendous influence on the social and economic life of the new and struggling commonwealth. Their generally favorable views, which reached a wide audience through countless hometown papers all over the country, helped to vindicate the Mormons in American public opinion.

III · CHRONICLES AND JUDGES

The following letters appeared originally in contemporary periodicals identified below. As here reprinted they are taken from Dale L. Morgan's "Letters by Forty-Niners" in Vol. 3 of the Western Humanities Review, *University of Utah (April, 1949). Their reproduction here is through the courtesy of the* Western Humanities Review.

I

[Great Salt Lake City]
8th July [1849]

We are now encamped in the Mormon City, fourteen hundred miles from the States. The city is laid off in a very handsome style, and is about five square.—The inhabitants number five thousand at this time, and are increasing in number every day. They have erected a fort, and are about commencing some fine buildings. The city is watered by two or three fine streams. They have to water their wheat and corn, and vegetables. They have now fifty thousand acres in wheat. Flour is scarce here; I do not know a single family in the city that has a supply. Every family was desirous to purchase from us, and offer from ten to fifteen cents per pound.—They do not want money here; they want sugar, coffee, tea and flour. I had my mules shod in the city, and they charged me four dollars per mule. Coffee is selling at 50 cents per pound, and rice at 25 cents. If you can accomplish the plan of a Rail Road from the States to the Salt Lake City, this will be one of the greatest places of trade in the known world. They have one of the finest warm springs for bathing, and the most healthy that is known. There is a boiling spring and a tar spring, and a cold spring also; and salt water in abundance. They have the finest salt here you ever saw, and any amount of saleratus; they gather it up in a pure state, and it makes splendid bread. The city of the Lake has appropriated $5,000 for the purpose of making a good road from the city to the North Fork of the Platte river, which will be the means of turning a great number of the emigrants in this direction. I find the Mormons very accommodating, and willing to extend to the emigrants all the hospitality they possibly can. We leave Sunday Morning for the gold diggings, with a fine prospect before us. One man can raise from fifty to a hundred dollars per day. They are packing dirt from fifteen to twenty miles on mules, from what they call dry diggings, to water. Tell the boys to come on— this is the only chance they will ever have to get rich. The gold dust is inexhaustible, if the representations here are correct. If we keep our health, we shall be home in eighteen months. I would advise all per-

234

sons who intend to emigrate to California this summer or next, to start with a light carriage and eight stout mules, from six to ten years old, and enough provisions to last four men through. Work four mules one day, and four the next, so as to rest them; and by travelling in that way, they can make forty miles per day, and not injure their mules. Start with a very light load; you can make the trip in 55 days.

After coming through the South Pass, the ridge that divides the waters of the Atlantic and Pacific, we had to ferry two streams, South Fork of Platte River, and Green River. A company built a boat on the Platte, and about the time they crossed, Mr. Armstrong, of Monroe, and another company, offered Capt. Finley, the owner of the boat, $250 for the boat. Capt. Finley told them that himself and company had crossed, and all others might go to hell; and then cut the boat in pieces before their eyes. This Captain Finley is from Illinois, and the wretch should be published in every newspaper in the U. States. A company from Pennsylvania, the Monroe company, and our company, built a boat and after our companies crossed we handed it over to the next train that arrived. This Capt. Finley is well known on the road from the Platte to California, and will be pointed out to every company and hissed at.

[John B. Hazlip]

[From the Palmyra *Missouri Whig*, October 4, 1849.]

II

City of the Great Salt Lake
Sunday, July 15th, 1849

Dear Wife:—

You will discover by the heading of this letter that we are in California and in the Mormon City.

. . . . The Mormons have had pretty hard times since they came here, but at this time they have got things pretty comfortable around them. They are just cutting their wheat, which is good; they also have corn, potatoes, etc., coming on; they also have cattle plenty; consequently cheese, butter, etc. Groceries are scarce. Coffee 50 cts. Sugar 37 cts. and other groceries in proportion. We can trade groceries for anything that they have, but they will not sell for money, for they have plenty and cannot buy what they want with it. The Mormons give very flattering accounts of the Gold Regions, and they are afraid that gold will be found in this valley. They say that it will ruin them, for they would starve if they should get the gold fever bad enough to call them from their farms. We expect to remain here until Tuesday to shoe some of our oxen. I went to hear a sermon today, and heard a very good Methodist sermon by a Mormon. They are going to have a great time here on the 24th of this month, celebrating the 2nd anniversary of the arrival of their President into this valley. They read the order of the day at the meeting to-day, and if I could get hold of it I would send it, so that you can see that they can do things up pretty strong out here. There is to be ringing of bells, firing of cannon, music from the band, &c, &c., 24 young men for something, I cannot recollect what; 24 young ladies dressed in white for something else; 24 Bishops for something else, etc. The United States Mail leaves here four times a year. It leaves next Tuesday or Wednesday, consequently you will get this letter pretty soon. You may get it sooner than the one I left at Fort Laramie, as that was to go by private conveyance.

I will now give you some kind of an idea of the Mormon City. It is laid out in an oblong square, four miles long and two miles wide; streets very wide; the size of the lots are 40 acres, and about one-half of these lots are occupied. The buildings are mostly small; they are built some of logs, but mostly of what they call *dobies* [adobes] (sun-dried brick). There are in the valley five Grist mills and eight or nine saw mills and two or three more building. Their lumber is pine and fir. They have to haul their firewood ten miles, for there is none grows in this part of the valley; consequently they have to go to the mountains for it. When the Mormons first settled here, they put their buildings in the shape of a fort; they built two rows of buildings three-fourths of a mile in length and [a] fourth of a mile apart, and shut up the ends by buildings across; inside of this they had three rows of buildings at equal distances across, forming four hollow squares, into which they could take all their cattle, wagons, etc., if they should be attacked by Indians, but they have never been bothered by Indians; consequently they have spread out over the country. The city is on a very pretty piece of ground, and if it was near a navigable stream it would be a great city, but there is no chance to get within four hundred miles of this with anything of the boat kind, and I think it is impossible to get a railroad into the valley, for it is surrounded with mountains that are almost impassable for anything. Here you can have plenty of ice all the year around, without the trouble of packing it away in ice houses; for eight miles from the city the tops of the mountains are covered with snow and ice. A few days ago I walked over snow that was ten feet deep. I would tell the depth of it by a channel that had been cut through it by the water.

A. P. Josselyn

[From the Zanesville (Ohio) *Courier*, reprinted in the Zanesville *Gazette*, October 3, 1849. The original letter is in the California State Library.]

"The Mormonee"

STRANGE TALES CAME out of the multifarious adventures of the Forty-Niners in their mad rush for gold. Few, if any, had a greater variety of experiences than William L. Manly, one of the survivors of the party whose tragic end gave the name to Death Valley.

On reaching the Green River, he and five or six others broke away from the company in which they had been traveling and embarked on the incredible plan of floating down the river to the Pacific Ocean. Their river-faring ended disastrously in what is now the Uinta Basin of eastern Utah. In an encounter with the famous Chief Walker and his hunting party, Manly's group learned of the friendly relations between the Indians and the Mormons, and, to obtain the good will of the redskins, passed themselves off as "Mormonee." With the aid and advice of the Indians, they made their way westward to the Mormon settlements, which they reached by what was then certainly the back door. Here they joined the California-bound company that later came to grief in the burning sands of Death Valley.

The excerpts below were taken from the reminiscent narrative written by Manly and edited by Milo M. Quaife under the title Death Valley in '49 *by William L. Manly (Chicago, 1927).*

There was some little talk, but I am sure we did not understand one another's language, and so we made motions and they made motions, and we got along better. We went with them down to the tepee, and there we heard the first word that was at all like English and that was "Mormonee," with a sort of questioning tone. Pretty soon one said "Buf-

237

falo," and then we concluded they were on a big hunt of some sort. They took us into their lodges and showed us blankets, knives, and guns, and then, with a suggestive motion, said all was "Mormonee," by which we understood they had got them from the Mormons. The Indian in the back part of the lodge looked very pleasant and his countenance showed a good deal of intelligence for a man of the mountains. I now told the boys that we were in a position where we were dependent on some one, and that I had seen enough to convince me that these Indians were perfectly friendly with the Mormons, and that for our benefit we had better pass ourselves off for Mormons, also. So we put our right hands to our breasts and said "Mormonee," with a cheerful countenance, and that act conveyed to them the belief that we were chosen disciples of the great and only Brigham and we became friends at once. The fine-looking Indian who sat as king in the lodge now, by motions and a word or two, made himself known as Chief Walker, and when I knew this I took great pains to cultivate his acquaintance.

I was quite familiar with the sign language used by all the Indians, and found I could get along pretty well in making him understand and knowing what he said. I asked him first how many "sleeps" or days it was from there to "Mormonee." In answer he put out his left hand and then put two fingers of his right astride of it, making both go up and down with the same motion of a man riding a horse. Then he shut his eyes and laid his head on his hand three times, by which I understood that a man could ride to the Mormon settlement in three sleeps or four days. He then wanted to know where we were going, and I made signs that we were wishing to go toward the setting sun and to the big water, and I said "California." The Country off to the west of us now seemed an open, barren plain, which grew wider as it extended west. The mountains on the north side seemed to get lower and smaller as they extended west, but on the south or east side they were all high and rough. It seemed as if we could see one hundred miles down the river, and up to the time we met the Indians we thought we had got through all our troublesome navigation and could now sail on quietly and safely to the great Pacific Ocean and the land of gold. . . .

I now had a description of the country ahead and believed it to be reliable. As soon after this as I conveniently could, I had a council with the boys who had looked on in silence while I was holding the silent confab with the chief. I told them where we were and what chances there were of getting to California by this route, and that for my part I had as soon be killed by Mormons as by savage Indians, and that I believe the best way for us to do was to make the best of our way to Salt Lake. "Now," I said, "those of you who agree with me can follow —and I hope all will."

An Oregon Emigrant

THE HIGHWATER MARK *in overland travel to the Pacific came in 1850. While the gold fields of California were the mecca for most of the travelers, not all set out for or arrived in that region. For more than a few Oregon remained, all during the gold rush, the end of the rainbow. While most Oregon-bound travelers turned north at Fort Bridger, moved down the Bear and thence to Fort Hall, thus by-passing the Utah region, an occasional traveler or company visited Salt Lake City before turning north to rejoin the main Oregon trail.*

Such a company arrived in the valley late in August, 1850. Solomon Zumwalt, who had been born in Missouri and was now emigrating to Oregon, spent the winter in Salt Lake Valley. Many years later, as an old man in Oregon, he wrote his reminiscences, and those portions dealing with his stay in Mormon country are here presented through the courtesy of Eugenia Learned James and the Missouri Historical Review, *in which they were originally published in July, 1954. Solomon's language, particularly his spelling, was interesting if not unique and adds flavor to his observations: "Thare war some men one evning camped on the crek ner the haus, said the war from Calafornia. Wm Crowe was at my haus that evning and a quantanc. He ses to my son Jackson les go too thar camp and hear Calaforna neus. They axt the bois what knd of people these mormens war. The bois bore doun hard on the mormens. The war mormens them selvs. The went to the sita and reported i had born doun on them. I new nothing ove it." To facilitate reading, this impossible spelling has been modernized.*

For want of better evidence to the contrary, Zumwalt's experiences as a winter "guest" among the Mormons must be accepted as typical of the treatment any law-abiding Gentile received during his sojourn in Zion.

239

So we soon came to the road that went to Salt Lake. My Company said they would go there to winter. McCabes said they hadn't provisions enough to go through to Oregon, so I reluctantly went with them to Salt Lake. We stayed several days at Fort Bridger, then left for Salt Lake, camped one evening in a valley now Parleys Park.

We saw a heap of bear sign. . . .

We next morning on the 19th of August started our teams across a divide went down a canyon camped on the canyon. Next day about noon we came out in the Great Salt Lake Valley. We rolled down to the city, camped on the west side of the city, turned our cattle off on Jordan [River]. The Mormon friends came to our camp to have a big talk with the newcomers. They told me the crickets were about to destroy their crops. God sent host of seagulls to eat the crickets and saved their crops. And that there was no grass in the valley till the Mormons came there. So I looked around and saw old turfs of grass on the ground. So I thought they were trying to spoof me and I believed just what I was aiming to. The next day 22nd of August we rolled out on the Utah road, went about 20 miles, camped on a stream called Dry Cottonwood, found plenty of water, grass, and wood. I stopped there to winter. The nearest settlers were 6 miles toward the city on Little Cottonwood. There was a settlement of Mississippians there that had some black people.

One of them came out to my camp and said I would do well to keep a herd of cattle. I had good range. He said it would help pay my expenses. He would help me get up a herd. His name was Smith. I soon got quite a herd and it was a great help to me. I had a boy Tolaver about 12 or 13 years old. I had bought him a small rifle. I fixed him on a horse. He was my herd boy. I put up a house and made me a corral, cut quite a lot of hay. The winter was favorable, did not need it much. There were several snows but the wind would blow it off the benches that the cattle could get at the bunch grass. They seemed to like it better than hay. Mr. Smith told me I could get plenty of vegetables if I would put up Bishop Crosby's vegetables. I took a wagon and team and put up a large lot of potatoes and turnips and beats and cabbage. The Bishop told me to take all the family would need through the winter and I must say to the credit of them Mormon friends they treated me like a gentleman.

I got along well with the Mormons generally I thought. They were often at my house getting their work cattle out of the herd. These large white wolves were bad when I first stopped. They killed some cows.

An Oregon Emigrant

I had a band of large steers. They would run like a thunder storm. Where there was a small animal attacked they wouldn't relieve it. Something I never knew in Missouri, the Mormons got strychnine and killed them all off. This was the first I knew of strychnine.

We were living comfortably there for emigrants. One evening there came a Mormon preacher one of the Seventy. We had a heap of talk that evening. I didn't bear down on his religion. We got along well. He started in the morning. Old Mr. McCabe was cutting wood before his cabin. He went there to convert him. Mc bore down bad on Mormonism, said Brigham Young had no more religion than his wagon. The preacher he said there was some hopes for me but none for McCabe, stamped the dust off his feet, and left.

There were some men one evening camped on the creek near the house, said they were from California. Wm. Crowe was at my house that evening an acquaintance. He says to my son Jackson let's go to their camp and hear California news. They asked the boys what kind of people these Mormons were. The boys bore down hard on the Mormons. They were Mormons themselves. They went to the city and reported I had bore down on them. I knew nothing of it. In a few days there came some emigrants from Utah told me the Mormons talked of running my cattle off. It made me feel very indignant that they would draw something from boys to get a row with me. I went over to Little Cottonwood and gave the case just as it was. They made light of it, said there were as bad people in the Mormon Church as there were anywhere. So I was all right again.

Mr. Goodal came around hunting up the emigrants that were going to Oregon. We selected a stream called Boxelder. It is between Ogden and Bear River. We were to collect about the 20th of March. I got my herd off of my hands and started for our rendezvous. I had to pass through the city. They levied a tax on me of $19.80. I got to Boxelder. I found a goodly number collected there bound for Oregon. We made a raise of 24 wagons.

━━━━━

A Soldier and Surveyor

AMONG THE EARLIEST VISITORS who came to Utah to appraise
the newly settled region and incidentally its people were several official
expeditions of more or less a military nature. Whereas the federal officials, who came to run the civil government, early and regularly got
themselves embroiled with the Mormon citizenry, the soldiers with some
exceptions managed to maintain peaceful relations, at least outwardly
and on the command level. The soldiers lived on the periphery of
settlement and concerned themselves with obvious services like surveying and exploration. The civil officials, on the other hand, of necessity
lived in the Mormon communities, becoming intimately involved with
the daily life of a social order they could not accept. The result was
nearly continual conflict caused by suspicion and distrust on the part
of the Mormons, misunderstanding and contempt on the part of the
officials.

The soldiers came first, and the first of these was Captain Howard
Stansbury of the Corps of Topographical Engineers, who, in the spring
of 1849, had been ordered by the War Department to conduct an exploration and survey of the Valley of the Great Salt Lake. He and his
party spent a year making an extended reconnaissance of the Salt Lake
region from Fort Hall on the north to Utah Valley on the south, including a survey of the Great Salt Lake, its islands, and all the lands immediately surrounding it. This survey was the first really scientific examination of the region, the work of the renowned John C. Frémont
not excepted.

Captain Stansbury's official report, Exploration and Survey of the Valley of the Great Salt Lake of Utah (Philadelphia, 1852), excerpted below, is more than a scientific record. It is frequently an absorbing trave-
logue, a detailed narrative of his experiences, and not least, an astute
interpretation of Mormon society. He had ample opportunity to observe
the Mormons. From late November until April, 1850, hard weather
forced him to winter in Salt Lake City. With the land, its people, and
their past he was sympathetic. He even had a good word to say about

242

polygamy. *The Mormons count him among such other early friends as Philip St. George Cooke, John W. Gunnison, and the little colonel, Thomas L. Kane.*

Descending the pass [on August 27, 1849] through dense thickets of small oak-trees, we caught the first glimpse of the GREAT SALT LAKE, the long-desired object of our search, and which it had cost us so many weary steps to reach. A gleam of sunlight, reflected by the water, and a few floating, misty clouds, were all, however, that we could see of this famous spot, and we had to repress our enthusiasm for some more favourable moment. I felt, nevertheless, no little gratification in having at length attained the point where our labours were to commence in earnest, and an impatient longing to enter upon that exploration to which our toils hitherto had been but preliminary. . . .

Before reaching Great Salt Lake City, I had heard from various sources that much uneasiness was felt by the Mormon community at my anticipated coming among them. I was told that they would never permit any survey of their country to be made; while it was darkly hinted that if I persevered in attempting to carry it on, my life would scarce be safe. Utterly disregarding, indeed giving not the least credence to these insinuations, I at once called upon BRIGHAM YOUNG, the president of the Mormon church and the governor of commonwealth, stated to him what I had heard, explained to him the views of the Government in directing an exploration and survey of the lake, assuring him that these were the sole objects of the expedition. He replied, that he did not hesitate to say that both he and the people over whom he presided had been very much disturbed and surprised that the Government should send out a party into their country so soon after they had made their settlement; that he had heard of the expedition from time to time, since its outset from Fort Leavenworth; and that the whole community were extremely anxious as to what could be the design of the Government in such a movement. It appeared, too, that their alarm had been increased by the indiscreet and totally unauthorized boasting of an *attaché* of General Wilson, the newly-appointed Indian Agent for California, whose train on its way thither had reached the city a few days before I myself arrived. This person, as I understood, had declared openly that General Wilson had come clothed with authority from the President of the United States to expel the Mormons from the lands which they occupied, and that he would do so if he thought proper. The Mormons very naturally supposed from such a declaration that there must be some understanding or connection between General Wilson and myself; and that the arrival of the two parties so nearly together was the result of a concerted and combined movement for the ulterior purpose of breaking up and destroying their colony. The impression was that a survey was to be made of their country in the same manner that other public lands are surveyed, for the purpose of dividing it into townships and sections, and of thus establishing and recording the claims of the Government to it, and thereby anticipating any claim the Mormons might set up from their previous occupation. However unreasonable such a suspicion may be considered, yet it must be remembered that these people are exasperated and rendered almost desperate by the wrongs and persecutions they had previously suffered in Illinois and Missouri; that they had left the confines of civilization and fled to these far distant wilds, that they might enjoy undisturbed the religious liberty which had been practically denied them; and that now they supposed themselves to be followed up by the General Government with the view of driving them out from even this solitary spot, where they had hoped they should at length be permitted to set up their habitation in peace.

Upon all these points I undeceived Governor Young to his entire satisfaction. I was induced to pursue this conciliatory course, not only in justice to the Government, but also because I knew, from the peculiar organization of this singular community, that, unless the "President" was fully satisfied that no evil was intended to his people, it would be useless for me to attempt to carry out my instructions. He was not only civil governor, but the President of the whole Church of Latter-Day Saints upon the earth, their prophet and their priest, receiving, as they all firmly believed, direct revelations of the Divine will, which, according to their creed, form the law of the church. He is, consequently, profoundly revered by all, and possesses unbounded influence and almost unlimited power. I did not anticipate open resistance; but I was fully aware that if the president continued to view the expedition with distrust, nothing could be more natural than that every possible obstruction should be thrown in our way by a "masterly inactivity." Provisions would not be furnished; information would not be afforded; labour could not be procured; and no means would be left untried, short of open opposition, to prevent the success of a measure by them deemed fatal to their interests and safety. So soon, however, as the true object of the expedition was fully understood, the president laid the subject-matter before the council called for the purpose, and I was informed, as the result of their deliberations, that the authorities were much pleased that the exploration was to be made; that they had themselves contemplated something of the kind, but did not yet feel able to incur the expense; but that any assistance they could render to facilitate our operations would be most cheerfully furnished to the extent of their ability. This pledge, thus heartily given, was as faithfully redeemed; and it gives me pleasure here to acknowledge the warm interest manifested and efficient aid rendered, as well by the president as by all the leading men of the community, both in our personal welfare and in the successful prosecution of the work. . . .

The winter season in the valley was long and severe. The vicinity of so many high mountains rendered the weather extremely variable; snows fell constantly upon them, and frequently to the depth of ten inches in the plains. In many of the cañons it accumulated to the depth of fifty feet, filling up the passes so rapidly that, in more than one instance, emigrants who had been belated in starting from the States, were overtaken by the storms in the mountain gorges, and forced to abandon every thing, and escape on foot, leaving even their animals to perish in the snows. All communication with the world beyond was thus effectually cut off; and, as the winter advanced, the gorges became more and more impassable, owing to the drifting of the snow into them from the projecting peaks.

We remained thus shut up until the third of April. Our quarters consisted of a small unfurnished house of unburnt brick or adobe, unplastered, and roofed with boards loosely nailed on, which, every time it stormed, admitted so much water as called into requisition all the pans and buckets in the establishment to receive the numerous little streams which came trickling down from every crack and knot-hole. During this season of comparative inaction, we received from the authorities and citizens of the community every kindness that the most warmhearted hospitality could dictate; and no effort was spared to render us as comfortable as their own limited means would admit. Indeed, we were much better lodged than many of our neighbours; for . . . very many families were obliged still to lodge wholly or in part in their wagons, which, being covered, served, when taken off from the wheels and set upon the ground, to make bedrooms, of limited dimensions it is true, but yet exceedingly comfortable. Many of these were comparatively large and commodious, and, when carpeted and furnished with a little stove, formed an additional apartment or back building to the small cabin, with which they frequently communicated by a door. It certainly argued a high tone of morals and an habitual observance of good order and decorum, to find women and children thus securely slumbering in the midst of a large city, with no protection from midnight molestation other than a wagon-cover of linen and the aegis of the law. In the very next enclosure to that occupied by our party, a whole family of children had no other shelter than one of these wagons, where they slept all the winter, literally out of doors, there being no communication whatever with the inside of their parents' house. . . .

The provisional State government, with all the machinery of executive, legislative, and judicial functionaries, was in regular and harmonious action, under the constitution recently adopted. The jurisdiction of the "State of Deseret" had been extended over and was vigorously enforced upon all who came within its borders, and justice was equitably administered alike to "saint" and "*gentile*"—as they term all who are not of their persuasion. Of the truth of this, as far at least as the gentiles were concerned, I soon had convincing proof, by finding, one fine morning, some twenty of our mules safely secured in the public pound, for trespass upon the cornfield of some pious saint; possession was recovered only by paying the fine imposed by the magistrate and amply remunerating the owner for the damage done to his crops. Their courts were constantly appealed to by companies of passing emigrants, who, having fallen out by the way, could not agree upon the division of their property. The decisions were remarkable for fairness and impartiality, and if not submitted to, were sternly enforced by the whole power of the community. Appeals for protection from oppression, by those passing through their midst, were not made in vain; and I know of at least one instance in which the marshal of the State was despatched, with an adequate force, nearly two hundred miles into the western desert, in pursuit of some miscreants who had stolen off with nearly the whole outfit of a party of emigrants. He pursued and brought them back to the city, and the plundered property was restored to its rightful owner. . . .

In their dealings with the crowds of emigrants that passed through their city, the Mormons were ever fair and upright, taking no advantage of the necessitous condition of many, if not most of them. They sold them such provisions as they could spare, at moderate prices, and such as they themselves paid in their dealings with each other. In the whole of our intercourse with them, which lasted rather more than a year, I cannot refer to a single instance of fraud or extortion to which any of the party was subjected; and I strongly incline to the opinion that the charges that have been preferred against them in this respect, arose either from interested misrepresentation or erroneous information. I certainly never experienced any thing like it in my own case, nor did I witness or hear of any instance of it in the case of others, while I resided among them. Too many that passed through their settlement were disposed to disregard their claim to the land they occupied, to ridicule the municipal regulations of their city, and to trespass wantonly upon their rights. Such offenders were promptly arrested by the authorities, made to pay a severe fine, and in some instances were imprisoned or made to labour on the public works; a punishment richly merited, and which would have been inflicted upon them in any civilized community. In short, these people presented the appearance of a quiet, orderly, industrious, and well-organized society, as much so as one would meet with in any city of the Union, having the rights of personal property as perfectly defined and as religiously respected as with ourselves; nothing being farther from their faith or practice than the spirit of *communism*, which has been most erroneously supposed to prevail among them. The main peculiarity of the people consists in their religious tenets, the form and extent of their church government (which is a theocracy), and in the nature especially of their domestic relations. . . .

It is in their private and domestic relations that this singular people exhibit the widest departure from the habits and practice of all other denominating themselves Christian. I refer to what has been generally termed the "spiritual wife system," the practice of which was charged against them in Illinois, and served greatly to prejudice the public mind in that State. It was then, I believe, most strenuously denied by them that any such practice prevailed, nor is it now openly avowed, either as a matter sanctioned by their doctrine or discipline. But that polygamy does actually exist among them cannot be concealed from any one of the most ordinary observation, who has spent even a short time in this community. I heard it proclaimed from the stand, by the president of the church himself, that he had the right to take a thousand wives, if he thought proper; and he defied any one to prove from the Bible that he had not. At the same time, I have never known any member of the community to avow that he himself had more than one, although that such was the fact was as well known and understood as any fact could be.

If a man, once married, desires to take him a second helpmate, he must first, as with us, obtain the consent of the lady intended, and that of her parents or guardians, and afterward the approval of the seer or president, without which the matter cannot proceed. The woman is then *"sealed"* to him under the solemn sanction of the church, and stands, in all respects, in the same relation to the man, as the wife that was first married. The union thus formed is considered a perfectly virtuous and honourable one, and the lady maintains, without blemish, the same position in society to which she would be entitled were she the sole wife of her husband. Indeed, the connection being under the sanction of the only true priesthood, is deemed infinitely more sacred and binding than any marriage among the gentile world, not only on account of its higher and more sacred authority, but inasmuch as it bears directly upon the future state of existence of both the man and the woman; for it is the doctrine of the church, that no woman can attain to celestial glory *without the husband,* nor can *he* arrive at full perfection in the next world without at least one wife: and the greater the number he is able to take with him, the higher will be his seat in the celestial paradise.

All idea of sensuality, as the motive of such unions, is most indignantly repudiated; the avowed object being to raise up, as rapidly as possible, "a holy generation to the Lord," who shall build up his kingdom on the earth. Purity of life, in all the domestic relations, is strenuously inculcated; and they do not hesitate to declare, that when they shall obtain the uncontrolled power of making their own civil laws, (which will be when they are admitted as one of the States of the Union,) they will punish the departure from chastity in the severest manner, even by death. . . .

Upon the practical working of this system of plurality of wives, I can hardly be expected to express more than a mere opinion. Being myself an "outsider" and a "gentile," it is not to be supposed that I should have been permitted to view more than the surface of what is in fact as yet but an experiment, the details of which are sedulously veiled from public view. So far, however, as my intercourse with the inhabitants offorded me an opportunity of judging, its practical operation was quite different from what I had anticipated. Peace, harmony, and cheerfulness seemed to prevail, where my preconceived notions led me to look for nothing but the exhibition of petty jealousies, envy, bickerings, and strife. Confidence and sisterly affection among the different members of the family seemed pre-eminently conspicuous, and friendly intercourse among neighbours, with balls, parties, and merry-making at each others' houses, formed a prominent and agreeable feature of the society. In these friendly reunions, the president, with his numerous family, mingled freely, and was ever an honoured and welcome guest, tempering by his presence the exuberant hilarity of the young, and not unfrequently closing with devotional exercises the gayety of a happy evening.

There are many other curious points contained in their religious creed, but it is not my purpose here to write a theological treatise upon their views. The effect of the system, as may be well supposed, is to render the people in a high degree separate and peculiar; and to prevent, not only all amalgamation, but even any intimate association, with other communities.

To this irreconcilable difference, not in speculative opinions only, but in habits, manners, and customs necessarily growing out of them, may, I think, in a great measure, be attributed the bitter hostility of the people among whom they formerly dwelt, and which resulted in their forcible expulsion. The same causes of social incompatibility which existed then, exist now, and in much greater strength—the community being freed from the pressure of public opinion that then surrounded them; and, although the freest toleration is (no doubt sincerely) proclaimed toward any who may choose to settle among them, yet I do not see how it is possible for the members of any other Christian societies, all of which are theoretically and practically opposed to their views, to exist among them, without constant collision, jealousy, and strife. The result, therefore, must be the establishment here of a people of one faith, the fundamental principles of whose civil government will, under the lead of the ecclesiastical hierarchy, be framed to accord with that faith, to build up and support it, and to exclude from all participation in its administration every element that does not fully coincide with its requirements. When what is now but a Territory shall have become a sovereign State, with the uncontrolled power of making its own laws, this will undoubtedly be done; and we shall then see in our midst a State as different from the rest of the Union in faith, manners, and customs, as it is widely separated by the vast plains and inhospitable deserts that surround it.

The Runaway Judges

FEW STATES HAVE HAD *such a hectic career in political apprenticeship as Utah. Its experiences in government, prior to the establishment of the territory, were unique in one respect and typically American in another. For the first two years of settlement the Mormons relied on their already existing and well-functioning theocratic organization, which they long had been used to obeying. In 1849 they created a more formal government, the provisional State of Deseret, which continued to operate for about two years. Deseret's successor, the Territory of Utah, was created by the organic act of September 9, 1850, which formed part of that larger legislation known as the Compromise of 1850. The staffing and organization of the new government, however, were not complete until nearly a year later with the arrival in August, 1851, of the last of the three federal judges, Perry E. Brocchus of Alabama.*

Almost immediately the government, at least the judiciary, began to disintegrate. In late September, Chief Justice Lemuel G. Brandebury of Pennsylvania, Brocchus, B. D. Harris of Vermont, territorial secretary, and Henry R. Day, Indian agent, packed their carpetbags and hurried east, deserting the territory and the offices to which they so recently had been appointed. The runaways leveled a blast of criticism at the Mormons which set the tone and pattern for Gentile-Mormon conflict for much of the long territorial period. Their irresponsible incriminations dissolved the good opinion of the Mormons the early overland travelers had given the country and created instead an image of Utah as lawless and seditious—an image that died hard.

The details of the clash and the reasons, at least from the Perry Brocchus point of view, are colorfully expressed in a letter he addressed to the President just prior to his departure from Great Salt Lake City. This letter and other related material, including a lengthy communication to the President signed by the runaway officials, can be found in the Congressional Globe, *32nd. Congress, 1st. session, Appendix (XXV).*

[Great Salt Lake City,
September 20, 1851.]

I shall leave for the States on the 1st October, and most gladly will I go, for I am sick and tired of this place— of the fanaticism of the people, followed by their violence of feeling towards the *"Gentiles,"* as they style all persons not belonging to their Church. I have had a feeling and personal proof of their fanatical intolerance within the last few days. I will give you a cursory view of the circumstances and the scene.

As soon after my arrival here as my illness would permit, I heard from Judge B. and Mr. Secretary H. accounts of the intolerant sentiments of the community towards Government officers and the Government itself, which filled me with surprise. I learned that not only were the officers sent here treated with coolness and disrespect, but that the Government of the United States, on all public occasions, whether festive or religious, was denounced in the most disrespectful terms, and often with invectives of great bitterness. I will mention a few instances. The 24th July is the anniversary of the arrival of the Mormons in this valley. It was on that day of this year that they assembled to commemorate that interesting event. The orator of the day, on that occasion, spoke bitterly of the course of the United States toward the Church of *"Latter Day Saints,"* in taking a battalion of their men from them for the war with Mexico, while on the banks of the Missouri river, in their flight from the mob at Nauvoo. He said the Government of the United States had devised the most wanton, cruel, and dastardly means for the accomplishment of their ruin, overthrow, and utter extermination.

His Excellency Governor Young, on the same occasion, denounced, in the most sacrilegious terms, the memory of the illustrious and lamented General and President of the United States, who has lately gone to the grave, and over whose tomb a nation's tears have scarcely ceased to flow. He exclaimed, *"Zachary Taylor is dead and gone to hell, and I am glad of it!"* and his sentiments were echoed by a loud amen from all parts of the assembly. Then, rising in the excess of his passion to his tiptoes, he vociferated, *"I prophesy, in the name of Jesus Christ, by the power of the priesthood that is upon me, that any other President of the United States, who shall lift his finger against this people, will die an untimely death and go to hell."* This kind of feeling I found pervading the whole community, in some individuals more marked than in others.

You may remember that I was authorized by the managers of the Washington National Monument Society to say to the people of the Territory of Utah, that they would be pleased to receive from them a block of marble or other stone to be deposited in the monument *"as an offering at the shrine of patriotism."* I accordingly called on Governor Young and apprised him of the trust committed to my hands, and expressed a desire to address the people upon the subject, when assembled in their greatest number. He replied that on the following Monday the very best opportunity would be presented. Monday came, and I found myself at their Bowery, in the midst of at least three thousand people. I was respectfully and honorably introduced by *"His Excellency"* to the vast assemblage. I made a speech, though so feeble that I could scarcely stand, and staggered in my debility several times on the platform.

I spoke for two hours, during which time I was favored with the unwavering attention of my audience. Having made some remarks in reference to the judiciary, I presented the subject of the National Monument, and *incidently thereto* (as the Mormons supposed) I expressed my opinions in a full, free, unreserved, yet respectful and dignified manner, in regard to the defection of the people here from the Government of the United States. I endeavored to show the injustice of their feelings towards the Government, and alluded boldly and feelingly to the sacrilegious remarks of Governor Young towards the memory of the lamented Taylor. I defended, as well as my feeble powers would allow, the name and character of the departed hero, from the unjust aspersions cast upon them, and remarked that, in the latter part of the assailant's bitter exclamation that he *"was glad that General Taylor was in hell,"* he did not exhibit a Christian spirit, and that if the author did not early repent of the cruel declaration, he *would perform that task with keen remorse upon his dying pillow.* I then alluded to my nativity; to my citizenship; to my love of country; to my duty to defend my country from unjust aspersions wherever I met them, and trusted that when I failed to defend her, my tongue, then employed in her advocacy and praise, might cling to the roof of my mouth, and that my arm, ever ready to be raised in her defence, might fall palsied at my side. I then told the audience if they could not offer a block of marble in a feeling of full fellowship with the people of the United States, as brethren and fellow-citizens, they had better not offer it at all, but leave it unquarried in the bosom of its native mountain. At the close of my speech the Governor arose and denounced me and the Government in the most brutal and unmeasured terms.

The ferment created by his remarks was truly fearful. It seemed as if the people (I mean a large portion of them) were ready to spring upon me like hyenas and destroy me. The Governor, while speaking, said that some persons might get their hair pulled or *their throats cut on that occasion.* His manner was boisterous, passionate, infuriated in the extreme; and if he had not been afraid of final vengeance, he would have pointed his finger at me, and I should *in an instant* have been a dead man. Ever since then the community has been in a state of intense excitement, and murmurs of personal violence and assassination towards me have been freely uttered by the lower order of the populace. How it will end I do not know. I have just learned that I have been denounced, together with the Government and officers, in the Bowery again today by Governor Young. I hope I shall get off safely. God only knows. I am in the power of a desperate and murderous set. I however feel no great fear. So much for defending my country.

I expect all the officers of the Territory, at least Chief Justice B.,

Secretary Harris, and Captain Day, Indian Agent, will return with me, *to return here no more.*

Jedediah Grant Strikes Back

THE CHARGES OF the "Runaway Judges" against the Mormons could not go unanswered. Jedediah Morgan Grant, first mayor of Salt Lake City and later one of the two chief advisors to Brigham Young, was chosen to give the official reply. After repairing to the East he addressed a series of three letters to James Gordon Bennett, who published the first one in his New York Herald. All three were later gathered into a pamphlet and, as "a rare bit of vigorous English, in masterful, biting style, bold, free, enjoyable," were given wide circulation. Brigham Young said they "were written in a humorous, readable style; for which they were principally indebted to the versatile pen of our friend Colonel Thomas L. Kane." If vigor and pungency of tone are any criterion, the Mormons won the battle of words.

The first set of officials quickly disappeared from the scene to be replaced by a succession of others, some of them as misfit in the Mormon environment as their unhappy predecessors. In any event the executive department in Utah continued in Mormon hands until Brigham Young was replaced by Alfred Cumming in 1858.

The first of the Grant letters, reproduced in part below from the New York Herald of March 9, 1852, carries the burden of the Mormon argument and affords, besides, an entertaining, often satirical picture of personalities and events worthy of Dickens.

JAMES GORDON BENNETT, ESQ.

Sir:—I will thank you to print, as soon as you can, the substance of this letter. Considered only as news, it ought to be worth your while. There is a great curiosity everywhere to hear about the Mormons, and eagerness to know all the evil that can be spoken of them. . . .

I will begin with the original and beginning of our troubles, found, to my mind, in the notion that, unlike other populous communities, we

III · CHRONICLES AND JUDGES

are not fit, or have not the right, to furnish our own rulers. . . . At the very outset of our national career, we had to have strangers sent to govern us. Who of worth and standing at home would venture out to our distant and undescribed country? Accordingly, the offices went begging among all the small-fry politicians who could be suspected of being fit to fill them. And (as I have heard, after sundry nominations were refused) the following were picked up:—

No. 1.—A Mr. Brandebury, who brought his recommendation, saying he had studied law in the office of a Pennsylvania county-court lawyer renowned for successful high and lofty tumbling in the support of the United States Bank through a bloodless civil war, but who, in every other respect, exaggerated the recommendation of a Presidential candidate, of being perfectly and entirely unknown.

No. 2.—Zerubbabel Snow, of Ohio, a lawyer practicing in the interior of that State—qualifications rather ahead of the others—willing to come out probably, having kinsfolk among us.

No. 3.—Mr. P. E. Brocchus, of Alabama, of whom I have again to speak—character unknown, I hope, to the President—in the lower purlieus of the District of Columbia by no means entitled to that recommendation.

No. 4.—B. D. Harris, a smart youngster—from a Vermont printing office, I think—for Secretary.

And for Indian Agent, No. 5, a lazy little fellow named Day—with half the head of a Yankee, for he was all the time thinking of a "trade," and half the heart of a woman, for he would have run from a squaw. . . .

The first we knew of our becoming a Territory was the account of the passage, September, 1850, of the law organizing Utah, which reached us before the year was out. Nothing could exceed the clamorous joy of our citizens at learning that they were thus invited into the family party by their brethren of the Union. Our national flags went up, hailed by huzzas, all over the settlement, and when we hoisted our large one on the liberty pole at Temple Block, in Great Salt Lake City, the artillery saluted it with one hundred rounds, rammed home.

The first actual appearance among us, by personal representative, of the government majesty of the United States, was the arrival of No. 1, as above, which came as much as half a year after (the 7th of June, I think), with a limited amount of personal luggage, including one remarkably large black umbrella, and put up at a boarding house on the outskirts of the town, resorted to by traders and carriers passing through the settlement. We welcomed this from our hearts. We did not fire the cannon at it, having saved this honor for our country's standard, or its enemies. Nor did we attend to appearances as well as the French, who made ready for their king by putting white kid gloves on the guide-posts' fingers, and a clean cambric ruffled shirt and silk stockings on the body of a criminal hanging in irons. Our means, after all, were limited; but we cordially did our best. As it was the Chief Justice, numbers of us paid him our respects; and, though our calls were not returned, proceeded to get up, after our custom, a Ball in his honor. . . .

We had not unmixed cause to be pleased with our new officials. Their speech and conduct, somehow, from the first, created and spread the impression that they wanted to get extra advantage out of us. They complained, not without reason, of the lowness of their salaries; and it was intimated to some that a vote, by ourselves, of a certain increase would be agreeable. They would not organize court, or go to work, but— an ill example to our youth—lived indolent together in their boarding houses, day after day—the only utterly idle persons in our whole community. Yet, at the same time, they assumed airs and graces, and various manners of condescension and superiority; in which, rest assured, they made a very great mistake. It is an error, the prevalent opinion that we all cleanse the nasal orifice with the big toe, and make tea with holy water. We have among us women who play on the piano and mix French with their talk, and men who like tight boots, and who think more of the grammar than the meaning of what they are saying; and who would ask nothing better than to be fed by other people for squaring circles and writing dead languages all their lives—albeit we would not give one good gunsmith's apprentice for the whole of them. And, though we are all out-and-out democrats, in spirit and in substance, we have plenty of the hard-to-comb curly-pates of people, of whom the saying is true, that we "have seen better days"; so that if there is any thing we can do, it is to take the measure of sham, half-cut pretensions, and write down their figures. There was one personal infirmity of Judge Brandebury, I am sure, was as much remarked upon with us as it could be anywhere— even the boarding-house folks were not content with it.

> *Affect in things about thee cleanliness,*
> *That all may gladly board thee as a flower.*

May I hope your readers understand? You see, with our score of spring streams rushing through the city plat, our fresh water lakes, our hot springs, baths and Jordan river, more cleansing than Abana and Pharphar rivers of Damascus—we think so much of washing—And soap is not very dear with us either! And we read the scriptures, including Zechariah iii., 3 and 4, where we are taught that the angel would not speak with Joshua before he changed his linen.—And; whistle! that shirt the Judge had on at our 24th of July celebration, where we did our best to make a dignity figure of him, was the greatest—it came about as near to being *the* great unwashed—considering there were ladies present, it was on the whole, I may say, the most Disrespectful Shirt, ever seen at a celebration. The Judge never stirred out without his big umbrella, not so much to keep the sun off, as to hide out people, no account of his being shy; but, after, this, whenever he was seen dragging about under it, it used to be the joke that he was afraid of rain water getting in on to that shirt. But, of course, no notice was taken of such trifles; and everything went on smooth and glassy as the pool of indolence itself, till after the 17th day of August.—This day, arrived out from the States, Mr. P. E. Brocchus, and in one short six weeks after that this man staid among us, he was the means of stirring up all the evil report that we have had since to encounter. . . .

To our people at Kanesville, where he stopped for other purposes than outfitting, he proclaimed his intention of running as delegate to Congress. He provided intoxicating liquors gratuitously to those in his company who would listen to his discourse on this subject. He said it was his only purpose in going out to Utah; and that, his election secured, he should return at once. He alluded darkly to dangers impending over us at Washington that only he could avert, and declared that he had come out to enable him to be our saviour. Thus he spoke and electioneered with the people of the train till he met a return company, who conveyed intelligence to the States of the election of Dr. John M. Bernhisel. His tone then changed! As soon as he arrived, he announced his intention of returning to the States. He said he was sick, and supported the character in the eyes of his fellow-lodgers by eating enormously, without taking any outdoor exercise. He was hale and busy enough, to our cost. He must have obtained his influence over the others almost immediately after his arrival. They soon removed to the boarding house in which he was quartered; and there evidently, as we think we can see now, concerted their schemes and courses of molestation and mischief. We heard now distinctly more of discontent and dissatisfaction, and more of the insufficient compensation and the rest. . . .

One day Brocchus reminded the Governor that he was going away very soon, and asked him to do him the favor of procuring him as large an audience of the people as possible, as he was very anxious to set before them in style the claims of the Washington monument fund. I do not know how he made out his case; but, as he was always specious and smiling, the Governor, willing to show him a pleasure, said, "I will invite you, sir, to speak at our approaching conference. It is a religious meeting, I suppose you are aware; but I wish well to your cause." One of the first buildings we ever raised at Salt Lake, was our Bowery, or gallery of rough timber and wattles, for public assemblies. Around it then was all naked ground, though it now stands in the heart of the business part of the city. Our semi-annual conferences have always met in it; and our Fall one assembling here by stated appointment, September the 6th; at its opening day, a handsome representation of the people from all quarters being in attendance, Governor Young took the first opportunity of fulfilling his promise. "I was respectfully and honorably introduced," says the published statement of Judge Brocchus. . . .

I am certain no one of his acquaintance at Salt Lake City was prepared for such a speech as he made on this occasion. In its way it beat Brandebury's shirt. I would give a hundred dollars for the sake of our cause, to have had a phonographer[*] to take down the stupendous effort. I can only now profess to remember a few points of it, recalled to my memory by the use that has been made of them since. He began by stating that he had read our history with deep interest, particularly that part relating to our sufferings in winter quarters, on the Missouri River, during the severe winter of '47. I intended to have visited winter quarters, he said, but, alas, was not able. A friend of mine brought me these flowers; here they are; it is all I can present you of that sainted place! At this sympathetic display he forced a tear, and, the careless observer would have said, wiped it from his cheek, but Deseret eyes saw the handerkerchief pass to the right and left, while the tear remained on the cheek by an overcast of the head. His reception was next referred to. I was a stranger and you took me in; sick, and you visited me, &c. Even a kind lady brushed the flies from my forehead; her kindness I can never forget.—Another tear was forthcoming, and wiped as before. Twenty minutes of this sort of thing quite naturally introduced the consideration of his personal merits. In the course of an able and flattering autobiography, he displayed all his advantages of experience and public service in important imaginary capacities. This sort of thing took up an hour more, by which the patience of the company was pretty nearly worn out, though they remained quiet. "For more than two hours," he writes, "I was favored with the unwavering attention of my audience."

---

[*] A shorthand reporter (*Ed. note*).

257

But a changed tone then came on him, with a change of subject. He began a studied assault upon his introducer, Governor Young, and an argument to the people against allowing the man so much influence as he possessed, the sum of it being that so long as this continued we would have no party divisions, and without party divisions we could not be a worthy object of the notice or favor of politicians. Soon, however, he found he could do nothing on this head. "Oh ladies, sweet ladies," he cried, "why do you 'go in' for such a man? Your smiles should be turned on the contemplation of men who can handle the sword—George Washington, and Zachary Taylor, the second Washington. Oh, Governor Young can't handle a sword!" Even such soft appeals as this were thrown away. From bad to worse, disapprobation rose till the orator was groaned. He tried a few insinuations more, and was groaned again, groaned with a will. At this, instead of taking his seat, he changed his ground, and made a direct and undisguised attack upon the audience itself, men and women, without distinction, accusing them of want of patriotism and attachment to the laws, and reproaching and insulting them to their face. General D. H. Wells, of Illinois, an impulsive and hot spoken man, but I am bound to say one of our most liberal and public spirited citizens, had delivered an oration on the 24th of July, severely condemning the course of the federal government towards us. Producing an imperfect report of this speech and commenting on it, Brocchus proceeded to attribute its sentiments to the people, and make them answerable for it, thereupon threatening them with destruction by the whole army and navy of the United States. In the same way he brought up remarks of Governor Young upon General Taylor, threatening the people with destruction for them also, and declaring that his (Brocchus's) influence should break him from office, the instant he arrived in Washington. Finally, the women hissing him here, he mentioned Washington, for the first time in connection with the monument, and as if merely incidentally. "It reminds me, *by the way*," he said, "that I have commission from the Washington Monument Association, to ask of you (the ladies) a block of marble, as the test of your citizenship and loyalty to the government of the United States. But in order for you to do it acceptably, you must become virtuous, and teach your daughters to become virtuous, or your offering had better remain in the bosom of your native mountains."

At this climax of insult, the meeting rose as one man, and their cries and uproar compelled the speaker to take his seat. The tumult continuing, we looked to the other officers of the United States, who had been

258

invited to the stand, to reply; but, as they failed to do so, the Governor being loudly called for, rose and spoke in substance (for I cannot imitate or remember successfully his peculiar style), as follows:—"But for this man's personalities, I would be ashamed not to leave him to be answered by some of our small spouters—sticks of his own timber. Such an orator, I should suppose, might be made by down-east patent, with Comstock's phonetics and elocution primers; but, I ask you all; have we ever before listened to such trash and nonsense from this stand? Are you a Judge, (he said, turning to him), and can't even talk like a lawyer, or a politician, and haven't read an American school history? Be ashamed, you illiterate ranter, (said he), not to know your Washington better than to praise him for being a mere brutal warrior. Washington was called first in war; but he was first in peace, and first in the hearts of his countrymen. He had a big head and a great heart. Of course, he could fight. But, Lord! What man can't? What man here will dare to say, with women standing by, that he is a bit more a coward than Washington was? Handle a sword! I can handle a sword as well as George Washington. I'd be ashamed to say I couldn't. But you, standing there, white and shaking now, at the hornets'-nest you have stirred up yourself—you are a coward; and that is why you have cause to praise men that are not; and why you praise Zachary Taylor. President Taylor you can't praise— you find nothing in him. Old General Taylor! what was he?—a mere soldier, with regular army-buttons on; no better to go at the head of brave troops than a dozen I could pick up between Leavenworth and Laramie. And, for one, I'll not have Washington insulted by having him compared to Taylor, for a single breath of speech. No, nor what is more, President and General Andrew Jackson crowed down and forgotten, while I am with this people—even if I did not know that one is in one place (of punishment), and the other in another (of reward)." Brigham Young spoke this out of his knowledge by the priesthood.

"What's the meaning," continued the Governor, but more at large than I can give it here, "what's the meaning of this insult of our patriotism? Is it the place of miserable vermin that feed upon its sacred body, to teach us the value of the Union? Sense enough you have to see we are bound to be its best friends. But you shall not go home to say you were never told so. Against the Union, are we? We want to have Saint Francisco on one side of us, and Saint Louis on the other, fighting and scratching like any other two saints of different denominations, do we? And the tax on the foreign goods we use isn't enough, to be sure, but we must want to pay one set of duties at a custom-house in New York or New Orleans, and then another at Jefferson City, may be, and another set again at Council Bluffs! That will help us, won't it? No, sir; we're not nailed to North or South, or any other point of the compass, here. We have come out from the North and South as well as East and West, and we want our old States to stick together, because we intend to stick to the whole of them. And we are just the very people to know what tomfool's nonsense it is, the notion of a minority that expects to get into a tight place, going off for safety into close partnership with its next neighbors. Who does not know that there is more bother with a quarrelsome neighbor than with a dozen that live further off. And what is a man's chance if, with a neighbor on each side of him, bent upon mischief, he has no other neighbors to help him keep them straight? It is just the same with States. Let the devil of persecution get abroad against any single one of them, as it did against us at home, and let it be Georgia or Illinois on one side, and North Carolina and Tennessee, or Missouri and Iowa on the other, all ready to join, if one is not enough, to put Charleston or Nauvoo down—and where is Charleston, or South Carolina either, going to be, if she hasn't then one outsider to help her? Now, tell all this, when you return, to some of your folks in Alabama, where you say you belong;—though, if you tell them instead, the Mormons want to get up a union with Selkirk's Settlement, or the Hudson Fur Company, or be annexed by the Mexican half-breeds, or the Indians, (say the Crows, or the Blackfeet, or the Snakes), I know they'd rather believe it.—Snake stories are about all they will believe of the Mormons!" After defining very fully his views after this wise, the Governor concluded, I remember, about as follows:—"What you have not been afraid to intimate about our morals, I will not stoop to notice, except to make my particular personal request of every brother and husband present, not to give your back what such impudence deserves. You talk of things 'you have on hearsay,' since your coming among us. I'll talk of hearsay then—the hearsay that you are discontented and will go home, because we cannot make it worth your while to stay. What it would satisfy you to get out of us I think it would be hard to tell; but I am sure it is more than you'll get. If you or any one else is such a baby-calf, we must sugar your soap to coax you to wash yourself of Saturday nights: go home to mammy straight away, and the sooner the better!"

This is the whole of Governor Young's speech, of which so much to-do has been made. What to make of the strange speech of Brocchus, to this day I am not clear. . . . We could not go on with the church business after the disgraceful occurrence, and our meeting had to be dismissed and dispersed.

After the Brocchus outrage, the story of the misconduct of other officers is soon related. First, we found out, to our astonishment, that neither Brandebury nor Harris were at pains to condemn or disavow his course. Soon we were threatened that Harris would return with Brocchus; not long after we heard the same ill of Brandebury, and soon after this . . . their purpose of doing so was formally announced to us, The Governor, upon this, fearing they might be as good as their word, and leave the territory to legal anarchy, called a special session of the Legislature to consider of the exigency. There was a rupture at once. They would not communicate with that body or notice its existence. The Assembly passed a joint resolution directing the United States Marshal to take into his custody the papers, seals and funds of the Secretary, as about to abscond. He disregarded it, and applying to Judge Brandebury, who, for this special purpose, constituted a United States Court for the first time, obtained an injunction on the marshal against interfering with him. The two houses passing also a resolution directing an order to be drawn for $500 on account of mileage, stationery, &c., out of the $24,000 placed in the Secretary's hands for such expenses; he refused to accept it, and on the contrary, wrote them back an insulting letter, in which he pronounced his (the Secretary's) opinion that they were illegally elected and constituted. This letter, dated September 25, came to the Assembly next day, or Friday, Sept. 26. What they would have done, or what would have been the course of their debates it would be hard to say. But the officers, as if they feared the Assembly really might take the Secretary's objections for more than they were worth, and resign and be reconstituted, which could have been done in a week—the next thing we knew, they were off—Sunday morning, bright and early, September 28, A.D., 1851. . . .

I have concluded my narrative. How far it contains cause of offence, perhaps, I am unable to see; but I am sure it will surprise every one that has perused it, to know that, wretched stitching together of trivialities as it appears, it covers the whole ground of the charges made against us. . . .

I am your very obedient servant,

JEDEDIAH M. GRANT.

261

════════

Critic in Crinoline

BENJAMIN G. FERRIS, *Secretary of the Territory of Utah, and his wife arrived in Salt Lake City late in October, 1852, about the same time as Justice Leonidas Shaver. They managed to stay through the winter— perhaps there was nothing else they could do—and then departed early in May with a company headed for California. Both wrote books dealing with their experiences in Utah. The one by Mrs. Ferris,* The Mormons at Home (*New York, 1856*), *brought together a series of letters originally published in* Putnam's Monthly Magazine *as "Life among the Mormons."*

Fortunately for the peace of Zion, Mrs. Ferris and her husband did not find kindred spirits in the incumbent officials, and soon departed for a more congenial clime. The sophisticated Mrs. Ferris was preoccupied with polygamy. After reading her phrenological vignettes of Mormon characters, who usually are either members of a "harem" or its master, one becomes satiated with terms like "vile institution," "licentious villains," "sinister look," and "wretched specimen." Her tale finally comes to sound like a cracked record.

A still valid appraisal of Mrs. Ferris and her book appeared in Littell's Living Age for June 7, 1856: "Mrs. Ferris, whose book we opened with expectation, is evidently not a fair witness. . . . That Mrs. Ferris, who prides herself on having played the 'fine lady in the prairie,' is not a very philosophical observer—is not very nice in her manners—is not very delicate in her feelings—every page of this odd book bears witness. But, as she professes to state what she saw and heard among the Mormons, we must take her with her faults, and make the best we can of her evidence, with all its drawbacks of vanity, inconsequence, and ill taste."

Her opinionated book, widely advertised and read in its day, but tiresome now in its unrelieved and narrow condemnation, is only briefly sampled here.

April 5 [1853]. I did not intend to say another word about the saints, male or female, but I was tempted yesterday to attend a meeting of the

Council of Health, and am so full of what I saw and heard, that it will be a relief to give a brief account of it. This Council of Health, as it is called, is a sort of female society, something like our Dorcas societies, whose members have meetings to talk over their occasional various aches and pains, and the mode of cure. There are a few who call themselves physicians in the place, and they are privileged to a seat in this important assemblage.

The meeting was in one of the ward school-houses. There were from forty to fifty present, old and young, and, judging from physiognomical indications, they all, with two or three exceptions, belonged to the lowest class of ignorance. There seemed to be no redeeming qualities. The elder were destitute of those mild, refined, and softened feelings, which often form such an agreeable relief to old age. The specimens before me were of the wrinkled, spiteful, hag-like order—time had evidently laid a rough and relentless hand upon them. The younger portion were to me, if anything, more repulsive still—there was no youthful vivacity of appearance or manner. They were stupid, and sensuality had swallowed up all pure womanly feelings.

The meeting was called to order by Dr. Richards, a hoary-headed old sinner, whose looks were sufficiently sanctified to remind you of some of our good deacons at home—but you must not fancy a further resemblance. He made a strange opening for a Council of Health. He said they were in midst of dangerous times—that trouble was brewing for the saints, by disaffected spirits, and, if they were not cut off before their plans ripened, the devil would reign again. At this interesting climax, he brought his hand down as though he intended, then and there, to punch a hole through the heads of one of these spirits. He managed to get up so much ferocity of expression, that I was relieved when he sat down.

A Dr. Sprague, a man having a look of vulgar dissipation, then rose and made a few common-place remarks about health. In the mean time, the women began to manifest much uneasiness, twisting, weaving, and rocking to and fro, as though they intended to do something effective when they got a chance. As soon as Dr. S. sat down, sister Newman bounded up like a cork, and in spiteful and sharp tones said that Mormon women ought not to be subject to pain, but that disease and death must be banished from among them and go to the gentiles, where they belonged; that God would soon glorify his name by cutting off the rotten nations of the earth; and then the women would obey their husbands, love them, wait on them, and, if they wanted more wives, help to get them. It was a rambling tirade, and there was enough more of the same kind, but I can only report the substance. She was succeeded by sister Susanna Lippincot, one of Dr. Richard's houris, and a fair specimen of the degraded class of spiritual wives. One of the sisters near me whispered, "She is full of the Spirit." I could easily see that she was full of spirits that came from the distillery. She advocated pouring down lobelia until the devils were driven out of the body. She fastened her red, gooseberry eyes upon me, and made some ill-natured remarks about the gentiles. She finally broke forth into an unknown tongue, and, as near as I can recollect, these were the words: "Eli, ele, elo, ela—come, coma, como—reli, rele, rela, relo—sela, selo, sele, selum." This gibberish was repeated over two or three times.

Sister Sessions then arose and translated these mysterious words. The interpretation proved to be a mere repetition of what the inspired Susanna had before said in murdered English. Sister Sessions took her seat, and sister Gibbs got up, fully possessed, to overflowing, with the notion of healing, even to the mending of broken limbs, by faith and the laying on of hands. By some unlucky mishap, her arm had been dislocated, and she roundly asserted that it had been instantaneously put into its place by this divine process. But alas! exercise had put her arm out of joint a second time, and she piteously bemoaned her fate with tears, lest the Lord might not condescend to heal her again. She was a wretched case of crazy fanaticism. Others poured forth incoherent nonsense in the same strain.

One woman had a daughter present, who was badly afflicted with scrofula, and expressed a wish to have the remedy applied. The sisters crowded around, and, with the two brothers, laid their right hands upon her, and prayed very much like the Catholics repeating their Aves and Pater Nosters over their heads. Dr. Sprague was then moved by the spirit to bless the patient in an unknown tongue, pronouncing, in a blatant tone, words something like these: "Vavi, vava, vavum—sere, seri, sera, serum." The same sister, who had already acted as interpreter, gave the meaning to these oracular utterances. They proved to be the invocation of great blessings, both temporal and spiritual; she was to have everything that heart could desire; her seed was to outnumber the hosts of Abraham, Isaac, and Jacob. Poor thing, she looked as though she needed some better guaranty for temporal comforts than these empty sounds. She could not have been over eighteen; had a large baby in her lap and another child at home; was poorly clad, and undoubtedly half fed.

My guide-book, Aunty Shearer, was with me. She, too, made some remarks, which, to do her justice, were a good deal more to the purpose.
Sister Sessions again took the floor, and related a dream of the night before, of a remarkable fight between the Lord and the devil. His sooty
majesty came pretty near obtaining the mastery, but was finally overcome, and, as the moral of the affair, the Lord advised her to use lobelia
in curing disease, as that would drive the devil away. With this crowning
dose the meeting adjourned.

This is a faithful account of the meeting, except that I have been compelled to soften down some of the expressions used, which were too gross
to be repeated. It has given me the horrors. I begin to have a superstitious
dread that we may be in some way prevented from leaving at the time
appointed, and our stay in this place indefinitely prolonged.

April 30. To-morrow we turn our backs upon the Mormon capital,
with its wretchedness, abominations, and crimes. We have formed a few
friendly acquaintances, with whom we part with regret; but oh! how rejoiced to escape from a region of human depravity, the terrible features
of which have opened more and more distinctly to view the longer our
sojourn has continued.

Frémont's Artist Observer

ONE OF THE MOST SENSITIVE and articulate observers of the early
Mormon scene in Utah was the Jewish artist and daguerreotypist Solomon Nunes Carvalho. A member of the fifth and final western exploring
expedition of John C. Frémont, Carvalho, with others in the party, arrived
in the Mormon community of Parowan on February 8, 1854, after incredible and nearly tragic hardships crossing the snowbound mountains
of southern Utah. Because of illness Carvalho left the expedition at
Parowan and proceeded north to Salt Lake City to recuperate. From here
early in May he traveled with Brigham Young's entourage south through
the territory, keeping a journal as he went. He continued on to California
and eventually returned to his home in the east.

Carvalho was an artist-photographer of considerable talent; yet it is as
an observer and chronicler of Mormon country that social historians are

most indebted to him. His sympathetic yet objective word pictures of Deseret, its people, and characteristic scenes are most readable, at times poignant. His explanation and appraisal of Mormon institutions, religious and civil, are accurate and believable. He was present at the peace conference between Ute Chief Walker and Brigham Young and has left an historic account of the treaty.

The following extracts from Carvalho are taken from his Incidents of Travel and Adventure in the Far West; with Col. Fremont's Last Expedition *(New York, 1858). The book was originally published in 1856, coincidentally with Frémont's presidential bid, and has gone through five subsequent printings, the latest in 1954.*

I

March 30th [1854].—The weather is very cold, and snow lies on the ground to the depth of six inches.

A stream of living water, twelve feet wide, fresh from the mountains, runs along between the sidewalk and the road—the Temple Block. Seeing a crowd assembled, I approached the spot, and found twelve persons, some of whom had already undergone the ceremony of baptism, and others patiently awaiting. The first immersion I saw was of a lady about 18 years of age. The priest who officiated, was standing up to his waist in the stream, with his coat off, and his sleeves rolled up to his elbows. The lady was handed in, and I noticed the shock on her system which a sudden plunge into cold freezing water must naturally have produced. The baptizer placing one hand on her back, the other on her head, repeated the following words: "I am commissioned by Jesus Christ to baptize you, in the name of the Father, and Son, and of the Holy Ghost. Amen."

He then pushed her over on her back, allowing the water to cover her. She struggled to get out of the water, but her husband remarked that the whole of her head had not been submerged, and insisted that "his wife should be properly baptized." She was consequently dipped effectually a second time, and the poor woman finally made her escape, almost frozen.

The next subject was an old lady of seventy-five years. She tottered into the stream by the aid of her crutch, and underwent the same ceremony. Query: would persons submit to those extraordinary tests if they did not possess faith?

The third person was a young man of about twenty years, with a calm, placid countenance. He underwent the operation without flinching. His face was the impersonation of faith and purity. I should have liked to have painted him as a study for a "St. John." They went each on their respective ways, many of them, I dare say, with the seeds of consumption sown at this moment, fully determined to live a life of piety and virtue.

II

The camp-ground or village where Wakara [Chief Walker] permanently resides, when not travelling, is situated about one mile off the main road, from the city of Nephi, to the Sevier River. Gov. Young made extensive preparations for this treaty. A large cavalcade accompanied him from Great Salt Lake City, composed of Heber C. Kimball, Woodruff, John Taylor, Ezra T. Benson, Lorenzo Young, Erasmus [Erastus] Snow, Parley Pratt (his apostles and advisers), together with about fifty mounted men, and one hundred wagons and teams filled with gentlemen, with their wives and families. This was an imposing travelling party, all following in regular succession; taking the word of command from the leading wagon, in which rode Gov. Brigham Young. One of his wives, an accomplished and beautiful lady, who made her husband's coffee, and cooked his meals for him at every camp, thus making herself a most useful appendage to the camp equipage, as well as an affectionate and loving companion to her spiritual lord while travelling. I sometimes formed a third party on the road, and frequently had my seat at their primitive table, which was, in fine weather, a clean white cloth, spread over the grass; or, in rainy weather, a movable table was arranged in the wagon. Venison, beef, coffee, eggs, pies, etc., were served at every meal.

I have often stopped at the top of some commanding eminence, to see this immense cavalcade, lengthened out over a mile, winding leisurely along the side of a mountain, or trotting blithely in the hollow of some of the beautiful valleys through which we passed, to the sound of musical choruses from the whole party, sometimes ending with

> *"I never knew what joy was*
> *Till I became a Mormon,"*

to the tune of "bonny breastknots." Certainly, a more joyous, happy, free-from-care, and good-hearted people, I never sojourned among. When the cavalcade arrived on the road, opposite to Walker's camp, Gov. Young sent a deputation to inform Wakara that he had arrived, and would be ready to give him an audience at a certain hour, that day.

Wakara sent word back to say, "If Gov. Young wanted to see him, he must come to him at his camp, as he did not intend to leave it to see any body."

When this message was delivered to Gov. Young, he gave orders for the whole cavalcade to proceed to Wakara's camp—"If the mountain will not come to Mahomet, Mahomet must go to the mountain."

The Governor was under the impression that Wakara had changed his mind, and intended to continue the war, and for that reason declined to meet him. But old Wakara was a king, and a great chief. He stood upon the dignity of his position, and feeling himself the representative of an aggrieved and much injured people, acted as though a cessation of hostilities by the Indians was to be solicited on the part of the whites, and he felt great indifference about the result.

Gov. Young, at the expense of the people of Utah, brought with him sixteen head of cattle, blankets and clothing, trinkets, arms and ammunition. I expressed much astonishment, that arms and ammunition should be furnished the Indians. His excellency told me that from their contiguity to the immigrant road, they possessed themselves of arms in exchange and trade, from American travellers. And as it was the object of the Mormons to protect, as much as possible, their people from the aggressions of the Indians, and also from the continual descent upon their towns—begging for food, and stealing when it was not given, he thought it more advisable to furnish them with the means of shooting their own game. The Utah Indians possess rifles of the first quality. All the chiefs are provided with them, and many of the Indians are most expert in their use.

When we approached Wakara Camp, we found a number of chiefs, mounted as a guard of honor around his own lodge, which was in the centre of the camp, among whom were Wakara and about fifteen old chiefs, including Ammon, Squash-Head, Grosepine, Petetnit, Kanoshe (the chief of the Parvains), a San Pete chief, and other celebrated Indians. The Governor and council were invited into Wakara's lodge, and at the request of his excellency, I accompanied them. Wakara sat on his buffalo-robe, wrapped in his blanket, with the old chiefs around him; he did not rise, but held out his hand to Gov. Young, and made room for him by his side.

After the ceremony of shaking hands all round was concluded, our interpreter, Mr. Huntington, made known the object of the Governor's visit, and hoped that the calumet of peace would be smoked, and no more cause be given on either side, for a continuation of ill-feeling, etc.

For five minutes intense silence prevailed, when an old grey headed Utah chief got up, and in the effort, his blanket slipped from his body, displaying innumerable marks of wounds and scars. Stretching aloft his almost fleshless arm, he spoke as follows:—

"I am for war, I never will lay down my rifle, and tomahawk, Americats have no truth—Americats kill Indian plenty—Americats see Indian woman, he shoot her like deer—Americats no meet Indian to fight, he have no mercy—one year gone, Mormon say, they no kill more Indian—Mormon no tell truth, plenty Utahs gone to Great Spirit, Mormon kill them—no friend to Americats more."

The chief of the San Pete Indians arose, and the tears rolled down his furrowed cheeks as he gave utterance to his grievances:

"My son," he said, "was a brave chief, he was so good to his old father and mother—one day Wa-yo-sha was hunting rabbits as food for his old parents—the rifle of the white man killed him. When the night came, and he was still absent, his old mother went to look for her son; she walked a long way through the thick bushes; at the dawn of day, the mother and the son were both away, and the infirm and aged warrior was lonely; he followed the trail of his wife in the bush, and there he found the mother of his child, lying over the body of Wa-yo-sha, both dead from the same bullet. The old woman met her son, and while they were returning home, a bullet from the rifle of Americats shot them both down." He added, "old San Pete no can fight more, his hand trembles, his eyes are dim, the murderer of his wife, and brave Wa-yo-sha, is still living. San Pete no make peace with Americats."

The old warrior sank down exhausted on his blanket.

Wakara remained perfectly silent.

Gov. Young asked him to talk, he shook his head, "No," after the rest had spoken, some of whom were for peace, Wakara said, "I got no heart to speak—no can talk to-day—to-night Wakara talk with great spirit, to-morrow Wakara talk with Governor."

Gov. Young then handed him a pipe, Wakara took it and gave one or two whiffs, and told the Governor to smoke, which he did, and passed it around to all the party; this ended the first interview.

An ox was slaughtered by the orders of Gov. Young and the whole camp were regaled with fresh beef that evening. I made a sketch of Wakara during the time that he sat in council. I also made a likeness of Kanoshe, the chief of the Parvain Indians.

The next morning the council again assembled, and the Governor commenced by telling the chiefs that he wanted to be friends with all the

Indians; he loved them like a father, and would always give them plenty of clothes, and good food, provided they did not fight, and slay any more white men. He brought as presents to them, sixteen head of oxen, besides a large lot of clothing and considerable ammunition. The oxen were all driven into Wakara's camp, and the sight of them made the chiefs feel more friendly.

Wakara, who is a man of imposing appearance, was, on this occasion, attired with only a deer-skin hunting shirt, although it was very cold; his blue blanket lay at his side; he looked care-worn and haggard, and spoke as follows:

"Wakara has heard all the talk of the good Mormon chief. Wakara no like to go to war with him. Sometimes Wakara take his young men, and go far away, to sell horses. When he is absent, then Americats come and kill his wife and children. Why not come and fight when Wakara is at home? Wakara is accused of killing Capt. Gunnison. Wakara did not; Wakara was three hundred miles away when the Merecat chief was slain. Merecats soldier hunt Wakara, to kill him, but no find him. Wakara hear it; Wakara come home. Why not Merecats take Wakara? he is not armed. Wakara heart very sore. Merecats kill Parvain Indian chief, and Parvain woman. Parvain young men watch for Merecats, and kill them, because Great Spirit say—'Merecats kill Indian'; 'Indian kill Merecats.' Wakara no want to fight more. Wakara talk with Great Spirit; Great Spirit say—'Make peace.' Wakara love Mormon chief; he is a good man. When Mormon first come to live on Wakara's land, Wakara give him welcome. He give Wakara plenty bread, and clothes to cover his wife and children. Wakara no want to fight Mormon; Mormon chief very good man; he bring plenty oxen to Wakara. Wakara talk last night to Payede, to Kahutah, San Pete, Parvain—all Indian say, 'No fight Mormon or Merecats more.' If Indian kill white man again, Wakara make Indian howl."

The calumet of peace was again handed around, and all the party took a smoke. The council was then dissolved.

Gov. Young intended to visit all the settlements south, to Harmony City. Wakara told his excellency that "he and his chiefs would accompany him all the way and back, as a body-guard." Grosepine, Ammon, Squash-head, Wakara and his wife, Canoshe and his wife, and about thirty Indian young men, all mounted on splendid horses, got ready to accompany the Governor's party. During the day, a great many presents were distributed among the tribe.

When I returned to our camp, I saw a crowd around the Governor's wagon. I approached, and found that his excellency had just concluded a purchase from the Utahs of two children, about two to three years of age. They were prisoners, and infants of the Snake Indians, with whom the Utahs were at war. When the Governor first saw these deplorable objects, they were on the open snow, digging with their little fingers for grassnuts, or any roots to afford sustenance. They were almost living skeletons. They are usually treated in this way—that is, literally starved to death by their captors. Gov. Young intended to send them to Salt Lake City, and have them cared for and educated like his own children. I never saw a more piteous sight than those two *naked infants,* in bitter cold weather, on the open snow, reduced by starvation to the verge of the grave—no, not the grave; for if they had died, they would have been thrown on the common for the wolves to devour!

III

The morning after my arrival [at Cedar City], I arose very early, and taking my sketch-book along, I sauntered around the city; in the course of my peregrinations, I saw a man walking up and down before an adobe shanty, apparently much distressed; I approached him, and inquired the cause of his dejection; he told me that his only daughter, aged six years, had died suddenly in the night; he pointed to the door, and I entered the dwelling.

Laid out upon a straw mattress, scrupulously clean, was one of the most angelic children I ever saw. On its face was a placid smile, and it looked more like the gentle repose of healthful sleep than the everlasting slumber of death.

Beautiful curls clustered around a brow of snowy whiteness. It was easy to perceive that it was a child lately from England, from its peculiar conformation. I entered very softly, and did not disturb the afflicted mother, who reclined on the bed, her face buried in the pillow, sobbing as if her heart would break.

Without a second's reflection I commenced making a sketch of the inanimate being before me, and in the course of half-an-hour I had produced an excellent likeness.

A slight movement in the room caused the mother to look around her. She perceived me, and I apologized for my intrusion; and telling her that I was one of the Governor's party who arrived last night, I tore the leaf out of my book and presented it to her, and it is impossible to describe the delight and joy she expressed at its possession. She said I was an angel sent from heaven to comfort her.

She had no likeness of her child.

I bid her place her trust in Him "who giveth and taketh away," and left her indulging in the excitement of joy and sorrow. I went out unperceived by the bereaved father, who was still walking up and down, buried in grief. I continued my walk, contemplating the strange combination of events, which gave this poor woman a single ray of peace for her sorrowing heart.

When I was about starting the next day, I discovered in the wagon a basket filled with eggs, butter, and several loaves of bread, and a note to my address containing these words—"From a grateful heart."

The Gallant Lieutenant

LATE IN THE SUMMER of 1854 Lieutenant Colonel E. J. Steptoe, in command of a body of troops on orders for California, arrived in Salt Lake City. Apparently his primary duty was to deliver a group of Dragoon recruits to posts on the Pacific coast. En route, however, he received a commission as governor of the Territory of Utah. This prospect, together with collateral duties directing him to deal with the Indians responsible for the killing of Captain John W. Gunnison the year before, caused Steptoe and his troops to spend the winter of 1854–5 in the territory. A critical situation was relieved when Steptoe declined the governorship and, along with other Gentile officials, joined the Mormons in urging the reappointment of Brigham Young.

History and the Saints themselves remember Steptoe as a gentleman. But the soldiers since time immemorial have been the bane of civilians, and many of Steptoe's officers and men were no exception. The troops had their eyes on the women, designs the Mormons could hardly approve.

Among Steptoe's officers was young and debonair Lieutenant Sylvester Mowry, who, in the eyes of Zion's young ladies, no doubt cut a fancier figure than the local boys. He was, to put it mildly, somewhat careless in his morals. And he was careless enough to say so. The gallant lieutenant's letters to a friend Edward J. Bicknall of Providence, Rhode Island, add a rare page to Mormon social history. In three letters written from Salt Lake City during the winter, Mowry told his friend, without guile or subterfuge and with candor to spare, about his relations with the civilians, particularly the women, freely admitting he did what his hosts feared he would do. His "conquests" were not empty brags. Mormon pulpits warned the Saints all winter against consorting with the soldiers. Brigham Young himself bore witness that the worst fears were realized: in a sermon in June, 1855, in language as unabashed as Mowry's, he fulminated against the soldiers and the girls who had chosen to leave with them earlier in the spring.

The letters printed here, never before published, were obtained through the courtesy of C. Corwith Wagner of St. Louis, Missouri, a collector of rare correspondence.

I

Salt Lake City U. T.
Sept 17th 1854

My Dear Bicknall

We are here in the heart of the Mormon city. Encamped in Union Square. This letter I send to California to be mailed to you from there as we have reports from the Fort Laramie that the Indians have blockaded the road to the States. . . .

Since I wrote you of our arrival we have been down the Valley south and West to Rush Valley where our animals are to be wintered. While there by order of Colonel Steptoe, my company was mounted and organized as Mounted Rifles so the subscriber doesn't go on foot any more for some time. My own horses (I keep two) are as pretty specimens of horse flesh as you could wish to see, one of them *"Pet"* kicked a man's under jaw to pieces the other day but he is usually pretty quiet.

I·may as well tell you here that it is more than probable we shall have Indian difficulties this winter and as all things are uncertain in this world, before I go out to do any fighting I am going to make my *will*.

I don't expect to be killed but as I have a good head of hair some Indian might be inclined to lift it, if he got a chance. I shall leave my will in safe hands to be forwarded to you. Should anything happen to me with the exception of a few little presents all I have I shall give to Celia. I write you this that there may be no misunderstanding about my wishes among my friends. And now let us turn to a more pleasant subject.

All you have ever heard about polygamy here is true and a damned sight more. Brigham Young has a great number of wives. . . . No one can tell how many, about fifty seems to be the general opinion. The other dignitaries in proportion. The Governor (Young) is as keen as the Devil.

He is an absolute Dictator here and is regarded as the direct delegate of God on Earth. I was at the Tabernacle last Sunday and the preaching was richer in some phases and more disgusting in others than you could well imagine. The Tabernacle holds about three thousand people and it was jammed full. Heber C Kimball the second man in the Mormon Church spoke. He openly advocated implicit obedience to Brigham Young and himself and denounced any one disobeying in the slightest degree. His *"Speech"* was full of such expressions as *"We are white folks."* *"You can't come it"* addressed to us. Speaking of our coming into the Valley of G. S. Lake he said we should be treated better than we were ever before, but we must keep our "hands off" the women. Then he said "Women, don't break the commandment. Keep yourself pure" &c &c. . . . Brigham's daughter in law is the prettiest woman I have seen yet. Her husband is on a mission and she is as hot a thing as you could wish. I am going to make the attempt and if I succeed and don't get my head blown off by being caught shall esteem myself some.

There are a great many disaffected persons here. Many women who rebel against the plurality wife system. Brigham's daughter among others. . . . The fact is the system on the surface and superficially examined looks well enough but within it is as corrupt as hell. To see one man openly parading half a dozen or more women to church with as many more "confined" at home is the devil according to my ideas of morality virtue and decency. . . . The big men of the Church are all rich and getting richer. The lower classes poor and doing no better fast. They pay one tenth of all property owned or made into the Church. If any man becomes troublesome he is ordered off on a mission—and he has to go. Brigham's son, husband of the pretty woman I mentioned, raised hell so he was sent off to arrest the scandal of his debaucheries and so presently he is a missionary. More anon.

For ourselves, we go into winter quarters from here if the Indians do not require our presence. For the officers one of the finest houses in the City has been hired. It was built to accommodate a number of wives, I believe, and makes good bachelor's quarters. At present I am living at the Union Hotel. Sleeping in Camp. Some of the gentlemen are boarding in private families—but we have made no permanent arrangements as yet except about the horses. The men's quarters are fine new buildings and we can be very comfortable.

The people here are social, gay and like every thing like parties. There are to be three dancing parties this week. Good music and pretty dancers.

By the way I forgot to tell you that the Church music consisted of half a dozen violins and a clarinet.

Many pretty women well dressed on occasion give a charming air to all their assemblies at the Tabernacle or Chamber and if it were not for their damnable system of espionage—better than that of the old Inquisition or Napoleon's police—we could get along well. They are jealous lecherous and revengeful in all that concerns women I believe. It will require tact and shrewdness on the part of woman and man to conduct an intrigue successfully, but I think it can be done. Write me often. Send me papers particularly the Journal. With very warmest regards to all at home believe me

Ever yours,
Sylvester Mowry

II

G. S. L. City U. T.
December 31st 1854

My Dear Bicknall

I write you via California as the direct mail route to the States is probably cut off by the Indians. They are raising hell all through the new Territories and we anticipate a severe Indian war during the next year.

Since I wrote you, we have gone on quietly here in quarters, in perfect harmony with our friends the Mormons except on two occasions. A week or two ago at the Theatre (which by the way is a very good one), one of the soldiers was drunk. He got into a fight with a Mormon, and it gave promise to be a very pretty little "muss." The officers were promptly on hand however, and succeeded in stopping it. I "went in" and was knocked down early in the action but not hurt. On Christmas the quarrel broke out again in the Streets. Quite a mob collected (three hundred about) stones were thrown, shots fired from pistols and rifles. Fortunately, owing to the coolness of Lieut Allston who was "officer of the day" and of the Mayor, the mob was dispersed with no greater injury than a few black eyes and "banged up" faces. We were all absent in another part of the city but soon arrived on the spot. The men were sent to their quarters and kept there. It is generally believed that this last affair was commenced by the citizens.

We have every reason to believe that the authorities and the well judging part of the community are favorably disposed towards us and have done and will do every thing in their power to make our stay pleasant—except in the case of admitting us quickly to the society of their women. In this they are inflexible and perhaps wisely so for gallantry and polygamy are congenial associates.

Chief Justice Kinney of the Supreme Court gave a complimentary party on Tuesday evening last to Col Steptoe and the officers of his command. It was a very pleasant affair. The Governor Brigham was there with part of his family—four or five very pretty women. All the principal men of the Church were there some with daughters some with first wives some with "Spirituals." To give you an idea of the richness of this favourite institution Elder Woodruff—one of the Twelve Apostles took me up to an old lady about fifty and introducing me said this is Mrs. Woodruff, then turning to a pretty plump girl about fifteen years old said—This is—um—ah—*also* Mrs. Woodruff.

There were many very pretty well dressed clean girls. I danced with the Gov's daughters and a few others.

Tomorrow the Gov. Brigham—gives us a great party. It is expected to be a fine affair. I wrote you about my being in love with the Gov's daughter in law Mary Young and that her husband was on a mission. The affair went on quietly but swimmingly for several weeks. I met her privately. She owned "the soft impeachment" and I was just about to congratulate myself on my victory when Brigham found it out. A damned infamous report was circulated in the city that I had been "caught in the act" by several persons. Here was hell. Mary was at home—not allowed to go out, frightened nearly to death and this cursed story in everybody's mouth. I had only one course to pursue. I could not trace the story to its source so I resolved to go to Brigham and tell him the story was an infamous lie. Well I called on him—had a long talk in private, which I will tell you sometime and succeeded in getting Mary very gracefully out of the scrape.

At the party the other night, I asked Brigham if he objected to my dancing with her. He replied "No"—and carried his politeness so far as to ask me to take her down to supper—which of course I did with much pleasure. So the affair stands now. I am waiting like Micawber for something to "turn up." Meanwhile my reputation is ruined among the females or rather among those who have the care of the females. They think me *dangerous* and I can't get a woman to look at me scarcely except in the ballroom. They will walk or ride perhaps with another officer but the old people although they treat me with much politeness advise the young ladies not to go with me anywhere. With the greatest difficulty I persuaded a pretty girl and a great favorite with us to let me take her home from Judge Kinneys party and when I had got her into the carriage she laid down in my arms let me feel her bust &c &c—Showing that the difficulty is not with the women but with their keepers. Now Ned, if I had done anything to establish such a reputation I would not care a damn—but to be called a "dangerous man" having accomplished nothing is rather steep—because it ruins my chance for the future I am afraid entirely. Mary is accessible if I can get the opportunity but "theres the rub." The other little piece that I took home from the party can be got down I believe, but *alas,* there appears to be no chance.

In default of more legitimate amusement Capt Ingalls, myself and three gentlemen have been playing "Draw Poker" for the last three weeks. . . .

Pray give my love to Charles if he is with you—and all my friends

Believe me best wishes
Ever yours
Sylvester Mowry

III

Camp Rush Valley
Utah Territory April 27th/55

My Dear Ned

. . . Mary Young I had to give up. Brigham sent me word that if I took her away he would have me killed before I could get out of the Territory. He is a man of his word in little matters of this sort and I concluded I had better not do it, although I went back to the city purposely to get her. We wrote each other affectionate notes. She swears she will run away and join me in California—and so it ends for the present if not for ever.

You have no idea what excitement has been created about Mary and myself. Everybody talks about it. Colonel Steptoe sent me an order not to come to the City again and privately sent me word that it would not be safe as Brigham was raving mad about it. Some damned scoundrel had written to him that Mary was going with me and that I had come after her. Mary knew it would be unsafe and at the last moment told me so and said she would wait. I am afraid I should have been fool enough to have tried to carry her off if she had said "go" and it would have ended in her being brought back and my "hair being raised." Better as it is. . . .

Col. Steptoe has not yet occupied the governorship of Utah. He will have a happy time if he does accept.

This is a great country. More than half of the women want to leave with us or with somebody. Everybody has got one except the Colonel and Major. The Doctor has got three—mother and two daughters. The mother cooks for him and the daughters sleep with him.

The Lord go with the fellows of the other party for they are hombres de bien. It was hard work saying goodbye.

One of our party Captain Ingalls has been indicted and is now being tried in the City for *abducting* a pretty little girl—but it is damned absurd. She wanted to go. Her brother drew a six shooter on the Captain and your friend the subscriber stepped in front of it until Ingalls could get out of the way. There was some talk about my coolness saving his life &c &c but I knew damned well that he would not shoot me—and I didn't believe he would shoot at all. Nor did he. Write to me at Benicia.

With warm regard
Ever yours
S Mowry

═════════

A French Botanist Attends a Mormon Conference

FOREIGN OBSERVERS *soon found their way to the Mormon capital, whose fame, thanks to energetic Mormon missionaries, spread far and wide. Mormon periodicals like the* Millennial Star *in Liverpool,* Skandinaviens Stjerne *in Copenhagen, and* Etoile du Deseret *in Paris gave intriguing news of the American far west. In the fall of 1855, Jules Remy, the French botanist, and his scholar companion, Julius Brenchley, came to see for themselves, traveling to Salt Lake City by way of California and the Humboldt route. The result of their month's stay was Remy's* Voyage au Pays des Mormons, *which appeared in Paris in 1860, and an English edition in two imposing volumes titled* A Journey to Great Salt Lake City, *by both Remy and Brenchley, which appeared the next year in London, with an "Introduction on the Religious Movement in the United States" by Remy.*

Ponderous disquisitions on the history, religion, and customs of the Mormons, not always based on intimate knowledge, interlard their per-

278

sonal observations, though a contemporary reviewer judged that Remy's work would "secure him no mean place among the speculative moralists of his country." While critical of things the pair did not like or understand, they were more sympathetic than many American contemporaries.

In the excerpt below from the 1861 edition of A Journey to Great Salt Lake City, *they attend the October general conference of the church. They describe it to the advantage of the Saints, though they could find little to praise in some of the sermons.*

The general affairs of the Church are regulated twice a year in the temple of the Great Salt Lake City, in the months of April and October, at public conferences which last several days. We were fortunate enough to assist at one of these oecumenical meetings, that which opened on the 6th of October, 1855. More than ten thousand of the faithful, convoked by an epistle from the Great Council, had come together from all parts of the Territory, to hear and receive the word of the Prophet-President and of the other ecclesiastical leaders. The Jerusalem of the American desert displayed an animation and life resembling the movement in the Eternal City during the Carnival and Holy Week, but then, in this case, the solemn business of the moment was, it must be acknowledged, unmixed with any profane amusements. Everywhere were to be seen rustic wagons, drawn by mules, oxen, or horses, going on fast or slow, and filled with Saints of both sexes, whose costume—varied without any attempt at show, picturesque in its simplicity—would have attracted the pencil of an artist. We most gladly availed ourselves of so favorable an opportunity to study the Mormon worship in its teaching and practice. The pope of the Saints did us the favor of inviting us to form part of his retinue on the pontifical platform; but while fully sensible of this attention, we preferred, in order to get a better notion of what was going on, to remain in the crowd. It was in the Bowery, already alluded to, that the conference took place. The faithful were expected to assemble twice a day, just as they do on Sundays. At each meeting, the religious exercises began as soon as the president announced that the business of the day was to begin. Then the choristers and band belonging to the choir executed a piece of one of our greatest masters; and we feel bound to say that the Mormons have a feeling for sacred music, that their women sing with soul, and that the execution is in no notable degree surpassed by that which is heard either under the roof of Westminster, or the frescoes of the Sistine chapel. The music finished, the officiating priest extemporizes a prayer, often long enough, in which he returns thanks to God for his mercies, and makes known to him the wants of the people. At the end of the prayer all the faithful respond "Amen." Then the choir sing a hymn, after which one or more sermons follow. When the preachers have done, the choristers sing a Psalm, accompanied with music, at the close of which, the officiating priest pronounces a blessing on all present, and so the service ends. Such invariably is the order of the religious services. When the communion is celebrated, the ceremony takes place immediately after the Psalm.

One of the peculiarities of the Mormon service which most struck us was, that the officiating priests and high dignitaries, dressed in the customary way, generally kept their hats ° on, the people remaining uncovered. We did not observe that Brigham Young uncovered himself once during the service, but he rose whenever he spoke; and while pronouncing the blessing, he held his arms raised and the hands extended just as a Catholic priest does when he intones the preface.

The sermons or discourses have no precise limits either in length or number. The head officiating priest, who has the title of President, allows any one to speak who desires it, according to his caprice or good pleasure. It is at the close of the sermon that the affairs of the Church are treated of, that they proceed to the appointment of the high functionaries and to the choice of the persons who are to be sent on distant missions into the five parts of the world. The Mormons have few preachers who can be considered accomplished speakers. The two brothers Pratt, Orson and Parley, are beyond dispute the best, and, we should say, the only orators that we heard; what with their easy elocution, their agreeable delivery, purity of language, knowledge of the laws of composition, consecutiveness of ideas, logical deduction from the principles they lay down, they possess whatever is requisite for real rhetorical excellence. Hence they may be listened to with interest, and without weariness; but this is by no means the case with the other preachers, whose strange ramblings appear to be more to the taste of the hearers. Brigham Young . . . is not without a certain kind of natural eloquence which is very pleasing to his people; and though he has had but little experience, he easily maintains a position among the Mormon orators immediately after the two brothers we have mentioned.

° However, Kimball [Heber C. Kimball, counselor to Brigham Young] said one day before a numerous audience, "I never feel disposed to remain with my hat on in the presence of Brigham. It seems to me that the *master ought to keep on his hat,* or rather to hang it on the peg which God has made for this purpose, which is, of course, his head."

Handcarts to Zion

MORMON PROSELYTES IN EUROPE and in the eastern United
States were usually impatient to "gather to Zion." Despite the distance
and the difficulties of travel by sailship and ox-team, eighty thousand
converts made their way to Utah by 1869, when the transcontinental
railroad ended pioneer hardships. Meanwhile, teams and wagons to
carry Mormon immigrants from the frontier terminal to the Salt Lake
Valley were costly, taxing every resource. The Perpetual Emigrating
Fund, a revolving fund founded in 1849 to help poor converts from
the states and abroad come to Zion, found itself temporarily exhausted
in 1855—crops had failed, the ensuing winter proved severe, and stock
died off in great numbers. Brigham Young proposed a cheaper mode
of transportation, a plan that would reduce the cost of passage from
Liverpool to Salt Lake to as little as ten pounds: "Let them come on
foot with handcarts or wheelbarrows; let them gird up their loins and
walk through and nothing shall hinder or stay them."

Early in 1856 word went to England, where 1,300 Saints eagerly responded to the first handcart call. They crossed the Atlantic in chartered
sailing vessels, like so many Mormon emigrants before them, but at the
railroad terminal in Iowa City in May they formed into five handcart
companies. The first three companies, made up of a hundred carts, with
nine hundred men, women, and children serving as wheel teams, leaders,
and pushers, arrived in the Salt Lake Valley late in September without
mishap, to be greeted with music and great rejoicing. In good health
and spirits, they felt themselves superior to the ox-trains:

> Who cares to go with the wagons?
>   Not we who are free and strong;
> Our faith and arms, with a right good will,
>   Shall pull our carts along.

But disaster overtook the remaining two companies—four hundred
English, Scots, Scandinavians, and Germans under James G. Willie and
Edward Martin. Their carts, crudely constructed of green lumber that
shrank in the heat and wooden axles that wore out, needed frequent

repairs. Blind faith prevailed over experienced counsel and they set out late from Florence, Nebraska, only to be caught in the highlands of Wyoming by early storms. With rations used up and strength failing, they were in pitiful condition when rescue teams from the Salt Lake Valley reached them. Some sixty-seven lost their lives. Others lost their frost-bitten limbs, to live on as crippled reminders of the grimmest ordeal in Mormon immigration history. "When those persons arrive," said Brigham Young, making the handcart survivors the subject of his Sunday sermon, ". . . I want them distributed in this city among the families that have good, comfortable houses; and I wish the sisters now before me, and all who know how and can, to nurse and wait upon them. . . . Prayer is good, but when baked potatoes, and pudding, and milk are needed, prayer will not supply their place."

The tragedy dampened the high hopes for what had begun as a bold and imaginative experiment. Yet ten companies—nearly three thousand people—traveled by handcart between 1856 and 1860. Thereafter "church teams" from the Valley fetched the convert-immigrants from the advancing railroad terminal.

Mormon handcart travel, a unique episode in American overland history, has been labeled both failure and success. The John Chislett narrative, reproduced here in part from T. B. H. Stenhouse, Rocky Mountain Saints *(New York, 1873), sees it as a terrible mistake. A British convert, he traveled with the ill-fated Willie company in 1856. His story, written after he fell out with the church, is an unrelieved recital of suffering brought on by poor leadership and worse luck. Mary Ann Hafen, Swiss immigrant in a later company, fared better. Her girlhood remembrance, excerpted through the courtesy of L. R. Hafen as the second selection below from* Recollections of a Handcart Pioneer *of 1860 (Denver, 1938; copyright 1938 by L. R. Hafen), is more typical.*

I

As we travelled along [across Iowa], we presented a singular, and sometimes an affecting appearance. The young and strong went along gaily with their carts, but the old people and little children were to be seen straggling a long distance in the rear. Sometimes, when the little folks had walked as far as they could, their fathers would take them on their carts, and thus increase the load that was already becoming too heavy as the day advanced. . . . The most affecting scene, however, was to see a mother carrying her child at the breast, for mile after mile, until nearly exhausted. The heat was intense, and the dust suffocating, which rendered our daily journeys toilsome in the extreme. . . .

A little less than four weeks' travelling brought us to the Missouri river. We crossed it on a steam ferry-boat, and encamped at the town of Florence, Nebraska, six miles above Omaha, where we remained about a week, making our final preparations for crossing the plains.

The elders seemed to be divided in their judgement as to the practicability of our reaching Utah in safety at so late a season of the year, and the idea was entertained for a day or two of making our winter quarters on the Elkhorn, Wood river, or some eligible location in Nebraska; but it did not meet with general approval. A monster meeting was called to consult the people about it.

The emigrants were entirely ignorant of the country and climate—simple, honest, eager to go to "Zion" at once, and obedient as little children to the "servants of God." Under these circumstances it was natural that they should leave their destinies in the hands of the elders. . . . These men prophesied in the name of God that we should get through in safety. Were we not God's people, and would he not protect us? Even the elements he would arrange for our good, etc. But Levi Savage used his common sense and his knowledge of the country. He declared positively that to his certain knowledge we could not cross the mountains with a mixed company of aged people, women, and little children, so late in the season without much suffering, sickness, and death. He therefore advised going into winter quarters without delay; but he was rebuked by the other elders for want of faith, one elder even declaring that he would guarantee to eat all the snow that fell on us between Florence and Salt Lake City. Savage was accordingly defeated, as the majority were against him. . . .

We started from Florence about the 18th of August, and travelled in the same way as through Iowa, except that our carts were more heavily laden, as our teams could not haul sufficient flour to last us to Utah; it was therefore decided to put one sack (ninety-eight pounds) on each cart in addition to the regular baggage. Some of the people grumbled at this, but the majority bore it without a murmur. Our flour ration was increased to a pound per day; fresh beef was issued occasionally, and each "hundred" had three or four milch cows. The flour on the carts was used first, the weakest parties being the first relieved of their burdens. . . .

We reached Laramie about the 1st or 2d of September, but the provisions, etc., which we had expected were not there for us. Captain

Willie called a meeting to take into consideration our circumstances, condition, and prospects, and to see what could be done. It was ascertained that at our present rate of travel and consumption of flour, the latter would be exhausted when we were about three hundred and fifty miles from our destination! It was resolved to reduce our allowance from one pound to three-quarters of a pound per day, and at the same time to make every effort in our power to travel faster. We continued this rate of ration from Laramie to Independence Rock. . . .

We had not travelled far up the Sweetwater before the nights, which had gradually been getting colder since we left Laramie, became very severe. . . . Cold weather, scarcity of food, lassitude and fatigue from over-exertion, soon produced their effects. Our old and infirm people began to droop, and they no sooner lost spirit and courage than death's stamp could be traced upon their features. Life went out as smoothly as a lamp ceases to burn when the oil is gone. At first the deaths occurred slowly and irregularly, but in a few days at more frequent intervals, until we soon thought it unusual to leave a camp-ground without burying one or more persons.

Death was not long confined in its ravages to the old and infirm, but the young and naturally strong were among its victims. Men who were, so to speak, as strong as lions when we started our journey, and who had been our best supports, were compelled to succumb to the grim monster. These men were worn down by hunger, scarcity of clothing and bedding, and too much labor in helping their families. Weakness and debility were accompanied by dysentery. This we could not stop or even alleviate, no proper medicine being in the camp; and in almost every instance it carried off the parties attacked. It was surprising to an unmarried man to witness the devotion of men to their families and to their faith, under these trying circumstances. Many a father pulled his cart, with his little children on it, until the day preceding his death. I have seen some pull their carts in the morning, give out during the day, and die before the next morning. These people died with the calm faith and fortitude of martyrs. Their greatest regret seemed to be leaving their families behind them, and their bodies on the plains or mountains instead of being laid in the consecrated ground of Zion. . . . When we pitched our camp in the evening of each day, I had to lift the sick from the wagon and carry them to the fire, and in the morning carry them again on my back to the wagon. When any in my hundred died I had to inter them; often helping to dig the grave myself. . . .

284

As we were resting for a short time at noon a light wagon was driven into our camp from the west. It occupants were Joseph A. Young and Stephen Taylor. They informed us that a train of supplies was on the way, and we might expect to meet it in a day or two. More welcome messengers never came from the courts of glory than these two young men were to us. They lost no time after encouraging us all they could to press forward, but sped on further east to convey their glad news to Edward Martin and the fifth handcart company who left Florence about two weeks after us, and who it was feared were even worse off than we were. As they went from our view, many a hearty "God bless you" followed them.

We pursued our journey with renewed hope. . . . We finally, late at night, got all to camp—the wind howling frightfully and the snow eddying around us in fitful gusts. But we had found a good camp among the willows, and after warming and partially drying ourselves before good fires, we ate our scanty fare, paid our usual devotions to the Deity and retired to rest with hopes of coming aid.

In the morning the snow was over a foot deep. Our cattle strayed widely during the storm, and some of them died. But what was worse to us than all this was the fact that *five persons* of both sexes lay in the cold embrace of death. . . . We buried these five people in one grave, wrapped only in the clothing and bedding in which they died. We had no materials with which to make coffins, and even if we had, we could not have spared time to make them, for it required all the efforts of the healthy few who remained to perform the ordinary camp duties and to look after the sick—the number of whom increased daily on our hands, notwithstanding so many were dying.

The morning before the storm, or, rather, the morning of the day on which it came, we issued the last ration of flour. On this fatal morning, therefore, we had none to issue. We had, however, a barrel or two of hard bread which Captain Willie had procured at Fort Laramie in view of our destitution. This was equally and fairly divided among all the company. Two of our poor broken-down cattle were killed and their carcasses issued for beef. With this we were informed that we would have to subsist until the coming supplies reached us. All that now remained in our commissary were a few pounds each of sugar and dried apples, about a quarter of a sack of rice and a small quantity (possibly 20 or 25 lbs.) of hard bread. The brother who had been our commissary all the way from Liverpool had not latterly acted in a way to merit the confidence of the company; but it is hard to handle provisions and suffer hunger at the same time, so I will not write a word of condemnation. These few scanty supplies were on this memorable morning turned over to me by Captain Willie, with strict injunctions to distribute them only to the sick and to mothers for their hungry children, and even to them in as sparing a manner as possible. . . .

Being surrounded by snow a foot deep, out of provisions, many of our people sick, and our cattle dying, it was decided that we should remain in our present camp until the supply-train reached us. It was also resolved in council that Captain Willie with one man should go in search of the supply-train and apprise its leader of our condition, and hasten him to our help. When this was done we settled down and made our camp as comfortable as we could. As Captain Willie and his companion left for the West, many a heart was lifted in prayer for their success and speedy return. They were absent three days—three days which I shall never forget. The scanty allowance of hard bread and poor beef, distributed as described, was mostly consumed the first day by the hungry, ravenous, famished souls.

We killed more cattle and issued the meat; but, eating it without bread did not satisfy hunger, and to those who were suffering from dysentery it did more harm than good. This terrible disease increased rapidly amongst us during these three days, and several died from exhaustion. Before we renewed our journey the camp became so offensive and filthy that words would fail to describe its condition, and even common decency forbids the attempt. . . . During that time I visited the sick, the widows whose husbands died in serving them, and the aged who could not help themselves, to know for myself where to dispense the few articles that had been placed in my charge for distribution. Such craving hunger I never saw before, and may God in his mercy spare me the sight again.

As I was seen giving these things to the most needy, crowds of famished men and women surrounded me and begged for bread! Men whom I had known all the way from Liverpool, who had been true as steel in every stage of our journey, who in their homes in England and Scotland had never known want; men who by honest labor had sustained themselves and their families, and saved enough to cross the Atlantic and traverse the United States, whose hearts were cast in too great a mould to descend to a mean act or brook dishonor; such men as these came to me and begged bread. I felt humbled to the dust for my race and nation, and I hardly knew which feeling was strongest at that time, pity for our condition, or malediction on the fates that so humbled the proud Anglo-Saxon nature. . . .

The weather grew colder each day, and many got their feet so badly frozen that they could not walk, and had to be lifted from place to place. Some got their fingers frozen; others their ears; and one woman lost her sight by the frost. These severities of the weather also increased our number of deaths, so that we buried several each day.

A few days of bright freezing weather were succeeded by another snow-storm. The day we crossed the Rocky Ridge it was snowing a little—the wind hard from the northwest—and blowing so keenly that it almost pierced us through. We had to wrap ourselves closely in blankets, quilts, or whatever else we could get, to keep from freezing. Captain Willie still attended to the details of the company's travelling, and this day he appointed me to bring up the rear. My duty was to stay behind everything and see that nobody was left along the road. I had to bury a man who had died in my hundred, and I finished doing so after the company had started. In about half an hour I set out on foot alone to do my duty as rearguard to the camp. The ascent of the ridge commenced soon after leaving camp, and I had not gone far up it before I overtook a cart that the folks could not pull through the snow, here about knee-deep. I helped them along, and we soon overtook another. By all hands getting to one cart we could travel; so we moved one of the carts a few rods, and then went back and brought up the other. After moving in this way for a while, we overtook other carts at different points of the hill, until we had six carts, not one of which could be moved by the parties owning it. I put our collective strength to three carts at a time, took them a short distance, and then brought up the other three. Thus by travelling over the hill three times —twice forward and once back—I succeeded after hours of toil in bringing my little company to the summit. The six carts were then trotted on gaily down hill, the intense cold stirring us to action. One or two parties who were with these carts gave up entirely, and but for the fact that we overtook one of our ox-teams that had been detained on the road, they must have perished on that Rocky Ridge. . . .

We travelled along with the ox-team and overtook others, all so laden with the sick and helpless that they moved very slowly. The oxen had almost given out. Some of our folks with carts went ahead of the teams, for where the roads were good they could out-travel oxen; but we constantly overtook some stragglers, some with carts, some without, who had been unable to keep pace with the body of the company. We struggled along in this weary way until after dark, and by this time our "rear" numbered three wagons, eight handcarts, and nearly forty persons. . . .

We finally came to a stream of water which was frozen over. We could not see where the company had crossed. If at the point where we struck the creek, then it had frozen over since they passed it. We started one team to cross, but the oxen broke through the ice and would not go over. No amount of shouting and whipping could induce them to stir an inch. We were afraid to try the other teams, for even should they cross we could not leave the one in the creek and go on. There was no wood in the vicinity, so we could make no fire, and were uncertain what to do. We did not know the distance to the camp, but supposed it to be three or four miles. After consulting about it, we resolved that some men should go on foot to the camp and inform the captain of our situation. I was selected to perform the duty, and I set out with all speed. In crossing the creek I slipped through the ice and got my feet wet, my boots being nearly worn out. . . .

After some time I came in sight of the camp fires, which encouraged me. As I neared the camp I frequently overtook stragglers on foot, all pressing forward slowly. I stopped to speak to each one, cautioning them all against resting, as they would surely freeze to death. Finally, about 11 p.m., I reached the camp almost exhausted. I had exerted myself very much during the day in bringing rear carts up the ridge, and had not eaten anything since breakfast. I reported to Captains Willie and Kimball the situation of the folks behind. They immediately got up some horses, and the boys from the Valley started back about midnight to help the ox-teams in. It was 5 a.m. before the last team reached the camp. . . .

There were so many dead and dying that it was decided to lie by for the day. In the forenoon I was appointed to go round the camp and collect the dead. I took with me two young men to assist me in the sad task, and we collected together, of all ages and both sexes, *thirteen corpses, all stiffly frozen.* We had a large square hole dug in which we buried these thirteen people, three or four abreast and three deep. When they did not fit in, we put one or two crosswise at the head or feet of the others. We covered them with willows and then with the earth. When we buried these thirteen people some of their relatives refused to attend the services. They manifested an utter indifference about it. The numbness and cold in their physical natures seemed to have reached the soul, and to have crushed out natural feeling and affection. Had I not myself witnessed it, I could not have believed that suffering would have produced such terrible results. But so it was. Two others died during the day, and we buried them in one grave, making *fifteen in all buried on that camp ground.* It was on Willow creek, a tributary of the Sweetwater river. I learned afterwards from men who passed that way the next summer, that the wolves had exhumed the bodies, and their bones were scattered thickly around the vicinity. . . .

It had been a practice among us latterly, when a person died with any good clothes on, to take them off and distribute them among the poor and needy. One of the men I buried near South Pass had on a pair of medium-heavy laced shoes. I looked at them and at my own worn-out boots. I wanted them badly, but could not bring my mind to the "sticking-point" to appropriate them. I called Captain Kimball up and showed him both, and asked his advice. He told me to take them by all means, and tersely remarked: "They will do you more good than they will him." I took them, and but for that would have reached the city of Salt Lake barefoot.

Near South Pass we found more brethren from the Valley, with several quarters of good fat beef hanging frozen on the limbs of the trees where they were encamped. These quarters of beef were to us the handsomest pictures we ever saw. The statues of Michael Angelo, or the paintings of the ancient masters, would have been to us nothing in comparison to these *life-giving pictures.*

After getting over the Pass we soon experienced the influence of a warmer climate, and for a few days we made good progress. We constantly met teams from the Valley, with all necessary provisions. Most of these went on to Martin's company, but enough remained with us for our actual wants. At Fort Bridger we found a great many teams that had come to our help. The noble fellows who came to our assistance invariably received us joyfully, and did all in their power to alleviate our sufferings. May they never need similar relief!

From Bridger all our company rode, and this day I also rode for the first time on our journey. The entire distance from Iowa City to Fort Bridger I walked, and waded every stream from the Missouri to that point, except Elkhorn, which we ferried, and Green river, which I crossed in a wagon. During the journey from Bridger to Salt Lake a few died of dysentery, and some from the effects of frost the day we crossed the fatal Rocky Ridge. But those who weathered that fatal day and night, and were free from disease, gradually regained strength and reached Salt Lake City in good health and spirits.

II

The first night out the mosquitoes gave us a hearty welcome. Father had bought a cow to take along, so we could have milk on the way. At first he tied her to the back of the cart, but she would sometimes hang back, so he thought he would make a harness and have her pull the cart while he led her. By this time mother's feet were so swollen that she could not wear shoes, but had to wrap her feet with cloth. Father thought that by having the cow pull the cart mother might ride. This worked well for some time.

One day a group of Indians came riding up on horses. Their jingling trinkets, dragging poles and strange appearance frightened the cow and sent her chasing off with the cart and children. We were afraid that the children might be killed, but the cow fell into a deep gully and the cart turned upside down. Although the children were under the trunk and bedding, they were unhurt, but after that father did not hitch the cow to the cart again. He let three Danish boys take her to hitch to their cart. Then the Danish boys, each in turn, would help father pull our cart.

Of course we had many other difficulties. One was that it was hard for the carts to keep up with the three provision wagons drawn by ox teams. Often the men pulling the carts would try to take shortcuts through the brush and sand in order to keep up.

After about three weeks my mother's feet became better so she could wear her shoes again. She would get so discouraged and down-hearted; but father never lost courage. He would always cheer her up by telling her that we were going to Zion, that the Lord would take care of us, and that better times were coming.

Even when it rained the company did not stop traveling. A cover on the handcart shielded the two younger children. The rest of us found it more comfortable moving than standing still in the drizzle. In fording streams the men often carried the children and weaker women across on their backs. The company stopped over on Sundays for rest, and meetings were held for spiritual comfort and guidance. At night, when the handcarts were drawn up in a circle and the fires were lighted, the camp looked quite happy. Singing, music and speeches by the leaders cheered everyone. I remember that we stopped one night at an old Indian camp ground. There were many bright-colored beads in the ant hills.

At times we met or were passed by the overland stage coach with its passengers and mail bags and drawn by four fine horses. When the Pony Express dashed past it seemed almost like the wind racing over the prairie.

Our provisions began to get low. One day a herd of buffalo ran past and the men of our company shot two of them. Such a feast as we had when they were dressed. Each family was given a piece of meat to take along. My brother John, who pushed at the back of our cart, used to tell how hungry he was all the time and how tired he got from pushing. He said he felt that if he could just sit down for a few minutes he would feel so much better. But instead, father would ask if he couldn't push a little harder. Mother was nursing the baby and could not help much, especially when the food ran short and she grew weak. When rations were reduced father gave mother a part of his share of the food, so he was not so strong either.

When we got that chunk of buffalo meat father put it in the handcart. My brother John remembered that it was the fore part of the week and that father said we would save it for Sunday dinner. John said, "I was so very hungry and the meat smelled so good to me while pushing at the handcart that I could not resist. I had a little pocket knife and with it I cut off a piece or two each half day. Although I expected a severe whipping when father found it out, I cut off little pieces each day. I would chew them so long that they got white and perfectly tasteless. When father came to get the meat he asked me if I had been cutting off some of it. I said 'Yes, I was so hungry I could not let it alone.' Instead of giving me a scolding or whipping, father turned away and wiped tears from his eyes."

Even when we were on short rations, if we met a band of Indians the captain of our company would give them some of the provisions so the Indians would let us go by in safety. Food finally became so low that word was sent to Salt Lake City and in about two weeks fresh supplies arrived.

At last, when we reached the top of Emigration Canyon, overlooking Salt Lake, on that September day, 1860, the whole company stopped to look down through the valley. Some yelled and tossed their hats in the air. A shout of joy arose at the thought that our long trip was over, that we had at last reached Zion, the place of rest. We all gave thanks to God for helping us safely over the plains and mountains to our destination.

When we arrived in the city we were welcomed by the people who came out carrying baskets of fruit and other kinds of good things to eat. Even though we could not understand their language, they made us feel that we were among friends.

━━━━━

Carpetbag Crisis: Drummond and his Trollop

THE INTERMITTENT TROUBLES with the federal officials which marked the long territorial period and which began with the first set of "Runaway Judges," came to a serious climax in 1855–7 with the appointment of the third group headed by Chief Justice John F. Kinney and Associate Justices George P. Stiles and W. W. Drummond.

Stiles became embroiled with a group of Mormon lawyers who apparently threatened him with violence and capped it off by entering his office and making a bonfire of his books and papers. Hosea Stout, one of the participants, recorded in his journal the details of the event: "Last night the law library of Judge Stiles & T. S. Williams was broken open and the books and papers thereof taken away. A privy near by was filled with books a few thousand shingles and laths added and the concern set on fire and consumed. Sic transit Lex non Scripti." The court records were in safekeeping, but Stiles, when he returned to Washington, reported that they had all been destroyed. The report greatly deepened public prejudice against the Mormons.

However, the man most responsible for precipitating the clash variously known as the "Utah War," "Johnston's Army," and "Buchanan's Blunder" was Judge Drummond. Contemporaries called him a "gambler and a bully," and a "man of not very estimable character, being notorious for the immorality of his private life," and agreed that he was a disgrace to the judiciary of the United States and an insult to the people of Utah. He allowed no opportunity to pass to insult the local laws, customs, and institutions, and soon found it expedient to return east, going by way of California and Panama. In a letter of resignation to

Carpetbag Crisis: Drummond and his Trollop

the Attorney General on March 30, 1857, he listed all sorts of hearsay charges against the Mormons which were often repeated in other clashes with them and formed "Exhibit A" in the government's case against Utah in 1857. The letter as presented here is taken from House Executive Document No. 71, 35th Congress, 1st. session.

After Drummond's departure the Deseret News *for May 20, 1857, published a letter from Mrs. Drummond disclosing that the judge had picked up one Ada Carroll in Washington and had passed her off in Utah as his wife. In view of the scandalous reports which the judge, clothed in "robes of hypocrisy," had published against the Mormons and polygamy, the* News *roasted his "predilection . . . for the 'scarlet lady' or one of her daughters . . . who sat with him on the Judicial Bench."*

These revelations concerning the dissolute Drummond came too late; the "Utah Expedition" was on its way and the Mormons were faced with another great crisis.

MARCH 30, 1857.

MY DEAR SIR: As I have concluded to resign the office of justice of the supreme court of the Territory of Utah, which position I accepted in A.D., 1854, under the administration of President Pierce, I deem it due to the public to give some of the reasons why I do so. In the first place, Brigham Young, the governor of Utah Territory, is the acknowledged head of the "Church of Jesus Christ of Latter Day Saints," commonly·called "Mormons"; and, as such head, the Mormons look to him, and to *him alone,* for the *law* by which they are to be governed: therefore no law of Congress is by them considered binding in any manner.

Secondly. I know that there is a secret oath-bound organization among all the male members of the church to resist the laws of the country, and to acknowledge no law save the law of the "Holy Priesthood," which comes to the people through Brigham Young direct from God; he, Young, being the vicegerent of God and Prophet, viz: successor of Joseph Smith, who was the founder of this blind and treasonable organization.

Thirdly. I am fully aware that there is a set of men, set apart by special order of the Church, to take both the lives and property of persons who may question the authority of the Church; the names of whom I will promptly make known at a future time.

Fourthly. That the records, papers, &c., of the supreme court have been destroyed by order of the Church, with the direct knowledge and approbation of Governor B. Young, and the federal officers grossly insulted for presuming to raise a single question about the treasonable act.

Fifthly. That the federal officers of the Territory are constantly insulted, harassed, and annoyed by the Mormons, and for these insults there is no redress.

Sixthly. That the federal officers are daily compelled to hear the form of the American government traduced, the chief executives of the nation, both living and dead, slandered and abused from the masses, as well as from all the leading members of the Church, in the most vulgar, loathsome, and wicked manner that the evil passions of men can possibly conceive.

Again: That after Moroni Green had been convicted in the district court before my colleague, Judge Kinney, of an assault with intent to commit murder, and afterwards, on appeal to the supreme court, the judgment being affirmed and the said Green being sentenced to the penitentiary, Brigham Young gave a full pardon to the said Green before he reached the penitentiary; also, that the said Governor Young pardoned a man by the name of Baker, who had been tried and sentenced to ten years' imprisonment in the penitentiary, for the murder of a dumb boy by the name of White House, the proof showing one of the most aggravated cases of murder that I ever knew being tried; and to insult the court and government officers, this man Young took this pardoned criminal with him, in proper person, to church on the next Sabbath after his conviction; Baker, in the meantime, having received a full pardon from Governor Brigham Young. These two men were Mormons. On the other hand, I charge the Mormons, and Governor Young in particular, with imprisoning five or six young men from Missouri and Iowa, who are now in the penitentiary of Utah, without those men having violated *any criminal law in America*. But they were anti-Mormons—poor, uneducated young men *en route* for California; but because they emigrated from Illinois, Iowa, or Missouri, and passed by Great Salt Lake City, they were indicted by a probate court, and most brutally and inhumanly dealt with, in addition to being summarily incarcerated in the saintly prison of the Territory of Utah. I also charge Governor Young with constantly interfering with the federal courts, directing the grand jury whom to indict and whom not; and after the judges charge the grand juries as to their duties, that this man Young invariably has some member of the grand jury advised in advance as to his will in relation to their labors, and that *his charge thus given is the only charge known, obeyed, or received by all the grand juries of the federal courts of Utah Territory.*

Again, sir, after a careful and mature investigation, I have been compelled to come to the conclusion, heart-rending and sickening as it may be, that Captain John W. Gunnison, and his party of eight others, were murdered by the Indians in 1853, under the orders, advice, and direction of the Mormons; that my illustrious and distinguished predecessor, Hon. Leonidas Shaw [Shaver], came to his death by drinking poisoned liquors, given to him under the order of the leading men of the Mormon Church in Great Salt Lake City; that the late secretary of the Territory, A. W. Babbitt, was murdered on the plains by a band of Mormon marauders, under the particular and special order of Brigham Young, Heber C. Kimball, and J. M. Grant, and not by the Indians, as reported by the Mormons themselves, and that they were sent from Salt Lake City for that purpose, and *that only;* and as members of the Danite Band they were bound to do the will of Brigham Young as the head of the church, or forfeit their own lives. These reasons, with many others that I might give, which would be too heart-rending to insert in this communication, have induced me to resign the office of justice of the Territory of Utah, and again return to my adopted State of Illinois. . . .

In conclusion, sir, I have to say that, in my career as justice of the supreme court of Utah Territory, I have the consolation of knowing that I did my duty, that neither threats nor intimidations drove me from that path. Upon the other hand, I am pained to say that I accomplished little good while there, and that the judiciary is only treated as a farce. The only rule of law by which the infatuated followers of this curious people will be governed, is the law of the church, and that emanates from Governor Brigham Young, and him alone.

I do believe that, if there was a man put in office as governor of that Territory, who is not a member of the church (Mormon), and he supported with a *sufficient* military aid, much good would result from such a course; but as the Territory is now governed, and as it has been since the administration of Mr. Fillmore, at which time Young received his appointment as governor, it is noonday madness and folly to attempt to administer the law in that Territory. The officers are insulted, harassed, and murdered for doing their duty, and not recognizing Brigham Young as the only law-giver and law-maker on earth. Of this every man can bear incontestable evidence who has been willing to accept an appointment in Utah; and I assure you, sir, that no man would be willing to risk his life and property in that Territory after once trying the sad experiment.

With an earnest desire that the present administration will give due and timely aid to the officers that may be so unfortunate as to accept situations in that Territory, and that the withering curse which now rests upon this nation by virtue of the *peculiar* and heart-rending institutions of the Territory of Utah, may be speedily removed, to the honor and credit of our happy country, I now remain your obedient servant,

W. W. DRUMMOND,
Justice Utah Territory.

Hon. JEREMIAH S. BLACK,
Attorney General of the United States, Washington City, D.C.

━━━━━━━

The Coming of Johnston's Army

UTAH'S FORTY-YEAR STRUGGLE *for statehood was marked by a series of crises and disputes with federal officials sent to govern the territory. None was quite so serious or dramatic as the rupture occasioned by the appointment, in the spring of 1857, of a new governor to replace Brigham Young and the dispatching of a military force to escort him to Utah and quell a supposed rebellion.*

Under the command of Colonel, later Brigadier General, Albert Sidney Johnston, an army of 2,500 men assembled at Fort Leavenworth for the March on Utah. An advance unit left in the middle of July, followed by other units at intervals of several weeks. News of the approaching army reached the Mormons while they were in Big Cottonwood Canyon celebrating the tenth anniversary of their entry into Great Salt Lake Valley. The ten years of peace they had wanted were up, and now it looked like Missouri and Nauvoo all over again. The army seemed to them only an organized mob. They were determined to resist.

They mobilized the territorial militia and sent guerrillas out to escort incoming Mormon immigrant trains and, without shedding blood, to burn and harass the supply trains of the United States troops. The fiery Heber C. Kimball vowed to send his enemies "to hell across lots."

296

Said he: "Send 2500 troops here, our brethren, to make a desolation of this people! God Almighty helping me, I will fight until there is not a drop of blood in my veins. Good God! I have wives enough to whip out the United States, for they will whip themselves: Amen."

Luckily for the Mormons, the federal troops made a tardy departure from the frontier, and winter brought them near disaster in the mountains. The Second Dragoons, the rear element of the expedition, under Colonel Philip St. George Cooke did not leave Leavenworth until September 17, 1857, acting as an escort to Governor Alfred Cumming, his wife, and other officials. Bad weather overtook Cooke's regiment, and it was not until November 19, after undergoing severe hardship, that he was able to reach the main body of the troops at winter quarters near Fort Bridger. Winter won the Mormons a reprieve until time and cooler heads could bring a peaceful solution of the crisis.

Meanwhile, on September 15, 1857, Brigham Young declared martial law. The prophet-governor's unique proclamation has been called Brigham Young's declaration of war. It is reproduced here from House Executive Documents, *No. 71, 35th Congress, 1st session.*

CITIZENS OF UTAH: We are invaded by a hostile force, who are evidently assailing us to accomplish our overthrow and destruction.

For the last twenty-five years we have trusted officials of the government, from constables and justices to judges, governors, and Presidents, only to be scorned, held in derision, insulted, and betrayed. Our houses have been plundered and then burned, our fields laid waste, our principal men butchered while under the pledged faith of the government for their safety, and our families driven from their homes to find that shelter in the barren wilderness, and that protection among hostile savages, which were denied them in the boasted abodes of Christianity and civilization.

The Constitution of our common country guarantees unto us all that we do now, or have ever claimed. If the constitutional rights which pertain unto us, as American citizens, were extended to Utah, according to the spirit and meaning thereof, and fairly and impartially administered, it is all that we could ask; all that we have ever asked.

Our opponents have availed themselves of prejudice existing against us, because of our religious faith, to send out a formidable host to accomplish our destruction. We have had no privilege or opportunity of defending ourselves from the false, foul, and unjust aspersions against us before the nation. The government has not condescended to cause an investigating committee, or other person, to be sent to inquire into and ascertain the truth, as is customary in such cases. We know those aspersions to be false; but that avails us nothing. We are condemned unheard, and forced to an issue with an armed mercenary mob, which has been sent against us at the instigation of anonymous letter writers, ashamed to father the base, slanderous falsehoods, which they have given to the public; of corrupt officials, who have brought false accusations against us to screen themselves in their own infamy; and of hireling priests and howling editors, who prostitute the truth for filthy lucre's sake.

The issue which has thus been forced upon us compels us to resort to the great first law of self-preservation, and stand in our own defence, a right guaranteed to us by the genius of the institutions of our country, and upon which the government is based. Our duty to ourselves, to our families, requires us not to tamely submit to be driven and slain, without an attempt to preserve ourselves; our duty to our country, our holy religion, our God, to freedom and liberty, requires that we should not quietly stand still and see those fetters forging around us which are calculated to enslave, and bring us in subjection to an unlawful military despotism, such as can only emanate, in a country of constitutional law, from usurpation, tyranny, and oppression.

Therefore, I, Brigham Young, governor and superintendent of Indian affairs for the Territory of Utah, in the name of the people of the United States, in the Territory of Utah forbid:

First. All armed forces of every description from coming into this Territory, under any pretence whatever.

Second. That all the forces in said Territory hold themselves in readiness to march at a moment's notice to repel any and all such invasion.

Third. Martial law is hereby declared to exist in this Territory from and after the publication of this proclamation, and no person shall be allowed to pass or repass into or through or from this Territory without a permit from the proper officer.

Given under my hand and seal, at Great Salt Lake City, Territory of Utah, this fifteenth day of September, A.D. eighteen hundred and fifty-seven, and of the independence of the United States of America the eighty-second.

BRIGHAM YOUNG

A Deserted City

WHILE THE TROOPS of Johnston's command suffered through the winter at Fort Bridger, Brigham Young planned a drastic step in his "scorched earth" policy. As early as September he had served warning that he would evacuate Salt Lake City and destroy everything behind him should the army attempt to enter. "Before I will suffer what I have in times gone by, there shall not be one building, nor one foot of lumber, nor a stick, nor a tree, nor a particle of grass and hay that will burn, left in reach of our enemies. I am sworn, if driven to extremity, to utterly lay waste this land, in the name of Israel's God, and our enemies shall find it as barren as when we came here."

During the winter, however, the efforts of Colonel Thomas L. Kane, an old friend of the Mormons, and the good judgment and tact of Governor Alfred Cumming brought about a rapprochement of the contending parties. President Buchanan, on April 6, 1858, found it expedient to issue a proclamation of pardon to the inhabitants of Utah, provided they would submit to the laws and assist the officers in the performance of their duties. Two commissioners, Ben McCulloch and L. W. Powell, brought the proclamation and at a conference on June 11 and 12 concluded a peace, assuring the people that the army would not in any way infringe on the person or property of anyone and would not locate near any settlement.

In spite of the rapidly evolving solution to the conflict, the Mormons meanwhile proceeded with their long-threatened exodus from their capital city. Late in March the "move south" began, which put virtually the whole of Salt Lake City's population on the road and in temporary settlements in Utah Valley. Mexico, it was rumored, was their ultimate destination. When the army marched through on June 26, it was greeted by a deserted city. The evacuation was a dramatic way to elicit the sympathy of the country and heap scorn on "Buchanan's Blunder."

Captain Albert Tracy, commanding officer of Company H, 10th Infantry, a component of Johnston's army, left a most vivid description of the march through the deserted Mormon capital. Two entries from his journal are reproduced below from "The Utah War, Journal of Captain

III · CHRONICLES AND JUDGES

Albert Tracy, 1858–60," originally printed in Vol. 13 of the Utah Historical Quarterly *(1945). The entries are reprinted here through the courtesy
of the Utah State Historical Society.*

June 25, 1858

We get off as early as five in the morning, and after a long and toilsome ascent in the course of which we pass additional fortifications of
the Mormons, reach at last the bald and rocky crest of "Big Mountain."
The view from this point is little less than magnificent—opening out
between rocky and snow-clad peaks and ridges, to the veritable valley
of Salt Lake in the distance, with even a partial glimpse of the lake
itself, at the right. It brought to mind our view from the chain of the
Popocatepetl, of the valley of Mexico, though to appearance less fertile.
We are allowed, however, little leisure for the contemplation of the
grand, our more immediate attention being drawn to the difficulties of
the descent—at our feet. So steep, so smooth, and so rocky was this
descent, that a mule or horse might scarcely keep his footing going
down, while in spite of drags, wagons, or ambulances, could only be
gotten to the base by means of ropes held hard by the men, who
stacked arms, and were all put upon fatigue to this end. Some of the
heavier wagons got to dragging pretty rapidly the parties put upon
them, and one at least went down with a rush, oversetting at the foot
of the descent, a wreck and a ruin—tongue, wheels, mess-chests, camp-
kettles and all. This being a Dragoon wagon the Infantry boys laughed
—which proceeding the Dragoons regarded as unfitting and disrespectful. It was long before the men and trains were gotten over, and when
at last they were, and we had descended from the glorious vision at the
crest, we found, going down the farther side of Big Mountain, such
clouds and density of dust as well nigh brought us to an open suf-
focation. Neither was the condition of things improved by a drove of
the Commissary's cattle, which had preceded us, leaving in the air a
mass of itself sufficient to our keenest vexation and misery. It is a fact
that the dust settled so thickly upon Clinton's cheeks and beard, that
I could not identify him until he had spoken. About sixteen miles we
make of it today; and tonight, at retreat, is read the proclamation of
Governor Cumming informing us that peace is had with the foe. Letter
to Sarah, to go by a mail tomorrow.

June 26, 1858

So early as three of the morning, the wild peaks and canons of the
Wasatch chain, rang and echoes to the notes of our bugles and reveille.

A Deserted City

The men are in due time upon their feet, and breakfast is had, and tents struck, and with the filing out of our wagons, we are again ready for the road. "Little Mountain" it was, in chief, that lay within our pathway today. We had, however, already overcome in our course so many that were larger, that, with perseverance, we reach at last the top of this one—a little blown it is true, but the top. Descending now the farther slope, which is rapid, and tries the muscles of your legs in an opposite way, by the extensors—we enter at a few miles from camp, Emigration Canyon. A very defensible place is this Canyon, and at a given abrupt angle of the road, a fort, well fortified, might have stood against thousands. It is likely, however, the place could be turned, rendering it thus of less value. Opening out from the last rough gorge, we entered upon a broad plateau, or bench, and Salt Lake City lay at our feet. We are surprised and refreshed with its general appearance of neatness and order. The buildings were almost entirely of adobe, giving them the appearance of grey cut stone. They were set well apart, nearly each by itself, and within the enclosures about them one saw that which one so longs to see from long familiarity with these deserts —perfectly bright green and luxuriant trees and shrubbery. The streets, as we viewed them from our height, are straight and wide, crossing each other generally at right angles. Beyond the city the Jordan River, running north and south. Beyond this the gray of the eternal desert, hemmed remotely by picturesque peaks and mountains. But soon colors flying again the regiment falls in, and with the Band at front and the whole in column of Companies, we enter, after a short descent, the City of the Saints of our Latter Day. And now came a spectacle not common. With the exception of a picked few of his "destroyers" of decidedly rough and sinister aspect, left as a police, and with orders to fire the city in case we offered to occupy it, every man, woman, and child, had, under the direction of the prophet, departed—fled! In place of the usual crowd to gather and gaze at, or hang upon the heels of troops, no single living soul, beyond the lounging vagabonds named, appeared—and these only by twos and threes, at corners, or from behind fence, glowering from beneath their hat-brims, with clubs in their hands, and pistols ready slung at their belts. It was substantially a city of the dead, and might have been depopulated by a pest or famine. The rich strains of our Band, then were wasted somewhat except to our own ears, upon these echoing, empty streets and tenements. The buildings of Brigham appear constituted mainly of a series of gables within the enclosure of a wall of adobe, having a wide gateway and a beehive above it. There are also images of lions, grim of aspect at the right and left. Why so many gables should appear, is explained upon the ground of the abundance of wives of our modern Turk of the Valley, together with their reputed steadily increasing families. It was when too, we arrived abreast with these buildings, that the adjutant, to break the monotony of more regular marches, directed the Band to strike up that most inspiring, if less reputable air y'clept "One-Eyed Riley." The men, not unfamiliar with the notes now given to the breeze, kept step as they had rarely done before, and general sense of "the humor of the thing" came to prevail. Our delights, however, were of comparatively short duration; for in place of halting soon, and beside the city, we were marched out westward miles away wholly without its limits, across the bridge of the Jordan and thence southward along the banks of that river, for at least three miles, before reaching ground for camp. There came again, too, the dust of the bottoms, rising thick and yellow about us, till we halted in a cloud, scarcely knowing one from another, or being able to discern a pace before us. It is nearly a year since we started, but we have reached, and even passed the grand goal of all our marchings—Salt Lake City. My faithful old hickory arm chair, with a plint-bottom, brought all the way from Leavenworth, was wrecked today, in an upset of the officer's wagon at the rear, and being condemned to fuel, is used to bid the kettle boil withal, and make our tea! Sic transit, etc.

Letters from the Governor's Lady

NOT THE OFFICIAL REPORTS but a charming woman's observant letters provide the most interesting glimpses of episodes in the "Utah War." Elizabeth Wells Randall Cumming, wife of Utah's first Gentile governor, came west with him subject to all the discomforts which beset the military train, but she displayed a patience and understanding, a sense of humor and even enjoyment of her experiences which the diaries and letters of the soldiers and officers lack. Daughter of Dr. John Randall of Boston and granddaughter of Samuel Adams of Revolutionary fame, she was a woman of considerable intelligence, discernment, and education, as her letters testify.

Letters from the Governor's Lady

Four of the letters reproduced here were addressed to Anne Eliza Cumming (Mrs. Peter Sken Smith) and one to Sarah Cumming, sisters of the Governor, whose home was Georgia. Two of the letters were written from the vicinity of Fort Bridger, where the army had wintered. They provide an interesting commentary on her husband's entry, with mediator Colonel Thomas L. Kane, into Mormon country ahead of the army, much to the annoyance of Cumming's associate officials and the military, who objected to his sympathy for the Mormons and his attempts to resolve the difficulties without force. Mrs. Cumming hints at a serious cabal. But the pound of flesh demanded of the Mormons by lesser souls for the miseries of the winter was denied, and when President Buchanan issued a proclamation of pardon in effect sustaining the earlier efforts of the governor, Mrs. Cumming had cause to be jubilant.

The letter dated April 22, 1858, contains a significant excerpt from the journal of Governor Cumming, in which he describes his encounter with the Mormon sentries and his ultimate reception in Salt Lake City: "I have every where been recognized as the Govr. of the Terrt."

Three letters from Salt Lake City itself, besides describing Mrs. Cumming's own arrival and her domestic contentment among the Mormons, provide intimate footnotes to history—the army's march through the deserted city on June 26, certain incidents of ill-feeling between the Mormons and the army, and the return of the people to their homes after the "move south" earlier in the spring. The final letter, written on September 24, is a far cry from the out-of-hand condemnations of Mrs. B. G. Ferris. Mrs. Cumming is rational and sympathetic. Of belief and action she dislikes or with which she disagrees she remarks simply that "these last qualities are their own business, not mine." Had Utah been sent only federal officials like Alfred Cumming and his wife Elizabeth, the incessant conflict of the long territorial period might have been avoided.

The letters which follow form part of the Alfred Cumming Collection in Duke University Library and are used here by permission of its Manuscripts Division.

I

Near Fort Bridger—Utah Terrt.
22d April 1858.

Dear Anne,

An express arrived here the day before yesterday, bringing me letters from Alfred. He had arrived safely at Salt Lake City, & been *received*

303

as *Governor* & was very busy. It was so long since he had left here (more than a fortnight,) that his *friends* here had begun to fear he might be imprisoned, thinking that if he had been recd. *peaceably*, he would have the power of course, to send me word—but just as they had begun to talk about anxiety, the express arrived here. I told you in what doubt he left here—& the having succeeded so much better than he had dared even to hope, has put him in excellent spirits—but the backbiting & defaming him that is going on here is astounding. I will not now go into details—but you will see enough against him in the eastern papers. A large party here persist in believing that all his reception was prearranged, that an amicable understanding had existed between him & Brigham Young—& some have written thus to Washington. But I will copy for you an acct of the first part of his journey, from a journal he sent me.

Alfred C. "Col. Kane & I, accompanied by the two drivers Jim & Petty, proceeded to a well-known spring _____ on our first day's journey. About sunset I sent Jim back to aid Petty in getting his wagon along. (This wagon contained provisions, & all the mules of both wagons were some of our poor creatures just alive after the cold & starvation of the winter.) *Col. Kane rode forward to reconnoitre in the vicinity of our proposed camp.* . . . [The next day] There was no excitement—no Mormons—no Indians. Suddenly, there appeared upon a neighboring eminence a tall, fine looking man, mounted upon an elegant horse—and armed Cap a pie—indicating by his manner that he desired to have a conference. Col. Kane advanced, pistol in hand to the conference. The horseman placed his hand upon his holster, as if he would give a gentle hint that two could play at that game. Horseman: Who are you?—Kane gives his name, & asks, who are *you?*—Horseman: Who is your friend—Kane: Are you alone?—Horseman: no, I am surrounded by friends.—Kane: Are you in command?—Horseman: No—Kane: I will communicate with your officer—Horseman: Let your friend remain where he is till I return. So—as in duty bound I remained, resting upon a pile of carriage cushions. Suddenly, I heard the invitation to advance. Meantime Jim & Petty had come up with the wagon. Soon we met a band of most splendid looking horsemen who received me as Governor of Utah—and treated me with marked consideration—changed my mules—assigned me a body guard. We urged forward with speed, and soon arrived at the Yellow where we found an excellent dinner prepared—[In] the wilderness I pitched my tent. It commenced snowing very hard—

covered the ground several inches. We opened our buffalo robes—and I almost envy myself the great enjoyment of sleeping after the fatigue and exposure of the previous night.

"I have every where been recognized as the Govr. of the Terrt. have entered upon the performance of my duties, and live in the hope of doing some good in my generation—but do not forget my *troubles* are now only beginning."

The rest of his letter relates to Mormon matters "to be kept strictly private."

The express will return to him to-day. I send him many dispatches from Washington which ought to have been received long ago—& have had the unpleasant task (acting by the advice of his best friends here) to tell him of what is being said & done to injure him—that he may know where to defend himself.

I trust Mr Smith & yourself are well. We have only heard *once* from you since we came here! . . .

always afftly, yr sister   Elizabeth.

II

28 May—1858
near Camp Scott

Dear Anne,

It is nearly one-o-clk—at night. The mail was to have left day after to morrow, but sent to us this morng. that it would leave at seven, a.m. tomorrow. I have had many callers to-day & have been obliged to see several Mormon women on business (there are some hundreds here now, since Alfred declared peace). I have been preparing for Maj. Powell & Major McCullough, who arrive here day after tomorrow, & at intervals packing glass, knives & forks &c for our journey to Salt Lake. Then at eleven-o-clk p.m. I began my letters. I write voluminous ones home, of course, a large eight-paged one I have just finished—& now I must say a few words to you. The mail leaves here now every week—& the letters arrive here now from the states in less than five weeks. The summer mail *expects* to come through in *eighteen* days.

As I told you Alfred went alone to Salt Lake, with Col Kane as Aide de Camp, & two servants (a driver & cook). They called him here *Quixotic* &c &c. & envy has told many falsehoods about him—that he tried to make a dishonorable compromise.

Now to-day comes from Washington, a proclamation of Mr. Buchanan

& a copy of governmental instructions to the Commissioners appointed to confer with Govr. C. as to the best mode of making peace—of avoiding a war—& they are recommended to do, just what Alfred *has* done, alone & unaided—I am *so glad*. Eckels, Chief Justice, as soon as Alfred had left for Salt Lake, made a charge (to the grand jury assembled here) against polygamy, two hours after A. had left. Col Kane said on hearing it on their return "Good God! His life has been in danger every hour, every minute, since he left here—nothing but his own undaunted courage & firmness has saved him. He has gone unaided into all the settlements, through bands sworn to take his life, & has come out safe—but had a rumor of this action of Eckels reached there, he would have had a hundred bullets in him in less than ten minutes."

And did not Alfred over & over tell the Judge, "Sir, the government does not meddle with their 'peculiar institutions'—Congress *cannot* do it—*I* have, *you* have no business with it. To enforce the U.S. laws is all we have to do." Then too the Judge sent out the marshal, sheriff, Justice of Peace, Secretary of State McCormick, & 10 others, under pretense of buying beef (where would they buy, when the country was under martial law, & only large bands of mormon soldiers on the road) in reality, furnished with writs for the arrest of "B. Young & sixty six others" indicted for treason, wherever they might find any of them—to bring them to camp & iron them. This, when Alfred had gone to try to induce them to submit to U.S. laws—to tell them, personally, the whole truth of their position, to show them how desperate was resistance, how terribly their people, their women & children would suffer in a civil war —to tell them what the policy of his own administration would be &c &c.

I wrote back by the express which brought me Alfred's first letter. I have been his only secretary since we came to Utah. So all his dispatches to Washington, I recd. & had to copy—so knew all he was doing. I saw what terrible work was being done here—& wrote to A. by return express warning him how his civil officials were marring endeavouring to mar [sic] his course of action—annoying & exasperating at the very moment they ought to wait. There were no mails of course between here & Salt Lake—armed bands of several hundreds along the road or rather trail to Echo Canon. So I could not tell him how much worse (daily) matters went. The party formed against Alfred here was very strong. Bets made in every direction, about different phases of the matter. The civil party were fortunately turned back by thirteen hundred men—ran back for dear life, not firing one shot.

Alfred sent me second express & many dispatches—& I was to tell *no one* what was in them—& oh so much *was* in them.

& here they said, "oh Cumming is in Salt Lake, & Brigham has placed his creatures around him, & C. does not stir except with these guards, *called* an escort, in reality his *keepers*." &c &c &c &c—& all the while I knew, he had had his office open *day* & *night* to receive complaints from the timid & disaffected, when he was in the city, that he had been to the northern settlements & rallied the people, had placed guards over their abandoned dwellings & fields—had been west & examined the military (proposed) stations, & south to over take the masses travelling southward they knew not where. He had been to the white mountains &c &c—& had taken possession of seals of office. & I did *long* for Alfred to come back, & that all should be known. How angry he was, when he found all out—I had told him comparatively little in my letters, only what was *necessary* for him to know. There were many to tell him on his return of other things, which I will not write—but he was furious. He made some of the officers resign their commissions at once. Sec. of State & Justice of Peace, whom he had appointed himself—& then resigned himself to wait *after his fashion*. We prepare to go to Salt Lake in a few days—but shall wait the arrival of the commissioners, whose instructions have been forwarded to Alfred, & who are ordered to do, just what Alfred *has* done—all alone.

Col Kane staid here, three or four hours on his return with Alfred. He then proceeded to Washington instantly, with dispatches telling of some of the doings here—& before you receive this, you will probably have seen in the papers the two sides of the question All is well so far.

Whether the people of Utah will "stay put" as the children say—remains to be proved. Brigham & the other leaders have agreed to submit to arrest & to trial, if they may be tried by a jury of their peers, & not by camp followers & teamsters—the only jury which *can* be formed *here* and I think they are very right. This Alfred demanded—but Mr. Buchanan offers *pardon on submission*.

Alfred likes some of the Mormons there—some of the leaders—not their Mormonism—but their courage, intellect, "admirable horsemanship" such as he has never seen equalled &c &c—but it is very late—& I am tired out. Farewell love to all friends

afftly yr sister
Elizabeth

Great Salt Lake City—17th June 1858

Dear Sarah,

As I have not written to you for a long time, I shall direct this letter to you, instead of to Anne, to whom I often write & trust to receive an answer from you, telling "all about" old friends & faces & yourself. The mail leaves here now once a week. I have so *much* to do & see & think, that writing *letters* to friends, instead of talking, seems very ineffectual to convey any idea of our lives.

We left Fort Bridger on the 3d of June. . . .

8 June—We were ready late this morn. A gentleman from Salt Lake City arrived about nine-o-clk, & begged us not to cross the next mountain, but go round by a Canon road, which wound round its foot. He left & we left an hour after. We did not see any road but the one over the next mountain—so we took that. I mended shoes & gloves & frock, which my adventures of the day before had caused to look somewhat like the clothes of the ugly Ute Indians—but I could get no others—& hoped that we should get into the city quietly. Though as Alfred had "conquered a peace" a few days before, & had made friends, *positive friends* of thorough going enemies, I thought there might be a reception—a *small* one, I knew—for the city was to be abandoned by its inhabitants, until after the army had passed through. This had been agreed upon—but I was *not* prepared for the death like stillness which existed. A large, beautiful city, the houses all separate—each with its garden— wide streets, with a pebbly stream running on each side—city capable of containing twenty thousand inhabitants—as level as Augusta, Georgia —houses mostly about two stories high, built of adobes, which are like bricks in shape & size, but a grey stone colour instead of red—the gardens full of flowers & vegetables & promise of fruit—but the doors of all houses closed—not a window to be seen—only boards instead—not a carriage or wagon or mule or horse or man to be seen. Mountains all around us, looking in the clear atmosphere, but a few *feet* from us— snow on the tops, green below—& the rushing of the water on each side the only sound. The valley city covers a level area of several miles —& one wondered when one should wake from a dream—or tried to look away from the pictured place. It did not seem *real*—but you could not look away. The mountains shut you in all around. The gorge through which we approached was no longer visible.

By & bye, Dr. Forney (who had preceded us) came up to my carriage, which was in advance:—he got in, & told Dundie to drive to Staines's house which had been left all ready for us. It was at this house that Col Kane & Alfred had remained when here before. I wish I had a picture of it for you—for it is very pretty. It stands about 130 feet back from the street—flowers etc in front—peach & other small trees on each side of the house & extending to the street—a large garden behind & on each side. The house built like an English cottage— a piazza in front, with flat open work pillars, for vines—& a piazza above the first, with heavy carved work all around it ornamented windows &c &c. I went into the large parlour. *There* was a really magnificent & monstrous piano—London make—& new eight octaves—sent for my use by Heber C. Kimball—some handsome chairs, sent for my use by Brigham Young—& other furniture, carpets &c. sent by other church dignitaries. Then in a china closet, near a large dining room, were cups & saucers & other table furniture, tablecloths, every thing had been thought of, for me to use, so that I need not be obliged to unpack, till matters were further settled. Mr. Staines's wives were at Provo, & were to continue there. He *may* rent us his house, is ready to do so if he does not burn it—but if there is any trouble when the army enters, the whole city is to be burned. The houses are now all emptied but this & an eating house—a little one at the other extremity of the city.

In the aftn several of the magnates of the church called. They had (about twenty of the leading men) come in from Provo City, & gone by the Canon road to meet us & escort us to our home—but we had taken the other road & so missed them. They were full of politeness, & with one of them, in especial, I was *very* much pleased—Wm Kimball, Heber Kimball's eldest son. Genl West & Col Ferguson—then Mr. *Cumming* & another apostle, called _____. Nearly all those of rank in the church have been missionaries in various parts of Europe—Paris, London, Stockholm, Copenhagen, are their frequent places of visiting, & their manners are polished & the conversation of these gentlemen is very varied & interesting—my favorite visitor was Wm Kimball, as they call him, (he has many brothers). His face is full of character & feeling —his air reserved, but very *truthful*—about thirty years old apparently. The others were generally agreeable. The next calls were from two gentlemen, appointed by Brigham Young to confer with Alfred. Brigham & his counsellors will come to the City from Provo to-morrow. B. Y. says that he & Gov. Cumming have settled matters, & seems to think it superfluous to see the Commissioners—but the gentlemen comms bring a proclamation & pardon from the President, & it is thought better there should be a conference with them—also, the time & manner of the entrance of the army is to be settled.

On 10th June—B. Young had a long private interview with the Gov in which they talked over all the matters to be discussed at the conference. In the aftn B. Young, Heber Kimball, Genl Wells, Mr. Armstrong, Hooper, late Secy State, & several others called, having come in in the morn from Provo. In H. Kimball's reported speeches, he is coarse, vulgar, denunciatory. In conversation he is plain, sensible, straight forward & gentlemanly—full of humor & sometimes witty but nothing coarse or disagreeable as I saw him.

Alfred says I must close my letter—that the mail bags will be closed in half an hour. I have partly copied this from my journal—& have much more to tell of course—but of *persons* I have thought I should not say a great deal—but wait till I see you—& again wait till I know them better. I have no time to read my letter over—as the postoffice (just opened) is a mile hence. So good bye in a great hurry & believe me always afftly yr Sister

Elizabeth

Alfred sends love, & says he is going to convert Mormons to some good *ism*.

IV

Friday 9th July—1858
Salt Lake City.

Dear Anne,

. . . My last letter from this place was dated somewhere about the 25th of June, I believe. On Saturday 26th the army passed through in excellent order. Tired, & dusty & hot, yet not a man nor a mule stepped out of place. They encamped about two miles beyond the city—on the Jordon [Jordan]—nearly 6000 animals (I am told) they have with them —& at their camp there is very little grass, a great deal of dust, full of soda & their Jordon water for drinking is full of saleratus—an unpleasant place for a camp—no wood, bad water & little grass—nothing to be bought in the city *at all*—for no one is here to sell. We have had all winter & spring at the camp, not only *as much* as we wanted, but a great deal more—& yet I have seen letters in the newspapers telling of our soon in camp being obliged to live on mules flesh. Our rations were limited when we first arrived there; limited in quality, & somewhat in quantity—but more than anyone could consume, I should think

310

unless the appetite was very inordinate. I speak of soldiers as well as the rest of us—but here in the city, we buy, *can* buy nothing—except in the garden of the house where I am, (the owner having recd. permission to remain in the city, & by profession a gardener) are vegetables & strawberries. One other man remained, who kept open a room for the strangers to eat in, & he sent out of the city twice a week for meat, & obtained his vegetables from this garden. We have lived on what we brought from camp with us—part of the day, & we take *dinner* at this room, together with the other civil officers, who unlike ourselves, could get no houses or rooms—& slept in their travelling vehicles —as did Gvr Powell & Major McCullough, the Commr. As soon as the army are "settled down" Alfred will go to Provo, & see Brigham Young and the other leading men, & send a proclamation to all the settlements that the army has passed through, nothing has been molested, & that all may return to the city in safety. Then stores will be re-opened & things will partially return to the old routine.

On Sunday 27—June—Genl. Johnston & staff, & nearly all the military officers called on us. Fortunately, the strawberries were not yet over, & I had enough for all. The proprietor of the eating [room] I have alluded to, had (in expectation of their dining with him) made a great effort & obtained *two* kinds of meat. So all were satisfied. Capn. Alfred Cumming [a nephew of the Governor] had called early in the morng. but "the Queen was in the kitchen" hulling strawberries. However, the "King" who was smoking a pipe, shared a pipe with the Captain, who promised to call again—after the formal calls were over.

Monday 28. Alfred left for Provo. Several officers called in the day to say good bye, for they said no one could stay any longer at that camp. The dust was so intolerable, they had not had dinner cooked at all, the little grass all gone, & the camp was to be moved early in the morng. first twelve, then six miles—then a halt for a few days & then to move again. It is well they go—much as I like some of the gentlemen, yet the feeling of the army is anything but friendly to the Mormons, & the last reciprocate the feeling, & even in these two days, notwithstanding the absence of the citizens & the good discipline of the army, half a dozen quarrels have been commenced, which threaten the "peace" so lately concluded. For instance, one mormon gentleman, who had come down from Provo on business, was introduced by a Gentile citizen to an army officer, a Lieut. though 45 years old—old enough to know better. The officer folded his arms, & declined the introduction— & thereupon ensued some words which would have led to difficulty, but that the parties were separated by those who were interested in the continuance of the peace. They were reminded Alfred *had* entered into certain engagements for the Mormons, & Genl. Johnston for his officers —at this present crisis—& so the matter stopped short—but it only shows the *feeling*. It is well to have some distance put between the fire & the gunpowder. Captn. Cumming passed the evening with me— is well—Some of the people in Provo were kind enough to send me three music books to aid me in passing the time while I am all alone here. . . .

Thurs. 1st. July—We have all been amused with the New York & other papers to-day. The *quantity* of news about Utah—but amid all the falsehoods, it is strange that *not one single truth* should be told— yet such is the fact. "The army are starving" "the Govr. is expelled"— "No news was recd. in camp while the Govr. was in Salt Lake" "Govr. C. applied to Genl. Johnston for an escort of twenty men—The Genl. answered 'No sir, the army came out as your escort, & you shall be accompanied by the whole or none'" "The Govr. was escorted to Salt Lake City by a party headed by the notorious O. P. Rockwell. This looks as though treachery were intended" "The Govr. was *induced* by Col Kane to visit Salt Lake—Govr. C. *says* he had no negotiations with Brigham—but facts are stubborn things—*we* know to the contrary— & rich developments are ahead" &c &c—The chief peculiarity of all these stories lies in the fact that there is not even a *foundation* for any of them.

Monday 5. July—Rode 18 miles to the camp to bid *the* four ladies good bye. They leave for Cedar valley, 22 miles farther from the city than they now are—too far to visit. The people are pouring into the city. Roads filled with waggons—but stores &c will not be opened for several days.

As soon as the people have cleaned their own houses, I hope to get some one to wash the walls & put in order the garden of the house we have taken.

7th. July—We are all quiet now. People still thronging in—& to-day they are working at our house.

Mail comes in now once a week—& goes out once a week. It averages 20 days from the states—at this season. We have newspapers to-day bearing date 15th June. Alfred's dispatches have been recd. in Washington. A message from the President congratulates the house upon the peaceable termination of difficulties.

Good night, dear Anne—I must close in haste, or the mail will be closed.

May God bless & keep you. Alfred is very well. If he were here, he would send love—but he is out—

always afftly yr sister—Elizabeth.

v

G.S.L. City—U.T.'y.
24th Sept. 1858.

We received your last letter, dear Anne, dated 9th Aug. about a fortnight since—and were glad to hear you had recovered from your recent illness—about the same time came a letter from Cornelia, dated some time in *March* last! . . .

Cornelia, like yourself, talks of "perils" & "discomfort." The newspapers (some of them) told sad stories about us, & so it is not wonderful absent friends should have been uneasy, especially when the mail was so irregular on account of snow &c—but I must say for myself, I think, (the last few weeks excepted) I have passed the happiest & pleasantest months of my life, after I left Leavenworth till we came to housekeeping here—and Alfred says to me just now, as I was speaking about the matter "Tell my friends when you write that I am safer here than I ever was in my life—for in other places I have been sometimes ill, & in this climate, it is next to impossible to get sick. Give them my love, & tell Anne I shall try to write to her soon."

Alfred is very well, and is very busy, of course. He has some annoyances, now & then, from "Gentiles" who (certain ones of them) endeavor to bring on quarrels with Mormons—desiring to bring on a war here—men without a profession or business, who live, nobody knows how. One of these gentry was arrested last week, offering the most unprovoked insults to each mormon who approached, & at last proceeding to assaults. Alfred has had *no* trouble from Mormons. The community, en masse, seem to be thankful, that if they cannot have their adored Brigham Young, for governor, they have, in his stead, one, who they *all* seem to regard as a *just & honorable* man, who will not *betray* their interests. Feeling thus, all that a people *can* do to make his stay here comfortable, they do—from Brigham Young, down to the most humble member of the community. I do not mean by pleasant words, & festivities &c—but by entering into, & endeavouring to carry out his views. I see Mrs Young two or three times a week, & she scarcely ever omits saying *something* about "we are much obliged to Govr. Cumming, we feel he is interested in the welfare of this people." Alfred has begged the *young men* to bear and forbear—to remember how recently the threatening cloud of war has passed over them & to remember the *object* of the unprincipled men who are trying to irritate & wound. The older men are not so exposed to this evil. Alfred has insisted on restitution being made by the Mormons to all Gentiles, who have complained of losses at their hands. They have never yet refused to make it—when restitution was possible—& if there has been any hesitation about it, in consequence of the enormously high prices of many articles here at this time, Brigham signs an order, which *must* be obeyed, as *salvation* depends on Brigham—(as the Pope can excommunicate a Catholic—so Brigham "cuts off" from "the church").

The Mormons, as a community, seem peaceable and well disposed. I have been here several months, and have never yet heard noise or oaths in the street, by night or by day. It is quiet here as in a New England village. I have seen only one Mormon man intoxicated—& that was during a public holiday—and such an industrious community is this, that strangers always speak of it with admiration. This is the side that touches *us*. As for themselves personally they are, so far as my observation goes, generally ignorant, fanatical, superstitious, & possessing a profound disdain for the religious belief of the rest of the world—but all these last qualities are their own business, not mine. So far as we are concerned, they are all that we ought to ask.

Such devotedness to their religion as they evince is instructive in more ways than one. The spirit of martyrdom here lives and has its being. Here one sees the power of *faith*—and how faith may be abused.

The Mormon ladies talk a great deal about their religion. They live it. They feel it. Every act almost of their lives is mormonized. They talk much of their happiness in having found the only true gospel—of their past sufferings in Nauvoo, & during their exodus—of their strong love for "The Holy City" "the chosen city of God."—"the *only* place, in this age of the world where God holds *direct intercourse* with human beings, as he did with Moses on the Mount.". . .

I intended, when I commenced this letter, to give an account of a three days picnic we had in Cottonwood Canon; invited by Prest. Young —but I have other letters to write, & this is already very long. Alfred never had entered a Mormon house, as guest, since he came here—but I, who came, with an ardent desire to see the country, & become *acquainted* with mormon homes (& *hearts,* if possible) go everywhere I

314

am invited—I am invited the oftener I believe *because* he does not go with me. These walled establishments here, contain women, not men —& they are best visited by women. So I feel at least—& I think he sees it as I do.

But to the picnic at the canon, he went. We had, like the rest, our own tents & wagons & private table—& mixed with the rest, when and as we pleased.

A visitor has just called—so I close at once—Love to enquiring friends.

Always afftly,
Elizabeth W. C.

Please give my love to Cornelia when you write, & thank her for her letter. I shall try to write soon.

P. S. A Gentile gentleman called on me to-day. He introduced himself. Not hearing the name, when he left I requested to be told it again. "Knight," said he "well known *in the States* as the man the Mormons *killed,* a few months since, under circumstances of peculiar atrocity."

Massacre at Mountain Meadows

IN SEPTEMBER, 1857, while Salt Lake City fearfully awaited the coming of Johnston's troops, events in one of the outlying settlements took a melancholy turn. In a small hill-girt valley of southwestern Utah known as the Mountain Meadows a band of white men and Indians fell upon more than a hundred disarmed overland travelers and massacred them, sparing only a few children. A horrified nation blamed the Mormons. The Mormons blamed the Indians. Twenty years later John D. Lee, once a familiar of Joseph Smith and Brigham Young, was executed on the dark and bloody ground for the crime, he alone paying the penalty for a mass murder no single man could have perpetrated. In Mormon country, his name has been a hiss and a by-word from that day to this.

For nearly a century a true understanding of the affair remained in the mists of secrecy, half-truths, and innuendo. Then in 1950, after years of painstaking research, Juanita Brooks brought out The Mountain

Meadows Massacre, *published by the Stanford University Press. A native of the region of the Meadows, herself a Mormon, and a trained and understanding historian, Mrs. Brooks succeeded in breaking the ice of silence surrounding the affair.*

The bitterness generated over the long years by the massacre has been two-fold: the hatred of the survivors, their heirs, and the families of the slain toward Utah and its people; and the deep resentment within the Mormon people themselves. Truth and understanding were lost in untempered charges and countercharges. But time has worked a reconciliation. If the years have obscured the details, making it difficult to reconstruct exactly what happened, time has also brought an understanding of why it happened.

In September, 1955, the Richard Fancher Society of America and the families of other victims of the massacre invited Mrs. Brooks to speak at the dedication of a memorial monument they had erected at Harrison, Boone County, Arkansas, where a hundred years ago the emigrant train assembled before starting its long journey toward a rendezvous with death. Here Mrs. Brooks delivered a brief but moving explanation of why it all happened. A Mormon speaking in Arkansas to the descendants of the dead fittingly closed one of the deepest wounds in Mormon history. Her remarks, reproduced below through the courtesy of the Utah State Historical Society, appeared originally in Vol. 24 of the Utah Historical Quarterly *(January, 1956). Mrs. Brooks is also co-editor, with Robert G. Cleland, of* A Mormon Chronicle: The Journals of John D. Lee.

My dear friends:

My text for today comes from Proverbs 4:7—"And with all thy getting, get understanding."

I should like to preface my remarks with an incident which will show why I selected this text.

When I was in my eighteenth year, I left home to teach school. In the town where I worked was a fine old man who seemed to me to exemplify Old Age at its best. There was a dignity about him, an aura of wisdom, and with it all a gentleness. I used to wonder what he was like as a young man—how big and handsome he must have been who now was like a shock of grain, ripe unto the harvest.

One day as I closed my school he came to my schoolroom, and after the customary greetings, he said, "I have something I would like you to do for me. My eyes have witnessed things that my tongue has never uttered, and before I die, I want them written down."

I promised that I would do it; I really intended to. But as eighteen is more interested in young men than in old ones, I put it off. There were last-day-of-school programs and reports to attend to; there were dates and dances. Soon after school closed a neighbor came to say that my old friend was ill, and that he kept asking for the little school ma'am.

I went at once and stayed by, the three days until he died. It was the first time I had witnessed the passing of a human soul, and I was shaken by it, but more shaken by the last hours in which this ninety-two-year-old patriarch tossed in delirium. He sang bits of Indian songs, he preached in the Indian tongue, he mumbled incoherent bits. Once he opened his eyes wide to the ceiling and shuddered. "Blood! Blood! Blood!" he said, in a voice that made my hair crawl.

I turned to my uncle who stood by. "What troubles him?" I asked. "He seems to be haunted."

"Maybe he is. He was at the Mountain Meadows massacre, you know."

No, I didn't know. Nor could I understand how such a man could possibly have been involved in anything so horrible. Surely here was no man of violence, no murderer! It was my attempt to understand that led to research in this subject, and which in the end produced the book *The Mountain Meadows Massacre*.

The history of the west is so often marked by tragedy and death, death for individuals and for groups. When we look back at them, we see how, by the slightest chance, each could have been avoided.

Take for example the Donner Party. When they broke from the larger train of which they were a part on that July day in 1846, they thought they would save five hundred miles in distance and make the Hastings Cut-off the regular California route. Had they been a week earlier, they might have got through before the snows fell. Or had winter not been premature that year, they might have made it. Or, better still, had the letter written by Edwin Bryant warning all trains to avoid this route been delivered, they would never have gone at all.

But how idle now to speculate. The fact was that the company tried the new, direct route and were overtaken by winter in the mountain pass which now bears their name. Their suffering, their survival, is a story of horror which has no parallel in American history, a story of people forced to subsist upon human flesh, of parents devouring the

317

bodies of their own children, of men casting lots for life. Of the 87 who took the Hastings Cut-off on July 20, 1846, only 47 reached their destination, and they only because they were rescued by relief parties from the coast.

A second example was the Sandwalking Train which left Great Salt Lake City on October 1, 1849, to follow the southern route, then only a faint trail. This company was loosely organized of a number of independent groups, among them the Jayhawkers, the Bug Smashers, the Wolverines, and others who were identified by family names such as the Bennetts and Wades.

They had hired Jefferson Hunt to pilot them through, but en route someone produced a map of a direct route west to the coast. In vain did their captain tell them it was too good, too easy, that lines on paper meant nothing where country had not been explored. In vain did he remind them that only a few men had passed over the route they were following: Jedediah Strong Smith in 1826, John C. Frémont in 1844, and some of the returning Mormon Battalion men in 1847. At the last camp he told them to choose, each teamster, which way he would go. As for himself he would take the beaten track though only one wagon went with him.

The next morning the Jayhawkers led out boldly for the short cut; wagon after wagon followed them, until of the total of 107 wagons that started, only 12 followed Captain Hunt.

Again the details do not belong here. Some of the wagons returned to the crossroads to follow the captain later, others made their way back to the road. Only *one* wagon of the 37 who went on finally reached its destination. And it was by this group that Death Valley received its name.

But there has been no tragedy like that of the Fancher train. Like the Donner Party, had it been a week or two earlier, it would have passed in safety, with supplies purchased from the Mormons. But after military law was declared and the people were told to prepare for war, possibly for a long siege, and not to sell a kernel of wheat to any passing emigrant train, complications set in.

In our effort to understand, let us pause here for a glance at Mormon history, for the dark happenings on the Mountain Meadows were made possible only by what had gone before.

The story of the rise of the Mormon Church is one of persecutions and drivings. Three times these people had been forced to leave their homes. There had been whippings and tar-and-feather parties, burning of homes and pillaging. At Haun's Mill in Missouri, a mob rode into the village; the Mormons took refuge in an old blacksmith shop, where they were killed like trapped animals, their bodies thrown into a dry well.

At last they established their city, Nauvoo, Illinois, where more than fifteen thousand of them gathered. This time their trouble grew into a local civil war, with both sides appealing to the government for aid.

Finally a truce was agreed upon, in which the Mormons were to evacuate Nauvoo in May, and their enemies were to leave them unmolested until that time. But the Missouri boys grew impatient, and in February began what they called "Wolf Hunts," or depredations of Mormon homes.

Now the Mormons were forced to leave before they were ready. On February 14, the first wagons crossed the river west, the thermometer fell to below zero and a heavy storm arose. In this first temporary shelter 19 babies were born in one night. During the first season, 600 Mormon graves were left on the prairies of Iowa—600 victims of exposure and hunger and disease. . . .

Another thing which must be taken into account was the love of the Mormon people for their prophet, Joseph Smith. When he was killed in the jail at Carthage, Illinois, there were many young men who, viewing his dead body, promised God that if they ever had an opportunity to avenge his death, they would do it.

Now given this much by way of background, is it too hard to understand how men who had suffered repeatedly, whose brothers had been killed at Haun's Mill, who just ten years before had taken the vow of vengeance, should be glad when their leaders said, "We will not run again! This time we will defend our homes!"

Word of an approaching army reached Utah on July 24; the Fancher train arrived in Salt Lake City on August 3 and 4. To the Mormons, the army was only another armed mob. They had learned by sad experience how far they could trust an army.

As with the Donner Party and the Sandwalking Train, the Fancher group was composed of more than one unit. There were also the "Missouri Wildcats," often described as being rough and ready and fearless. Now for any man, even in time of peace, to come into a Mormon village and boast that he carried the gun that had "shot the guts out of old Joe Smith" was to invite Mormon retaliation. Now when the wave of patriotic fervor was at its height, it was doubly dangerous.

Another element in the situation which was most important in the final tragedy was the Indians. The oldest settlement in this area was but five years old; the youngest scarcely three. In the southern part of the state beyond Cedar City there were seventy-nine families widely scattered in eleven small villages. Outnumbered more than two to one by the Indians, the Mormons had sought in every way to gain their friendship and confidence. Now with war declared, they must have the natives for allies. Here was a wealthy train which would mean loot and horses, both of which the Indians would be glad to have.

I shall not go into the details of the horrible affair. It would do none of us any good now. The Indians had gathered from miles around and were stirred up by the fact that some of their men had been killed. Like a fire started in a small patch of weeds that may get out of control when a wind comes up, they posed a real problem. Some of the white men did not approve, but in the army who talks back to his commanding officer? Some, remaining silent, did not carry out the orders.

So there was carried out one of the most despicable mass murders of history. It was tragic for those who were killed and for the children left orphans, but it was also tragic for the fine men who now became murderers, and for their children who for four generations now have lived under that shadow.

Many of them moved away. Not that they feared the law, but that they could not face their neighbors. They wanted their children to grow up so far away that they would not hear of this or become connected with it. Within a year, the population of Cedar City had decreased almost half.

Nearly twenty years later one man was executed on the scene of the massacre. Some of you may know what it is like to hang the wrong man—it can so easily be done; it has been done in more places than one. This man chose to be shot, and took death voluntarily rather than involve anyone else.

Let me come back now to my text: "With all thy getting, get understanding." Socrates said, "To understand all is to forgive all." It is given to God alone to understand *all*, but as His children we may strive toward understanding, and that is our only purpose here today.

Horace Greeley Interviews Brigham Young

IN THE SUMMER OF 1859 *Horace Greeley, founder and crusading editor of the New York* Tribune, *followed his own advice to young men and went west. He spent ten days among the Mormons en route to California and held what in the history of professional journalism may be considered "the first formal interview with a famous man." He gave an illuminating question-and-answer report of his visit with Brigham Young on July 13 in one of six letters he wrote from Salt Lake City to his* Tribune, *part of the series of running accounts in which he described his overland journey.*

"A perfect walking budget of facts, tables, and statistics," as Whitman found him, the eccentric Greeley seemed "all brain and little body." Alive to every reform question of the day—abolitionism, Fourierism, temperance, women's rights, homestead legislation, the protective tariff —he found much to arouse his conscience and curiosity among the Mormons. His interview reflects his foremost concern with slavery and candidly records Brigham Young's rather startling proslavery views. In other letters, Greeley, amid much moralizing, reports the hearsay about the Mountain Meadows Massacre and describes his impressions of Mormon preaching, polygamy, land use and irrigation, iron and sugar beet manufacture, and the doctrine of popular sovereignty as applied to Utah.

He did not find Mormon preaching very edifying: "I do not think good men delight in this assumption of an exclusive patent for the grace of God. . . . It is too well calculated to puff up its disciples with self-conceit and spiritual pride."

Greeley predicted that polygamy as the "graft on the original stock of Mormonism, will be outlived by the root." And he proved prophetic of the way Utah's boundaries were shortly to be reduced by the creation of Nevada and Colorado: he recommended that Carson Valley be cut off on the one side and a Rocky Mountain Territory be made on the other. Then, if popular sovereignty was to be more than a farce, let Brigham Young be reappointed governor and "Let the Mormons have the Territory to themselves—it is worth very little to others." As things

stood, Brigham Young carried the Territory "in his breeches pocket"
anyway, rendering "the Federal Judiciary, the Federal Executive, and
the Federal Army, as now existing in Utah . . . three transparent
shams." To Greeley these measures seemed the "safest and best mode
of dealing with the difficulties already developed and daily developing
here, unless the notion of 'Popular Sovereignty' in the Territories is to
be utterly exploded and given up."

The following selection reporting the interview with Brigham Young
is Greeley's letter of July 13. Captioned "Two Hours with Brigham
Young," it was published in the New York Daily Tribune *on August 20,*
1859, from which it is taken here rather than from the revised collec-
tion of the summer's letters which he issued in 1860 as An Overland
Journey. *The "Dr. Bernhisel, M. C.," who arranged the interview was*
John M. Bernhisel, Utah's delegate to Congress.

SALT LAKE CITY, UTAH, July 13, 1859.

My friend Dr. Bernhisel, M. C., took me this afternoon, by appointment, to meet Brigham Young, President of the Mormon Church, who
had expressed a willingness to receive me at 2 p.m. We were very cordially welcomed at the door by the president, who led us into the
second-story parlor of the largest of his houses (he has three), where
I was introduced to Heber C. Kimball, Gen. Wells, Gen. Ferguson,
Albert Carrington, Elias Smith, and several other leading men in the
Church, with two full-grown sons of the President. After some unim-
portant conversation on general topics, I stated that I had come in quest
of fuller knowledge respecting the doctrines and polity of the Mormon
Church, and would like to ask some questions bearing directly on these,
if there were no objection. President Young avowed his willingness to
respond to all pertinent inquiries; the conversation proceeded substantially as follows:

H. G.—Am I to regard Mormonism (so-called) as a new religion, or
as simply a new development of Christianity?

B. Y.—We hold that there can be no true Christian Church without
a priesthood directly commissioned by and in immediate communication with the Son of God and Saviour of mankind. Such a church is
that of the Latter-Day Saints, called by their enemies Mormons; we
know no other that even pretends to have present and direct revelations of God's will.

H. G.—Then I am to understand that you regard all other churches
professing to be Christian as the Church of Rome regards all churches

not in communion with itself—as schismatic, heretical, and out of the way of salvation?

B. Y.—Yes, substantially.

H. G.—Apart from this, in what respect do your doctrines differ essentially from those of our Orthodox Protestant Churches—the Baptist or Methodist, for example?

B. Y.—We hold the doctrines of Christianity, as revealed in the Old and New Testaments—also in the Book of Mormon, which teaches the same cardinal truths, and those only.

H. G.—Do you believe in the doctrine of the Trinity?

B. Y.—We do; but not exactly as it is held by other churches. We believe in the Father, the Son, and the Holy Ghost, as equal, but not identical—not as one person [being]. We believe in all the bible teaches on this subject.

H. G.—Do you believe in a personal devil—a distinct, conscious, spiritual being, whose nature and acts are essentially malignant and evil?

B. Y.—We do.

H. G.—Do you hold the doctrine of Eternal Punishment?

B. Y.—We do; though perhaps not exactly as other churches do. We believe it as the bible teaches it.

H. G.—I understand that you regard baptism by immersion as essential.

B. Y.—We do.

H. G.—Do you practice Infant Baptism?

B. Y.—No.

H. G.—Do you make removal to these valleys obligatory on your converts?

B. Y.—They would consider themselves greatly aggrieved if they were not invited hither. We hold to such a gathering together of God's people as the bible foretells, and that this is the place, and now is the time appointed for its consummation.

H. G.—The predictions to which you refer have usually, I think, been understood to indicate Jerusalem (or Judea) as the place of such gathering.

B. Y.—Yes, for the Jews—not for others.

H. G.—What is the position of your Church with respect to Slavery?

B. Y.—We consider it of divine institution, and not to be abolished until the curse pronounced on Ham shall have been removed from his descendants.

H. G.—Are any slaves now held in this territory?

B. Y.—There are.

H. G.—Do your Territorial laws uphold Slavery?

B. Y.—Those laws are printed—you can read for yourself. If slaves are brought here by those who owned them in the States, we do not favor their escape from the service of those owners.

H. G.—Am I to infer that Utah, if admitted as a member of the Federal Union, will be a Slave State?

B. Y.—No; she will be a free state. Slavery here would prove useless and unprofitable. I regard it generally as a curse to the masters. I myself hire many laborers and pay them fair wages; I could not afford to own them. I can do better than subject myself to an obligation to feed and clothe their families, to provide and care for them in sickness and health. Utah is not adapted to Slave Labor.

H. G.—Let me now be enlightened with regard more especially to your Church Polity: I understand that you require each member to pay over one-tenth of all he produces or earns to the Church.

B. Y.—That is a requirement of our faith. There is no compulsion as to the payment. Each member acts in the premises according to his pleasure, under the dictates of his own conscience.

H. G.—What is done with the proceeds of this tithing?

B. Y.—Part of it is devoted to building temples and other places of worship; part to helping the poor and needy converts on their way to this country; and the largest portion to the support of the poor among the saints.

H. G.—Is none of it paid to Bishops, and other dignitaries of the Church?

B. Y.—Not one penny. No Bishop, no Elder, no Deacon, or other church officer, receives any compensation for his official services. A bishop is often required to put his hand in his own pocket, and provide therefrom for the poor of his charge; but he never receives anything for his services.

H. G.—How, then, do your ministers live?

B. Y.—By the labor of their own hands, like the first apostles. Every Bishop, every Elder, may be daily seen at work in the field or the shop, like his neighbors; every minister of the Church has his proper calling by which he earns the bread of his family; he who cannot or will not do the church's work for nothing is not wanted in her service; even our lawyers (pointing to Gen. Ferguson and another present, who

324

are the regular lawyers of the Church), are paid nothing for their services; I am the only person in the Church who has not a regular calling apart from the church's service, and I never received one farthing from her treasury; if I obtain anything from the tithing-house, I am charged with and pay for it, just as any one else would; the clerks in the tithing-store are paid like other clerks, but no one is ever paid for any service pertaining to the ministry. We think a man who cannot make his living aside from the Ministry of Christ unsuited to that office. I am called rich, and consider myself worth $250,000; but no dollar of it was ever paid me by the church, not for any service as a minister of the Everlasting Gospel. I lost nearly all I had when we were broken up in Missouri and driven from that State; I was nearly stripped again when Joseph Smith was murdered and we were driven from Illinois; but nothing was ever made up to me by the Church, nor by any one. I believe I know how to acquire property and how to take care of it.

H. G.—Can you give me any rational explanation of the aversion and hatred with which your people are generally regarded by those among whom they have lived and with whom they have been brought directly in contact?

B. Y.—No other explanation than is afforded by the crucifixion of Christ and the kindred treatment of God's ministers, prophets and saints, in all ages.

H. G.—I know that a new sect is always decried and traduced—that it is hardly ever deemed respectable to belong to one—that the Baptists, Quakers, Methodists, Universalists, &c., have each in their turn been regarded in the infancy of their sect as the off-scouring of the earth; yet I cannot remember that either of them were ever generally represented and regarded by the older sects of their early days as thieves, robbers, murderers.

B. Y.—If you will consult the contemporary Jewish account of the life and acts of Jesus Christ, you will find that he and his disciples were accused of every abominable deed and purpose—robbery and murder included. Such a work is still extant, and may be found by those who seek it.

H. G.—What do you say of the so-called Danites, or Destroying Angels, belonging to your Church?

B. Y.—What do *you* say? I know of no such band, no such persons or organization. I hear of them only in the slanders of our enemies.

H. G.—With regard, then, to the grave question on which your doctrines and practices are avowedly at war with those of the Christian world—that of a plurality of wives—is the system of your Church acceptable to the majority of its women?

B. Y.—They could not be more averse to it than I was when it was first revealed to us as the Divine will. I think they generally accept it, as I do, as the will of God.

H. G.—How general is polygamy among you?

B. Y.—I could not say. Some of those present [heads of the church] have each but one wife; others have more: each determines what is his individual duty.

H. G.—What is the largest number of wives belonging to any one man?

B. Y.—I have fifteen; I know no one who has more; but some of those sealed to me are old ladies whom I regard rather as mothers than wives, but whom I have taken home to cherish and support.

H. G.—Does not the Apostle Paul say that a bishop should be "the husband of one wife?"

B. Y.—So we hold. We do not regard any but a married man as fitted for the office of Bishop. But the Apostle does not forbid a bishop having more wives than one.

H. G.—Does not Christ say that he who puts away his wife, or marries one whom another has put away, commits adultery?

B. Y.—Yes; and I hold that no man should ever put away a wife except for adultery—not always even for that. Such is *my* individual view of the matter. I do not say that wives have never been put away in our Church, but that I do not approve of the practice.

H. G.—How do you regard what is commonly termed the Christian Sabbath?

B. Y.—As a divinely appointed day of rest. We enjoin all to rest from secular labor on that day. We would have no man enslaved to the Sabbath, but we enjoin all to respect and enjoy it.

—Such is, as nearly as I can recollect, the substance of nearly two hours' conversation, wherein much was said incidentally that would not be worth reporting, even if I could remember and reproduce it, and wherein others bore a part; but, as President Young is the first minister of the Mormon Church, and bore the principal part in the conversation, I have reported his answers alone to my questions and observations. The others appeared uniformly to defer to his views, and to acquiesce fully in his responses and explanations. He spoke readily, not always with grammatical accuracy, but with no appearance of hesitation or

326

reserve, and with no apparent desire to conceal anything, nor did he repel any of my questions as impertinent. He was very plainly dressed in thin summer clothing, and with no air of sanctimony or fanaticism. In appearance, he is a portly, frank, good-natured, rather thick-set man of fifty-five, seeming to enjoy life, and be in no particular hurry to get to heaven. His associates are plain men, evidently born and reared to a life of labor, and looking as little like crafty hypocrites or swindlers as any body of men I ever met. The absence of cant or snuffle from their manner was marked and general; yet, I think I may fairly say that their Mormonism has not impoverished them—that they were generally poor men when they embraced it, and are now in very comfortable circumstances—as men averaging three or four wives apiece certainly need to be.

If I hazard any criticisms on Mormonism generally, I reserve them for a separate letter, being determined to make this a fair and full expose of the doctrine and polity, in the very words of its prophet, so far as I can recall them. I do not believe President Young himself could present them in terms calculated to render them less obnoxious to the Gentile world than the above. But I have a right to add here, because I said it to the assembled chiefs at the close of the above colloquy, that the degradation (or, if you please, the restriction) of woman to the single office of childbearing and its accessories, is an inevitable consequence of the system here paramount. I have not observed a sign in the streets, an advertisement in the journals, of this Mormon metropolis, whereby a woman proposes to do anything whatever. No Mormon has ever cited to me his wife's or any woman's opinion on any subject; no Mormon woman has been introduced or has spoken to me; and, though I have been asked to visit Mormons in their houses, no one has spoken of his wife (or wives) desiring to see me, or his desiring me to make her (or their) acquaintance, or voluntarily indicated the existence of such a being or beings. I will not attempt to report our talk on this subject, because, unlike what I have above given, it assumed somewhat the character of a disputation, and I could hardly give it impartially; but one remark made by President Young I think I can give accurately, and it may serve as a sample of all that was offered on that side. It was in these words, I think exactly: "If I did not consider myself competent to transact a certain business without taking my wife's or any woman's counsel with regard to it, I think I ought to let that business alone." The spirit with regard to Woman, of the entire Mormon, as of all other polygamic systems, is fairly displayed in this avowal. Let any such system become established and prevalent, and woman will soon be confined to the harem, and her appearance in the street with unveiled face will be accounted immodest. I joyfully trust that the genius of the Nineteenth Century tends to a solution of the problem of Woman's sphere and destiny radically different from this.

―――――

A British Adventurer in the City of the Saints

FIVE YEARS AFTER the visit of the Frenchmen Jules Remy and Julius Brenchley, a Kiplingesque British adventurer traveled to America expressly to observe the Mormons. Scholar, linguist, soldier, diplomat, and explorer, Sir Richard Burton in 1860 at thirty-nine had already served a military career in India, had been on a pilgrimage to Mecca disguised as a Mohammedan, and had spent several years in Africa, four of them exploring the sources of the Nile. Inevitably he saw Islamic parallels among the Mormons. "It was an appropriate design," said the Edinburgh Review, *"on the part of the English Hadjee to visit the Mormon city. It may not have required that wonderful endurance of physical hardships, which in Captain Burton is combined with so much sensitiveness of character and delicacy of perception, to accomplish this journey, any more than his varied knowledge and literary requirements were needed to describe the common manners and unlettered life of this bastard result of American civilization; but there is enough of analogy between the novel notions and revived customs of the people of Utah, and the ideas and institutions of that elder world, with which he is so familiar, to make the comparison interesting to himself and to others."*

Sir Richard, eventually the author of some fifty books and translator of The Arabian Nights, *published in London in 1861 his American observations in* The City of the Saints and across the Rocky Mountains to California. *A "genial work," with a style that "ambles along like a well-trained horse with the bridle loose upon his neck," as one contemporary review found it, it is perhaps the most widely remembered travel book about the Mormons. Later observers criticized it as altogether too favorable. They objected to Burton's approval of polygamy. (His wife had to explain publicly that his practice did not follow his teaching.) Much of the book describes the journey to and from Utah, but more than half is devoted to the City of the Saints itself, where he tarried from August 25 to September 20, 1860. Every traveler became rhapsodic at first sight of the Salt Lake Valley and its mountain approaches, but Burton's descriptions are particularly lyric. He found Echo Canyon so sublime he feared it would make all similar features "look tame." He sensed the feelings of the Mormon converts as they caught their first glimpse of the Holy Valley: "Even I could not . . . gaze upon the scene without emotion."*

The following portrait of Salt Lake City is taken from the New York edition of 1862.

In due time, emerging from the gates, and portals, and deep serrations of the upper course, we descended into a lower level: here Big, now called Emigration Kanyon, gradually bulges out, and its steep slopes of grass and fern, shrubbery and stunted brush, fall imperceptibly into the plain. The valley presently lay full before our sight. At this place the pilgrim emigrants, like the Hajjis of Mecca and Jerusalem, give vent to the emotions long pent up within their bosoms by sobs and tears, laughter and congratulations, psalms and hysterics. It is indeed no wonder that the children dance, that strong men cheer and shout, and that nervous women, broken with fatigue and hope deferred, scream and faint; that the ignorant should fondly believe that the "spirit of God pervades the very atmosphere," and that Zion on the tops of the mountains is nearer heaven than other parts of earth. In good sooth, though uninfluenced by religious fervor—beyond the natural satisfaction of seeing a bran-new Holy City—even I could not, after nineteen days in a mail-wagon, gaze upon the scene without emotion.

The sublime and the beautiful were in present contrast. Switzerland and Italy lay side by side. The magnificent scenery of the past mountains and ravines still floated before the retina, as emerging from the gloomy depths of the Golden Pass—the mouth of Emigration Kanyon is more poetically so called—we came suddenly in view of the Holy Valley of the West. . . .

The city revealed itself, as we approached, from behind its screen, the inclined terraces of the upper table-land, and at last it lay stretched before us as upon a map. At a little distance the aspect was somewhat Oriental, and in some points it reminded me of modern Athens without the Acropolis. None of the buildings, except the Prophet's house, were whitewashed. The material—the thick, sun-dried adobe, common to all parts of the Eastern world—was of a dull leaden blue, deepened by the atmosphere to a gray, like the shingles of the roofs. The number of gardens and compounds—each tenement within the walls originally received 1.50 square acre, and those outside from five to ten acres, according to their distance—the dark clumps and lines of bitter cottonwood, locust, or acacia, poplars and fruit-trees, apples, peaches, and vines—how lovely they appeared, after the baldness of the prairies!—and, finally, the fields of long-eared maize and sweet sorghum strengthened the similarity to an Asiatic rather than to an American settlement. The differences presently became as salient. The farm-houses, with their stacks and stock, strongly suggested the Old Country. Moreover, domes and minarets—even churches and steeples—were wholly wanting, an omission that somewhat surprised me. The only building conspicuous from afar was the block occupied by the present Head of the Church. The court-house, with its tinned Muscovian dome, at the west end of the city; the arsenal, a barn-like structure, on a bench below the Jebel Nur of the valley—Ensign Peak; and a saw-mill, built beyond the southern boundary, were the next in importance.

On our way we passed the vestiges of an old moat, from which was taken the earth for the bulwarks of Zion. A Romulian wall, of puddle, mud, clay, and pebbles, six miles—others say 2600 acres—in length, twelve feet high, six feet broad at the base, and two and three quarters at the top, with embrasures five to six feet above the ground, and semi-bastions at half musket range, was decided, in 1853–54, to be necessary, as a defense against the Lamanites, whose name in the vulgar is Yuta Indians. . . .

The road ran through the Big Field, southeast of the city, six miles square, and laid off in five-acre lots. Presently, passing the precincts of habitation, we entered, at a slapping pace, the second ward, called Denmark, from its tenants, who mostly herd together. The disposition of the settlement is like that of the nineteenth century New-World cities—from Washington to the future metropolis of the great Terra Australis—a system of right angles, the roads, streets, and lanes, if they can be called so, intersecting one another. The advantages or disadvantages of the rectangular plan have been exhausted in argument; the new style is best suited, I believe, for the New, as the old must, perforce, remain in the Old World. The suburbs are thinly settled; the mass of habitations lie around and south of Temple Block. The streets of the suburbs are mere roads, cut by deep ups and downs, and by gutters on both sides, which, though full of pure water, have no bridge save a plank at the *trottoirs*. In summer the thoroughfares are dusty, in wet weather deep with viscid mud.

The houses are almost all of one pattern—a barn shape, with wings and lean-tos, generally facing, sometimes turned endways to the street, which give a suburban look to the settlement; and the diminutive casements show that window-glass is not yet made in the Valley. In the best adobes the adobe rests upon a few courses of sandstone, which prevent undermining by water or ground-damp, and it must always be protected by a coping from the rain and snow. The poorer are small, low, and hut-like; others are long single-storied buildings, somewhat like stables, with many entrances. The best houses resemble East Indian bungalows, with flat roofs, and low, shady verandas, well trellised, and supported by posts or pillars. All are provided with chimneys, and substantial doors to keep out the piercing cold. The offices are always placed, for hygienic reasons, outside; and some have a story and a half —the latter intended for lumber and other stores. I looked in vain for the out-house harems, in which certain romancers concerning things Mormon had informed me that wives are kept, like any other stock. I presently found this but one of a multitude of delusions. Upon the whole, the Mormon settlement was a vast improvement upon its contemporaries in the valleys of the Mississippi and the Missouri.

The road through the faubourg was marked by posts and rails, which, as we advanced toward the heart of the city, were replaced by neat palings. The garden-plots were small, as sweet earth must be brought down from the mountains; and the flowers were principally those of the Old Country—the red French bean, the rose, the geranium, and the single pink; the ground or winter cherry was common; so were nasturtiums; and we saw tansy, but not that plant for which our souls, well-nigh weary of hopes of juleps long deferred, chiefly lusted—mint. The fields were large and numerous, but the Saints have too many and various occupations to keep them, Moravian-like, neat and trim; weeds overspread the ground; often the wild sunflower-tops outnumbered the heads of maize. The fruit had suffered from an unusually nipping frost in May; the peach-trees were barren; the vines bore no produce; only a few good apples were in Mr. Brigham Young's garden, and the watermelons were poor, yellow, and tasteless, like the African. On the other hand, potatoes, onions, cabbages, and cucumbers were good and plentiful, the tomato was ripening every where, fat full-eared wheat rose in stacks, and crops of excellent hay were scattered about near the houses.

The people came to their doors to see the mail-coach, as if it were the "Derby dilly" of old, go by. I could not but be struck by the modified English appearance of the colony, and by the prodigious numbers of the white-headed children.

Presently we debouched upon the main thoroughfare, the centre of population and business, where the houses of the principal Mormon dignitaries and the stores of the Gentile merchants combine to form the city's only street which can be properly so called. It is, indeed, both street and market, for, curious to say, New Zion has not yet built for herself a bazar or market-place. Nearly opposite the Post-office, in a block on the eastern side, with a long veranda, supported by trimmed and painted posts, was a two-storied, pent-roofed building, whose sign-board, swinging to a tall, gibbet-like flag-staff, dressed for the occasion, announced it to be the Salt Lake House, the principal, if not the only establishment of the kind in New Zion. In the Far West, one learns not to expect much of the hostelry; I had not seen aught so grand for many a day. Its depth is greater than its frontage, and behind it, secured by a *porte cochère,* is a large yard for corraling cattle. A rough-looking crowd of drivers, drivers' friends, and idlers, almost every man openly armed with revolver and bowie-knife, gathered round the doorway to greet Jim, and "prospect" the "new lot"; and the host came out to assist us in transporting our scattered effects. We looked vainly for a bar on the ground floor; a bureau for registering names was there, but (temperance, in public at least, being the order of the day) the usual tempting array of bottles and decanters was not forthcoming; up stairs we found a Gentile ballroom, a tolerably furnished sitting-room, and bed-chambers, apparently made out of a single apartment by partitions too thin to be strictly agreeable. The household had its deficiencies; blacking, for instance, had run out, and servants could not be engaged till the expected arrival of the hand-cart train. However, the proprietor, Mr. Townsend, a Mormon, from the State of Maine—when expelled from Nauvoo, he had parted with land, house, and furniture for $50—who had married an Englishwoman, was in the highest degree civil and obliging, and he attended personally to our wants, offered his wife's services to Mrs. Dana, and put us all in the best of humors, despite the closeness of the atmosphere, the sadness ever attending one's first entrance into a new place, the swarms of "emigration flies"—so called because they appear in September with the emigrants, and, after living for a month, die off with the first snow—and a certain populousness of bedstead, concerning which the less said the better. . . .

A British Adventurer in the City of the Saints

Walking in a northward direction up Main, otherwise called Whisky Street, we could not but observe the "magnificent distances" of the settlement, which, containing 9000—12,000 souls, covers an area of three miles. This broadway is 132 feet wide, including the side-walks, which are each twenty, and, like the rest of the principal avenues, is planted with locust and other trees. There are twenty or twenty-one wards or cantons, numbered from the S.E. "boustrophedon" to the N.W. corner. They have a common fence and a bishop apiece. They are called after the creeks, trees, people, or positions, as Mill-Creek Ward, Little Cottonwood, Denmark, and South Ward. Every ward contains about nine blocks, each of which is forty rods square. The area of ten acres is divided into four to eight lots, of two and a half to one and a quarter acres each, 264 feet by 132. A city ordinance places the houses twenty feet behind the front line of the lot, leaving an intermediate place for shrubbery or trees. This rule, however, is not observed in Main Street. . . .

Main Street is rapidly becoming crowded. The western block, opposite the hotel, contains about twenty houses of irregular shape and size. The buildings are intended to supply the principal wants of a far-Western settlement, as bakery, butchery, and blacksmithery, hardware and crockery, paint and whip warehouse, a "fashionable tailor"—and "fashionable" in one point, that his works are more expensive than Poole's—shoe-stores, tannery and curriery; the Pantechnicon, on a more pretentious style than its neighbors, kept by Mr. Gilbert Clements, Irishman and orator; dry-goods, groceries, liquors, and furniture shops, Walker's agency, and a kind of restaurant for ice-cream, a luxury which costs 25 cents a glass; saddlers, dealers in "food, flour, and provisions," hats, shoes, clothing, sash laths, shingles, timber, copper, tin, crockery-ware, carpenters' tools, and mouse-traps; a watchmaker and repairer, a gunsmith, locksmith, and armorer, soap and candle maker, nail-maker, and venders of "Yankee notions." On the eastern side, where the same articles are sold on a larger scale, live the principal Gentile merchants, Mr. Gilbert and Mr. Nixon, an English Saint; Mr. R. Gill, a "physiological barber"; Mr. Godbe's "apothecary and drug stores"; Goddard's confectionery; Messrs. Hockaday and Burr, general dealers, who sell every thing, from a bag of potatoes to a yard of gold lace; and various establishments, Mormon and others. Crossing the street that runs east and west, we pass on the right hand a small block, occupied by Messrs. Dyer and Co., sutlers to a regiment in Arizona, and next to it the stores of Messrs. Hooper and Cronyn, with an ambrotype and daguerrean room behind.

333

The stores, I may remark, are far superior, in all points, to the shops in an English country town that is not a regular watering-place.

Charles Dickens Describes a Mormon Emigrant Ship

IN 1863 Charles Dickens as the "Uncommercial Traveller" briefly boarded the sailship Amazon *to see for himself what was already a common sight in a number of European ports: a company of departing Mormon converts bound for Utah. Mormon emigration was then at high tide. By 1860 thirty thousand proselytes, largely from Scandinavia and the British Isles, had left for Zion. Nearly ten thousand more would leave England in the ensuing decade. They were part of Mormonism's "gathering," an extensive church-directed program of emigration to the place of refuge for the righteous in the last days.*

The gathering's organization amazed contemporaries. It included a shipping agency in Liverpool, chartered vessels, wholesale outfittings on the frontier, veteran leadership, and a Perpetual Emigrating Fund which pooled the resources of rich and poor to make the most of self-help and timely assistance. Mormon arrangements made the Atlantic crossing a humane experience instead of the usual nightmare. Lord Houghton, writing for the Edinburgh Review *in January, 1862, noted that "The Select Committee of the House of Commons on emigrant ships for 1854 summoned the Mormon agent and passenger-broker before it, and came to the conclusion that no ships under the provisions of the 'Passengers Act' could be depended upon for comfort and security in the same degree as those under his administration. The Mormon ship is a Family under strong and accepted discipline, with every provision for comfort, decorum, and internal peace."*

Dickens confirmed this view. His lively sketch "Bound for the Great Salt Lake" is reprinted here from The Uncommercial Traveller *in the Gadshill Edition of his works (Scribner's, 1898). The Uncommercial Traveller is a collection of essays, on occasion autobiographical, which Dickens began writing in 1860 for his serial* All the Year Round *and continued during the remainder of his life. "Dickens is here," says Andrew Lang, ". . . still the man who began by 'Sketches by Boz.' The*

Charles Dickens Describes a Mormon Emigrant Ship

lover of the open air, the un-bookish naturalist of human life, the student of tramps, cheap-jacks, sailors on shore, and plyers of odd trades in shy neighborhoods. . . . [The Uncommercial Traveller] *is an epitome of Dickens; none of his greater qualities, scarcely one of his blemishes, is absent."*

Behold me on my way to an Emigrant Ship, on a hot morning early in June. My road lies through that part of London generally known to the initiated as "Down by the Docks." Down by the Docks is home to a good many people—to too many, if I may judge from the overflow of local population in the streets—but my nose insinuates that the number to whom it is Sweet Home might be easily counted. Down by the Docks is a region I would choose as my point of embarkation aboard ship if I were an emigrant. It would present my intention to me in such a sensible light; it would show me so many things to be run away from. . . .

Pleasant whispers of there being a fresher air down the river than down by the Docks, go pursuing one another, playfully, in and out of the openings in its spire. Gigantic in the basin just beyond the church, looms my Emigrant Ship: her name, the *Amazon*. Her figure-head is not disfigured as those beauteous founders of the race of strong-minded women are fabled to have been, for the convenience of drawing the bow; but I sympathise with the carver:

> A flattering carver who made it his care
> To carve busts as they ought to be—not as they were.

My Emigrant Ship lies broadside-on to the wharf. Two great gang-ways made of spars and planks connect her with the wharf; and up and down these gangways, perpetually crowding to and fro and in and out, like ants, are the Emigrants who are going to sail in my Emigrant Ship. Some with cabbages, some with loaves of bread, some with cheese and butter, some with milk and beer, some with boxes, beds, and bundles, some with babies—nearly all with children—nearly all with bran-new tin cans for their daily allowance of water, uncomfortably suggestive of a tin flavor in the drink. To and fro, up and down, aboard and ashore, swarming here and there and everywhere, my Emigrants. And still as the Dock-Gate swings upon its hinges, cabs appear, and carts appear, and vans appear, bringing more of my Emigrants, with more cabbages, more loaves, more cheese and butter, more milk and beer, more boxes, beds, and bundles, more tin cans, and on those shipping investments accumulated compound interest of children.

III · CHRONICLES AND JUDGES

I go aboard my Emigrant Ship. I go first to the great cabin, and find it in the usual condition of a Cabin at that pass. Perspiring landsmen, with loose papers, and with pens and inkstands, pervade it; and the general appearance of things is as if the late Mr. Amazon's funeral had just come home from the cemetery, and the disconsolate Mrs. Amazon's trustees found the affairs in great disorder, and were looking high and low for the will. I go out on the poop-deck, for air, and surveying the emigrants on the deck below (indeed they are crowded all about me, up there too), find more pens and inkstands in action, and more papers, and interminable complication respecting accounts with individuals for tin cans and what not. But nobody is weeping, and down upon the deck in every corner where it is possible to find a few square feet to kneel, crouch, or lie in, people, in every unsuitable attitude for writing, are writing letters.

Now, I have seen emigrant ships before this day in June. And these people are so strikingly different from all other people in like circumstances whom I have ever seen, that I wonder aloud, "What *would* a stranger suppose these emigrants to be!"

The vigilant bright face of the weather-browned captain of the *Amazon* is at my shoulder, and he says, "What, indeed! The most of these came aboard yesterday evening. They came from various parts of England in small parties that had never seen one another before. Yet they had not been a couple of hours on board, when they established their own police, made their own regulations, and set their own watches at all the hatchways. Before nine o'clock, the ship was as orderly and as quiet as a man-of-war."

I looked about me again, and saw the letter-writing going on with the most curious composure. Perfectly abstracted in the midst of the crowd; while great casks were swinging aloft, and being lowered into the hold; while hot agents were hurrying up and down, adjusting the interminable accounts; while two hundred strangers were searching everywhere for two hundred other strangers, and were asking questions about them of two hundred more; while the children played up and down all the steps, and in and out among all the people's legs, and were beheld, to the general dismay, toppling over all the dangerous places; the letter-writers wrote on calmly. On the starboard side of the ship, a grizzled man dictated a long letter to another grizzled man in an immense fur cap: which letter was of so profound a quality, that it became necessary for the amanuensis at intervals to take off his fur cap in both his hands, for the ventilation of his brain, and stare at him who dictated, as a man of many mysteries who was worth looking at. On the larboard side, a woman had covered a belaying-pin with a white cloth to make a neat desk of it, and was sitting on a little box, writing with the deliberation of a bookkeeper. Down upon her breast on the planks of the deck at this woman's feet, with her head diving in under a beam of the bulwarks on that side, as an eligible place of refuge for her sheet of paper, a neat and pretty girl wrote for a good hour (she fainted at last), only rising to the surface occasionally for a dip of ink. Alongside the boat, close to me on the poop-deck, another girl, a fresh well-grown country girl, was writing another letter on the bare deck. Later in the day, when this self-same boat was filled with a choir who sang glees and catches for a long time, one of the singers, a girl, sang her part mechanically all the while, and wrote a letter in the bottom of the boat while doing so.

"A stranger would be puzzled to guess the right name for these people, Mr. Uncommercial," says the captain.

"Indeed he would."

"If you hadn't known, could you ever have supposed——?"

"How could I! I should have said they were in their degree, the pick and flower of England."

"So should I," says the captain.

"How many are they?"

"Eight hundred in round numbers."

I went between-decks, where the families with children swarmed in the dark, where unavoidable confusion had been caused by the last arrivals, and where the confusion was increased by the little preparations for dinner that were going on in each group. A few women here and there, had got lost, and were laughing at it, and asking their way to their own people, or out on deck again. A few of the poor children were crying; but otherwise the universal cheerfulness was amazing. "We shall shake down by to-morrow." "We shall come all right in a day or so." "We shall have more light at sea." Such phrases I heard everywhere, as I groped my way among chests and barrels and beams and unstowed cargo and ring-bolts and Emigrants, down to the lower-deck, and thence up to the light of day again, and to my former station.

Surely, an extraordinary people in their power of self-abstraction! All the former letter-writers were still writing calmly, and many more letter-writers had broken out in my absence. A boy with a bag of books in his hand and a slate under his arm, emerged from below, concentrated himself in my neighbourhood (espying a convenient skylight for his purpose), and went to work at a sum as if he were stone deaf. A father and mother and several young children, on the main deck below me, had formed a family circle close to the foot of the crowded restless gangway, where the children made a nest for themselves in a coil of rope, and the father and mother, she suckling the youngest, discussed family affairs as peaceably as if they were in perfect retirement. I think the most noticeable characteristic in the eight hundred as a mass, was their exemption from hurry.

Eight hundred what? "Geese, villain?" EIGHT HUNDRED MORMONS. I, Uncommercial Traveller for the firm of Human Interest Brothers, had come aboard this Emigrant Ship to see what eight hundred Latter-day Saints were like, and I found them (to the rout and overthrow of all my expectations) like what I now describe with scrupulous exactness.

The Mormon Agent who had been active in getting them together, and in making the contract with my friends the owners of the ship to take them as far as New York on their way to the Great Salt Lake, was pointed out to me. A compactly-made handsome man in black, rather short, with rich-brown hair and beard, and clear bright eyes. From his speech, I should set him down as American. Probably, a man who had "knocked about the world" pretty much. A man with a frank open manner, and unshrinking look; withal a man of great quickness. I believe he was wholly ignorant of my Uncommercial individuality, and consequently of my immense Uncommercial importance.

UNCOMMERCIAL. These are a very fine set of people you have brought together here.

MORMON AGENT. Yes, sir, they are a *very* fine set of people.

UNCOMMERCIAL (looking about). Indeed, I think it would be difficult to find eight hundred people together anywhere else, and find so much beauty and so much strength and capacity for work among them.

MORMON AGENT (not looking about, but looking steadily at Uncommercial). I think so.——We sent out about a thousand more, yes'day, from Liverpool.

UNCOMMERCIAL. You are not going with these emigrants?

MORMON AGENT. No, sir. I remain.

UNCOMMERCIAL. But you have been in the Mormon Territory?

MORMON AGENT. Yes; I left Utah about three years ago.

UNCOMMERCIAL. It is surprising to me that these people are all so cherry, and make so little of the immense distance before them.

Charles Dickens Describes a Mormon Emigrant Ship

MORMON AGENT. Well, you see; many of 'em have friends out at Utah, and many of 'em look forward to meeting friends on the way.

UNCOMMERCIAL. On the way?

MORMON AGENT. This way 'tis. This ship lands 'em in New York City. Then they go on by rail right away beyond St. Louis, to that part of the Banks of the Missouri where they strike the Plains. There, wagons from the settlement meet 'em to bear 'em company on their journey 'cross—twelve hundred miles about. Industrious people who come out to the settlement soon get wagons of their own, and so the friends of some of these will come down in their own wagons to meet 'em. They look forward to that, greatly.

UNCOMMERCIAL. On their long journey across the Desert, do you arm them?

MORMON AGENT. Mostly you would find they have arms of some kind or another already with them. Such as had not arms we should arm across the Plains, for the general protection and defence.

UNCOMMERCIAL. Will these wagons bring down any produce to the Missouri?

MORMON AGENT. Well, since the war broke out, we've taken to growing cotton, and they'll likely bring down cotton to be exchanged for machinery. We want machinery. Also we have taken to growing indigo, which is a fine commodity for profit. It has been found that the climate, on the further side of the Great Salt Lake suits well for raising indigo.

UNCOMMERCIAL. I am told that these people now on board are principally from the South of England?

MORMON AGENT. And from Wales. That's true.

UNCOMMERCIAL. Do you get many Scotch?

MORMON AGENT. Not many.

UNCOMMERCIAL. Highlanders, for instance?

MORMON AGENT. No, not Highlanders. They ain't interested enough in universal brotherhood and peace and good will.

UNCOMMERCIAL. The old fighting blood is strong in them?

MORMON AGENT. Well, yes. And besides, they've no faith.

UNCOMMERCIAL (who has been burning to get at the Prophet Joe Smith, and seems to discover an opening). Faith in——!

MORMON AGENT (far too many for Uncommercial). Well,—in anything!

Similarly on this same head, the Uncommercial underwent discomfiture from a Wiltshire laborer: a simple fresh-colored farm-laborer, of eight-and-thirty, who at one time stood beside him looking on at new arrivals, and with whom he held this dialogue:

UNCOMMERCIAL. Would you mind my asking you what part of the country you come from?

WILTSHIRE. Not a bit. Theer! (exultingly) I've worked all my life o' Salisbury Plain, right under the shadder o' Stonehenge. You mightn't think it, but I haive.

UNCOMMERCIAL. And a pleasant country too.

WILTSHIRE. Ah! 'Tis a pleasant country.

UNCOMMERCIAL. Have you any family on board?

WILTSHIRE. Two children, boy and gal. I am a widderer, I am, and I'm going out alonger my boy and gal. That's my gal, and she's a fine gal o' sixteen (pointing out the girl who is writing by the boat). I'll go and fetch my boy. I'd like to show you my boy. (Here Wiltshire disappears, and presently comes back with a big shy boy of twelve, in a superabundance of boots, who is not at all glad to be presented.) He is a fine boy too, and a boy fur to work! (Boy having undutifully bolted, Wiltshire drops him.)

UNCOMMERCIAL. It must cost you a great deal of money to go so far, three strong.

WILTSHIRE. A power of money. Theer! Eight shillen a week, eight shillen a week, eight shillen a week, put by out of the week's wages for ever so long.

UNCOMMERCIAL. I wonder how you did it.

WILTSHIRE (recognizing in this a kindred spirit). See theer now! I wonder how I done it! But what with a bit o' subscription heer, and what with a bit o' help theer, it were done at last, though I don't hardly know how. Then it were unfort'net for us, you see, as we got kep' in Bristol so long—nigh a fortnight, it were—on accounts of a mistake wi' Brother Halliday. Swaller'd up money, it did, when we might have come straight on.

UNCOMMERCIAL (delicately approaching Joe Smith). You are of the Mormon religion, of course?

WILTSHIRE (confidently). O yes, I'm a Mormon. (Then reflectively.) I'm a Mormon. (Then, looking round the ship, feigns to descry a particular friend in an empty spot, and evades the Uncommercial for evermore.)

After a noontide pause for dinner, during which my Emigrants were nearly all between-decks, and the *Amazon* looked deserted, a general muster took place. The muster was for the ceremony of passing the

Government Inspector and the Doctor. Those authorities held their temporary state amidships, by a cask or two; and, knowing that the whole eight hundred emigrants must come face to face with them, I took my station behind the two. They knew nothing whatever of me, I believe, and my testimony to the unpretending gentleness and good nature with which they discharged their duty, may be of the greater worth. There was not the slightest flavor of the Circumlocution Office about their proceedings.

The emigrants were now all on deck. They were densely crowded aft, and swarmed upon the poop-deck like bees. Two or three Mormon agents stood ready to hand them on to the Inspector, and to hand them forward when they had passed. By what successful means a special aptitude for organization had been infused into these people, I am, of course, unable to report. But I know that, even now, there was no disorder, hurry, or difficulty.

All being ready, the first group are handed on. That member of the party who is entrusted with the passenger-ticket for the whole, has been warned by one of the agents to have it ready, and here it is in his hand. In every instance through the whole eight hundred, without an exception, this paper is always ready.

INSPECTOR (reading the ticket). Jessie Jobson, Sophronia Jobson, Jessie Jobson again, Matilda Jobson, William Jobson, Jane Jobson, Matilda Jobson again, Brigham Jobson, Leonardo Jobson, and Orson Jobson. Are you all here? (glancing at the party, over his spectacles).

JESSIE JOBSON NUMBER TWO. All here, sir.

This group is composed of an old grandfather and grandmother, their married son and his wife, and *their* family of children. Orson Jobson is a little child asleep in his mother's arms. The Doctor, with a kind word or so, lifts up the corner of the mother's shawl, looks at the child's face, and touches the little clenched hand. If we were all as well as Orson Jobson, doctoring would be a poor profession.

INSPECTOR. Quite right, Jessie Jobson. Take your ticket, Jessie, and pass on.

And away they go. Mormon agent, skilful and quiet, hands them on. Mormon agent, skilful and quiet, hands next party up.

INSPECTOR (reading ticket again). Susannah Cleverly and William Cleverly. Brother and sister, eh?

SISTER (young woman of business, hustling slow brother). Yes, sir.

INSPECTOR. Very good, Susannah Cleverly. Take your ticket, Susannah, and take care of it.

341

And away they go

INSPECTOR (taking ticket again). Sampson Dibble and Dorothy Dibble (surveying a very old couple over his spectacles, with some surprise). Your husband quite blind, Mrs. Dibble?

MRS. DIBBLE. Yes, sir, he be stone-blind.

MR. DIBBLE (addressing the mast). Yes, sir, I be stone-blind.

INSPECTOR. That's a bad job. Take your ticket, Mrs. Dibble, and don't lose it, and pass on.

Doctor taps Mr. Dibble on the eyebrow with his forefinger, and away they go.

INSPECTOR (taking ticket again). Anastatia Weedle.

ANASTATIA (a pretty girl, in a bright Garibaldi, this morning elected by universal suffrage the Beauty of the Ship). That is me, sir.

ANASTATIA (shaking her curls). I am with Mrs. Jobson, sir, but I've got separated for the moment.

INSPECTOR. Oh! You are with the Jobsons? Quite right. That'll do, Miss Weedle. Don't lose your ticket.

Away she goes, and joins the Jobsons who are waiting for her, and stoops and kisses Brigham Jobson—who appears to be considered too young for the purpose, by several Mormons rising twenty, who are looking on. Before her extensive skirts have departed from the casks, a decent widow stands there with four children, and so the roll goes.

The faces of some of the Welsh people, among whom there were many old persons, were certainly the least intelligent. Some of these emigrants would have bungled sorely, but for the directing hand that was always ready. The intelligence here was unquestionably of a low order, and the heads were of a poor type. Generally the case was the reverse. There were many worn faces bearing traces of patient poverty and hard work, and there was great steadiness of purpose and much undemonstrative self-respect among this class. A few young men were going singly. Several girls were going two or three together. These latter I found it very difficult to refer back, in my mind, to their relinquished homes and pursuits. Perhaps they were more like country milliners, and pupil teachers rather tawdrily dressed, than any other classes of young women. I noticed, among many little ornaments worn, more than one photograph-brooch of the Princess of Wales, and also of the late Prince Consort. Some single women of from thirty to forty, whom one might suppose to be embroiderers, or straw-bonnet-makers, were obviously going out in quest of husbands, as finer ladies go to India. That they had any distinct notions of a plurality of husbands or wives, I do not believe. To suppose the family groups of whom the majority of emigrants were composed, polygamically possessed, would be to suppose an absurdity, manifest to any one who saw the fathers and mothers.

I should say (I had no means of ascertaining the fact) that most familiar kinds of handicraft trades were represented here. Farm-laborers, shepherds, and the like, had their full share of representation, but I doubt if they preponderated. It was interesting to see how the leading spirit in the family circle never failed to show itself, even in the simple process of answering to the names as they were called, and checking off the owners of the names. Sometimes it was the father, much oftener the mother, sometimes a quick little girl second or third in order of seniority. It seemed to occur for the first time to some heavy fathers, what large families they had; and their eyes rolled about, during the calling of the list, as if they half misdoubted some other family to have smuggled into their own. Among all the fine handsome children, I observed but two with marks upon their necks that were probably scrofulous. Out of the whole number of emigrants, but one old woman was temporarily set aside by the doctor, on suspicion of fever; but even she afterwards obtained a clean bill of health.

When all had "passed," and the afternoon began to wear on, a black box became visible on deck, which box was in charge of certain personages also in black, of whom only one had the conventional air of an itinerant preacher. This box contained a supply of hymn-books, neatly printed and got up, published at Liverpool, and also in London at the "Latter-Day Saints' Book Depot, 30, Florence-Street." Some copies were handsomely bound; the plainer were the more in request, and many were bought. The title ran: "Sacred Hymns and Spiritual Songs for the Church of Jesus Christ of Latter-Day Saints." The Preface, dated Manchester, 1840, ran thus:—"The Saints in this country have been very desirous for a Hymn Book adapted to their faith and worship, that they might sing the truth with an understanding heart, and express their praise, joy and gratitude in songs adapted to the New and Everlasting Covenant. In accordance with their wishes, we have selected the following volume, which we hope will prove acceptable until a greater variety can be added. With sentiments of high consideration and esteem, we subscribe ourselves your brethren in the New and Everlasting Covenant, BRIGHAM YOUNG, PARLEY P. PRATT, JOHN TAYLOR." From this book—by no means explanatory to myself of the New and Everlasting Covenant, and not at all making my heart an understanding one on the subject of that mystery—a hymn was sung, which did not attract any

343

great amount of attention, and was supported by a rather select circle. But the choir in the boat was very popular and pleasant; and there was to have been a band, only the cornet was late in coming on board. In the course of the afternoon, a mother appeared from shore, in search of her daughter, "who had run away with the Mormons." She received every assistance from the Inspector, but her daughter was not found to be on board. The saints did not seem to me particularly interested in finding her.

Towards five o'clock, the galley became full of tea-kettles, and an agreeable fragrance of tea pervaded the ship. There was no scrambling or jostling for the hot water, no ill humor, no quarrelling. As the *Amazon* was to sail with the next tide, and as it would not be high water before two o'clock in the morning, I left her with her tea in full action, and her idle steam tug lying by, deputing steam and smoke for the time being to the tea-kettles.

Mark Twain Makes Some Wisecracks

SAMUEL CLEMENS *of Hannibal, Missouri, tramp printer and river pilot, was twenty-six and not yet Mark Twain when in 1861 he came west with his brother Orion, who had accepted an appointment as territorial secretary for Nevada. They stayed only two days in Salt Lake en route to Carson City, long enough to provide Twain with some humorous recollections when he came to write* Roughing It *ten years later. By then he was already famous as "The Wild Humorist of the Pacific Slope," pictured in the advertisements astride a jumping frog in mid-air; and his* Innocents Abroad, *published in 1869, was a national bestseller. He was editor of the Buffalo* Express, *married to a genteel New Englander, and destined for immortality with his greatest books yet to come.*

In Roughing It, *full of anecdotes about his six years of vagabonding in Nevada and California, he gave the public the drolleries they expected. "This book," he wrote, "is merely a personal narrative, and not a pretentious history or a philosophical dissertation." He apologized for any "information" in it. "The more I calk up the sources, and the tighter I get, the more I leak wisdom." He could hardly be expected to suppress a few*

Mark Twain Makes Some Wisecracks

jokes about the Mormons, to whom he devoted five brief and very un-
even chapters in his book. The following samples are taken from the
original subscription edition of 1872.

As the night closed in we took sanctuary in the Salt Lake House and
unpacked our baggage. We had a fine supper, of the freshest meats and
fowls and vegetables—a great variety and as great abundance. We
walked about the streets some, afterward, and glanced in at shops and
stores; and there was fascination in surreptitiously staring at every crea-
ture we took to be a Mormon. This was fairy-land to us, to all intents
and purposes—a land of enchantment, and goblins, and awful mystery.
We felt a curiosity to ask every child how many mothers it had, and if
it could tell them apart; and we experienced a thrill every time a dwelling-house door opened and shut as we passed, disclosing a glimpse of
human heads and backs and shoulders—for we so longed to have a good
satisfying look at a Mormon family in all its comprehensive ampleness,
disposed in the customary concentric rings of its home circle. . . .

Next day we strolled about everywhere through the broad, straight,
level streets, and enjoyed the pleasant strangeness of a city of fifteen
thousand inhabitants with no loafers perceptible in it; and no visible
drunkards or noisy people; a limpid stream rippling and dancing through
every street in place of a filthy gutter; block after block of trim dwellings, built of "frame" and sunburned brick—a great thriving orchard and
garden behind every one of them, apparently—branches from the street
stream winding and sparkling among the garden beds and fruit trees—
and a grand general air of neatness, repair, thrift and comfort, around
and about and over the whole. And everywhere were workshops, factories, and all manner of industries; and intent faces and busy hands were
to be seen wherever one looked; and in one's ears was the ceaseless
clink of hammers, the buzz of trade and the contented hum of drums
and fly-wheels.

The armorial crest of my own State consisted of two dissolute bears
holding up the head of a dead and gone cask between them and making
the pertinent remark, "United, We Stand—(hic!)—Divided, We Fall."
It was always too figurative for the author of this book. But the Mormon
crest was easy. And it was simple, unostentatious, and fitted like a glove.
It was a representation of a Golden Beehive, with the bees all at
work! . . .

Salt Lake City was healthy—an extremely healthy city. They declared
there was only one physician in the place and he was arrested every

week regularly and held to answer under the vagrant act for having "no visible means of support." They always give you a good substantial article of truth in Salt Lake, and good measure and good weight, too. Very often, if you wished to weigh one of their airiest little commonplace statements you would want the hay scales. . . .

The second day, we made the acquaintance of Mr. Street (since deceased) and put on white shirts and went and paid a state visit to the king. He seemed a quiet, kindly, easy-mannered, dignified, self-possessed old gentleman of fifty-five or sixty, and had a gentle craft in his eye that probably belonged there. He was very simply dressed and was just taking off a straw hat as we entered. He talked about Utah, and the Indians, and Nevada, and general American matters and questions, with our secretary and certain government officials who came with us. But he never paid any attention to me, notwithstanding I made several attempts to "draw him out" on federal politics and his high handed attitude toward Congress. I thought some of the things I said were rather fine. But he merely looked around at me, at distant intervals, something as I have seen a benignant old cat look around to see which kitten was meddling with her tail. By and by I subsided into an indignant silence, and so sat until the end, hot and flushed, and execrating him in my heart for an ignorant savage. But he was calm. His conversation with those gentlemen flowed on as sweetly and peacefully and musically as any summer brook. When the audience was ended and we were retiring from the presence, he put his hand on my head, beamed down on me in an admiring way and said to my brother:

"Ah—your child, I presume? Boy, or girl?". . .

Our stay in Salt Lake City amounted to only two days, and therefore we had no time to make the customary inquisition into the workings of polygamy and get up the usual statistics and deductions preparatory to calling the attention of the nation at large once more to the matter. I had the will to do it. With the gushing self-sufficiency of youth I was feverish to plunge in headlong and achieve a great reform here—until I saw the Mormon women. Then I was touched. My heart was wiser than my head. It warmed toward these poor, ungainly and pathetically "homely" creatures, and as I turned to hide the generous moisture in my eyes, I said, "No—the man that marries one of them has done an act of Christian charity which entitles him to the kindly applause of mankind, not their harsh censure—and the man that marries sixty of them has done a deed of open-handed generosity so sublime that the nations should stand uncovered in his presence and worship in silence.". . .

All men have heard of the Mormon Bible, but few except the "elect" have seen it, or, at least, taken the trouble to read it. I brought away a copy from Salt Lake. The book is a curiosity to me, it is such a pretentious affair, and yet so "slow," so sleepy; such an insipid mess of inspiration. It is chloroform in print. If Joseph Smith composed this book, the act was a miracle—keeping awake while he did it was, at any rate. If he, according to tradition, merely translated it from certain ancient and mysteriously-engraved plates of copper, which he declares he found under a stone, in an out-of-the-way locality, the work of translating was equally a miracle, for the same reason.

The book seems to be merely a prosy detail of imaginary history, with the Old Testament for a model; followed by a tedious plagiarism of the New Testament. The author labored to give his words and phrases the quaint, old-fashioned sound and structure of our King James's translation of the Scriptures; and the result is a mongrel—half modern glibness, and half ancient simplicity and gravity. The latter is awkward and constrained; the former natural, but grotesque by the contrast. Whenever he found his speech growing too modern—which was about every sentence or two—he ladled in a few such Scriptural phrases as "exceeding sore," "and it came to pass," etc., and made things satisfactory again. "And it came to pass" was his pet. If he had left that out, his Bible would have been only a pamphlet. . . .

At the end of our two days' sojourn, we left Great Salt Lake City hearty and well fed and happy—physically superb but not so very much wiser, as regards the "Mormon question," than we were when we arrived, perhaps. . . . All our "information" had three sides to it, and so I gave up the idea that I could settle the "Mormon question" in two days. Still I have seen newspaper correspondents do it in one.

———

Glimpses of Mormon Society

A YOUNG LITERARY BOHEMIAN from New York with an addiction to strange drugs and recondite books traveled overland to California in 1863 and paused long enough in Salt Lake City to record some vivid impressions. Fitz Hugh Ludlow had fascinated the country six years before, at twenty-one, with a shocking account of his sensations and sufferings in The Hasheesh Eater, *a work which made him known during his*

brief but brilliant career as the American De Quincey. In San Fran-
cisco, where Ludlow stayed four months and contributed to the Golden
Era, *he stimulated Mark Twain to try something better than mere jour-*
nalism.

Sensitive and highstrung, the bookish Ludlow was far from the disso-
lute person the public supposed. He was hardly blasé when the sight of
two wives of one Mormon living peacefully together could make him
blush and stare. He was, on the contrary, "a slight, boyish-looking chap,
with quick, bright eyes, who eagerly saw and delighted in everything
about him." On the long trip west he rode day and night at the stage-
coach driver's elbow, "not frightened, but too nervous, too keenly stim-
ulated by the new sights, the new experiences, the new sensations, to
sleep." The geologic wonders of the approaches to Zion overwhelmed
him as they had Burton. The canyon defiles of the Wasatch made the
Palisades of the Hudson seem "insignificant as a garden fence." No less
acutely does he describe Mormon society. His report of the Mormon
view of the Civil War, then in progress, is particularly revealing.

With Albert Bierstadt, the noted landscape painter, along drawing
sketches, Ludlow made notes on their journey for a series of articles
which appeared in the Atlantic Monthly *in 1864. In 1870 these were*
published, together with Bierstadt's illustrations, in a single volume, The
Heart of the Continent. *The following passages are taken from Ludlow's*
article "Among the Mormons," which appeared in the Atlantic *for April*
1864.

Though Mormondom is disloyal to the core, it still patronizes the Fourth
of July, at least in its phase of festivity, omitting the patriotism, but keeping the fireworks of our Eastern celebration, substituting "Utah" for "Union" in the Buncombe speeches, and having a ball instead of the Declaration of Independence. All the saints within half a day's ride of the city
come flocking into it to spend the Fourth. . . .

Last Fourth of July, it may be remembered, fell on a Saturday. In
their ambition to reproduce ancient Judaism (and this ambition is the
key to their whole puzzle) the Mormons are Sabbatarians of a strictness
which would delight Lord Shaftesbury. Accordingly, in order that their
festivities might not encroach on the early hours of the Sabbath, they
had the ball on Fourth-of-July eve, instead of the night of the Fourth. I
could not realize the risk of such an encroachment when I read the following sentence printed on my billet of invitation:—

"Dancing to commence at 4 p.m."

Bierstadt, myself, and three gentlemen of our party were the only Gentiles whom I found invited by President Young to meet in the neighborhood of three thousand saints. . . . I sought out our entertainer, Brigham Young, to thank him for the flattering exception made in our Gentile favor. He was standing in the dress-circle of the theatre, looking down on the dancers with an air of mingled hearty kindness and feudal ownership. . . . Like any Eastern partygoer, he is habited in the "customary suit of solemn black," and looks very distinguished in this dress, though his daily homespun detracts nothing from the feeling, when in his presence, that you are beholding a most remarkable man. . . .

Brigham's manners astonish any one who knows that his only education was a few quarters of such common-school experience as could be had in Ontario County, Central New York, during the early part of the century. There are few courtlier men living. His address is a fine combination of dignity with the desire to confer happiness—of perfect deference to the feelings of others with absolute certainty of himself and his own opinions. He is a remarkable example of the educating influence of tactful perception, combined with entire singleness of aim, considered quite apart from its moral character. His early life was passed among the uncouth and illiterate; his daily associations, since he embraced Mormonism, have been with the least cultivated grades of human society —a heterogeneous peasant-hord, looking to him for erection into a nation: yet he has so clearly seen what is requisite in the man who would be respected in the Presidency, and has so unreservedly devoted his life to its attainment, that in protracted conversations with him I heard only a single solecism ("a'n't you" for "aren't you,") and saw not one instance of breeding which would be inconsistent with noble lineage. . . .

Brigham began our conversation at the theatre by telling me I was late—it was after nine o'clock. I replied, that this was the time we usually set about dressing for an evening party in Boston or New York.

"Yes," said he, "you find us an oldfashioned people; we are trying to return to the healthy habits of patriarchal times."

"Need you go back so far as that for your parallel?" suggested I. "It strikes me that we might have found four-o'clock balls among the *early* Christians."

He smiled, without that offensive affectation of some great men, the air of taking another's joke under their gracious patronage, and went on to remark that there were, unfortunately, multitudinous differences between the Mormons and Americans at the East, besides the hours they kept.

349

"You find us," said he, "trying to live peaceably. A sojourn with people thus minded must be a great relief to you, who come from a land where brother hath lifted hand against brother, and you hear the confused noise of the warrior perpetually ringing in your ears."

Despite the courtly deference and Scriptural dignity of this speech, I detected in it a latent crow over that "perished Union" which was the favorite theme of every saint I met in Utah, and hastened to assure the President that I had no desire for relief from sympathy with my country's struggle for honor and existence.

"Ah!" he replied, in a voice slightly tinged with sarcasm. "You differ greatly, then, from multitudes of your countrymen, who, since the draft began to be talked of, have passed through Salt Lake, flying westward from the crime of their brothers' blood."

"I do indeed."

"Still, they are excellent men. Brother Heber Kimball and myself are every week invited to address a train of them down at Emigrant Square. They are honest, peaceful people. You call them 'Copperheads,' I believe. But they are real, true, good men. We find them very truth-seeking, remarkably open to conviction. Many of them have stayed with us. Thus the Lord makes the wrath of man to praise Him. The Abolitionists —the same people who interfered with our institutions, and drove us out into the wilderness—interfered with the Southern institutions till they broke up the Union. But it's all coming out right—a great deal better than we could have arranged it for ourselves. The men who flee from Abolitionist oppression come out here to our ark of refuge, and people the asylum of God's chosen. You'll all be out here before long. Your Union's gone forever. Fighting only makes matters worse. When your country has become a desolation, we, the saints whom you cast out, will forget all your sins against us, and give you a home."

There was something so preposterous in the idea of a mighty and prosperous people abandoning, through abject terror of a desperate set of Southern conspirators, the fertile soil and grand commercial avenues of the United States, to populate a green strip in the heart of an inaccessible desert, that, until I saw Brigham Young's face glowing with what he deemed prophetic enthusiasm, I could not imagine him in earnest. Before I left Utah, I discovered, that, without a single exception, all the saints were inoculated with a prodigious craze, to the effect that the United States was to become a blighted chaos, and its inhabitants Mormon proselytes and citizens of Utah within the next two years—the more sanguine said, "next summer."

To resume Brigham for the last time. After a conversation about the Indians, in which he denounced the military policy of the Government, averring that one bale of blankets and ten pounds of beads would go farther to protect the mails from stoppage and emigrants from massacre than a regiment of soldiers, he discovered that we crossed swords on every war-question, and tactfully changed the subject to the beauty of the Opera-House. . . .

The Opera-House [the Salt Lake Theater] was a subject we could agree upon. I was greatly astonished to find in the desert heart of the continent a place of public amusement which for capacity, beauty, and comfort has no superior in America, except the opera-houses of New York, Boston, and Philadelphia. It is internally constructed somewhat like the first of these, seats twenty-five hundred people, and commodiously receives five hundred more, when, as in the present instance, the stage is thrown into the *parquet*, and the latter boarded up to the level of the former for dancing. Externally the building is a plain, but not ungraceful structure, of stone, brick, and stucco. My greatest surprise was excited by the really exquisite artistic beauty of the gilt and painted decorations of the great arch over the stage, the cornices, and the moulding about the *proscenium*-boxes. President Young, with a proper price, assured me that every particle of the ornamental work was by indigenous and saintly hands.

"But you don't know yet," he added, "how independent we are of you at the East. Where do you think we got that central chandelier, and what d' ye suppose we paid for it?"

It was a piece of workmanship which would have been creditable to any New York firm—apparently a richly carved circle, twined with gilt vines, leaves, and tendrils, blossoming all over with flaming wax-lights, and suspended by a massive chain of golden lustre. So I replied that he probably paid a thousand dollars for it in New York.

"Capital!" exclaimed Brigham. "I made it myself! That circle is a cartwheel which I washed and gilded; it hangs by a pair of gilt ox-chains; and the ornaments of the candlesticks were all cut after my patterns out of sheet-tin!"

I talked with the President till a party of young girls, who seemed to regard him with idolatry, and whom, in return, he treated with a sage mixture of gallantry and fatherliness, came to him with an invitation to join in some old-fashioned contradance long forgotten at the East. I was curious to see how he would acquit himself in this supreme ordeal of dignity; so I descended to the *parquet*, and was much impressed by the aristocratic grace with which he went through his figures. . . .

There was very little ostentation in dress at the ball, but there was also very little taste in dressing. Patrician broadcloth and silk were the rare exceptions, generally ill-made and ill-worn, but they cordially associated with the great mass of plebeian tweed and calico. Few ladies wore jewelry or feathers. There were some pretty girls swimming about in tasteful whipsyllabub of puffed tarlatan. Where saintly gentlemen came with several wives, the oldest generally seemed the most elaborately dressed, and acted much like an Eastern chaperon toward her younger sisters. (Wives of the same man habitually besister each other in Utah. Another triumph of grace!) . . .

Heber Kimball . . . took a vivid interest in Bierstadt's and my own eternal welfare. He quite laid himself out for our conversion, coming to sit with us at breakfast in our Mormon hotel, dressed in a black swallowtail, buff vest, and a stupendous truncate cone of Leghorn, which made him look like an Italian mountebank-physician of the seventeenth century. I have heard men who could misquote Scripture for their own ends, and talk a long while without saying anything; but he so far surpassed in these particulars the loftiest efforts within my former experience, that I could think of no comparison for him but Jack Bunsby taken to exhorting. Witness a sample:

"Seven women shall take a hold o' one man! There!" (with a slap on the back of the nearest subject for conversion). "What d' ye think o' that? Shall! *Shall* take a hold on him! That don't mean they *sha'n't*, does it? No! God's word means what it says. And therefore means no otherwise—not in no way, shape, nor manner. Not in no *way*, for He saith, 'I am the *way*—and the truth and the life.' Not in no *shape*, for a man beholdeth his nat'ral *shape* in a glass; nor in no *manner*, for he straightway forgetteth what manner o' man he was. Seven women *shall* catch a hold on him. And ef they *shall*, then they *will!* For everything shall come to pass, and not one good word shall fall to the ground. You who try to explain away the Scriptur' would make it fig'rative. But don't come to ME with none o' your spiritooalizers! Not *one* good word shall fall. Therefore *seven* shall not fall. And ef seven shall catch a hold on him— and, as I jist proved, seven *will* catch a hold on him—then seven *ought* —and in the Latter-Day Glory, *seven,* yea, as our Lord said un-tew Peter, 'Verily, I say un-tew you, not seven, but seventy times seven,' these seventy times seven shall catch a hold and cleave. Blessed day! For the end shall be even as the beginnin', and seventy-fold more abundantly. Come over into my garden."

This invitation would wind up the homily. We gladly accepted it, and I must confess, that, if there ever could be any hope of our conversion, it was just about the time we stood in Brother Heber's fine orchard, eating apples and apricots between exhortations, and having sound doctrine poked down our throats with gooseberries as big as plums, to take the taste out of our mouths, like jam after castor-oil.

IV · LAMENTATIONS

IV · Lamentations

Conflict and Accommodation in Zion

═══════

FOR NEARLY TWENTY YEARS, despite the threats and skirmishes of the 1850's, the Mormons were masters in their own land. In Mormon eyes it was still Deseret, though Congress had reduced it from a regional empire to the arbitrary boundaries of the Territory of Utah. It was a Bible commonwealth, making no distinction between temporal and spiritual affairs under the strong central direction of Brigham Young and his apostles. Their regular visitations gave isolated settlements the sense of a wider and intimate community. Brother Brigham's voice and handshake were a living experience among his people, who put their resources at his disposition to build their exclusive Kingdom. It was a closed society, where every social and civil difference amounted to a religious difference and could not be abided. It was comfortable for the believers, hard on the discontented, who, like heaven's rebel angels, were soon cast out. Zion's strength depended on unity, unchallenged either from within or without.

But the world outside saw in Zion only an oppressive society. With the Civil War over, the nation took stock of its reunited continent and found Utah, once willingly abandoned to the Mormons, worth saving. The speculators went after its minerals; the reformers went after its soul. The scarlet woman, redeemed and purified, might in time be welcomed into the sisterhood of states. Bent on this double mission, the Gentile came to Utah, and with him the world. He had come on the scene with the Forty-Niners, the soldiers, and the first federal appointees, but now he came to stay, forming a society within a society. After 1869, the transcontinental railroad brought him in numbers, as merchant, denominational missionary and schoolteacher, miner and investor, carpetbagger, and at last as federal marshal armed with warrants to conduct raids on Mormon homes in search of polygamists.

The Mormons, determined to preserve their solidarity, met the infiltration with enterprise and stiffened resistance: they met the Gentile merchants with Zion's Cooperative Mercantile Institution, and growing economic inequality with the communal forms of a United Order; they met sectarian schools with church academies, and worldly fashions with retrenchment associations; they countered the Gentile lobby's Liberal party with a People's party and gave the women the vote; they opposed anti-polygamy legislation, like the Anti-Bigamy Act of 1862, with petitions and mass meetings and a test case that made its way to the Supreme Court; and they met "cohab" raids with the "underground" and refugee colonies in Arizona, New Mexico, Colorado, and across the borders in Canada and Mexico. Meanwhile, in an unabated program of proselyting and immigration they went on winning souls of their own. But a major schism in 1869–70 known as the Godbeite movement, responding to the pressures from without, opposed Brigham Young's temporal power and argued that Utah's salvation lay in developing her mines. It shocked Mormondom, and Gentiles hailed it as a sign of change.

The "Mormon Question" became a national preoccupation, filling the vacuum left by the victory over slavery. Voices on both sides grew shrill. The Mormons firmly believed that fifty million people were calling for their destruction. Extremist reformers as firmly believed that Utah faced the country with another bloody struggle. Some factions were ready to overrun the Territory with Gentile colonists who would outvote the Mormons or with an army of occupation and carpetbag rule until the Mormons yielded. Moderates advocated moral persuasion in vain. One punitive bill after another in Congress sought to make the Anti-Bigamy Act of 1862 effective, culminating in severe legislation in the 1880's which stripped Utah probate courts of their power, outlawed the Mormon militia, disfranchised the Mormons, disincorporated the church, confiscated its property, and subjected Utah to control by a federal commission.

The legislation only hastened what changing conditions were already accomplishing. Social and economic realities foreshadowed the end for Mormonism's unique society as they had for the slave interests in the South. In 1890 the Mormons capitulated in a manifesto vetoing the heavenly revelation on polygamy of nearly fifty years before. A generation of conflict ended in strategic retreat and accommodation to the conforming forces of life in America.

The accounts that follow compress a turbulent history. From Speaker Schuyler Colfax fearing an "irrepressible conflict" in 1865 to Delegate Charles S. Varian congratulating the state constitutional convention on its harmony in 1890, the observers have left vivid impressions of the "Mormon Question," the coming of the railroad, the denominational inroads, the opening of the mines, the signs of nonconformity and change, the retrenchment, the co-operatives, the polygamy crusade and counter-crusade, and the final rapprochement of Mormon and Gentile. The period begins with alarm, proceeds with something of Emerson's amazement at the Mormons as "an after-clap of Puritanism," and closes with the chastened Mormons welcomed into the Union. Zion's lamentations give way at length to Gentile psalms about her comeliness and virtue.

The Irrepressible Conflict

IN THE SUMMER OF 1865, *with the Civil War over and the "Republic saved, reunited, bound together as never before," Samuel Bowles of Massachusetts, editor of the Springfield* Republican, *crossed the continent by rail and stage to measure "the national breadth" and report on "those great, pressing public themes of the Pacific Railroad, the Mormons, and the Mines." In his party were Speaker of the House Schuyler Colfax, Lieutenant-Governor Bross of Illinois, and Albert D. Richardson of the New York* Tribune, *who later wrote his own account of the journey. "Our party," recorded Bowles, "were almost the first who had ever travelled Across the Continent simply to see the country, to study its resources, to learn its people and their wants. . . ."*

In thirty-two letters to his paper—seven of them on the Mormons— Bowles digested for a curious East "the materials of half a Continent," the "interests and hopes of the West." In one mood he felt that in Utah "The conflict of sects and civilization . . . will soon solve the polygamous problem—rightly and without bloodshed—if the Government will make itself felt in it with a wise guardianship, a tender nursing, a firm principle." But in a different mood, he saw the Mormons facing the nation with another "irrepressible conflict." Bowles was prone to misread events. He saw militia drilling and being provided with arms "under the auspices and authority of the Mormon church" and absurdly thought "an open conflict with the representatives of the Government is apparently braved, even threatened." The militia was in fact simply organiz-

ing for the defense of the southern settlements in Utah's Black Hawk Indian war.

In October, 1869, Bowles and Colfax, by then Vice-President of the United States, visited Utah again, only to refuse Mormon hospitality because the Vice-President believed a rumor that Brigham Young had called him and President Grant "gamblers and drunkards." Colfax archly lectured the Mormons on polygamy, arguing that it was not a religious principle. Apostle John Taylor countered in an exchange widely reprinted in the eastern press. It was part of the running and edgy debate between the Mormons and the rest of the country that marked the whole period.

The following impressions of the first and happier visit come from Across the Continent *(Springfield, Mass., 1866), a collection of the letters Bowles had published serially in his* Republican.

I

Great Salt Lake City, Utah, June 14 [1865]

. . . No internal city of the Continent lies in such a field of beauty, unites such rich and rare elements of nature's formations, holds such guarantees of greatness, material and social, in the good time coming of our Pacific development. I met all along the Plains and over the mountains, the feeling that Salt Lake was to be the great central city of this West; I found the map, with Montana, Idaho, and Oregon on the north, Dacotah and Colorado on the east, Nevada and California on the west, Arizona on the south, and a near connection with the sea by the Colorado River in the latter direction, suggested the same: I recognized it in the Sabbath morning picture of its location and possessions; I am convinced of it as I see more and more of its opportunities, its developed industries, and its unimproved possessions.

Mr. Colfax's reception in Utah was excessive if not oppressive. There was an element of rivalry between Mormon and Gentile in it, adding earnestness and energy to enthusiasm and hospitality. First "a troop cometh," with band of music, and marched us slowly and dustily through their Camp Douglas. Then, escaping these, our coach was waylaid as it went down the hill by the Mormon authorities of the city. They ordered us to dismount; we were individually introduced to each of twenty of them; we received a long speech; we made a long one—standing in the hot sand with a sun of forty thousand lens-power concentrated upon us, tired and dirty with a week's coach-ride; was it wonder that the mildest of tempers rebelled?—transferred to other carriages, our hosts drove us through the city to the hotel; and then—bless their Mormon hearts—they took us at once to a hot sulphur bath, that nature liberally offers just on the confines of the city, and there we washed out all remembrance of the morning suffering and all the accumulated grime and fatigue of the journey, and came out baptized in freshness and self-respect. Clean clothes, dinner, the Mormon tabernacle in the afternoon, and a Congregational ("Gentile") meeting and sermon in the evening, were the other proceedings of our first day in Utah.

Since, and still continuing, Mr. Colfax and his friends have been the recipients of a generous and thoughtful hospitality. They are the guests of the city; but the military authorities and citizens vie together as well to please their visitors and make them pleased with Utah and its people. The Mormons are eager to prove their loyalty to the government, their sympathy with its bereavement, their joy in its final triumph—which their silence or their slants and sneers heretofore had certainly put in some doubt—and they leave nothing unsaid or undone now, towards Mr. Colfax as the representative of that government, or towards the public, to give assurance of their rightmindedness. Also they wish us to know that they are not monsters and murderers, but men of intelligence, virtue, good manners and fine tastes. They put their polygamy on high moral and religious grounds; and for the rest, anyhow, are not willing to be thought otherwise than our peers. And certainly we do find here a great deal of true and good human nature and social culture; a great deal of business intelligence and activity; a great deal of generous hospitality—besides most excellent strawberries and green peas, and the most promising orchards of apricots, peaches, plums and apples that these eyes ever beheld anywhere. They have given us a serenade; and Mr. Colfax has addressed them at length with his usual tact and happy effect, telling them what they have a right to expect from the government, and reminding them that the government has the right to demand from them, in turn, loyalty to the Constitution and obedience to the laws, and complimenting them on all the beauty of their homes and the thrift of their industry. Governor Bross and Mr. Richardson also made happy addresses, and the crowd of the evening, and the "distinguished guests" gave every sign of being mutually pleased with each other. . . .

In Mormon etiquette, President Brigham Young is called upon; by Washington fashion, the Speaker is also called upon, and does not call —there was a question whether the distinguished resident and the distinguished visitor would meet; Mr. Colfax, as was meet under the situation of affairs here, made a point upon it, and gave notice he should not call; whereupon President Brigham yielded the question, and graciously came to-day with a crowd of high dignitaries of the church, and made, not one of Emerson's prescribed ten minute calls, but a generous, pleasant, gossiping sitting of two hours long. He is a very hale and hearty looking man, young for sixty-four, with a light gray eye, cold and uncertain, a mouth and chin betraying a great and determined will—handsome perhaps as to presence and features, but repellent in atmosphere and without magnetism. In conversation, he is cool and quiet in manner, but suggestive in expression; has strong and original ideas, but uses bad grammar. He was rather formal, but courteous, and at the last affected frankness and freedom, if he felt it not. To his followers, I observed he was master of that profound art of eastern politicians, which consists in putting the arm affectionately around them, and tenderly inquiring for health of selves and families; and when his eye did sparkle and his lips soften, it was with most cheering, though not warming, effect—it was pleasant but did not melt you.

Of his companions, Heber C. Kimball is perhaps the most notorious from his vulgar and coarse speech. He ranks high among the "prophets" here, and is as unctuous in his manner as Macassar hair oil, and as pious in phrase as good old Thomas a Kempis. He has a very keen, sharp eye, and looks like a Westfield man I always meet at the agricultural fairs in Springfield. Dr. Bernhisel has an air of culture and refinement peculiar among his associates; he is an old, small man, venerable, and suggestive of John Quincy Adams, or Dr. Gannett of Boston, in his style. Two or three others of the company have fine faces—such as you would meet in intellectual or business society in Boston or New York—but the strength of most of the party seems to lie in narrowness, bigotry, obstinacy. They look as if they had lived on the same farms as their fathers and grandfathers, and made no improvements; gone to the same church, and sat in the same pew, without cushions; borrowed the same weekly newspaper for forty years; drove all their children to the West or the cities; and if they went to agricultural fairs, insisted on having their premiums in pure coin.

But the hospitality of Utah is not confined to the Mormons. The "Gentiles" or non-Mormons are becoming numerous and influential here, and, citizens and soldiers, comprise many families of culture and influence. They are made up of officers of the federal government, resident representatives of telegraph and stage lines, members of eastern or California business firms having branches here, and a very fair proportion, too, of the merchants of the city. Some of the more intelligent of the disgusted and repentant Mormons swell the circle. They have organized a literary association, established a large and growing Sunday school, largely made up of children of Mormon parents, have weekly religious services led by the chaplain at Camp Douglas, conduct an able and prosperous daily paper (the *Union Vedette*), and in every way are developing an organized and effective opposition to the dominant power here. These people, united, earnest and enthusiastic as minorities always are, claim a share in entertaining Mr. Colfax and his friends, and gave them a large and most brilliant social party last night. They are not reluctant to show us their ladies, as the Mormons generally seem to be, and their ladies are such, in beauty and culture, as no circle need be ashamed of.

II

SALT LAKE CITY, June 18.

. . . Ultimately, of course, before the influences of emigration, civilization and our democratic habits, an organization so aristocratic and autocratic as the Mormon church now is must modify its rule; it must compete with other sects, and take its chance with them. And its most aristocratic and uncivilized incident or feature of plurality of wives must fall first and completely before contact with the rest of the world—marshalled with mails, daily papers, railroads and telegraphs—ciphering out the fact that the men and women of the world are about equally divided, and applying to the Mormon patriarchs the democratic principle of equal and exact justice. Nothing can save this feature of Mormonism but new flight and a more complete isolation. A kingdom in the sea, entirely its own, could only perpetuate it; and thither even, commerce and democracy would ultimately follow it. The click of the telegraph and the roll of the overland stages are its death-rattle now; the first whistle of the locomotive will sound its requiem; and the pickax of the miner will dig its grave. Squatter sovereignty will speedily settle the question, even if the government continues to coquette with it and humor it, as it has done.

But the government should no longer hold a doubtful or divided position toward this great crime of the Mormon church. Declaring clearly both its want of power and disinclination to interfere at all with the church organization as such, or with the latter's influence over its followers, assuring and guaranteeing to it all the liberty and freedom that other religious sects hold and enjoy, the government should still, as clearly and distinctly, declare, by all its action and all its representatives here, that this feature of polygamy, not properly or necessarily a part of the religion of the Mormons, is a crime by the common law of all civilization and by the statute law of the Nation, and that any cases of its extension will be prosecuted and punished as such.

―――――

A Humanitarian Looks at the "Mormon Question"

IN 1866 William Hepworth Dixon, then editor of the influential Athenaeum in London, came to the United States to see what power those "master passions" of liberty and religion were exercising on American life. In the Mormons, the Shakers, the Spiritualists, and the Oneida Perfectionists he found "the most singular doctrines, the most audacious experiments," and he fully and philosophically reported them the next year in New America, a work that went through many editions and was widely translated in Europe.

He devoted nearly a third of the book to the Mormons, whom he treated so indulgently that later observers mistrusted him. But Dixon was an open-minded humanitarian sympathetic to all sorts of social experiments. He wrote on prison reform and championed the common people. Widely traveled, biographer of Penn and Bacon, novelist, playwright, prodigious contributor to numerous periodicals, he could not resist the fascination of "the changes now being wrought in the actual life of man and woman on the American soil." He described them all, including the problems of race and reconstruction in the reborn Union, with equal insight.

In the following dialogue he evaluates the growing "Mormon Question." It is taken from the chapter called "The Republican Platform" in the Philadelphia edition (1867) of New America.

"We mean to put that business of the Mormons through," says a New England politician; "we have done a bigger job than that in the South; and we shall now fix up things in Salt Lake City."

"Do you mean by force?" asks an English traveller.

364

"Well, that is one of our planks. The Republican Platform pledges us to crush those Saints."

This conversation, passing across the hospitable board of a renowned publicist in Philadelphia, draws towards itself from all sides the criticism of a distinguished company of lawyers and politicians; most of them members of Congress; all of them soldiers of the Republican phalanx.

"Do you hold," says the English guest, "you as a writer and thinker—your party as the representatives of American thought and might—that in a country where speech is free and tolerance wide, it would be *right* to employ force against ideas—to throw horse and foot into a dogmatic quarrel—to set about promoting morality with bayonets and bowie-knives?"

"It is one of our planks," says a young member of Congress, "to put down those Mormons, who, besides, being infidels, are also Conservatives and Copperheads."

"Young is certainly a Democrat," adds an Able Editor from Massachusetts, himself a traveller in the Mormon land; "we have no right to burn his block on account of his politics; nor, indeed on account of his religion; we have no power to meddle with any man's faith; but we have made a law against plurality of wives, and we have the power to make our laws respected everywhere in this Republic!"

"By force?"

"By force, if we are driven by disloyal citizens to the use of force."

"You mean, then, that in any case you will use force—passively, if they submit; actively, if they resist?"

"That's our notion," replies our candid host. "The government must crush them. That is our big job; and next year we must put it through."

"You hold it right, then, to combat such an evil as polygamy with shot and shell?"

"We have freed four million negroes with shot and shell," replies a sober Pennsylvanian judge.

"Pardon me, is that a full statement of the case? That you have crushed a movement of secession by means of military force is true; but is it not also true that, five or six years ago, every one acknowledged that slavery was a legal and moral question, which, while peace and order reigned in the slave-states, ought not to be treated otherwise than on legal and moral grounds?"

"Yes, that is so. We had no right over the negroes until their masters went into rebellion. I admit that the declaration of war gave us our only standing."

"In fact, you confess that you had no right over the blacks until you had gained, through the rebellion, a complete authority over the whites who held them in bondage?"

"Certainly so."

"If, then, the planters had been quiet; keeping to the law as it then stood; never attempting to spread themselves by force, as they tried to do in Kansas; you would have been compelled, by your sense of right, to leave them to time and reason, to the exhaustion of their lands, to the depopulation of their States, to the growth of sound economical knowledge—in short, to the moral forces which excite and sustain all social growths?"

"Perhaps so," answers the Able Editor. "The Saints have not yet given us such a chance. They are very honest, sober, industrious people, who mind their own business mainly, as men will have to do who try to live in your barren plains. They are useful in their way, too; linking our Atlantic states with the Pacific states; and feeding the mining population of Idaho, Montana, and Nevada. We have no ground of complaint, none that a politician would prefer against them beyond their plural households; but New England is very sore just now about them; for everybody in this country has got into the habit of calling them the spawn of our New England conventicles, simply because Joseph Smith, Brigham Young, Heber Kimball, all the chief lights of their church, happen to be New England men."

"When New England," adds a representative from Ohio, with a laugh, "goes mad on any point, you will find that she contrives in this Republic to have her way."

"When her way is just and open—sanctioned by moral principle and by human experience—it is well that she should have her way. But will Harvard and Cambridge support an attack by military power on religious bodies because they have adopted the model of Abraham and David? You have in those western plains and mountains a hundred tribes of red-men who practise polygamy; would you think it right for your missionary society to withdraw from among them the teacher and his Bible, and for General Grant to send out in their stead the soldier and his sword? You have in those western territories a hundred thousand yellow men who also practise polygamy; would you hold it just to sink their ships, to burn their ranches, to drive them from your soil, with sword and fire?"

"Their case is different to that of the Saints," rejoins the Able Editor; "these red-skins and yellow-skins are savages; one race may die out, the

366

other may go back to Asia; but Young and Kimball are our own people, knowing the law and the Gospel; and whatever they may do with the Gospel, they must obey the law."

"Of course, everybody must obey the law; but how? Those Saints, I hear, have no objection to your law when administered by judge and jury, only to your law when administered by colonels and subalterns."

"In other words," says the Pennsylvanian judge, "they have no objection to our law when they are left to carry it out themselves."

"We must put them down," cries the young member of Congress.

"Have you not tried that policy of putting them down twice already? You found them twelve thousand strong at Independence, in Missouri; not liking their tenets (though they had no polygamy among them then), you crushed and scattered them into thirty thousand at Nauvoo; where you again took arms against religious passion, slew their Prophet, plundered their city, drove them into the desert, and generally dispersed and destroyed them into one hundred and twenty-seven thousand in Deseret! You know that some such law of growth through persecution has been detected in every land and in every church. It is a proverb. In Salt Lake City, I heard Brigham Young tell his departing missionaries, they were not to suggest the beauty of their mountain home, but to dwell on the idea of persecution, and to call the poor into a persecuted church. If you want to make all the western country Mormon, you must send an army of a hundred thousand troops to the Rocky Mountains."

"But we can hardly leave these pluralists alone."

"Why not—so far at least as regards bayonets and bowie-knives? Have you no faith in the power of truth? Have you no confidence in being right? Nay, are you sure that you have nothing to learn from them? Have not the men who thrive where nobody else can live, given ample evidence that, even though their doctrines may be strange and their morals false, the principles on which they till the soil and raise their crops, are singularly sound?"

"I admit," says the Able Editor, "they are good farmers."

"Good is a poor term, to express the marvel they have wrought. In Illinois, they changed a swamp into a garden. In Utah, they have made the desert green with pastures and tawny with maize and corn. Of what is Brigham Young most fond? Of his harem, his temple, his theatre, his office, his wealth? He may pride himself on these things in their measure; but the fact of his life which he dwelt upon most, and with the noblest enthusiasm, is the raising of a crop of ninety-three and a half bushels of wheat from one single acre of land. The Saints have grown rich with a celerity that seems magical even in the United States. Beginning life at the lowest stage, recruited only from among the poor, spoiled of their goods and driven from their farms, compelled to expend millions of dollars in a perilous exodus, and finally located on a soil from which the red-skin and the bison had all but retired in despair, they have yet contrived to exist, to extend their operations, to increase their stores. The hills and valleys round Salt Lake are everywhere smiling with wheat and rye. A city has been built; great roads have been made; mills have been erected; canals have been dug; forests have been felled. A depot has been formed in the wilderness from which the miners from Montana and Nevada can be fed. A chain of communication from St. Louis to San Francisco has been laid. Are the Republican majority prepared to undo the progress of twenty years in order to curb an obnoxious doctrine? Are they sure that the attempt being made, it would succeed? What facts in the past history of these Saints permit you to infer that persecution, however sharp, would diminish their number, their audacity, and their zeal?"

"Crushing them! No; none. I see no way of dealing with any moral and religious question except by moral means employed in a religious spirit. Why not put your trust in truth, in logic, in history? Why not open good roads to Salt Lake? Why not encourage railway communication; and bring the practical intellect and noble feeling of New England to bear upon the household of many wives? Why not meet their sermons by sermons; try their science by science; encounter their books with books? Have you no missionaries equal to Elder Stenhouse and Elder Dewey? You must expect that while you act on the Saints, the Saints will react upon you. It will be for you a trial of strength; but the weapons will be legitimate and the conclusions will be blessed. Can you not trust the right side and the just cause, to come out victoriously from such a struggle?"

"Well," says the judge, "while we are divided in opinion, perhaps, as to the use of physical force, we are all in favor of moral force. Massachusetts is our providence; but, after all, we must have one law in this Republic. Union is our motto, equality our creed. Boston and Salt Lake City must be got to shake hands, as Boston and Charleston have already done. If you can persuade Brigham to lie down with Bowles, I am willing to see it."

Denominational Inroads

WHILE POLITICAL EXTREMISTS CALLED for Sherman to march *through Utah as he had marched through Georgia, the moderates had more faith in education and the changes time and the railroad would bring. "If you really have the interests of Utah at heart," one Gentile wrote his pastor in 1869, "just send here about twenty-five earnest Methodist preachers, that can sing and pray, and turn them loose; it would do more good than all the Cullom bills* Congress could pass." Brigham Young, secure in his advantage, had always invited visiting clergymen to speak in the Tabernacle. By turns he indulged and embarrassed them. But after the Civil War scores of dedicated denominational workers took up the cause of Utah's redemption in earnest. Among the American churches, benighted Utah took priority over heathen Africa as a field for Christian martyrs.*

As early as 1867 the Episcopalians sent thirty-year-old Rt. Rev. Daniel Sylvester Tuttle west as the first missionary bishop of Montana with jurisdiction in Idaho and Utah. "As to companions," he was instructed, "get as many clergymen as you can find, and take them along. Leave one by all means at Salt Lake City, where there is a remarkable opening for our services at this time. . . . You need not wait for your consecration before you cast about for a good missionary, not to the Mormons, but to others among the Mormons. I suppose that an open attempt to convert Brigham Young's followers w'd be followed by very unpleasant consequences."

Except for a year in Virginia City, Bishop Tuttle made Salt Lake City his headquarters until 1886, when he became bishop of Missouri. At his

---

* The abortive Cullom bill, first presented to the House in 1869, sought to subject Utah to complete federal control. The attempt stirred Mormondom to its center and occasioned a mammoth protest meeting in the Tabernacle in Salt Lake City to petition the Senate not to pass it. It was one of a series of Congressional bills directed against polygamy when it became apparent that the Anti-Bigamy Act of 1862 could not be enforced. In 1867 the Cragin bill sought to abolish jury trials in polygamy cases; in 1874 the Poland bill and in 1876 the Christiancy bill would disqualify Mormon jurors; in 1882 the Edmunds Act made "unlawful cohabitation" a punishable offense, empowered federal marshals to hunt polygamists, and establish a federal commission to regulate Utah elections; in 1887 the Edmunds-Tucker Act disincorporated the Mormon Church and disfranchised the women (*Ed. note*).

IV · LAMENTATIONS

departure, the Deseret News *paid him tribute: "So far as we are aware he has not, like many of his cloth, used his ecclesiastical influence towards the oppression and spoliation of the Latter Day Saints. . . . We respect a consistent antagonist." One of Bishop Tuttle's missionaries, Rev. H. L. Foote, held Salt Lake City's first Episcopalian service in May, 1867, in Independence Hall, with 150 present. Independence Hall, which a Young Men's Literary Association had built two years before as a Gentile center, had also served Rev. Norman McLeod, Congregationalist chaplain at Fort Douglas, before he left to lecture in the East on the Mormon problem.*

The following letter from Warren Hussey, a Salt Lake Gentile banker, to Bishop Tuttle before he left New York to his new assignment is taken from Tuttle's Reminiscences of a Missionary Bishop *(New York, 1906).*

Mr. Warren Hussey wrote me from Salt Lake City. . . . I confirmed him and his wife in the first confirmation class presented in Salt Lake City. During his entire residence there he was senior warden of the parish. To him, more than any other layman resident, was due the prompt and vigorous upbuilding of our work in Utah. . . . It will be noticed that Mr. Hussey, from his business association, and perhaps from the reactionary state of mind induced by resentfulness at unfair statements and unjust dealings, is inclined to take a favorable view of the Mormons:

Banking House of Hussey, Dahler & Co.,
Salt Lake City, March 13, 1867.

Rev. Dan'l S. Tuttle, Morris.
Dear Sir:

Your valued favor of the 11th February forwarded me by our mutual friend, Rev. H. B. Hitchings, is duly at hand, and for and in behalf of the friends of the church here I will try and answer your inquiries to the best of my ability.

I am quite intimate with Prest. Young and have very frequently heard him express himself concerning other churches coming in here; and am very sure they will meet a hearty welcome from him, *under certain circumstances.* He is not at all prejudiced against other religions, but is most in favor of his own of course. Have frequently heard him say that the Mormons were not the only people to be saved. Other denominations would also be redeemed, but they must all, his and every other Christian Church, work and pray, practice and live the religion they profess, etc., etc. They *do profess to live and practice their religion* to greater perfection than other denominations, and have great grounds for making such assertions. In a conversation had with Prest. Young since receipt of your letter he has only reiterated former statements, and assured me no minister, nor any one else, who w'd come here and mind their own business, need have the slightest fear of being disturbed by Mormons.

There are very few communicants here, some ½ Doz. or so to my knowledge. Other Gentiles who are not communicants, however, would be very glad indeed to see a church established here, and are willing to aid in supporting a minister, provided he is the right kind of a man.

I was out with a subscription paper yesterday afternoon and readily raised a subscription of over $1,200 for the support of a minister one year and can increase it to $1,500 or more. A large amount would be required to support a married clergyman. Rents and living are high, and it is very expensive traveling here. If any one comes it must of necessity be a single man. The latter can obtain a good room and excellent board here at $22 per week, including lights, fuel and washing; and at $1,500 per year could get along very nicely indeed. While it would require almost this amount merely to rent a house for a married clergyman. All are anxious for a clergyman at once, and the sooner a start is made the sooner we will get under headway, and the more liberally we can get subscriptions. There is no other church in operation here now but the Mormons. The Catholics will be here during the spring or summer, and probably the Methodists; and the first here will get the most support. . . .

This comes somewhat near answering your inquiries, and in addition to doing so I desire to give also my ideas of our wants here. Prest. Young and the Mormon Church are, in my opinion, the worst lied about, if I may use this expression, of any people living. Parties here who are at enmity with them, and others who desire large government contracts are exceedingly anxious to bring about if possible a collision between them and our government, in hopes of bringing on another Mormon War. No abuse seems too low to heap upon them by these friends of Christianity; no story too big to tell and publish to the world. The Mormons would be a very different people from any I ever saw to *like* such treatment. They seem to be just foolish enough to desire *justice* done them if possible, and that the truth is enough to tell at all times.

Prest. Young said to me, he did not expect anything of this abuse and

371

detraction from an Episcopal bishop. "They are men of education and better sense; they are gentlemen, and any gentleman is welcome here, no matter what his creed," were about his words.

The supporters of your church here will be Gentile business men generally—men who are daily mingling, in business and socially, with the Mormons and their leaders, and who are determined to live here in peace and harmony and do justice to all; and they are utterly and absolutely unwilling to give money and support to any minister who will come here and get himself and friends into trouble. Our minister, if we are so fortunate to get one, should be a young man of ability, and a good Christian; a man willing to work for his cause and build up his church on its merits and not expect to tear down an opposing cause to build on. Such a man will undoubtedly prosper here, I think, and receive a general support from the Gentile population. I trust you will pardon my long digression from your inquiries, when I say that it was upon my promising to write you as I have that parties were induced to subscribe to a minister's support as they did. "We are willing to give, but we want a man to come here who will preach the gospel, and attend to his discreet duties," was the usual answer to my soliciting subscriptions. Such a man if he possesses fair ability and is a good Christian, I feel must succeed. I think the Sabbath collections, aside from amt. subscribed for a salary, will give quite a revenue, above paying all expenses for rents, fuel and lights, as the audience will be large aside from church members, especially if we get a smart, able man. The better the man the more can be raised for him. I shall continue soliciting and raise the amount as high as I can.

Hoping it is God's will that we may meet you here in June, and that all will work for the good and advancement of His cause and the improvement of His creatures,

I am sincerely yours,
Warren Hussey.

The Lord's Co-op

SALT LAKE CITY *in the late 1860's, with a population of 20,000 and about to boom with the railroad at its gates and the mines opening up all around it, was a thriving commercial mart. Immigrant converts arriving from Europe, overlanders passing through on their way to California, miners wintering over, soldiers on leave from nearby army camps, and the Saints coming in from the settlements eager to see what the latest wagon trains had brought in from the East, kept business lively. With goods scarce and in great demand, enterprising merchants freighted their stores a thousand miles from the Missouri River and made fortunes. They charged all the traffic would bear.*

Brigham Young denounced the price gougers, Mormon as well as Gentile. Their wealth at the expense of the common welfare irritated him. He accused the four Walker brothers, Mormons, of paying an insufficient tithe and called for $30,000 outright. The Walker brothers refused and left the church, to become wealthier still. The growing affluence of the Gentile businessmen seemed a particular threat. Brigham Young bore down on them from the pulpit, hoping to drive them out. In 1866 twenty-two non-Mormon firms signed an open letter "To the Leaders of the Mormon Church" offering to leave the territory if the church would buy them out. Brigham Young gave them a resounding no.

In 1868 he proposed that the people become their own merchants, a proposal which led to the birth of Zion's Cooperative Mercantile Institution—Z. C. M. I.—as a parent wholesaler, with retail branches in all the settlements. Independent Mormon merchants received notice they were expected to merge with the church co-op, taking shares in it for their stock. Supporting Z. C. M. I. became a religious obligation. Trading with the Gentiles was a sign of apostasy. The Lord's all-seeing eye, painted over the portals of the parent store and all its branches, became Z. C. M. I.'s trademark, symbolizing the co-operative's intent to preserve Mormon social and economic unity.

Edward W. Tullidge, prominent writer and editor of the time, and an associate of the men who created Z. C. M. I., describes the founding of this great mercantile establishment, which still flourishes today, though

not as a co-operative. His account, almost too tactful, is taken from his
History of Salt Lake City (*Salt Lake City, 1886*).

Early in our commercial history, there grew up a conflict between the
merchants and the Church. To become a merchant was to antagonize
the Church and her policies; so that it was almost illegitimate for Mormon men of enterprising character to enter into mercantile pursuits;
and it was not until Jennings, Hooper and Eldredge redeemed Utah
from this conflict by resigning to the Church their own basis that Utah
commerce developed into proper forms and became inspired with the
true genius of mercantile enterprise. . . .

Early in 1868, the merchants were startled by the announcement "that
it was advisable that the *people* of Utah Territory should become their
own merchants"; and that an organization should be created for them
expressly for importing and distributing merchandise on a comprehensive plan. When it was asked of President Young, "What do you think
the merchants will do in this matter; will they fall in with this cooperative idea?" he answered, "I do not know, but if they do not we shall
leave them out in the cold, the same as the Gentiles, and their goods
shall rot upon their shelves."

This surely was implacable; but . . . Brigham Young and the Mormons as a peculiar community had in 1868 come face to face with implacable necessities. They had, in fact, to cease to be a communistic
power in the world and from that moment exist as a mere religious sect,
or preserve their temporal cohesiveness. The Mormons from the first
have existed as a society, not as a sect. They have combined the two
elements of organization—the social and the religious. They are now a
new society-power in the world and an entirety in themselves. They are
indeed the only religious *community* in Christendom of modern birth.
They existed as such in Ohio; in Missouri, in Illinois, and finally in Utah;
and to preserve themselves as a community they made an exodus to the
isolation of the Rocky Mountains. They intend forever to preserve themselves as a community; that was the plain and simple meaning of Brigham Young's answer concerning the merchants in 1868. It was not an
exodus which was then needed to so preserve them, but a Zion's Cooperative Mercantile Institution. . . . To appreciate the radical necessity
of such a combination of the Mormon moneyed classes at that time will
be to understand . . . the immense service which three or four of the
chief commercial and moneyed men of the Territory did to the commu-

nity in resigning their own basework to a Zion's Institution, thus setting the example to the lesser mercantile powers throughout the Territory.

The cooperative plan having been sufficiently evolved in the mind of President Young and his apostolic compeers, the President called a meeting of the merchants in the City Hall, October, 1868. It was there and then determined to adopt a general cooperative plan throughout the Territory to preserve the commerce and money resources of the people within themselves, and thus also to preserve the social unity. As yet, however, the methods of cooperation were not perfected nor the idea of a Z. C. M. I. completely evolved. It was necessary for the merchants themselves to work out the idea into practical shape, it being their special movement, though inspired by the Church. . . . Of themselves the merchants never would have reconstructed themselves upon a cooperative plan. The inspiration of the movement was from the Church, while its *success* was in such men as Jennings, and Hooper and Eldredge and Clawson; but especially was the commercial basework of Mr. Jennings, with his Eagle Emporium, required for the foundation of an Institution colossal enough to represent a community. Brigham Young was wise enough to know the necessary parts of the combination.

The initial movement of cooperation having been made, meeting followed meeting; a committee was appointed to frame a constitution and by-laws, and, without seeing the end from the beginning, their part of the program was carried out, and an institution formed on paper; subscriptions were solicited, and cash fell into the coffers of the Treasurer *pro tem.* This was during the winter months of 1868. With the turn of the year a committee was appointed to commence operations. They waited upon the President for advice, who, in his quiet but decided way, said: "Go to work and do it." After a little conversation, the question was again suggested: "What shall we do?" With the same sententious brevity, the reply came, "Go to work and do it." "But how?" the questioners continued; "we haven't enough money; we haven't the goods; we have no building; we haven't sufficient credit." "Go to work and do it, and I will show you how," was the President's finality to those who came to seek counsel. . . .

Review the commercial and financial combination as defined in Brigham Young's mind at that moment. There was, perhaps, first, the Hon. William H. Hooper. He had served the people faithfully in Congress ever since the "Utah War," and the President esteemed him as the keystone of the commercial arch. As a far-seeing, watchful politician, also

375

William H. Hooper could perfectly comprehend at once the political and commercial complications of the times and foresee that, as the people's Delegate, he would soon have to grapple in Congress with the same essential problem that Brigham Young had to grapple with at home. This was, to preserve the community intact and sufficiently resistive toward all antagonistic forces; and scarcely a year had passed ere the Hon. William H. Hooper fully realized this in his defence of the Mormons against the Cullom Bill. . . .

There was, probably, next in the President's mind, Horace S. Eldredge. He had been with the people in their troubles in Missouri and Illinois, had conducted their emigrations and was one of the commercial founders of the Mormon commonwealth in Utah. Therefore Horace S. Eldredge was a proper foundationstone of Z. C. M. I.

The third—and in some respects the most important man defined in the President's mind—was William Jennings. In 1869, he could have carried a million dollars to either side in means and credit. He had the goods at that moment in Salt Lake City; he had built his Eagle Emporium, which was quite worthy of Zion's Cooperative Mercantile Institution to open business in, and he had abundance of commercial credit either East or West to sustain the President in his great design. . . .

To the everlasting honor of William Jennings be it said, he did not betray the President and the people in their cooperative movement. Mr. [T.B.H.] Stenhouse treats his act as a shrewd piece of business policy; but the true historian can only consider it as an act commensurate with the needs of those times. William Jennings resigned his business basis to Z. C. M. I., sold his stock to it for over $200,000, and rented his Eagle Emporium for three years to the institution at an annual rental of $8,000. Eldredge & Clawson also sold their stock and resigned their business basis to Z. C. M. I., and other leading firms followed the example.

The organization of Z. C. M. I. was at length effected in the winter of 1868–69. It consisted of a president, vice-president, secretary, treasurer and seven directors. Brigham Young was very properly chosen president. . . .

The policy which had been wisely and considerately pursued in purchasing the stock of existing firms, or receiving them as investments at just rates, shielded from embarrassment those who would otherwise have inevitably suffered from the inauguration and prestige of the Z. C. M. I.

Simultaneously with the framing of the parent institution, local organizations were formed in all the settlements of the Territory; each feeling itself in duty bound to sustain the one central depot and to make their purchases from it. The people with great unanimity, became shareholders in their respective local cooperatives, and also in the parent institution; so that they might enjoy the profits of their own investment and purchases. Thus, almost in a day, was effected a great reconstruction of the commercial relations and methods of an entire community which fitted the purposes of the times and preserved the temporal unity of the Mormon people as well as erecting for them a mighty financial bulwark.

The Mormons and the Mines

IN THE EARLY 1860's Col. Patrick E. Connor's soldiers, the California Volunteers stationed at Camp Douglas, prospected in the mountains surrounding Salt Lake Valley and soon confirmed what had long been suspected—they were rich in valuable minerals. "Utah," Lincoln predicted, "will become the treasure house of the nation," and he urged Speaker Schuyler Colfax to go and investigate the mineral resources of the territory. By 1882 local historian Edward Tullidge could say that in another quarter century Utah would be less renowned as Zion than as the greatest mining state in America.

From the outset Brigham Young had warned the Saints to tend their farms and develop home industries and to keep hands off the mines. The strength and glory of England, he said, lay in coal and iron and industry; the weakness and corruption of Spain in silver and gold. Gold was good for ornament, perhaps, but not as a foundation for Zion's economy. The Saints sold their flour and meat and produce to the mines and gained indirectly. Even some Forty-Niners envied the Mormon way: "I almost wished," wrote one, "I could awake from my golden dream . . . while I pursued my domestic duties as quietly, as happily, and contentedly as this strange people."

The mining threat had once been distant, as far away as California or Carson City or Leadville. Utah lost ribs in the creation of Colorado and Nevada as Gentiles took over the eastern and western extremes of the original territory. Now, in the early 1870's the mountains ringing Salt Lake City itself blossomed with exotic names like Ophir and Eureka. The miners and speculators peopled Main Street, hustling with a new excitement. Along broad Brigham Street arose the elegant mansions of the mining magnates, who joined the federal officials, the military, the denominational missionaries and school teachers to form a Gentile elite in the heart of Zion.

In the following selection Charles Marshall, an English traveler, describes Salt Lake's quickened tempo and Brigham Young's attitude toward the latest infiltration from outside. The excerpt is taken from "Salt Lake City and the Valley Settlements," which appeared in Fraser's Magazine (London), in July, 1871.

The only novelty [on Main Street] in the busy scene of buying and selling likely to attract the notice of the traveller is the inscription, repeated on almost every shopfront, "Zion Cooperative Mercantile Association," with the universal motto, "Holiness to the Lord," with an ill-painted large eye looking out of a chevaux-de-frise of rays. From two of the principal stores, Dr. Godby's [Godbe's] on one side of the way, and Messrs. Walkers' on the other, this inscription is conspicuously absent. These gentlemen became recusant on the determination of the church executive to impose the cooperative principle on the whole trading community.

For a year past Main Street has been growing constantly more bustling and animated. It had long been whispered that rich mines existed in the Territory of Utah. Mormon policy, however, delayed as long as possible an open discovery of the position and richness of these mines. But within the past few months the secret has blazed abroad. Already miners, by scores, by hundreds, and even by thousands, have poured into the Territory, and commenced operations. The whole Gentile population is mad with the excitement of the gold fever, and the Mormons feel the contagion. A "rush" to Utah comparable with that to California and to British Columbia is likely to take place, and if so will seriously affect, and probably simplify, the Mormon political difficulty.

The town feels the change. Business has grown active. The picturesque, lumbering, excellently-built Concord stages, leather-hung, constructed expressly to endure the prodigious jolting of roughly-made mountain roads, come in and go out for the new mining canyons at full speed with their fine teams of four horses. Shaggy-looking, roughly-dressed, dare-devil miners hang about the hotel doors and street corners, and spit, and chew, and smoke, and talk with mouthfuls of quaint oaths, or jostle the quiet-looking Mormon men and women in the street-walks. Every second shop in Main Street has heaps of specimen ores on shelves within, or deposited in the windows.

The Mormons and the Mines

The population of Salt Lake City is estimated by the Mormons at 20,-000, though the United States census makes it considerably less. Of these perhaps a couple of hundred are Gentiles. The numbers in the whole Territory of Utah are estimated by the Mormons at 150,000, among whom there may be a couple of thousand of Gentile miners. Utah has long possessed sufficient population to entitle it to become a State. But the Mormons would control all elections for governor, judges, all minor official appointments, the members of both houses of the State Legislature, and the Senators and Representatives in Congress, and would, of course, have the powerful protection of their own State rights in defence of their religious and social order. Congress, therefore, persistently refuses to sanction the admission of Utah into the Union as a State. It is confidently predicted by the resident Gentiles that the mining rush will bring in twenty thousand people before the close of 1871, and an increasing proportion later, until the Mormon votes are swamped. . . .

From Salt Lake City a broad, roughly-made roadway runs along the upward "benches" or terraces of the plains of Great Salt Lake and Utah southward for three or four hundred miles, through a perpetual succession of Mormon settlements. Branch roads to the right and left strike away through the passes, or canyons as they are called, to more isolated communities. Lines of stage coaches run on these roads to carry mails and passengers. A singular variety of wagons, "buggies," and ox-carts, sometimes of picturesquely primitive construction, are everywhere encountered.

I took my place with the mail one morning by the driver's side on the stage going south. I speak literally, for the leathern mailbags, curiously strengthened with metal rivets, were pushed under my feet, and I did myself the pleasure of assisting to change these at our various stopping-places. . . .

At an early point in our journey a rough hand holding a whiskey bottle was struck out from behind, and we all "liquored up." My fellow-passengers were four miners, who had hunted fortune with the pickaxe with varying success in California, Columbia, Montana, and Colorado. The accounts they willingly gave of their brawls, Indian fights, escapes, and spells of good and ill luck, were entertaining, and possibly trustworthy. All agreed that Utah surpassed every mining country they had known, and all were happily confident of now achieving fortune.

"Jess look at me," said one of them, a powerful-looking fellow, with an immense mass of dark hair, putting his big hands complacently on the spruce suit of clothes in which he was dressed to give point to his talk, which was ornamented with a profusion of big Western oaths. "I come into Salt Lake a fortnight ago not worth a live cent. My clows was mostly composed of holes, jined together with dirt, and I had jest about forgot what the sight of a squr' meal was. Wal, darn *me* if I'd sell my claims now for fifty thousand dollars. Stranger, take another pull.". . .

At Payson, seventy miles below Salt Lake, I presented letters of introduction to the Mormon President, Brigham Young. He was travelling by easy stages to visit the southern settlements, and to pass the winter in a mild climate; and also with the purpose of deciding on the future direction of Mormon settlement—a matter of increasing concern since the threatened irruption of Gentile miners.

The President was attended by two wives, one of whom, with some children, was to be left at St. George as her constant residence. It was a preaching tour as well as a journey of observation. George A. Smith, a cousin of the martyred Joseph, and the second in rank of the three presidents of the Mormon Church, and Brigham, junior, as the people call him, the second son of the great Brigham, each with one or two wives, and a servant or two for the horses, completed the numbers of the unpretentious cortege.

The President was staying at the house of one of the few well-to-do men of the place. The room into which I was shown was furnished handsomely and with some taste. Almost all the travelling party were assembled here, the ladies dressed with an elegance beyond what I had then seen among the Mormons. The President received me courteously, drew a chair for me at his side, and talked willingly on a variety of subjects.

I was invited to stay to breakfast, a substantial meal served in another apartment. In some respects Brigham Young's tastes are very simple; he took only bread-and-milk. Noticing that I did not eat the hot rolls universally supplied at all meals in America, he asked for stale bread, and remarked with approval that he had never seen hot bread eaten in England during his visit there in early years. During the past few months, under his immediate influence, a number of his wives and many of the Mormon ladies have commenced a Retrenchment Society, with the view of opposing a growing tendency among the leading families to an ostentation and luxuriousness of living. The retrenchment is to be made at the table, in the furnishing of the house, and especially in dress. But the movement is not a popular one.

The Mormon President is seventy years of age: he is hale, stout, and strong, and it would not be impossible to mistake him for sixty. In appearance, dress, and style of speech he resembles a rough, burly English farmer. . . .

One of the most interesting subjects on which we talked was the probable effect on the community of the influx of miners. Some of the President's remarks were characteristic enough to be repeated.

"This is no doubt a good mining country for spending money in," he said, "and we shall get it. A few fortunes will be made here by the Gentiles; but more will be lost. For every dollar made here there will be ten dollars sunk, I am quite sure."

He did not appear to have any great fear of an evil influence being exercised on his people by the incoming mass of lawless men.

"They will entice away, or marry, our wives and daughters? Let them if they can. We don't want any women among us who are not convinced of the authority and excellence of our system. We can well spare all who can be perverted."

George A. Smith talked with me afterwards on this subject freely.

"We don't anticipate any trouble," he said. "The miners have always got on with us singularly well. We have supplied them with everything they wanted forth and back from California. It is in fact we who have made Nevada and Montana with our beef and bread. If the miners are let alone, they will certainly not make any difficulty with us. The only danger is that they may be tampered with by politicians. But we shall find the means for managing them."

It was Bishop Fairbanks, I think, who explained to me the Mormon view of their President's policy in interdicting mining enterprises. In the earlier years the chief need of the settlement was a sufficiency of food. Every man's labor was of consequence in preparing and securing the harvest. What would have been the value of silver ores to a starving people remote from markets? Then, a little later, the immense demand for their produce for the supply of the miners and immigrants presented a surer means of profit than digging for gold. The purpose of the President was simply to restrain the people until the fitting time should come. . . .

I remained with Mr. Young until about noon, when the whole party set off on their next stage south. The wagons started in succession as they were ready. . . . Mr. Brigham Young brought up the rear. He drove a spring "buggy" with a folding leather top, drawn by a couple of solemn-looking mules. The vehicle was very roomy, but was well filled when the President and his favorite wife, an elegantly-dressed lady, sat in it. To Gentile eyes the clumsy figure of the head of the new religion, stooping slightly with age, shapeless and wide, in great encompassing overcoats, mounting with difficulty the open buggy, was a sight not exactly imposing. A group of men and boys, hands in pockets, watched the operation with grave interest. Mr. Young drew up over his knees, and over the lady by his side, a magnificent otter-skin robe, and placed in her lap a large apple. Then he took the reins. The chief hierarch in the new church dispensed with any sort of patriarchal or apostolic blessing. "I am much obliged to you friends, for your hospitality," was all he said, addressing no one in particular; "I wish you all good-day," and off he went.

"An After-Clap of Puritanism"

ON APRIL 18, 1871, *Ralph Waldo Emerson, then in his sixty-eighth year, arrived in Salt Lake City with a party of friends in a private Pullman car en route to San Francisco. The next morning they called on Brigham Young. Emerson noted in his memorandum book simply "Apr. 19, Called on B. Young   Salt Lake City   Tabernacle   Left Ogden." He evidently wrote home of the meeting, for his daughter Ellen wrote him in May that "Elizabeth Ripley laughed to hear he had called on Brigham Young." Brigham Young did not make anything of the occasion either. The* Deseret News *did not report the visit. The two great Yankees seem to have made little impression on each other. Happily, James B. Thayer, a member of the party, published a charming reminiscence in 1884 in* A Western Journey with Mr. Emerson, *source of the brief selection reproduced below.*

Emerson first mentioned the Mormons in 1842 apropos of a Chardon Street Bible Convention where, along with "mad men and mad women" and "all the fanaticism of all shades and forms" also "Mormons came and spoke." In 1853 he mentioned them again: "Fatalism, foolish and flippant, is as bad as Unitarianism or Mormonism." And in 1862, when his son Edward was traveling through the West, an apprehensive Emerson hoped that the emigrants were strong enough to "keep the ways open against spiteful Mormons. . . . I shall be glad to get a letter from the boy next week, from Salt Lake." Finally, in 1872, on the S. S. Wyoming *bound*

*for Egypt, he sat at table next to "a speechless young Mormon woman
from Utah with an untidily stuffed head of reddish hair; but she soon
disappeared. . . ." Emerson wrote home that his "well-known orthodoxy
. . . is walled round by whole families of missionaries. . . . But the liberal ocean sings louder, & makes us all of one church."*

In the forenoon most of the men of our party called upon Brigham
Young; the ladies declined, with thanks. Young's carriage was waiting
for him at the door, but a card was sent in, and we were admitted.
"The President" soon entered the room arrayed for his drive, his long
cloak on, and his hat in hand. He was a man of not over medium
height, full-blooded, and with the look of some stout stage-driver who
had prospered and been used to authority. His face was smooth, except
for whiskers of a reddish cast touched with gray. His hair, rather thick
and of a like color, seemed wet, and was parted behind and brushed or
rather rolled up on the top, in a cheap way that one might see on a
teamster at a ball, or on a teamster's child that had just left the hands of
its mother. He shook hands all round with a stolid sort of dignity, and
sat down. His mouth was close, his nose somewhat aquiline, his eye
quiet but cunning, his manner good, and steady. A little talk sprang
up—not without its difficulties. Some one spoke to Young of what we
had liked about his town, and said that he had had an excellent
opportunity to show what combined labor could do, and the directing
power of a single man; and he unluckily used the phrase, "the one-man
power." "Yes," said Young, quickly, "the one-man power! It's easy to
talk about that! We have no more of it than they have elsewhere!"
Alas, we had not begun well.* But this was smoothed over, and we
tried again. Much excitement was existing just then about newly discovered mines in Utah. He intimated that he cared little about them,
and did not expect much from them. Mr. Emerson asked him what
books there were from which one could get a correct impression of their
opinions. He said, shortly: "There were none. They didn't print any-

---

* We found afterwards that he had lately preached a sermon, printed that very day,
in which he had touched upon the "one-man power." "Is it our ability," he said, "that
has accomplished what we see here in building up a colony in the wilderness? Is it
the doings of man? No. To be sure, we assist in it, and we do as we are directed. But
God is our captain; he is our master. He is the '*one man*' that we serve. . . . What do
you suppose I think when I hear people say, 'Oh, see what the mormons have done in
the mountains. It is Brigham Young. What a head he has got! What power he has got!
How well he controls the people!' The people are ignorant of our true character. It is
the Lord that has done this. It is not any one man or set of men; only as we are led
and guided by the Spirit of truth."

thing." But his secretary, a thin, pallid young man, intervened, and suggested to Young that there *was* a book, "Answers to Questions." "Yes," Young replied, "that was good; as good as anything." He gave no sign of knowing who Mr. Emerson was; but the secretary soon turned to one of us, and with a motion towards Mr. Emerson, inquired, in a public way: "Is this the justly celebrated Ralph Waldo Emerson?" and then to Mr. Emerson: "I have read a great many of your books." We were then desired to enter our names in a register, and so took our leave.

We afterwards found a copy of "The Deseret News" of that same day, April 19, containing Young's sermon to which I referred before. It was a strange discourse—patriarchal, giving much homely good advice, marked by quaint sense, and yet flavored also with a revolting mixture of religious fanaticism and vulgar dishonesty. Mr. Emerson was a good deal interested by a certain power in the address, and a certain homespun sense.

We left Salt Lake City in the afternoon, returned to Ogden, and started westward again at once. It was still nearly nine hundred miles to San Francisco, and we should reach it in two days. At sunset we were scudding along close by the Great Salt Lake. The northern edge of its large expanse (it is about a hundred and twenty six miles long), lay right under the car windows; ducks in profusion were flying and settling on the water, purple mountains were in the distance, and behind these the sun was setting in majesty. Presently we were running along under a snow-covered range of mountains; and the soft tints and changes of light on these engaged every one's attention. And then it was over. Mr. Emerson had dropped his writing to see it all, and now turned to one of the ladies: "Well, what are you going to *do* about this—all this beauty?" She answered: "You say somewhere that it is better to die for beauty than to live for bread." At which he murmured a little, good-naturedly, and was silent. Then he began to talk of the Mormons. Some one said, "They impress the common people, through their imagination, by Bible names and imagery." "Yes," he said; "it is an after-clap of Puritanism. But one would think that after this Father Abraham could go no further."

A Visit with Amelia Folsom Young

"I LOVE my wives," said Brigham Young, "respect them, and honor them, but to make a queen of one and peasants of the rest I have no such disposition, neither do I expect to do it." But when he met and married Harriet Amelia Folsom, it was apparent that he had found a favorite. Brigham Young was sixty-one when he married Amelia, an English girl of twenty-five. The daughter of William Folsom, architect and builder who had helped construct the Tabernacle and the Salt Lake Theater, was tall and handsome and refined. Brigham Young curled his hair and changed his homespun for broadcloth when he courted her. Amelia was not easily won, for there were rivals. But in 1863 she accepted the will of the Lord and married the courtly Brigham, stipulating conditions: a house and carriage of her own, fine clothes, a place in the box of honor at the theater. Of all his twenty-seven wives, he deferred most to her, and it was she who accompanied him on his tours of inspection about the settlements. Spiteful Ann Eliza Young, the last of Brigham's marriages, and the only one to come to grief, wrote: "Polygamist as he professes to be, he is, under the influence of Amelia, rapidly becoming a monogamist in all except the name."

The following description of a visit to Amelia's is taken from "A Week among the Mormons," which appeared in Lippincott's Magazine *(Philadelphia) in 1871. It was written by a woman who signed herself "A.M.," a member of one of the first parties to come west all the way by train.*

One bright morning we started on a short exploring expedition around the city, meaning to return some of the visits that to our great surprise had been made to us by various Mormon women. Turning down the street opposite the "Gable House" [today the Lion House] with the "Eagle Gate," where Brigham Young has his abode, and where each gable is said to testify to the presence of a wife, we came to a pleasant-looking house, on whose porch stood a remarkably fine-looking woman, of whom we inquired for Mr. Joseph Young's house. With much suavity and courtesy we were directed opposite. Some one said, "That woman can never be a *Mormon:* she must belong to a Gentile family." During the call on "Mrs. Joe" we asked, "Who is your very handsome neighbor?" "Why," in some astonishment, "that is Amelia, and she wants your party to go to the President's with her." So the party adjourned to Mrs. Amelia Young's house, to be introduced to the favorite wife of Brigham—the only woman, it is reported, who has any influence over him, and who is considered to be "the power behind the throne." The house itself externally is very like all the Salt Lake buildings, being constructed of sun-dried brick, or "adobe," and painted to suit individual taste; low in structure—only a story and a half high—with a hall running through the middle. But this house and its surroundings were in fine order: paint fresh, fences straight and trim, and a general air of neatness and finish that was often wanting in other buildings. The furnishings in-doors was the best we had seen; a fine "Steinway" stood open, the walls bore some pleasant pictures; the aspect was more familiar than any before encountered, and Mrs. Amelia became the surroundings: tall and grace-ful, with a commanding figure and a head worthy of better things, it was hard to realize her position. A daughter of Brigham, about twenty, was also in the room, seemingly on the best of terms with "Aunt Amelia," this being the avowed relationship held by the children of one wife to all the other wives. After the first few moments the talk flowed into Mormon channels. We noticed that on all occasions they *would* talk of themselves, assert their superiority over the rest of the world, and endeavor by vehement self-assertion to prove how much better was their condition than that of others. Mrs. Joe said, "Amelia, are you going to the President's?" "That will not be necessary. I have sent for the Pres-ident!" But a few moments elapsed ere the President's own handsome carriage, drawn by a pair of black horses, drew up to the door, with a message that its owner was engaged at a business meeting, but had sent Mrs. Amelia the carriage, and would come himself at a later hour. Amelia offered to show the ladies some of their best families, and our party, just filling the carriage, moved off. . . .

We were amused at the commotion created by Mrs. Amelia's appear-ance in the stores on the street. Evidently she was recognized as a power. We watched her closely, curiously. Aware of her history, of the months of sueing that Brigham had undergone ere he could bring her to consent to be Mrs. Young No. 40 or 50, or thereabouts, we looked and marveled. After the progress was over, the question was put: "What do you think of polygamy *now?* Is it what people have represented it to be?" "Not exactly," was the response, "but much worse." "Ah, well! I suppose your minds are not educated up to this point, but the day will come when you will see that we are in the right. I am not the only wife of my husband, but I consider myself the *equal, if not the superior, of ANY woman in the United States.*" And she evidently did. "A kinder, more indulgent, more affectionate husband than mine cannot be seen." "No," chimed in *Miss Young,* "nor a better, kinder father than mine is." We were glad to hear it, but somehow it did sound a little dubious.

Retrenchment: Brigham Young's Doctrine on Dress

"ALL ISRAEL," *Brigham Young told his household on November 28, 1869, "are looking to my family and watching the example set by my wives and children. For this reason I desire to organize my own family first into a society for the promotion of habits of order, thrift, industry, and charity; and above all things I desire them to retrench from their extravagance in dress, in eating and even in speech. . . . I am weary of the manner in which our women seek to outdo each other in all the foolish fashions of the world." He formed his daughters, at first unhappy at being denied their ribbons and hair frizzes, into a Retrenchment Association. It proved to be the forerunner of a churchwide Young Ladies Mutual Improvement Association still in existence, along with a similar association for the young men.*

The retrenchment of the 1870's was another aspect of Zion's determination to remain socially aloof and, as far as possible, economically independent of the Gentile. Brigham Young's warning voice rose as the threat from outside mounted. In 1872 he made dress a prominent theme in his sermons up and down the state, calling on the Saints to economize and "Retrench in everything that is not good and beautiful."

The following passages come from stenographic reports of his sermons published in the Deseret News *for June 5 and October 23, 1872.*

I wish to say to some of my sisters, not to all, that if I were my own tailor, I should cut my own coat to suit myself. "What would be your fashion?" says one. I will tell you. I have a coat here which you can see; if I were to take hold of a swillpail, this part of the skirt must drop in; and if I took hold of a milkpail I must take the coat around by the other end, and hold it, or else it is in the milk. I see no convenience or beauty in it. That which is convenient should be beautiful; and I want my coat cut so that when I lift a pail of water, or a milk or swillpail the skirts shall not fall into it; and so with the pockets, I would have them convenient. If I were a lady and had a piece of cloth to make me a dress, I would cut it so as to cover my person handsomely and neatly; and whether it was cut according to the fashion, or not, custom would soon make it beautiful. I would not have eighteen or twenty yards to drag behind me, so that if I had to turn round I would have to pick up my dress and throw it after me, or, just as a cow does when she kicks over the milk pail, throw out one foot to kick the dress out of the way. That is not becoming, beautiful or convenient; all such fashions are inconvenient. Take that cloth and cut you a skirt that will be modest and neat; that does not drag in the dirt, nor show your garters; but cut it so that it will clear the ground when you walk, when you are passing over the floor it will not drag everything on the floor, or in the street as you pass along. Put enough into the skirt to look well, and if we are to go into particulars, of course, we would have to say, we must use enough to cover the person. I do not expect mother Eve even did this.

We could relate some little incidents of our past experience, that perhaps would not entertain the people, and still, perhaps, they might learn something from them. For instance, in some circles it has been fashionable for a lady to wear, perhaps, twelve yards in the skirt of her dress, but when it came to the waist, I guess three-quarters of a yard would have been enough. I will relate a circumstance of which I heard, that took place in the metropolis of our country. A gentleman, a stranger, was invited to a grand dinner party there. The ladies, of course, were dressed in the height of fashion, their trails dragging behind them, and their——well, I suppose there was a band over the shoulder to the waist, but I do not recollect whether the gentleman said there was or not; but one gentleman present, who knew this gentleman was a stranger, said to him, with all the loveliness and elegance in his heart that one could imagine: "Is not this beautiful? Did you ever see the like of this?" "No sir," said the party questioned, "never since I was weaned." Well, all this, you know, is custom and fashion. . . .

We have the ability to tell what looks well, just as well as anybody else. We need not go to New York, London, or Paris to tell whether a coat looks well if it has a collar half an inch wide. Do you recollect when the collars were not more than that? I do, and I recollect when they were about six or seven inches in width. Now we need not go to Paris to ask them whether a coat looks just right with a half inch or a five inch collar; we are the judges, and can decide that just as well as anybody else on the face of the earth. . . . This, I say, to my sisters. Pause, reflect, look at the facts in the case as regards the folly and expense of fashion. Take the people of this city, and, if you can, form a correct estimate of the cost of the useless articles they wear. . . . Just take these useless articles that do no good to the body of the persons who use them, and we would find that the means expended in their purchase would enable us to relieve many poor, suffering, distressed creatures abroad in the nations of the earth, and bring them here and put them in a situation in which they would be healthy, wealthy and happy. If we make a calculation on this subject we shall find that the waste of the Latter-day Saints is immense. . . .

The time will come when Babylon will fall. If it should fall now, it would leave us pretty destitute. We would soon wear out our head dresses and fine clothing, and what would we do? Why, we should be as badly off as the saints were when they came into this valley, twenty-five years ago. They picked up a few buckskins, antelope skins, sheepskins, buffalo skins, and made leggings and moccasins of them, and wrapped the buffalo robes around them. Some had blankets and some had not; some had shirts, and I guess some had not. One man told me that he had not a shirt for himself or family. If Babylon should happen to tip over, so that we could not reach out and gather the necessaries of life, we should be in a bad condition. I want to put you in mind of these things, and it is my duty to say to the Latter-day Saints that they should take measures to sustain themselves—they should lay a foundation for feeding and clothing themselves. . . . Latter-day Saints should dress in that plain, neat, comely manner that will be pleasing and prudent, in every sense of the word, before the Lord, and try and please him that we serve, the Being that we acknowledge as our God. Not flaunting, flirting and gossiping, as a great many are, and thinking continually of their dresses and of this, that and the other that will minister to and gratify their vanity. Such women seldom think of their prayers.

Through Utah with Captain Codman

IN THE SUMMER and autumn of 1874, John Codman and his wife traveled 400 miles by wagon and horseback down the length of Utah from Logan to Cove Fort, looping back by way of western and little visited settlements. They reported the northern part of their trip to the New York Evening Post, the southern and western to Galaxy magazine. It was their second sojourn among the Mormons. Captain Codman (he had been to sea) published his account of the previous year's visit in The Mormon Country. A Summer with the Latter-day Saints (*New York, 1874*). *Critics found it so favorable they warned him he had not seen the real Mormonism. In the settlements, they said, he would encounter only ignorance, poverty, and degradation. But the Codmans, indulgent of back-country crudities and discomforts, remained as friendly as at first.*

Codman made it clear he was equally opposed to polygamy and the legislation attempting to abolish it. Such efforts only kept it alive. He inveighed heavily against the Gentile "ring," which made the attack on polygamy a screen for its own political ambitions. The best way to solve the Mormon question, he argued, was to leave polygamy to "the omnipotent jurisdiction of railroads and fashions and to the common sense of the rising and more cultured generation." He found Mormon society gradually overcoming the prejudices of Eastern capitalists who had been afraid investments in Mormon country were unsafe.

The following miscellany samples Codman's observations of 1874 as they were published serially in the Galaxy *during 1875.*

This little village [Tooele], now so peaceful and quiet, was lately the scene of intense political excitement; the newspapers have been full of the election quarrels at Tooele. They have not related to Republicanism or Democracy. Such trifling issues did not affect votes in any degree. . . . The great question was, shall Judge Rowberry, the Mormon bishop, who for years had presided at the Probate Court, retain his office, or shall the Gentile Brown occupy his place? In short, it was a religious fight. Bunyan's "Holy War" and Milton's "Paradise Lost" could only approach in prose or poetry to an idea of the fury of the battle. Mormon hosts were marshalled against the Gentile cohorts, the one considering themselves the armies of the Lord, and the others willing to be called the soldiers of Lucifer, so that they might gain the victory. Mormonism pressed every man and woman into its service, and the Gentile element ransacked all the mining camps of the country for its supplies. It was Lowlander against Highlander—the saints dwelling on the plains against the irreverent "cusses" of the mountains who had invaded the soil, heretofore sacred to the religion of the prophet.

It was the first organized attempt to gain a Gentile foothold in any part of the territory. The means used for the assault were as unscrupulous as those wielded for the defence. Governor Woods descended from the dignity of his office to mingle in the broil, threatening, when he was interrupted in his speech, to "punch the head" of his assailant and to "boot out" the county clerk if he did not "dry up." Parson Smith, of the Methodist persuasion, is such a muscular Christian that when he was damned by some devout Mormons, he replied to them that he was not allowed to swear, but, suiting the action to the words by throwing off his coat, he "would lick the whole crowd, three at a time." Per contra, in a rather more quiet style of warfare, when they found the election was going against them, the Mormon Judge and his clerk carried off the records of the court, which were not recovered without much difficulty. There was doubtless a great deal of illegal voting on both sides, from Mormon women who paid no taxes, and from Gentile miners who constituted themselves residents of two or three different camps at the same time.

The end attained was a Gentile victory. The Probate Court is now in Gentile hands, and as Salt Lake City is in the same district, it is proposed to bring Brigham Young and all the great polygamists of that city to trial in Tooele; and to put down by this decisive blow the "twin relic of barbarism," which has so heavily weighed upon the consciences of those virtuous mining Gentiles, so that they can henceforward drink their whiskey without molestation, and use their pistols and bowie knives in peace. This must be accomplished before the next election, for in the meantime Brigham, warned by the disastrous results of this campaign, will not fail to pour a sufficient Mormon reinforcement into Tooele County to insure a victory for the Church, by reinstating the deposed judge and his clerk. . . .

President George A. Smith, next in council to Brigham Young himself . . . is my favorite apostle. We have often heard him preach at the

Tabernacle in Salt Lake. His views are more liberal than those advocated by many of his coreligionists, and his plain, practical teachings are instructive to Gentiles as well as to Mormons. He is fifty-seven years of age, of tall, portly figure, with a face of infinite jollity and expressive humor. This crops out so frequently that the audience always expects to be entertained when "Brother George A." holds forth. . . .

On the occasion of [our] visit to Richfield we attended the crowded meeting and listened to the discourses of Mr. Smith and several others. . . . He gave the people some very good advice: "Make the most of materials at hand, without procuring luxuries from abroad. Skin every dog or cat that dies or is killed. If that don't give you leather enough for shoes besides what you get from cattle, make the soles of wood; wooden soles are preventatives of rheumatism. They are better than the sponge soles you import from the East. Raise your own sheep. Manufacture your own wool. Make your women useful as well as ornamental. Work outside, and they will be encouraged to work inside. You have got everything you want right here at home—the best of land, the best of cattle, the best of religions, the best of everything. Thank God for his continual mercies. Pray to Him morning and evening, and at every meal. When the railroad is completed you can have some luxuries you cannot now procure, and you can pay for them in the abundant excess of your own productions. Pay up your tithing like good Latter-Day Saints; not a particle of it shall be misappropriated. We want more temples for the Lord, and whatever excess there is shall go to bringing people from all parts of the earth to participate with you in your blessings. Never get into debt. When you take up land pay for it as soon as you can, whether obliged to do so or not; for I have always noticed that people get into debt when they are flush and have to pay up when money is scarce. To those of you who were so unfortunate as to have come to this country with your clothes on I would say, Get clothed at once with all the rights of an American citizen. You have a judge in this district who is a just and honorable man, and who does not consider himself a missionary sent here expressly to convert you. If you lived in Salt Lake City I would tell you to see Judge McKean and his whole "ring" in perdition before taking the false oath he seeks to impose. If you are drawn on a jury don't shirk your duty. Don't lie before God or man. If a man is indicted for polygamy entered into since the law of 1862, and it is proved, convict him accordingly. We know that law is unconstitutional, and we can beat them in their own courts. Don't be nervous about it.

Take a little valerian tea and put your trust in God. Everything will come out all right. Show to the world that you are a quiet, law-abiding people. We have stood a good deal, and we can stand it to the end. May every blessing attend you. I ask it of the Eternal Father in the name of Jesus Christ. Amen."

We have listened to worse sermons than this. . . .

Kanosh is supposed to be the dwelling place of the chief of that name. Here he owns an adobe hut, where he keeps a squaw, while he ranges the mountains and valleys in an independent way, on his own account. Considering that he is alive, he comes near to being a good Indian. Phil Sheridan says that the only really good Indian is a dead Indian, and upon the whole I think Phil is generally correct in his estimate of their moral character.

Kanosh is a devout Mormon. He preaches to his tribe "to love God, and not to drink whiskey, or tea and coffee: to love God because he is good, to hate whiskey because it is bad, and to abstain from tea and coffee because they are dear." Not a bad Indian that, General Phil, after all!

The Orderville Brethren

THE MORMON CO-OPERATIVES of the late 1860's were only prelude to more sweeping economic reforms in the 1870's. The hard times following the panic of 1873 complicated Mormon efforts to remain self-sufficient despite the railroad and its influence. In the winter of 1873–4 Brigham Young preached the United Order, a plan which admonished the Saints to foster equality by mobilizing their resources for the common good. In most communities the Order became primarily a share-holding union of certain enterprises—members of the Order carried on farming, herding, merchandizing, and small manufacturing co-operatively, but continued to own their houses and lands privately. But in a few settlements, the Order practiced an apostolic communism, a return to an old ideal in Mormonism—the Order of Enoch.

Most of the United Orders were short-lived. But Orderville, in Long Valley, which lies between Bryce and Zion National Parks, lasted ten years. Founded in 1874 primarily by veteran Mormon colonists from the cotton mission on the Muddy River, by 1880 it numbered over 700. Completely communitarian, the people even ate as one big family. Phil Robinson, British journalist, visited the settlement in 1882. He predicted a vigorous life for it, provided it could include greater provision for individual stewardships.

But within three more years the Order, though not the settlement, had to be dissolved. The younger generation felt growing dissatisfactions (Robinson hints at them); even fellow Mormons considered Orderville queer and unprogressive; and in 1884 federal deputies began relentless prosecution of the Edmunds Act, which provided fines and punishment for "unlawful cohabitation." Many of the Orderville brethren were polygamists, and the prosecution of 1884 sent them underground or to prison, disrupting the normal life of the community. In 1885 the Order was dissolved. Some eighty families divided up the assets valued at $100,000 by bidding at auction for the community's goods to the extent of their "credits." It was another crack in Mormonism's unique and united front. Today Orderville is a rural community of 400 people engaged in farming and raising livestock. A few landmarks in ruins remain of the old communal establishments.

The following selection is taken from the Boston edition (1883) of Phil Robinson's Sinners and Saints, *a work most favorable to the Mormons.*

Travelling through the settlements, I have seen in a considerable number of homes the Rules of the [United] Order framed upon the walls. At any time these would be curious; *to-day,* when the morality of the principles of Mormonism is challenged, they are of special interest:—

"RULES THAT SHOULD BE OBSERVED BY MEMBERS OF THE UNITED ORDER.

"We will not take the name of the Deity in vain, nor speak lightly of His character or of sacred things.

"We will pray with our families morning and evening, and also attend to secret prayer.

"We will observe and keep the Word of Wisdom according to the spirit and the meaning thereof.

"We will treat our families with due kindness and affection, and set before them an example worthy of imitation. In our families and intercourse with all persons, we will refrain from being contentious or quarrelsome, and we will cease to speak evil of each other, and will cultivate a spirit of charity towards all. We consider it our duty to keep from acting selfishly or from covetous motives, and will seek the interest of each other and the salvation of all mankind.

"We will observe the Sabbath day to keep it holy, in accordance with the Revelations.

"That which is committed to our care we will not appropriate to our own use.

"That which we borrow we will return according to promise, and that which we find we will not appropriate to our own use, but seek to return it to its proper owner.

"We will, as soon as possible, cancel all individual indebtedness contracted prior to our uniting with the order, and, when once fully identified with said order, will contract no debts contrary to the wishes of the Board of Directors.

"We will patronize our brethren who are in the order.

"In our apparel and deportment we will not pattern after nor encourage foolish and extravagant fashions, and cease to import or buy from abroad any article which can be reasonably dispensed with, or which can be produced by combination of home labor. We will foster and encourage the producing and manufacturing of all articles needful for our consumption as fast as our circumstances will permit.

"We will be simple in our dress and manner of living, using proper economy and prudence in the management of all intrusted to our care.

"We will combine our labor for mutual benefit, sustain with our faith, prayers, and works those whom we have elected to take the management of the different departments of the order, and be subject to them in their official capacity, refraining from a spirit of fault-finding.

"We will honestly and diligently labor and devote ourselves and all we have to the order and to the building up of the Kingdom of God."

Under these general regulations a great number . . . enrolled themselves. . . . The Kings of Kingston planted their family flag on the windswept Circleville plain. At Sunset another communistic colony was established, and in Long Valley, in the cañons of the Rio Virgin, was inaugurated the "United Order of Orderville.". . .

If a man wished to join the Order, he gave in to the Bishop a statement of his effects. It was left to his conscience that this statement should be complete and exhaustive; that there should be no private reservations. These effects—whatever they might be, from a farm in another part of the Territory to the clothes in his trunk—were appraised by the regular staff, and the equivalent amount in stock, at $10 a share, was issued to them. From that time his ownership in his property ceased. His books would perhaps go into the schoolhouse library, his extra blankets next door, his horse into a neighbor's team. According to his capacities, also, he himself fell at once into his place among the workers, going to the woollen factory or the carpenter's shop, the blacksmith's forge or the dairy, the saw-mills or the garden, the grist-mill or the farm, according as his particular abilities gave promise of his being most useful. His work here would result, as far as he was personally concerned, in no profits. But he was assured to a comfortable house, abundant food, good clothes. The main responsibilities of life were therefore taken off his shoulders. The wolf could never come to his door. He and his were secured against hunger and cold.

But beyond this? There was only the approbation of his companions, the reward of his conscience. With the proceeds of his labor, or by the actual work of his own hands, he saw new buildings going up, new acres coming under cultivation. But none of them belonged to him. He never became a proprietor, an owner, a master. While therefore he was spared the worst responsibilities of life, he was deprived of its noblest ambitions. He lived without apprehensions, but without hopes too. If his wife was ill or his children sickly, there were plenty of kind neighbors to advise and nurse and look after them. No anxieties of such matters need trouble him. But if he had any particular taste—music, botany, anything—he was unable to gratify it, unless these same kindly neighbors agreed to spend from the common fund in order to buy him a violin or a flower-press—and they could hardly be expected to do so. Quite apart from the fact that a man learning to play a new instrument is an enemy of his kind, you could not expect a community of graziers, farmers, and artisans to be unanimously enthusiastic about the musical whims of one of their number, still less for his "crank" in collecting "weeds"—as everything that is not eatable (or is not a rose) is called in most places of the West.

Tastes, therefore, could not be cultivated for the want of means, and any special faculties which members might individually possess were of necessity kept in abeyance. Amid scenery that might distract an artist, and fossil and insect treasures enough to send men of science crazy, the community can do nothing in the direction of Art or of Natural History, unless they all do it together. For the Order cannot spare a man who may be a good ploughman, to go and sit about in the cañons painting pictures of pine-trees and water-falls. Nor can it spare the money that may be needed for shingles in buying microscopes for a "bughunter." The common prosperity, therefore, can only be gained at a sacrifice of all individual tastes. . . .

The settlement itself is grievously disappointing in appearance. For as you approach it, past the charming little hamlet of Glendale, past such a sunny wealth of orchard and meadow and corn-land, past such beautiful glimpses of landscape, you cannot help expecting a scene of rural prettiness in sympathy with such surroundings. But Orderville at first sight looks like a factory. The wooden shed-like buildings built in continuous rows, the adjacent mills, the bare, ugly patch of hillside behind it, give the actual settlement an uninviting aspect. But once within the settlement, the scene changes wonderfully for the better. The houses are found, the most of them, built facing inwards upon an open square, with a broad side-walk, edged with tamarisk and mulberry, box-elder and maple-trees, in front of them. Outside the dwelling-house square are scattered about the school-house, meeting-house, black-smith and carpenters' shops, tannery, woolen-mill, and so forth, while a broad roadway separates the whole from the orchards, gardens, and farm-lands generally. Specially noteworthy here are the mulberry orchard—laid out for the support of the silk-worms, which the community are now rearing with much success—and the forcing-ground and experimental garden, in which wild flowers as well as "tame" are being cultivated.

Among the buildings the more interesting to me were the school-houses, well fitted up, and very fairly provided with educational apparatus; and the rudimentary museum, where the commencement of a collection of the natural curiosities of the neighborhood is displayed. What this may some day grow into, when science has had the chance of exploring the surrounding hills and cañons, it is difficult to say; for Nature has favored Orderville profusely with fossil strata and mineral eccentricities, a rich variety of bird and insect life, and a prodigious botanical luxuriance. Almost for the first time in my travels, too, I found here a very intelligent interest taken in the natural history of the locality; but the absence of books and of necessary apparatus, as yet of course prevents the brethren from carrying on their studies and experiments to any standard of scientific value.

Though staying in Orderville so short a time, I was fortunate enough to see the whole community together. For on the evening of my arrival there was a meeting at which there was a very full gathering of the adults—and the babies in arms. The scene was as curious as anything I have ever witnessed in any part of the world. The audience was almost equally composed of men and women, the latter wearing, most of them, their cloth sunbonnets, and bringing with them the babies they were nursing.

Brigham Young used to encourage mothers to bring them, and said that he liked to hear them squalling in the Tabernacle. Whether he really liked it or not, the mothers did as he said, and the babies too, and the perpetual bleating of babies from every corner of the building makes it seem to this day as if religious service was being held in a sheep-fold. Throughout the proceedings at Orderville babies were constantly handed across from mother to neighbor and back from neighbor to mother. Others were being tossed up and down with that jerky, perpendicular motion which seems so soothing to the very young, but which reminded me of the popping up and down of the hammers when the "lid" of a piano is lifted up during a performance. But the baby is an irrepressible person, and at Orderville has it very much its own way. The Apostle's voice in prayer was accepted as a challenge to try their lungs, and the music (very good, by the way) as a mere obligato to their own vocalization. The patient gravity of the mothers throughout the whole performance, and the apparent indifference of the men, struck me as very curious— for I come from a country where one baby will plunge a whole church congregation into profanity, and where it is generally supposed that *two* crying together would empty heaven. Of the men of Orderville I can say sincerely that a healthier, more stalwart community I have never seen, while among the women, I saw many refined faces, and remarked that robust health seemed the rule. . . .

Unfortunately one of the most characteristic features of this family community was in abeyance during my visit—the common dining-table. For a rain-flood swept through the gorge above the settlement last winter and destroyed "the bakery." Since then the families have dined apart or clubbed together in small parties, but the wish of the majority is to see the old system revived, for though they live well now, they used, they say, to live even better when "the big table" was laid for its 200 guests at once.

Self-supporting and well-directed, therefore, the Orderville "communists" bid fair to prove to the world that pious enthusiasm, if largely tempered with business judgment, can make a success of an experiment which has hitherto baffled all attempts based upon either one or the other alone.

———

Mormon Households

FROM THE TRAGIC DAYS of their exodus from Nauvoo, Thomas L. Kane of Philadelphia maintained a lifelong interest in the Mormons. He had explained their plight to the nation in 1846 and had interceded for them in the crisis of 1857. In the fall of 1872, accompanied by his wife and two sons, Colonel Kane came to Utah to visit his old friend Brigham Young. Early in December they traveled together to St. George, Brigham Young's winter home in southern Utah, where they spent several months. Sarah Wood Kane, the colonel's wife, wrote her impressions of Mormon households visited on the way down. Her father, William Wood, published them in 1874 as a means of winning understanding for the Mormons, who were being subjected to renewed prosecution under hostile national legislation aimed at polygamy.

Twelve Mormon Homes Visited in Succession on a Journey through Utah to Arizona (*Philadelphia, 1874*), *from which the selections below are taken, is a charming description of home life among the Mormons, particularly outside the capital city. The cultured Mrs. Kane's insights and sympathy are a far cry from the unbridled criticisms the professional reformers indulged in. The Kanes, of course, were traveling with Brigham Young and consequently were entertained by the best Mormon society.*

In Provo] we entered the grounds of . . . a villa built in that American-Italian style which Downing characterizes as indicating "varied enjoyments, and a life of refined leisure." On its broad piazza our hostess stood ready to greet us; a buxom, black-haired, quick-eyed dame, who gave us a becoming welcome, and hailed the rest of the party with many a quip and merry jest as she led the way into her large parlor. In two minutes she had flitted up the stairway to show me my rooms; in two more she had committed my entertainment, so far as talking to me went, to another of her husband's wives, also a guest; and in about fifteen more she had all of our large party seated at a table, which was so abundantly spread that there was no more than room left for our plates. To be sure— New England fashion—we had, big and little, glass and china, about nine apiece.

399

IV · LAMENTATIONS

We had a brave long grace before meat. I noticed that before uttering it President Young's eye had wandered over the table, to see every corner lifted, even the glass top of the butter-dish. The stoppers were taken from the decanters of homemade wine. (I once saw, at a Mormon dinner-party in the city, the corks drawn from the champagne-bottles which effervesced an accompaniment to the speaker!) I don't know why the covers were taken off; it would have made an epicure wish the grace— a full-fledged prayer—shorter, with such savory viands cooling.

What had we for dinner? What had we not! Turkey and beef, fresh salmon-trout from the lake, wild duck, chicken-pie, apple-fritters, wild-plum-, cranberry-, and currant-jellies, a profusion of vegetables; and then mince-pies (drawn from the oven *after* the grace was said!), smoking plum-puddings for *us*, and wholesome plain ones for the children (who preferred the *un*wholesome!); pears, peaches, apples, and grapes, pitchers of cream and scarcely less creamy milk, cakes, preserves, and tarts numberless, and tea and coffee. All were served and pressed upon us by our active hostess, for whom a seat was reserved at President Young's right hand—to which she was invited about once in five minutes, replying, "Immediately, Brother Young," "Directly, Sister Lucy," as she flew off, to reappear with some fresh dainty.

Such a busy woman! That she looked well to the ways of her household, no one could doubt who heard her prompt, cheery replies to the queries addressed her from time to time by President Young and her husband (he was also a guest, if a man can be a guest under his wife's roof!) respecting the welfare of the cows, and calves, and sheep, and hired boys, the winter's provision of wood and coal, and the results of the summer's husbandry.

She conducted me over her house afterward, with a justifiable pride in its exquisite neatness and the well-planned convenience of its arrangements. She showed me its porte-cochère for stormy weather, its covered ways to barn and wood-shed, and the never-failing stream of running water that was conducted through kitchen and dairy. I noticed the plump feather-beds in the sleeping-rooms, the shining blackness of the stoves (each with its teakettle of boiling water), that no speck dimmed her mirrors, and not a stray thread littered her carpets. It was not only here, but everywhere else in Utah, that I rejoiced in the absence of—well— spittoons, and of the necessity for them. I saw neither smoking nor chewing among the Mormons.

This Provo house was the very foppery of cleanliness. Small wonder that, with but one young girl to help her, its mistress had little leisure for reading. I had asked for books, meaning to judge of the character of the household by their aid. There was only the Bible, the Book of Mormon, a photograph album, and Worcester's Dictionary in all that big house—except in a carefully-locked closet, where were the story- and lesson-books of her one child, a son, gone now to Salt Lake City to study a profession. When she opened this door and lovingly handled the volumes, speaking of her loneliness without him, tears gathered in her eyes. I thought myself of a home that I knew of, not half so tidy it must be confessed, over-flowing with books and music, playthings, and children's happy voices, where boys and girls gathered round their mother with their paintings, drawing, and sewing, while their father read aloud; and my own tears came as I thought how solitary her life must be when each day's work was done; how much more solitary it would be when the evening of her life closed in. No "John Anderson" to be her fireside companion, none of the comfort that even a lonely widow finds in the remembrance of former joys and sorrows shared with the one to whom she has been best and nearest. This woman would have only her model house, so clean and so white, so blank and vacant—even of memories!

However, my pity seemed for the present uncalled for. My hostess was soon jesting with her guests. I must admit that she appeared to be a happy and contented woman. . . .

At every one of the places we stayed on this journey, we had prayers immediately after the dinner-supper, and prayers again before breakfast. No one was excused; wives, daughters, hired men and women, all shuffled in. The Mormons do not read from the Bible, but kneel at once, while the head of the household or an honored guest prays aloud, beginning, as I noticed on this occasion, instead of ending, "In the name of Thy Son our Savior Jesus Christ, Father, we ask," etc. I do not think they as often say, "If it be Thy Will," as we do, but simply pray for the blessings they want, expecting they will be given or withheld, as God knows best. Though I do remember Brigham Young's once praying for the restoration and healing of the sick "if not appointed unto death." They spend very little time in ascriptions, but ask for what they need and thank Him for what He has given—with surprising fluency and detail.

It interested me and my children, too, though they could scarcely repress a start and titter, when they and their absent brother and sister were alluded to by name. At home, when, for no greater audience than my children, I venture to extemporize the prayer at family worship, I am sometimes puzzled whether to introduce the names and individuals, or to adhere prudently to generalities. But the Mormons take it for granted that God knows our familiar names and titles, and will ask a blessing on "Thy servant, Colonel Jonathan P. Hitchcock, jr.," where I would spend a minute or two in devising a periphrasis. I liked this when I became used to it, and could join in with some knowledge of the circumstances of those we prayed for. . . .

[Parowan.] In the southern Mormon settlements at least, there is no distinction made between mistress and servant. The younger "sisters" think it no degradation to go to live in the houses of the married ones and help them with their work, and when work is over, they sit down to meals or "go to parties" together. I am not speaking of the rougher sort alone. I have met a wealthy bishop's daughter at a dance, dressed in white muslin, who has opened the door for me next morning with arms fresh from the wash-tub, when I went to call upon her mistress. It did me no harm when she shook hands on leaving me in the parlor, apologizing for being unable to remain with me.

Such girls sometimes marry their masters. A nice possibility for the wife hiring "help" to keep before her eyes! I met one woman who had claimed from her *mistress* the fulfillment of a jesting promise—that if she served her faithfully for seven years, she would give her to her husband to wife. At the end of the seven years, she jilted a man to whom she was affianced, recalled the forgotten promise to her mistress's mind, and became her master's plural wife. There was no question of affection on either side. I believe she merely wished to share in his glory in heaven, with a modest competence here below. I give her up to you, father, to abuse to your heart's content. Apparently, she angled for a rich man quite as much as if she had not been a Saint. It is not for such as she that I ask your pity and sympathy. It is for those women who have become "plural wives" from a sense of duty, and who think their lot happy because they deem that God's blessing rests upon is hard conditions. I would have you pity Delia J., for instance, the wife of a man double her age. Of her the first wife said to me, "Delia is the blessing of my life. It is true that she has had trouble in polygamy. She could not bring her mind for a long time to see it to be her duty. But she is reconciled now. I thank the Lord every day that now that I am infirm, Brother Samuel and his health and comfort are attended to as he is growing old."

Childless herself, this Delia is dearly loved by all the other wives' children, some of them older than she is. That first wife's eldest daughter said to me unaffectedly one day, when we happened to interrupt an earnest conference between her mother and Delia, Mother loves her better than any of us, and admits her into her inmost confidence; "because of course, she is nearer to pa than we can be."

Pity her! I pitied Delia from the depths of my soul! I saw her wince once at an allusion to her childlessness, and thought how happy that devoted, affectionate nature might have made a home where she ruled sole mistress of the heart of a husband worthy of her.

Yet Delia was one of those who spoke most earnestly to me of polygamy as of divine institution, and rejected with horror the solution of the Mormon difficulty which I advocated: that Congress should forbid any further polygamous marriages, but legalize those that already existed, seemed to me both just and merciful.

"Secure my social position!" she once repeated after me. "How can that satisfy me! I want to be assured of *my position in God's estimation.* If polygamy is the Lord's order, we must carry it out in spite of human laws and persecutions. If our marriages have been sins, Congress is no vicegerent of God; it cannot forgive sins, nor make what was wrong, right. 'Hard for me if polygamy were abolished without some provision for women situated as I am!' Yes, but how much harder to bring myself to accept such a law as you speak of, and admit, as I should be admitting, that all I have sacrificed has not been for God's sake! I should feel as if I were agreeing to look upon my past life as a—as a worthless woman's—upon which I had never had His blessing. I'd rather die!"

How I detested her husband as she spoke! I felt sure *he* could not believe that that was a divine ordinance which sacrificed those women's lives to his. I heard him say that when "Joseph" first promulgated the Revelation of Polygamy he "felt that the grave was sweet! All that winter, whenever a funeral passed,—'and it was a sickly season,'—I would stand and look after the hearse, and wish I was in that coffin! But that went over!"

I should think it *had* gone over! He has had more than half a dozen wives.

Crusade and Countercrusade

BRIGHAM YOUNG died in 1877—an event headlined in the nation's press, which expected Mormonism to disintegrate. But the Mormons flourished, as did polygamy. On a rising tide of public feeling against the Mormons, one Congressional bill after another sought the formula that would at last check Utah's waywardness. Hardly an annual message of the President failed to allude to the "Mormon Question." Extremists throughout the country called for cannon of the biggest bore to thunder the seventh commandment into the Mormons; they wanted to dissolve the legislature and govern Utah by commission; and they clamored for enforceable legislation that would disfranchise polygamists and prohibit Mormon immigration, which fed all the other iniquities.

Congress had passed an Anti-Bigamy Act in 1862, but reform efforts under it had been desultory and abortive for years. Wives would not testify against their husbands and no Mormon jury would convict a polygamist. The late 1870's, however, marked the beginning of a fierce and widespread crusade which did not relent until the Mormons had been brought to their knees. Brigham Young himself, just before his death, had been put under house arrest. On November 7, 1878, some two hundred Gentile women in Salt Lake City held a mass meeting in the Congregational Church and addressed an appeal to "the Christian women of the United States" to join in urging Congress to take more drastic action. They enlisted the aid of Mrs. Rutherford B. Hayes, wife of the President, and sent a circular letter to the clergy throughout the country asking them to read the resolutions to their congregations and forward signed petitions to Congress.

In a counter demonstration, two thousand Mormon women gathered in Salt Lake Theater a week later to pass resolutions of their own endorsing polygamy as a religious practice and claiming the Constitution's guarantees of religious freedom on its behalf. But in January of the following year, the United States Supreme Court upheld the constitutionality of the anti-bigamy law in the test case of George Reynolds, former secretary to Brigham Young. The decision robbed the Mormons of what had been their strongest argument and gave their foes a powerful weapon for the ensuing climactic campaign.

Crusade and Countercrusade

John M. Coyner, Salt Lake journalist and an anti-Mormon, attended the demonstrations of 1878 and described them in his "Letters of Mormonism." The excerpt below is taken from the letter of January 28, 1879, as reprinted in his Hand-Book on Mormonism *(Salt Lake City, 1882). An extremist, he echoed the sentiment Samuel Bowles had expressed thirteen years before, that there was "an irrepressible conflict" between the Mormons and the nation which only force could settle.*

When . . . I attended, as a reporter, the mass-meeting of the Mormon women held in the theatre in this city and called to defend polygamy against the so-called crusade of the Gentile women, who had sent out an appeal to the Christian women of America against polygamy, I went with the determination to reach, if possible, bottom facts. When I was a young man, I read a book entitled, "Fifteen Years among the Mormons." * I was led to believe, from what I there read, that the women of Utah were held by the men in a kind of captivity, not being able to escape from their degradation, on account of the mountain fastnesses and the extended desert that intervened between them and civilization; and I supposed that, as soon as the railroad, with all its non-Mormon influences, had reached Utah, the most of the women would gladly embrace the opportunity of fleeing the country to escape thralldom. But in this I was much mistaken.

The history of Mormonism, from its beginning, shows that the women have been more devoted than the men; and to-day there is more true devotion to Mormonism from principle's sake among the women than among the men. I was, therefore, not surprised to find the theatre packed from pit to dome with some two thousand women, the most of whom, as shown by the uplifted hands when a vote was taken, were devoted Mormons. It was the most remarkable meeting I ever attended. There were the aged mothers of seventy, who, amid storm and privation, had emigrated among the first to this desert wilderness. There was the grown-up matron, whose life marks the growth of the Mormon power in the Territory. There were also many buxom lassies, some brought up in the Territory, others the last importations from the Old World, many of whom had lately become the third, fourth or tenth wife of an aged elder. There was no excitement, no enthusiasm, but seemingly that fixed

---

* Nelson Winch Green, *Fifteen Years among the Mormons* (New York, 1858). An anti-Mormon work, it claimed to be the story of Mary Ettie V. Smith, "a sister of one of the Mormon high priests; she having been personally acquainted with most of the Mormon leaders and long in the confidence of the 'Prophet,' Brigham Young." Ed. note.

determination that causes one to do, suffer, and, if need be, die for what he considers right. The meeting was regularly organized. The president, who was dressed in silk material entirely made in this Territory, spoke readily and fluently for more than half an hour. Among other things, she said: "Polygamy is as essential to woman's happiness as her salvation."

Mormon theology teaches that all those who are faithful Mormons, living up to the privileges of their religion in this world, and having many wives and numerous children, will be kings in the celestial world, and their wives queens; while those who are not married at all are compelled to be the slaves of those kings. Just think of the Apostle Paul being the servant of Brigham Young throughout the ages of eternity. Those who have but one wife, if they are faithful to the priesthood and pay tithing, will have a home in the celestial world, but will not occupy any place of honor. Hence, if any ambitious woman wishes a place of honor in the celestial world, she must be a polygamous wife. Another, who said she was seventy years of age, said: "I thank God that I am a polygamous wife, that my husband is a polygamist," and she had a "feeling of great pity for those who did not enjoy this good blessing." One old lady said: "I would not abandon it (meaning polygamy) to exchange with Queen Victoria and all her dependencies." The secretary of the meeting said: "The women of this country want to crush us, but it will be diamond cut diamond." And thus for nearly three hours one speaker after another defended polygamy, all believing it to be an inspired doctrine, given by God to aid in redeeming a sinful world from a condition of sin and pollution to one of holiness and purity.

The following Resolution, among others, was unanimously adopted by the meeting:

"*Resolved,* That we solemnly avow our belief in the doctrine of the patriarchal order of marriage, a doctrine which was revealed to, and practiced by, God's people in past ages, and is now re-established on earth by divine command of Him who is the same yesterday, to day and forever—a doctrine which, if lived up to and carried out under the direction of the precepts pertaining to it, and of the higher principles of our nature, would conduce to the long life, strength and glory of the people practicing it; and we therefore endorse it as one of the most important principles of our holy religion, and claim the right of its practice.". . .

A similar meeting of the Mormon women of Provo City was held on the 7th of December. The chairman of the meeting said:

"The day will come when temples will be more numerous than our

406

enemies can imagine, and when the people of God, by the practice of such heavenly institutions as the patriarchal order of marriage will cover the whole face of the land, from sea to sea. That day will assuredly dawn on the land of America."

One of the leading speakers said:

"Shall we, the wives and daughters of the best men on earth, submit to the dictation of unholy, licentious and wicked men? No, never! I feel that it is high time for the women of Utah to stand up and defend this Heaven-revealed principle. I am a polygamous wife, and am proud to say it. I regard those women who are my husband's wives to be so as much as I am. Our husbands are virtuous and noble men, and are the friends of all mankind.". . .

Mrs. Zina Y. Williams was introduced to the meeting as a polygamous daughter of Brigham Young. This descendant of a prophet declared herself a child of polygamy and the widow of a polygamist—one of God's noblemen. She considered herself blessed among women in being permitted to come upon earth through the lineage of a polygamous servant of God. "I regard this privilege," said the ecstatic Zina, "as the richest diadem a mortal ever possessed." She inquired of her hearers if she could stand there—a daughter of President Brigham Young, the wife of a good man, and a daughter of Zion, and let the daughters of the United States trample upon her right? Perish the thought. "They may well be afraid of us," said this daughter of the covenant, "for we are gaining strength while they are getting weaker; we are increasing, while they are diminishing; and the sons and daughters of Zion are spreading over the whole land."

Now, what does all this mean? Simply this, and nothing less, that it is the settled policy of the Mormon hierarchy to spread their peculiar system of society all over America. Being religious fanatics, they have now come to such a point in their growth and power that they feel justified in throwing down the gauntlet before the American nation, and their battle-cry is, "Polygamy, or Death.". . .

There is an irrepressible conflict between the Mormon power and the principles upon which our free institutions are established, and one or the other must succumb. The arguments, the dogmas, and the whole line of defence of this system are so similar to those used years gone by, by the defenders of the system of slavery, that it is, indeed, well named the "Twin Sister." And now I say to the American people that, if something is not done soon to stop the development of this law-breaking, law-defying fanaticism, either our free institutions must go down beneath its power, or, as with slavery, it must be wiped out in blood. For facts go to show that the Mormons will not obey the laws of the land. Polygamous marriages are going on just the same since the Reynolds decision as before. The Mormons are very bitter against the Government, and, when the proper opportunity comes, will not hesitate to draw the sword and fight for their religion. As American citizens we must meet this thing.

Senator Brown of Georgia Defends the Mormons

THE NATIONAL CLAMOR for Utah's reform mounted with each passing year. The most radical proposals came from the churches. With the zeal of abolitionists they would free Utah from the moral blight of polygamy as they had once kept Kansas and Nebraska free from the moral blight of slavery. "Let the lands and tenements of the Mormons be thrown open to original entry by civilized settlers," urged the Presbyterian Chicago Interior. "There are enough young men in the west and south who are seeking homes to finish up the pest, fumigate the territory, and to establish themselves in ninety days after the word 'go' is given." But Boston's Congregationalist did not think wholesale robbery very Christian, and warned that the proposal would only attract "all the ruffians in the west." The Methodist felt that "Ten millions of dollars, wisely expended, would probably settle the Mormon question." The moralists besieged Congress with bills and petitions.

The agitation found its most effective voice in New England, leaving the South, still smarting from carpetbag rule, to sympathize with the Mormons. In 1882 Senator George F. Edmunds of Vermont introduced a bill designed to put teeth into the Anti-Bigamy Act of 1862: it made polygamy a crime and "unlawful cohabitation"—much easier to prove— a misdemeanor. Polygamy drew a penalty of $500 or five years' imprisonment, or both, and unlawful cohabitation drew a fine not to exceed $300 and imprisonment not to exceed six months. It excluded polygamists and anyone who believed in polygamy from jury service; and it declared all registration and election offices in Utah vacant, their duties to be performed by a board of five federal commissioners. The Utah Com-

mission, as it came to be called, spelled complete carpetbag control for the territory and delivered the Mormons into the hands of the Gentile lobby.

The Edmunds bill became law in March, 1882, but not without some strong opposition to what seemed its violation of the right of trial by jury and its denial of the cherished principle of local self-government. During the debate in the Senate, Joseph E. Brown of Georgia declared the bill so drastic that he considered Reconstruction "mildness itself compared with what is in store for Utah." His eloquent objections echoed arguments the Mormons themselves often employed. The following passages from his speech are taken from the report of the Senate debates of February 15 and 16, 1882, in the Congressional Record.

The bill proposes to apply a religious test to the Mormons. In so far as it punishes the Mormon for his opinions, it is a religious test applied. He believes that Joseph Smith was a prophet as much as I believe that Jeremiah was a prophet; and while I think he is in an egregious error, I have no right to proscribe him because of his belief as long as he does not practice immorality. And I have no right to do more as a legislator than to prescribe rules to punish him for his immoralities, and leave him to the full enjoyment of his religious opinions, just as I claim the right to enjoy my own opinions. If we commence striking down any sect, however despised or however unpopular, on account of opinion's sake, we do not know how soon the fires of Smithfield may be rekindled or the gallows of New England for witches again be erected, or when another Catholic convent will be burned down.

We do not know how long it will be before the clamor would be raised by the religious institutions of this country, that no member of a church who holds the infallibility of the Pope or the doctrine of transubstantiation should hold office or vote in this country. We do not know how long it would be before it would be said that no member of a church who believed in close communion and baptism by immersion as the only mode, should vote or hold office in this country. You are treading on dangerous ground when you open this floodgate anew. We have passed the period where there is for the present any clamor on this subject, except as against the Mormons; but it seems there must be some periodical outcry against some denomination. Popular vengeance is now turned against the Mormons. When we are done with them, I know not who will next be considered the proper subject of it.

To accomplish this great object the Territorial practices of half a century are to be blotted out, local self-government is to be destroyed, the church is to be plundered, and the prosperous region of Utah is to be subjected to the rule of satraps whose unlimited power will enable them to rob and pillage the people at pleasure. If this system is once inaugurated, bitter as was our experience in the South during the late reconstruction period when our affairs were being regulated, it was mildness itself compared with what is in store for Utah as long as the wealth accumulated by the Mormons is not exhausted.

Mr. President, I shall be a party to no such proceedings. Other sections of the Union have frequently run wild in keeping up with New England ideas and New England practices on issues of this character. I presume they will do so again, but I, for one, shall not be a party to the enactment or enforcement of unconstitutional, tyrannical, and oppressive legislation for the purpose of crushing the Mormons or any other sect for the gratification of New England or any other section. The precedents which we are making, when the persons and parties in the States who feel it their duty to regulate the affairs of others find themselves unemployed and the regulation of Mormonism no longer profitable, will be used against other sects. Whether the Baptists, or the Catholics, or the Quakers will be selected for the next victim does not yet appear. But he who supposes that this spirit of restless and illegal intermeddling with the affairs of other sections will be satiated or appeased by the sacrifice of the Mormons has read modern history to little advantage.

The Mormon sect is marked for the first victim. The Constitution and the practices of the Government are to be disregarded and if need be trampled down to gratify the ire of dominant intermeddling.

And such is the fanaticism now prevalent in reference to the Mormon sect, that when it is clearly shown the regulation which they desire can not take place within the Constitution and laws, the restless regulators will doubtless be ready to follow the example of Mr. Stevens and regulate Mormonism outside of the Constitution. But why should Southern men become camp-followers in this crusade?

The Mormons, may, however, be consoled by the reflection that their privileges need not be curtailed if they are obedient, nor the present practice diminished, but they must change the name and no longer conduct the wicked practice in what they call the "marriage relation."

The Government considers this no great hardship, as it freely permits in the Mormons, if called by the right name, what it does not punish in other people. For, without violating the policy of the Government in so

410

far as it has been proclaimed by its Utah Commission, if the Mormons will conform to its requirements as to the mode, the practice of prostitution in Utah need not in the slightest degree be diminished. The clamor is not against the Mormon for having more than one woman, but for calling more than one his wife. And the Mormons will do well to remember that the policy of putting the whole population, men, women, and children to the sword, and filling the whole land with wailing, blood, and carnage will not be wanting in advocates if a portion of them still continue, each to cohabit with more than one woman in what they call "the marriage relation."

The Government and people of the United States have deliberately determined that they must call it by the proper name. Let the Mormon who has a plurality of women remember that he must conform to the practice elsewhere and call but one of them his wife.

This, Mr. President, is the point we have reached. This is the distinction we have drawn. This is our present policy and practice as applied to the Territory of Utah. What consummate statesmanship!

The Cohabs Go Underground

UNTIL THE PASSAGE of the stringent Edmunds Act of 1882, only two Mormon polygamists in twenty years had been indicted under the anti-bigamy law of 1862. The "unlawful cohabitation" provision of the Edmunds Act finally enabled the courts to secure convictions. Arrests increased and convictions jumped from 4 in 1884 to 55 the following year, 132 in 1886, and 220 in 1887, the year an even more severe measure, the Edmunds-Tucker Act, disfranchised the Mormon voters, disincorporated the church, and confiscated its property. By the end of 1888, nearly 600 Mormons had been fined or imprisoned. Altogether some 1,300 paid the penalty of the law, so many Rolands fighting a hopeless rearguard action. They considered themselves "prisoners for conscience' sake," their sentence for "doing the works of Abraham" an honor rather than a stigma.

Utah after 1884 swarmed with federal marshals and their deputies, some of them Mormon turncoats, "spotters" who spied on their neighbors *to obtain evidence of plural cohabitation. Their surprise raids kept Mormon households in constant suspense and challenged whole communities to outwit them. "So many went to prison," commented one villager, "that it seemed as if it had become more popular, and there was not so much excitement when a person was arrested. . . . A man would rather suffer than have his family brought before these courts to testify and often [be] asked indecent questions. To the praise of the Heroes they stood it in nearly all cases bravely, a few recanted, but their numbers were small."*

Many polygamists took to the "underground," hiding out among friends in outlying settlements or exiling themselves for a while in Mexico or Canada, where the Mormons founded refugee colonies. Mormon folklore and family tradition are replete with stories about the "cohab hunts" and running from the "feds." The head of the church himself, John Taylor, and most of the apostles went into hiding, not only to save themselves but to save the church in the name of a divine principle. John Taylor died "on the underground," a martyr in the eyes of his people and faithful to his sacred trust.

The story of Atkinville, a one-family village on the Virgin River in Utah's Dixie, is both typical and unusual. It enjoyed a momentary greatness as the hideout of Wilford Woodruff, chief of the Mormon apostles. Out of her own family tradition, Grace Atkin Woodbury of Salt Lake City recalls the times in the late 1880's when Atkinville harbored the man who became the leader of the Mormons in 1887 and who issued the famous manifesto ending polygamy in 1890. The editors are grateful to Mrs. Woodbury for allowing them to use her manuscript reminiscences.

Uncle Joseph Walker once remarked: "It was certainly no small honor, even as it was a heavy responsibility, to have such an eminent man's safety and welfare entrusted to this family. . . . His residency there lent luster and added importance to the place far beyond anything else that could have happened to the village. . . ." Here came the church mail, hundreds of letters which he answered. Most of his time was devoted to church business. To paraphrase Isaiah, out of Mormon Dixie went forth the law of the church and the word of the Lord from Atkinville.

While Apostle Woodruff used St. George as headquarters, he leaned heavily upon Thomas P. Cottam for advice and guidance in finding safe places to stay and avoid detection. One of the places that he found safe and congenial was the home of William Squires and his son John. Emma

Squires said that when Woodruff lived at her place he had a room upstairs where he always retreated before she opened the door when someone knocked. She had to be very careful not to let anyone know he was there.

The home was near the red hill and in those days had orchards and vineyards at the rear of the house where Woodruff occasionally went hunting quails. To disguise him while out hunting, Emma made him a sunbonnet and a mother hubbard dress. One day an inquisitive neighbor met and recognized him in the rear of the house as he was returning from a hunt. He had to find a new place to live immediately. This may have been the impelling reason that sent him to Atkinville.

Atkin family tradition supplies the best explanation of his visits and retreats to Atkinville. It was the safest place he could find in the region. He developed confidence in the hospitality, dependability and loyalty of the family. Besides, there were thickets of tamarix lining the river bottoms and the tules [cattails and rushes] of the pond into which he could quickly flee with little fear that the marshals could find him. In addition, most of the people of the region were loyal Latter-day Saints who faithfully entered the conspiracy to assist the harassed brethren. They felt no guilt and no embarrassment in thus helping "the work of the Lord." A few malcontents and unsympathetic non-members aided the marshals, but the Saints quickly passed word of their whereabouts by grapevine. Emma Squires said that her father, William Thompson, regarded himself as Woodruff's bodyguard and was especially vigilant in keeping track of the marshals. Young Will Thompson passed urgent information between St. George and Atkinville, traveling on horseback on little-known trails to avoid the marshals.

Woodruff's journal hints why he visited or moved to Atkinville on given dates. On January 31, 1885: "I rode to Brother Atkin's visited his pond; 2 boys set fire to his rushes and flags and burned things all around his pond so there was no hiding places to get the wild fowl or for any other purpose." He did not visit Atkinville again until June 29, after the tules had re-grown. On February 23, 1887, he wrote: "Marshal Armstrong arrived in the evening in St. George." And three days later, February 26: "I took my bed and luggage with Brother Thompson and went to Wm. Atkin's to stop awhile." He stayed more than three months. On September 2, 1887, the marshals raided St. George after Woodruff had left: "Early this morning, one of James G. Bleak's homes was visited by deputy marshals. Then they went to D. D. McArthur's home and one went in; the others kept watch outside. From there . . . to A. R. White-

413

head's home and searched. . . . Then to Ed. A. Hendrix and searched; then to James Booth's; no arrests; left the city without waiting for breakfast."

In his journal, Woodruff referred to forty visits to the Atkin pond, twelve from St. George, twenty-eight from Atkinville. Some of these were doubtless for hunting and fishing only, but there is no certain way of distinguishing them from the trips for hiding, for he often fished or hunted to while away the time of waiting. Usually, he indicated the number of fish or ducks that he took during his visits to the pond, even if he got nothing. On March 8, 1887, he remarked, perhaps significantly: "I went on to the pond with my boat a part of the day"; and on March 24: "I went on to the pond in the afternoon."

An alert at Atkinville started a chain reaction. Aunt Nellie says that she was dispatched to the hilltop east of the house where she could watch the approach roads. If she spotted the marshal's buggy coming around the dugway above Bloomington or coming down the Price road, it was a signal for the next step. Hyrum says there was then a rush to get Brother Woodruff, his bed roll, food and water, his books and fishing tackle into the large boat (14 x 5 feet) on the pond where he could remain safely concealed in the heavy cattails and rushes. . . . When the danger was passed, William went out to the pond, made a noise like a duck and Woodruff quacked back in reply. . . .

Most of Apostle Woodruff's days at Atkinville were busy ones, filled with incessant letter writing, visiting with church emissaries or conducting other indoor activities. For exercise, he consistently interrupted his church duties once or twice a week to hunt in the hills and fields or fish and hunt waterfowl from the boat on the pond. For a man eighty years of age, he was unusually active although, occasionally, he recorded that he came home very tired. A good night's sleep seemed to restore his vigor. On days when groups of people from town came to Atkinville for picnics he had to stay in his room, a virtual prisoner. That grieved him very much.

While Woodruff was in Atkinville, the Atkin family was very solicitous about his welfare. "All of us children knew he was in the home and we . . . were proud to have our home selected for this purpose of . . . keeping [him] in seclusion. . . . We would have stood almost any torture before we would have exposed President Woodruff." They used to call him Grandpa Allen. . . .

On his two- to four-day trips to St. George during his stay at Atkinville, Apostle Woodruff usually spent most of his time in the St. George

Temple in a room prepared for his use, fitted with a trap door under his desk which led to secret hiding places. . . .

These were grim and desperate times. Charles L. Walker was the night guard at the temple from the time of its completion in 1877 until his death in 1904. He possessed a beautiful Colt's revolver and powder horn that he had purchased in St. Louis on his way to Utah in 1855. . . . Joseph Walker remembers: "My father was a good shot . . . at 30 paces . . . [he could] place a slug between the eyes of a fattened hog . . . [or] pick a chicken hawk off the tall ash trees at the back of the lot. . . . Father's revolver always lay at hand beside the big Bible in his hut at the Temple. When the 'Feds' were on the loose in town, he often told me as we walked around the Temple at night, 'I have my orders.' He went into no further detail.

"Whenever Wilford Woodruff or other 'high authorities' were on the 'underground' in St. George, his trusty Colt's must always be in place behind his waist band . . . on the left side just beyond the mid-line where his right hand could most quickly grasp it . . . and loaded.

"He often told me that when Wilford Woodruff came from his rendezvous at Atkinville to spend some time in the temple . . . to get exercise [he] would walk around the temple building while father patrolled. . . . They timed their walking speed so that each was . . . opposite the other . . . [so that] if a prowling 'Fed' [should come] upon Woodruff, he [would be] within easy range of the deadly Colt's revolver."

Capitulation: Wilford Woodruff Issues a Manifesto

YEARS OF PROSECUTION—to the Mormons persecution—under the various anti-polygamy laws finally sent hundreds of men to prison and other hundreds into hiding and exile. The Edmunds-Tucker Act of 1887 heaped more coals on Mormon heads. The courts prevented Mormon immigrants from obtaining citizenship, and the impending Cullom-Struble bill proposed a test oath which would disfranchise the whole Mormon population of Utah. Not only was a religious principle at stake but the whole social order, all civil and political rights, as well. The people wearied of the struggle. B. H. Roberts, Mormon historian, acknowl-

edged that "There were murmurings and complainings among the people on account of the long continued controversy, which gave no promise of coming to an end."

Wilford Woodruff, who at eighty succeeded to the leadership of the church in 1887, faced the severe measures of the Edmunds-Tucker Act and saw the end. He had spent enough time on the underground. At last he capitulated. On September 24, 1890, he issued an "Official Declaration," since known as the Manifesto, calling for submission to the will of the United States. The October general conference of the church unanimously sustained it. The document which officially ended nearly fifty years of plural marriage and perverse resistance is reproduced below from the Doctrine and Covenants of the Church of Jesus Christ of Latter-day Saints *as it was presented to the conference on October 6, 1890.*

OFFICIAL DECLARATION

To Whom it may Concern:

Press dispatches having been sent for political purposes, from Salt Lake City, which have been widely published, to the effect that the Utah Commission, in their recent report to the Secretary of the Interior, allege that plural marriages are still being solemnized and that forty or more such marriages have been contracted in Utah since last June or during the past year, also that in public discourses the leaders of the Church have taught, encouraged and urged the continuance of the practice of polygamy—

I, therefore, as President of the Church of Jesus Christ of Latter-day Saints, do hereby, in the most solemn manner, declare that these charges are false. We are not teaching polygamy or plural marriage, nor permitting any person to enter into its practice, and I deny that either forty or any other number of plural marriages have during that period been solemnized in our Temples or in any other place in the Territory.

One case has been reported, in which the parties allege that the marriage was performed in the Endowment House, in Salt Lake City, in the Spring of 1889, but I have not been able to learn who performed the ceremony; whatever was done in this matter was without my knowledge. In consequence of this alleged occurrence the Endowment House was, by my instructions, taken down without delay.

Inasmuch as laws have been enacted by Congress forbidding plural marriages, which laws have been pronounced constitutional by the court of last resort, I hereby declare my intention to submit to those laws, and to use my influence with the members of the Church over which I preside to have them do likewise.

There is nothing in my teachings to the Church or in those of my associates, during the time specified, which can be reasonably construed to inculcate or encourage polygamy; and when any Elder of the Church has used language which appeared to convey any such teaching, he has been promptly reproved. And I now publicly declare that my advice to the Latter-day Saints is to refrain from contracting any marriage forbidden by the law of the land.

WILFORD WOODRUFF
President of the Church of Jesus Christ
of Latter-day Saints.

President Lorenzo Snow offered the following:

"I move that, recognizing Wilford Woodruff as the President of the Church of Jesus Christ of Latter-day Saints, and the only man on the earth at the present time who holds the keys of the sealing ordinances, we consider him fully authorized by virtue of his position to issue the Manifesto which has been read in our hearing, and which is dated September 24th, 1890, and that as a Church in General Conference assembled, we accept his declaration concerning plural marriages as authoritative and binding."

The vote to sustain the foregoing motion was unanimous.

Salt Lake City, Utah, October 6, 1890.

———

Utah Joins The Union

WITH POLYGAMY OFFICIALLY DEAD, a reformed Utah seemed at last unsullied enough to be admitted to the Union. The years had seen six appeals for statehood, years which meanwhile saw all the surrounding territories but Arizona received into the Union—Nevada as early as 1864, Colorado in 1876, Idaho and Wyoming in 1890. But the Gentile-Mormon struggle for power, in which polygamy was but the most sensational issue, had brought Utah Territory's appeals to an impasse and left deep scars. With the wounds of the religious conflict healing, the time seemed finally ripe for amicable home rule.

417

IV · LAMENTATIONS

Events moved quickly after the Manifesto of 1890. In the spring of 1891, the Mormons dissolved their People's party and, on the advice of their leaders, divided along national party lines. In 1893 the Liberal party, instrument of the Gentiles, disbanded. In 1894 Congress passed an enabling act looking to statehood. Under its provisions, 107 delegates met in Utah's last constitutional convention. By May 8, 1895, after two months of deliberation, they gave Utah a constitution. The national government promptly accepted it. In November the people chose their first state officers and ratified the constitution by an overwhelming vote. On January 4, 1896, President Grover Cleveland issued the proclamation of statehood, and Utah's nearly half century of struggle to be master in its own house was over.

A delegate who had been in the forefront of the anti-Mormon crusade sounded the note of reconciliation that made the work of the convention so fruitful. Charles S. Varian, one-time United States District Attorney for Utah Territory and relentless in his prosecution of polygamy, represented Salt Lake County and was by far the most active member of the assembly. In the closing moments of the convention he took the floor to move for adjournment and to congratulate the delegates on the harmonious conclusion of their efforts. His brief speech signalized the coming era of good feeling. The president of the convention, Mormon apostle John Henry Smith, responded with equal good will and called for a benediction. It was a good beginning for the new state.

Charles S. Varian's remarks are reproduced here from the Official Report of the Proceedings and Debates of the Convention Assembled at Salt Lake City on the Fourth Day of March, 1895, to Adopt a Constitution for the State of Utah *(Salt Lake City, 1898).*

Mr. President, I simply want to say, before that motion shall be made, which I shall withhold, if necessary, for other gentlemen to present any remarks that they may have to make, that in my judgment, we may well take a minute of time before finally concluding our labors, by adopting the order of final adjournment in congratulating each other because of the fact that this Convention has demonstrated, beyond the peradventure of a doubt, that all that was needed here in this Territory of Utah, in order to unify its people, was to bring together its representatives from every section and locality in the commonwealth, that they might look into each other's faces, ascertain each other's motives, learn to judge and believe in each other, as members of one common family. I believe that this result has been accomplished by this Convention. I believe that every

418

man who has been a member here, has been liberalized in his views, has been taught by his fellowmen that, after all, we are very much alike, that the same passions, and the same motives, actuate us all.

We have been taught also that underlying everything here has been the one idea of duty—duty born of the circumstances, fraught with great consequences, which has impelled every man on this floor, during the past two months, to give his best endeavors toward the sought-for-result. I do not believe that any gentleman that has participated in the labors of this Convention can possibly carry away with him any other conviction than that it is his bounden duty to stand by and support the results of the joint labors of the Convention. Called together for this especial purpose, building up and lifting up a commonwealth, all the dead past has been buried, nothing remains but to set our faces toward the rising sun of the future, using all our endeavors to carry on the work set before us, conscious that if we fail in the end, nevertheless that we at least can say, we have labored diligently and faithfully, we have fought the good fight, we have kept the faith. In this fraternal spirit towards all of you, gentlemen, I now move that this Convention do adjourn *sine die*.

V · PSALMS

V · Psalms

An Era of Good Feeling

THE COUNTRY GREETED Mormon capitulation and Utah's admission to the Union with mixed approval and suspicion. After 1890, the year of the Manifesto, Mormon society was in transition, seeking the good opinion of the nation. Some observers insisted that polygamy had simply gone underground and that Mormon authority was still unchallenged. Mormonism, they charged, still spelled treason and was simply marking time to revive old practices. The Mormons were the nation's Boers, said Lord Rosebery, Utah another Transvaal, a thorn in the side of Uncle Sam. But in view of the facts, the rhetoric of a few alarmists was unconvincing. When in 1907 a widely publicized Senate investigation of Apostle Reed Smoot, Senator-elect from Utah, concluded without scandal, the crusade and conflict gave way to an era of good feeling.

Zion, no longer a closed society, accommodated itself to the times. For an earlier generation of Mormons Zion had meant primarily a place, a dedicated homeland—first Missouri, then Illinois, and finally Deseret. The doctrine had been preached with passion and commitment and had directed Mormonism's great energies into proselyting, immigration, and colonization. But as outside influences broke in upon the harmony of one faith, one Lord, and one people, Zion became less provincial. Zion meant "the pure in heart," a people and a condition, and the ideal expanded to mean any place where the pure in heart dwell. It means today permanent Mormon congregations and temples in Europe, once abhorred as Babylon. The great events of millennium and the Second Coming which had seemed so imminent to the early Mormons retreated into a future comfortably remote. Mormonism spiritualized its message and no longer frightened the nation as an *imperium in imperio*. Insisting less on building a literal Kingdom, it joined hands with eastern capital to build instead a greater Utah. The Mormons quickly won national respect. It was good business now to treat them well.

The capitulation is more apparent than real. Once openly theocratic,

423

the Mormons are now content to run the legislature and send their senators and congressmen to Washington. Utah is still the Mormon homeland, though the Saints in California may soon outnumber those in Utah, and Los Angeles already rivals Salt Lake City as a Mormon stronghold—part of the great dispersion which today marks Mormonism and which finds growing Mormon congregations all over the United States and in many lands. All over the world Mormon missionaries and Mormon Fulbright scholars and Mormon Point Four experts by word and deed still preach an America they feel has a special promise for mankind. The old energies persist in an extraordinary activism within the church and in a multitude of good works in which the Mormons love to engage. Their long heritage of crisis leads some to fill Welfare cellars against a day of need; their heritage of hope leads others to work for causes such as the United Nations. Their sense of mission finds expression in high places as outstanding Mormon personalities answer calls to public service.

Though the Mormons still regard theirs as the one true authoritative church indispensable to salvation, the church is very much in the world and increasingly of it. Combining strong central direction with considerable local initiative, the institution is strong and solvent. The Mormons are collectively very prosperous. The Council of the Twelve Apostles, serving as a corporate board of directors, manages a wealthy philanthropy. A venerable church president such as David O. McKay, mildest of men, is at the same time president or director of banks, insurance companies, air lines, railroad companies, hotels and department stores, and investment and security corporations. "Zion prospers, all is well," runs a favorite Mormon hymn, though as it moves from an agrarian tradition into a life dominated by industry and the city, modern Mormonism must grapple with the same community challenges that face modern America.

The following selections review the changes of half a century. They are by turns openly admiring, ironical, and critical, but always appreciative. The observers are now mostly professional writers and trained reporters. Neither reformers nor eulogists, they come simply curious to see how a people with a rich and distinctive past are making out in the troubled present.

━━━━━━

Elegy: A Summer in a Mormon Village

AN INDULGENT CURIOSITY and kindly appreciation marked Florence A. Merriam's brief stay among the Mormons. From New York she came west sometime in the early 1890's with an ornithologist girl friend "for the birds and the climate" and spent a summer in an unnamed Utah village shouldering the Wasatch Mountains and overlooking the Great Salt Lake. It was very likely Bountiful, about eight miles north of Salt Lake City, today a commuters' suburb. Becoming more interested in the people than in birdlife, she recorded what she saw of the quaint and the picturesque in an elegiac prose reminiscent of the genteel local colorists who were sketching byways of life all over the country before urban and industrial changes caught up with them. Her quiet passages are a sharp contrast to the self-righteous polemic of her crusading sisters of a few years before.

The excerpts below are taken from her charming little book, My Summer in a Mormon Village *(Boston, 1894). "Grandma," a Mormon widow, sweet-souled and devout, figures in conversations throughout the book as her chief informant. Florence Merriam (sometimes known as Florence Merriam Bailey) also wrote* Birds Through an Opera-Glass, *a book for young people.*

From my rocking-chair under the trees of our yard I looked out upon the village street with interest and curiosity; for the sights and sounds of a village street in Utah differ widely from those of a New York or New England town.

The sound of galloping hoofs was as common as that of wheels. Men passed in saddles, and boys bareback—two on a horse—doing errands and driving home the cows, or running races, tearing madly up the streets. Even the little boys whose feet reached only half way down the horses' sides seemed as much at home on an unruly pony as on a seesaw. For almost every one raises horses in Utah. Nearly every wagon that passed was followed by one or more colts. . . .

On Decoration Day, the whole town passed by our yard. There were no soldiers buried in the village, but the people observed the day by

425

decorating the graves of their own dead. When on the mountain side in the morning, I found men as well as children gathering flowers in the sage-brush. In our family, our sweet-faced school-teacher arranged flowers for the grave of the old grandfather who had recently died; and the little grandchildren filed out of our gate with their arms full of flowers, taking them first across the street to the desolate old grandmother, and then carrying them on to the village cemetery to lay reverently upon the newly made mound.

Almost all the villagers went out to the graveyard, though it was a long walk in the hot sun. Mothers passed, wheeling their baby carriages; men, women, and children went by with their arms full of blossoms; while some walked past carrying great clothes-baskets full of flowers. . . .

Not long after this, the village had another event to talk over—this time of a less saddening nature. It was the "Old People's Party." It seems that the Mormons have adopted the interesting custom of giving an annual "party" to all the old people of Utah. This year it was at Og-den, and there were said to be twelve hundred there over seventy years of age. The old people wore badges of different colors according to their ages—seventy, eighty, or ninety. The governor and many of the principal citizens were present, speeches were made, prizes given to the oldest, and refreshments served to the old people by the young people. A number went from our village.

But as a rule our neighbors did not travel much. Outside life touched ours mainly in passing. . . . Most of our "transients" were mild traveling men on their way through the Territory. Drummers brought their trunks to the house, spreading their goods on beds, tables, and chairs for the in-spection of the village shop-keepers, who came in their shirt sleeves to look over the stock. Dentists came out from Salt Lake, and all the town flocked to have its aching teeth pulled. . . .

Our village bore the title of "city," but in our lanes downy yellow duck-lings waddled up the banks of the puddles through stems of ballooning dandelions; humming-birds darted about the white tops of the blossom-ing locust-trees on the main streets, and I let my horse drink from pools in the mountain brooks along the chief highways. . . .

One morning we breakfasted with a man of so much more intelligence than the ordinary "transient," that I inquired his name and business. "He is a whitewasher, and has come to do the kitchen," the mother told me; concluding: "He has just come back from a mission to England"! After that I often saw him on a Sunday, in a black broadcloth suit, returning from the Mormon "meeting-house."

Elegy: A Summer in a Mormon Village

We were continually having surprises of this kind to remind us where we were. When I bought a bottle of ammonia, I read with a start the mystic letters on the label, "Z. C. M. I."—Zion's Coöperative Mercantile Institution. Over the door of one of the principal stores in town this was shortened to "COÖP," and every one spoke familiarly of "the Coöp." The building next door to the Coöp bore the mysterious sign of "Bishop's Store House"; it proved to be the village tithing house. . . .

To an outsider, one of the most appalling features of Mormonism is the rooted opposition of the people to medical science, their distrust of the skilled physician, and their faith in the Biblical ceremonials of anointing and laying on of hands. In the younger generation both the prejudice and the faith are being modified, even Brigham Young having taught that the church ceremonials should be supplemented by medicine; but in talking with grandma I found the old faith unshaken. She told me with reverent memories of the help she had received. At one time when she had been ill so long that she had lost all courage and hope, the Mormon sisters had her brought into Salt Lake. As she was too sick to go through the Temple to be healed, they said that they would "administer" to her; and taking sacred oil they bathed and anointed her, praying over her during the ceremony. "Oh, the words was beautiful," she exclaimed, with an exalted look in her dear old eyes.

When the administration was concluded they said to her impressively, "Sister, your mission is not ended yet. If this does not make you well, something will come to you that will help you." And the dear soul, full of unquestioning faith, told me how she went home and soon after found a patent medicine circular on the floor—no one ever knew where it came from, and she believed it was "sent." So father went down the street and got a bottle for her, and that was the first thing that helped her. . . .

When a christening occurred in the village, grandma explained to me the rites of baptism. She said, "We don't call it christening, we call it blessing the babies." It seems that, according to the Mormon customs, when the child is eight days old its father ought to bless and name it. Then on a fast day—they come on the first Thursday of every month—the baby is blessed and named by the Elders, with laying on of hands. At eight years old, the child is baptized and confirmed.

Baptism with the Mormons means immersion, and grandma told me that young girls were often baptized in the village pond when the ice had to be broken for them; and that afterwards they had to drive two or three miles in their wet clothing. When I exclaimed in horror, she explained that they were "wrapped in shawls and quilts" and the men

427

"drove as fast as they could"; and she assured me that "none of them ever catches a bit of cold.". . .

Baptism and the ceremonies of the church, such as confirmation and marriage, are often held in the Temple now. Grandma's face lit up with a holy light when she spoke of the sacred edifice. When I asked her what it was like, she said, "I can't *describe* it, but it is the *beautifullest* place— white—with correspondences—so beautiful!". . .

In describing the work to me, her face took on its most beautiful expression. She said the workers all wear Temple robes of white—men and women all are robed in white as they form in procession, walking two by two, up to the great baptismal font, that is upheld by the golden oxen. Sometimes hundreds of white-robed workers will be standing around the font waiting to be baptized. She said devoutly, "It makes me think of the Judgment Day."

The Plural Widows of St. George

ST. GEORGE, in the red rock country of Utah's southwestern extremity, now on a busy highroad to Las Vegas and Los Angeles, was once as isolated as Sarah Comstock found it in 1909. Colonized in 1861 as part of the Cotton Mission, and ever since called Utah's Dixie, it was Brigham Young's wintering place, his darling among the settlements. His home there still stands. In St. George, seedbed and proving ground for a number of his ideas, he first introduced the United Order and dedicated the first temple in Utah. St. George produced the hardiest pioneers, the most orthodox Saints who, away from Gentile influence, kept many of the old ways and the old temper longer than other communities.

Sarah Comstock, coming fresh to St. George from the outside, wrote about it with evident sympathy. Her two-part article "The Mormon Woman," which appeared in Collier's for October 2 and November 9, 1909, and from which the excerpts below are taken, provides an open-minded, reflective, and intimate glimpse of the past in plural households as the widows themselves recalled it.

There was a day of dust and sage-brush and gray splotches of sheep and angular mountains, and by the time we reached Chadbourne's ranch, where "Ma Chaddy," a motherly old Latter-Day Saint, sets forth a meal, we were ready to remain forever in the desert rather than return to the crippled, palsied, wobegone old United States mail stage in which this seventy-mile drive must be made. Night was falling.

"The worst third of the drive is ahead," said the driver, with apparent pride in what he was about to produce.

But at the end of it! I was to find the very heart of old-time Mormonism, the site of the first of all the temples, the alleged vision-born city of Brigham Young, the spot where few "Gentiles" have ever set foot. To be one of those rare Gentiles, about to penetrate to the valley in the wilderness as that little band of the faithful penetrated to it a half-century ago, holds one in a suspense such as the relic-hunter knows when he approaches the lost city of a lost tribe. For Mormonism elsewhere is beginning to be stirred by the unrest of a modern world. Railroads shriek in its ears, commercial interests disturb its repose, political squabbles fret it, churches of many denominations are whispering questions to its rising generation. But in Saint George, known throughout Utah as "Dixie Land," I was to come upon Mormonism unadulterated, the Mormonism of those earliest pioneers whom the Prophet led. The passion of the relic-hunter overcame every ache.

The flat desert reaches were past now, the road was precipitous. The stage pitched furiously, and its old hold rattled beneath us. Uncanny shapes loomed: dead volcanoes, thrusting their black cones against the slightly less black sky. Walls of rock stood out, all of a color with the night until a rising moon showed them red and added to the weirdness of it all. The thin, far-off cry of a coyote cut the desolation.

"You've lost the road; I know you have," I told the driver. "Nobody ever came into a wilderness like this and built a town of two thousand people. Towns don't grow where they have no reason for being."

"The command of the Lord is reason enough."

The solitude bore down more and more heavily. Even the coyote's voice vanished. The shapes grew more grotesque as the moon rose, the walls grew redder. The world looked like a planet where man has never trod. It was terrifying, primeval, chaotic.

"There's some mistake," I insisted. "There can't be any civilization in such a place."

And then the looming rocks parted suddenly upon a picture which was as unreal in that desert place as the mirage itself. Straight little streets lay before us, bordered with trees which were feathery in the moonlight. Tiny cottages appeared, rows of them snuggled among bushes

429

and flower-beds. There was a steady tinkle of trickling water; save for this the place was as still as a city of the peaceful dead.

"Curfew rung an hour ago," said the driver. "It's ten o'clock now and everything's quiet. There—that's the hotel just ahead."

And we dismounted at a rambling, two-story adobe building where the stranger in a strange land may abide.

The pantry had been locked long before; but no truly Mormon heart could harden itself against the picture of dustiness, weariness, and hunger that we presented. I heard the click of a key in a lock and then came a tower of bread and butter, another tower of chocolate cake, and a giant pitcher of milk.

"It's a rather tiresome trip," I remarked, trying to put it with polite moderation.

Somebody laughed. "They call it a hard trip now," he said. "What would you have called it if you'd been one of those pioneer women who helped the men ferret out the place half a century ago with nothing to eat but pine nuts for days at a time, and with nothing over their heads but a willow wickiup, and with their babies sickening and dying on their hands?"

I paused guiltily in the midst of my chocolate cake feast. "Have any of them survived?" I asked.

"Survived? Why, the town's full of 'em. In most cases they seem to have outlived the men, somehow. I don't know how it is—seems like women can stand more. You'll meet pioneer women at every turn."

"Whatever did they come for?" I reflected.

"Why, because they were called," was the simple answer. I knew later that this was the key to the Mormon woman's strange, to us inexplicable, life. Unswerving faith in the priesthood has made all things possible to her, from conquering a wilderness to accepting polygamy. . . .

Seen by day the town had proved to be a basin encircled by rock: red sandstone on the north, black volcanic rock for the rest. In the center of the basin stands the glittering white temple, so dazzling, so impressive, in that vivid air, against that red background, that it is said many of the faithful have broken down and wept when it first burst upon their vision. The cottages are mostly of adobe, sometimes of red rock; they are old, half smothered in November by a mass of roses, chrysanthemums, and brown tamarach plumes. Many of them display the two or three front doors, relic of polygamy's reign. A few old men, many old women, some children, and chickens potter about in the red dust of the streets—for Saint George has not a sidewalk. At the edge of every street runs the ditch full of clear water guided down from the heights above to make the desert rejoice. In early days this rejoicing took the form of cotton, whence the name "Dixie Land." These streams persistently fill the ear with their gentle trickle through the quiet streets.

Day after day I wandered through the red dust, stopping now to gossip over a gate, again to enjoy some quaint picture. Here would be a huge soap kettle swinging in a yard, an old woman bending over it, stirring with a stick. There walked another old woman, knitting as she walked. At a door a widow stopped to gossip with another of her husband's widows. . . .

Little Mrs. D———, a woman of more than seventy, was the first one who ever talked with me intimately on that subject which has made the Mormon woman's life a matter of interest and wonder for so many years. "Now I'll tell you about polygamy," she volunteered one day, after explaining to me many points of doctrine, all the way from "Our father Adam, whose hair is white like the pure wool," to the most mysterious subject in Mormonism, that of the marriage of the dead.

"Do," I said, moving up a little closer and trying to keep back a squirm of anticipation.

"There's three of us," she went on. "He's dead. I was the first one, and the second lives up in Iron County, and the third lives here. We love each other and we always did, even when he was alive, and we all lived together. And we hardly knew our children apart, it was so much like one family. They called their own mothers 'Mother,' but they all called me 'Ma' whether they was mine or not."

"Were you married long before your husband went into plural marriage?"

"Quite a long time. But at last we decided he ought to, so he says to me: 'Who shall it be?' He didn't want another wife and he didn't want to pick her out."

It struck me that the simplest way of solving this difficulty would have been to remain monogamous, and I said so.

"My dear, you don't understand," she responded. "Many's the man 'as walked the floor the night through because the priesthood was urgin' polygamy upon 'em and they felt they must do their duty, but they didn't want no more wives. Many of 'em's glad to take advantage of the manifesto nowadays and have only one to support.". . .

"We talked it over," the little woman said, "and we talked it over, and at last I told him I wanted Vilate for the second wife. She was my best friend and I loved her. 'Don't you like her?' I asked him. 'Oh yes, I like all the girls in the choir,' he said. She sung in the choir where he was choirmaster. So he married her, and later on he married Hannah.

"It's real convenient sometimes to be in polygamy. Now there was once he wanted to go to Georgia, and he says to me: 'Come along; let's go.' But I didn't want to: my babies was little then, and they'd be such a bother. So I says: 'Oh, I don't want to go. Take Hannah; she'll keep you company,' And he did.". . .

The high gate creaked, and I found myself within the yard of Mrs. Caroline Y———, the tall, thin, meek, forlorn old lady whom I had seen at the ward reunion. Her great brown cat did picket duty at her door, but I found favor, knowing the weaknesses of cats, and Sister Caroline received me kindly, though mournfully. She was dipping her brush in the wash-basin, the better to plaster back her sparse hair. She did this earnestly, as if fearing lest a rebellious lock might appear to symbolize a rebellious soul. As she stooped meekly from her great height, the very foolish and fantastic thought occurred to me that her spirit had been plastered back with a damp brush all her life.

While she combed and brushed herself and tidied her little room she talked about the old days when she had come to Dixie in one of those first wagons which were let down by ropes over the red rock wall.

"We ate bread and molasses and beef and squash, and we raised cotton and danced and went to meetin'. I helped, but I wasn't fulfillin' a woman's duty accordin' to the Lord's command, and the years kept goin' on and I was gettin' to be an old maid. Then Brother Y——— decided to go into polygamy, and he chose me for the second wife."

"And you wanted to marry him?"

"I knew it was the right thing to do. Polygamy was practised by Abraham and others in them days, and it was the will o' the Lord."

"And were you happy in it?"

Old Caroline looked out toward the black and red wall which has shut in the many emotions of many women. "It was right," she said drearily.

"I was always shy with 'em," she went on slowly. "You see he'd married her when she was sixteen, and they was attached. And then, long afterward I come into their home. I never could feel anyways but shy with 'em."

"Then you took up polygamy wholly as a matter of religion?"

"Yes, religion, that was what it meant to me. I wouldn't have no courtin'. Before we was married he used to want me to go out walkin', but I wouldn't have it. 'No courtin',' I says to him. 'If you've got anything to say to me, you know how to say it and where. Come to the house and say it out straight, no strollin' around like young lovers. I don't go walkin' with any woman's husband.'

"And I wouldn't have no signs of affection from him in her presence, neither. I wouldn't have anything that might hurt her feelin's. There was some did, but none o' that, I told him. But polygamy was religion to me. And I was always shy before her, anyway.". . .

On a day when the holidays were not far off, I strolled in the old cemetery where Saint George has laid away its dead for half a century. Tamarisks purr over the graves of the old polygamists. Here men are gathered unto their wives, for even in death the Mormon woman must share the man of her choice. On a stone I read the name of a long-dead saint; on each side of his a stone bore the name of one of his wives. In another lot a stone bore the names of children of two wives. In still another a somewhat ornate monument displayed three columns rising from one base; the first wife's name is on one of these, the other two are reserved for the husband and the second wife, who are still living. . . .

I wondered if the Mormon woman's "tragedy" were not about the same as everybody's else tragedy—all a matter of how you take it. The practical little lady will find polygamy convenient, and the lugubrious one will find it dreary, and the petty one will find it annoying, and the spiritual one will find it exalting. But back of all these temperamental differences is the belief among all the old-school Latter-Day Saints and many of the younger ones that it is right; and that unswerving belief has made polygamy possible to these women. Probably that accounts for their cheerfulness; I believe Sister Caroline is the only really mournful woman in Dixie Land. Now that they have been through their ordeal, they are passing into an old age made content by faith in the glory soon to be theirs.

Reed Smoot, Apostle in Politics

THE ELECTION OF REED SMOOT, Mormon apostle, to the United States Senate in 1903 brought a storm of national protest. Americans could not believe that he was the husband of only one wife and that his church loyalties would not dictate his political activities. But the fears

433

*proved unfounded. The Senate Committee on Privileges and Elections
after an exhaustive investigation found him blameless. The most intensive snooping into his personal and public affairs went unrewarded. The
Republican Senator was a Puritan, devoted to a sober, industrious, and
patriotic economic orthodoxy that was as American as it was Mormon.
During five unbroken terms he was able to serve both his church and
country without loss of personal integrity because nothing in their ma-
terialistic creeds conflicted. Smoot's long tenure—by 1930 he was "dean
of the Senate"—saw the Mormons achieve eminent respectability.*

*Nels Anderson, mingling satire and respect, gives a revealing portrait
of the Apostle-Senator in "Pontifex Babbitt," reproduced in part here
from the* American Mercury, *October, 1926 by permission. Senator Smoot
was then in full career as chairman of the powerful Finance Committee,
though the Smoot-Hawley Tariff, which he considered his greatest
achievement, was not to come until 1931. In 1932 he was decisively defeated at the polls by a fellow Mormon but a Democrat, Elbert D.
Thomas, a professor of political science at the University of Utah. The depression undid Smoot politically and financially. In his apostleship he rose
in seniority until he was but one step removed from the church presidency, but the last eight years of his life seemed an anti-climax. He died
on February 9, 1941, at the age of seventy-nine.*

*Nels Anderson was teaching in the New School for Social Research
in New York when he wrote "Pontifex Babbitt." He went on to make
the Mormons the subject of a doctoral study,* Desert Saints: The Mormon
Frontier in Utah (*Chicago, 1942*).

Senator Slocum has the floor. "Mr. President," he says, "I ask unanimous
consent to print in the *Record* a communication in the nature of a petition
from the Giles County Corn Growers' Association, protesting against the
morals of a mechanical age." And then:

> Senator Smoot: I would suggest that the Senator refer the matter
> to the Committee on Printing. I should like to add for the benefit of
> other Senators that yesterday the *Record* contained twenty-one col-
> umns of such material, and the total cost of printing it was $834.55.

Senator Slocum: Does that mean that the Senator from Utah objects?
Senator Smoot: I feel it my duty to object.
Whereupon Senator Slocum, refusing to desert his constituents, and
taking advantage of a time-honored right, proceeds to read the memorial
into the *Record*. Five minutes pass and Senator Smoot begins to squirm
with impatience. Ten minutes pass and he looks worried, as well he

may, for the valuable time of more than sixty learned Senators is being wasted. But the persistent Slocum reads on and fifteen minutes pass. Still he is only half finished. Then Smoot yields, Slocum sits down smiling and the communication goes into the *Record*.

What would the morning hour be in the United States Senate without a scene like that, with the eagle-eyed Smoot as the principal actor? For twenty years, as self-appointed censor of the *Record*, he has waged his war against this printing of slush. For twenty years he has been powerfully and assiduously on the job. How different this Smoot from the lamb-like novice who came to the Senate in 1903, and for two years thereafter was the butt of anti-Mormon virtue! He is still tall and soberly garbed, and still he wears the high poke collar that threatens to lacerate his throat should he turn his head quickly. He is still grave and unsmiling, and the years have dried him out and left him lean and gray. He is still as sparing of words as he ever was. But in his voice there is now a ring of authority. He is no longer lamb-like, no longer meek and timid. The uncertain, furtive air of a hunted man has been shuffled off, and in its stead has come the self-confident mien and manner of a master.

Reed Smoot, Apostle of the Mormon Church, on his first appointment to the Senate was the object of a hurricane of protest. All the old pious rage against the Latter Day Saints flared up again, and Christian pastors and political opponents left no stone unturned in their zeal to oust him from office. But he stayed on, working, and waiting. He said nothing, but sawed wood. Today, it is probable, he has more real power in his hands than any other man in Washington, not even excepting Dr. Coolidge. He knows more about the actual workings of the government than any of his colleagues. In all national legislation, and especially when it relates to finance, he has become a dominating influence. No important bill dealing with revenue or expenditures can go on the books before he has left upon it the impress of his dour and suspicious personality.

The exponent of a harsh and unyielding economy in government house-keeping, he is the son of a frugal, unimaginative race among whom thrift and hard work are the chief virtues of this life and the only assurances of salvation in the life beyond. His father, a Mormon who crossed the plains with Brigham Young and the other pioneers, became one of the first mayors of Salt Lake City. He was its mayor when the United States Army came to destroy it, when the people fled to the mountains and left a few men behind to apply the suicidal torch. Later the elder Smoot became the leader of the region around Provo, where Reed was born in 1862. The brunt of pioneering had passed by then, and the Indians had ceased to trouble. But the Mormons were still having clashes with the Federal government over polygamy, and their struggle with the forces of Nature had only begun.

The elder Smoot became the ecclesiastical head of the Provo region He was a devout man and the Lord blessed him in his stock and store. He became the owner of woolen mills, and a merchant, and later a banker and real estate man. He was a worker and a praying man. In Zion he was the *Stammvater* of the royal dynasty of Smoot. Young Reed, while he never showed any startling ability, was from the beginning a patient worker. At the age of seventeen he graduated from the Brigham Young Academy at Provo, now the Brigham Young University, and his father gave him his choice of studying medicine, becoming a lawyer or going into business. He chose the last, and took a petty job in the Provo Woolen Mills. In Provo the story still floats about that on one of the walls he wrote: "I will yet be superintendent of these mills." He became superintendent. Forty years later while battling for raw wool in the Senate, he declared with no little pride: "I don't care what happens to me financially. I know that I can go into a woolen mill, and I can run a woolen mill."

It was evident to the future Senator that a good business man ought to know something about politics, just as now he insists that a politician ought to know something about business. A good business man ought to have a political party. So he subscribed to two New York newspapers, one Republican and the other Democratic, and these he read religiously for more than a year before making up his mind. He finally concluded that a business man could sleep with greater comfort in the Republican bed. He then proceeded to put his house in order, and so carefully did he plan that no detail was missing when the call came. His first move was to step into his father's shoes in business. Then he proceeded to don his father's ecclesiastical pants by following him in the leadership of the Provo branch of the Mormon Church. Here he was so useful and efficient that he soon outstripped his father. Presently he was elected to the august Quorum of the Twelve Apostles. He became a sort of Mormon cardinal. Getting so far at thirty-nine was no small achievement, but Smoot, the go-getter, was still out for more. He found that the financial affairs of the Church had dropped into a dreadful rut. For thirty years only dreamers had been at the helm. So he set himself to straightening out the tangles, and it was not long before he had completed the job. Out of gratitude his brethren in authority, finding Utah in need of a Senator, saw to it that he received the appointment.

For a Mormon to be sent to the Senate at that time was akin to being nominated for martyrdom, and it was in this spirit that he took the call. The halo he won in the struggle he still wears out in Utah. The fruits still drop at his feet. But he entered the Senate a very humble man. His ambition was to learn what all Senators are supposed to know and what a Republican Senator is expected to do. He came in like an office boy in a big firm. He sat at the feet of those great and good men, Lodge, Penrose, Aldrich and Platt. They found him an apt pupil, safe, sober and steady. They recognized that he was a lion for efficiency, a tiger for economy and a wolf for detail. But for a number of years he floundered. He was like an untrained man at the mechanic's bench, not knowing just how to take hold of the tools. He was put to carrying water for the players and lent occasional aid in rubbing down the stars. Sometimes he would try to get the floor, but he was slow of speech and *gauche*. The opposition Senators razzed him and the newspapers kidded him. The Mormon haters still glared at him, eager for a chance to undo him.

But all that is now past. Today he is on top. The public no longer thinks of him as Smoot the Mormon. He has become somebody. A word from him gets more press attention than an hour of the best eloquence found in the two chambers on the hill. He is chairman of the Finance Committee, ranking member and virtually chairman of the Committee on Appropriations, the watch dog of the Treasury, a militant proponent of economy in government, and one of the chief financial advisors to the President. Eloquence in the Senate is becoming a lost art, a sort of vestigial hangover from the Daniel Webster days. Government is more and more a matter of patient grinding in committee rooms—and here Smoot excels. In these committee rooms laws are made, mutilated or killed; appointments are made, deals are made, and men are made. In them there is no playing to the galleries, no beating of tom-toms. Work is the chief thing—and Smoot is the most untiring worker in all Washington.

Yet he is also conspicuous for other reasons. For example, for his romantic, almost voluptuous guardianship of wool, for his veneration for the sugar beet, and for his dogged attempts to inject what he regards as efficiency into the administration of the government. His adoration of wool scarcely needs explaining. All the time he was an owner of woolen mills a bloody war was being waged between the cattle and sheep interests in Utah. In spite of the trusty rifles of Mormon cowboys, Mormon sheepherders overran the hills of Zion—and the change was surely not unwelcome to the operators of woolen mills. His relation to sugar is hardly more subtle. He is loyal to sugar for sentimental as well as for material reasons. It was beet sugar stock that saved the Mormon Church financially. The first beet sugar mill west of the Mississippi his father imported from Germany. By this precedent the whole surrounding region was committed to beet growing. He is loyal first to beet sugar, and then to any sugar produced in the continental United States. . . .

He grew up in the stern and sobering shadows of the Wasatch Range and in the society of toil lovers. The Mormons are the super-Puritans of American culture. To them the earth is only a place to prepare for Heaven, and Heaven is simply a place of eternal order. Life on earth must be a thing of serious effort, a sort of tuning up for the life beyond. To them there is no virtue like keeping one's lamp trimmed, and no joy in this life or the next that does not come from work. Thus Smoot instinctively busies himself with keeping the national house in order.

Other Senators work at the eternal problem of reelection, and need to turn to one another for aid and comfort. Smoot, who can stay as long as he wants, has been free to turn his attention to other things. It has never been necessary for him to exchange favors. He doesn't have to court his voters by inserting their communications in the *Record*. He never goes on baby-kissing or hand-shaking tours. He is never found at teas, nor does he address women's clubs or graduating classes. He never invades the White House on social calls. He is sure of his job.

True to his clerical background, he believes in the sanctity of authority and in fidelity to leadership. There must be leaders and followers, and it is the business of the followers to follow. There are two classes of followers, the common folks and the subordinate leaders. When harmony prevails between followers and leaders one always knows what is going to happen next. Such a perfect relationship maintains itself between Smoot and his constituency. He always gets from them what is his due as their faithful leader. They constitute his flock, politically and ecclesiastically.

At the lower end of Provo, in an area of the city no longer inhabited by the best people, stands a monument to the loyalty of these sheep. This is the Smoot family home, which has stood vacant for years, with the windows boarded and the grass growing tall in the yards. The natives accept it unquestioningly as the sign of a sacrifice. They believe that during all the years that Brother Smoot has been in Washington serving them he has been denying himself the comforts of home. He has never sought to disillusion them. When he spoke at Provo in the last Presidential campaign he even gave them a gentle reminder. He was forced to move very near the light to read some documents from which he was quoting. "Fellow citizens," he said, "you will pardon me, I am sure. I have nearly ruined my eyes working for the good people of Utah." [*Applause.*]

Having this view of loyalty and believing in the divinity of the American government, it is natural for him to regard its management as a solemn and even religious business. He takes his senatorship no less seriously than he does his apostleship. In both roles he brings to bear the same habits of mind. In his orthodox fidelity to the one he is no more immovable than in his orthodox fidelity to the other. For his theological loyalty he has been persecuted, but for his senatorial loyalty to party and the *status quo* the Babbitt press has never ceased to extol him. To show how much both these roles are one, it is needful only to recall how, during the strained days of April, 1917, while the Senate was deliberating on war, he halted the proceedings long enough to make what he termed "this simple but earnest appeal: God bless and approve the action to be taken by the Senate this day. Our Father, preserve our government and hasten the day when liberty will be enjoyed by all the peoples of the earth." Saints and Gentiles rejoiced at his piety, and the day will come when loyal Utah will cast this prayer in bronze and chisel it in stone. Smoot has never had reason to doubt his home folks. He holds them in the palm of his hand. . . .

In Utah Smoot is considered a great statistician and the most able economist in Washington, with the possible exception of Andy Mellon. They remember with pride how he once talked against time for thirty-three hours, and didn't have to read any poetry or tell any funny stories: he talked only facts. Smoot, in truth, is so much the statistician that he has almost ceased to be a human being. His devotion to numbers has converted him into an adding-machine. He never smiles; he is devoid of humor. They say he loves children, as do all Mormons, but if he loves adults he never shows it. His apostolic face never lights up except when he goes into the parks to feed the birds. Here for the moment he becomes a man of flesh and blood, but even this diversion he indulges in solitude. He burns the mid-night oil over columns and percentages, over deficits and surpluses, always and ever with one end in view: to prove his side right and the other wrong. He is a Republican statistician.

When he confronts a good debater in the Senate he is a sorry spectacle. At repartee he is a failure; the words clog in his throat or he flies into a rage that anyone should impeach his word. But give him his own weapons, his charts and curves, and the tide of battle comes his way. When he turns on the enemy with: "Let us take the facts; not windjamming, but the facts," it is rarely that he is beaten. But it is hard to qualify him as a political economist. If protecting large incomes and rushing to the defense of vested interests is sufficient to justify such a rating his reputation is secure. Unfortunately for his Utah admirers, scientists are not rated that way. The *laissez faire* political economy, alas, is rapidly passing from the world. It is only found in the most antiquated universities. But even the most ardent *laissez faire* economists would not accept Smoot. He leans so far toward the let-it-alone philosophy that he becomes the champion of an almost theological *laissez faire*. Things are as they should be by divine arrangement. Providence will see to it that everything stays on the track, and the world isn't going to go haywire. Man must not throw monkey-wrenches into the machinery. With this naïve philosophy Smoot would solve all the social and economic problems of the world. He would tell the crook to be honest, the unemployed to go to work, and all people to practice clean living, prayer, and loyalty to their leaders.

No one has ever heard the chairman of the Finance Committee raise his apostolic voice in the interest of what is called humanity. He never thinks of people in the concrete. He is above and beyond the groveling masses. The mines in his own State are veritable mantraps. Most mines in the West are bad, but nowhere can a worker get leaded, gassed, crushed, or poisoned with arsenic or copper water more readily than in Utah. Yet let a Senator try to start an investigation of mining conditions out there, and at once Smoot finds his voice—the same voice that is heard when sugar probes and other such villainies are suggested. The uplifters never go to him for favors, nor have they ever sent him any bouquets.

Alarmists point to the possibility that Apostle Smoot may one day become the President of his Church, and so begin to speak directly and familiarly to God. According to precedent, when the head of the Church dies the senior Apostle in point of service takes his place. Heber J. Grant, the present head of the Church, is an old man, but hale. Rudger Clawson, the president of the Quorum of the Twelve Apostles, is next in line. He too is old, but also hale. Both these men must die before Smoot can be elevated to the dizzy splendors of the presidency, which will make him God's personal representative on earth. The alarmists fear for the rest of us if he should one day hold in one hand the keys to the Everlasting Kingdom, and in the other the keys to the Committee on Finance. The Lord would then whisper to Brother Reed and Brother Reed would whisper to Brother Calvin. But I don't believe there is any cause for real alarm. Smoot, as Apostle, would not get any disturbing revelations. His head doesn't work that way. He knows that we already

440

have the kind of government that God wants, that the Constitution is an inspired document, and that the Heavens are most tranquil when the Republicans are in the saddle. The Heavens are most tranquil then because he, Smoot, holds a front seat on the band-wagon. He would be very loath to uproot anything or change anything. His God likes to sit tight.

Thus, if he were President of the Mormon Church his habits of life and manner of thinking would be altered very little. He would plod on as usual, gathering the right brand of stand-pat Republican statistics and piling them high in his encyclopaedic mind. He might become more austere and his vote would probably change to a benediction, but nothing else would happen. He has been too long in the game to get the voices mixed. He knows the still small voice of the Holy Spirit, but he also knows the still small voice in the White House. Both are authoritative and they never contradict each other. Smoot would never confuse them.

———

Vachel Lindsay Encounters the Mormons in Canada

AMERICA'S TROUBADOUR POET VACHEL LINDSAY often traded rhymes for bread. Determined to return poetry to the people as a spiritual antidote to vulgarity and materialism, he tramped about the countryside giving sonorous recitations of original verses like "The Congo" and "General William Booth Enters into Heaven." In 1921 with the English writer Stephen Graham he made a long summer's walk through the Rockies and western Canada. By campfire or sitting on rocks in the sun, Graham wrote thirty-two letters for the New York Evening Post *describing their glorious adventure. Graham later compiled these letters into a book, from which the chapter on the Mormons in Cardston, Alberta, is excerpted below (from* Tramping with a Poet in the Rockies *by Stephen Graham. Copyright 1922, D. Appleton & Co. Reprinted by permission of the publishers Appleton-Century-Crofts, Inc.). One reader commented that* "Tramping with a Poet *will someday stand on the shelf of open-air literature beside* Travels with a Donkey."

As the selection below opens, Graham and Lindsay have just visited the Dukhobors or "spirit wrestlers," a Russian religious community who came to western Canada in 1898. The Mormons had been there since the spring of 1887, when a company from Cache Valley, Utah, established a

colony on Lee's Creek, tributary of St. Mary's River, and called it Card-
ston for its founder, Charles O. Card. Other settlements quickly followed,
providing a refuge for polygamous households anxious to avoid federal
prosecution in Utah, Idaho, and Arizona. Mormon colonies in Mex-
ico, at Juarez and Dublan, were being founded at the same time and for
the same purpose. In Canada they prospered, in time forming several
stakes (permanent territorial divisions of the church) and constructing
at Cardston the first Mormon temple outside the United States. The most
cordial relations have existed between the Mormons and the provincial
and dominion governments of Canada.

We were regaled at farmhouses by sweet Mormon brides, who gave
us bannocks, who gave us of their simmering greengages out of the great
cauldron on the stove. Elders on horseback very politely, and with many
details, showed us the way to Cardston and the Mormon Temple. We
were happily and sympathetically disposed towards the Mormons, and
Vachel, who has taught the Salt-Lake City girls to dance whilst he
chanted to them "The Queen of Sheba," has a soft spot in his heart for
the sect. . . .

Cardston, which at length we reached, is largely a Mormon city. The
Temple, a remarkable structure, exteriorly chaste and beautiful, domi-
nates the scene, and the clouds rest upon it, obscuring its upper storeys
in cloudy weather. It is not used for general worship; for that purpose
there is a sufficiently ugly tabernacle. It is almost exclusively for the
Mormon sacraments, the sealing of wives and children, and for the medi-
tational recreation of the elders. Once the building has been completed
and consecrated it will remain inaccessible to outsiders, but in order to
avert suspicion, visitors are shown over it until that time. We were lucky,
as the Temple is very nearly finished, and it is a rare experience for an
outsider to gain access. There are only eight Mormon Temples in the
world, and the rites performed therein are entirely secret. . . .

We walked up to the Temple at three in the afternoon, the designated
time when visitors are shown round, and punctually at that hour the
doors were opened and the curious were admitted.

"Wherever we locates we builds temples," said the guide a curious old
fellow, so illiterate that he strewed the temple floor with his aitches, an
Englishman from the provinces, squat, confidential, insinuating. "This,
is the eighth Mormon Temple," said he. "The ninth is now rising in Phoenix, Arizona."

The visitors were mostly farm-women, and Vachel and I looked like a couple of tramps in their midst. Our clothes hung on us; we held in our hands a couple of the most weather-beaten of old hats. I was the "big un" and Vachel was the "little un." We looked to have a little less intelligence than gopherrats.

"The 'ole edifiss is of stone," said the guide, "and the foundation is of rock and concrete. There's not five dollars' worth of wood in the construction. All the wood you see is haksessories."

"Are all the temples built of stone only?" I asked cautiously, with the air of a stone-mason out of a job.

"No," said he. "Each is built on a seprit plan."

"'Ere," said he, turning to the rest of the company, "'ere we seals. This 'ere room is for ordinances only. No, we don't worship in the Temple. It's not used for public worship. You see the red-brick building as you came up to the Temple. That is the Tabernacle where public worship is held, and that is free to all. But 'ere in the Temple we 'as the ordinances and the meditations."

The guide was naturally a Mormon, and as he showed us around I thought his main objects were to tell us nothing while pretending to tell us all, and yet at the same time to make converts among the women. He did all he could to interest the latter in the cooking and lighting and warming and washing arrangements.

"You 'ave 'ere the electric stoves to cook the meals. You couldn't keep running in and out of the Temple in yer sacred garments to get meals at resterongs, so we cooks 'ere. But there can be no smell of cooking— as this exhaust takes all the smell away out of the building. Very convenient, eh, ain't it? We've had over ten thousand applications from women to come and cook in the Temple."

The farm-women giggled appreciatively. The guide led them on to the laundering establishment. As the Mormons wear secret underlinen with signs, they naturally don't care to send their laundry out to wash. And in the Temple we were given to understand every man and woman wore special white garments. Consequently there would be much laundering. But all was to be done by the latest machinery, driven by electric power. "No hand-work, no scrubbing, no drudgery and gettin' your fingers red and 'ard," said the guide. "Then, when the wash is done, hup, in they go to the drying chamber, and in a few seconds they are sufficiently dry to be taken out and ironed on the electric irons."

For a moment it was like being at an ideal home exhibition. "Then the radiators," said the guide, "you see, they don't project into the rooms, but are fixed in the walls dead level with the surface of the walls."

"Of course the Temple 'asn't got its upolstery in yet, but in every room the furniture will be all of a piece with the inlay wood of the walls. If the walls is oak the furniture will be oak to match; if it's bird's-eye maple, the furniture'll be bird's-eye maple; if it's Circassian mahogany the furniture will be Circassian mahogany too. Every room will have its color scheme. 'Ere you see the thermometer. Now the temperature of the building will be regulated. It won't matter wot the weather is like outside, it will be controlled inside. The engineer will 'ave 'is orfice outside the Temple and don't never need come in. All they 'as to do is telephone 'im to raise the temperature ten degrees or lower it five and he'll do it."

"We comes to the baths" (they are pretty elaborate). "'Ere's the men's section, over there's the women's. You natcherally bathe first of all when you enter the Temple and remove every speck of dust or dirt from your body. And 'ere are the robing-rooms where spotless garments is waiting you to put on. You walks all in white wherever you go in the Temple, and when it 'as been consecrated no more folks will ever go in it in ordinary clothes like as you and me to-day."

The Temple proved to be the last word in luxury and modern convenience. In the most elegant club in London, Paris, or New York I have not seen such luxury and sensual comfort as was in this Temple in the rough wild west. Every room was inlaid with precious woods. The baths and robing-rooms were worthy of a Sultan, the lounge and one-piece carpets all suggested a material heaven. The guide showed us the vast font reposing on the life-size figures of twelve oxen, the symbols of the twelve tribes of Israel. This font was the centre of a stately chamber with galleries running round it. From the galleries the friends of the candidates could watch the ceremony of immersion. The font was large enough to baptize families at once.

"And you can be baptized many times," said the guide. "For yourself, then for your friends, and then for the dead—for any one you would like to have saved."

"Baptized for the dead?" said one of the women in horror. "Yes," said he. "You think it strange, but the early Christians all used to do it. Just turn up First Corinthians, chapter fifteen. 'What shall they do which are baptized for the dead, if the dead rise not at all? Why are they then baptized for the dead?' which shows plainly that the apostles recommended it."

"Is the water cold?" asked a farm-girl, timorously.

"Cold," said the guide ingratiatingly, "oh, no! It's warmed. It's just *nice*. I should say about the temperature of warm milk."

"Oh!" "Oh!" There was chorus of approval from the women, who had been considering the whole matter from a purely personal point of view.

We were then led to the Creation Room, the Garden of Eden Room, and the Earth-natural Room, all adorned with works of art. There were pictures of the world before Creation, and then of each stage in the process of Creation.

"God don't love chaos. 'E's a great organiser. 'E organised it, and 'e divided the water from the hearth and gave us light and made the hanimal creation—yes, all that lives and breeves," said the guide. " 'Ere we meet to meditate on the Creation. Isn't it a beutiful room?"

Some one asked him if the artists were Mormons. "Yes, all of them," said he, and then went on—

"You'd think it get stuffy in 'ere. But no; we 'as the hair taken out and washed and then returned. It's a new device for washing the hair."

We passed to Eden. Here were pictures of the whole animal creation in benevolent and sentimental happiness; the tiger browsing beside the lamb, and the lion and the giddy goat frisking around.

The guide purveyed the story of the Garden of Eden, but left out Adam and Eve, and I walked away from him to wander round and seek the portraits of our first parents. They were not included. But I found that the painting of the Tree of Knowledge of Good and Evil and the Tree of Life were concave at the base, and that there was a recess and an alcove to each. So there was a place for a living Adam and Eve to sit, side by side, when the meditation on the Garden was going on. My idea is that Eve would be seated in the Tree of Life and Adam in the Tree of Knowledge. But that is surmise. The guide would not tell us what the alcoves were for, but in the eye of curious imagination I saw Adam and Eve sitting there in primitive innocence whilst the hearts of the elders were inditing of a good matter.

From Eden we went to the Earth-natural, which was a hideous place where every animal was depicted with a vicious expression. A large mad coyote or, was it a hyena? seemed to control the atmosphere of the chamber.

" 'Ere we 'ave the Hearth after sin 'as crept in," said the guide. " 'Ere is life as we know it, full of sin which you can't escape. You can all learn a great deal from them pictures. Think of Hadam and Eve. 'Ave you ever thought of it—'ow God gave them the garden of Eden, and of the 'experience' 'e made them 'ave there. Isn't it true about us? 'E didn't mean that nothin' should ever 'appen to us. 'E brought us into the world that we might 'ave an experience."

445

So we went on to the Marriage Room, which was entirely bare, and no one could say what it would be like when the decorations and the furniture had been added. I judged it time for me to cease being Simple Simon, so I asked the guide as humbly as I could whether the marriages were legal when the ceremony was performed.

"Yes," said he. "You 'ave a legal marriage."

"But polygamy?" I queried, and I saw his eyes flame.

"Polygamy 'as been done away with long ago when Utah was received into the Union," he answered in a gruff way. . . .

The guide hurried us to the door. "I've some pictures of the Temple for sale," said he to the farm-women. But they seemed all to have been scared by my question about polygamy. Vachel and I stopped to look at the pictures. After all, they were only picture-postcards of the exterior. We bought three. . . .

Vachel and I went up to the Temple at night. It looked like a place produced by enchantment—the highest thing on the highest eminence of the widespread but low-built city of Cardston. Clouds hid the top of it. There was no one near but ourselves, apparently not even a watchman. The massive gates were locked and barred, and above them gleamed electric lanterns in large and graceful M's.

We have learned an elementary lesson about them.

"Remember that, Vachel," said I. "M for Mormon."

"The guide said a true word," said the poet. "God sent us into the world that we might have an experience."

Sin Comes to Ogden

THE VITRIOLIC BERNARD DE VOTO was never more caustic than when chastising his own land and people. Born in Ogden, Utah, of a Gentile father and a Mormon mother, he personally dramatized the conflict of cultures. He attended the University of Utah for a year, long enough to contribute an early piece to its literary magazine The Pen, *but departed in 1915 in protest at the dismissal of a bevy of professors too liberal for the times. He exorcised his unease in Zion by writing illtempered essays about a society he was not sure he hated or admired*

446

*until at length, absorbed in Western history, he mellowed to write one
of the most sympathetic accounts ever accorded the Mormon role in a
significant moment of the nation's history, a moment De Voto called "the
year of decision."*

*In going east to Harvard he turned to other quarrels: the professor's
house was not for him and he badgered academicians as he had badgered
the Mormons. For a while he edited the* Saturday Review of Literature,
*charging it with his own vitality and crusades, this time literary. He is
best remembered for his long occupancy of the Editor's Easy Chair in
Harper's and for his stirring contributions to Western history in such
books as* Across the Wide Missouri *and* The Year of Decision. *He was,
moreover, a militant conservationist and a conscience for the times on
issues of deep moral import, whether they involved McCarthy, the FBI,
or God himself. He was novelist as well as critic and historian. As John
August he even wrote detective potboilers.*

*The selection below is taken from "Ogden: The Underwriters of Sal-
vation," which was included in Duncan Aikman's anthology* The Tam-
ing of the Frontier (New York, 1925). *Written over thirty years ago, it
shows the neophyte De Voto at his waspish best, a characteristic mingling of contemporary observation with history as De Voto felt it in his
blood.*

The Overland Limited stops at Ogden for fifteen minutes. The tourist,
a little dizzy from altitude but grateful for trees after miles of desert,
rushes out to change his watch and see a Mormon. He passes through
a station that is a deliberate triumph of hideousness and emerges at the
foot of Twenty-fifth Street. Beyond him are the peaks, the Wasatch at
more than their usual dignity, but in the foreground are only a double row
of shacks far gone in disintegration, stretching upward in the direction
of the hills. The gutters, advertised as sparkling with mountain water,
are choked with offal. The citizenry who move along the sidewalks are
habituated to the shanties, but the newcomer, who whether from east
or west believes in a decent bluff of progress, is invariably appalled. What
manner of folk, he wonders, what kind of Digger Indians, can suffer
this daily assault upon the credo of Kiwanis? He thinks of the First National in Kokomo, or the Biltmore in Racine. He shudders. He hurries
back to the train, pausing on the way to buy a postcard to which is
attached a bag of table salt from Great Salt Lake. That at least is up to
date.

Robert Louis Stevenson, the one poet known to have passed through

Ogden, faced these same shanties when they had withstood some forty fewer years of drouth. His only contribution to the booster-literature of the city was a note on the Chinese immigrants, who, he observed, displayed a far greater personal cleanliness than the natives.

Lest an Ogden spirit be offended, let me make amends. It is true that the one new building on Twenty-fifth Street since 1900 is the Pullman porters' club. But let us take the tourist blindfolded through the city, past the Cornville Center palaces of the wealthy and the bungalow-warrens of the bourgeoisie, to Ogden Canyon. Past that, still blindfolded against the Keep Kool Kamps and the Dewdrop Inns, to some ridge whence he may see the joists and rafters of a continent, with the city insignificant on the plain. Here he will see Ogden as it is, an oasis, a garden in the desert, with the peaks splendid above it—lines that sweep the eye irresistibly onward, distances and colors that carry the breath with them, the mountains in which the gods of the Utes walked in the cool of the day. For majesty, he will be willing to forget the measles of the street.

Better still, let him arrive on one of the three or four midwinter days when the smoke has drifted westward and left the sky clean. Then, emerging in a heliotrope twilight, he will not see the shanties or the filth. The city is blotted out and there are only ridges deep in snow, saintly and whitened peaks with collars of mist half way down their slopes—mist slowly burning to its core of tourmaline, with sapphires winking at the edge. Night brings its erasure of hideousness, the good folk ride homeward in the world's worst trolleys, and presently they are fed and stalled. But almost till the time they are abed, the eastern peaks, above their chasubles of mist, are luminous with a garnet flame that tints the snow against the night. Infinitely cold, the mist and the darkness; but warm the glow—a fire burning on the very hearth of heaven.

But do not conclude, because the city is resolute in shabbiness beneath the peaks, that it is leading a schism from the faiths of Rotary and Mr. Bok. Its hideousness, its squalor, are no protest against *The Ladies' Home Journal*. Your Ogdenite, instead, sees his city as those dreams come true. He peoples these streets with the chaos of State and Madison, lines them with Wrigley Twins, roofs them with elevateds. To him the Eccles Block is sixty stories high, and the constable at the corner, who is flapping a hand at three Fords and an Overland, is waving back six rows abreast of Packards as far as the traffic towers stretch toward the Chicago River.

Or if not now, at least by to-morrow noon. An idealist, he sees the illusion in front of the fact of dirt and mediocrity. A dreamer, he dwells for ever in the city of his hopes. Besides, when you come down to it, he asks, turning his back on the Broom Hotel, what city its size?—etc. Follows a list of statistics from the Weber Club, of mines and sugar beets, of warehouses and factories, of jobbers and railroads and farms. . . . And so on—a small backwater American city, less immaculate than most, less energetic, less comfortable, but at one with its fellows in drowsiness, in safety.

Yet once, even the tourist must remember, once the frontier marched through Ogden with its chariots and its elephants. Once there were demigods and heroes. Once there was desire and splendor—something of courage and adventure, something of battle, life a hot throbbing in the veins. Where now there are culture clubs and chiropractors, there was a city shouting its male-ness to the peaks.

Ogden was a settlement of pious Mormons who tilled their fields and obeyed the prophet, who looked at the mountains but saw the meadows of Jerusalem. And then word came that the Pacific Railroad was not disposed to adopt the prophet's suggestion. "Why," said the engineers, "should we build over an extra divide merely to get to Salt Lake City when we can follow a water-level route through Weber Canyon?" And Weber Canyon debouched a mile or so from Ogden. Then suddenly there was a freight-line from Zion, and a little later came the surveyors from the east and from the west. Then a new goldfield, poised on the present boundary between Idaho and Wyoming, opened up. An adventurous Gentile made a trail to it, shortened its line of supplies two hundred miles, and the first affluence Ogden had ever seen began.

There were two streets—then three, then four. Saloons came, bringing progress—bright lights, tablecloths, store shirts, flowered vests, the etiquette of the Colt. The miners came, and scarlet women; such women as Ogden had never seen. Women with laces and silks, with rouge and rice powder. Women who were all that Mr. Service has declared their Alaskan sisters to be, but who brought civilization to this cowpath settlement. Women who, it may be, troubled the souls of their Mormon sisters. For Mark Twain, looking impartially at the evidence, has said that a man who married a dozen of them was a large-scale benefactor of the human race.

Strange sights by day in the streets that had seen nothing more extraordinary than a drove of pigs. Ox teams by the dozen plodding ahead of a freighter's wagon with seven-foot wheels and a bullwhacker snaking his whip above their ears. Mules singly or in tandem packed with the

449

outfits of prospectors, their owners trudging in their dust. Gamblers, set-tlers, bartenders, Mexicans, Chinks, remittance men. And by night what sounds! In the saloons, the roar of good men singing, the fellow-ship of males, the debate of a hundred disputants at once, each one an authority. Above them the seduction of fiddles where the women con-sorted with their prey. In the streets, strayed revelers taking the long way home, the clop-clop of horses as belated ones arrived, the click of dice, sometimes the voice of the Colt. . . . It was a little different from discussions as to the true nature of Satan's fur, or from the hymns with which the Mormon dances had begun. Sin had come to Ogden.

And now descended on Ogden the Hartigans and the McCarthys and the Flahertys. Through the mouth of Weber Canyon, racing against its ten-mile day and the Chinks of the C. P., the Union Pacific burst like a spring flood. Now came Hell on Wheels to Mormonry.

Not long did it pause, this mobile terminal, but never again would righteousness be quite the same. The Irish roared and sang and ham-mered, like happy devils assaulting the earth, and laid their steel and passed on. On to Corinne they went, on to Promontory Point, and met the Chinks and sniped at them from behind ties or seized them bodily, when the scientific spirit was strong, and took them apart. Those last eighty miles of railroad building, both companies roaring for land and fame, were a romancer's dream of strength and trickery and violence. They ended; dignitaries came to drive their golden spike; and the Cen-tral Pacific built on into Ogden any way, in the hope that it could swindle the government of fifty thousand acres more. And the Irishmen all came back. For Ogden was now a railroad town. . . .

Came too, not only Bret Harte's gambler, but his aristocratic cousin, the confidence man, of derringer and long-tailed coat, who worked the passenger trains and fleeced his traveling companions at faro or sold them mountain peaks or rivers or franchises to build ferries in the desert. The good and the great came, to see what the railroad was doing in the waste places. And now that other symbol of the west began to come —the cowboy making his long drive northward from Texas, his face hidden in his bandana, his lungs choked with alkali. Ogden was as far west as the Long Trail ever came, as far west as the dionysiac joy of the buckaroo ever set the peaks echoing.

One and all they made their way from bar to bar but ended at the Chapman House. French Pete, other and true name unknown, was the civilizing influence that turned many a man toward the arts. Here is a menu of French Pete's, preserved to this smaller age. Turtle soup, crack-

450

ers; mountain trout, Columbia river salmon, oysters San Francisco; antelope steak, shoulder of venison, beef Chicago; breasts of sage hen, prairie chicken in cream, quail, mourning doves, Canada goose; southern yams in candy, peas, celery, watercress, potatoes O'Brien; hot biscuits, cornpone; honey, watermelon, peaches and cream. The little slip indicates that one was expected, not to make a choice from this ecstasy, but to down it all from the first to the last. The other side is an equally heroic list; cocktails named after railroad presidents, Indian chiefs, and mining camps; punches, cordials, highballs, fizzes, rickies, Juleps; it ends, "Irish whiskey, fifteen cents a glass." And one line reads, "Champagne: California, $1.00. Imported, $2.00." A pint? No, a half-gallon.

To the Chapman House came the mining and railroad millionaires, the English cattle-barons, actors and singers making continental tours, and more than one princeling from Graustark or beyond. The register, if it could be recovered, would be a miniature history of the frontier. . . .

Near the Chapman House was Gentile Kate's brothel, incomparably the leader of its kind. Kate was herself a respected part of the business life of the town, a speculator in real estate, the most liberal customer of the stores; she was, too, an unofficial great lady. When a railroad dignitary or a visiting Cabinet member was to be banqueted, she was always bidden to provide conversation and fine raiment above the reach of Ogden. No one was ever swindled at her establishment; no one was ever disorderly there, twice. A person of dignity was Gentile Kate, and of more than a little wit. But her annoyance was Mormons—perhaps because she disliked their colorlessness, perhaps because she felt that their multiple marriages were sabotage against her profession, perhaps because she had knowledge of certain patriarchs and bishops who, by day, denounced her in their meeting-houses. Doing almost a bank's business in loans and mortgages, she never lent a penny to a Mormon; and the one unladylike expression in her vocabulary coupled a vivid genealogy with the name of Joseph Smith.

Early in her career, Brigham Young died of overeating, and soon there was an auction of his effects. Of late years he had taken to parading the streets of Salt Lake in a new carriage—a barouche made for him in the East. One sees the picture: Brigham at his portliest, at his most benignant, leaning back in the wine-colored cushions, one arm bracing his paunch, his eyes straying over the multitudes who uncovered and bowed their heads as the right hand of God went by. An equipage of splendor, behind gray stallions, on one side the all-seeing eye, carved and glistening, on the other side the beehive of Deseret, and on the rear

451

the angel Moroni ascending to heaven from audience with Joseph Smith. But only a carriage, after all.

The Utah Central, one day, bore it up to Ogden. Next day, behind the same gray stallions, bearing the same insignia of Mormonry, it rolled up and down the streets of Ogden, and haughty in its cushions was Gentile Kate.

Meanwhile, following the Irish, other people were settled in Ogden, putting up their stores, shipping their freight to the multitudes of little towns that had germinated in the railroads' wake. Much money was being made in Ogden—and this, as it was Gentile money, gravelled the Mormons' souls. Now begins the last protracted struggle between the faithful and the damned. As always, it gave the Mormon more than his native color. Unmolested, he is only a fanatic worshiping outrageous gods; but fighting the Gentile, he is laved with all the high-lights of martyrdom and sanctity and desperation. . . .

A merry decade it was, these ten years of the People's Party and the Liberal Party—ten years of plot and counterplot, of stuffed ballot boxes and bribed judges, of scandals built to order and set off at the right moment; of broken heads, of oratory and defiance. From Mormon pulpits streamed curses that had for their model the chapters of Deuteronomy which raise cursing to an art. From Irish bar-rooms streamed the laughter of men. Sometimes a Gentile Machiavelli was set upon by night in an alley and his head was bashed. Sometimes one was bought outright or another caught with the goods. In the last case he would be tried by Mormon jury before a Mormon judge, with his comrades—who wasted no sympathy on a man who could get caught—swearing him into centuries of prison.

Sometimes a madness would come upon the Irish, and they would go out for entertainment. Bishop Jones, hurrying to priesthood meeting, would find himself captive to a dozen brawlers who would, perhaps, drag him to the new steam laundry, strip him, and immerse him in a vat of soap with lewd parodies of the Temple ordinances. Did he believe Brigham Young had taken to wife Semiramis and Cleopatra and the Queen of Sheba? Down with him into the suds! Did he expect to beget souls in heaven? Let the soap cover him! And so on till the bishop, recanting Mormonism, precept by precept, emerged a bishop of the black mass.

They went forth to battle, these Irish, but they always died. Till one November the auguries pointed the other way and the Irish swaggered down the middle of the streets. Election day saw two machines perfected. One by one, in the out-lying districts where no Gentiles lived, the Mormons filed in, voting for themselves, for their wives, their children, their great grandparents, and the legions they had taken to wife in celestial marriage. A Gentile election-judge nodded jovially and called them by their first names. All day long till the polls closed. Then, out of nowhere, came rigs galloping; hard men descended on the polls, lifted the ballot box, and disappeared with the Gentile judge. Down the Weber and Ogden rivers flowed streams of ballots sanctified by the Lord's chosen.

Word had reached the Liberal headquarters that special trains had come up from Salt Lake City and that the Mormons were voting all the names on the tombstones. Headquarters grinned and consulted watches. A special arrived from as far north as the Idaho line—and northward there were only Mormons. The upper floor of the city hall filled with a reserve to be called into action ten minutes before the polls closed. A Gentile leader made to go up the stairs. No less a man than Porter Rockwell, now aging, and soon to die, tapped him on the shoulder.

"My orders," Porter said, "is to shoot anybody that goes up them stairs."

The Gentile nodded and beckoned two deputy marshals who happened, very casually, to be standing nearby. "Your orders," he informed them, "is to shoot anybody that comes down them stairs."

An hour before the polls closed all the locomotives in the railroad yards began to whistle. Two specials roared in from Echo, Wasatch, Evanston, and points east. How many Irish clambered down from cars and roofs and tenders history does not estimate. But they streamed uptown and began to vote. They voted the payrolls of the U. P., the registers of the Chapman House and the Broom Hotel, the tax-lists of Evanston, and every other document that bore names. Then, reversing first and last names, they voted again. . . .

That night the planets knew that Gentile Ogden was delivered from the oppressor's heel. How much firework was burned, how much firewater drunk, it is a melancholy business to calculate. . . .

The Mormons have dwelt their eighty years among the mountains and never seen them. And, because they have won their battle, they have kept the Gentiles from seeing them as well. . . . Down the streets of Ogden to-day go the Mormon Buicks and the Gentile Fords, equally intent on the matter at hand. No dominant energy is apparent. The frontier is buried deep beneath this crumbling asphalt. By day or night

453

there is no dust of mule teams, no roar of miners' chorus or shout of Irish going forth against the Chink or the Mormon. Even the transient color of the tourist flees away.

Why not? Since frontiers must fall Ogden could not be Hell on Wheels for ever. Not even its ghosts will walk for it but emigrate westward to Hollywood where at times they lift another squalid art to moments of insight. And if Ogden is not an American city, if it will not bustle or erupt, if it is dingy and penurious and sleeping—why, for that too it has a recompense. It is an outpost of the New Jerusalem, concentrated on the things that pay.

Depression: "Perhaps the Mormons Are Pointing the Way"

IN HIS NEWSPAPER DAYS, Senator Richard L. Neuberger of Oregon made his beat the Northwest, "a frontier so vast that France could be put into it twice and there yet would be many miles of forests and ravines and uplands left over." It was to him the last great outpost region of a country that, despite a demoralizing depression, was still full of promise. Out of his dynamic faith in this region—faith in its inhabitants and in the land itself—he wrote a series of articles for Harper's, *the* New Republic, The New York Times, *the* Portland Oregonian, *and others, which he gathered into a book called* Our Promised Land *(New York, 1939). His chapter "The Saints in the Promised Land" is excerpted below through Senator Neuberger's courtesy and by permission of The Macmillan Co. (copyright 1938 by Richard L. Neuberger).*

In it he describes with enthusiasm the efforts of the Mormons to help themselves as opposed to accepting the dole. What was first called the Church Security Program, now the Church Welfare Program, was the Mormons' own New Deal. Onlookers at first made extravagant claims for its success, to the embarrassment of the Mormons themselves, who were well aware that by no means all their members had voluntarily marched off relief. Reporter Neuberger makes the proper qualifications, at the same time paying high tribute to the idea, the effort, and the long tradition of co-operation behind it.

Depression: "Perhaps the Mormons Are Pointing the Way"

The program as he describes it still flourishes, with benefits in brotherhood as much a premium as the tangible assistance rendered the handicapped, the widowed, and the momentarily destitute. Mormon households are officially advised to keep a two-year supply of foodstuffs on hand, constantly refreshed and replenished, against a day of need they feel sure is coming. Mormon farmers have recently been urged to keep horsepower—real horses—in reserve against the oil shortage and paralysis of mechanized farming the next war will bring.

Out along the interurban line in a tree-shaded section of Salt Lake City stands a sturdy brick-and-timber building. Deep bins in its basement hold five thousand sacks of potatoes, four thousand sacks of apples, and two thousand sacks of onions. Men in mackinaws and overalls trudge in all day long with additional sacks and crates. On the floor above, they leave heaping armloads of fruits and vegetables still moist with rain and dew.

In a spacious kitchen at the rear of the building, kettles of pears and peaches and tomatoes boil merrily as nimble-fingered women in white aprons preserve this array of products of the orchard and field. More than two hundred thousand jars and cans already have been stacked ceiling-high in countless rows. Up a flight of wooden stairs other women are sewing dresses, stuffing quilts, and cutting patterns. Above them on the wall hangs a hand-lettered sign. Here is what it says:

> It ain't the guns or armaments
> Or the tunes the band can play,
> But the close coöperation
> That makes us win the day.

Coöperation means a lot to these people, and to many others like them in two hundred twenty-one such storehouses throughout the Far West. Not so long ago most of the men carrying sacks and armloads of vegetables and the women canning fruits and stitching shirts were dependent upon government relief, or possibly on private charity. Now they have become self-supporting. They are doing useful work. The food they preserve and the clothes they sew provide not only for themselves, but for thousands of other persons engaged in the various phases of the Security Program of the Mormon Church. This program is America's most unique attempt to answer the grim question of unemployment and relief. . . .

At the April conference of the church in 1936, the tall, patriarchal Heber Grant said that coöperation and hard work and the intelligent use of Nature's bountifulness could end the evils of the dole. Mormons from metropolitan Salt Lake City to the lonely foothills of the Uintas and Cascades voiced eager agreement. They eagerly helped set the program in motion. Idle church members were given a chance to harvest crops, cut trees, mine coal, sew petticoats and jackets, and provide other necessities. People once indigent and destitute became self-sustaining and independent. Work replaced idleness. Excess goods were stacked in abundance in bins, cellars, and storehouses.

This unique plan of the Mormons is based on the belief that every able-bodied person can do some useful task, if only given the chance. Why not make that chance available? There are plenty of natural resources in the Promised Land of the Far West waiting only work and development. The church, financed by tithes and "fast days," is obtaining farms, building storehouses, setting up sewing projects, and making other arrangements to provide the necessities of life for thousands of men and women. The work is done by the people taken off Federal relief rolls or private charity lists. Each Mormon is put at the job for which he is best fitted. The idle lumberjack fells trees or chops wood. The destitute farmer plows a loamy field. The housewife in a hungry family cans vegetables or patches clothes. The products of all these tasks are pooled in the storehouses. From there they are distributed to the people engaged in the program. . . .

Under this coöperative, nonprofit system wilderness fastnesses have been cleared, farms cultivated, storehouses built, and Temples erected. Thousands of men being given work and supplies by the Security Plan have helped add new buildings to the estimated $16,000,000 worth of edifices already owned by the Mormon Church. Last year [1937] the Security Program encouraged a building outlay of $3,000,000, the greatest annual expenditure in the history of the Latter-day Saints. Much of the work and materials that went into this undertaking was provided coöperatively by once idle Mormons in communities scattered all the way from the Coast to the fringe of the Dust Bowl. . . .

Exactly how is the Security Program being worked out? What methods and ways have taken twenty-two thousand Mormons off relief and made them independent citizens once more? How are the Latter-day Saints of the present applying to modern economic problems the persistence and vigor of their fathers and grandfathers who settled Utah's rough-and-ready frontier?

The Church Security Program is made up of a number of different phases. Here they are:

1. Keeping a complete index and record of all Mormons who are unemployed or destitute, and making an intensive effort to find jobs for these people in industry and business in their communities.

2. The prompt payment of tithes, the observance of special "fast days," and the contribution of volunteer work by every Mormon able to do so, in order that the church may carry on and finance the Security Program.

3. Investigating thoroughly the agricultural conditions in all sections of Utah, Idaho, Colorado, California, Oregon, and other States where Mormons are located, and placing needy families on farms that are productive and fertile—farms they can pay for in extra produce and surplus goods.

4. Promoting and planning church building projects, irrigation undertakings, mining operations, and similar enterprises, and letting the local communities supply their share in labor and materials.

5. Encouraging a coöperative spirit that will make possible the rehabilitation and recovery—spiritually, as well as materially—of many families through the aid and assistance of their friends and neighbors.

The whole country watches closely as this plan is put into effect. . . . In the spacious kitchen of the Mormon storehouse at Salt Lake City, I talked with a slender woman who was watching a boiling kettle of tomatoes. She must have been forty-four or forty-five years old, and wisps of gray streaked her dark hair. Every now and then she picked up a wooden ladle and stirred the vat in which the tomatoes plopped and steamed like bubbling lava in some incipient valcano. Splashes from the kettle red-flecked the woman's white apron.

"Pretty hot work?" I ventured.

She smiled. "Sure, but I don't mind it. Don't you know it's fun for a woman to be in a kitchen—especially when it's the first kitchen she's been in for a long, long time?"

That was a lead. So I asked, "What do you mean?"

She told me her story. The depression had taken away her job as cashier in a tearoom. She had worked on and off in stores, but three months in a millinery shop had been the longest at any one place. Finally she had been forced to go on relief. Most of the time she had lived in rooming houses and dingy hotels. Occasionally she had gone hungry. The WPA had been a last refuge. Now, she was preserving fruits and vegetables in one of the Mormon storehouses. From the storehouse she also was drawing blankets, clothing, shoes, towels, soap, pillow slips—and even books and magazines from a little library that occupied part of the crowded upper floor.

I asked her if she was happy.

"Happier than I've ever been since the crash in 1929," she replied. "I lost my job right at the start of the depression. This is the first time in almost ten years that I've felt any security. All of us here who work in the kitchen"—she pointed around the big room where other women were peeling and boiling golden pears and ruddy apples—"feel that we have a real chance to come back. We're also much happier in our social life. The church is helping that way, too. Some of us are going to move into a home that a prominent church member has just given to the Security Program. Won't that be grand?"

And she turned back to her steaming pot of tomatoes—tomatoes that would feed the Mormon families whose mothers stitched the clothes and whose fathers chopped the wood that the slender woman at the kettle wore and used. . . .

Beautification of the various church buildings—temples, chapels, and storehouses—has given employment to a large number of Mormons. Two vast new temples are under way, one in Los Angeles and the other in Idaho.* Under the Security Program the Mormons are erecting buildings in every State on the sundown side of the Rocky Mountains. . . .

The mainstay of the Church Security Program is farming. The coal mines, the timber groves, the carpentry shops, the sewing tables, the building enterprises: they all are important, but secondary to the farms. A venerable Mormon Elder in Boise said to me: "We have plenty of land out West. The Lord has provided it. Why shouldn't our unemployed brothers and sisters be cultivating that land, making good things grow? As long as we have idle land there is no need for idle people." The Mormons are putting into practice this bit of hinterland philosophy. On hundreds of Security Program farms, produce is being raised to feed thousands of families.

The sole criticism that I heard directed against the church's program came from some adherents of the New Deal who insisted that the denunciations of the dole and relief were thrusts at the Roosevelt administration. I asked several Mormon leaders about this. They denied the contention and pointed out that in November of 1936—when the Security Program was well under way—Utah with its three hundred thousand Mormons gave the President the largest proportionate majority over Landon that he received in any State outside the South except Nevada. Church and State, these men assured me, are separate in Utah.

---

* Both have since been completed (*Ed. note*).

A few years back Reed Smoot, high-ranking member of the Mormon Council of Twelve Apostles, was defeated decisively for reëlection to the United States Senate by a University of Utah professor of political science named Elbert Duncan Thomas.

The successor to the conservative Smoot has become one of the aggressively liberal supporters of the New Deal. He delivered the most scholarly Senate speeches in defense of the President's plan to renovate the Supreme Court, and he earned a place on the *Nation's* honor roll by upholding the National Labor Relations Board against its host of vituperative critics. Placid, calm, and sad-faced, Senator Thomas has brought to Capitol Hill both the learning and the imperturbability of the typical college professor. He argues for civil rights and economic security with the mild demeanor of the pedagogue rather than the vigor of the politician. In Washington he represents the best and most humanitarian traditions of the Mormon religion and proves that, regardless of what anti-New-Deal tendencies may purportedly be latent in the Security Program, the Latter-day Saints of Utah enjoy being represented by a thoroughgoing disciple of the President.

Tourist Holiday

NO ONE SEEMS to have more fun with Utah's vestigial peculiarities than the expatriate returning home for a visit after making good in the outside world. No talented native son knows Utah better than Samuel W. Taylor or writes about it so gaily and so aptly. An acute commentary runs beneath the airy Taylorisms of his article on Utah for Holiday *magazine of August, 1953.*

Sam Taylor, now of California, is the grandson of John Taylor, third president of the church and successor to Brigham Young. His father was Apostle John W. Taylor, among the last of the great individualists in Zion. A handsome, energetic, adamant idealist who helped promote Mormon refugee colonies in Mexico and Canada, John W. refused to knuckle under to the manifesto forbidding polygamy, married six wives, and was "cut off" for his pains. Sam has told his father's story in Family Kingdom. *The following excerpts from his article provide a quick tour of Mormon country in the boom times of oil, uranium, and scenery. First published in* Holiday, *copyright 1953 by the Curtis Publishing Company, it is excerpted here through the courtesy of Mr. Taylor.*

You get your suit pressed at a While-U-Wait shop, and when paying for it automatically slide a dime tip across the counter. The proprietor pushes the dime back. "I make a profit from my business," he says. "I don't want anything extra."

You pocket the dime, wondering if you've been away too long. You should have known better than to affront the dignity of a Mormon businessman.

You're on a tour of Utah, to see the state as a tourist might. You're talking with motel owners, gas-pump jockeys and hash slingers, and you're interested in what makes it Utah—things typical or peculiar, like the rainbow cliffs, the "hope" houses, and Salt Lake City during a Latter-day Saints Conference. . . .

Nothing better illustrates the Mormon horror of going into debt than the hope house. It consists of a concrete basement roofed over and used for living quarters. By largely doing the work himself, the canny native can get a roof over his head; and when he has saved the cash he'll build himself a house atop the basement—so he hopes, hence the name. You count hundreds of hope houses throughout the state, many with TV antennas sticking from the low roofs, or with brand-new cars alongside.

Often you'll carry away and remember the little things. You'll forget that, at Bingham, the biggest open-cut copper mine in North America has forty-two power shovels scooping up 200,000 tons a day, but you'll remember the hairbreadth approach to the mine through the town's single street, so narrow that the dogs proverbially wag their tails up and down. Everyone knows that a swimmer can't sink in the brine of Great Salt Lake, but what impresses you is that the granite boulders of the railroad embankment weigh so little in the dense water they literally float away during storms.

You are impressed with the primitive wilderness of much of Utah, but what drives it home is the news that the only doctor of Blanding was drafted into the Army. Blanding, with 1178 people, is the largest city of San Juan County, into which could be dropped Delaware, Connecticut and Rhode Island. You ask a waitress if Blanding is a Mormon town. "Well, no, it isn't," she says. "There are six Gentiles here.". . .

You get to Blanding (from Salt Lake City, of course—everything begins and ends there) south and east on U.S. Highway 50. . . . You go through big country, where nothing stops the eye and you can see forever, country so big it seems the rim of the world, but after you turn south at Crescent Junction you go over the rim and enter a new world. It's something from the moon. It's a stage set. It's fairyland. You accept it as you do Mickey Mouse, as fantasy.

You take the first branch road to the right, rough going over sand and slickrock, one-way road, thirty miles down and thirty back, and your destination has the enticing name of Dead Horse Point. But as you drink in the vista of the Colorado gorge, tier upon tier of rainbow cliffs to the end of vision, watching the living color of the stone bloom and fade and change with the time of day, you forget the name and the road and even that the natives unconsciously damn it with assertions it beats the Grand Canyon view. (Is a rose more beautiful than an Easter lily?) Now you're within gunshot range of Monument Canyon (not to be confused with Monument Valley), the Needles, Chesler Park, and other Technicolor fantasies, though you'll see them by Jeep, pack-horse or airplane—not passenger car.

You think natural bridges are something, so you turn east to Arches National Monument. Here, at last count, were eighty-eight natural arches, or bridges—there is a technical difference between an arch and a bridge, though whatever it's called, Landscape Arch is the longest natural *span* in the world, at this writing. When you stand below this tremendous arch you wonder if it will be there tomorrow, for its time is running out and any day can be its last. It spans 291 feet and the enormous weight of this almost flat arch is supported by a ribbon of soft sandstone shaved by the cutting wind to barely six feet thick. Other spans have fallen in; you see their skeletons. Of those that remain there are double ones side by side and one atop the other, and twins that look like the ruins of an enormous pair of eye-glasses. The same erosive forces of wind and rain and frost that enlarge and eventually destroy an old arch are at work creating new ones. Natives watched the birth of the youngest arch here just fifteen years ago. Natural forces are one thing, vandalism another. The Goblet of Venus, down near Blanding, is now nothing but a picture on a post card. As a joke, a deer hunter shot its slender base away and it was a big laugh when it toppled.

You've thought of uranium as rare and exotic, a fearful thing from far reaches, and it seems a matter of course that in this fairyland uranium is the biggest industry. The towns of Moab, Monticello and Blanding are booming, mining uranium, trucking it, processing it, building roads to get it out. You watch the blasting at the painted cliffs high on the rim of a breathless canyon as a road is carved where no road could possibly be, except for uranium. There's oil down here, too, in country so wild they had to float sketchy drilling equipment down the deep gorge of the treacherous Colorado, and then cap off the oil because they had no equipment for getting it out. With roads going in they'll get the oil now, but eventually they'll dig more gold from the tourists, because of those roads, than from either oil or uranium.

There is no east-west road across Southern Utah, and by now nobody has to tell you why not. You leave the blacktop of Monticello, and from Blanding you continue south over slickrock and quicksand. You stop for a watermelon at Bluff, a ghost town of decaying sandstone mansions haunted by strangers; the Mormon founders moved on when the San Juan ate away their farmland and the Government gave their rangeland to the Indians. "Take your pick, four bits apiece, any size," says the old codger selling them. You ask if he's L.D.S. "No," he says, "you see, we raise melons; we don't have no time for religion." As you stagger to the car with the watermelon (the map says "Carry Water" doesn't it?) he calls, "Seen the Goosenecks? Well, you're seeing the sights, ain't you? Then, by God, see the Goosenecks!"

So you see the Goosenecks, the great convolutions of the San Juan, fifteen hundred feet below where you stand. And then, despite the big sign which warns against it, you fight the sand traps and the bottomless holes left by the last cloudburst and head south through Monument Valley, where the huge stone sentinels rise from the floor of the terrible plain one after another into the violet haze, impossible, unforgettable; you grow smaller and more puny by the mile.

Now you've crossed into Arizona, and you have to make a 250-mile triangle—west and north—to get back into Utah. You come north over the ridge in the Kaibab Forest on U.S. 89 and the trees fall away to the desert floor below, and ahead is the border of Utah. *Now, wait a minute,* you think, *this can't be.* For the boundary between Arizona and Utah is an arbitrary line ruled on the map by politicians in Washington. Yet ahead, running right along that accidental line, are tiers of the great painted cliffs.

You enter the cliffs and the state at Kanab, just a hop, skip and jump from the two best-known scenic attractions, Zion Park and Bryce Canyon. They're all you expected—Zion's Great White Throne rising a sheer 3000 feet out of the red cliffs, and the living kaleidoscope of Bryce's fiery city of stone. You can take in Cedar Breaks the same afternoon. This is your dish, if you want your scenery laid out for you on a platter. But if you want to fight for it a little, to see something not *every* tourist does, you detour from the main drag and head out State 24, southeast through Loa and Bicknell to the Wayne Wonderland, with its natural bridges, its weird sculpture and its Great Organ, a symphony of color. Here is Capitol Reef, with Chimney Rock rising blood red from the cream-plastic slopes. And from here, if you really want to earn your scenery, you make trips to the cream-and-yellow buttresses of Cathedral Valley or nature's gargoyles in the grotesque Valley of the Goblins. . . .

As far back as you can remember, there have been oil booms. . . . You have suspected promotion, but now they seem to be getting actual oil, so you decide to see what the boom looks like in the Uintah Basin, over in the northeastern corner of the state.

You go east along Daniels Canyon from Heber, on U.S. 40, and the aspen leaves shimmer butter-yellow against the deep green conifers. Daniels is just one of a dozen canyons that could be promoted as tourist attractions, except that Utah has so much scenery. Where the country opens up near Strawberry Reservoir a line of double-decked trucks comes barreling out of the mountains on a yellow dirt road. Here is the reason you've missed what used to be one of the characteristic features of Utah travel, the sheep herds trailing the highways. The trucks are packed with sheep, transporting an entire herd from mountain range onto winter range in the desert. . . .

The Basin is another area where a few sketchy roads peter off into nowhere. U.S. 40 runs along the north rim of the wild tangle of plateaus and canyons and mesas that extends south the entire length of the state and into Arizona, country so broken that just one all-weather highway crosses its expanse (U.S. 50, which you traveled on the way to Blanding). This enormous wasteland, one quarter of the entire state, is drained sterile by the deep gorges of the Green and the Colorado.

To the north of U.S. 40 are the Uinta Mountains, claimed to be the only range running east-and-west in the nation. Here are Utah's highest mountains, rising from the immense desert, cradling dense timber and a thousand lakes. This is the proverbial sportsmen's paradise; at least 100 of the lakes have never been fished. The high Uintas have been preserved in their original state as a wilderness area without roads or houses. Here is the great watershed of Utah, the source of its best rivers. Ironically, much of the water of this desert state is wasted, running from the slopes of the Uintas into the sterile trap of the Green River gorge. Utah is 96 per cent scenery—only 4 per cent of its land can be cultivated— yet so determined is the state to keep the high Uintas primeval that the

Central Utah Project, which would reclaim 200,000 acres from the desert by using some of the Uinta water, is opposed because it would injure the scenery.

At Roosevelt you find the Indians eating T-bones and the whites ordering hamburgers. The Utes not only nicked the Great White Father for thirty-two million bucks on an old land claim but the've got oil on the reservation besides. The whites gnaw their hamburgers and really pity those poor Utes, getting all this jack and not knowing how to spend it. They tell of Indians buying refrigerators and vacuum cleaners and washing machines without having electricity to run them, about big new cars. With a wink they point out squaws with permanents, walking down the street in evening dress at high noon. "The Government shouldn't give them money until they've been taught how to spend it," you're told. You hear of Indians driving blind drunk, and that they can't handle liquor, which is something the whites could give lessons on. . . .

Dinosaur National Monument straddles the Utah-Colorado line next door to Vernal, and after peering at a barren ledge containing vague outlines of what once were bones and now are rock like the rest of the ledge, you sympathize with the lady tourist alongside you. "Did we," she asks bleakly, "come 350 miles to see *this?*" For once Utah doesn't live up to its billing. But if it's scenery you want, Split Mountain, right next door, can make you forget the so-called bones. Split Mountain is exactly what its name implies. The gorge of the Green cuts through its middle from peak to base. And here you're in color again.

Vernal is like Blanding—the only surfaced road is back the way you came. But you can "earn" your scenery north on State 44 over the Uintahs to Manila. Red Canyon and Horseshoe Canyon, on the way, make you feel it was effort well spent. And you wonder if the Utah genius for prosaic names for breath-taking scenes might have a sly system behind it. Perhaps Dinosaur Monument fell on its face for you because its name had fired your imagination. No amount of previous build-up can spoil a spectacle named Goosenecks, Dead Horse Point, or Horseshoe Canyon; these take you completely and delightfully by surprise. . . .

You learn that Utah has gained 25 per cent in population in the last decade, as people poured into the Wasatch Oasis, the narrow strip of fertile land that runs down the center of the state from above Ogden to below Provo. Here in north-central Utah there's an industrial boom, and if you were born in Provo it's a shock to return to the country town of memory to find it such a bustling industrial city that there's a smog problem. . . .

Tourist Holiday

When you feel a bit pensive about the passing of a country town you're told, "My hell, it's gone anyhow now; let's look ahead." Provo is proud of its $21,000,000 annual payroll. "But now we're geared to industry," the city editor of the *Herald* tells you. "We used to go along in our small-town way and nothing much affected us. Now the first rumor of a steel strike throws business into a tailspin."

You find a curious rivalry between industry and education. Until a decade ago, Provo was The University City. Then with the arrival of Geneva Steel it became The Steel City, and the Brigham Young University was relegated to a seat far in the rear, behind a post. Then the brethren reached out and plucked a Mormon lawyer from Washington, D.C., to be president of the Church university, and things began happening. Ernest L. Wilkinson is an executive, hard worker, a driver, a man who gets things done, rather than a lofty intellectual. He represented the Utes in putting the bite on the Great White Father for thirty-two million. Utah natives stand in awe of success like this; by now the story's grown, it was sixty-five million and his fee the largest in history. "When he wants a new building for the campus he just goes to Salt Lake and comes back with the money," you're told. "He knows where the bear sleeps.". . .

You go up on the hill to see what is happening and are absolutely lost on the campus of your Alma Mater. The new buildings have dwarfed and misplaced the old ones. There are no landmarks left. The biggest and most prominent building on the campus in your day was the library, and now you can't find it; an undergrad (a mere boy; they sure go to college *young* these days) has to show you the way. The throb of jackhammers fills the academic air as workmen swarm over three and a quarter million dollars of additional construction.

When you attended these hallowed halls there were about 1500 students and a chilling rumor that the Church was going to turn the school over to the state or back to the Indians. Now they enroll a freshman class of 3000. . . .

The BYU admits students of all faiths, on condition they observe the Mormon moral code and take a two-hour class in religion each quarter. The base of religious instruction is broad, and a student can select courses in psychology of religion, religious philosophy, the Old Testament, history of religion and kindred subjects without being exposed to Mormon doctrine. Thus any Gentile may, at his own risk, enroll if he meets the academic standards. But the risk is real, for some 25 per cent of the Gentile students are baptized as converts before graduation, and there is

465

the added hazard of marrying a Mormon gal met at school and joining the Church eventually. The Y is one of the most marryin' schools in the world. Last year every member of the student body executive council got married—in fact, they all married each other.

Along with the frank recognition that gals do wear bras and Pantie Girdle P-17's, you find more evidence of religious consciousness than there was back in the cynical 30's. The athletic teams now pray before each contest, a custom initiated by the players, not their elders. Students used to attend Church, if at all, in town. Now the school has two branches of religious services, and 1200 devout undergrads crowd into Campus Branch, their desire to bear testimony so great that the procedure has been put on an assembly-line basis. All those who feel impelled to tell of their personal conviction of the Gospel's truth and the Divine agency of its Prophet are asked to stand, and from the young army that arises are selected a lucky two dozen who receive numbered cards. There are two traveling microphones, and as holder of card No. 1 bears his testimony the holder of card No. 2 gets ready at the other mike, every moment being utilized, bearing testimony by the numbers.

You leave the campus with one more evidence of size and change. They now have campus police, who have given you a parking ticket. And as you complete your tour of the state you notice that education has vanquished industry. The new signs urge tourists to visit "Provo, The University City."

You head west to leave the state, through Grantsville and past the corner of stone wall sticking from the sagebrush that once was the house where your mother grew up in a plural family during the brief flowering of the Principle in Utah. You look back for a last glimpse of the trade mark of the old Mormon towns, the Lombardy poplars, and then you head west over the salt flats, the great and bitter barrier upon which for thousands of square miles there is no bush nor twig nor weed nor blade of grass nor living thing (but have you seen it bloom pink at the sunset and violet at the dawn?). The salt flats isolate the state on the west as do the Uinta Mountains and Great Salt Lake on the north, the broken canyon and mesa country on the east, and the Grand Canyon on the south. You are leaving this physical island with its strange mental wall, in which a peculiar people live their religion as a way of life. . . .

On either side as you cross the salt flats you see the mirage of the floating mountains sailing on their peaks. At Bonneville, where the fastest things on wheels have sped, you turn onto the blinding surface and open

466

your car up. It's rough up to fifty, then it begins smoothing out and then you're floating over the vast table of salt and it's just a question of time and nerve and gasoline. You head back to the highway dismayed that you couldn't crack ninety, and soon you're in Wendover, the state line, and spraddling the line is the biggest mannikin in the world, greeting your entrance into Nevada with the sign, "Where the West Begins."

At first this seems strange, but after you get into Nevada you realize how right it is. You haven't been in the West. In physical layout the villages of Utah are New England. You haven't found Western clothes, customs, language or mental attitude. You have been in an island fairyland of enormous beauty, peopled by a unique brand of tightly-knit Puritans.

The Contemporary Scene

ONE OF THE BEST in the American Guide Series produced by state writers' projects under WPA is Utah: A Guide to the State *(New York, 1941). It was edited by Dale L. Morgan, whose introduction to the volume appears below through the courtesy of Mr. Morgan, the Utah State Institute of Fine Arts, and Hastings House (copyright 1941 by the Utah Institute of Fine Arts). Few essays achieve its sane awareness of both the colorful past and the significant present of Mormon society. Its tone of critical appreciation is characteristic of Morgan as historian.*

Dale L. Morgan, of Mormon extraction, is at present attached to the research staff of Bancroft Library at the University of California. He has written scores of essays and a number of definitive books about the West, including The State of Deseret, The Great Salt Lake, The Humboldt, Jedediah Smith and the Opening of the West, *and the text for a centennial edition of pioneer maps for Rand McNally. He has projected a dozen other works, not the least a three-volume history of the Mormons.*

The Mormon habitat has always been a vortex of legend and lie. Even today, as the state settles down to gray hairs, there lingers something wonderful and outrageous about Utah, a flavor of the mysterious and strange. Many still journey to Utah to see a Mormon.

Even if there had been no background of Joseph Smith, Angel Moroni, and the *Book of Mormon,* Utahns would have been incomprehensible, misunderstood and lied about, because they set down in the book of Western history the most stubbornly cross-grained chapter it contains. All the conventions of Western life in Utah went haywire. Only late, and briefly, did Utahns turn feverish, like their neighbors, with get-rich-quickness. Wars of cattle baron and homesteader dissolved at Utah's borders, because farmers had come first to the creeks. Lynch law wandered into the bishops' courts to sit in the back pews and watch, bemused, the quiet sanity of theological justice. Immaculate woman and scarlet woman together lifted their petticoats to take flight before family migrations and polygamy. Utah has always had a way of doing things different. The rest of the country has never quite got over it.

Much of that pioneer distinctiveness survives in Utah life, although the forces of twentieth century civilization have shaped Utah into patterns of conformance, so that there are fewer outward stigmata to a Utahn, and somewhat less wild speculation about him. Most visitors now betray no disappointment at finding Mormons hornless.

"Utahn" is regarded as almost synonymous with "Mormons," although there have always been those who would quarrel fiercely with this assumption. Although the total Church membership ("Church" meaning always *the* Church) numbers perhaps only three-fifths of the population, the particular quality of Utah life is almost wholly Mormon. Whatever there is of substance to the "gentile" influence represents, if native to Utah, a reaction to Mormon culture rather than anything distinctive in its own right. Two blocks in Salt Lake City stand as the tangible heart and center of Mormon Utah—Temple Square and the adjacent eastern block where stand the modern Church offices and the pioneer structures raised by Brigham Young. But the vital texture of Mormon culture is something much more broad spread—the honest old adobe houses, the villages nestling in the valley bottoms, the people themselves.

Mormon Utah is primarily that fertile strip of occupied land, down through the north-central part of the state, lying at the foot of the Wasatch mountain rampart. Four-fifths of the population lives here, in towns that vary from metropolitan Salt Lake City to humble villages that are distinguishable as towns only by their general store and sturdy "meeting house." This densely populated area, said to sustain more persons to the acre than even crowded Japan, is the great monument to Mormon endeavor, although the log or adobe houses built by Utah's founding fathers rise from creek bottoms all over the state.

Even in this richest and oldest-settled area, the stamp of a pioneer culture is everywhere manifest. Grandsires built too sturdily, albeit of such building materials as wood and mud, for the pioneer period to have lost its substance. Even in Salt Lake City old adobe houses stand up indomitably to the years, the very earth of their dooryards seeming to have crumbled sooner. In smaller towns these houses retain their pioneer flavor of accomplishment; often they are still the best houses in town, despite modern structures of pressed brick, whitepainted wood, or stone. There are few flourishes to such building. They stand upon the earth, compact and designed to live in, the bare high walls weathered native gray. Almost always these houses are shadowed by trees. If houses could not stand as monuments to a culture, trees, gardens, and sheer greenness could. The cities themselves, almost universally set four-square to the directions, reflect an ideal of spacious and noble planning. Exigencies of one kind and another have invaded the grand sweep of pioneer planning, but nothing is more quickly remarkable to visitors than the breadth and straightness of the streets, the width of the sidewalks, and the length of blocks in Utah cities. And all the cities are tree-grown, comfortable with homes and lawns and gardens and flowering shrubs.

Not in this greenest area but in the outlands most nearly survives the old Mormon society. Few "gentiles" have found that hard land to their liking; they have settled instead in the cities, and cast there the social and physical weight of their differentness. The Mormon "wards," or local congregations, in the rural villages comprise from ten to a hundred families living on terms of social intimacy unknown in the cities. Every man is every man's neighbor; all the children go to the same school; the families go together on Sunday to meeting, or to the canyons on outings. Perhaps the sons and daughters sing in the choir; certainly they go together to the dances, bazaars, and banquets held in the meeting house. Only the richer communities have church buildings sufficiently elaborate to boast chapel and "amusement hall" both; characteristically the meeting house serves all community purposes unless the school building is called into use. Until "gentile" accessions to political power in the late eighties, the meeting house served also for school.

Always the most important person in the ward is the bishop. He may also be mayor or justice of the peace or some other officer of civil distinction, but to the people his authority stems first of all from his bishopric, because he there most nearly satisfies their daily needs. He may settle a dispute, officiate at a dance, preside at a marriage, or sign a "recommend" for a member planning temple work for his dead. On Sunday nights at Sacrament meeting, he has words of advice for the brethren, advice temporal as much as spiritual. The bishop is heart and center of a way of living, as close to the earth and the people as his grandfather, who may conceivably in his own time have served as bishop.

Something of this close-knit social fabric is common also to the cities, but the very size of the cities has broken down the completeness of intimacy. Schools are numerous, and school districts do not conform to ward boundaries; life is more complex generally; and "gentiles" live intermingled with Mormons. In the cities, indeed, "gentile" has become almost a word of lost significance, though in the outlying areas it is still a term of sharp differentiation. Yet Mormon feels closer to Mormon always, out of the long community of tradition, despite the forces of depression, and intermarriage, which have worked quietly to break down all distinctions among Utahns.

It is surprising how little of color survives out of the years of turmoil. The violent days of struggle between Mormon and anti-Mormon, polygamist and anti-polygamist, have faded almost to nothing. Polygamy has become almost legendary; the generation coming now of age marvels almost as greatly as outsiders that polygamy was once a part of the Utah way of life. There are a very few polygamists still alive, patriarchs looking back over the full years, but even among the Mormons there are few who number a polygamist among their acquaintances. In ordinary living, polygamy survives chiefly in a consciousness of relatives. Utah families are larger today than the national average—larger than Utah's apparent capacity to retain the increase—but even monogamic families in times past ran to far greater size, and Utahns have relatives enough in the straight line of descent; the genealogical ramifications consequent upon polygamy—half-granduncles and grandaunts, half second- third- fourth- and fifth-counsins—are such that the typical Utahn of old Mormon descent never inquires into the full extent of his relationships, content to stipulate vaguely that he may be distantly related to a tenth of the population of the state.

Mormons live perhaps more comfortably in Utah than non-Mormons, because the major pattern of the state's life is Mormonmade; Mormons are not, like "gentiles," under the necessity of challenging the structure of their social life. Probably in no other state is there so acute a religious consciousness as in Utah; there continues, not obviously, an undercurrent social antagonism that is, however, only a vestigial feeling out of the long warfare. Some of the anti-Church feeling derives also from the idealogical developments affecting other churches in other states, in the iconoclastic attitudes taken by the younger generation toward all churches

470

and religions; if it is stronger here, the feeling grows out of greater help-lessness toward a more strongly integrated church. The Church stands likewise as an embodiment of convention, in a time when convention and tradition are being broken upon the distress of American society; inevitably there are rebels to speak against it. For most Utahns, however, the Church contributes to a more comfortable life—it is itself a whole way of living.

The West, in popular argot, has always been radical—and Utah especially so. That is in part an Eastern egotism, which finds outrageous that which for excellently good reasons does not conform to the Eastern idea of how things should be done. But it is in the nature of Utah contrariety, perhaps a consequence in part of the strong New England breed which shaped Mormon beginnings, that Utahns in general are pronouncedly conservative, though lately consistent Democrats. In part this conservation stems from the binding forces of Church convention and Church morality, and the homogeneity of the racial stock, which is not only more than 99 per cent white, but is almost wholly Anglo-Scandinavian; there has been no social conflict of racial groups to facilitate unrest. There is probably a greater emphasis upon the family in Utah than generally in the country; there is probably less drinking, less smoking, and perhaps less card-playing; certainly there is a greater disposition to stay put. Yet this conservationism certainly is not insularism. Probably there is a greater cosmopolitan leavening to Utah society, urban and rural, than anywhere in the country; there is hardly a village that does not contain one or more persons who have served upwards of two years as a Church missionary in distant lands—Europe, Africa, South America, Australia, or even Japan.

Utah's neighborliness is often remarked by visitors; here the years tell their own tale, for outlanders frequently, in early days, were viewed with a chill and suspicious eye. Utah socially is not large enough, or complex enough, to have mastered wholly the art of minding its own business—an art which can be carried to extremes. Many have settled in Utah for no other reason than this over-the-fence sort of friendliness, although there are those who have left the state in a wholehearted quest for more privacy. The state is also too close to its pioneer beginnings for the social amenities to come with entire grace. Art has been backward, and literature and music have been subordinated to religious ends. Education has been a pride of Utahns, who point to one of the highest literacy ratings in the country, but the state has not been sufficiently rich either economically or socially to attract from outside the mature, reflective

471

minds that enrich popular living; indeed, Utah has lost many of its own sons and daughters to areas of greater opportunity. In a state where seven of twenty-nine counties lack a bank, eight a railroad, and several a telegraph line, it is inevitable that there should be some social lags.

Utah has its own characteristic symbolisms. Most omnipresent is the beehive. It occurs on the state seal, on the university seal, on the Beehive House in Salt Lake City, on the masthead of newspapers, on the Mormon-owned Hotel Utah in Salt Lake City, on top of policemen's call boxes, on every conceivable interior decoration, on places of business. Four names, drawn direct from Utah history, occur in probably every city of size in the state—there are Beehive laundries, Seagull loan companies, Deseret cafes, and Zion stores, or any imaginable reshuffling of the four. *Book of Mormon* names are widespread, both for places and persons. The state has towns named Deseret, Lehi, Manti, Moroni, and Nephi; Lehi, Moroni, and Nephi are still current as names of individuals, though now more rarely seen. Frequently occurring first names of historical significance are Orson, Heber, Parley, and Hyrum, though there are few Brighams in these latter years. Names of Biblical flavor are probably more numerous in Utah than anywhere outside tradition-bound New England, while Ute and Paiute place names also add their own distinctive flavor to the state.

Mormon Church conferences, the annual meeting in the spring, and the semi-annual conference in the fall, bring thousands of people from all over the state, and from many adjoining states, into Salt Lake City. The annual conference, normally including April 6, is, sartorially and socially, the Mormon Easter. There are more flower-trimmed hats, more pastel topcoats, at conference time than on Easter proper—and it nearly always rains. "Conference weather" is proverbial. In the 67-year period from 1874 to 1940, only once, 1916–1918, was there a period of successive conference weeks free of measurable precipitation, the average precipitation being about half an inch, although in 1929 there fell 15.4 inches of snow. In a desert state, "conference rains" are put up with gladly.

In Utahns there is universally a consciousness of the earth, in part because of the recency of its pioneering, but principally because Utah is an uncertainly subdued land, instinct with hardship. A Utahn who goes to New England or to Oregon looks at the broad rivers almost bitterly. It is unnatural that rivers should waste into the sea, just as it is unnatural that farmers should mature crops by rain alone. Rivers should be dammed at canyon mouths, and their waters carried in canals to the thirsting land. Water in Utah is precious, savored as champagne might be in another land. Life does not come easy. Perhaps some of the especial flavor of Utah comes from this quality of things coming hard. Its beauty is not wholehearted; always there is something withheld. Utah's loveliness is a desert loveliness, unyielding and frequently sterile; its one sea, Great Salt Lake, is lethal and worthless. This kind of country does not appeal to everyone; some have fled it in hatred. Yet many Utahns have not really loved the land of their nativity until they have ventured into more prodigal areas, into the lush green Northwest, the fertile Middle West, or the granite-ribbed East.

The state is immense and varied, almost beyond belief. The band of irrigated green, west of the Wasatch Mountains, extends from north central Utah southward, curving gently west to a corner with Arizona and Nevada. West of this band is the gray-green Great Salt Lake, gray desert, and peaked mountains. Eastward is the red desert country of the Colorado Plateau, yellowing as it approaches the Uinta Mountains on the north, ever reddening as it extends southward and eastward to the Arizona and Colorado lines—a country of flat-topped mountains and violent color. These dessicated gray and red deserts, and these mountains, represent more than 90 per cent of Utah. The tremendous weight of the land lies upon everything. The mountains climb into the skies; the deserts ache with sheer empty immensity. Utah is many things at once: Utah is green-carpeted vales lying peacefully under the shadow of the Wasatch; Utah is a wide solitude of rolling dry valleys, with hills marching beyond hills to blue horizons; Utah is unearthly white desert; Utah is tall snow-crowned mountains; Utah is blue lakes; Utah is canyon and plateau wonderfully fragrant with pines.

Its aspect changes with the sharp progression of the seasons. Winter is a time of hibernation. In summer much of the state is bled by the sun to an inhospitable dun and gray. But in spring the flowering desert has a surpassing loveliness, and in autumn the canyons choke with color.

In Salt Lake City, in Ogden and Provo and Logan, the immensity of the state is circumscribed, and the world is as near as the front page of the daily newspapers. Yet the quiet hills bespeak something alien and impermanent to this urban reality of steel and stone, aspirin and cashiers' registers. One can almost start out of a dream to see these things perished and the land returned to the hills—green-gray with sage or tawny with dry June grass under the blue-drifting smoke of Indian campfires. Out in the desert the world changes; sheep and cattle graze in a land out of time and space, and even the radio in the sheepherder's

473

wagon does not convince one that cities can exist in a world where the sun shines so brilliantly in the deep blue sky while the warm wind rustles in the sage.

In the red deserts are Utah's scenic and scientific marvels, its dinosaur bones, its cliff-dwellings, its multicolored canyons, its Indians, more natural arches and bridges than anybody knows—two more were discovered in 1940—its cow-country frontier, its vast tracts of unmapped, unexplored country. Cardeñas discovered the canyon of the Colorado, but his reports use no single adjective of color. Mormon pioneers, cowboys, and sheepherders have looked upon marvels of natural color to see them as "piles of rocks" that couldn't sprout a kernel or feed a beast. Utah has been, historically, a detoured country; the Oregon Trail went north of it, other cross-country travel south of it. Utah's deserts wait still, wrapped in multicolored serenity, for their full measure of appreciation.

It is fitting that the worthless dry deserts nevertheless should begin, profitably for Utah, to instill in popular consciousness some other definition of the state than Mormonism, for the richer land has been pressed almost to its uttermost by the Mormon struggle with the earth. Mormon enterprise was a powerful force that wrought greatly with a hostile environment; but Utah today is supported by its mines and its livestock far more importantly than by its farms, despite the national reputation of its celery and its fruit, and despite its alfalfa, wheat, sugar beets, and garden vegetables. The fertility of the land has been outstripped by the fertility of the people. The sons and daughters born so strangely stalwart from the loins of Eastern and European converts who left urban homes to wrestle with unfamiliar Utah deserts, today are migrating from the state, bringing their strength, their vigor, and their eager ambition to the great cities of either coast. They go like a lifeblood, from wounds that Utah hopes one day to close.

―――――――

Hometown Revisited

OVER A CENTURY separates Joseph Smith's own story from Wallace Stegner's nostalgic reminiscence, but the first Mormon's visions founded the city which a latter-day Gentile finds a sanctuary. Wallace Stegner

Hometown Revisited

tells below how, after many wanderings, he discovered that Salt Lake City is his spiritual hometown. Salt Lake City is today the home, not of any single or singular people, but of any questing spirit who lives, or has lived, there deeply. As Stegner says, "Home is what you can take away with you." He speaks for Saint as well as Gentile and fittingly closes this collection.

Wallace Stegner's contributions to American literature and history are legion. The Big Rock Candy Mountain, Beyond the Hundredth Meridian, *and* Mormon Country *suggest the variety. Teacher and writer, after experience at the University of Utah, the University of Iowa, and Harvard, he now directs the Creative Writing Center at Stanford.*

The following selection is reprinted through the courtesy of Mr. Stegner from the February, 1950, number of Tomorrow *magazine, which published a series called "Hometown Revisited."*

I have always envied people with a hometown. They always seem to have an attic, and in the attic albums of pictures, spellers used in the third grade, gocarts and Irish mails with the scars of young heels and teeth on them. In the homes of these fortunate ones there is always some casual friend of thirty or forty years' standing, someone who grew up next door, some childhood sweetheart, some inseparable companion from primary days. Some people even live in the houses their fathers and grandfathers used; and no matter how wide they may scatter from the hometown, always behind them is a solid backstop of cousins and grandmothers and relatives once or twice removed, maintaining the solidarity and permanence of the clan.

None of these forms of moss cling to a rolling stone, and I was born rolling. If I met a playmate of thirty years ago we would not recognize each other even as names. Since I left them to move elsewhere, I have never again encountered a single one of the children I knew in any of my various dwelling places. The things that accumulate in others' attics and in their memories, to turn up again in their futures, have been cleaned out of mine five dozen times to simplify moves. Since I was born in Iowa forty years ago (my hometown held me six weeks) I have lived in twenty places in eight different states, besides a couple of places in Canada, and in some of these places we lived in anywhere from two to ten different houses and neighborhoods. This is not quite the same thing as traveling extensively; it involves having no permanent base whatever. Until my wife and I built a house this year I am sure no member of my family had ever owned one.

The absence of roots has always seemed to me a deprivation both personally and professionally. Personally, I was condemned to friendships that were always being sharply cut off and rarely renewed, so that for a time they tried to live by mail and then lamely dwindled out. Professionally, as a writer, I considered myself unequipped with the enduring relationships from which the deepest understanding of people might have come. I have always thought of myself as a sort of social and literary air plant, without the sustaining roots that luckier people have. And I am always embarrassed when well-meaning people ask where I am from.

That is why I have been astonished, on a couple of recent trips through Salt Lake City, to find a conviction growing in me that I am not as homeless as I had thought. At worst, I had thought myself an Ishmael; at best, a half-stranger in the city where I had lived the longest, a Gentile in the New Jerusalem. But a dozen years of absence from Zion, broken only by two or three short revisitings, have taught me different. I am as rich in a hometown as any one, though I adopted my home as an adolescent and abandoned it as a young man.

A Gentile in the New Jerusalem: certainly I was. Salt Lake City is a divided concept, a complex idea. To the devout it is more than a place; it is a way of life, a corner of the materially-realizable heaven; its soil is held together by the roots of the family and the cornerstones of the temple. In this sense Salt Lake City is forever foreign to me, as to any non-Mormon. But in spite of being a Gentile I discover that much of my youth is there, and a surprising lot of my heart. Having blown tumbleweed-fashion around the continent so that I am forced to *select* a hometown, I find myself selecting the City of the Saints, and for what seems to me cause.

It has such a comfortable, old-clothes feel that it is a shock to see again how beautiful this town really is, quite as beautiful as the Chamber of Commerce says it is; how it lies under a bright clarity of light and how its outlines are clean and spacious, how it is dignified with monuments and steeped in sun, tempered with shade, and how it lies protected behind its rampart mountains, insulated from the stormy physical and intellectual weather of both coasts. Serenely concerned with itself, it is probably open to criticism as an ostrich city; its serenity may be possible only in a fool's paradise of isolationism and provincialism and smugness. But what is a hometown if it is not a place you feel secure in? I feel secure in Salt Lake City, and I know why. Because I keep meeting so many things I know, so many things that have not changed since I first saw the city almost thirty years ago.

True, it has grown by at least fifty thousand people since then, new roads have been built and new industries imported, new streets of houses are strung out from the old city limits. But there were people and roads and industries and houses there before; these new ones have not changed the town too much, and seem hardly to have affected its essential feel at all.

It was an amazement to me, returning, to realize how much I know about this city, until I remembered that I had lived there off and on for nearly fifteen years; that as a Boy Scout I had made an elaborate and detailed map of its streets in order to pass some test or other; that as a high-school student I had solicited advertisements among all its business houses; that while I was in college I had worked afternoons in a store that was always in need of somebody to double as a truck driver, so that I delivered parcels lengthwise and endwise over the city. There is no better way to learn a place; I have known no place in that way since.

Moreover, Salt Lake is an easy town to know. You can see it all. Lying in a great bowl valley, it can be surmounted and comprehended and possessed wholly as few cities can. You can't possibly get lost in it. The Wasatch comes with such noble certitude up from the south and curves so snugly around the "Avenues" that from anywhere in the city you can get your directions and find your way. And man has collaborated with nature to make sure that you can't get lost. The streets are marked by a system so logical that you can instantly tell not merely where you are but exactly how far you are from anywhere else. And when your mind contains, as I found recently that mine did, not merely this broad plot but a great many of the little lost half-streets with names like Elm and Barbara and Pierpont, then you have blocked off one of the great sources of nightmare.

You can't get lost. That is much. And you can always see where you are. That is even more. And you can get clear up above the city and look all the way around and over it, and that is most. Looking into the blank walls of cities, or staring up at them from dirty canyon sidewalks, breeds things in people that eventually have to be lanced.

Sure and comfortable knowledge is one thing. Association, which often amounts to love and always involves some emotional relationship, is another. Mere familiarity, I suppose, generates an emotional attachment of a kind, but when years of the most emotionally active time of one's

477

life have been spent among certain streets and houses and schools and people and countrysides, the associational emotion is so pervasive that it may be entirely overlooked for years, and comprehended only in retrospect. Nostalgia, the recognition of old familiarity, is the surest way to recognize a hometown.

In a way, my family's very mobility helped to make this town peculiarly mine, for we lived in many neighborhoods. We lived at Fifth South and Fifth East under old cottonwoods behind a mangy lawn; we lived on Seventh East across from Liberty Park so that I knew intimately the rats in the open surplus canal; we lived in a bungalow on Eighth East, an old brick ruin on Twenty-first South and State, a pleasant house on Fifteenth East above the high school I attended. We lived on Ninth East and Fourth South, on Seventh South and Eleventh East, in an apartment on First Avenue, in an ancient adobe down near the heart of town by the post office. I beat my way to school across lots from many different directions, and my memory is tangled in the trees on certain old streets and involved in the paths across many vacant lots and impromptu baseball fields.

The mere act of writing them down amplifies and extends the things that remain with me from having lived deeply and widely in Salt Lake City. I suppose I played tennis on almost every public and private court in town, and I know I hiked over every golf course. For three or four winters, with a club basketball team, I ran myself ragged in the frigid amusement halls of a hundred Mormon ward houses and took icy showers and went home blown and rubber-legged late at night. With a team in the commercial league, or with the freshman squad at the university, I hit all the high-school gyms, as well as the old rickety Deseret Gymnasium next door to the Utah Hotel, where cockroaches as big and dangerous as rollerskates might be stepped on behind the dark lockers. From games and parties I ran home under dark trees, imagining myself as swift and tireless as Paavo Nurmi, and the smell and taste of that cold, smoky, autumnal air and the way the arc lights blurred in rounded golden blobs at the corners is with me yet. It makes those streets of twenty and twenty-five years ago as real as any I walk now; those are the streets I judge all other city streets by, and perhaps always will.

This, I discover belatedly, is the city of many firsts: the first car, the first dates, the first jobs. No moon has ever swum so beguilingly up over mountains as it used to swim up over the Wasatch; none has ever declined so serenely as it used to decline sometimes when we came home at two or three after a date and twenty-mile drive out to Taylors-

478

ville or Riverton to take our girls home. No friends have ever so closely
and effortlessly touched the heart. No sandwiches have ever since had
the wonderful smoky flavor that the barbecued beef used to have at
the old Night Owl on Ninth South, by the ball park. No heroes have ever
walked so tall as Willie Kamm and Tony Lazzeri and Lefty O'Doul and
Duffy Lewis and Paul Strand and Fritz Coumbe of the old Salt Lake
Bees in the Pacific Coast League. The year Tony Lazzeri hit sixty home
runs, most of them over the short left field fences at Bonneville Park, I
haunted State Street, outside that fence, and risked death in traffic a hundred times to chase batting-practice balls and get a free seat in the
left field bleachers. And when Coumbe, who had pitched (I believe)
for the Athletics and played against Babe Ruth (Ruth hit the first ball he
threw him over the center field fence) came to live in the other half of
a duplex from us, and brought other heroes home with him, and gave me
a left-handed first-base mitt that had belonged to George Sisler, I grew
twelve inches overnight.

Here for the first time I can remember triumphs, or what seemed
triumphs then. In Salt Lake I wrote my first short story and my first
novel. In Salt Lake I fell in love for the first time and was rudely jilted
for the first time and recovered for the first time. In Salt Lake I took my
first drink and acquired a delightful familiarity with certain speakeasies
that I could find now blindfold if there were any necessity. I experi-
mented with ether beer and peach brandy and bathtub gin and survived them all, as I survived the experience of driving an automobile at
sixteen or seventeen, by hairbreadth but satisfactory margins.

It seems to me now that in the course of one activity or another, driven
by that furious and incomprehensible adolescent energy which lies dead
somewhere in Salt Lake and which I wish I could bring back as readily
as I bring back its memory, I surged up and down and across New Jerusalem from Murray to Beck's Hot Springs, and from Saltair to Brighton
and Pinecrest. And how it was, its weathers and its lights, is very clear
to me.

So is the country that surrounds the city and that gives the city so much
of its spaciousness and charm and a large part of its nostalgic tug.

Salt Lake lies in the lap of mountains. East of it, within easy reach of
any boy, seven canyons lead directly up into another climate, to fishing
and hunting and camping and climbing and winter skiing. Those canyons opened out of my backyard, no matter what house I happened to
be living in. City Creek and Dry Canyon were immediate and walkable.
Parley's could be penetrated by the judicious who hung around on the

tracks behind the state penitentiary and hooked onto D & RG freights as they began to labor on the grade. Sometimes we rode a boxcar or a gondola; sometimes an indulgent fireman let us ride on the coal in the tender. Up in the canyon we could drop off anywhere, because even with two engines the train would only be going ten or fifteen miles an hour. South of Parley's was Mill Creek, and this we reached on more elaborate expeditions with knapsacks. In spring there were lucerne fields and orchards to go through toward the canyon's mouth, and the lucerne patches could always be counted on to provide a racer snake or two, and the orchards a pocketful of cherries or apricots or peaches. On a hot day, after a climb, cherries chilled in the cold water of Mill Creek and cherished, one by one, past teeth and palate and throat, were such cherries as the world has not produced since.

And the other canyons: the little swale of Hughes, where in late April the dogtooth violets were a blanket under the oakbrush; Big Cottonwood, up which ore trucks used to give us a lift to the Maxwell or the Cardiff mines, and where the peaks went in a granite whorl around the lakes and cottages of Brighton; Little Cottonwood, with the ghost town of Alta at its head, since famous for ski slopes; and Bell's, a glacial 'U' with waterfalls and hanging glacial meadows lifting in a long steep southward curve toward Long Peak and the point of the mountain, from which we could look down on the narrows where the Jordan River slipped between alluvial gravel slopes toward the dead sea.

Knowing Salt Lake City means knowing its canyons too, for no city of my acquaintance except possibly Reno breaks off so naturally and easily into fine free country. The line between city and mountains is as clean as the line between a port city and salt water. Up in the Wasatch is another world, distinct and yet contributory, and a Salt Lake boyhood is inevitably colored by it.

There is a limit to the indulgence of recollection, for fear nostalgia should be overcome by total recall. But it is clear to me, now that I have chosen a hometown, that I do not believe unqualifiedly in a "most impressionable age" between five and ten. The lag between experience and the kind of assimilation that can produce nostalgia is considerable, I suppose. In our early maturity we have just come to realize how much our tender minds absorbed in early childhood. But later we may have other realizations. Other recollections brighten as the first ones fade, and the recognition that now makes me all but skinless as I drive down Thirteenth East Street in Salt Lake City is every bit as sharp and indelible as the impressions my blank-page senses took as a child. Not all experience, not even all romantic and nostalgic experience, is equivalent to Wordsworth's.

Any place deeply lived in, any place where the vitality has been high and the emotions freely involved, can fill the sensory attic with images enough for a lifetime of nostalgia. Because I believe in the influence of places on personalities, I think it somehow important that certain songs we sang as high-school or college students in the twenties still mean particular and personal things. "I'm Looking Over a Four-leaf Clover" is all tied up with the late-dusk smell of October on Second South and Twelfth East, and the shine of the arc light on the split street tipping up the Second South hill. "When Day Is Done" has the linseed-oil smell of yellow slickers in it, and the feel of the soft corduroy cuffs those slickers had, and the colors of John Held pictures painted on the backs. "Exactly Like You" means the carpet, the mezzanine, the very look and texture and smell, of the Temple Square Hotel.

Salt Lake is not my hometown because my dead are buried there, or because I lived certain years of my youth and the first years of my marriage there, or because my son was born there. Duration alone does not do it. I have since spent half as many years in Cambridge, Massachusetts, without bringing from that residence more than a pitiful handful of associations. I was not living in Cambridge at the pace and with the complete uncritical participation that swept me along in Salt Lake. To recall anything about Cambridge is an effort, almost an act of will—though time may teach me I took more from there too than I thought I did. But Salt Lake City, revisited either in fact or in imagination, drowns me in acute recognitions, as if I had not merely sipped from but been doused with Proust's cup of reminding tea.

From its founding, Salt Lake City has been sanctuary: that has been its justification and its function. And it is as sanctuary that it persists even in my Gentile mind and insinuates itself as my veritable hometown. Yet there are darker and more ambiguous associations attached to it, and it is strange to me, returning, to find myself looking upon Salt Lake as the place of my security. It never was at the time I lived there. I suppose no age of man is less secure than adolescence, and more subject to anguishes, and I think I do not exaggerate in believing that my own adolescence had most of the usual anguishes and some rather special ones besides. Certainly some of the years I lived in Salt Lake City were the most miserable years of my life, with their share of death and violence and more than their share of fear, and I am sure now that off and on for considerable periods I can hardly have been completely sane.

481

There are houses and neighborhoods in Salt Lake whose associations are black and unhappy, places where we lived which I thought of at the time as prisons. Yet revisiting the city I am warmed by this flood of recollection, the unhappiness dwindles into proportion or perspective, even unimportance. Or perhaps the unhappiness takes on a glow in retrospect, and perhaps the feeling of security and well-being which Salt Lake gives me now is partly satisfaction at having survived here things that might have destroyed me. Or perhaps it arises from the pure brute satisfaction of having experienced anything, even misery, with that much depth and sharpness. Or perhaps, like the discomforts of a camping trip that become hilarious in telling, the verbal formulation of distress has the capacity to cure it. So Emerson, after flunking a mathematics examination in college, could go home and triumph over all the arts of numbers by writing a destructive essay on the subject.

I suppose that may come close to the core of my feeling about Salt Lake. Returning is a satisfactory literary experience; the present has power to evoke a more orderly version of the past. And what is evoked, though it may be made of unpleasant or unhappy elements, is satisfactory because it *is* a kind of vicarious thing, a literary product.

Whether it says with the Anglo-Saxon poet, "That have I borne, this can I bear also," or whether it says, "There, for a while, I lived life to the hilt, and so let come what may," my hometown, late discovered, is not a deprivation or a loss or a yearning backward. I recently had the experience of recognizing, and with pleasure, what the city meant to me, but I was not heartbroken to leave either it or that youth of mine that it embalms, and I do not necessarily yearn to return to either. It does not destroy me with a sense of lost green childhood or of any intimation of immortality long gone and irrecoverable. There is only this solid sense of having had or having been or having lived something real and good and satisfying, and the knowledge that having had or been or lived these things I can never lose them again. Home is what you can take away with you.

Index

INDEX

INDEX

INDEX

INDEX